D0204340

QUANTITATIVE MANAGEMENT
AN INTRODUCTION

Note to the Student

Dear Student,

If you winced when you learned the price of this textbook, you are experiencing what is known as "sticker shock" in today's economy. Yes, textbooks are expensive, and we don't like it anymore than you do. Many of us here at Kent have sons and daughters of our own attending college, or we are attending school part time ourselves. However, the prices of our books are dictated by the cost factors involved in producing them. The costs of paper, designing the book, setting it in type, printing it, and binding it have risen significantly each year along with everything else in our economy. You might find the following table to be of some interest.

Item	1967 Price	1984 Price	The Price Increase
Monthly Housing Expense	$114.31	$686.46	6.0 times
Monthly Automobile Expense	82.69	339.42	4.1 times
Loaf of Bread	.22	1.00	4.6 times
Pound of Hamburger	.39	1.48	3.8 times
Pound of Coffee	.59	2.45	4.2 times
Candy Bar	.10	.35	3.5 times
Gasoline	.35	1.20	3.4 times
Men's Dress Shirt	5.00	25.00	5.0 times
Postage	.05	.22	4.4 times
Resident College Tuition	294.00	1,581.00	5.4 times

Today's prices of college textbooks have increased only about 2.8 times 1967 prices. Compare your texts sometime to a general trade book, i.e., a novel or nonfiction book, and you will easily see significant differences in the internal design, quality of paper, and binding. These features of college textbooks cost money.

Textbooks should not be looked on only as an expense. Other than your professors, your textbooks are your most important source for what you hope to learn in college. What's more, the textbooks you keep can be valuable resources in your future career and life. They are the foundation of your professional library. Like your education, your textbooks are one of your most important investments.

We are concerned, and we care. Please write to us at the address below with your comments. We want to be responsive to your suggestions, to give you quality textbooks, and to do everything in our power to keep their prices under control.

Wayne Barcomb

Wayne A. Barcomb
President

Kent Publishing Company
20 Park Plaza
Boston, MA 02116

QUANTITATIVE MANAGEMENT
AN INTRODUCTION

Second Edition

Michael Q. Anderson
UNIVERSITY OF NEW MEXICO

R. J. Lievano
UNIVERSITY OF NEW MEXICO

KENT PUBLISHING COMPANY

A Division of Wadsworth, Inc.
BOSTON, MASSACHUSETTS

Senior Editor: John B. McHugh
Production Editor: Carolyn Ingalls
Interior and Cover Designer: Outside Designs
Manufacturing Manager: Linda Siegrist

Kent Publishing Company

A Division of Wadsworth, Inc.

©1986 by Wadsworth, Inc., 10 Davis Drive, Belmont, California 94002. All rights reserved. No part of this book may be reproduced, stored in a retrieval system, or transcribed, in any form or by any means, electronic, mechanical, photocopying, recording, or otherwise, without the prior written permission of the publisher, Kent Publishing Company, 20 Park Plaza, Boston, Massachusetts 02116.

Printed in the United States of America
1 2 3 4 5 6 7 8 9—90 89 88 87 86

Library of Congress Cataloging-in-Publication Data

Anderson, Michael Q.
  Quantitative management.

  Rev. ed. of: Quantitative management decision making, with models and applications. c1982.
  Bibliography: p.
  Includes index.
  1. Decision-making—Mathematical models.
2. Operations research.   3. Management science.
I. Lievano, R. J.   II. Anderson, Michael Q.   Quantitative management decision making, with models and applications.
III. Title.
HD30.23.A473   1986   658.4′034   85-23169
ISBN 0-534-05958-9

TO KATHY

TO MALINDA AND GILBERTO

PREFACE

Management-science techniques are finding wide use in the business world, and the number of graduates in the discipline is increasing. For these techniques to be useful, however, there must be effective communication between management and technical staff—which means that managers themselves must become at least somewhat familiar with management-science methods.

This text was written with the following objectives in mind:

- To acquaint general business or management students with the most widely used management-science techniques.
- To explain these management-science techniques, using mathematics no higher than college-level algebra.
- To show the wide applicability of management-science techniques through the liberal use of examples and applications.
- To enrich the treatment of standard topics by including applications-oriented material beyond that found in current management-science texts.

This text is designed primarily for undergraduate students of business and for graduate-level and executive-management courses in which students have only a minimal background in mathematics. The prerequisite is a knowledge of college algebra. A basic knowledge of probability is also helpful, although Appendixes E and F will provide basic information in this area.

The text differs from most management-science texts in that it includes the following:

- A large number of practical examples and applications. (See, for example, Section 7 of Chapter 2, Section 5 of Chapter 4 and Chapter 12, Section 3 of Chapter 14, and Section 5 of Chapter 15. In addition, the chapter exercises are almost entirely applications oriented.)
- End-of-section problems, with solutions provided in Appendix B.
- Two categories of topics not typically addressed in texts at this level: The first consists of advanced topics; the second includes topics that specifically

address practical implementation of the techniques. (For example, see Section 8 of Chapter 6; Sections 4 and 7–12 of Chapter 8; Sections 3 and 5 of Chapter 9; Sections 7–10 of Chapters 10, 13, and 14; Section 5 of Chapter 15; and Sections 3 and 5 of Chapters 17 and 18.)

Each special topic is presented at the same basic level; that is, it is intended for students with minimal math background (in contrast with other texts, which relegate such material to incongruous chapter appendices). In addition, we have tried to maintain as much independence as possible between various chapters and sections within chapters. Thus, some or all of the added material may be assigned without concern for level of presentation.

The following interdependencies should be observed:

1. Chapter 3 requires Chapter 2.
2. It is desirable that Chapter 6 precede Section 2 of Chapter 18.
3. Chapter 7 requires Chapter 6.
4. Chapters 13 and 14 require Chapter 2.
5. Section 3, Chapter 17, requires Chapter 2.
6. Appendixes E and F review probability theory.

The inclusion of computer solutions in this revised edition is intended to acquaint students and instructors with the availability and characteristics of computational aids. SAS/OR was chosen because it is comprehensive, simple to use, and available at a relatively modest cost for many different kinds of computers in both batch and interactive versions. Since it is a mainframe software, it is accessible to a larger number of people and is much more powerful than that available for microcomputers. The format shown in the examples is that of a file prepared for batch computation, but the interactive version of SAS/OR has essentially the same syntax.

ACKNOWLEDGMENTS

Many people contributed to the development and completion of this revised edition. Our editor, John B. McHugh, and his able assistant editor, Ms. Katherine Murray, kept us at a coordinated pace and provided information, encouragement, and enthusiasm. The following reviewers provided many helpful comments and suggestions: Kathy Fitzpatrick (Appalachian State University), David Pentico (Virginia Commonwealth University), and H. Ray Souder (Northern Kentucky University). Mr. Michael Morse took primary responsibility for the preparation of the Solutions Manual, improving on the fine work done for the first edition by Mr. John Loucks. Mr. Morse improved upon the completeness of the solutions, designed photocopy-ready formats, and prepared professional-quality graphics. Also, our wives, Kathy Anderson and Malinda Lievano, as well as Messrs. Adrian and Julian Lievano, provided valuable moral and physical support.

Any errors are, of course, our responsibility. We welcome any comments and suggestions for improving the book.

Note to the Student

It is our belief that the greatest satisfaction in studying management science comes when you can successfully solve various problems that you will typically encounter as a working manager. Accordingly, we have tried to provide substantial numbers of interesting examples and applications of problem-solving techniques.

The key to solving quantitative management problems is *practice*. Practice will improve your accuracy and speed, help you gain insight into the basic nature of management problems, and permit you to develop a feel for choosing the correct techniques to solve particular problems. To help you develop problem-solving skills, we have included several completely solved example problems in each section, and, at the end of certain sections, there are sets of problems that you must solve using the techniques described in the examples. (Solutions to these problems are given in Appendix B.) Finally, many exercises follow each chapter, in order to give you the opportunity to practice the skills that you have learned.

The best way to become familiar with this text is to thumb through it—and don't neglect to look at the appendixes. You will note that we have tried to keep the use of scientific notation and Greek letters to a minimum, but Appendix C explains those that (for unavoidable reasons) have been used. If you find a chapter particularly interesting, you may wish to check the references in Appendix A for additional reading on the topic it covers.

MICHAEL Q. ANDERSON
R. J. LIEVANO

CONTENTS

CHAPTER 3   Linear Programming: The Simplex Method   63

SECTION THREE: PROBABILISTIC MODELS   405

CHAPTER 10   Decision Theory   407

CHAPTER 18   Heuristics in Management Science   645

1   INTRODUCTION

CONTENTS

1. WHAT IS MANAGEMENT SCIENCE?

There have been various definitions of the term **management science.** The reason for this is partly due to the fact that management science professionals (1) come from varied backgrounds and disciplines (business, engineering, operations research, and the sciences) and (2) tend to disagree on the nature of their profession.

In this text we will use the term management science (MS) to mean the formal study of quantitative (or mathematical) models and their implementation or use in managerial decision making. Several terms are used interchangeably with management science, including the following: **operations research** (OR), **quantitative business analysis, quantitative methods,** and **decision science.**

2. HISTORICAL BACKGROUND OF OR/MS

In this section we briefly outline a few historical notes on the recent origins of operations research/management science. There is evidence of the use of systematic quantitative analysis as early as World War I, in Thomas Edison's antisubmarine warfare studies, which analyzed the effectiveness of zigzagging movements in protecting merchant ships.

During World War II, operations research was firmly established as an effective problem-solving method. The British were the first to organize formal operations research groups. In 1939, G. A. Roberts with Bawdsey Research Station and Dr. E. C. Williams independently developed early warning communications systems studies for the Royal Air Force. The two were brought together by A. P. Rowe, the superintendent of Bawdsey Research Station, which became the Telecommunications Research Establishment. Under H. Larnder their work became the basis for other British operational research activities. (**Operational research** is the British term for operations research.)

P. M. S. Blackett, professor at the University of Manchester, Fellow of the Royal Society, Nobel laureate, and former naval officer, formed an interdisciplinary team to study radar-equipped gun sites. This group, which became known as Blackett's Circus, was given the name Anti-Aircraft Command Research Group and consisted of two mathematicians, a surveyor, a physicist, three physiologists, two mathematical physicists, an army officer, and an astrophysicist. The group evolved into what is today the Army Operational Research Group. After the war, British civilian OR gained considerable popularity.

Soon after the United States entered the war, the U.S. Air Force and Navy also began to develop organized OR efforts. In 1942 the air force established the Operations Analysis Division of the Office of Management Control. The Office of Scientific Research and Development trained analysts for the air force at Princeton University and the Massachusetts Institute of Technology. The air force developed successful bombing tactics in destroying underground oil storage depots in Italy. It was also successful in developing sighting techniques used in formation bombing, bombing accuracy studies, jungle warfare, and amphibious operations.

The U.S. Navy established the Operations Research Group in 1943 to analyze antisubmarine warfare. This interdisciplinary group later became the Operations Evaluation Group. At the Naval Ordnance Laboratory (NOL), Dr. Ellis A. Johnson directed seminars in mining operations and used war gaming to study strategy, tactics, and technology. The NOL Operational Research Group was established and included Drs. John Von Neumann and J. L. Doob. In Operation Starvation, headed by Johnson, 12,000 mines were successfully set in Japanese waters against 1.2 million tons of enemy shipping, with only one percent B-29 aircraft losses. The navy also developed methods for maneuvering ships against kamikaze attacks and was able to reduce by over 60 percent the number of ships hit. Successful search techniques for enemy ships and submarines were also developed against German blockade runners.

After the war, operations research activities were continued in Britain as a war office under the name Army Operational Research Group. In the United

States the navy established the Operations Evaluation Group in 1947, and the air force established the Operations Analysis organization. In 1946 the air force also initiated Project RAND (an abbreviation for Research and Development) to formulate air force decisions on research and development and to coordinate relations with the aviation industry. Two years later Project RAND became the nonprofit RAND Corporation, originally financed by the Ford Foundation. The army, in 1949, formed the Operations Research Office.

Nonmilitary OR activities were also going on before and after the war. However, one of the distinguishing features of military OR was the use of the multidisciplinary approach, and only recently has this approach been revived and employed in industrial OR groups to include not only scientific activity but also the various business disciplines.

The first operations research periodical, entitled *The Operational Research Quarterly*, appeared in Britain in 1948, published by the Operational Research Society. The Operations Research Society of America (ORSA), established in 1951 with Dr. Philip M. Morse as its first president, the following year published the first issue of *Operations Research*. A sister organization, The Institute of Management Sciences (TIMS), established in 1952, publishes *Management Science*. ORSA and TIMS now conduct several OR activities jointly, including publication of *Interfaces*, an applications-oriented professional journal. The American Institute of Decision Sciences, established in 1971, publishes *Decision Sciences*.

3. COMPUTERS AND OR/MS

Computers and OR have long been associated. The principal motivation for the development of digital computers arose from their potential ability to solve major real-life problems. Some of the most computationally demanding problems are those to which OR techniques are applied. Without the digital computer, many of those techniques would be of little practical importance. Computers and OR thus developed together. Since 1952, when the first large-scale OR application was successfully accomplished on a digital computer, the use of computerized OR techniques has continued to grow. Dramatic as this growth has been, it may be small in comparison to future potential. In today's competitive domestic and international environment, productivity is the key, and OR is an essential productivity tool. The relative inaccessibility, difficulty of use, and expense of large computers limited the application of OR in the past. The personalization of the computer, providing accessibility and ease of use and emphasizing decision support, promises unprecedented expansion in the application of OR. Thousands of organizations, both large and small, are engaged in the development of computer software to assist in assignment, budgeting, distribution, financial planning, forecasting, inventory control, scheduling, and many other activities. At the core of these products are OR techniques. For the first time, OR has the opportunity to become a mass-market product, generating interest in and resources for its continued development.

4. MATHEMATICAL MODELS AND DECISION MAKING

Decision making is the major responsibility of management. Managers typically go through the following steps in dealing with a given problem:

1. They recognize a problem exists; that is, they define the problem.
2. They then identify various parameters of the problem, such as the variables that are under the control of the decision maker. The objectives or goals are defined, for example: "to maximize profit," "to minimize cost," or "to maintain stable employment." They must recognize the practical constraints on the problem's solution, such as budget, labor requirements, and machine capacity.
3. They systematically examine the alternatives for a solution to the problem—that is, a solution that satisfies the stated objectives.
4. They put the solution into practice.

This natural sequence of steps taken in the decision-making process provides us with a solid framework for specifying the role of management science. (See Figure 1.1.)

The Process of Operations Research Modeling

In studying the quantitative management science models in this text, you should keep the following framework in mind. Applying mathematical modeling to management entails substantially more responsibility than simply formulating equations.

1. PROBLEM DEFINITION.
As a management scientist, you must first clearly define and delineate the problem confronting management. It is extremely important at this step to interact with and involve management and other members of the organization. The eventual success of your recommendations will perhaps depend as much on human factors as on the accuracy and elegance of your mathematical model. The best way to sell people on your efforts is to involve them in the formulation of your ideas. Get the input of people in management. Determine their concerns, expectations, and roles relative to the problem. Stimulate their interest in your involvement. These actions will at the same time help to establish your credibility with management.

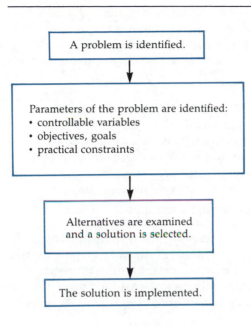

FIGURE 1.1   *Steps in a manager's decision-making process.*

2. MODEL FORMULATION. Once you have defined the problem, formulate a model. A **model** is an abstract representation of the problem situation. In this text we will use the term *model* to mean a quantitative or mathematical representation.

In formulating a model, you must determine which assumptions to employ. In doing so, your interaction with management must be kept clearly in mind, for it is important that the model accurately represents the problem confronting management. However, here lies the difficulty in model formulation. The more realistic the assumptions applied to the problem, the more difficult it will be to formulate a model. As a management scientist, you must resolve this problem with careful judgment. On the one hand, a model should be as simple as possible in order that it be *tractable*, or usable, in obtaining answers to questions. On the other hand, a model should incorporate the *essential* realistic assumptions drawn from the problem definition. Typically, the greater the degree of realism incorporated into a model, the less tractable the model will be. (There are, of course, exceptions to this generality.)

The main *components* of a model are the following:

A. Decision Variables. What variables are under the control of management, the decision maker? For example, in a bank service system, management may be able through employment policy to determine the number of tellers available to serve customers. The number of tellers would be a decision variable for a problem in which improving the customer service level is a stated goal. Thus in formulating a model, the decision variables must be clearly defined.

B. Objective. What is the stated objective or objectives of management? The goal must be clearly identified as part of the model formulation. Is it to maximize monthly profits, to provide satisfactory customer service, to minimize costs, to maintain employee satisfaction? Are there multiple or conflicting goals? If so, can they be reduced to a single goal? If not, is a special modeling technique, such as goal programming (Chapter 13), appropriate?

C. Constraints. What practical considerations constrain, or limit, the decision maker's choices in achieving the stated objective? There may be resource constraints, such as a finite availability of people, financing, or productive capacity. Or there may be certain minimum requirements that must be met. For example, in designing a low-cost feed mix, it may be stated that the mix must meet minimum nutritional requirements, which will add to the cost.

3. VALIDATION. Does the model accurately represent the real problem situation? The process of determining whether the model is an accurate representation is called **validation.** At this stage you may need to collect data and test the model. If the model does not appear to give reasonable results, you may have to return to step 2 above, model formulation; the assumptions and parameters may require revision.

4. IMPLEMENTATION. After validation, you implement the model, which then becomes a component of the managerial decision-making process. Model implementation consists of the following steps:

A. "Sell" the Model. You must present the model to management and attempt to gain acceptance of it. Again, human factors play an overriding role here. In order to ensure acceptance of the model, you should maintain management involvement and input throughout the modeling process. *Primary focus should be placed on what interests and concerns management.* Effective communication between you and management is extremely important.

B. Use of the Model. The mathematical operation, or use, of the model can be described as follows: A model is used systematically to evaluate alternative solutions to the problem. Alternative solutions are generated by varying the values of the decision variables. Solutions that satisfy the constraints of the problem are then evaluated according to the extent to which they meet the stated objective. The best solution is then selected.

This solution does not automatically or necessarily become the solution to management's problem. It becomes an *input* to the decision-making process.

C. Decision Making. Management now uses the output of the model as an input to its decision-making process, along with other relevant inputs *selected by management*. In a nonquantitative judgmental process, management then makes a decision.

It is important that you as a management scientist maintain your involvement and interest during the implementation phase. Successful application of management science techniques depends critically upon following the decision-making process through this implementation phase and maintaining effective interpersonal communications throughout. You may be required by management to conduct a **sensitivity analysis,** systematically observing the response of model output to specified variations of model parameters. For example, management may wish to observe the effects on profits if the manufacturing capacity of one of the firm's facilities is increased 10 percent. You should be prepared to use the model to provide an answer to such management questions.

Furthermore, the implementation phase should be considered to extend beyond the immediate problem requirements into the future, when conditions may change. Ideally, *flexibility should be built into the management scientist's model*. The model should be adaptable and applicable to conditions as assumptions change dynamically over time. In a sense we are saying that an ideal model essentially should *have the capacity to plan for change*. To date, management science models have generally not posessed this capacity, although recently such a feature has received attention as a desirable, if not a necessary, requirement. (See Figure 1.2.)

5. AN OUTLINE OF THE TEXT WITH DESCRIPTION OF TOPICS

In this text we will use the term **algorithm** to mean a step-by-step, well-defined procedure for finding an optimal solution to a problem. You will find examples of algorithms in chapters 5–6, 7, 9–10, 12, 14, 17, and 20.

The models presented in this text can be classified as being either deterministic or stochastic. A **deterministic model** is one in which the parameters of the model are assumed to be constant. A **stochastic** (or **probabilistic**) **model** is one in which some or all of the parameters are random variables subject to chance events. Figure 1.3 classifies the models of this text according to this scheme.

Section One: Mathematical Programming

CHAPTERS 2 AND 3—LINEAR PROGRAMMING. Linear programming is a method of determining the most efficient use of limited resources in maximizing some measure of benefit. For example, a firm manufactures two products, each of which requires different amounts of machine- and labor-hours as well as raw

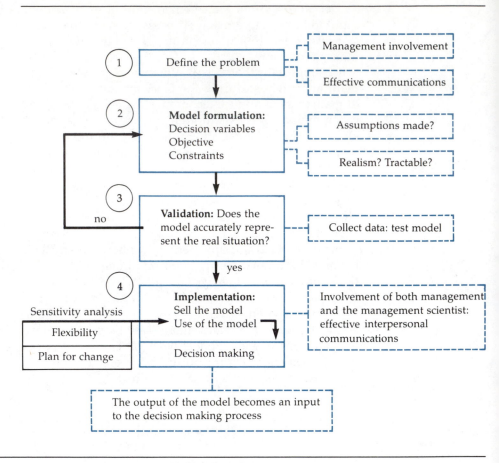

FIGURE 1.2   *The decision-making process in management science.*

materials. Each product is associated with a profit. Assuming available machine-hours, labor-hours, and raw materials are limited, what quantities of each of the two products should be produced in order to maximize profits? In Chapter 2 graphical methods are presented for solving such problems. Several applications are also discussed in detail. In Chapter 3 an algebraic method for solving such problems (called the simplex method) is presented.

CHAPTER 4—THE TRANSPORTATION PROBLEM. This chapter presents a method for determining the most profitable distribution pattern for transporting products from factories to markets.

CHAPTER 5—THE ASSIGNMENT PROBLEM. A method is presented for determining the best way to assign n objects to n other objects, such as worker-to-job assignments or vendor selection for product purchases.

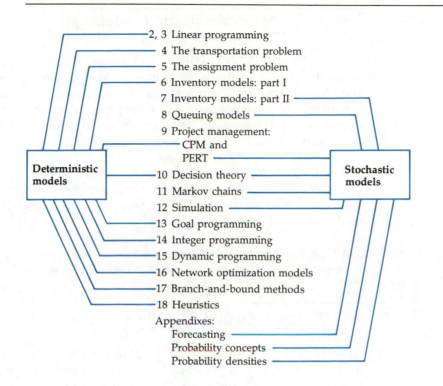

FIGURE 1.3   *A classification of models of this text.*

Section Two: Operations Models

CHAPTERS 6 AND 7—INVENTORY MODELS. Well-known management science models are given for determining the minimum-cost inventory-ordering policy for a firm.

CHAPTER 8—QUEUING MODELS. Various interesting models are presented for studying the basic phenomenon of customers lining up and waiting to be served by a service facility.

CHAPTER 9—PROJECT MANAGEMENT: CPM AND PERT. Methods are discussed for the systematic management of large projects involving several interrelated activities.

APPENDIX TO SECTION TWO—TIME-SERIES FORECASTING. Basic, classical models are discussed for forecasting the level of some variable over time, such as sales or college enrollments.

Section Three: Probabilistic Models

CHAPTER 10—DECISION THEORY. Models are presented for making decisions when the payoff to the decision maker depends on (1) the decision made and (2) an event that occurs *after* the decision is made. Deciding whether or not to drill for oil is an example of a decision theory problem. If the decision is made to drill, the payoff depends on whether or not oil is found and in what quantities.

CHAPTER 11—MARKOV CHAINS. Markov chain models are useful in studying systems that follow known probabilistic changes over time. The long-run behavior of such systems can easily be analyzed using Markov chain methods.

CHAPTER 12—SIMULATION. Simulation is a technique for studying complex systems that are subject to chance and change over time.

Section Four: Advanced Topics

CHAPTER 13—GOAL PROGRAMMING. Models similar to the linear programs of chapters 2 and 3 are presented. Linear programming applies only to problems having a single objective. Goal programming is applicable to problems that have multiple, even conflicting, objectives.

CHAPTER 14—INTEGER PROGRAMMING. An integer program is simply a linear program in which the values of the decision variables must be whole numbers (integers).

CHAPTER 15—DYNAMIC PROGRAMMING. Dynamic programming is a method of solving problems that lend themselves to a special stage-by-stage series of subproblem solutions.

CHAPTER 16—NETWORK OPTIMIZATION MODELS. Models are presented that provide a systematic framework for determining shortest travel routes, minimum-cost communications systems, and maximum use of distribution systems.

CHAPTER 17—BRANCH AND BOUND METHODS. Specialized solution methods for solving the assignment problem (Chapter 5) and integer programs (Chapter 14) are discussed.

CHAPTER 18—HEURISTICS IN MANAGEMENT SCIENCE. Problems in transportation analysis and inventory theory are solved using heuristic methods. A heuristic method is a solution procedure that is easy to use and that gives good *approximate* solutions, not necessarily *optimal* solutions.

I

MATHEMATICAL
PROGRAMMING

2

LINEAR PROGRAMMING:
FORMULATION AND GRAPHICAL METHOD

CONTENTS

1. INTRODUCTION

Linear programming (LP) is a mathematical method for solving a large class of special problems. Typically it applies to problems in which one is attempting either to maximize benefits while using limited resources or to minimize cost while meeting certain requirements.

The list of useful applications to which linear programming applies is both large and impressive. Some examples of these applications are presented below.

PRODUCT MIX PROBLEMS. How many units of each product should a firm manufacture to maximize profits while observing certain marketing and production constraints or limitations?

THE DIET PROBLEM. From what sources should nutrients be extracted to make a food product at minimum cost while observing certain minimum nutritional requirements?

13

BLENDING PROBLEMS. Suppose a firm has a given group of substances that it can blend together to make a new substance. What quantities of each existing substance should we use in order to make the new substance at minimum cost and yet ensure that it has certain desirable properties? This class of problems includes the diet problem but also includes more general blending problems such as the manufacture of metal alloys.

ADVERTISING/PROMOTION PLANNING. How much money should be spent in various advertising media to promote a product with maximum effectiveness while observing certain market goals, budget limitations, and limits placed on the use of each medium?

INVESTMENT PLANNING. How much money should be placed in each of several investment alternatives in order to maximize yearly return while observing constraints on the amount of investment funds available and restrictions on each investment alternative?

PRODUCTION/INVENTORY PLANNING. How much product should a firm plan to manufacture in each of several upcoming months in order to meet forecasted demand while minimizing costs of carrying inventory, hiring, firing, overtime wages, and subcontracting?

OPTIMAL CARGO SHIPMENT. How many units of each of several products should a firm ship in a limited-capacity carrier in order to maximize profit while satisfying certain demand constraints and physical capacity constraints? The carrier might be a semitrailer truck, a train boxcar, or an air-cargo plane. The limited physical capacity of the carrier might be expressed in terms of a limit on the weight or volume of product the carrier is designed to transport.

The preceding examples of applications for LP modeling certainly do not constitute a complete list of useful applications. Recently, linear programming has been applied to problems in wastewater management, plant location, school busing, oil refining, factory assembly-line balancing, and trim loss minimization (e.g., when several patterns must be cut out of a rolled sheet of material such as steel). In Section 7 of this chapter we shall state and formulate the above applications more precisely as linear programs.

The following example will be used throughout this chapter and the next as a model to demonstrate linear programming concepts and solution methods.

EXAMPLE 2.1. *Sue's Product Mix Problem.* Sue's Crackpot Pottery Company is a one-person operation (headed by Sue) set up to manufacture small items of handcrafted pottery. Sue has designed two products, a turned plant pot and a free-sculpted ashtray. The plant pot is turned on a pottery wheel, which she rents from a local co-op, and the ashtray must be made entirely by hand. Sue estimates that in the upcoming week, the pottery wheel will be available a maximum of 30 machine-hours, and the time she will have to spend working in her business is limited to 50 labor-hours. It takes her 1-1/4 hours to make a plant pot and 2 hours to make an ashtray. Her profit on each plant pot is $5, and her profit on each ashtray is $12. On the basis of past demand, Sue projects sales of ashtrays to be a *maximum* of 15, while sales of pots are not restricted. Her problem is to determine how many units of each product she should make in the upcoming week.   ▲

2. LP FORMULATION AND ASSUMPTIONS

In this section we shall formulate Sue's product mix problem (Example 2.1) as a linear program and discuss the details of the formulation. The basic concepts introduced here are important for a general understanding of LP problem formulation.

APPLICATIONS

The following applications appear in this chapter in text, examples, or problems:

Advertising/promotion planning
  Media mix

Blending
  Metal-alloy design

Cargo shipment/loading applications

Facilities expansion

Government regulations—analyzing the effect of safety regulations on product mix

Investment planning
  Financial mix
  Portfolio selection

Product distribution

Product mix problems
  A woodworker
  A potter
  Manufacturer of scaffolds
  A bakery
  Kitchenware manufacturer
  A toy manufacturer
  A baby-care products manufacturer

Production/inventory planning
  A multiperiod problem with subcontracting options

Strategic military-effectiveness analysis

Formulating Sue's Product Mix Problem

At this point, reread the verbal description of Sue's situation as given in Example 2.1. Can you state exactly what Sue's problem is? What is she attempting to do or to decide? Is she trying to minimize cost, maximize profit or revenue, or does she have some other goal in mind? Are there any factors that restrict her decision-making options? Developing an ability to answer these questions in a precise manner is perhaps more an art than a science and is the essence of successful LP formulation. We answer these questions in the following manner: Sue must determine (1) how many pots and how many ashtrays to make (decision variables) in order to (2) *maximize* her weekly profit (objective function) (3) *subject to* the following restrictions (constraints):

a. a machine-hour limit on the pottery wheel (30 hours/week),
b. a labor-hour constraint (50 hours/week),
c. a sales (or marketing) constraint on ashtrays (sales of ashtrays will be between 0 and 15).

You will note that we have identified three components in Sue's problem. Each of these components will in turn correspond directly to a component of a linear program that will solve the problem. The three components are referred to as (1) the **decision variables,** (2) the **objective function,** and (3) the **constraints** of the linear program.

The Decision Variables

The decision variables in a given problem correspond to the decisions that must be made in order to specify a solution to the problem. In Sue's case, she must specify two things: how many pots to make and how many ashtrays to make. The first decision variable, denoted x_1, is the number of pots to make; the second decision variable, denoted x_2, is the number of ashtrays to make.

There is nothing special about our choice of notation. You would be just as correct to denote the two decision variables by any two symbols such as P and A, or x_P and x_A, or N_1 and N_2.

The Objective Function

The objective function in a given problem corresponds to the goal of the decision maker who is solving the problem. The objective function is expressed mathematically in terms of the decision variables. For Sue's problem the objective is to maximize profit for the week. The unit profit per pot is $5, and the unit profit per ashtray is $12. If Sue makes x_1 pots and x_2 ashtrays, her profit per week is $5x_1$ from pots plus $12x_2$ from ashtrays. If we denote the objective function by Z, we have $Z = 5x_1 + 12x_2$ ($ profit/week).

The Constraints

The constraints of a given problem are mathematical expressions of the limitations imposed on the possible choices of values for the decision variables. Each constraint will be expressed in terms of some or all of the decision variables. In Sue's problem there are three constraints. First, the total number of machine-hours available on the pottery wheel is 30, and it takes 1-1/4 hours (5/4 hours) to make each pot. It would take Sue $[(5/4) \times x_1]$ hours to make x_1 pots, and this amount cannot exceed the total machine-hours available. That is, the first constraint can be expressed mathematically in terms of the decision variables as $[(5/4) \times x_1] \leq 30$.

Second, there is a constraint on total number of labor-hours Sue has available—namely, 50 hours. If Sue decides to make x_1 pots and x_2 ashtrays, it will require $(5/4)x_1$ plus $2x_2$ hours of her time. We can now express the second constraint as $(5/4)x_1 + 2x_2 \leq 50$.

Third, since Sue feels that she could not sell more than 15 ashtrays, we must impose another constraint, which we can express as $x_2 \leq 15$.

In addition to the above three constraints, we impose two more. Since Sue would not make a negative quantity of product, to be precise we must also require that x_1 and x_2 be nonnegative, that is, greater than or equal to zero units each ($x_1 \geq 0$ and $x_2 \geq 0$). These last two constraints are referred to as **nonnegativity constraints.**

A Mathematical Statement of the LP

The linear program formulated for Sue's problem is stated mathematically as follows.

Definition of the decision variables:
Let x_1 = number of pots to make this week
x_2 = number of ashtrays to make this week
Z = dollars of profit per week
LP formulation
Maximize $Z = 5x_1 + 12x_2$ ($ profit/week)

Subject to:

(1) $\quad \dfrac{5}{4}x_1 \qquad\qquad \le 30 \quad$ (machine-hours)

(2) $\quad \dfrac{5}{4}x_1 + 2x_2 \le 50 \quad$ (labor-hours)

(3) $\qquad\qquad\quad x_2 \le 15 \quad$ (sales)

(4) $\qquad x_1 \qquad\quad \ge 0$
(5) $\qquad\qquad\quad x_2 \ge 0$ $\Big\}$ (nonnegativity)

The problem is to choose values of x_1 and x_2 that will maximize Z, subject to satisfying the constraints.

From Sue's problem we can make certain observations that are common to many practical situations. For example, suppose for a moment that there were *no* constraints in Sue's problem. Then the solution would be simple: Sue would make an infinite quantity of pots and ashtrays, and her profit would be infinite. As we know, such a solution is not realistic because Sue *would not have the time* to make an infinite number of items. But this is precisely what constraint (2) says—namely, that Sue's time is limited to 50 labor-hours.

From a conceptual viewpoint we see that Sue is faced with the problem of maximizing profits (a measure of benefit) while using a limited amount of resources (machine-hours, labor-hours, and potential sales prospects).

Try to analyze each linear program you study in this chapter and the next by using such a conceptual perspective. In Table 2.1 we identify the decision variables, the objective function, and the constraints for each of the examples listed in Section 1 of this chapter. These problems will be formulated more precisely in Section 7.

Assumptions Underlying a Linear Program

Examine the linear program formulated for Sue's problem. You will notice that the decision variables appear in the objective function and the constraints in a special form. A decision variable may be multiplied by a constant number and may be combined with other decision variables only in an **additive** manner; that is, in a linear program, the following kinds of expressions are *not* permitted: x_1^2, $x_1 \cdot x_2$, x_1/x_2, $\log x_1$, e^{x_1}, and so forth. Only expressions of the form $c_1 \cdot x_1$ and $c_1 \cdot x_1 + c_2 \cdot x_2$, where c_1 and c_2 are given numbers, are permitted. You will observe that these rules are satisfied in the LP for Sue's problem. Technically, we say that the decision variables must appear *only* in **linear relationships** in a linear program. In general, a linear relationship involving the n decision variables $x_1, x_2, \ldots, x_n$ is an expression of the form $c_1x_1 + c_2x_2 + \cdots + c_nx_n$, where $c_1, c_2, \ldots, c_n$ are n given numbers. Note that negative numbers are not excluded from this definition. For example, $2x_1 - 3x_2 + x_3$ is a linear expression in three decision variables (x_1, x_2, and

TABLE 2.1   *Identifying the Components of an LP*

Example	Decision Variables	Objective Function	Constraints
Product mix problems	The number of units of each product to make	To maximize profit	Subject to limits on machine hours, labor hours, and sales
Diet problem	The quantity of each food source to use to make a new food product	To minimize the cost of the new food product	Subject to meeting certain nutritional requirements
Blending problems	The amount of each existing substance to mix into the blend to make a new substance	To minimize the cost of the new substance	Subject to the condition that the new product must possess certain desirable properties
Advertising/ promotion planning	The levels of use of each of several advertising/ promotion alternatives	To maximize advertising effectiveness	Subject to a budget limitation, to goals of reaching certain target markets, and to limits placed on the use of media by management
Investment planning	How much money to invest in each investment alternative	To maximize return on investment	Subject to a budget constraint and to limits on the amount of money to be tied up in each investment alternative
Production/ inventory planning	How much product to produce each period	To minimize total inventory, production, and procurement costs	Subject to meeting customer demand and other limitations placed on the production and inventory system
Optimal cargo shipment	How many units of each product to ship in the carrier	To maximize profit from sales of the products shipped	Subject to meeting certain sales requirements and certain physical limitations on storage/weight placed on the carrier

x_3), where $c_1 = 2$, $c_2 = -3$, and $c_3 = 1$. The expression could also be written as $2x_1 + (-3)x_2 + x_3$.

Implications of Linearity

In Sue's problem we formulated the objective function as $Z = 5x_1 + 12x_2$, a linear expression in x_1 and x_2. What does linearity mean in terms of the objective Z? Suppose we decide to make 3 pots, so $x_1 = 3$. The profit *from pots* is then $5x_1 = 5(3) = \$15$. Now suppose $x_1 = 4$ pots. Then the profit from pots is $5(4) = \$20$—that is, profit has increased by \$5. In general, we see that the profit from pots is *linear* in x_1 or, to put it another way, profit from pots increases at the constant rate of \$5 per pot for each pot sold. This means that there are no economies of scale that would cut production costs and, correspondingly, increase profits above \$5 per pot.

This may not be entirely accurate in a given problem. For example, Sue may be able to get quantity discounts on materials purchased for larger output levels of pots. Also, as she prepares a production run on pots, she will certainly increase her efficiency and decrease scrap from mistakes after some point. All of these factors would cut costs and increase the unit profit on each pot produced. However, such economies of scale are not accounted for in the LP model for this problem. In Sue's problem, we would argue that these cost differentials are not significant and that profit is linear, or *very close* to linear.

Note also that to calculate total profit, we must add the profit from pots ($5x_1$) to that from ashtrays ($12x_2$) in order to arrive at total profit—$5x_1 + 12x_2$. Thus we are assuming that there are *no interactions* between the sales of the two products; that is, sales of pots do not affect sales of ashtrays one way or the other.

In problems where these linearity assumptions are not accurate approximations of the real situation, it may not be possible to formulate a linear program. In such cases, so-called *nonlinear* programming methods must be employed to solve the problem.

Divisibility

In the mathematical statement of the LP for Sue's product mix problem, there is nothing to prevent the decision variables x_1 and x_2 from having **noninteger values.** (A noninteger value is a number that includes a fractional or decimal part; for example, 1, −2, 0, 10, and 120 are **integers** and 1.2, −2.633, 0.5, and 10.7 are noninteger values.) In fact, it is entirely possible for the solution to the LP to be noninteger valued. When the solution to the LP involves large values of the decision variables, one remedy to this problem is to round the decision variables to the nearest integer. In smaller problems where rounding may not produce accurate results, another solution method called **integer programming** is employed (see Chapter 14).

For Sue's LP we will see that the optimal solution has both x_1 and x_2 as integers. This will happen purely by coincidence.

Summary of Steps in Formulating a Linear Program

The sequence of steps you should follow in formulating a problem as a linear program is listed below.

STEP 1. Read the verbal statement of the problem. Identify the essential objective—that is, what is the decision maker trying to determine and what factors limit his or her choice of decisions and alternatives.

STEP 2. From your initial analysis in step 1, precisely define the *decision variables*. The decision variables should be defined in such a way that specifying *the best combination of them would solve the decision maker's problem*. Include the appropriate units of measurement in your definitions, for example, "units of pots," "shares of stock A," "pounds of corn," and "number of radio commercials."

STEP 3. From your analysis of the decision maker's objective, state precisely *in words* what the objective function is. For example, "to maximize total profit per week," "to maximize total dividend return per year," "to minimize the cost per pound of animal feed," and "to maximize total number of person-exposures to our product per month through advertising."

Now write your stated objective as a linear relationship of the decision variables defined in step 2. This becomes the *objective function* of the LP.

STEP 4. From step 1 you determined what resources and other factors limit the choice of permissible values of the decision variables. List these restrictions in writing. For each restriction, use the decision variables to write a corresponding linear expression and constraint. For example, in Sue's problem we went through this reasoning to write the resource limit on machine-hours as $(5/4)x_1 \le 30$. In that example, all the constraints of the problem were of the form "$\le$" (except the two nonnegativity constraints). In the problems you will encounter in this chapter and the next, you will also find the need to employ "$\ge$" constraints as well as "$=$" constraints.

The steps involved in successful LP formulation are summarized as follows: (1) write an accurate description of the problem; (2) define the decision variables; (3) express the objective function in terms of the decision variables (using linear expressions); then (4) express the constraints in terms of the decision variables (using linear expressions).

What Can Go Wrong?

Many things in general! For our purposes you should make it a habit to question at least the following points:

In step 1, is enough information given? Can all the costs, profits, and other numbers be determined or estimated?

In steps 2, 3, and 4, it is often the case that your choice of decision variables (step 2) will not be the best choice for expressing the objective function and/or constraints simply; that is, another choice of decision variables might lead to an easier LP formulation. The point to be made is that steps 2, 3, and 4 often interact with each other to arrive at the final formulation; therefore, your initial choice of decision variables in step 2 oftentimes will not work at all when you reach steps 3 and 4.

In step 2, be *aware* of the divisibility assumption.

In steps 3 and 4, are the assumptions implicit in linearity *reasonable*? They may not be *exactly* satisfied in your formulation, but they should be reasonably approximated.

EXAMPLE 2.2. *Nancy and Bob's Machine Shop.* Nancy and Bob run a small machine shop operation in which they manufacture two products, using two machines. Each product must be processed first through machine *A* and then machine *B*. Product 1 requires 2 hours/unit on machine *A* and 1-1/2 hours/unit on machine *B*. Product 2 requires 1 hour/unit and 1.8 hours/unit on machines *A* and *B*, respectively. Per-unit profit on products 1 and 2 is $25 and $40, respectively. The capacity of machine *A* is 30 hours/week, and machine *B* is available for 45 hours/week. Analyze the situation of Nancy and Bob's operation.

Solution. Following the steps outlined above we briefly record our analysis as follows:

STEP 1. Nancy and Bob are attempting to maximize weekly profits from their business. They must determine the number of units of products 1 and 2 to produce. Their decisions are limited by a stated machine-hour capacity.

STEPS 2, 3, AND 4. Definition of the decision variables:

Let x_1 = number of units of product 1 to make per week
    x_2 = number of units of product 2 to make per week
LP formulation:
Maximize $Z = 25x_1 + 40x_2$ ($ profit/week)
Subject to:
(1) $2x_1 + x_2 \leq 30$ (capacity of machine *A*, hours/week)

(2) $\dfrac{3}{2}x_1 + 1.8x_2 \leq 45$ (capacity of machine B, hours/week)

(3) $x_1 \geq 0$
(4) $ x_2 \geq 0$ $\quad$ (nonnegativity)

Note how constraint (1), for example, is derived: Each unit of product 1 requires 2 hours on machine A; thus if we decide to make x_1 units of product 1, we would use $2x_1$ hours of machine A time. Each unit of product 2 requires 1 hour on machine A, so producing x_2 units of product 2 would use $1x_2 = x_2$ hours of machine A time. Therefore, if we make x_1 units of product 1 and x_2 units of product 2, the total time required on machine A is $2x_1 + x_2$, and since the weekly capacity of machine A is 30 hours, we must require that $2x_1 + x_2 \leq 30$. Similarly, you should reason through constraint (2). In Problem 2 of Section 3 you will be asked to solve the above LP. Do you recognize this problem as a product mix problem?   ▲

Problems

1. Modify the LP of Example 2.2 (Nancy and Bob's machine shop) to include the following additional information:
   a. Because of a raw material shortage this week, production of product 2 cannot exceed 21 units. Formulate the LP to account for this.
   b. In the same week Nancy and Bob have received an order for five units of product 2 and are committed to producing at least this amount. Formulate the LP to account for this *in addition to* the information in part (a) above.
2. The Woodbutcher is a one-man operation, owned and run by Roberto Gomez, that specializes in large-volume production of high-quality basic wood products. Currently Gomez makes a three-by-five-foot, three-shelf bookcase and a traditional-style writing desk. Gomez uses three main heavy tools: a table saw, a router, and a belt sander. A bookcase requires 1 hour on the table saw, 1-1/4 hours on the router, and 15 minutes on the belt sander. A desk takes 2 hours on the table saw, 45 minutes on the router, and 6 minutes on the belt sander. Profit on a bookcase is $18, and profit on a desk is $30. Gomez works 10 hours per day, Monday through Friday, cutting, operating the router, and sanding. He spends 12 hours on Saturday on final assembly and finishing. Gomez has found it convenient to organize the work into four operations: (1) Monday, Tuesday, and Wednesday are spent entirely with the table saw, cutting out all the pieces for both products for the week's output; (2) all of Thursday and half of Friday (15 hours) are spent using the router; (3) the rest of Friday is spent running the belt sander; and (4) final assembly and finishing is done on Saturday. At this point it takes Gomez 30 minutes to assemble a bookcase and 1 hour to assemble and finish a desk.
   Formulate Gomez's problem as a linear program.

3. GRAPHICAL LP SOLUTION

In this section we shall present a graphical method for solving linear programs. This method will work only if the number of decision variables does not exceed two. Example 2.1 (Sue's product mix problem) will be used to demonstrate the graphical method. In Chapter 3 we shall explain the *simplex solution* method for linear programs, which will work on any size LP. At that time Sue's problem will again be used to demonstrate how the simplex method works. Furthermore, we shall refer back to the graphical method as the simplex method is explained. Thus it is important that you study the present chapter carefully.

The graphical method is organized into the three steps listed below.

The Graphical Method: Maximization Problems

STEP 1. Graphing the constraints (identifying the feasible solution space).

STEP 2. Graphing objective function values.

STEP 3. Finding the optimal solution; that is, finding the values of the decision variables that give the best value of the objective function.

For ease of reference here is Sue's LP problem again:

Find x_1 and x_2 (number of pots and ashtrays) to
Maximize $Z = 5x_1 + 12x_2$ ($ profit/week)

Subject to:

(1) $\dfrac{5}{4}x_1 \leq 30$ (machine-hours)

(2) $\dfrac{5}{4}x_1 + 2x_2 \leq 50$ (labor-hours)

(3) $x_2 \leq 15$ (sales)

(4) $x_1 \qquad \geq 0$
(5) $\qquad x_2 \geq 0$ (nonnegativity)

Step 1—Graphing the Constraints

The main purpose of step 1 is to represent graphically the set of values (x_1, x_2) that satisfy *all* the constraints. This set is called the **feasible solution space.** It gives all combinations of x_1 and x_2 that are feasible in terms of meeting all the constraints.

For example, let $x_1 = 4$ and $x_2 = 6$ (4 pots and 6 ashtrays). Such a combination is feasible; that is, it will be contained in the feasible solution space.

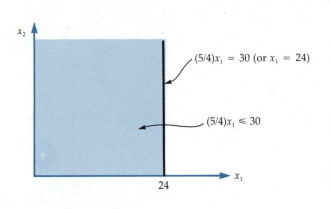

x_2

$(5/4)x_1 = 30$ (or $x_1 = 24$)

$(5/4)x_1 \leq 30$

x_1

24

FIGURE 2.1(a) $(5/4)x_1 \leq 30$.

To see this, simply test each of the five constraints to see that each constraint is *satisfied*. Constraint (1) becomes $(5/4)x_1 = (5/4)(4) = 5 \leq 30$, which is satisfied; constraint (2) becomes $(5/4)(4) + 2(6) = 5 + 12 = 17 \leq 50$; constraint (3) becomes $x_2 = 6 \leq 15$, which is also satisfied. Constraints (4) and (5) are obviously satisfied, since $4 \geq 0$ and $6 \geq 0$.

On the other hand, is it feasible to make 20 pots and 15 ashtrays? The answer is "no." The reasoning is as follows: First, constraint (1) becomes $(5/4)(20) = 25 \leq 30$, so the available machine-hours are sufficient. Try constraint (3): $x_2 = 15 \leq 15$ clearly holds; in fact, constraint (3) becomes an equality. Constraints (4) and (5) are obviously satisfied. Now look at constraint (2). The number of labor-hours required to make 20 pots and 15 ashtrays is $(5/4)(20) + 2(15) = 25 + 30 = 55$, which is *not* less than or equal to 50 (the total Sue has available). Thus constraint (2) is not satisfied, and therefore the combination $(x_1 = 20, x_2 = 15)$ is not in the feasible solution space.

We shall now show how to construct a graph of the feasible solution space.

CONSTRAINT (1). To graph $(5/4)x_1 \leq 30$, first graph the equality $(5/4)x_1 = 30$, which is equivalent to $x_1 = 30(4/5) = 24$. This is a line parallel to the x_2 axis crossing the x_1 axis at 24, as shown in Fig. 2.1(a). Every point on this vertical line satisfies the equation $x_1 = 24$. To graph the inequality $(5/4)x_1 \leq 30$, simply shade the region to the left of the vertical line, including the vertical line. This is shown in Fig. 2.1(a). Every point in this shaded region has an x_1 coordinate that satisfies the inequality $(5/4)x_1 \leq 30$.

CONSTRAINT (2). To graph $(5/4)x_1 + 2x_2 \leq 50$, first graph the line corresponding to the equality $(5/4)x_1 + 2x_2 = 50$. An easy way to do this is to find the two points at which the line crosses the axes. To find the point at which the line crosses the x_1 axis, set $x_2 = 0$. Then solve for x_1 as follows:

$$\frac{5}{4}x_1 + 2(0) = 50$$

$$\frac{5}{4}x_1 = 50$$

$$x_1 = 40$$

To find the x_2 intercept, set $x_1 = 0$ and solve for x_2 as follows:

$$\frac{5}{4}(0) + 2x_2 = 50$$

$$2x_2 = 50$$

$$x_2 = 25$$

Connect the two intercepts by drawing a straight line from one to the other, as shown in Fig. 2.1(b). Every point on this line satisfies the equation $(5/4)x_1 + 2x_2 = 50$. For example, for $x_1 = 20$ and $x_2 = 12.5$, we have the point $(20, 12.5)$, which is on the line and also satisfies the equation

$$\frac{5}{4}(20) + 2(12.5) = 25 + 25 = 50$$

To graph the inequality $(5/4)x_1 + 2x_2 \leq 50$, simply shade the region lying on and under the line, as shown in Fig. 2.1(b). You should convince yourself that this region does contain all points (x_1, x_2) that satisfy constraint (2). Try various points to see that this is true. We already know that points

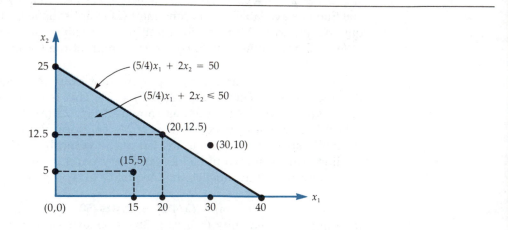

FIGURE 2.1(b) $(5/4)x_1 + 2x_2 \leq 50$.

lying *on* the line satisfy the constraint with equality. Points under the line will satisfy the constraint with strict inequality. For example, try the point (15, 5). We have

$$\frac{5}{4}(15) + 2(5) = 28.75 < 50$$

and we do see in Fig. 2.1(b) that (15, 5) is contained in the region. Try (30, 10), which does not fall in the region

$$\frac{5}{4}(30) + 2(10) = 57.5 \nleq 50$$

(The symbol $\nleq$ is read "*not* less than or equal to.")

CONSTRAINT (3). Graphing $x_2 \leq 15$ is similar to graphing constraint (1). This region consists of the horizontal line $x_2 = 15$, together with all points under the line, as shown in Fig. 2.1(c).

CONSTRAINTS (4) AND (5). These constraints specify that only the first quadrant is to be considered, that is, only the quadrant bounded by the positive x_1 axis and the positive x_2 axis.

THE FEASIBLE-SOLUTION SPACE. The feasible-solution space consists of the points that satisfy *all* five constraints. One way to obtain this region is to put each of the regions shown in Figs. 2.1(a)–2.1(c) on the same graph and then find the area that is contained in each of the three shaded regions (the intersection of the three regions).

The result of such a procedure is shown in Fig. 2.2. In this figure we have shown each *constraint line* and drawn an arrow to indicate the direction of

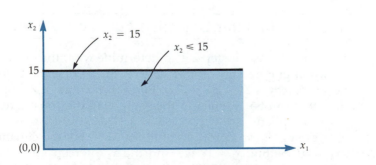

FIGURE 2.1(c) $x_2 \leq 15$.

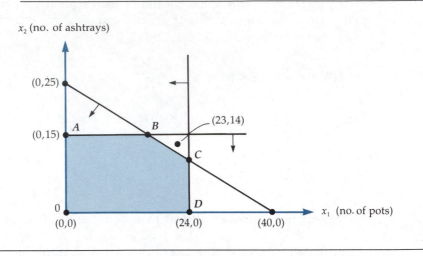

x_2 (no. of ashtrays)

(0,25)

(0,15) A B (23,14)

C

0
(0,0)   (24,0)   (40,0) x_1 (no. of pots)

D

FIGURE 2.2   *The feasible-solution space for Sue's product mix.*

shading for the given constraint. The feasible-solution space is the shaded region on, and bounded by, *OABCD*. The points in this region satisfy each of the five constraints. A point *not* in the region fails to satisfy one or more of the five constraints. Again, convince yourself of the truth of this statement.

For example, the point (23, 14) satisfies constraints (1), (3), (4), and (5) but fails to satisfy (2) and, therefore, is excluded from the feasible-solution space. In other terms, we can say that (23, 14)—that is, $x_1 = 23$ pots and $x_2 = 14$ ashtrays—is a feasible product mix if we have to satisfy only the machine-hours limit and the sales limit. However, there are not enough labor-hours available to produce this product mix. (Check to see that it would take 56.75 hours to make 23 pots and 14 ashtrays.)

Step 2—Graphing Objective Function Values

The main purpose of step 2 is to determine what the objective function looks like when graphed in the x_1–x_2 plane. Recall that the objective function for Sue's problem is $Z = 5x_1 + 12x_2$. For a *fixed* value of Z, this equation defines a line that can be graphed in the same way the constraint line of constraint (2) was graphed.

For example, for a profit level of $60, Z = 60, the equation becomes $5x_1 + 12x_2 = 60$. Setting $x_1 = 0$, we find the x_2 intercept to be 5, and setting $x_2 = 0$, the x_1 intercept is 12. This line is shown in Fig. 2.3. All (x_1, x_2) combinations on this line will yield a profit of $60. For example, (5, 35/12) falls on the line and yields a $60 profit, since 5(5) + 12(35/12) = 25 + 35 = 60.

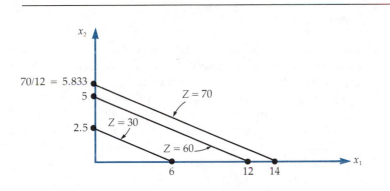

FIGURE 2.3

The lines Z = 5x₁ + 12x₂.

As another example, to find all points that yield a profit of $30, set $Z = 30$ and graph the line $5x_1 + 12x_2 = 30$. This line is also shown in Fig. 2.3. The intercepts are found as usual. To find the x_1 intercept, set $x_2 = 0$ and solve for x_1:

$$5x_1 + 12(0) = 30$$

$$5x_1 = 30$$

$$x_1 = 6$$

To find the x_2 intercept, set $x_1 = 0$ and solve for x_2:

$$5(0) + 12x_2 = 30$$

$$12x_2 = 30$$

$$x_2 = 2.5$$

As a final example, for a profit of $70, set $Z = 70$ and graph the line $5x_1 + 12x_2 = 70$ (see Fig. 2.3).

Note that the general equation $Z = 5x_1 + 12x_2$ defines a *family of lines*. Different values of Z give different lines in this family. However, each line of the family has the same *slope* (in this case the common slope is $-5/12$). This means that each line in the family is *parallel* to every other line of the family.

Thus from the results of step 2 you should now know:

1. Different profit levels (values of Z) correspond to different lines.
2. These lines are all parallel to each other.
3. The greater the value of Z, the farther the line is away from the origin $(0, 0)$, as shown in Fig. 2.3.

Step 3—Finding the Optimal Solution

Essentially, step 3 combines the results of steps 1 and 2. Graphically, we now combine Figs. 2.2 and 2.3 to obtain Fig. 2.4. We have labeled each constraint equation in Fig. 2.4 by number.

Recall that the objective of the problem is to find the combination (x_1, x_2) that yields the maximum profit or, in other terms, the maximum value of Z. We have graphed the set of points that yields $Z = 60$ in Fig. 2.4. We know that larger profit values for Z correspond to lines parallel to the line $Z = 60$ and lying farther away from the origin $(0, 0)$.

Now place a straightedge on the line $Z = 60$ (a pencil or ruler will do). Move the straightedge in a northeasterly direction, moving the straightedge parallel to the $Z = 60$ line. Go as far as possible until you reach the outermost edge of the feasible solution space. Doing this, you can go as far as the line shown passing through point B. The (x_1, x_2) combination corresponding to point B is the *optimal solution* to the problem, and the Z value represented by the line labeled Z^* is the maximum obtainable profit.

To find the (x_1, x_2) coordinates of point B, we note that point B is the intersection of constraint lines (2) and (3), so we solve (2) and (3) simultaneously for x_1 and x_2:

(2) $\qquad \dfrac{5}{4}x_1 + 2x_2 = 50$

(3) $\qquad\qquad\quad x_2 = 15$

Put (3) into (2) to obtain:

$$\frac{5}{4}x_1 + 2(15) = 50$$

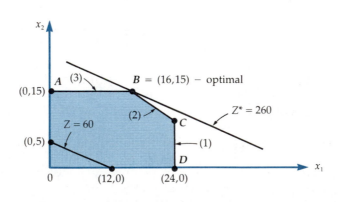

FIGURE 2.4   *Finding the optimal solution to Sue's product mix problem.*

$$\frac{5}{4}x_1 = 50 - 30 = 20$$

$$x_1 = 20\left(\frac{4}{5}\right) = 16$$

Thus the optimal values of x_1 and x_2 are 16 and 15, respectively, and are shown in Fig. 2.4 as the coordinates of point B. The optimal value of the objective function, denoted by Z^* in Fig. 2.4, is easily found by substituting $x_1 = 16$ and $x_2 = 15$ in the equation for Z:

$$Z^* = 5(16) + 12(15)$$

$$= 80 + 180$$

$$= 260$$

After performing such an analysis, it is good practice to summarize your results concisely as follows: The optimal product mix is to produce 16 pots and 15 ashtrays per week, yielding a maximum weekly profit of $260.

Comments

1. In the above problem are you convinced that $Z = \$260$ is the maximum achievable profit? If not, try to achieve a larger profit, such as $270. The graph of $5x_1 + 12x_2 = 270$ is shown in Fig. 2.5, together with the feasible solution space for the problem ($OABCD$). You may very well have graphed such a line, but can you find a point on the line $Z = 270$ that *also* lies in

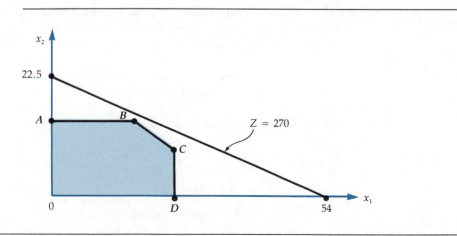

FIGURE 2.5

the feasible solution space? The answer is "no." In other words, because of the practical constraints of the problem, it is not feasible to attain a profit greater than $260 per week.
2. In practice, when you solve linear programs using the graphical method, you will develop the ability to perform steps 1, 2, and 3 on a single graph.
3. Note that in Fig. 2.4 we chose $Z = 60$ as a starting value of Z. The number 60 was selected somewhat arbitrarily, although it is a *convenient* number to pick. Recall that $Z = 5x_1 + 12x_2$. To locate the x_1 and x_2 intercepts (in order to graph a Z line), the value of Z must be divided by 5 to find the x_1 intercept and by 12 to find the x_2 intercept. By choosing $Z = 60$, these intercepts are easy to compute (60/5 and 60/12 both divide evenly), and thus the starting value of Z is easy to graph.

EXAMPLE 2.3. *Graphical LP Solution: Maximization.* A–1 Shaky Frames manufactures scaffolding for construction work. The phase of its operations prior to final assembly involves cutting and threading the steel tubing. Shaky Frames manufactures two basic models of scaffold units, a 2-meter unit using 2.5-cm. tubing and a 3-meter unit using 3.75-cm. tubing. The profits on these two units are $60 and $80, respectively.

Cutting operations are performed on machine A, and threading operations are performed on machine B. These machines have yearly capacities of 4,000 hours each—two 8-hour shifts per day, 5 days a week, 50 weeks a year (two weeks are allowed for planned maintenance).

The 2-meter scaffold unit requires 1 hour on machine A and 2 hours on machine B. The 3-meter unit requires 1-1/2 hours on machine A and 1 hour on machine B (more cutting is required, but the joints are less complex than for the 2-meter unit).

How many scaffold units of each kind should A–1 Shaky Frames manufacture per year?

Solution. (First note that this is a product mix problem.) The LP formulation of Shaky Frames's problem can be stated as follows.
Definition of the decision variables:

Let x_1 = number of 2-meter scaffold units/year
   x_2 = number of 3-meter scaffold units/year
LP formulation:
Maximize $Z = 60x_1 + 80x_2$ ($ profit/year)
Subject to:

(1) $x_1 + \dfrac{3}{2}x_2 \leq 4{,}000$ (machine-hour capacity constraint for machine A)

(2) $2x_1 + x_2 \leq 4{,}000$ (machine-hour capacity constraint for machine B)

(3) $x_1 \geq 0$
(4) $x_2 \geq 0$ (nonnegativity)

In Fig. 2.6 we have graphed each constraint *equation* as a line. Attached to each of the two constraint lines is an arrow indicating the direction of the

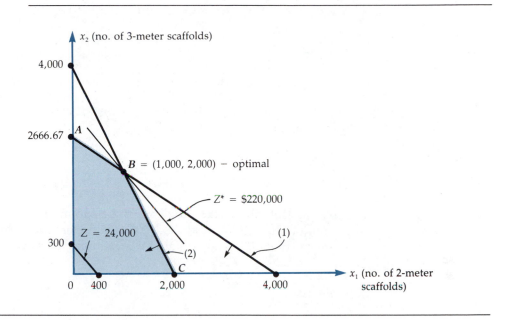

FIGURE 2.6   *A–1 Shaky Frames.*

region represented by the constraint. The resulting feasible solution space is shown as the shaded area including and bounded by *OABC*.

The line representing all points that yield a profit of $24,000—namely, $60x_1 + 80x_2 = Z = 24,000$—is also shown. (The value $Z = 24,000$ was chosen arbitrarily as a convenient figure to use.) Moving parallel to this line and outward, we find that it is possible to go as far as the line labeled Z^*.

Thus the (x_1, x_2) coordinates of point *B* correspond to the optimal levels of production of the two products. To find the coordinates of point *B*, we note that *B* is the intersection of lines (1) and (2); thus we must solve constraint equations (1) and (2) simultaneously for x_1 and x_2:

(1) $x_1 + \dfrac{3}{2}x_2 = 4{,}000$

(2) $2x_1 + x_2 = 4{,}000$

Multiply (2) by 1/2, subtract the resulting equation from (1), and solve for x_2:

$$(1) - \frac{1}{2} \times (2) \qquad x_1 + \frac{3}{2}x_2 = 4{,}000$$

$$- \left(x_1 + \frac{1}{2}x_2 = 2{,}000 \right)$$

$$\overline{\qquad\qquad x_2 = 2{,}000 \qquad}$$

Now put $x_2 = 2,000$ back into (1) and solve for x_1:

$$x_1 + \frac{3}{2}(2,000) = 4,000$$

$$x_1 = 4,000 - 3,000 = 1,000$$

To find the maximum yearly profit Z^*, substitute $x_1 = 1,000$ and $x_2 = 2,000$ into the equation for Z:

$$Z^* = 60(1,000) + 80(2,000)$$

$$= \$220,000/\text{year}$$

The optimal solution to the problem can be summarized as follows: The optimal product mix is to produce 1,000 two-meter units per year and 2,000 three-meter units per year, yielding a maximum yearly profit of $220,000. ▲

Problems

1. Solve the problem facing A–1 Shaky Frames (Example 2.3) if the profit on the 2-meter unit increases from $60 to $70. (Remember to specify the optimal x_1 and x_2 values as well as the resulting maximum value of Z.)
2. Refer to Example 2.2—Nancy and Bob's Machine Shop. Solve the LP for this product-mix problem.
3. Refer to the version of Example 2.2 given in Problem 1(b) of Section 2. Solve this product-mix problem.
4. Refer to Problem 2 of Section 2—The Woodbutcher. How many desks and bookcases should Roberto Gomez make per week? How much profit can he realize from this product mix?
5. Solve the product-mix problem of A–1 Shaky Frames (Example 2.3) if the profit on the 2-meter unit is $60 but the profit on the 3-meter unit increases to $100.

4. SOLVING MINIMIZATION PROBLEMS

The graphical method for solving minimization problems is the same as that for maximization problems except for one change in step 3. The three steps for solving LP minimization problems involving two decision variables are listed below.

Graphical Method: Minimization Problems

STEP 1. Graph the constraints (same as for maximization problems.)

STEP 2. Graph objective function values (same as for maximization problems).

STEP 3. Find the optimal solution. This step is similar to step 3 for maximization problems *except* in determining the optimal Z line (which we denoted by Z^* in Figs. 2.4 and 2.6. We first graph a convenient Z line and then move this line in a downward direction *toward* the origin (0, 0). We stop with Z^* at the last point touched in the feasible solution space.

EXAMPLE 2.4. GRAPHICAL LP SOLUTION—MINIMIZATION: THE DIET PROBLEM

In the introduction to this chapter, Section 1, and again in Table 2.1, the diet problem was briefly described. Now we give a simple version of the problem, involving just two decision variables.

Consider the problem of preparing a school-lunch menu. There are two basic foods that can be combined into an oven-baked casserole. The school dietician, Jackson, is responsible for ensuring that the students receive certain government-specified minimum nutritional requirements. The lunch casserole must contain at least 10 units of protein, at least 7 units of vitamin A, and at least 8 units of iron.

As was mentioned, Jackson will use two basic food substances to make the casserole. We will call these substances F1 and F2. Each ounce of F1 contains 2 units of protein, 2 units of vitamin A, and 1-1/3 units of iron. Each ounce of F2 contains 2 units of protein, 1 unit of vitamin A, and 2 units of iron. The cost per ounce of F1 is 3¢ and the cost per ounce of F2 is 4¢. Jackson's problem is to determine how to mix the two foods into a casserole so that each student will receive the specified nutritional requirements and yet keep the lunch cost to a minimum. Can you assist?

Solution. If you have some difficulty approaching this problem, you should review the summary of steps in formulating a linear program presented in Section 2 of this chapter.

Jackson must decide how many ounces of F1 and F2 to use *per serving* in the casserole. Thus the two decision variables are x_1 = number of ounces of F1 and x_2 = number of ounces of F2 to use per serving.

Jackson's objective is to minimize the cost of food preparation or, more specifically, to minimize the cost per serving, which in our notation would be $Z = 3x_1 + 4x_2$ (cents per serving).

However, Jackson is constrained in his efforts to minimize costs, since he must make sure that each serving meets the minimum nutritional requirements specified by the government. If he were not so constrained, the solution to his problem would be (disastrously) simple—namely, he would set $x_1 = x_2 = 0$ and have a zero cost and no school lunch at all.

To derive the constraint for protein, suppose a single serving is made up of x_1 ounces of F1 and x_2 ounces of F2. How many units of protein would the serving contain? Since each ounce of F1 would contribute 2 units of protein, the serving would contain $2x_1$ units of protein from F1. Since each ounce of $F2$ also contains 2 units of protein, the serving would contain $2x_2$ units of protein from $F2$. Since the serving must meet the minimum requirement of 10 units of protein, $2x_1 + 2x_2$ must be at least 10; that is, $2x_1 + 2x_2 \geq 10$ becomes a constraint for the LP.

Using a similar line of reasoning, you should be able to derive the other constraints for the problem. The LP can be stated as follows:

Definition of the decision variables:

Let x_1 = number of ounces of $F1$ per serving
$\quad x_2$ = number of ounces of $F2$ per serving
LP formulation:
Minimize $Z = 3x_1 + 4x_2$ (cents per serving)
Subject to:

(1)	$2x_1 + 2x_2 \geq 10$	(units of protein)
(2)	$2x_1 + x_2 \geq 7$	(units of vitamin A)
(3)	$\dfrac{4}{3}x_1 + 2x_2 \geq 8$	(units of iron)
(4)	$x_1 \qquad \geq 0$	(nonnegativity)
(5)	$\qquad x_2 \geq 0$	

To solve this LP graphically, follow the three steps outlined at the beginning of this section.

For example, in step 1 (graphing the constraints) we illustrate how to graph constraint (1). As usual, first graph the *constraint equation* $2x_1 + 2x_2 = 10$ by finding the x_1 intercept ($x_2 = 0$ implies $x_1 = 5$) and the x_2 intercept ($x_1 = 0$ implies $x_2 = 5$), as shown in Fig. 2.7. All points on this line, labeled (1) in Fig. 2.7, correspond to quantities of $F1$ and $F2$ that, when combined, will yield exactly 10 units of protein. All points above the line will yield more than 10 units of protein. Instead of shading the entire region above line (1), we have placed an arrow on the line pointing in the direction of shading.

The other constraints are similarly represented in Fig. 2.7. The region that is common to each of the five regions represented by the five constraints is shown shaded and denotes the feasible-solution space.

Step 2 involves graphing a convenient Z line. Recall that $Z = 3x_1 + 4x_2$. In Fig. 2.7 we have graphed $Z = 36$.

In step 3 we are concerned with finding the minimum value of Z that can be obtained by a point in the feasible-solution space. Starting with $Z = 36$, we can decrease the cost by moving this line parallel to itself and toward the origin. We go as far as possible toward the origin until we reach the last attainable point in the feasible solution space (labeled point B in Fig. 2.7; the corresponding optimal Z line is labeled Z^*).

The optimal (x_1, x_2) combination is given by the coordinates of point B. Noting that B is the point of intersection of constraint lines (1) and (3), we must solve these two constraint equations simultaneously for x_1 and x_2:

(1) $2x_1 + 2x_2 = 10$

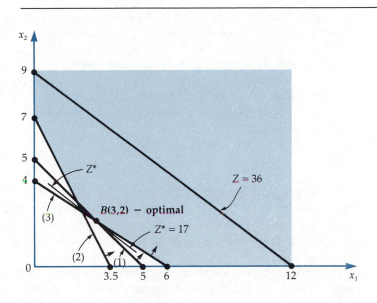

 FIGURE 2.7   *The diet problem.*

(3) $\dfrac{4}{3}x_1 + 2x_2 = 8$

Subtract (3) from (1) and solve for x_1:

$$\left(2 - \dfrac{4}{3}\right)x_1 + (2 - 2)x_2 = 10 - 8$$

$$\dfrac{2}{3}x_1 + 0x_2 = 2$$

$$x_1 = 2\left(\dfrac{3}{2}\right) = 3$$

Put $x_1 = 3$ into (1) and solve for x_2:

$$2(3) + 2x_2 = 10$$

$$2x_2 = 4$$

$$x_2 = 2$$

The corresponding minimum cost Z^* is found by substituting $x_1 = 3$ and $x_2 = 2$ into the equation for Z:

$$Z^* = 3(3) + 4(2) = 17$$

The optimal amounts of *F1* and *F2* to combine per serving are 3 ounces and 2 ounces, respectively. The resulting minimum cost per serving is 17¢ for a 5-ounce serving.

Note: Suppose a serving of 5 ounces is considered too small to satisfy a student's appetite. For example, let us assume that Jackson plans to serve 8 ounces of the casserole per student. The way to handle this problem is to formulate a new LP that is identical to the LP above except that it will include a sixth constraint:

$$x_1 + x_2 = 8$$

If you graph this constraint in Fig. 2.7 and solve for Z^*, you will find the optimal solution to be $x_1 = 8$, $x_2 = 0$, $Z^* = 24¢$. *Mathematically*, we have done nothing wrong. However, student tastes might indicate that a casserole consisting of a single food ingredient is not a casserole at all; it might not even taste very good.

Jackson might decide that in order for a serving of the casserole to have any culinary appeal it should contain at least 2 ounces of *F1* and at least 3 ounces of *F2*. We can handle this requirement mathematically by imposing the following additional constraints on the original problem:

$$x_1 + x_2 = 8$$

$$x_1 \quad\;\; \geq 2$$

$$x_2 \geq 3$$

You are asked to solve this modified LP in Problem 1 below.   ▲

Problems

1. Solve Jackson's Diet Problem (Example 2.4), imposing the three additional constraints, $x_1 + x_2 = 8$, $x_1 \geq 2$, and $x_2 \geq 3$.
2. Suppose Jackson (Example 2.4) *in addition* to including the constraints in Problem 1 also stipulates that too much *F1* would spoil the taste and too much *F2* would cause the casserole to bake too quickly and possibly burn. Specifically, Jackson feels that the amounts of *F1* and *F2* per serving should not exceed 5 ounces and 6 ounces, respectively. Formulate an LP to determine the optimal ingredient mix, and solve graphically.
3. Solve the following linear program:

   Minimize $Z = 10x_1 + 3x_2$
   Subject to:
   (1) $x_1 \quad\quad\;\; \leq 20$
   (2) $3x_1 + 4x_2 \leq 96$
   (3) $x_1 + \;\; x_2 \geq 15$

(4) $3x_1 + x_2 \geq 30$
(5) $x_1 \qquad \geq 0$
(6) $\qquad x_2 \geq 0$

4. Solve the LP in Problem 3 if Z is changed to $Z = 8x_1 + 3x_2$.
5. Solve the LP in Problem 3 if Z is changed to $Z = 10x_1 + 20x_2$.

5. GENERAL PROPERTIES OF LINEAR PROGRAMS

The special linear properties of linear programs were noted in Section 2. The fact that both the objective function and the constraints are linear expressions has certain geometric implications for the optimal solutions to linear programs. In this section we shall present the general properties of linear programs.

Corner Points

As we found in Fig. 2.4, the optimal solution to Sue's product mix problem (Example 2.1) turned out to be $x_1 = 16$ pots and $x_2 = 15$ ashtrays. If you refer to that graph, you will note that this solution occurs at a **corner point** of the feasible-solution space. In that example the corner points are labeled O, A, B, C, and D.

The optimal solution to an LP will always occur at a corner point of the feasible-solution space.

If you refer to Fig. 2.6, you will note that the optimal solution to A–1 Shaky Frames's problem (1,000; 2,000) occurs at a corner point. In the minimization problem illustrated in Fig. 2.7 (the diet problem), we see once again that the optimal solution, point $B = (3, 2)$, occurs at a corner point.

This special property of the optimal solution is a result of the linearity assumptions and is one of the primary ideas behind the simplex solution method in Chapter 3.

Combinatorial Analysis of the Solution Space

The special properties of corner points discussed above should give you an idea for a possible means of solving linear programs.

Let us assume that you must solve an LP involving two decision variables and have constructed a graph similar to the one in Fig. 2.4. One method for finding the optimal solution is to test each feasible corner point—O, A, B, C, and D—to see which one(s) yield the highest value of Z. First, we must find the coordinates of each of these points. Locating each corner point for this problem involves solving two simultaneous equations.

For example, to find point O we must solve $x_1 = 0$ and $x_2 = 0$ to get (0, 0). To find point A we solve $x_1 = 0$ and $x_2 = 15$ to get (0, 15); to find point B we solve $x_2 = 15$ and $(5/4)x_1 + 2x_2 = 50$ to get (16, 15); to find point C we solve $(5/4)x_1 + 2x_2 = 50$ and $x_1 = 24$ to get (24, 10); and finally, to find point D we solve $x_1 = 24$ and $x_2 = 0$ to get (24, 0).

After finding the x_1 and x_2 coordinates of each point, we must evaluate Z at each of these points. Since $Z = 5x_1 + 12x_2$ for Sue's problem, we have:

At (0, 0) $Z = 5(0) + 12(0) = 0$

At (0, 15) $Z = 5(0) + 12(15) = 180$

At (16, 15) $Z = 5(16) + 12(15) = 260$

At (24, 10) $Z = 5(24) + 12(10) = 240$

At (24, 0) $Z = 5(24) + 12(0) = 120$

We then select (16, 15) as the optimal solution, since it is the corner point that yields the maximum value of Z. Note that in order to solve the problem in this way it was necessary to (1) graph the feasible-solution space, (2) solve five sets of two simultaneous equations, (3) compute five values of Z, and (4) select the best Z value and (x_1, x_2) combination.

What if we had *not* first constructed the graph shown in Fig. 2.4? In other words, how would we solve the problem using the method of testing corner points if we did not have a picture of the feasible-solution space before us?

The original problem for Sue's product mix involved five constraint equations. We would have to solve each *pair* of the five for (x_1, x_2), test to see if the solution was feasible, then compute the value of Z at the solution. For example, in addition to the original five pairs of equations, we would have to solve the following pairs:

$x_2 = 0$ and $\frac{5}{4}x_1 + 2x_2 = 50$

$x_1 = 0$ and $\frac{5}{4}x_1 + 2x_2 = 50$

$x_1 = 24$ and $x_1 = 0$ (No solution here.)

$x_2 = 15$ and $x_2 = 0$ (No solution here.)

$x_1 = 24$ and $x_2 = 15$

Suppose we solve $x_1 = 0$ and $(5/4)x_1 + 2x_2 = 50$ to get (0, 25). We must then test to see if (0, 25) lies in the feasible region. Remember we are assuming that we do not have the visual aid of Fig. 2.4. Testing (0, 25) for feasibility involves substituting $x_1 = 0$ and $x_2 = 25$ into each of the original five constraints of the LP to see if all five are satisfied. In this case $x_1 = 0$ and $x_2 = 25$ violates the constraint $x_2 \le 15$, so we must discard (0, 25) as a possibility.

In a problem having ten decision variables and four constraints, it can be proven that we would have to solve 210 systems of equations each involving four equations in four unknowns. If the problem involved twenty decision variables and five constraints, we would have to solve 15,504 systems of eight equations in eight unknowns. This is clearly not computationally practical. The power of the simplex method, which will be explained in the next chapter, is that it *greatly* reduces the computational burden encountered when the number of decision variables is two or more.

6. SPECIAL SITUATIONS THAT MAY ARISE IN LINEAR PROGRAMMING

In this section we discuss some of the exceptional cases one may encounter when attempting to solve a linear program. These will arise once again as special considerations in the next chapter.

Multiple Optimal Solutions

An LP may have more than one optimal solution. This is illustrated in the following example:

EXAMPLE 2.5. *Multiple Optimal Solutions.* Consider the linear program:

Maximize $Z = 2x_1 + 4x_2$
Subject to:
(1) $\quad x_1 \qquad \leq \; 8$
(2) $\qquad\quad x_2 \leq \; 3$
(3) $\quad 3x_1 + 6x_2 \leq 30$
(4) $\quad x_1 \qquad \geq \; 0$
(5) $\qquad\quad x_2 \geq \; 0$

The constraint equations, feasible-solution space, and line $Z = 8$ are shown in Fig. 2.8. If we proceed, in an attempt to find the maximum value of Z, by moving the line $Z = 8$ outward, we see that the optimal Z line, Z^*, will *coincide* with constraint equation (3). This is because line (3) is parallel to line $Z = 8$ (see Fig. 2.8).

Thus since both corner point A and corner point B are optimal, we have *multiple optimal* solutions.

To find point A, solve (2) and (3):

(2) $\qquad\qquad x_2 = 3$

(3) $\qquad 3x_1 + 6x_2 = 30$

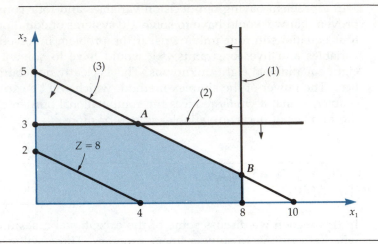

FIGURE 2.8 *Multiple optimal solutions (Example 2.5).*

Put (2) into (3) and solve for x_1:

$$3x_1 + 6(3) = 30$$

$$3x_1 = 12$$

$$x_1 = 4$$

So $A = (4, 3)$ and $Z^* = 2(4) + 4(3) = 20$.

Let us find point B and see if it also gives $Z^* = 20$. We must solve (1) and (3):

(1) $x_1 = 8$

(3) $3x_1 + 6x_2 = 30$

Put (1) into (3) and solve for x_2:

$$3(8) + 6x_2 = 30$$

$$6x_2 = 6$$

$$x_2 = 1$$

So $B = (8, 1)$ and $Z^* = 2(8) + 4(1) = 20$.

Are there other (x_1, x_2) combinations that will yield the maximum Z value of 20? The answer is "yes." In fact, *every* point on the line segment connecting A and B will be an optimal solution to the LP. It is known mathematically that every point on the line segment can be written as a combination of points A and B. More precisely, if (x_1, x_2) is a point on segment

AB, then there is a number α between zero and one such that $x_1 = \alpha(4) + (1 - \alpha)(8)$ (recall that the x_1 coordinate of $A = 4$; the x_1 coordinate of $B = 8$) and $x_2 = \alpha(3) + (1 - \alpha)(1)$; that is, a combination of the x_2 coordinates of A and B.

As an example, let $\alpha = 0$. Then we have

$$x_1 = 0(4) + (1 - 0)(8) = 8$$

and

$$x_2 = 0(3) + (1 - 0)(1) = 1$$

which is point B. If $\alpha = 1$, we get point A. Let us try $\alpha = 1/4$. Then we have

$$x_1 = \left(\frac{1}{4}\right)(4) + \left(1 - \frac{1}{4}\right)(8) = 1 + 6 = 7$$

and

$$x_2 = \left(\frac{1}{4}\right)(3) + \left(1 - \frac{1}{4}\right)(1) = \frac{3}{4} + \frac{3}{4} = \frac{3}{2}$$

If we evaluate Z at $(7, 3/2)$, we get

$$Z = 2(7) + 4\left(\frac{3}{2}\right) = 14 + 6 = 20$$

Thus $(7, 3/2)$ is also an optimal solution to the LP. Similarly every point on the segment AB is optimal, yielding the maximum Z of 20.   ▲

MANAGERIAL IMPLICATIONS. *Mathematically,* the maximum value of Z is found to be 20 and can be obtained at any (x_1, x_2) combination on the line segment AB. From a *managerial perspective* this implies that there is some flexibility in the choices open to management in selecting the x_1 and x_2 values. Regardless of the point selected on segment AB, management is assured of achieving the maximum objective value of 20. The particular point selected for the decision variables x_1 and x_2 may then be based on other nonmathematical factors involving the firm's operations.

No Feasible Solutions

It may be found that there are no feasible solutions (or, in other terms, the feasible-solution space may be empty). If this happens, the problem should be reexamined to see if it was formulated properly. If the problem is formulated properly and the feasible-solution space is still found to be empty, the analyst will need to reexamine the constraints of the problem to see which constraints, if any, can be modified to make the problem solvable. This may require that the firm make more resources available (for example, increase the budget, increase machine-hours, or increase labor-hours).

EXAMPLE 2.6. *No Feasible Solutions.* Consider the following linear program:

Maximize $Z = 2x_1 + 5x_2$
Subject to:
(1) $x_1 + x_2 \leq 10$
(2) $2x_1 + 3x_2 \geq 48$
(3) $x_1 \qquad \geq 0$
(4) $\qquad x_2 \geq 0$

Constraints (1) and (2) are graphed in Fig. 2.9. You can see that there is no point (x_1, x_2) that can satisfy both constraints (1) and (2) at the same time. Thus there are no feasible solutions to this LP.   ▲

Unbounded Objective Function

Consider the following LP in which there is no maximum value of Z:

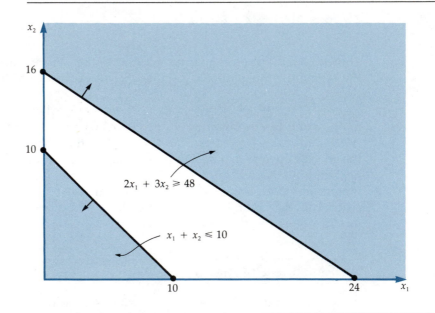

FIGURE 2.9   *No feasible solutions (Example 2.6).*

EXAMPLE 2.7. *Unbounded Objective Function.*

Maximize $Z = 3x_1 + 4x_2$
Subject to:
(1) $\quad 9x_1 + 3x_2 \geq 54$
(2) $\quad 3x_1 \quad\quad \leq 15$
(3) $\quad\quad x_1 \quad\quad \geq 0$
(4) $\quad\quad\quad x_2 \geq 0$

In Fig. 2.10 we have graphed the feasible-solution space and the line $Z = 12$. It can be seen from the graph that it is possible to increase Z without limit. For example, we have also graphed $Z = 48$ and $Z = 72$. In each case there are points in the feasible-solution space (shaded) that would yield these Z values. In fact, no matter how large a value we select for Z, there are points in the feasible-solution space that would yield the Z value selected. Thus we say that Z is **unbounded.** ▲

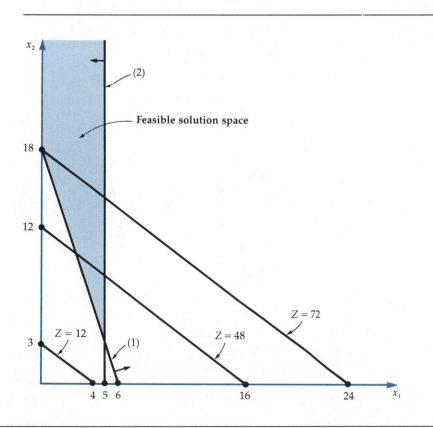

FIGURE 2.10   *Unbounded objective function (Example 2.7).*

In a problem where you find Z to be unbounded, this should be an indication that the problem is incorrectly formulated. If Z corresponds to profit, for example, we know from practical considerations that it is not possible to attain an infinite profit. Either you have incorrectly formulated one or more constraints or you have omitted one or more constraints. At this point, go back to the first step of problem formulation and make certain that you understand the verbal description of the problem and that the description is a complete and accurate one.

Problems

Classify each problem below as having multiple optimal solutions, having no feasible solution, or having an unbounded objective function. If possible, solve the problem.

1. Minimize $Z = 2x_1 + 3x_2$
   Subject to:
   (1) $x_1 + 1.5x_2 \geq 6$
   (2) $x_1 \qquad\quad \geq 4$
   (3) $\qquad\quad 3x_2 \leq 9$
   (4) $x_1 \qquad\quad \geq 0$
   (5) $\qquad\quad x_2 \geq 0$

2. Maximize $Z = x_1 + 5x_2$
   Subject to:
   (1) $3x_1 \qquad\quad \geq 4$
   (2) $\qquad\quad x_2 \leq 10$
   (3) $4x_1 + 2x_2 \geq 4$
   (4) $x_1 \qquad\quad \geq 0$
   (5) $\qquad\quad x_2 \geq 0$

3. Maximize $Z = 12x_1 + x_2$
   Subject to:
   (1) $2x_1 + x_2 \leq 6$
   (2) $\qquad\quad x_2 \leq 4$
   (3) $3x_1 + 4x_2 \geq 28$
   (4) $x_1 \qquad\quad \geq 0$
   (5) $\qquad\quad x_2 \geq 0$

4. Maximize $Z = 9x_1 + 8x_2$
   Subject to:
   (1) $x_1 + 2x_2 \leq 6$
   (2) $8x_1 \qquad\quad \geq 2$
   (3) $4.5x_1 + 2x_2 \leq 18$
   (4) $x_1 \qquad\quad \geq 0$
   (5) $\qquad\quad x_2 \geq 0$

7. LP APPLICATIONS—FORMULATION

In Section 1 of this chapter we presented a list of applications for which LP formulations might be appropriate. The classic product mix problem was illustrated in Example 2.1, and a simple version of the diet problem appears in Example 2.4.

In this section we shall present LP formulations for certain problems in optimal blending, advertising/promotion, financial investment, production/inventory, and cargo shipment.

This is a good chance for you to practice and develop your skill in formulating linear programs. Recall the four steps outlined in Section 2: (1) analyze the problem, (2) define decision variables, (3) express the objective function in terms of the decision variables, and (4) express the constraints of the problem in terms of the decision variables. Try to formulate each problem below as a linear program without looking ahead to the solutions given.

Optimal Blending: Metal-Alloy Design

Three metals—copper, nickel, and zinc—are to be combined to produce an alloy suitable for a new $1 coin being designed by the Bureau of the Mint and Engraving. The costs per pound of the three metals are $0.60, $1.10, and $0.85, respectively.

Chemical analysis determines the following design requirements for the new alloy: the percentage of copper must not exceed five times the percentage of nickel; the total percentage of nickel and zinc must exceed at least one-quarter the percentage of copper; the amount of zinc must not exceed 50 percent; copper must constitute at least 25 percent and nickel at least 30 percent of the new alloy. The bureau would like to produce the new alloy at minimum cost.

ANALYSIS. This is an example of a problem in which we must consider both the definition of the decision variables *and* the objective function at the same time. A reasonable objective would be to minimize the cost *per pound* of the new alloy. Thus imagine that you are designing the optimal (minimum cost) blend of *one* pound of new alloy. We can then define the decision variables as follows:

Let x_1 = pounds of copper *per pound* of new alloy
    x_2 = pounds of nickel *per pound* of new alloy
    x_3 = pounds of zinc *per pound* of new alloy

Note an interesting fact about the way we have defined the decision variables. Each decision variable is a value between zero and one. Because of this we also have a convenient correspondence between "percentage of composition" and the decision variables. For example, suppose $x_1 = 0.55$. We can view this in two ways: (1) there are 0.55 pound of copper per pound of new alloy, or (2) the proportion (or percentage) of copper in the new alloy is 55 percent.

We can now formulate the blending problem as a linear program:

Minimize $Z = 0.60x_1 + 1.10x_2 + 0.85x_3$

Subject to:

(1) $x_1 + x_2 + x_3 = 1$

(2) $x_1 \leq 5x_2$ (i.e., $x_1 - 5x_2 \leq 0$)

(3) $x_2 + x_3 \geq 0.25x_1$ (i.e., $-0.25x_1 + x_2 + x_3 \geq 0$)

(4) $x_3 \leq 0.5$

(5) $x_1 \geq 0.25$

(6) $x_2 \geq 0.3$

(7) $x_1 \quad\quad \geq 0$

(8) $x_2 \quad\quad \geq 0$

(9) $x_3 \geq 0$

In this LP, Z = cost ($) per pound of new alloy. Constraint (1) says that the total weight of copper, nickel, and zinc must add up to one pound. Constraint (2) says that either the weight of copper must be less than five times the weight of nickel or, since we can view x_1, x_2, and x_3 as *proportions*, the proportion (percentage) of copper cannot exceed five times the proportion (percentage) of nickel. Try to interpret the other constraints in this way.

Using a canned computer program that solves linear programs based on the simplex method (to be discussed in the next chapter), the optimal solution of this problem was found to be $x_1 = 0.70$, $x_2 = 0.30$, $x_3 = 0$, and $Z^* = \$0.75$ per pound.

Advertising/Promotion Planning

Coladrink is planning next month's advertising and promotion strategy for marketing one of its products. It has budgeted $30,000 for advertising and promotion.

Coladrink has four options available: (1) Place a single ad in the local newspaper at a cost of $350; this can be expected to reach an estimated 800 potential customers who will notice the ad and take time to look it over; (2) buy a single 30-second spot on one of the local radio stations at a cost of $1,500; this would reach an estimated 7,000 people; (3) place an ad in a local entertainment magazine at a cost of $1,000; this would reach an estimated 9,500 people; and (4) distribute free samples to local merchants. The samples would cost $100 per box of 200 and would reach an estimated 350 people (this would result if each of the 200 people who received free samples shared the product with members of their families and told their friends about the product).

Based on the number of potential merchants who would cooperate in placing the free samples, the number of boxes of free samples used is limited to 100. Coladrink's marketing manager indicates that as a trial test she would like to see at least 25 boxes of free samples placed with some of the more promising stores.

The one-month planning horizon consists of 30 days. Not more than six ads per day should appear in the newspaper (morning and evening editions combined), but at least one ad per day should be placed in both editions for at least half the month. The magazine comes out weekly (four times a month), and it is not considered effective to place more than one ad in each issue. The radio station has only 15 unsold spots left for next month. The president of Coladrink says he would like to use at least one radio spot per week to promote the product.

For every spot on the radio station it is considered wise to follow up by running at least a total of three ads in the newspaper and magazine combined.

What would you recommend to Coladrink for planning next month's advertising and promotion in order to reach as many people as possible?

ANALYSIS. Coladrink must decide to what extent it should use each of the four advertising/promotion options in order to reach as many potential customers as possible. How can we *measure* these levels of use? The description of the problem suggests the following definition of the decision variables:

Let x_1 = number of ads in the newspaper
x_2 = number of 30-second spots on the radio
x_3 = number of ads in the magazine
x_4 = number of boxes of free samples to distribute

In words, the objective function Z equals the total number of people reached by, or exposed to, the advertising/promotion program. From the exposure rates in the problem statement, is it possible to express Z in terms of the decision variables defined above? The answer is "yes": $Z = 800x_1 + 7,000x_2 + 9,500x_3 + 350x_4$. (Try formulating each constraint in terms of these decision variables.)

The appropriate LP formulation for Coladrink's problem is:

Maximize $Z = 800x_1 + 7,000x_2 + 9,500x_3 + 350x_4$
Subject to:

(1)	$350x_1 + 1,500x_2 + 1,000x_3 + 100x_4 \leq$	30,000
(2)	$x_4 \leq$	100
(3)	$x_4 \geq$	25
(4)	$x_1 \leq$	180
(5)	$x_1 \geq$	30

(6)				x_3		$\leq$	4
(7)		x_2				$\leq$	15
(8)		x_2				$\geq$	4
(9)	x_1		$+$	x_3		$\geq$	$3x_2$
(10)	x_1					$\geq$	0
(11)		x_2				$\geq$	0
(12)				x_3		$\geq$	0
(13)					$x_4 \geq$		0

The explanation of the constraints is as follows:

Constraint (1). This is the budget constraint: The total amount of money spent on the four alternatives must be within the $30,000 budget. This amount equals ($350 per newspaper ad times the number of newspaper ads) + ($1,500 per 30-second radio spot times the number of radio spots) + ($1,000 per magazine ad times the number of magazine ads) + ($100 per box of samples times the number of boxes of samples), which can be written as:

$$350x_1 + 1,500x_2 + 1,000x_3 + 100x_4 \leq 30,000$$

Constraint (2). This constraint says that the number of boxes of free samples cannot exceed 100.

Constraint (3). This constraint corresponds to the marketing manager's request to place at least 25 boxes of free samples with local merchants.

Constraint (4). This constraint limits the number of newspaper ads to 180 per month: 6 ads per day (maximum) times 30 days per month equals 180 ads per month maximum.

Constraint (5). This constraint ensures that at least 30 ads will be placed in the newspaper next month. Constraint (5) was derived from the statement in the problem that at least one ad per day should be placed in each of the two editions (morning and evening) for at least half the month (15 days); this amounts to placing a minimum of 2(15) = 30 ads.

Constraint (6). This constraint limits the number of magazine ads to a maximum of four per month.

Constraint (7). This constraint expresses the fact that the radio station has only 15 unsold spots left next month, so x_2, the number of radio spots, cannot exceed 15.

Constraint (8). This constraint reflects the president's request that at least one radio spot per week be utilized (one spot per week times four weeks per month equals four spots per month minimum).

Constraint (9). This constraint says that the total combined number of news-paper ads (x_1) and magazine ads (x_3) must be at least three times the number of radio spots (x_2).

Constraints (10)–(13). These are nonnegativity constraints.

Using a canned computer program, the solution to this media mix problem was found to be $x_1 = 30$, $x_2 = 8.67$, $x_3 = 4$, $x_4 = 25$, and $Z^* = 131,416.67$ people reached.

Investment Planning

Amtrex, Inc. has $100,000 available for investment and must decide how much of this is to be invested in each of three available alternatives: stock A, stock B, and bond X.

Stock A is priced at $50 per share and is expected to return $10 per share in annual dividends. Although this return is high, stock A is also considered somewhat risky. Stock B is priced at $25 per share and returns $3 per year. Bond X is quoted at $200 with an annual return of 9 percent.

Amtrex has decided to limit its investment in the riskier stock A to a max-imum of one-fourth its total investment. For every share of stock A pur-chased, Amtrex will purchase at least three shares of stock B. There are a maximum of 250 bonds available to Amtrex at the stated price. Amtrex also stipulates that the total investment in bonds must be at least as great as half its investment in stocks.

How do you recommend that Amtrex invest its funds?

ANALYSIS. What would be a reasonable objective? From the description of the problem we can assume that Amtrex's goal is to maximize its annual return from the three investment alternatives. This suggests the following definition of the decision variables:

Let x_1 = number of shares of stock A to purchase
   x_2 = number of shares of stock B to purchase
   x_3 = number of bonds to purchase

The objective function Z is defined to be the total annual return and, there-fore, is expressed in terms of the decision variables: $Z = 10x_1 + 3x_2 + 18x_3$. (Note that the return on bond X is computed as 9 percent of 200, or $18 per bond.)

Amtrex's first constraint is a budget constraint of $100,000. If Amtrex pur-chases x_1 shares of stock A, x_2 shares of stock B, and x_3 bonds, its total in-vestment will be $50x_1 + 25x_2 + 200x_3$. Since this cannot exceed the budget constraint, we can write:

$$50x_1 + 25x_2 + 200x_3 \leq 100,000$$

This is constraint (1) of the LP below.

What about other constraints placed on our choice of values for x_1, x_2, and x_3? From the problem statement there are four more such constraints, listed below as (2), (3), (4), and (5), in addition to the usual nonnegativity constraints.

The resulting LP becomes:

Maximize $Z = 10x_1 + 3x_2 + 18x_3$

Subject to:

(1) $50x_1 + 25x_2 + 200x_3 \leq 100{,}000$

(2) $50x_1 \leq (0.25)(50x_1 + 25x_2 + 200x_3)$

(3) $x_2 \geq 3x_1$

(4) $x_3 \leq 250$

(5) $200x_3 \geq (0.50)(50x_1 + 25x_2)$

(6) $x_1 \geq 0$

(7) $x_2 \geq 0$

(8) $x_3 \geq 0$

Constraint (1). This is the budget constraint already discussed.

Constraint (2). This constraint limits the total investment in stock A (which is $50x_1$ dollars) to one-fourth (0.25) the total investment [$(50x_1 + 25x_2 + 200x_3)$ dollars].

Constraint (3). This constraint states that the total number of shares of stock B (x_2) must be at least as great as three times the total number of shares of stock A (x_1).

Constraint (4). This constraint expresses the fact that, since there are only 250 bonds available to Amtrex, the number of bonds it decides to purchase cannot exceed this amount.

Constraint (5). This constraint states that the total investment in bonds ($200x_2$ dollars) must be at least as great as one-half (0.50) its total investment in stocks, which is $(50x_1 + 25x_2)$ dollars for stocks A and B combined.

Constraints (6), (7), and (8). These are the usual nonnegativity constraints.

Using a computer program, the solution to the LP was found to be:

$x_1{}^* = 500$ shares of stock A

$x_2{}^* = 1{,}666.67$ shares of stock B

$x_3{}^* = 166.67$ bonds

$Z^* = \$13{,}000$ annual return

Note that if you substitute $x_1 = 500$, $x_2 = 1{,}666.67$, and $x_3 = 166.67$ into the budget constraint (1), Amtrex will spend the entire $100,000—this is reasonable. The rate of return would be 13 percent.

Production/Inventory Planning

The product mix problem (Example 2.1) is one type of production problem. Similarly, both the blending problem and the diet problem (Example 2.4) can be viewed as production problems.

Another large class of production problems deals not only with production quantities but also with inventory planning, hiring, firing, overtime, subcontracting, and meeting forecasted demand with given production capacity. In this section we present a simple version of such problems. In Chapter 4, which deals with *the transportation problem*, we shall discuss production problems in more detail.

Computon, a manufacturer of pocket calculators, forecasts demand for its Model T1 calculator to be 1,500 units for period 1 (January–June) and 2,100 units for period 2 (July–December). The calculator requires a special integrated circuit or chip for the central processor module. Computon manufactures this chip in-house but also has a subcontractor available for supplying this special unit. The cost to manufacture the chip in-house is $4.50. Subcontracting costs (including shipping) are currently $5.25 for period 1 but are expected to increase to $6.25 for period 2.

The inventory holding cost to keep a single chip in inventory for one period is $1.90 (a somewhat high figure owing primarily to risk of obsolescence).

Computon's manufacturing capacity is 1,700 chips per period. Computon's subcontractor can provide 200 chips in period 1 and 300 chips in period 2.

How should Computon plan its inventory, production, and procurement for the coming year?

ANALYSIS. Computon's objective is to minimize the cost of meeting demand during the year. Computon has two means of meeting the forecasted demand—by in-house production and by procurement (subcontracting). The company could use any feasible combination of these options in each of the two periods.

We must distinguish between the period in which a chip is produced, or procured, and the period in which it is sold. Thus let x_{ij} denote a decision variable equal to the number of chips produced in-house in period i and sold in period j. We shall use y to denote procurement in a similar manner. Thus we have the following definition of decision variables:

Let x_{11} = number of chips produced in-house in period 1 and sold in period 1
x_{12} = number of chips produced in-house in period 1 and sold in period 2
x_{22} = number of chips produced in-house in period 2 and sold in period 2

y_{11} = number of chips procured in period 1 and sold in period 1
y_{12} = number of chips procured in period 1 and sold in period 2
y_{22} = number of chips procured in period 2 and sold in period 2

The objective function Z equals the cost to produce and procure the chips for the two periods. Suppose we produce x_{11} chips in-house in period 1 for sale in period 1. The production cost is \$4.50 per chip and the holding cost is 0, so the cost associated with x_{11} is \$4.50x_{11}. On the other hand, if we produce x_{12} chips in-house in period 1 to be sold in period 2, we must pay the production cost of \$4.50 per chip *plus* the cost to carry each chip in inventory for one period, \$1.90. Thus the cost associated with x_{12} is \$6.40x_{12}. The objective function Z is the sum of all such terms (see the LP formulation below).

What about the constraints? From the description of the problem we note that the following three factors must be considered: (1) demand must be met in each period, (2) in-house production cannot exceed the stated capacities, and (3) procurement quantities are limited to the stated available amounts.

Putting all of this information together, we formulate the following LP:

Minimize $Z = 4.50x_{11} + 6.40x_{12} + 4.50x_{22} + 5.25y_{11} + 7.15y_{12} + 6.25y_{22}$
Subject to:

(1) $x_{11} \quad\quad\quad + y_{11} \quad\quad\quad\quad\quad \geq 1{,}500$
(2) $\quad x_{12} + x_{22} \quad\quad + y_{12} + y_{22} \geq 2{,}100$
(3) $x_{11} + x_{12} \quad\quad\quad\quad\quad\quad\quad \leq 1{,}700$
(4) $\quad\quad\quad x_{22} \quad\quad\quad\quad\quad\quad\quad \leq 1{,}700$
(5) $\quad\quad\quad\quad\quad y_{11} + y_{12} \quad\quad \leq \quad 200$
(6) $\quad\quad\quad\quad\quad\quad\quad\quad y_{22} \leq \quad 300$
(7)   Each $x_{ij} \geq 0$
       and each $y_{ij} \geq 0$
       (six nonnegativity constraints)

You should try to understand how each constraint was derived. Constraint (1) is the demand constraint for period 1 (the total number of chips produced and procured in period 1 must be at least sufficient to meet the demand of 1,500 for period 1); constraint (2) is the demand constraint for period 2; constraints (3) and (4) express the in-house production capacities for periods 1 and 2, respectively; and constraints (5) and (6) state the procurement limits for periods 1 and 2, respectively. Also note the coefficients of the decision variables in the objective function. For example, the coefficient of y_{12} equals \$5.25 (procurement cost in period 1) plus \$1.90 (cost to carry one chip in inventory for one period).

The following optimal solution to the LP was found by using a computer program:

$x_{11}^* = 1{,}500$

$x_{12}^* = 100$

$x_{22}^* = 1,700$

$y_{11} = 0$

$y_{12} = 0$

$y_{22}^* = 300$

$Z^* = \$16,915$

Thus 1,500 chips should be produced in-house in period 1 and sold in period 1 to meet the demand of 1,500 for that period. In addition, 100 chips should be produced in-house in period 1 and carried in inventory for sale in period 2. (This uses up 1,600 units of the 1,700 unit in-house capacity for period 1.) The period 2 demand of 2,100 chips is met by combining the number of chips available from three sources: (1) 100 chips from period 1 inventory (x_{12}), (2) 1,700 chips from period 2 in-house production (x_{22}), and (3) 300 chips produced by the subcontractor (y_{22}). The total cost of this plan is $16,915.

Optimal Cargo Shipment

Radix, Inc., distributes three products to several markets. Radix is currently planning its shipments to the Midwest market for the first quarter of the year. For the first quarter, Radix must ship all products by truck (a railroad system will be available for use in the near future). There is no demand restriction on the products that can be sold in its Midwest market, so Radix is free to ship each of the three products in any quantity mix it chooses. Each truck's capacity is limited to 2,000 cubic feet (ft^3) of space and 8,000 pounds of product.

The volume and weight requirements of each unit of the three products are given in the following table:

Product	Volume (ft^3)	Weight (lb)
1	2	5
2	4	15
3	1	2

The unit profit on products 1, 2, and 3 is $5, $12, and $3, respectively. Determine the best amounts of each product to ship.

ANALYSIS. The objective is to maximize total profits, which can be done by maximizing the total profit per truckload. The decision variables should equal the number of units of each product to be shipped, and the constraints must account for the volume and weight restrictions of the truck. We are led to the following LP formulation.

Definition of decision variables:

x_1 = number of units of product 1 to ship per truckload
x_2 = number of units of product 2 to ship per truckload
x_3 = number of units of product 3 to ship per truckload
Maximize $Z = 5x_1 + 12x_2 + 3x_3$ ($ profit/truckload)
Subject to:
(1) $2x_1 + 4x_2 + x_3 \leq 2,000$
(2) $5x_1 + 15x_2 + 2x_3 \leq 8,000$
(3)   Each x_j $\geq$ 0
           (3 nonnegativity constraints)

Constraint (1). This is the volume constraint of the truck. Each unit of product 1 requires 2 cubic feet of space; therefore, if we ship x_1 units of product 1 per truckload, we will require a total of $2x_1$ cubic feet for product 1. Product 2 requires a total of $4x_2$ cubic feet and product 3 requires $1x_3$ cubic feet. Thus if we ship x_1 units, x_2 units, and x_3 units of products 1, 2, and 3, respectively, we will require a total of $2x_1 + 4x_2 + x_3$ cubic feet of truck space, and this must be less than or equal to 2,000.

Constraint (2). This is the weight constraint. It states that the total weight of shipping x_1, x_2, and x_3 units of the three products must not exceed the weight capacity of 8,000 pounds per truckload. The linear expression on the left side of constraint (2) is derived following reasoning similar to that for constraint (1) above.
    Results of a computer run on this LP are as follows:

$x^*_1 = 0$

$x^*_2 = 500$ units of product 2.

$x^*_3 = 0$

 $Z^* = \$6,000$ per truckload

(An alternate optimal solution is $x^*_1 = x^*_2 = 0$ and $x^*_3 = 2,000$.)

8. CONCLUDING REMARKS

The concept of a linear program (LP) has been introduced in this chapter. We have seen that a wide range of practical management problems can be formulated as LPs (see Section 1).
    The three steps in formulating an LP are as follows (see Section 2):

1. Study carefully a verbal statement of the problem facing management.
2. Define (in words) the decision variables.
3. Express the objective function in terms of the decision variables.
4. Express the constraints in terms of the decision variables (using linear expressions).

Be certain that the following underlying LP assumptions are reasonably satisfied:

1. Linearity assumptions
2. Divisibility assumption

In practice, LPs are solved by the simplex method, which is discussed in the next chapter. If the problem has only two decision variables, the graphical solution method can be applied, as follows:

1. Graph the constraints and shade the feasible solution space.
2. Graph the objective function (Z line).
3. By moving the Z line, determine the optimal solution.

It is a special property of LPs that an optimal solution can always be found at a corner point of the feasible-solution space.

Various special situations may arise in solving LPs (see Section 6), such as the following:

1. The LP may have multiple optimal solutions.
2. The LP may have no feasible solutions. In this case reexamine the constraints.
3. The LP may have an unbounded solution, such as an infinite profit. In this case the problem has been incorrectly formulated; check the constraints.

TERMINOLOGY

After studying this chapter you should be familiar with the following terms:

TERM	SECTION
constraints	2
corner points	5
decision variables	2
divisibility	2
feasible-solution space	3
graphical LP method	3
linear program	2
linear relationships	2
multiple optimal solutions	6
objective function	2
unbounded objective function	6

EXERCISES

1. *Product Mix—A Bakery.* Rustle's Bakery specializes in two pastries—donuts and cakes. Profit per dozen donuts is $0.60, and profit per cake is $3.25. It takes 1/6 labor-hour to make a dozen donuts (using special equipment) and 2 labor-hours to prepare a cake. Rustle's employs three people, each working 40 hours a week. Sales of donuts are not expected to exceed 500 dozen a week. Determine the optimal product mix for Rustle's Bakery.

2. *Product Mix—A Kitchenware Manufacturer.* Potsnpans manufactures two types of kitchenware pans, denoted the No. 10 pan and the No. 12 pan. Each pan is stamped from steel and then sent through an oven where a coating of enamel is applied. The stamping machine is available 50 hours a week for production (after normal maintenance is performed), and the oven operates 45 hours per week. Each No. 10 pan requires 5 minutes on the stamping machine and 10 minutes in the oven. A No. 12 pan requires 7 minutes on the stamping machine and 13 minutes in the oven. Profit runs $2.50 for the No. 10 pan and $4.55 for the No. 12 pan. Determine the optimal product mix for Potsnpans.

3. *Sensitivity Analysis.* This term refers to the process of analyzing changes in the optimal solution to a problem when some (or all) of the parameters of the problem change. Refer to Exercise 2 above (Potsnpans):
   a. Suppose the per unit profit on the No. 12 pan decreases to $4. Does the optimal product mix change?
   b. Assume that the per unit profit on the No. 12 pan decreases further to $3.50. Does the optimal product mix change?

4. *Metal-Alloy Design.* Metaltex manufactures two metal alloys, #1 and #2, and is currently working on the design and planning production of a third alloy, #3. Alloy #1 consists of 10 percent copper, 80 percent zinc, and 10 percent nickel. The composition of alloy #2 is 40 percent copper, 40 percent zinc, and 20 percent nickel. Alloy #1 costs $2 per pound, and alloy #2 costs $2.25 per pound. The new alloy (#3) is to be a blend of these two alloys. Design specifications require that alloy #3 consist of at least 25 percent copper and at least 60 percent zinc.
   a. Can you recommend to Metaltex the best way to mix alloys #1 and #2? How much per pound will the new alloy cost?
   b. *Sensitivity Analysis:* Would your recommendation change if Metaltex reports a 20 percent increase in the cost of alloy #1? How would this cost increase affect the cost to produce the new alloy?

5. *Optimal Feed-Mix Design.* Farmer Nancy runs a small Midwest farm, raising cattle and pigs. Although her cattle business has been very profitable, the profit on pigs has been low, and she suspects that costs for feeding pigs have been too high. Each pig requires three basic nutrients,

which we will refer to as $N1$, $N2$, and $N3$. Each pig requires a minimum of 10 units, 15 units, and 8 units per day of the nutrients $N1$, $N2$, and $N3$, respectively. Nancy mixes corn and a commercial feed together to form a pig feed for use on the farm. Each pound of corn provides 3 units, 4 units, and 4 units of $N1$, $N2$, and $N3$, respectively, and costs 80¢. Each pound of the commercial feed provides 5 units, 15 units, and 3 units of $N1$, $N2$, and $N3$, respectively, and costs 95¢.

   a. Can you design a minimum-cost feed mix? (*Hint:* Minimize the daily cost of feeding each pig.)

   b. *Sensitivity Analysis:* Suppose the cost of the commercial mix goes up to $1.30. How would you change your design in part (a)?

6. *Portfolio Selection.*   James has $1,000 to invest in either government bonds, which earn 6 percent per year, or gold, which he expects will increase 15 percent in value during the next year. James feels that gold might represent a somewhat risky investment, so he decides to invest not over 40 percent of his money in gold. However, James would like to put at least $100 in gold. For every dollar invested in gold he will invest at least $2 in bonds (as a diversification measure).

   a. How much should James invest in gold and bonds in order to maximize his wealth at the end of the year?

   b. *Sensitivity Analysis:* James would like to investigate the effect of a pessimistic gold market forecast on his portfolio. Specify how his portfolio and annual return would change if gold were expected to return only 5 percent (rather than 15 percent).

7. *Feed Mix.*   Margaret owns a small dog, Pepperschnitz, who currently enjoys two types of dog food—Ruffchow and Specialtreat. Ruffchow is a basic dog food for main meals and costs 5¢ per ounce. Ruffchow consists of 35 percent protein, 10 percent crude fiber, and 12 percent fat (the rest consists of minor ingredients). Specialtreat is a cheese-flavored cracker that costs 3-1/2¢ per ounce and consists of 25 percent protein, 12 percent crude fiber, and 8 percent fat. Margaret wants to be sure that her dog gets at least 7 ounces of protein, 4 ounces of crude fiber, and 3 ounces of fat per week from these two sources. How much of each type of dog food should Margaret feed Pepperschnitz per week in order to meet the nutritional requirements at minimum cost?

8. *Advertising Mix Design.*   The Pin Cushion, a newly established small retailer of fabrics and sewing items, is currently planning how best to spend its advertising budget of $200 this month. Two alternatives are being considered—the *Thrifty Dollar* (a local advertising publication) and the local newspaper. An ad in the *Thrifty Dollar* costs only $2.50 and would be read by approximately 50 people; an ad in the local newspaper costs $12 and would reach an estimated 600 people. To be effective, at least five ads should be placed in each publication. Not more than 30 ads can be placed in the local paper (one per day). An ad in the *Thrifty*

Dollar is good for three days; thus not more than 10 of these ads can be placed during the month. It is considered desirable that the number of ads in the local paper be at least twice the number placed in the *Thrifty Dollar*. Determine the advertising mix that maximizes the number of people exposed to the advertising during the current month.

9. *Ingredient Mix—A Catering Service.*   Cactus Catering Service regularly prepares a special punch for catered parties. The punch consists of a premixed fruit juice concoction and vodka. In an effort to cut costs, Cactus is reexamining the method of mixing the fruit juice used in the punch. Currently, one ounce of the fruit juice consists of 40 percent orange juice and 60 percent unsweetened grapefruit juice. The cost per ounce of each of these two juices is 4¢ and 3¢, respectively. The product development department at Cactus' main office feels it can improve the mix and reduce its cost at the same time. After performing some consumer research and product analysis, the following design specifications were agreed upon: The mix should consist of at least 30 percent orange juice and no more than 40 percent grapefruit juice. The ratio of orange juice to grapefruit juice should be at least 2:1 but no more than 4:1.
   a. Determine the minimum-cost (per ounce) design for the mix according to the above specifications.
   b. Can Cactus realize a cost savings over its current mix?
   c. What would happen if the cost of grapefruit juice increases to 4¢ per ounce? to 5¢ per ounce?

10. *Product Distribution.*   Heartwood operates two lumber mills, one in city A and the other in city B. Cut and surfaced white pine is shipped from these two mills to two markets, which we label as market 1 and market 2. The annual demand at these two markets is 10,000 board feet at market 1 and 15,000 bd ft at market 2. This demand must be met exactly. The capacity of mill A is 8,000 bd ft per year and annual capacity at mill B is 18,000 bd ft. Production costs run 50¢ and 55¢ per bd ft at mills A and B, respectively. Shipping costs depend primarily on distance and are given in the following table:

	Cents/bd ft/mile to market				Miles to market	
	1	2			1	2
From mill A	2¢	3¢		From mill A	10	15
From mill B	4¢	1¢		From mill B	9	13

Formulate an LP to determine the optimal distribution system for Heartwood. Can you solve this problem?

11. *Product Mix: Manufacturing.*   Kraftcorp manufactures two molded plas-
    tic saucer-like toys, T1 and T2. Each of these products must go through
    two manufacturing processes, A and B. Each unit of T1 requires one
    hour in process A and 1-1/2 hours in process B; each unit of T2 requires
    2 hours in process A and 3/4 hour in process B. The machinery sup-
    porting process A currently has a weekly machine-hour capacity of 100
    hours, and the weekly capacity of process B machinery is 90 machine-
    hours. Per-unit profits on T1 and T2 are $100 and $150, respectively.
    Determine the optimal product mix for Kraftcorp.

12. *Kraftcorp: Sensitivity Analysis for Facilities Expansion.*   (Refer to Exercise
    11 above.) Kraftcorp management is considering a major expansion of
    its operations. The plan involves doubling process A machine-hour ca-
    pacity to 200 hours per week. Including depreciation on the new facilities
    required and additional operating expenses, operating costs would in-
    crease $10,000 a week. At the same time it is recognized that the addi-
    tional capacity would allow production to be increased. What is your
    recommendation to Kraftcorp concerning its proposed expansion?

13. *Product Mix: Manufacturing.*   Tendercare Baby Products (TBP) manu-
    factures two types of unbreakable plastic baby bottles as part of its full
    line of baby-care products. Two primary machines are required to man-
    ufacture the bottles. The processing times (in hours) on the two ma-
    chines for the two products are given in the following table along with
    the per-unit profit on each bottle and the monthly capacity of each ma-
    chine in hours:

Bottle	Machine		Profit
	A	B	
1	2	1	75¢
2	1/2	3	50¢
Capacity	320 hr./mo.	300 hr./mo.	

    Determine the optimal product mix for TBP.

14. *Sensitivity Analysis: The Effect of Government Regulations on Tendercare
    Baby Products.*   (Refer to Exercise 13 above.) Due to a new government
    safety regulation, TBP must now modify its baby bottle to comply with
    set guidelines. This will require that each of the two bottles be run through
    a third machine process. Each bottle will require one hour on the new
    machine in addition to the processing times on machines A and B. The
    monthly capacity of the new machine is 200 machine-hours.
    a. Will this new regulation affect the product mix and profits at TBP?
    b. How much should TBP be willing to pay to expand the capacity of
       the new machine from 200 to 500 hours?

15. *A Cargo-Loading Application.* John and Robert are considering the possibility of selling products at a local weekend flea market to pick up some extra cash. Such a venture, if successful, could also serve as a base for starting a small business. They will use John's van to transport their merchandise. To start out they have selected two products to sell, pottery and plant stands. The pottery items can be purchased at wholesale prices from a friend, and the plant stands are available on a wholesale basis from a local importer. The wholesale prices of these products are $1.50 and $2 per item, respectively, and retail prices at the flea market should run $4 and $6. John and Robert together have $400 to invest in this venture for the coming weekend. The space capacity of the van is 80 cubic feet. Each pottery item requires 1/4 cubic feet, and each plant stand requires 1/2 cubic feet to ship. Due to the high customer traffic at the flea market, they should be able to sell as many as 200 pieces of pottery and 150 plant stands. How many of each type of product should John and Robert purchase to sell at the flea market?

16. *A Cargo-Loading Application.* Suzanne sells two newspapers, the *Journal* and the *Tribune,* in front of a shopping center after school each evening. She carries the newspapers in a canvas bag that has a capacity of 3 cubic feet. Each copy of the *Journal* weighs 1/4 pound, requires 1/10 cubic feet, and can be sold at a profit of 8¢ per copy. Each copy of the *Tribune* weighs 1/6 pound, requires 1/8 cubic feet, and has a profit of 6¢ per copy. Suzanne cannot comfortably carry over 20 pounds of newspapers.
   a. How many copies of each newspaper should Suzanne carry each evening?
   b. Suppose the available supply of the *Journal* is limited to 25 copies. Determine the optimal mix of newspapers Suzanne should carry.

17. *Strategic Military Effectiveness Analysis.* The government is currently studying the strike effectiveness of a new fighter jet. The jet is designed to carry two types of bombs for use on inanimate targets. The jet has a payload weight capacity of 2,000 pounds and a space capacity of 500 cubic feet. The rated damage effectiveness of bomb $B1$ is 10 and that of bomb $B2$ is 18. Each $B1$ bomb weighs 100 pounds and occupies 23 cubic feet; each $B2$ bomb weighs 150 pounds and occupies 45 cubic feet.
   a. How many of each type of bomb should the jet carry in order to maximize its total damage effectiveness?
   b. Assume that it is decided the jet should be equipped with at least nine $B2$ bombs in order to coordinate striking strategy with other defensive units. Determine the optimal loading of the jet.

3

LINEAR PROGRAMMING:
THE SIMPLEX METHOD

CONTENTS

1. INTRODUCTION

In Chapter 2 you learned a graphical method of solving linear programs. However, as was pointed out, the method only works for linear programs having two decision variables. It will not solve the larger problems that occur in practical management situations. In Section 5 of Chapter 2, we attempted to convince you that a direct combinatorial search of the corner points is computationally impractical in large problems.

So how are linear programs actually solved in practice? They are solved by canned computer programs (or packages). These programs are either written by resident experts in computing and management science techniques or supplied by the computer manufacturer or by independent software vendors.

The basic method on which these programs operate is called the **simplex method.** In actual practice the canned programs, which are generally modified versions of the simplex method, are computationally more efficient. Our aim in this chapter is to give you an *overview* of the basic simplex method so that you will have some understanding of how the available canned programs work. By studying the mechanics of the method, you will also gain insight into the economic interpretations of linear programs and their solutions. Thus there is some *qualitative* value in studying the simplex method.

It is not our intent that you become expert in manually solving LPs by using the simplex method. However, you should develop skill in *formulating* linear programs. Much of the previous chapter was directed toward this objective. Additional formulation problems are given at the end of this chapter.

2. AN OVERVIEW OF THE SIMPLEX METHOD

In the previous chapter we indicated that a linear program has associated with it a feasible-solution space and that the optimal solution to the linear program always occurs at a corner point. You might wish to review Section 5 of that chapter, "General Properties of Linear Programs."

An overview of how the simplex method operates to solve an LP is given in the **simplex algorithm,** as follows:

1. Establish an initial corner-point feasible solution to start the algorithm.
2. Is the current solution optimal? If so, STOP. You have solved the linear program. If not, go on to step 3.
3. Move to a *better* adjacent corner-point feasible solution. This new solution becomes the current solution. Return to step 2 to see if this solution is optimal.

In Fig. 3.1 we show the simplex algorithm in *flowchart form.* In the next section we shall illustrate how each of these steps is performed numerically.

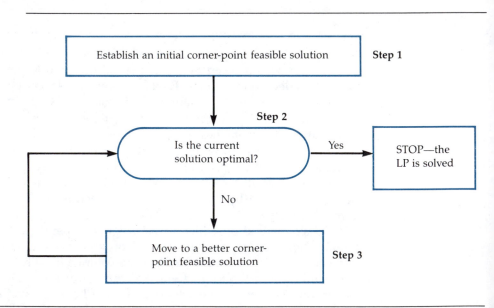

FIGURE 3.1   *The simplex algorithm.*

3. SIMPLEX SOLUTION OF THE PRODUCT MIX PROBLEM

In this section we shall demonstrate the simplex method by solving Sue's product mix problem (Example 2.1 of the previous chapter). For ease of reference we shall restate the problem:

Maximize $Z = 5x_1 + 12x_2$ ($ profit/week)
Subject to:

(1) $\dfrac{5}{4} x_1 \le 30$ (machine-hours)

APPLICATIONS

The following applications appear in this chapter in text, examples, or problems:

Advertising planning: media mix
Allocating sales effort: real estate application
Cargo loading: import product selection
Crime prevention
Feed mix for a cattle ranch
Investment management
Manufacturing equipment selection
Nurse scheduling for an urgent health care center
Product distribution: logistics
Product distribution: warehousing
Product mix problems
Production scheduling: routing
Recycling metal scrap for metal-alloy design
Subcontractor selection

---

(2) $\dfrac{5}{4} x_1 + 2x_2 \le 50$ (labor-hours)

(3) $\qquad\qquad x_2 \le 15$ (sales)

(4) $\qquad x_1 \qquad \ge 0$

(5) $\qquad\qquad x_2 \ge 0$

(Recall that x_1 equals the number of plant pots to make per week, x_2 equals the number of ashtrays to make per week, and the unit profit on these two products is $5 for each plant pot and $12 for each ashtray.)

Also, we shall reproduce the graphical representation of this problem that was shown in Chapter 2 (see Figure 2.4) and present it here as Fig. 3.2.

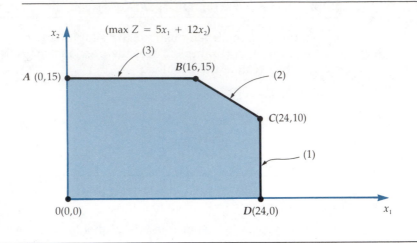

FIGURE 3.2   *Sue's product mix problem.*

The problem has five corner-point feasible solutions, labeled O, A, B, C, and D, having (x_1, x_2) coordinates as follows:

$O = (0, 0)$, the origin

$A = (0, 15)$

$B = (16, 15)$

$C = (24, 10)$

$D = (24, 0)$

In soving this problem by the simplex algorithm we shall key each step to one of the three steps of the simplex algorithm shown in Fig. 3.1. Also, we shall give the reason behind the computations made at each step. Before getting into the details of the simplex method, it is first necessary to discuss the notion of a **slack variable.**

Slack Variables

You may recall from Chapter 2 that an optimal solution to a linear program always occurs at a corner point of the feasible-solution space. Since the corner points are located on the boundary of the feasible-solution space, we would like to devise a method of systematically representing this boundary. In geometric terms, this is one of the main reasons for using slack variables (to be discussed shortly). Algebraically, you will recall from Chapter 2 that each corner point is the intersection of two constraint *equations*. To find such an intersection, you must solve the two equations simultaneously. We can do this by introducing slacks, variables that will allow us to convert each inequality to an equality.

To demonstrate the use of slack variables, let us take the second constraint as an example:

(2) $\dfrac{5}{4}x_1 + 2x_2 \leq 50$

A graph of the region represented by the constraint is shown in Fig. 3.3. Every point on the line satisfies constraint (2) with equality. Points lying under the line satisfy the constraint with strict inequality.

The method involves introducing a slack variable, s_2, to "take up any slack" between the left-hand and right-hand sides of constraint (2):

(2) $\dfrac{5}{4}x_1 + 2x_2 + s_2 = 50$

For example, take the point (10, 15) that represents the product mix (10 plant pots, 15 ashtrays). This product mix corresponds to $x_1 = 10$, $x_2 = 15$, and requires $(5/4)(10) + 2(15) = 42.5$ labor-hours to produce. Thus the slack variable s_2 for constraint (2) equals $50 - 42.5 = 7.5$ and *represents the number*

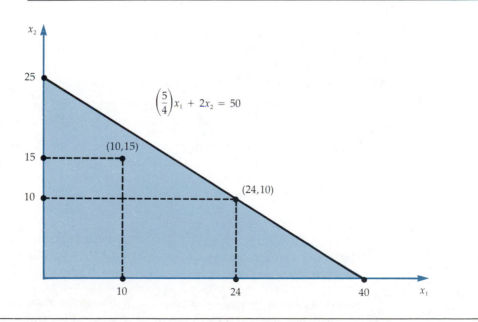

FIGURE 3.3

of unused labor-hours. On the other hand, the product mix (24 plant pots, 10 ashtrays) requires $(5/4)(24) + 2(10) = 50$ labor-hours to produce. In this case there is zero slack: $s_2 = 50 - 50 = 0$, meaning that the labor-hour resource is being fully used.

In general, any point lying *under the line* $(5/4)x_1 + 2x_2 = 50$ corresponds to a product mix in which the slack variable s_2 is positive, which in turn means that the 50 labor-hours resource is not fully used. A point lying *on the line* corresponds to a product mix requiring the full 50 labor-hours to produce.

We also note that the profit associated with a slack variable is zero. For example, at the point (10 pots, 15 ashtrays) the slack s_2 equals 7.5 labor-hours. Obviously, we receive no profit on these unused labor-hours.

Solving Sue's Problem: The Simplex Method

STEP 1. Establish an initial corner-point feasible solution.

Rule. Convert each constraint inequality into an equality and set up the initial *simplex tableau.*

Sue's Problem. Since each constraint in Sue's problem is of the form "≤," we can convert each constraint to an equality by adding slack variables, which we shall label s_1, s_2, and s_3, as follows:

$$(1) \qquad \frac{5}{4}x_1 + 0x_2 + \ s_1 + 0s_2 + 0s_3 = 30$$

$$(2) \qquad \frac{5}{4}x_1 + 2x_2 + 0s_1 + \ s_2 + 0s_3 = 50 \tag{3-1}$$

$$(3) \qquad 0x_1 + \ x_2 + 0s_1 + 0s_2 + \ s_3 = 15$$

Note that we have also explicitly introduced zero coefficients as needed. Slack variable s_1 makes constraint (1) an equality, s_2 makes constraint (2) an equality, and s_3 makes constraint (3) an equality. Since the profit associated with each of these is 0, we can also write Z as

$$Z = 5x_1 + 12x_1 + 0s_1 + 0s_2 + 0s_3 \tag{3-2}$$

The initial simplex tableau appears in Table 3.1. Study it carefully, comparing the entries to the coefficients of constraints (1), (2), and (3) and of Z.

Row 1. For ease of reference later on, the original Z coefficient of each variable is listed along the top row: 5, 12, 0, 0, and 0. This is called the c_j row. Thus $c_1 = 5$, $c_2 = 12$, $c_3 = 0$, $c_4 = 0$, and $c_5 = 0$.

Row 2. The corresponding variables are listed in the second row from the top: x_1, x_2, s_1, s_2, and s_3.

Rows 3, 4, 5. Study the three equations in Eq. (3–1). Do you see an obvious initial solution to these three equations? Suppose you set $x_1 = x_2 = 0$. Then you would have the following system:

$$s_1 + 0s_2 + 0s_3 = 30$$

$$0s_1 + s_2 + 0s_3 = 50$$

$$0s_1 + 0s_2 + s_3 = 15$$

This system has the obvious solution $s_1 = 30$, $s_2 = 50$, and $s_3 = 15$.

In Table 3.1 you will see that s_1, s_2, and s_3 are listed as basic variables. Their values are given as 30, 50, and 15, respectively, in the column headed "Right-hand side." The other entries in rows 3, 4, and 5 are the constraint coefficients.

A **basic variable** is a variable that is considered to be part of a solution to the LP. Note that our LP has three constraints, which are converted to three constraint equations. You may recall the fundamental fact from algebra that, given three equations, it is possible to solve for only three variables. In our example we set two variables equal to zero (x_1 and x_2) and solve for the remaining three variables, s_1, s_2, and s_3. The three variables we wish to solve for at any step of the simplex method are called the basic variables.

Row 6. If $x_1 = x_2 = 0$ and $s_1 = 30$, $s_2 = 50$, and $s_3 = 15$, then we find the value of Z from Eq. (3–2) as follows:

$$Z = 5(0) + 12(0) + 0(30) + 0(50) + 0(15) = 0$$

TABLE 3.1   *Initial Simplex Tableau for Sue's Problem*

(Row 1)	c_j	5	12	0	0	0	
(Row 2)	Basic variables	x_1	x_2	s_1	s_2	s_3	Right-hand side
(Row 3)	s_1	5/4	0	1	0	0	30
(Row 4)	s_2	5/4	2	0	1	0	50
(Row 5)	s_3	0	1	0	0	1	15
(Row 6)	Z						0
(Row 7)	z_j	0	0	0	0	0	
(Row 8)	$c_j - z_j$	5	12	0	0	0	

Note that we have written a 0 in row 6 of the right-hand column of the tableau.

Row 7. Now look at the z_j row. The leftmost z_j is z_1 and equals 0. This was obtained as follows: Multiply each objective function coefficient of the basic variables by the corresponding entry in the x_1 column of the table and sum the results. The objective function coefficients of the basic variables, s_1, s_2, and s_3 are listed in row 1 of the table (the c_j row) as 0, 0, and 0. The x_1 column coefficients are 5/4, 5/4, and 0. Thus

$$z_1 = 0\left(\frac{5}{4}\right) + 0\left(\frac{5}{4}\right) + (0) = 0$$

Similarly, z_2, the second entry from the left in row 7, is calculated as follows:

$$z_2 = 0(0) + 0(2) + 0(1) = 0$$

And continuing, we calculate

$$z_3 = 0(1) + 0(0) + 0(0) = 0$$

$$z_4 = 0(0) + 0(1) + 0(0) = 0$$

$$z_5 = 0(0) + 0(0) + 0(1) = 0$$

Row 8. This row is simply row 1 (the c_j row) minus row 7 (the z_j row). Thus

$$c_1 - z_1 = \ 5 - 0 = \ 5$$

$$c_2 - z_2 = 12 - 0 = 12$$

$$c_3 - z_3 = \ 0 - 0 = \ 0$$

$$c_4 - z_4 = \ 0 - 0 = \ 0$$

$$c_5 - z_5 = \ 0 - 0 = \ 0$$

Reasons Behind Step 1. The purpose of introducing the simplex tableau is simply to have a convenient "bookkeeping" device for performing the steps of the simplex algorithm. It would be entirely feasible to execute the simplex algorithm without using the organization of the simplex tableau. However, such an attempt would be confusing and more time-consuming.

In Table 3.1 you will note that we *should have* at this point an initial corner-point feasible solution. Do we? Of course! We have $x_1 = x_2 = 0$ as discussed above. This corresponds to the corner point labeled 0 in Figure 3.2.

An interpretation of the z_j and $c_j - z_j$ rows will be given in step 2 below.

STEP 2. Is the current solution optimal?

Rule. Examine the $c_j - z_j$ row (row 8). If *all* the entries of that row are less than or equal to 0, the current solution is optimal and we stop. Otherwise, we continue on to step 3.

Sue's Problem. The entries in the $c_j - z_j$ row are 5, 12, 0, 0, and 0, which are not all less than or equal to zero. Thus the current solution ($x_1 = x_2 = 0$, $s_1 = 30$, $s_2 = 50$, $s_3 = 15$) is not optimal, and we shall have to continue on to step 3.

Reasons Behind Step 2.

THE MEANING OF THE z_j's. Look at the initial tableau in Table 3.1. The current basic variables are s_1, s_2, and s_3. The *nonbasic* variables are x_1 and x_2 and are equal to 0. To interpret the meaning of z_1 (the leftmost entry of row 7), let us ask "What would happen if we let x_1 enter the basis and become positive?" To see what would happen to s_1, let us write row 3 in the following equation form:

$$\frac{5}{4}x_1 + 0x_2 + s_1 + 0s_2 + 0s_3 = 30$$

or

$$s_1 = 30 - \frac{5}{4}x_1$$

From this we can see directly that for each unit we increase x_1, the variable s_1 will have to give up (or decrease by) 5/4 units.

If you follow this same logic with row 4 and row 5, you will see that for each unit we increase x_1, we would have to give up 5/4 units of s_2 and 0 units of s_3. Since s_1, s_2, and s_3 each contribute zero profit (that is, have 0 coefficients in Z), the total profit we would have to give up by increasing x_1 one unit is

$$\left(\frac{5}{4} \text{ units of } s_1\right)\left(\$0 \text{ profit from } s_1\right)$$

plus

$$\left(\frac{5}{4} \text{ units of } s_2\right)\left(\$0 \text{ profit from } s_2\right)$$

plus

$$(0 \text{ units of } s_3)(\$0 \text{ profits from } s_3)$$

which equals $0. But this is exactly how we computed z_1 in Step 1.

Thus, in general, *the value of z_j equals the profit we would have to give up for each unit we increase the variable of column j.*

THE MEANING OF $c_j - z_j$. Again, take x_1 of column 1 as an example. How much profit would we *gain* by increasing x_1 one unit? The answer is c_1 (or the objective function coefficient of x_1), which equals \$5. The *net profit realizable by increasing* x_1 *one unit* is

(Profit gained) − (Profit given up) = $c_1 - z_1$

$$= 5 - 0$$

$$= \$5$$

Thus, in general, $c_j - z_j$ *equals the net profit realizable by increasing the variable of column j by one unit.*

BRINGING IT TOGETHER. Now the reason behind the rule of step 2 should become clear. If all the $(c_j - z_j)$s are less than or equal to 0, then no net profit can be gained by letting one of the nonbasic variables become basic. That is, the current basic variables yield the highest attainable profit and the current solution is optimal.

Substitution Rates. We noted above that for each unit x_1 increases, s_1 would have to decrease 5/4 units, s_2 would decrease 5/4 units, and s_3 would not be affected. The numbers 5/4, 5/4, and 0 comprise the column under x_1. We refer to these entries as **marginal substitution rates.** Let us examine these rates more closely in economic terms. The initial solution (shown in Table 3.1) corresponds to 0 production: $x_1 = 0$, $x_2 = 0$. As the slack variables indicate, this leaves 30 unused machine-hours, 50 unused labor-hours, and 15 units of sales potential for ashtrays.

Now suppose we increase production of pots from 0 to 1 unit. This unit would require 5/4 machine-hours to produce. Thus the 30 unused machine-hours would be decreased by 5/4, or equivalently, the slack variable s_1 would decrease by 5/4. In addition, the production of one pot would require 5/4 labor-hours, thus decreasing the slack variable s_2 by 5/4. Since there is no sales constraint on pots, the slack variable $s_3 = 15$ is not affected, as indicated by the 0 in row 5, column x_1.

In summary, to increase x_1 by one unit would entail substituting 5/4 units of s_1, 5/4 units of s_2, and 0 units of s_3 for the unit of x_1. The entries in the other columns (under x_2, s_1, s_2, and s_3) have similar economic interpretations.

STEP 3. Move to a better adjacent corner-point feasible solution.

Rule. This rule has three parts:

1. Determine the **entering variable;** that is, which nonbasic variable should enter the basis and become basic? The nonbasic variable that has the larg-

est $c_j - z_j$ value is the entering variable. The column of the simplex tableau corresponding to the entering variable is called the **pivot column.** If two or more nonbasic variables are tied for the largest $c_j - z_j$ value, break the tie arbitrarily.

2. Determine which of the variables in the basis should leave the basis. This variable is called the **leaving variable.** To determine the leaving variable, first divide each *positive* entry of the pivot column into the corresponding entry of the right-hand-side column. The row variable corresponding to the minimum ratio is the leaving variable.

3. Generate the new simplex tableau. The entry of the tableau that is at the intersection of the pivot column and the row of the leaving variable is called the **pivot element.** As illustrated below, this entry is used to bring the entering variable into the basis and to remove the leaving variable.

SUE'S PROBLEM. We now demonstrate the three parts of step 3 for Sue's problem.

1. The entering variable is x_2, since its $c_j - z_j$ value is 12 compared to x_1's $c_j - z_j$ value of 5. The pivot column is column 2 headed by x_2, as follows:

$$\frac{x_2}{\begin{matrix}0\\2\\1\end{matrix}}$$

2. Divide each *positive* entry of the pivot column into the right-hand side as follows:

$$50 \div 2 = 25$$

$$15 \div 1 = 15$$

(Ignore the *zero* entry of the pivot column.) The minimum ratio, 15, corresponds to the s_3 row; therefore, s_3 is the leaving variable.

3. The pivot element is "1," illustrated as follows:

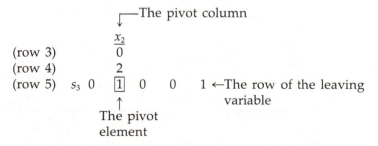

Our goal is to associate row 5 with the entering variable x_2. Look at Table 3.1, repeated on p. 74. As the pivot column shows, x_2 also appears in the

s_2 row (row 4). Thus, we must remove x_2 from that row. This is easily done by multiplying row 5 by 2 and subtracting the result from row 4 as follows:

5/4	2	0	1	0	50	(old row 4)
− (0	2	0	0	2	30)	−(2 × row 5)
5/4	0	0	1	−2	20	(new row 4)

Since the coefficient of x_2 in the s_1 row is 0, we do not have to eliminate x_2 from that row.

The new simplex tableau is given in Table 3.2. It shows the results of the first iteration of the simplex method on Sue's problem.

TABLE 3.1   *Initial Simplex Tableau for Sue's Problem*

		x_1	x_2	s_1	s_2	s_3	Right-hand side
(Row 1)	c_j	5	12	0	0	0	
(Row 2)	Basic variables						
(Row 3)	s_1	5/4	0	1	0	0	30
(Row 4)	s_2	5/4	2	0	1	0	50
(Row 5)	s_3	0	1	0	0	1	15
(Row 6)	Z						0
(Row 7)	z_j	0	0	0	0	0	
(Row 8)	$c_j - z_j$	5	12	0	0	0	

TABLE 3.2   *Results of Iteration 1*

		x_1	x_2	s_1	s_2	s_3	Right-hand side
(Row 1)	c_j	5	12	0	0	0	
(Row 2)	Basic variables						
(Row 3)	s_1	5/4	0	1	0	0	30
(Row 4)	s_2	5/4	0	0	1	−2	20
(Row 5)	x_2	0	1	0	0	1	15
(Row 6)	Z						180
(Row 7)	z_j	0	12	0	0	12	
(Row 8)	$c_j - z_j$	5	0	0	0	−12	

Note the changes made. Row 5 is now associated with the basic variable x_2. Row 4 is replaced by its new values as computed above. Z in row 6 is calculated from the solution represented by the new tableau.

$s_1 = 30$, $s_2 = 20$, $x_2 = 15$ (the basic variables)

$x_1 = s_3 = 0$ (the nonbasic variables)

Thus

$Z = \$0(s_1) + \$0(s_2) + \$12(x_2)$

$\quad = \$0(30) + \$0(20) + \$12(15)$

$\quad = \$180.$

As before, we obtain the z_j row by multiplying each basic variable objective function coefficient by the corresponding entry in the column. Each of these computations is given below, where the objective function coefficients of the basic variables are 0 (for s_1), 0 (for s_2), and 12 (for x_2). Thus

$z_1 = 0\left(\dfrac{5}{4}\right) + 0\left(\dfrac{5}{4}\right) + 12(0) = 0$ (using the x_1 column)

$z_2 = 0(0) \quad + 0(0) \quad + 12(1) = 12$ (using the x_2 column)

$z_3 = 0(1) \quad + 0(0) \quad + 12(0) = 0$ (using the s_1 column)

$z_4 = 0(0) \quad + 0(1) \quad + 12(0) = 0$ (using the s_2 column)

$z_5 = 0(0) \quad + 0(-2) + 12(1) = 12$ (using the s_3 column)

Row 8 is simply the c_j row minus the z_j row.

$c_1 - z_1 = 5 - 0 = 5$

$c_2 - z_2 = 12 - 12 = 0$

$c_3 - z_3 = 0 - 0 = 0$

$c_4 - z_4 = 0 - 0 = 0$

$c_5 - z_5 = 0 - 12 = -12$

Geometrically, the new corner-point feasible solution $(x_1, x_2) = (0, 15)$ corresponds to point A in Figure 3.2. Point $O = (0, 0)$ was the initial corner-point feasible solution. The value of Z at point O was 0 and the value of Z is now 180 at point A. Thus *we have moved to a better corner-point feasible solution,* as step 3 requires (see Figure 3.4).

Reasons Behind Step 3. We shall discuss each of the three parts in turn.

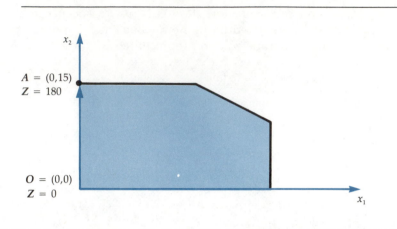

x_2

$A = (0,15)$
$Z = 180$

$O = (0,0)$
$Z = 0$

x_1

FIGURE 3.4

1. *Determining the entering variable.* Recall that $c_j - z_j$ measures the net amount that profit will increase if we increase the corresponding nonbasic variable by one unit. The entering variable is chosen on the basis of which nonbasic variable would increase Z at the fastest rate.

2. *Determining the leaving variable.* As we increase the new entering basic variable we will select one of the old basic variables to leave the basis. To see why we do this, note that there are three constraint equations in Sue's problem. You may recall from one of your math courses that given three equations you can solve for only three unknowns. Thus, if we introduce a new variable (the entering variable), we must remove one of the existing variables (otherwise we would be trying to solve for four variables, using three equations).

   So which variable should leave the basis? The rule we follow is to remove the variable which would go to 0 first as the entering variable is increased. Refer to Table 3.1. Let us solve each of the three equations for the corresponding *basic variables in terms of the entering variable x_2*, as follows:

   (the s_1 row) $s_1 = 30 - 0x_2$

   (the s_2 row) $s_2 = 50 - 2x_2$

   (the s_3 row) $s_3 = 15 - x_2$

   Look at s_1. What happens to s_1 as x_2 is increased? Since the coefficient of x_2 is 0, nothing happens to s_1 as x_2 increases. This is why the rule says to ignore 0 entries in the pivot column when computing the ratios (also ignore negative entries, since in such cases the corresponding current basic variable would only increase as the entering variable increases).

Note that s_1 measures unused machine-hours and currently equals 30. Since the production of ashtrays does not require the machine-hour resource, increasing x_2 will not affect the value of s_1.

Look at s_2. Since $s_2 = 50 - 2x_2$, s_2 first becomes 0 when x_2 is increased to 25. Beyond 25, s_2 would become negative, which is not permitted. Note that the number 25 is the ratio 50/2, computed according to the rule. (If x_2 is increased to 25 units, the labor-hour resource would be fully used up. This would be indicated by s_2 being driven to 0.)

Look at s_3. Since $s_3 = 15 - x_2$, s_3 first becomes 0 when x_2 is increased to 15. Beyond 15, s_2 would become negative. Note, too, that $15 = 15 \div 1$, as the rule indicates. (You should note that s_3 measures unused sales potential and currently equals 15. Each ashtray produced will decrease s_3 by one unit. Thus, when x_2 is increased to 15, the sales potential resource will be fully used up.)

Conclusion. We should remove s_3 from the basis, since it will first be driven negative as x_2 increases. If instead we remove s_2, there is a danger that s_3 would take on negative values as x_2 increases beyond 15, indicating that we would be exceeding the sales potential of ashtrays.

3. *Generate the new simplex tableau.* Once the entering and leaving variables are determined, a new simplex tableau must be generated that has the entering variable as a basic variable and the leaving variable as a nonbasic variable. The so-called Gauss-Jordan method of elimination is used to accomplish two things:

(a) Make the coefficient of the entering variable equal to 1 in the leaving variable row. This coefficient is the pivot element. In our example, looking at Table 3.1 again, you will recall that the pivot element is already 1. If it had not been 1, we would have divided the entire s_3 row by that pivot number; this division would then make the pivot element equal to 1.

(b) Make the coefficient of the entering variable 0 in every row except the leaving variable row. This is accomplished by subtracting appropriate multiples of the leaving row from each row. In our example, the x_2 coefficient in the s_1 row of Table 3.1 was already 0, so nothing was done to that row. In the s_2 row, the x_2 coefficient was 2. Thus to eliminate this 2, we multiplied the s_3 row by 2 and subtracted the result from the s_2 row.

General Gauss-Jordan Rule. In general, determine the entering and leaving variables and then divide the leaving variable row by the pivot element to make the pivot entry 1. Then for each of the other rows, if the coefficient of the entering variable is m, multiply the leaving varible row by m and subtract the result from that row.

An Insight. Look at the result of the first iteration in Table 3.2. The basic variables are s_1, s_2, and x_2. The nonbasic variables are $x_1 = s_3 = 0$. You will notice that each basic variable has a coefficient of 1 in its row and a coefficient of 0 in all the other rows. If we substitute $x_1 = s_3 = 0$ in the three equations of Table 3.2, we can write this system of equations as follows:

$$\frac{5}{4}(0) + 0x_2 + 1s_1 + 0s_2 + 0(0) = 30$$

$$\frac{5}{4}(0) + 0x_2 + 0s_1 + 1s_2 - 2(0) = 20$$

$$0(0) + 1x_2 + 0s_1 + 0s_2 + 1(0) = 15$$

or

$$s_1 = 30$$

$$s_2 = 20$$

$$x_2 = 15$$

Thus by following the simplex algorithm, solving the system of constraint equations is trivial.

Following the Simplex Algorithm

Look at the flowchart of the simplex algorithm in Fig. 3.1. We have just completed step 3. We must now go back to step 2 to test whether the current solution ($s_1 = 30$, $s_2 = 20$, $x_2 = 15$) is optimal, and the procedure starts all over again. We now perform these steps for Sue's problem.

Sue's Product Mix Problem:
Iteration 2 of the Simplex Algorithm

STEP 2. Is the current solution optimal? Since the entries in the $c_j - z_j$ row are *not* all less than or equal to 0, the current solution is not optimal, and we continue on to step 3.

STEP 3. Move to a better corner-point feasible solution. Three parts of this step are as follows:

1. *Determine the entering variable.* This would be x_1, since it has the largest $c_j - z_j$ value (which is 5). The pivot column is the x_1 column.
2. *Determine the leaving variable.* The ratios are

$$30 \div 5/4 = 24$$

$$20 \div 5/4 = 16$$

TABLE 3.3

Column	Old s_2 row entry $\div$ pivot element $=$ new entry				
x_1	$\dfrac{5}{4}$	$\div$	$\dfrac{5}{4}$	$=$	1
x_2	0	$\div$	$\dfrac{5}{4}$	$=$	0
s_1	0	$\div$	$\dfrac{5}{4}$	$=$	0
s_2	1	$\div$	$\dfrac{5}{4}$	$=$	$\dfrac{4}{5}$
s_3	-2	$\div$	$\dfrac{5}{4}$	$=$	$-\dfrac{8}{5}$
Right-hand side	20	$\div$	$\dfrac{5}{4}$	$=$	16

These were computed by dividing the *positive* entries of the pivot column into the corresponding entries of the right-hand side. Since 16 is less than 24, we select s_2 as the leaving variable.

3. *Generate the new simplex tableau.* The pivot element is 5/4 (the intersection of the x_1 column and the s_2 row; that is, the pivot column and the leaving variable row).

To make the coefficient of x_1 equal to 1 in the s_2 row, divide the s_2 row by the pivot element 5/4 to get a new row as shown in Table 3.3.

The constraint equation is now as shown in Table 3.4
We must use the Gauss-Jordan method to eliminate the coefficient (5/4)

TABLE 3.4

Row	Basic variable	x_1	x_2	s_1	s_2	s_3	Right-hand side
(3)	s_1	$\dfrac{5}{4}$	0	1	0	0	30
(4)	x_1	1	0	0	$\dfrac{4}{5}$	$-\dfrac{8}{5}$	16
(5)	x_2	0	1	0	0	1	15

of x_1 from the s_1 equation as follows:

$$s_1 \text{ row} - \left(\frac{5}{4} \times x_1 \text{ row}\right)$$

$$\frac{5}{4} \quad 0 \quad 1 \quad 0 \quad 0 \quad 30 \qquad s_1 \text{ row}$$

$$-\left(\frac{5}{4} \quad 0 \quad 0 \quad 1 \quad -2 \quad 20\right) \qquad -\left(\frac{5}{4} \times x_1 \text{ row}\right)$$

$$\overline{\quad 0 \quad 0 \quad 1 \quad -1 \quad 2 \quad 10 \quad} \qquad \text{new } s_1 \text{ row}$$

Using these new rows (equations) we can generate the new simplex tableau as shown in Table 3.5.

The values of z_j are calculated as follows:

$$z_1 = 0(0) \quad + 1(5) \quad + 0(12) = \quad 5 \quad (\text{using the } x_1 \text{ column})$$

$$z_2 = 0(0) \quad + 0(5) \quad + 1(12) = 12 \quad (\text{using the } x_2 \text{ column})$$

$$z_3 = 1(0) \quad + 0(5) \quad + 0(12) = \quad 0 \quad (\text{using the } s_1 \text{ column})$$

$$z_4 = -1(0) + \frac{4}{5}(5) \quad + 0(12) = \quad 4 \quad (\text{using the } s_2 \text{ column})$$

$$z_5 = 2(0) \quad + \left(-\frac{8}{5}\right)(5) + 1(12) = \quad 4 \quad (\text{using the } s_3 \text{ column})$$

TABLE 3.5   *Results of Iteration 2 (the final iteration)*

		x_1	x_2	s_1	s_2	s_3	
(Row 1)	c_j	5	12	0	0	0	
(Row 2)	Basic variables	x_1	x_2	s_1	s_2	s_3	Right-hand side
(Row 3)	s_1	0	0	1	−1	2	10
(Row 4)	x_1	1	0	0	$\frac{4}{5}$	$-\frac{8}{5}$	16
(Row 5)	x_2	0	1	0	0	1	15
(Row 6)	Z						260
(Row 7)	z_j	5	12	0	4	4	
(Row 8)	$c_j - z_j$	0	0	0	−4	−4	

The $c_j - z_j$ are

$$c_1 - z_1 = 5 - 5 = 0$$

$$c_2 - z_2 = 12 - 12 = 0$$

$$c_3 - z_3 = 0 - 0 = 0$$

$$c_4 - z_4 = 0 - 4 = -4$$

$$c_5 - z_5 = 0 - 4 = -4$$

and Z is calculated as shown in Table 3.6 ($s_2 = s_3 = 0$ are nonbasic).

This completes step 3 of iteration 2 of the simplex algorithm. Note that *geometrically* we have moved from point A of Fig. 3.4 where $Z = 180$, to a "better" adjacent point, B, where $Z = 260$ (see Fig. 3.5). According to the flowchart in Fig. 3.1, we must return to step 2 to test this new solution for optimality.

TABLE 3.6

Basic variable	Objective function coefficient ×		Value of the basic variable
s_1	0 ×	10 =	0
x_1	5 ×	16 =	80
x_2	12 ×	15 =	180
		Σ =	260

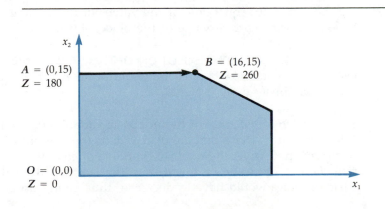

FIGURE 3.5

Sue's Product Mix Problem:
Iteration 3 of the Simplex Algorithm

STEP 2. Is the current solution optimal? Since all the $c_j - z_j$ entries of Table 3.5 are less than or equal to 0, the current solution is optimal. We now STOP—the LP is solved.

The solution to the LP is

$x_1 = 16$

$x_2 = 15$

$Z = 260$

This agrees with the result we obtained by using the graphical method of the previous chapter. (See Fig. 2.4 for a graphical summary.)

Summary of the Simplex Method

We have been using Fig. 3.1 as an overview of the simplex algorithm and have given detailed algebraic procedures for each step shown in the flow-chart. A brief summary of the algebraic procedure follows.

STEP 1. ESTABLISH AN INITIAL CORNER-POINT FEASIBLE SOLUTION. Convert each inequality constraint to an equality. For "≤" constraints, this requires introducing slack variables. The slack variables then become the initial solution that corresponds to the original variables' being 0. The other two types of constraints, "≥" and "=," are discussed in Section 4 of this chapter.

The simplex tableau is a convenient bookkeeping device for recording all the data of the problem. It shows the basic variables (the variables currently in the solution) and essentially handles the process of simultaneously solving the constraint equations for the values of the variables. In addition, the table shows the current value of the objective function Z.

STEP 2. IS THE CURRENT SOLUTION OPTIMAL? If all the $c_j - z_j$ entries are less than or equal to 0, the current solution is optimal and we STOP. Otherwise we must go on to step 3.

The Meaning of the z_j's. For the nonbasic variables (those not in the current solution; that is, those that are 0), z_j equals the amount of profit that would be given up if we let the nonbasic variable of column j enter the basis. This reduction in the value of Z is due to the fact that the value of the current basic variables would have to decrease, thus giving up profit.

The Meaning of the $(c_j - z_j)$'s. For the nonbasic variables, $c_j - z_j$ equals the *net profit* that can be gained by entering the nonbasic variables into the solution.

STEP 3. MOVE TO A BETTER ADJACENT CORNER-POINT FEASIBLE SOLUTION.

1. *Determine the entering variable;* that is, determine which nonbasic variable should enter the basis. This will be the nonbasic variable having the largest positive $c_j - z_j$ value. The column corresponding to the entering variable is called the *pivot column.*
2. *Determine the leaving variable.* This will be the basic variable that will be driven to 0 first as the entering variable increases. To find the leaving variable, compute the ratios of the right-hand-side entries to the corresponding *positive* entries in the pivot column. The basic variable in the row corresponding to the minimum ratio is the leaving variable.
3. *Generate the new simplex tableau.* The entry in the pivot column and row of the leaving variable is the *pivot element.* Using the Gauss-Jordan method of elimination, generate the new simplex tableau. The entering variable becomes the basic variable associated with the row of the leaving variable. Its coefficient in that row must be made equal to 1 (by dividing that row by the pivot element), and its coefficient in all other rows must be made equal to 0 (using Gauss-Jordan).

Now return to step 2.

Problems

1. Using the simplex algorithm, solve the following linear program:

Maximize $Z = 60x_1 + 80x_2$
Subject to:

$$(1) \quad x_1 + \frac{3}{2}x_2 \le 4{,}000$$
$$(2) \quad 2x_1 + x_2 \le 4{,}000$$
$$(3) \quad x_1, \quad x_2 \ge 0$$

This is the A-1 Shaky Frames problem (Example 2.3) that was solved graphically in the previous chapter. Compare each step of the simplex solution with the graphical solution (Fig. 2.6).

2. Solve the following linear program, using the simplex algorithm:

Maximize $Z = 4x_1 + 3x_2$
Subject to:

$$(1) \quad x_1 + 0.6x_2 \le 30$$
$$(2) \quad x_1 \quad\quad \le 25$$
$$(3) \quad\quad\quad x_2 \le 20$$
$$(4) \quad x_1, \quad x_2 \ge 0$$

Solve the same problem graphically, and use the graphical representation to interpret the successive simplex solutions.

3. Solve the following linear program, using the simplex method:

Maximize $Z = 2x_1 + 3x_2 + x_3$
Subject to:
(1) $x_1 + x_2 + x_3 \leq 9$
(2) $2x_1 + 3x_2 \qquad \leq 25$
(3) $\qquad x_2 + 2x_3 \leq 10$
(4) $x_1, \qquad x_2, \qquad x_3 \geq 0$

This is an example of a problem that cannot be solved by the graphical method.

4. ADAPTING TO OTHER LP FORMS

In Section 3 of this chapter we illustrated the simplex algorithm, using a maximization problem having all "≤" constraints. The simplex method is easily applied to other forms after making suitable modifications as described in this section.

Minimization Problems

Suppose we have an LP whose objective function is

Minimize $Z = 2x_1 + 3x_2$

There are two methods for handling this type of problem:

METHOD 1. Convert the LP to a maximization problem. This can be done by applying the simplex algorithm to the following objective function:

Maximize $Z' = -Z = -2x_1 - 3x_2$

If you maximize the negative of Z, then you will drive $-Z$ up through negative values as close to 0 as possible to $-Z^*$:

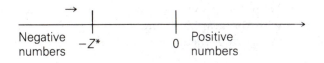

Now what has happened to $+Z$ as you have done this? It has been driven down through positive values as close to 0 as possible to Z^*:

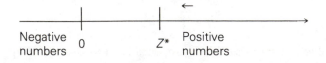

In summary, to minimize Z, apply the simplex algorithm to maximize $-Z$, obtain an answer $-Z^*$, then take the negative of this to obtain the answer to the minimization problem, Z^*. A mathematician would say that "minimizing Z is equivalent to maximizing $-Z$."

METHOD 2. Modify the simplex algorithm. In this method we do not negate Z but instead work directly with the objective of minimizing Z. To do so we must slightly modify the simplex algorithm as follows:

Step 1. Same as before.

Step 2. To see if the current solution is optimal, we must check the $c_j - z_j$ row for negative numbers. If there are no negative values of $c_j - z_j$, the current solution is optimal. Otherwise we continue to step 3. The reason behind this step derives from our interpretation of $c_j - z_j$ as net profit. If the net profit obtainable by entering a nonbasic variable is *negative*, this means that the objective function will *decrease* if that variable is allowed to enter the basis. If we are minimizing, this is precisely what we want.

It is more convenient (and makes more sense) in minimization problems to think of the c_j's as costs and to interpret $c_j - z_j$ as the amount by which the cost would increase if we enter the jth variable into the basis. If $c_j - z_j$ is negative, it would mean that the cost would decrease.

Step 3. Choose the nonbasic variable having the most negative $c_j - z_j$ value as the *entering variable*, since this variable would decrease Z the fastest. The other two parts of step 3 are the same as before.

Greater-Than-or-Equal-To Constraints

Suppose an LP has a constraint such as

$$2x_1 + 3x_2 + x_3 \geq 10$$

We can convert this to an equality by subtracting a **surplus variable** s from the left-hand side as follows:

$$2x_1 + 3x_2 + x_3 - s = 10 \quad (s \geq 0)$$

(The variable s measures the surplus between the left-hand side and the right-hand side.)

There is just one problem left to resolve. In step 1, which variable will be the initial basic variable? For "$\leq$" constraints we let the slack variables be the initial basic variables. But suppose we let the surplus variable s be the basic variable for the above equation. With x_1, x_2, and x_3 initially nonbasic,

$x_1 = x_2 = x_3 = 0$, and we would have

$$-s = 10$$
$$s = -10$$

which would give us a negative basic variable violating the nonnegativity requirement $s \geq 0$.

To resolve this difficulty, we simply introduce what is called an **artificial variable,** denoted a, into the equation as follows:

$$2x_1 + 3x_2 + x_3 - s + a = 10$$

and initially let a be the basic variable and $x_1 = x_2 = x_3 = s = 0$ be nonbasic. So $a = 10$ in the initial simplex tableau. In order to ensure that the artificial variable is eventually driven to 0, we "penalize" it by setting its coefficient in the objective function equal to a very negative number in the case of maximization (such as $-999,999$); or to a very large positive number in the case of minimization (such as $999,999$). The coefficient of the surplus variable in the objective function is 0. In practice, we usually let M denote a very large positive number and use either $-M$ or M as the objective function coefficient of an artificial variable.

Equality Constraints

An equality constraint is handled by using the artificial variable technique as described above. Thus the constraint

$$2x_1 + 4x_2 = 6$$

would become

$$2x_1 + 4x_2 + a = 6$$

and a would be the initial basic variable for this constraint. We would also use $-M$ or M as the objective function coefficient of the artificial variable a.

EXAMPLE 3.1. Suppose we have the following LP:

Maximize $Z = 2x_1 + 3x_2 + x_3$
Subject to:
(1) $\quad x_1 + 2x_2 + x_3 \leq 20$
(2) $\quad 2x_1 + x_2 \geq 4$
(3) $\quad x_2 + 4x_3 = 10$
(4) $\quad x_1, x_2, x_3 \geq 0$

To establish the initial simplex tableau, we use a slack variable s_1 in constraint (1), a surplus s_2 and an artificial variable a_1 in constraint (2), and an artificial variable a_2 in constraint (3). The resulting LP becomes

Maximize $Z = 2x_1 + 3x_2 + x_3 + 0s_1 + 0s_2 - Ma_1 - Ma_2$

Subject to:

(1)	$x_1 + 2x_2 + x_3 + s_1$	$= 20$
(2)	$2x_1 + x_2 \qquad - s_2 + a_1$	$= 4$
(3)	$x_2 + 4x_3 \qquad + a_2 = 10$	
(4)	$x_1, \quad x_2, \quad x_3, \quad s_1, \quad s_2, \quad a_1, \quad a_2 \geq 0$	

Since a_1 and a_2 have a very large negative "profit" of $-M$, we can be sure that, in the final solution to the LP, a_1 and a_2 will be 0. The *only* purpose in using a_1 and a_2 is to establish a convenient initial solution to the three constraint equations (1), (2), and (3), as shown in the initial simplex tableau (Table 3.7).

In Table 3.7 we have for the first iteration:

1. The initial corner-point feasible solution is $s_1 = 20$, $a_1 = 4$, $a_2 = 10$ (the other variables are nonbasic and therefore equal 0).
2. The value of Z is $-14M$, since

$$Z = 2x_1 + 3x_2 + x_3 + 0s_1 + 0s_2 - Ma_1 - Ma_2$$

$$= 2(0) + 3(0) + 0 + 0(20) + 0(0) - M(4) - M(10)$$

$$= -14M$$

TABLE 3.7   *Initial Simplex Tableau for Example 3.1*

(Row 1)	c_j	2	3	1	0	0	$-M$	$-M$	
(Row 2)	Basic variables	x_1	x_2	x_3	s_1	s_2	a_1	a_2	Right-hand side
(Row 3)	s_1	1	2	1	1	0	0	0	20
(Row 4)	a_1	2	1	0	0	-1	1	0	4
(Row 5)	a_2	0	1	4	0	0	0	1	10
(Row 6)	Z								$-14M$
(Row 7)	z_j	$-2M$	$-2M$	$-4M$	0	M	$-M$	$-M$	
(Row 8)	$c_j - z_j$	$2 + 2M$	$3 + 2M$	$1 + 4M$	0	$-M$	0	0	

3. The entering variable would be x_3, since $1 + 4M$ is the largest positive $c_j - z_j$ value.
4. The leaving variable would be a_2.   ▲

EXAMPLE 3.2. Suppose we have the following LP:

Minimize $Z = 2x_1 + 3x_2$
Subject to:

(1) $x_1 + x_2 \geq 10$
(2) $x_2 \leq 20$
(3) $30x_1 + 8x_2 = 240$
(4) $x_1, \quad x_2 \geq 0$

Using method 2 for minimization, we would have the following initial system:

Minimize $Z = 2x_1 + 3x_2 + 0s_1 + Ma_1 + 0s_2 + Ma_2$
Subject to:

(1) $x_1 + x_2 - s_1 + a_1 = 10$
(2) $x_2 + s_2 = 20$
(3) $30x_1 + 8x_2 + a_2 = 240$
(4) $x_1, \quad x_2, \quad s_1, \quad a_1, \quad s_2, \quad a_2 \geq 0$

Note the high "penalty cost" put on the artificial variables a_1 and a_2 in the objective function. This will assure us that in the final solution to the LP a_1 and a_2 will both be 0. Also note the use of the surplus variable s_1 and the slack variable s_2. If we use method 1 for minimization, the objective function would be

Maximize $-Z = -2x_1 - 3x_2 + 0s_1 - Ma_1 + 0s_2 - Ma_2$

(Since the coefficients of s_1 and s_2 are 0, we can write these terms as either $-0s_1, -0s_2$ or as $0s_1, 0s_2$.)   ▲

Problems

1. For Example 3.2, using method 1 for minimization problems:
   a. Construct the initial simplex tableau.
   b. Solve using the simplex algorithm for maximization problems.
   c. Solve the problem graphically.
2. For Example 3.2, using method 2 for minimization problems:
   a. Construct the initial simplex tableau.
   b. Solve using the simplex algorithm modified for minimization objectives.
   c. Solve the problem graphically.
3. Solve the following LP, using the simplex method:

Maximize $Z = 5x_1 + 4x_2$
Subject to:
(1) $\quad 4x_1 + 5x_2 \geq 100$
(2) $\quad 3x_1 + 2x_2 \leq 60$
(3) $\quad\qquad\quad x_2 \leq 15$
(4) $\quad x_1, \quad x_2 \geq 0$

Solve graphically, and interpret the iterations of the simplex algorithm.

5. SPECIAL SITUATIONS THAT MAY ARISE

In Section 6 of Chapter 2, we discussed three special situations that could arise in linear programs: (1) multiple optimal solutions, (2) no feasible solutions, and (3) unbounded solutions. Each of these was illustrated graphically by an example. In this section we indicate how each of these conditions is detected by the simplex algorithm.

Multiple Optimal Solutions

Let us suppose we apply the simplex algorithm to solve a linear program in which one of the *nonbasic* variables in the optimal tableau has a $c_j - z_j$ value of 0. This would mean that this variable could enter the basis *without changing* the optimal value of the objective function Z. Thus, instead of choosing to STOP in step 2 of the simplex algorithm, we could go on to step 3 and select this nonbasic variable as the entering variable. The result of doing this would be another set of basic variables that yield the same (optimal) value of Z. (See Problem 1 in this section.)

No Feasible Solutions

If one or more of the artificial variables in the final simplex tableau is a basic variable, the linear program has no feasible solutions.

Recall that an artificial variable is given an objective function coefficient that represents a high penalty for including the artificial variable in the solution. (For maximization problems, an artificial variable a appears as $-Ma$ in the objective function; for minimization it would appear as $+Ma$.) You will also recall that the only reason for introducing artificial variables into a linear program is to obtain a convenient initial feasible corner-point solution. The idea, then, is to drive the artificial variables to 0 while letting the "real" variables enter the solution. If we have not driven the artificial variable(s) in the final solution to 0, it is an indication that there are no feasible solutions to the original problem. (See Problem 2 at the end of this section.)

Unbounded Solutions

Suppose we are performing step 3 of the simplex algorithm; we select an entering basic variable and then begin to determine the leaving variable. If there are no positive entries in the pivot column (the column under the entering variable), the LP has an unbounded solution.

To see why this is true, recall that to determine the leaving variable we compute the ratios of the right-hand-side entries to the corresponding pivot column entries that are *positive*. The resulting minimum ratio pinpoints the current basic variable that would first be driven to 0 as the entering variable is increased. If there are no such positive ratios, then none of the current basic variables would be driven to 0 as we let the entering variable increase. We could thus let the entering variable come into the basis, increase it as much as we wanted, and increase the "profit" without bound, or in the case of minimization, we could decrease the "cost" Z without bound. (See Problem 3 in this section.)

Degeneracy

There is one additional special situation that may arise in performing the simplex algorithm. In determining the leaving variable, ties may occur in computing the ratios (of the right-hand-side entries to the positive corresponding pivot column entries). In such a case we break the tie arbitrarily and select one of the tied basic variables to leave the basis. The other tied basic variable, which is not chosen to leave the basis, will become 0 in the current iteration.

There is the theoretical possibility that the simplex method will "cycle" endlessly when such ties arise and never reach the optimal solution; however, in practice, this almost never happens. Thus when a tie occurs, it is usually sufficient simply to flip a coin to determine which variable should leave the basis.

Problems

1. *Multiple Optimal Solutions.* Apply the simplex algorithm to the LP of Example 2.5 in the previous chapter.
   a. Solve the LP.
   b. Specify three optimal solutions.
2. *No Feasible Solutions.* Apply the simplex algorithm to the LP in Example 2.6 of the previous chapter.
3. *Unbounded Solutions.* Apply the simplex algorithm to the LP in Example 2.7 of the previous chapter.

6. SENSITIVITY ANALYSIS

After the solution to a linear program is determined, it is often of interest to ask how the solution might change if some parts of the linear program change. For example, we might ask how the solution to a linear program would change if:

1. the value of one of the right-hand-side entries changes;
2. the value of one of the objective function coefficients changes;
3. the value of a constraint coefficient changes.

Varying the inputs to a linear program and then examining the corresponding changes in the optimal solution is referred to as **sensitivity analysis.**

As we pointed out in the introduction to this chapter, linear programs are solved in practice by canned computer programs. Most of these programs provide sensitivity analysis as part of the output report either automatically or as an option which the user can request.

In general, the mathematical treatment of sensitivity analysis can become, technically, beyond the scope of this introductory textbook. We shall, however, present a brief treatment (without mathematical details) of the first two types of changes listed above: (1) What happens to the optimal solution to a linear program if the value of one of the right-hand-side entries changes? (2) What happens if an objective function coefficient changes?

Let us discuss these cases of sensitivity analysis, using Sue's product mix problem.

Shadow Prices

Sue's product mix problem is stated mathematically as a linear program in Section 3 of this chapter, and the optimal simplex solution appears in Table 3.5. We see that $x_1 = 16$ (she should make 16 plant pots per week), $x_2 = 15$ (she should make 15 ashtrays per week), and $Z^* = 260$ (her weekly profit will then be $260).

Recall that Sue had 50 labor-hours per week available to make pots and ashtrays. Note that since the slack variable s_2 equals zero for the labor-hour constraint, Sue is using up all the available 50 labor-hours to produce the following optimal product mix:

Constraint (2) $\dfrac{5}{4}(16) + 2(15) = 50$

Thus $s_2 = 0$. This also follows from the fact that s_2 is nonbasic in the optimal solution (see Table 3.5). Or if you prefer a graphical reason why $s_2 = 0$, note in Fig. 3.2 that the optimal solution (16, 15) lies on the second constraint line, line 2, so the slack variable for constraint (2) must be 0 at that point.

What happens if we increase the available labor-hours to 51 per week? If you were to re-solve the LP with constraint (2) replaced by

$$\frac{5}{4}x_1 + 2x_2 \le 51$$

you would obtain as the optimal solution:

$x_1^* = 16.8$ pots

$x_2^* = 15$ pots

$Z^* = \$264$ per week

In other words, profit has increased by \$4—from \$260 to \$264 per week. Changing a right-hand-side value corresponds to changing the availability of a resource. In our case we have increased the labor-hour resource by one unit. Graphically, the effect on constraint line (2) can be illustrated as shown in Fig. 3.6.

Could we have predicted this without re-solving the entire linear program? Yes! To see how this is done, examine the optimal simplex tableau for Sue's original problem (Table 3.5). In that table, s_2 is nonbasic (= 0). What happens if we increase the slack variable s_2 in the optimal solution? For the s_2 variable, $c_j - z_j = -4$, which tells us that profit would decrease by \$4 if s_2 increases by one unit. Thus, the value of each labor-hour must be \$4. So if we increase the available labor-hours from 50 to 51, profit should increase by \$4, and this is exactly what happened.

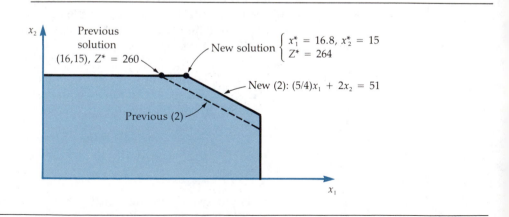

FIGURE 3.6

What about the other constraints? The current machine-hour capacity is 30 hours per week. The current solution (16, 15) uses 20 machine-hours, as follows:

Constraint (1) $(5/4)(16) = 20 \leq 30$

Since we are not fully utilizing the machine-hour resource availability of 30 hours, it stands to reason that it would be of no value to us if we had 31 hours available. Thus if we increase the machine-hour capacity from 30 to 31, we would find that $x_1^* = 16$, $x_2^* = 15$, and $Z^* = 260$ as before. If you do not believe this, you should re-solve the LP using a new constraint (1): $(5/4)x_1 \leq 31$. The value of an additional machine-hour is $0. But note that the $c_j - z_j$ value for the s_1 column is 0.

From the optimal simplex tableau, Table 3.5, can you now guess what would happen to total profit if we projected an additional sale for ashtrays? The answer appears in the $c_j - z_j$ entry for the s_3 column: If Sue could increase the sales of ashtrays from 15 to 16 per week, she would gain an additional $4 in profit. You might wish to check that if we were to re-solve the original LP with constraint (3) replaced by

Constraint (3)' $x_2 \leq 16$

we would obtain

$x_1^* = $ 14.4 pots

$x_2^* = $ 16 ashtrays

$Z^* = \$264$ per week

Graphically, this would give us the picture shown in Fig. 3.7.

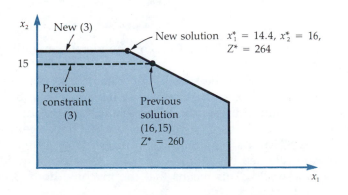

FIGURE 3.7

Thus we see that the value of each unit of resource (in our case, machine-hours, labor-hours, and sales potential) in the optimal LP solution is given by the negative value of $z_j - c_j$ in the columns corresponding to the slack variables for the resource constraints. In our case these values are seen to be 0, 4, and 4, respectively, for machine-hours, labor-hours, and sales potential. These entries in the optimal LP tableau are called **shadow prices**.

Economic Analysis

We have noted that by increasing the sales potential of ashtrays from 15 to 16 per week, an additional $4 in profit would be gained. But recall that the profit on an ashtray is $12. How do we account for this *apparent* discrepancy?

The reason derives from our discussion of substitution rates in Section 3. Look at column s_3 of Table 3.5 (the final simplex tableau for Sue's product mix problem). Suppose we increase s_3 by one unit; that is, we *increase the slack* in the sales constraint (3) for ashtrays. Increasing the slack s_3 by one unit means that we are decreasing the output of ashtrays by one unit, so Z will decrease by $12. So far, then, we note that if s_3 increases one unit, x_2 must decrease by one unit. This substitution rate of 1 for 1 is indicated by the 1 in column s_3, row x_2 of Table 3.5. Also note the $-8/5$ substitution rate in the x_1 row. This means that x_1 will *increase* by 8/5 units if s_3 increases one unit. Thus Z will *increase* by $8 (8/5 pots × $5/pot = $8). The net change in Z caused by increasing s_3 by one unit is

1 less ashtray $-12

$\dfrac{8}{5}$ additional pots   8

$$\overline{\$-\ 4}$$

or a $4 decrease in Z. Thus if we could generate an additional sale, Z would *increase* by $4.

Do you see where the substitution rate of two units of s_1 for one unit of s_3 comes from (row s_1, column s_3)? Constraint (1) is $(5/4)x_1 \leq 30$. If x_2 decreases one unit (in response to increasing s_3 one unit), 2(1) = 2 labor-hours are released, so s_2 increases by 2. But as we have seen, the output of pots increases 8/5 units. The production of 8/5 pots requires the 2 labor-hours that were released by ashtrays, and also requires an additional (8/5)(5/4) = 2 machine-hours. This means that the machine-hour slack variable s_1 must decrease by 2.

Similar interpretations apply to the $4 labor-hour shadow price.

Managerial Use of Shadow Prices

Shadow prices can be used by management to determine the value or desirability of increasing resource allocations to the operation being analyzed. The next example illustrates this.

EXAMPLE 3.3. *Use of Shadow Prices.* (Refer again to Sue's product mix problem.) Let us assume that Sue is considering the potential value of increasing her advertising efforts to promote the sales of her ashtrays. She has designed a one-page advertising leaflet showing an ink drawing of the ashtray design along with its price. After checking with local printers, she finds that the lowest bid to print the leaflets is $20 per 1,000, or 2¢ each. Based on her analysis of past marketing effectiveness of the leaflets, she estimates that one potential sale is generated for every 300 leaflets distributed.

Question. How many leaflets should Sue order?

Solution. In order to increase sales potential by *one* ashtray, Sue must distribute 300 leaflets, each costing 2¢, for a total cost of $6. But as we saw above, the shadow price of the sales potential constraint is only $4. Thus she should not order any leaflets to promote sales of ashtrays.

Question. What would be the break-even printing cost of the leaflets?

Solution. To answer this, simply solve the following break-even equation:

$300p = \$4$

$\quad p = \$0.0133$, or 1-1/3¢ per leaflet

Above 1-1/3¢ each, the total cost of the leaflets per sales potential generated would exceed the marginal profit of $4 per additional sales of ashtrays. However, if Sue can get the leaflets printed for less than 1-1/3¢ each, it would certainly be profitable for her to do so.　　　　　　　　　　　　　　▲

Right-hand-side Ranging

Over what range of values of the right-hand sides of the constraints are the shadow prices valid? For example, in Sue's problem, by how much could sales potential increase above 15 ashtrays per week and still result in a $4 shadow price per unit of sales potential?

　　The rules to follow to determine the range over which the shadow prices remain valid are:

1. In the optimal simplex tableau, divide the entries of the column corresponding to the shadow price into the corresponding entries of the right-hand-side values. Interpret any division by 0 to be $-\infty$ (negatively infinite—or arbitrarily small).
2. Now let x denote the least nonnegative quotient (so $x \geq 0$), and let y denote the least nonpositive quotient (so $y \leq 0$). Also, let b denote the current value of the right-hand side of the resource constraint.
3. Then the range of values over which the shadow price remains valid is from $b - x$ to $b - y$.

Note: If all quotients are strictly negative, set $x = b$; if all quotients are strictly positive, set $y = -\infty$. The above rules apply only to "≤" constraints. We shall not discuss the other two cases, "≥" and "=," since, as we have already noted, in actual practice the ranging will be performed as part of the output of a canned LP program. The discussion here is intended only to give you a general idea of what is involved.

EXAMPLE 3.4. *Shadow Prices: Right-hand-side Ranging.* Refer back to Example 3.3. Let us assume that Sue manages to find a printer who will print the leaflets at a cost of 1¢ each. Then, since 1¢ is less than the breakeven cost of 1-1/3¢, it is to Sue's advantage to purchase some leaflets. In fact, to generate one additional sale of ashtrays, she will spend (300 leaflets/sales potential) × (1¢/leaflet) = $3, which is less than the $4 shadow price of the sales constraint.

The current sales potential is 15. We now determine the range over which the shadow price of $4 per sales potential remains valid. Following the rules stated above, we write down the right-hand side of the optimal simplex tableau (Table 3.5) and divide each entry by the s_3 column as follows:

Right-hand side	÷	s_3 column	=	a ratio
10		2		5
16		$-\dfrac{8}{5}$		-10
15		1		15

Thus the least positive number is $x = 5$, the least negative number is $y = -10$, and the current value of the sales potential is $b = 15$ [the right-hand side of constraint (3) of the original problem]. The range over which the shadow price of $4 remains valid is from $b - x$ to $b - y$, or from $15 - 5$ to $15 - (-10)$, or from 10 to 25. Outside of this range, one or more of the other constraints will be violated, and the solution (and thus the shadow price) would change.

Getting back to the question of how many leaflets to have printed, we see that it is safe to generate an additional 10 sales for ashtrays (up to 25). Each sale requires a 300-leaflet advertising effort, so 3,000 leaflets should be purchased. The net gain in profit (over the $260) would be

(10 sales)($4/sale, shadow price) − (3,000 leaflets)($0.01/leaflet)

or $10 (per week). You might note that in practice the cost of distributing the leaflets should also be considered. Problem 1 at the end of this section asks you to perform sensitivity analysis on the other two resource constraints for Sue's product mix problem.   ▲

Changes in the Objective Function Coefficients

What happens to the optimal solution to a linear program if the coefficients of the objective function change? To answer this, two cases must be considered.

CASE 1. If the coefficient c_j of a *nonbasic* variable changes, then the current optimal solution to the linear program remains optimal as long as the $c_j − z_j$ value of the given nonbasic variable remains less than or equal to 0; that is, as long as $c_j \leq z_j$. By looking at the z_j given in the optimal simplex tableau, we can easily see what the upper limit on the permissible range of c_j is before the solution changes. If c_j is increased above z_j, $c_j − z_j$ becomes positive, and it is advantageous to enter this nonbasic variable into the solution. Thus, another iteration of the simplex method must be made. Obviously a decrease in the c_j of a nonbasic variable would only make it even less profitable.

CASE 2. Suppose the objective function coefficient c_j of a *basic* variable changes. Over what range of values of c_j will the current optimal solution remain optimal? In this case we list the $c_j − z_j$ row and the basic variable row of the final simplex tableau. Then divide each *nonbasic* $c_j − z_j$ entry by the corresponding basic row entry. The least positive ratio gives the upper limit to changes in c_j, and the least negative ratio gives the lower limit on changes in c_j. If there are no positive ratios, the upper limit on the c_j range is $+\infty$; if there are no negative ratios, the lower limit is $-\infty$; division by 0 is taken to be $+\infty$.

EXAMPLE 6.5. *Objective Function Coefficient Ranging.* Referring once again to Sue's product mix problem, suppose the unit profit on plant pots changes. Over what range can it change without affecting the current optimal solution?

Since x_1 = number of pots is a *basic variable*, we list the $c_j − z_j$ row and the x_1 row from the optimal simplex tableau, Table 3.5:

$$c_j - z_j \qquad 0 \quad 0 \quad 0 \quad -4 \quad -4$$

$$x_1 \qquad 1 \quad 0 \quad 0 \quad \frac{4}{5} \quad -\frac{8}{5}$$

$$\qquad\qquad\qquad\qquad\qquad \uparrow \quad \uparrow$$

$s_2 \quad s_3$ nonbasic
columns

In the $c_j - z_j$ row, the last two entries (-4 and -4) correspond to the nonbasic variables s_2 and s_3. Thus, we divide each of these by the corresponding entry in the x_1 row as follows:

$$-4 \div \frac{4}{5} = -5$$

$$-4 \div \frac{-8}{5} = 2.5$$

The least positive quotient is 2.5, the least negative quotient is -5; thus, the x_1 profit coefficient can range from $5 - 5$ to $5 + 2.5$ or from 0 to 7.5 and the current solution will remain optimal.

For example, suppose the profit on pots decreases from \$5 to \$3. Then the optimal solution will still remain

$x_1^* = 16$ pots

$x_2^* = 15$ pots

although the weekly profit will decrease:

$Z^* = 16(\$3) + 15(\$12) = \$228$ per week

Problem 2 at the end of this section asks you to determine the ranging of the profit on ashtrays. This sensitivity analysis is illustrated in Figure 3.8. ▲

EXAMPLE 3.6. *Advertising/Promotion Planning.* For this example refer back to Section 7 of the previous chapter, where we presented an advertising/promotion problem facing the Coladrink company. For the one-month planning horizon, the following optimal solution was found, using a canned computer program:

$x_1^* = 30$ newspaper ads

$x_2^* = 8.67$ 30-second spots on radio

$x_3^* = 4$ magazine ads

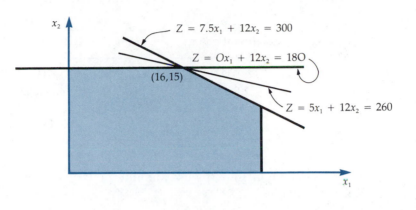

FIGURE 3.8

$x_4^* = 25$ boxes of free product samples

$Z^* = 131,416.67$ person-exposures for the month

(It took seven iterations and 7 seconds of computer time to generate this result.)

In addition to this output, shadow prices for each constraint, ranging for each constraint and ranging for the objective function coefficients of the basic variables, were computed and printed as part of the computer printout. These results are shown in Tables 3.8 and 3.9.

TABLE 3.8   *Sensitivity Analysis for Right-hand-side Constraints*

Constraint	RHS	Shadow price	Range From	Range To
(1)	30,000	4.6667	23,000	34,000
(2)	100	0.0	25	Unbounded
(3)	25	116.6667	0	95
(4)	180	0.0	30	Unbounded
(5)	30	833.3333	25.2941	50
(6)	4	4,833.3333	1.3333	11
(7)	15	0.0	8.6667	Unbounded
(8)	4	0.0	0	8.6667
(9)	0	0.0	0	8.0000

TABLE 3.9   *Sensitivity Analysis for Objective Function Coefficients*

Variable	Coefficient value	Range	
		From	To
x_1	800	0	1,633.3333
x_2	7,000	5,250.0000	14,249.9961
x_3	9,500	4,666.6680	Unbounded
x_4	350	0	466.6665

We can demonstrate the use and interpretation of sensitivity analysis with a few examples:

1. Constraint (1) is the budget constraint. At the optimal solution the shadow price indicates that for each dollar spent (at the current budget level of $30,000), 4.6667 person-exposures can be gained. This shadow price remains valid for budget levels ranging from $23,000 to $34,000. Thus, for example, if Coladrink is willing to increase its budget by $1,000 (to $31,000), an additional 4,666.7 person-exposures can be gained.

2. Constraint (6) states that the number of magazine ads cannot exceed four per month. The solution indicates that $x_3^* = 4$, so constraint (6) is "tight" (has 0 slack). The high shadow price 4,833.3333 (valid in the range from 1.3333 to 11 ads per month) might be an indication that management should reexamine its assumption that placing more than one ad per issue would not be effective.

3. Constraint (2) expresses the fact that a limited number of merchants would cooperate in placing the free product samples, so a maximum of 100 such samples could be used. Constraint (3) reflects the desire of the marketing manager to place at least 25 such samples. The optimal solution indicates that only 25 samples be used ($x_4^* = 25$). Note the 0 shadow price for constraint (2): there would be no value in increasing the 100 sample limit. In fact, the shadow price for constraint (3) tells us that we could *gain* 116.6667 person-exposures for every unit we could decrease the right-hand-side value (below 25). For example, if constraint (3) were $x_4 \geq 24$, the optimal solution to the LP would be 116.6667 person-exposures greater than the current value of Z^*. The reason for this is that, apparently, the free samples are not very effective relative to their cost *and* relative to the cost-effectiveness of the other three alternatives. Thus by decreasing the requirement that 25 samples be used, funds could be diverted to more effective promotional uses. The range for the objective function coefficient of x_4 indicates that these statements are valid for values of the x_4 coefficient ranging from 0 to 466.6665.

4. We see from the computer output that as long as the person-exposure rating of magazine ads remains above 4,666.6680, x_3 will always be a basic

variable; that is, Coladrink will employ such ads in their promotional strategy. Suppose, for example, that a company official says that he believes the effectiveness of magazine ads has dropped from 9,500 to 5,000 and, therefore, argues that Coladrink should cut back on its use of such ads. *According to the LP*, and all other factors remaining constant, the company official would be in error. Even if his estimate of 5,000 is correct, the optimal LP solution would not change—that is, the values of x_1^*, x_2^*, x_3^*, and x_4^* would not change, although Z^* would be decreased by $(9,500 - 5,000) \times 4 = 18,000$ person-exposures.   ▲

Problems

1. Perform a sensitivity analysis on the right-hand side of constraints (1) and (2) of Sue's product mix problem as follows:
   a. Specify the shadow prices on each resource.
   b. Determine the ranging of the resource levels over which the shadow prices remain valid.
2. Perform a ranging analysis on the profit coefficient of ashtrays for Sue's product mix problem.

7. THE DUAL LP

Associated with every linear program is another linear program called the **dual LP** of the first. (The original LP is termed the **primal LP.**) In this section we shall show how to derive the dual LP to Sue's product mix LP, point out the correspondence between the two LPs, and indicate the economic significance of the dual LP as well as its computational value.

The Dual LP for Sue's Product Mix LP

In Section 3 we gave the primal LP for Sue's problem. The dual LP is derived in the following way:

1. The number of variables of the dual equals the number of constraints of the primal. For Sue's problem, the dual thus has three variables (ignore the nonnegativity constraints of the primal LP). We shall label these variables y_1, y_2, and y_3.
2. The right-hand sides of the primal become the coefficients of the objective function of the dual. For Sue's LP, the objective function then is $Z = 30y_1 + 50y_2 + 15y_3$.
3. The columns of the primal become the rows of the dual; also the objective function coefficients of the primal become the right-hand sides of the dual.

Each "≤" of the primal is converted to "≥" in the dual. Thus for Sue's problem the constraints of the dual become

$$\frac{5}{4}y_1 + \frac{5}{4}y_2 + 0y_3 \geq 5$$

$$0y_1 + 2y_2 + 1y_3 \geq 12$$

4. The objective of maximizing is changed to minimizing. In summary, the dual LP to Sue's product mix primal LP is

Minimize $Z = 30y_1 + 50y_2 + 15y_3$
Subject to:
(1) $\quad \frac{5}{4}y_1 + \frac{5}{4}y_2 \qquad \geq 5$
(2) $\quad \qquad 2y_2 + y_3 \geq 12$
(3) $\quad y_1, \qquad y_2, \quad y_3 \geq 0$

Solving the Dual

To set up the initial simplex tableau for the dual, we introduce surplus and artificial variables to convert the dual to the following form:

Minimize $Z = 30y_1 + 50y_2 + 15y_3 + 0s_1 + Ma_1 + 0s_2 + Ma_2$
Subject to:
(1) $\quad \frac{5}{4}y_1 + \frac{5}{4}y_2 + 0y_3 - s_1 + a_1 + 0s_2 + 0a_2 = 5$
(2) $\quad 0y_1 + 2y_2 + y_3 + 0s_1 + 0a_1 - s_2 + a_2 = 12$

If you were to apply the simplex method to solve the dual, you would discover three things:

1. The values of the dual variables equal the shadow prices of the primal.
2. The shadow prices of the dual equal the values of the basic variables of the primal. In our case, we would find upon solving the dual that
   a. $y_1^* = 0$, $y_2^* = 4$, $y_3^* = 4$
      (Recall that in Table 3.5 the shadow prices of the primal were 0, 4, and 4.)
   b. The shadow prices of the dual are 16 and 15 (which are the values of x_1 and x_2 given in Table 3.5.
3. Z^* for the dual equals $260.

Thus to solve the dual, it is sufficient to solve the primal and to examine the shadow prices. And to solve the primal, it is sufficient to solve the dual and look at its shadow prices. In other words, solving one of the LPs automatically yields a solution to the other.

(Problem 1 at the end of this section asks you to solve the dual LP for Sue's primal LP.)

Computational Considerations

Even with the use of efficient canned computer programs for solving linear programs, computation times may be large. In general, the time it takes to solve a linear program depends quite heavily on the number of *constraints;* the number of variables the problem has does not appreciably affect computation time. Doubling the number of constraints may increase computation time by a factor exceeding two and, in fact, may increase computing time four- or eightfold.

Thus, for example, if a linear program has ten variables and thirty constraints, it might be more efficient to solve it by forming the dual having thirty variables and only ten constraints.

Economic Interpretation of the Dual

In our discussion of linear programming in Section 6 of this chapter, we gave an economic interpretation of shadow prices—namely, the shadow price corresponding to a constraint gives the value of each unit of resource represented on the right-hand side of that constraint. For Sue's LP (see Table 3.5), the first shadow price equals zero. Thus the value of an additional machine-hour is zero. The second shadow price equals 4, so the value of an additional labor-hour is $4. The third shadow price is 4, meaning that the value of an additional sales potential is $4. These statements are all made relative to the optimal (or final) simplex tableau of the primal.

In the notation given above, the optimal values of the dual variables y_1, y_2, and y_3 equal the three (primal) shadow prices. Thus we can interpret the first term of the dual objective function $30y_1^*$ as giving the total implicit or *imputed* value of the 30 machine-hours in the final solution as follows:

$30y_1^*$ = 30 machine-hours × y_1^*/machine-hour

A similar interpretation applies for the other two terms of the dual objective function. Since the dual objective is to minimize, we can interpret the dual objective as trying *to minimize the total imputed value of the resources used up in the primal*.

What about the dual constraints? To see how we might interpret their meaning in economic terms, look closely at the primal LP for Sue's problem. Suppose Sue makes one pot; that is, $x_1 = 1$. Then, from constraint (1), she will use up 5/4 of the machine-hour resource; from constraint (2), she will use up 5/4 of a labor-hour resource; and from constraint (3), she will use up zero sales potential. These three numbers—5/4, 5/4, and 0—are precisely the coefficients of constraint (1) of the dual LP. If we again interpret

y_1, y_2, and y_3 as the imputed unit values of each of the three resources, the dual constraint

(1) $(5/4)y_1 + (5/4)y_2 + 0y_3 \geq 5$

says that the total imputed value of the resources used up by producing each pot must be at least as great as the profit obtained from the sale of each pot. This is certainly a reasonable requirement for the dual to make.

In brief, the dual LP attempts to determine the most efficient allocations of the resources in the primal problem.

We shall not pursue the topic of duality further in this introductory text. Our purpose here is simply to give you a glimpse of the rich theory and application of duality in linear programming. Also, we have restricted the discussion to primal problems that have a maximization objective and "$\leq$" constraints. More complicated rules exist for finding the duals of other primal LPs.

Problem

Apply the simplex method to the dual LP of Sue's primal LP problem.

8. COMPUTER SOLUTION OF LP PROBLEMS

Were it not for the development of digital computers, the simplex method would be of little practical importance. As you have seen in the examples shown in this chapter (and particularly if you have tried to solve some problems yourself!), the simplex method requires tedious computation, even for small problems. The solution of a problem with as few as twenty constraints involves hundreds of computations. Maintaining correctness and accuracy in hand computation would be very difficult; therefore, a problem involving hundreds of constraints would be practically impossible to solve by hand.

The simplex method was developed by George B. Dantzig in 1947 and published in 1951. The first computerized solution of a linear program was conducted by the National Bureau of Standards in 1952. Computerized linear programming "packages" came into widespread use in the early 1960s with the development of MPS (Mathematical Programming System) for the IBM 360 series of computers.

Modern computer programs for linear programming are based on the revised simplex method, which uses streamlined matrix algebra methods to increase computing efficiency. In this section, we will show the use of two such programs: the linear programming option of MPSX (Mathematical Programming System Extended); and PROC LP in SAS/OR (Statistical Analysis System/Operations Research), a group of programs for solving assignment, network, scheduling, and transportation problems, in addition to linear programming. SAS/OR was developed by SAS Institute, Inc. (SAS Circle, P.O. Box 8000, Cary, NC 27511-8000), the developer of SAS (Statistical Analysis System), perhaps the most widely used data management and statistical computer package in the world. SAS products are available for a large variety of computers and operating systems.

Sue's Problem in MPS Format

A problem is set up for MPS linear programming in four parts: (1) A control section which specifies the names of the data sets to be used, the type of objective, and the kind of output desired; (2) a **ROWS** section, which lists the row (constraint) names and types; (3) a **COLUMNS** section, which lists the column (variable) names and nonzero coefficients; and (4) an **RHS** section which lists the names of the rows that have nonzero right-hand sides and the corresponding values.

The Control Program

```
 1   PROGRAM ('ND')
 2   INITIAL Z
 3   MOVE (XDATA 'SUEROWS')
 4   MOVE (XPBNAME 'SUEPM')
 5   MOVE (XOBJ 'PROFIT')
 6   MOVE (XRHS 'SUERHS')
 7   SETUP ('MAX')
 8   PRIMAL
 9   SOLUTION
10   EXIT
11   PEND
```

The **MOVE** commands identify the names of the data sets, which form the different parts of the linear program, and cause them to be read. The **SET UP** command identifies the objective (maximize), the **PRIMAL** statement specifies that the primal be solved, and **SOLUTION** initiates the calculation.

The ROWS Section

```
12   NAME        SUEROWS
13   ROWS
14    N   PROFIT
15    L   MACHRS
16    L   LABHRS
17    L   SALES
```

The names given to the section or to the rows can be up to eight characters long. Here we have the objective function (PROFIT), the machine-hours constraint (MACHRS), the labor-hours constraint (LABHRS), and the sales constraint (SALES). The letter to the left of a name denotes the constraint type (L—Less than or equal to; E—Equal to; G—Greater than or equal to; and N—Free).

The COLUMNS Section

```
18    COLUMNS
19        ASHTR      PROFIT        5.00
20        ASHTR      MACHRS        1.25
21        ASHTR      LABHRS        1.25
22        PLPOT      PROFIT       12.00
23        PLPOT      LABHRS        2.00
24        PLPOT      SALES        15.00
```

This section identifies the column-row intersections and the values to be inserted. As for the rows, column names can be up to eight characters long. Here, ASHTR identifies the product (variable) ashtrays, and PLPOT the product plant pots.

The RHS Section

```
25    RHS
26        SUERHS     MACHRS       30.00
27        SUERHS     LABHRS       50.00
28        SUERHS     SALES        15.00
29    ENDRHS
```

The purpose of naming the right-hand sides (RHS) is to permit the insertion of several different values (with different RHS names). Different sets of right-hand-side values could then be conveniently used by specifying the desired name in the control program.

With this data and specifications, MPS sets up the initial simplex tableau, inserting the coefficients in the appropriate rows and columns, and adding slack, surplus, and artificial variables, as appropriate. The standard output includes: 1) a **STATUS** section, which states whether an optimal solution was achieved, the number of iterations required, the value of the objective function, the name of the objective function used, and the name of the right-hand sides used; 2) a **ROWS** section, which gives the status (AT: BS-Basis, LL-Lower Limit, UL-Upper limit), the values (ACTIVITY), slack or surplus, lower and upper limits and shadow prices (DUAL ACTIVITY) of the resources and/or requirements represented by the rows; and 3) a **COLUMNS** section, giving the status (AT), the values (ACTIVITY), objective function coefficients, lower and upper limits, and the valuation of nonbasic variables at the optimal solution (REDUCED COST). The output for the solution of Sue's product mix problem is shown below.

Solution Output

```
SOLUTION    (OPTIMAL)
TIME =       0.01 MINS.   ITERATION NUMBER =      3
             ...NAME...        ...ACTIVITY...          DEFINED AS
             FUNCTIONAL              260.00            PROFIT
             RESTRAINTS                                SUERHS


SECTION 1--ROWS

NUM  ROW    AT  ACTIVITY  SLACK     LL      UL    DUAL ACTIVITY
1    PROFIT BS    260.00  260.00-  NONE    NONE           1.000
2    MACHRS BS     20.00   10.00   NONE    30.00
3    LABHRS UL     50.00     .00   NONE    50.00          4.000
4    SALES  UL     15.00     .00   NONE    15.00          4.000


SECTION 2--COLUMNS

NUM   COLUMN  AT   ACTIVITY INPUT COST  LL   UL   REDUCED COST
5     ASHTR   BS     16.00       5.00  .00  NONE
6     PLPOT   BS     15.00      12.00  .00  NONE
```

The solution can then be read from the appropriate row and column listings: produce 16 ashtrays (ASHTR) and 15 plant pots (PLPOT) for a profit (PROFIT) of $260. At this point there are ten slack machine hours (MACHRS), and the values of the scarce resources (DUAL ACTIVITY) are $4 per additional hour of labor and $4 per additional unit of plant pot sales potential.

Sue's Problem in SAS/OR PROC LP Format

Although PROC LP can read MPSX format with a procedure provided with SAS/OR, it has its own straightforward format. Problems are stated in a way similar to that in which the examples in this book are presented. Communication is through keywords, which identify the components and characteristics of a linear program.

The PROC LP Program

```
1   TITLE 'SUE S PRODUCT MIX PROBLEM';
2   DATA SUEPM;
3      INPUT ASHTR PLPOT T$ SRHS NAME$;
```

```
4          CARDS;
5     5.00  12.00   MAX                PROFIT
6     1.25   0.00   LE      30.00      MACHRS
7     1.25   2.00   LE      50.00      LABHRS
8     0.00   1.00   LE      15.00      SALES
9     ;
10    PROC LP DATA = SUEPM;
11        VAR ASHTR PLPOT;
12        ID NAME;
13        RHS SRHS;
14        TYPE T;
```

The **DATA** line tells SAS/OR that a data set is to be created and names it. The **INPUT** statement identifies the names of the variables to be read in (the $ after the T and NAME identifies them as nonnumeric) and the sequence in which they will be placed in the data lines (lines 5–8) following the statement **CARDS,** which tells SAS/OR to start reading data. The first data line is identified as the objective function by the keyword **MAX** (the value for T in that data line). Since the objective function has no right-hand-side value, the column for **SRHS** has the SAS missing-value symbol (a period). The next three data lines are identified as constraints by the keyword **LE** (for less than or equal to). Note that coefficients of zero for decision variables must be included. The PROC LP statement must be followed by the names of the decision variables after the keyword **VAR,** by the names chosen for the rows (optional) after the keyword **ID,** by the name of the right-hand-side values after the keyword **RHS,** and by the name of the type variables after the keyword **TYPE.** The semicolon at the end of each program line is a SAS convention meaning the end of a statement. The solitary semicolon on line 9 denotes the end of the data.

Solution Output

Output from PROC LP is in a format similar to that of MPSX. The **Problem Summary** lists several characteristics of the problem. The **Solution Summary** indicates the status of the solution, the value of the objective function, and details about the time and iterations required. The **Constraint Summary** shows details on the resources or requirements represented by the rows. Finally, the **Variable Summary** gives the values of the decision variables and their status. The output for the program described above is shown below.

```
               SUE'S PRODUCT MIX PROBLEM

    L I N E A R    P R O G R A M M I N G    P R O C E D U R E

                    PROBLEM SUMMARY

            MAX PROFIT          OBJECTIVE FUNCTION
            SRHS                    RHS VARIABLE
```

```
T                          TYPE VARIABLE
PROBLEM DENSITY                    0.467

VARIABLE TYPE                     NUMBER

STRUCTURAL
  NONNEGATIVE                          2


LOGICAL
  SLACK                                3

TOTAL                                  5

CONSTRAINT TYPE                   NUMBER

LE                                     3
FREE                                   1

TOTAL                                  4
```

```
                 SOLUTION SUMMARY



             TERMINATED SUCCESSFULLY

OBJECTIVE VALUE                   260.00

PHASE 1 ITERATIONS                     0
PHASE 2 ITERATIONS                     3
INITIAL B. F. VARIABLES                3
TIME USED (SECS)                    0.00
NUMBER OF INVERSIONS                   1
```

```
              CONSTRAINT SUMMARY
```

CONSTRAINT ROW ID	TYPE	S/S COL	RHS	ACTIVITY	DUAL ACTIVITY
1 MACHRS	LE	3	30.000000	20.000000	0
2 LABHRS	LE	4	50.000000	50.000000	4.000000
3 SALES	LE	5	15.000000	15.000000	4.000000
4 PROFIT	OBJECTIVE		260.000	260.000	0

VARIABLE SUMMARY

COL	VARIABLE NAME	STATUS	TYPE	PRICE	ACTIVITY	REDUCED COST
1	ASHTR	BASIC	NONNEG	5	16.000000	0
2	PLPOT	BASIC	NONNEG	12	15.000000	0
3	-ROW1-	BASIC	SLACK	0	10.000000	0
4	-ROW2-		SLACK	0	0	-4.000000
5	-ROW3-		SLACK	0	0	-4.000000

9. CONCLUDING REMARKS

In this chapter we have given a brief treatment of the simplex method. As we have seen, the algebraic details of the method have intuitive geometric and economic interpretations.

Existing computer codes are based on the simplex method or variations of it, such as the revised simplex method. The revised simplex method employs streamlined matrix algebra methods to increase computing efficiency.

We have touched on only a few of the several interesting topics in linear programming, and we encourage the interested student to consult the references for this chapter in Appendix A for more advanced topics.

Two major events related to linear programs have recently occurred. In 1979, the Russian mathematician L. G. Kachian presented a method based on a very different approach from that of the simplex method. His new method promises to be faster than the simplex method and applicable to some nonlinear problems; however, these promises have yet to be proven. In November, 1984, N. Karmarkar, a scientist with AT&T Bell Laboratories, presented yet another new linear programming algorithm at the national joint meeting of The Institute of Management Sciences and the Operations Research Society of America. Karmarkar's algorithm promises to be even faster. The following articles provide descriptions of these methods and their characteristics: Lynn Arthur Steen, "Linear Programming: Solid New Algorithm," *Science News* 116 (1979): 234–236; Gina Bara Kolata, "Mathematicians Amazed by Russian's Discovery," *Science* 206 (1979): 545–546; N. Karmarkar, "A New Polynomial-Time Algorithm for Linear Programming," paper presented at the national TIMS/ORSA meeting, November, 1984.

TERMINOLOGY

After studying this chapter you should be familiar with the following terms:

TERM	SECTION
artificial variable	4
basic variable	3

EXERCISES

1. Solve the following LP, using the simplex method. Interpret each step graphically.

   Maximize $Z = 3x_1 + 9x_2$
   Subject to:
   (1) $2x_1 + 4x_2 \leq 8$
   (2) $x_1 + 7x_2 \leq 7$
   (3) $x_1, \quad x_2 \geq 0$

2. Solve the following LP, using the simplex method. Interpret each step graphically.

   Minimize $Z = x_1 + 2x_2$
   Subject to:
   (1) $2x_1 + 3x_2 \geq 12$
   (2) $3x_1 + 7x_2 \geq 21$
   (3) $x_1, \quad x_2 \geq 0$

3. Given the LP

   Maximize $Z = 12x_1 + 6x_2 + 3x_3$
   Subject to:
   (1) $x_1 + x_2 + x_3 \leq 4$
   (2) $2x_1 + 3x_2 + x_3 \leq 10$
   (3) $x_1, \quad x_2, \quad x_3 \geq 0$
   a. Solve using the simplex method.
   b. Specify the values of the shadow prices.

4. Solve the following LP and interpret graphically.

   Maximize $2x_1 + 4x_2$
   Subject to:
   (1) $x_1 + 3x_2 \leq 12$

(2) $5x_1 + 6x_2 \geq 30$

(3) $x_1, \quad x_2 \geq 0$

5. *Manufacturing Equipment Selection.*   Snaptite, Inc., manufactures metal fasteners. The company currently is planning production of a new nut and bolt unit for fastening furniture legs. It has budgeted $100,000 for the project. The plant engineer has made 1,200 square meters of floor space in the existing plant available for the required production facilities.

Three machine types are available, M1, M2, and M3, having daily output capacities of 180 units, 250 units, and 150 units, respectively. M1 costs $6,000 and requires 40 square meters of floor space; M2 costs $8,000 and requires 60 square meters; M3 costs $4,800 and requires 50 square meters. (The floor space requirements include work area, storage area, and space for the machine.)

Formulate an LP to determine how many of each type of machine to purchase in order to maximize daily output.

6. *Product Distribution.*   Zertex manufactures paper products in each of its four plants, which we label P1, P2, P3, and P4, located in different states. One of its products is a special architectural drawing paper that it distributes to three major markets, which we label M1, M2, and M3. The costs to produce this paper vary from plant to plant, depending on local labor conditions, tax structures, utility rates, and availability of materials. These production costs are $7.50 per roll (100 feet) in P1, $7.25 per roll in P2, $8.30 per roll in P3, and $7.75 per roll in P4. Weekly capacities at these plants are 500 rolls, 400 rolls, 800 rolls, and 650 rolls, respectively. The market demands, which must be met exactly, are 700 rolls/week at M1, 800 rolls/week at M2, and 700 rolls/week at M3. Shipping costs differ between plant and markets and are given in Table 3.10 (in $/roll).

Formulate an LP model to determine the optimal product distribution pattern for Zertex.

7. *Subcontractor Selection.*   Compurong, a maker of solid-state electronic calculators, subcontracts the manufacture of three integrated circuit com-

TABLE 3.10

Plant	Market		
	M1	M2	M3
P1	0.25	0.30	0.20
P2	0.10	0.40	0.25
P3	0.15	0.20	0.15
P4	0.40	0.10	0.45

ponents. The company uses 200, 300, and 150 units of the three components each month. Compurong currently relies on four electronic component manufacturers for its subcontracting assignments. The cost to procure each of the three components from the four manufacturers and the maximum quantities the manufacturers can supply are given in Table 3.11.

For example, manufacturer 1 can supply a maximum of 100 units per month of all three components combined. Manufacturer 2 does not make component 2, and manufacturer 3 has no excess capacity available to provide component 3 to Compurong, even though it does produce the component for other firms.

Formulate an LP model to determine how Compurong should subcontract for the manufacture of the three components.

8. In Exercise 7 above, suppose Compurong is notified of the following changes in subcontractor policy: (1) Manufacturer 1 can provide at most 50 units of component 3, and (2) manufacturer 3 can provide at most 100 units of component 1. In addition, Compurong has agreed to purchase at least 75 units of component 2 from manufacturer 4.

Formulate an LP model to determine the optimal subcontractor selection.

9. *Cargo Loading: Import Product Selection.* Tradex Corporation has established commercial relations with a Japanese company to import products made by that company. Tradex will operate monthly air cargo flights to this Japanese company, which has offered three products to Tradex. We shall label these products P1, P2, and P3. The per-unit profit of each of these products to Tradex when sold in its national markets is $50, $100, and $75, respectively. The respective unit weights of the three products are 7 kg, 12 kg, and 15 kg, and corresponding unit shipping space requirements are 5 cubic meters, 11 cubic meters, and 8 cubic meters. The weight and space limitations of each flight are 1,000 kg and 900 cubic meters.

a. Formulate an LP model to determine which products Tradex should import.

TABLE 3.11

Manufacturer	Component 1	Component 2	Component 3	Maximum supply (units/month)
1	$1.20	1.10	0.90	100
2	1.05	-	1.00	150
3	0.90	1.25	-	300
4	0.95	1.07	1.05	200

b. How would you modify the LP if Tradex's Japanese affiliate offers a fourth product that has a $125 per-unit profit potential and requires 10 kg and 12 cubic meters of shipping weight and space, respectively?

10. *Allocating Sales Effort: Real Estate Application.* Betty, a real estate sales-person, is planning her sales objectives for the upcoming month. She has decided to concentrate her efforts on three client classes: (1) residential home buyers, (2) condominium prospects, and (3) investors in single-family dwellings. The commission per unit sale for each of these classes averages $800, $700, and $400, respectively, before business expenses are deducted. On the average, her expenses incurred per sale for the three categories run $50, $100, and $35, respectively, and include automobile expenses, office expenses, and entertainment. The amount of time Betty spends for each sale in the three categories is 20 hours, 8 hours, and 22 hours, respectively. Advertising expenditures required per sale run $100, $110, and $50, respectively, for the three classes. Her advertising budget is limited to a maximum of $1,800 for the upcoming month, and the time she will have available for selling is 250 hours (25 days × 10 hours per day). Betty currently has two residential accounts and one investment prospect that must be worked on in the coming month.

Formulate an LP to determine how many sales in each category Betty should set as her monthly goal.

11. *Sensitivity Analysis.* Hendrix Manufacturing produces two products, each of which must be processed on three machines. The profit per unit on the two products is $24 and $30, respectively. Product 1 requires 4 hours processing time on machine A, 8 hours on machine B, and 2 hours on machine C. The processing times for product 2 on the three machines are 6 hours, 4 hours, and 3 hours, respectively. The machine-hour capacities for the three machines in the upcoming month are 240 hours, 240 hours, and 150 hours for machines A, B, and C, respectively.

To determine the optimal product mix, the following LP was formulated:

Maximize $Z = 24x_1 + 30x_2$
Subject to:
(1) $4x_1 + 6x_2 \leq 240$
(2) $8x_1 + 4x_2 \leq 240$
(3) $2x_1 + 3x_2 \leq 150$
(4) $x_1, \quad x_2 \geq 0$

A canned computer program was used to solve this problem. The final (optimal) simplex tableau appearing in the computer printout is shown in Table 3.12 [s_1, s_2, s_3 are slack variables for constraints (1), (2), and (3), respectively].

a. Specify the optimal x_1, x_2, and Z values.

b. What are the shadow price values?

TABLE 3.12

c_j Basic variables	24 x_1	30 x_2	0 s_1	0 s_2	0 s_3	Right-hand side
x_2	0.0	1.0	0.250	−0.125	0.0	30
x_1	1.0	0.0	−0.125	0.188	0.0	15
s_3	0.0	0.0	−0.500	0.000	1.0	30
Z						1,260
z_j	24	30	−4.50	−0.75	0.0	
$z_j - c_j$	0	0	−4.50	−0.75	0.0	

c. Over what range of the right-hand-side values is each shadow price valid?

d. Over what range of unit profit on product 1 will the current product mix remain optimal?

e. Over what range of unit profit on product 2 will the current product mix remain optimal?

12. *Sensitivity Analysis: Hendrix Manufacturing.* (Refer to Exercise 11 above.)

a. Due to a rise in material costs, the profit per unit on product 1 decreases to $21 (from $24). How does this affect the optimal product mix? What about the monthly profit?

b. Suppose the profit per unit on product 2 increases from $30 to $33, due to the successful application of a new production process for that product. How does this affect the optimal product mix? What about the monthly profit?

c. Suppose the machine-hour capacity of machine A can be increased to 275 hours per month at a total monthly cost of $130. Would you recommend that Hendrix undertake the capacity expansion?

d. Suppose management can increase the machine-hour capacity of machine B from 240 hours to 350 hours at a total monthly cost of $88. Should the expansion be undertaken?

13. *Production Scheduling—Routing.* Magnux Industries manufactures four products that have net unit profits of $4.40, $6.60, $3.30, and $5.75. Each product must be processed first on a punch press and then on a drill press. Magnux currently owns three punch presses and two drill presses that have monthly capacities of 165, 130, 150, 155, and 140 hours, respectively, for punch presses 1, 2, 3 and drill presses 1 and 2.

The required processing time (in hours) for each product on the various machines is given in Table 3.13. A dash indicates that a machine is not suited to process the product.

Formulate a linear program to determine (1) the appropriate product mix, and (2) the routing of the scheduled production.

TABLE 3.13

	Punch presses			Drill presses	
Products	1	2	3	1	2
1	0.16	0.17	0.12	-	0.32
2	0.12	-	0.22	0.34	0.38
3	0.20	0.31	-	0.52	0.45
4	-	0.18	0.14	0.24	0.26

Hint: The output of the LP should indicate how many units of each product should be manufactured with each of the routing schemes. For example: How many units of product 1 should be processed first on punch press 1 and then on drill press 2?

14. *Feed Mix—Cattle Ranch.* A farmer is designing a feed mix for her cattle ranch. The feed mix must contain at least 10 units of vitamin A, 12 units of vitamin C, 13 units of protein, and 9 units of niacin. Three types of feed are available for creating the desired feed mix. The cost per pound of each of these feeds and the nutritional content of each (in units) are given in Table 3.14. Formulate an LP to determine the minimum-cost feed mix.

15. *Nurse Scheduling.* An urgent health care center, operated by the General Hospital, schedules nurses to come on duty every 3 hours for a 6-hour shift. The shift times and the minimum number of nurses required during each 3-hour time interval are given in Table 3.15. Determine the schedule that will minimize the total number of nurses employed by the clinic.

Hint: The output of the LP should specify how many nurses should show up for work at the start of each of the 3-hour time intervals.

16. *Product Distribution: Warehousing.* Cantric Corp. operates four factories that manufacture products for three warehouses. The weekly capacities

TABLE 3.14

	Nutrient				
Feed	A	C	Protein	Niacin	Cost ($/lb)
1	3	2	1	1	$0.50
2	4	1	0	3	0.42
3	1	3	2	4	0.48

TABLE 3.15

Time	Number of nurses needed
12:00 P.M. (midnight)– 3:00 A.M.	1
3:00 A.M.– 6:00 A.M.	2
6:00 A.M.– 9:00 A.M.	3
9:00 A.M.–12:00 M. (noon)	7
12:00 M. (noon)– 3:00 P.M.	9
3:00 P.M.– 6:00 P.M.	5
6:00 P.M.– 9:00 P.M.	4
9:00 P.M.–12:00 P.M. (midnight)	3

of the four factories are 70, 80, 50, and 60 units, respectively. Warehouse 1 has a weekly need for exactly 90 units of product. Warehouses 2 and 3 have indicated their minimum needs to be 80 and 60 units per week, respectively, but each of them will take any quantities over these minimum requirements. The shipping costs from factories to warehouses are given in Table 3.16 (in $/unit). Cantric would like to operate at full capacity and distribute the output to the warehouses at minimum cost.

Set up an LP to determine the optimal distribution.

17. *Recycling Metal Scrap for Metal-Alloy Design.*   Reran, Inc., a metal recycling plant, regularly takes in three kinds of metal scrap products to be recycled. The metal content of each of these products is given in Table 3.17.

Each month Reran can purchase up to 4 tons, 4 tons, and 10 tons of the three products at costs of $4, $7, and $3 per ton, respectively. The company is considering extracting the metal contents of the three products into two metal-alloy blends. These two new alloys and their percentage compositions are given in Table 3.18. Reran expects it could sell alloy 1 at a profit of $30 per ton and alloy 2 at a profit of $35 per ton.

TABLE 3.16

Factory	Warehouse 1	2	3
1	3	2	8
2	9	10	7
3	1	6	4
4	3	3	6

TABLE 3.17

Metal	Scrapped product (percentage composition)		
	1	2	3
Iron	20	0	50
Copper	40	45	15
Nickel	30	10	5
Zinc	10	45	30

TABLE 3.18

Metal	Alloy	
	1	2
Iron	40	5
Copper	50	50
Nickel	5	30
Zinc	5	15

Formulate an LP to determine the profit-maximizing procurement/production plan for Reran.

18. *Recycling Metal Scrap—A Modification.* Suppose Reran (Exercise 17) has the option of purchasing pure iron, copper, nickel, and zinc at prices of $15, $10, $30, and $35 per ton, respectively.

   Modify the LP of Exercise 17 to incorporate this option.

19. *Crime Prevention.* The city of Riversdale has recently experienced an increase in its crime rate. The mayor has expressed her concern over the matter to the chief of police, Janet Silvano. Chief Silvano has indicated that she could effect a 50 percent decrease in the crime rate if her police force were adequately staffed. The mayor has said that she will give some consideration to Chief Silvano's estimate of adequate staffing requirements but that she would expect Chief Silvano to come up with a minimal estimate.

   The police personnel come on duty at 4-hour intervals for 8-hour shifts. These reporting times and Chief Silvano's estimates of the minimum number of police personnel required for each 4-hour interval are given in Table 3.19.

   Formulate an LP to determine the minimum police-force size.

TABLE 3.19

Time	Number of police personnel
11:00 P.M.– 3:00 A.M.	40
3:00 A.M.– 7:00 A.M.	10
7:00 A.M.–11:00 A.M.	20
11:00 A.M.– 3:00 P.M.	25
3:00 P.M.– 7:00 P.M.	30
7:00 P.M.–11:00 P.M.	35

20. *Investment Management.* The Second National Bank of Kotterville is planning to place $700 million in the following investment categories at the corresponding rates of return:

TABLE 3.20

	Rate of return
Mortgages	11-1/8%
Signature loans	10%
Government securities	8-1/2%
Municipal bonds	11%
Cash reserves	0%

The following restrictions are placed on the allocation of the bank's funds:
a. At least 15 percent is to be retained in cash reserves.
b. To insure liquidity, the signature loans (which are typically 90-day notes) plus the cash reserves must comprise at least 25 percent of the allocation.
c. Not more than 55 percent should be placed in mortgages and signature loans.
Formulate an LP to determine how the money is to be allocated.

21. *Advertising Planning.* Mutual of Nebraska Life Insurance Company must determine the most effective means of allocating its advertising budget of $2.5 million for the coming year. The following table gives the alternatives it has decided to consider. For each medium, the cost per ad and the expected number of person-exposures per ad is given.

Medium	Cost per spot/ad	Person-exposures per ad	Notes
TV	$25,000	200,000	Cost per 30-second spot
Radio	1,000	4,000	Cost per 30-second spot
Magazine A	10,000	60,000	Cost per half-page ad
Magazine A	25,000	180,000	Cost per full-page ad
Magazine B	15,000	70,000	Cost per full-page ad
Major newspaper	2,000	20,000	Standard ad

The company is already committed to at least four ads in magazine B. Furthermore, it wishes to restrict the number of major newspaper ads to no more than twenty. The TV network indicates that only six spots are open, and the radio station indicates that it has only 500 spots left. Company executives stipulate that they want to see at least 30 percent of the budget spent on radio and television.

Formulate an LP to determine how the advertising budget should be spent in order to maximize the number of person-exposures.

4 THE TRANSPORTATION PROBLEM

CONTENTS

1. INTRODUCTION

In the previous two chapters we studied a special type of mathematical problem—linear programs. In practice, certain linear-programming problems arise that exhibit various special features. One such type of problem is the **transportation problem.** Because of the special nature of these problems, algorithms are available for solving transportation problems. This computational method is more efficient than the simplex method of linear programming and makes more sense intuitively. Another special type of linear program is called the **assignment problem.** In fact, the assignment problem is a special type of transportation problem. Once again, because of its special nature, more efficient algorithms exist for solving the assignment problem.

Figure 4.1 graphically shows these relationships. In this chapter we shall discuss the transportation problem. The assignment problem is discussed in Chapter 5.

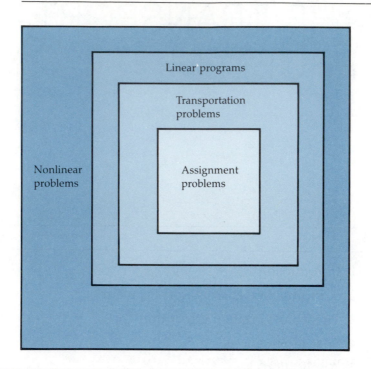

FIGURE 4.1

2. A PRODUCTION/DISTRIBUTION PROBLEM

Our first example is a standard transportation problem. It will serve to demonstrate the various ideas we shall discuss in this section and the next.

EXAMPLE 4.1. Whitny Stone and Gravel, Inc., operates three gravel pits, located in the geographically separate towns of Stonefall, Rockgate, and Bedrock. Gravel mined at these locations is distributed by truck to concrete plants, located in the towns of Mixer, Albuq, Jackson, and Torerel. The weekly production capacities of the three stone pits are 18, 26, and 20 truckloads, respectively. The weekly demands of the four "markets" are 19, 15, 12, and 18 truckloads, respectively. The production costs differ at the three quarries and are estimated to be $20 per truckload at Stonefall, $15 per truckload at Rockgate, and $25 per truckload at Bedrock. The transportation costs per truckload between each quarry and market are given in Table 4.1 (in dollars per truckload). (These costs are based on mileage and driver wage rates.)

Whitny Stone and Gravel must determine the best way to satisfy the weekly market demands for gravel. ▲

TABLE 4.1

	Market			
Quarry	Mixer	Albuq	Jackson	Torerel
Stonefall	20	20	25	15
Rockgate	5	10	15	10
Bedrock	25	15	5	10

Network Representation

We can graphically represent the Whitny problem as the network model shown in Fig. 4.2. Although such a model does not directly help to solve the problem, it does aid in visualizing the problem. The three sources and their respective capacities are shown at the left. The four destinations and their respective demands, given as "negative supplies," are shown at the right. (Destinations are sometimes, suggestively, called **sinks.**) The arrows from sources to destinations indicate the direction of flow of the supplies, and the costs per unit of flow (that is, per truckload) are shown next to each arrow. Note how these costs are computed: the production costs are added to the shipping costs. For example, to send one truckload from Stonefall to Mixer costs $20 (production cost at Stonefall) plus $20 (shipping cost from Stonefall to Mixer), for a total cost of $40.

APPLICATIONS

The following applications appear in this chapter in text, examples, or problems:

Assigning students to public schools

Capacity planning/expansion

Contract awarding

Distribution planning

Facilities planning

Marketing distribution

Municipal street maintenance: snow removal

Plant layout: tool-crib location

Plant location

Production/distribution

Production/inventory planning

Sales territory assignments

Scheduling resource requirements

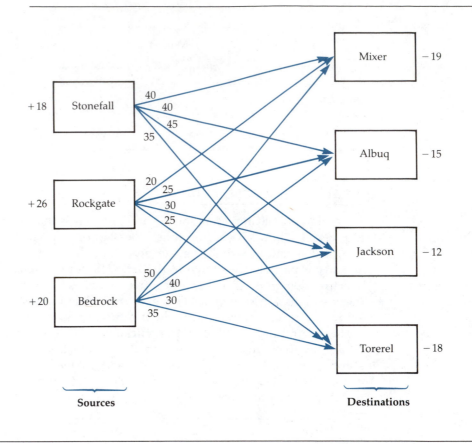

FIGURE 4.2   *Network representation of the Whitny problem.*

Linear-Programming Formulation

We mentioned in the introduction to this chapter that the transportation problem is a special type of linear program. Let us formulate the Whitny problem as an LP. To do so we must answer the following questions: (1) What is Whitny trying to decide or determine? (2) What is Whitny's objective? and (3) What are the constraints on Whitny's possible choices?

In response to the first question, Whitny must determine the number of truckloads to ship from each quarry to each market. Regarding the second question, Whitny's objective is to minimize total weekly costs. As for the third question, the available capacities at each of the three quarries cannot be exceeded, and the stated weekly demands of each of the four markets must be met.

To formulate the LP, we shall use the first letter of each source and destination as an abbreviation.

DECISION VARIABLES. Let the following equal the number of weekly truck-loads sent from the first to the second:

Let X_{SM} = Stonefall to Mixer
$\quad X_{SA}$ = Stonefall to Albuq
$\quad X_{SJ}$ = Stonefall to Jackson
$\quad X_{ST}$ = Stonefall to Torerel
$\quad X_{RM}$ = Rockgate to Mixer
$\quad X_{RA}$ = Rockgate to Albuq
$\quad X_{RJ}$ = Rockgate to Jackson
$\quad X_{RT}$ = Rockgate to Torerel
$\quad X_{BM}$ = Bedrock to Mixer
$\quad X_{BA}$ = Bedrock to Albuq
$\quad X_{BJ}$ = Bedrock to Jackson
$\quad X_{BT}$ = Bedrock to Torrel

OBJECTIVE FUNCTION

Minimize $Z = 40X_{SM} + 40X_{SA} + 45X_{SJ} + 35X_{ST} + 20X_{RM} + 25X_{RA}$
$$+ 30X_{RJ} + 25X_{RT} + 50X_{BM} + 40X_{BA} + 30X_{BJ} + 35X_{BT}$$

(Z = total weekly cost)

Subject to:

(1) $\quad X_{SM} + X_{SA} + X_{SJ} + X_{ST} = 18$

(2) $\quad X_{RM} + X_{RA} + X_{RJ} + X_{RT} = 26$

(3) $\quad X_{BM} + X_{BA} + X_{BJ} + X_{BT} = 20$

(4) $\quad X_{SM} \quad\quad + X_{RM} \quad\quad + X_{BM} = 19$

(5) $\quad X_{SA} \quad\quad + X_{RA} \quad\quad + X_{BA} = 15$

(6) $\quad X_{SJ} \quad\quad + X_{RJ} \quad\quad + X_{BJ} = 12$

(7) $\quad X_{ST} \quad\quad + X_{RT} \quad\quad + X_{BT} = 18$

(8) $\quad X_{SM}, X_{SA}, X_{SJ}, X_{ST}, X_{RM}, X_{RA}, X_{RJ}, X_{RT}, X_{BM}, X_{BA}, X_{BJ}, X_{BT} \geq 0$

Constraint (1) says that the total supply at the Stonefall quarry is 18 truck-loads per week. Constraints (2) and (3) similarly express the supplies at Rockgate and Bedrock, respectively. Constraints (4)–(7) are demand constraints for Mixer, Albuq, Jackson, and Torerel, respectively. For example, constraint (4) says that the total number of truckloads shipped to Mixer must equal its demand of 19 per week.

One way to solve Whitny's problem is to apply the simplex method (Chapter 3) to the above LP (or, more realistically, use a commercial LP computer program based on the simplex method). However, notice the presence of a large number of zeros in the constraints. For example, in constraint (1) there are eight zero coefficients. Also, note that the nonzero coefficients all equal 1. It is partly due to these facts that the transportation algorithm proves to be much more efficient than the simplex method for solving such problems. Besides the issue of computational efficiency, there is perhaps a better reason for taking a look at the transportation algorithm. Reexamine Fig. 4.2, then look again at the LP formulation. Which representation seems more "natural" or "intuitive"? We hope you feel that the network model is a more natural way of viewing Whitny's problem. As you will soon see, the transportation method structures the problem along the lines of Fig. 4.2.

3. THE TRANSPORTATION ALGORITHM

In this section we shall present one version of the transportation algorithm and apply it to solve Whitny's problem.

An Overview of the Algorithm

In Fig. 4.3 we give (in flowchart form) an overview of the transportation algorithm. You will note that it very closely resembles the simplex algorithm shown in Fig. 3.1. We should point out to you that there are really several "transportation algorithms." Each differs from the others in the manner in which the various steps are performed. Some of these well-known methods are listed below.

STEP 1. Four methods of establishing an initial feasible solution are:

1. The northwest-corner rule (NW-corner)
2. The least cost method
3. Vogel's approximation method (VAM)
4. Russell's method

STEP 2. Is the current solution optimal? Two methods employed in answering this question are:

1. The stepping-stone method
2. The modified distribution method (MODI)

In solving the Whitny problem, we shall use the NW-corner rule and the stepping-stone method. Later in this section we will indicate how to use two other methods of establishing an initial feasible solution. We shall then discuss MODI.

Solving the Whitny Problem

We shall now go through the steps of the transportation algorithm (Fig. 4.3), using the Whitny problem (Example 4.1) for illustration purposes.

STEP 1. TRANSPORTATION TABLE AND NW-CORNER RULE We first need to set up the transportation table. This table must show the sources (and their

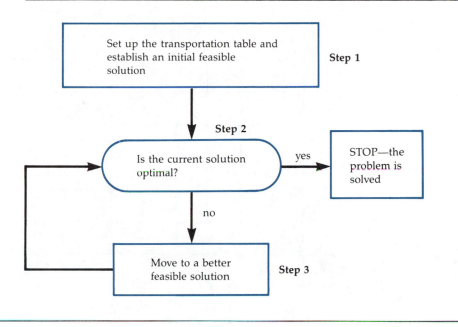

FIGURE 4.3   *The transportation algorithm.*

supplies), the destinations (and their demands), and the per-unit costs. Also, the table must be set up so that the total supply is equal to the total demand. (The case in which supply does not equal demand will be discussed in Section 4 of this chapter. For the Whitny problem, it so happens that supply = demand = 64.) We have set up the transportation table for Whitny in Fig. 4.4, using the abbreviations given earlier for names of sources and destinations. Note the placement of the costs per unit of flow (that is, per truckload). Also, note that total supply equals total demand, as required.

The next thing we must do in step 1 is to establish an initial feasible solution. A feasible solution must satisfy the following three criteria:

a. The supply of each source must be used.
b. The demand of each destination must be met.
c. The number of entries made in the transportation table must be equal to $r + c - 1$, where r = the number of rows in the table and c = the number of columns in the table. (The reason for this is somewhat technical, and we shall not concern ourselves with it here.)

We shall use the **northwest-corner rule** to establish an initial feasible solution. This rule states that we start in the northwest corner of the table (in our case square $S–M$) and allocate as many units as possible to that square while observing the supply and demand constraints. We then move to the

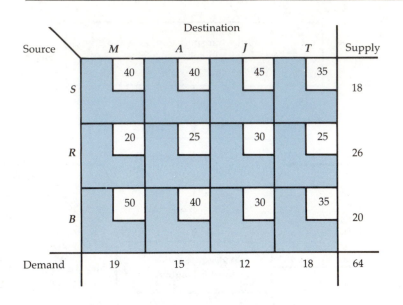

Source	Destination				Supply
	M	A	J	T	
S	40	40	45	35	18
R	20	25	30	25	26
B	50	40	30	35	20
Demand	19	15	12	18	64

FIGURE 4.4   *Transportation table for the Whitny problem.*

right, allocating units as we go, until row 1 supply is used up. Then we move down to row 2 and allocate as many units as possible along row 2 until the row 2 supply is used up. We continue in this manner until all row supplies are exhausted.

The NW-corner initial solution for the Whitny problem is given in Fig. 4.5. This solution was constructed as follows:

a. Start with square S–M (the northwest-corner square). Allocate as many units as possible to that square. Since the supply of row 1 (Stonefall) is 18 units and the demand of column 1 (Mixer) is 19 units, the maximum number of units we can allocate to square S–M is 18. (If we were to allocate more than 18 units, the supply constraint of row 1 would be exceeded.)

b. Since row 1 supply is used up, we move down to row 2, column 1 (square R–M). The remaining demand of column 1 is 1 unit (19 − 18 = 1). The supply of row 2 is 26 units, so we can allocate a maximum of 1 unit to square R–M.

c. Row 2 now has a remaining supply of 26 − 1 = 25 units. We move to the right to square R–A. Column 2 has a demand of 15 units, so we can allocate 15 units to square R–A.

d. Row 2 now has a remaining supply of 25 − 15 = 10 units. Column 3

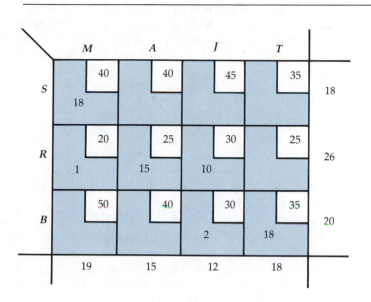

FIGURE 4.5   *Northwest-corner initial solution for the Whitny problem.*

has a demand of 12 units, so we can allocate the remaining 10 units to square R–J.

e. Since row 2 supply is used up, we move down to row 3, column 3 (square B–J). The *remaining* demand of column 3 is 12 − 10 = 2 units. The supply of row 3 is 20 units, so we can allocate 2 units to square B–J. This meets the column 3 demand of 12 units.

f. Row 3 has a remaining supply of 20 − 2 = 18 units, all of which we can allocate to square B–T. This completes the NW-corner initial solution.

Note that the NW-corner initial solution will always look like a stairway:

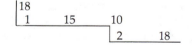

This completes step 1 of the algorithm. (You should continue to refer to Fig. 4.3 as we proceed through the solution of the Whitny problem.) How good is this initial solution? The total *weekly* cost of the NW-corner solution is easily computed, as follows:

18($40) + 1($20) + 15($25) + 10($30) + 2($30) + 18($35) = $2,105

In step 2 we shall determine whether or not this cost figure can be improved.

Note that the total number of allocations is six (squares S–M, R–M, R–A, R–J, B–J, and B–T), and check to see that the $r + c - 1$ criterion is satisfied:

$$r = 3$$

$$c = 4$$

$$r + c - 1 = 3 + 4 - 1 = 6$$

STEP 2. IS THE CURRENT SOLUTION OPTIMAL?

Since the "current solution" is the NW-corner initial solution, we must check to see whether the NW-corner solution is optimal. We shall use what is called the **stepping-stone method** for this purpose.

Before proceeding, let us introduce the following definitions to distinguish the "allocated" squares from the "nonallocated" squares:

a. An allocated square is called a **basic square.** (In Fig. 4.5 the basic squares are S–M, R–M, R–A, R–J, B–J, and B–T, which have respective allocations of 18, 1, 15, 10, 2, and 18 units.)
b. A nonallocated square is called an **open square.** (In Fig. 4.5, the open squares are S–A, S–J, S–T, R–T, B–M, and B–A, each of which has an "allocation" of *zero* units.)

Now, to answer the main question of step 2—Is the current solution optimal?—we examine each *open square* and ask the question: By how much would the total cost increase if one unit was allocated to this square?

For example, let us see what would happen if we were to allocate one unit to the open square S–A. Look at Fig. 4.5 (our current solution) and imagine placing a 1 in square S–A. What "chain-reaction" would this cause? If we put a 1 in square S–A, column 2 would then add up to $1 + 15 = 16$ units, exceeding the demand of 15. Thus to prevent this from happening we must *decrease* square R–A from 15 to 14. But then row 2 would add up to $1 + 14 + 10 = 25$ units, which is less than the supply of 26 for that row. Thus to maintain balance, we add one unit to square R–M, giving it $1 + 1 = 2$ units. But then column 1 would add up to $18 + 2 = 20$, which exceeds the column 1 demand of 19 units. So we adjust for this by subtracting one unit from square S–M, giving it $18 - 1 = 17$ units. Now we are back to where we started, namely square S–A, and we find that row 1 adds up to the required supply of 18 as follows:

S–M has 17 units
<u>S–A has　1 unit</u>
row 1 has 18 units

We can summarize this chain reaction graphically in Fig. 4.6. A plus sign means "allocate one additional unit," and a minus sign means "decrease the

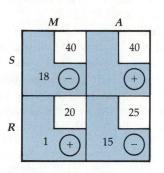

FIGURE 4.6

allocation by one unit." Note that a *closed path* is formed by the chain re-action. The path starts and ends at *S–A*, as shown in Fig. 4.7.

Now, by how much would the total cost increase if we were to allocate one unit to the open square *S–A*? To answer this, note that increasing the allocation to *S–A* by one unit would cost $40. However, decreasing the al-location to square *R–A* by one unit (from 15 to 14) would save $25. Increasing the allocation to square *R–M* by one unit would cost an additional $20. And, finally, decreasing the allocation to square *S–M* by one unit would save $40. The *net cost increase* would be

$$\$40 - \$25 + \$20 - \$40 = -\$5$$

The negative sign means that the cost would actually *decrease* by $5 per unit

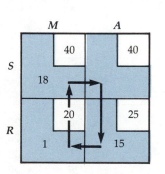

FIGURE 4.7

for every unit we could allocate to square S–A. This fact already tells us that the NW-corner solution is not optimal.

We continue to evaluate each of the remaining open squares in a similar manner. For each open square, we identify the closed path of plusses and minuses and compute the net cost increase. It is a fact that, for each open square, there is a *unique* closed path. The closed path must begin and end on the open square, and the plusses and minuses can only be placed on basic squares. It is permissible to skip over some basic squares in constructing the closed path. For example, the closed path associated with open square B–M is

$$+(B\text{–}M) - (R\text{–}M) + (R\text{–}J) - (B\text{–}J)$$

(we skipped over square R–A), and the net cost increase would be

$$\$50 - \$20 + \$30 - \$30 = \$30$$

for each unit allocated to square B–M, which clearly would not be desirable. The result of evaluating each open square is summarized in Table 4.2. (Make sure you see how square S–T was evaluated.)

The test for optimality (step 2, Fig. 4.3) is: When minimizing costs, if all cost increase evaluations of open squares are positive or 0, the current solution is optimal. If at least one open square has a negative evaluation, the current solution is not optimal.

In our case, the current solution is clearly not optimal, so we continue to step 3 of the algorithm.

STEP 3. MOVE TO A BETTER FEASIBLE SOLUTION. In this step we must do the following three things:

a. Determine which open square is to become a basic square; that is, determine the **entering open square.**

TABLE 4.2

Open square	Closed path	Net cost increase ($)
S–A	$+SA - RA + RM - SM$	$40 - 25 + 20 - 40$ $= -5$
S–J	$+SJ - RJ + RM - SM$	$45 - 30 + 20 - 40$ $= -5$
S–T	$+ST - BT + BJ - RJ + RM - SM$	$35 - 35 + 30 - 30 + 20 - 40 = -20$
R–T	$+RT - BT + BJ - RJ$	$25 - 35 + 30 - 30$ $= -10$
B–M	$+BM - RM + RJ - BJ$	$50 - 20 + 30 - 30$ $= +30$
B–A	$+BA - RA + RJ - BJ$	$40 - 25 + 30 - 30$ $= +15$

b. Determine which of the current basic squares is to become an open square; that is, determine the **exiting basic square.**
c. Generate a new feasible solution.

Determining the Entering Open Square. The rule for determining the entering open square is to select the open square having the highest per-unit cost decrease (as computed in the net cost increase column, step 2). Thus we select the open square having the *most negative* net cost increase, which is square $S–T$ (with a –$20).

Determining the Exiting Basic Square. The rule for determining which basic square is to become an open square is to examine the closed path associated with the entering square. Make a list of the basic squares on this path which have minus signs on them. These squares are called **donors.** The exiting basic variable is the donor that has the smallest current allocation made to it. It is generally helpful to trace out the closed path of the entering square on the current table, showing the "+" and "−" squares. In our case we have traced the closed path shown in Fig. 4.8. This makes it easy to spot the donors, the exiting variable, and what must be done to generate the new solution. Thus we have Table 4.3, and we see that the exiting basic square is $R–J$.

Generate a New Feasible Solution. To generate a new feasible solution, we let the entering square become a basic square and force the exiting square to become an open square. The number of units originally allocated to the

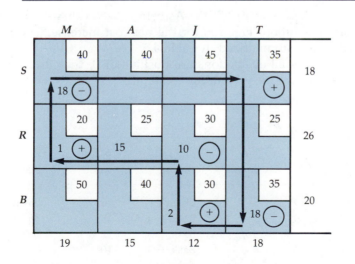

FIGURE 4.8

TABLE 4.3

Donor (on the path of S–T)	Allocated units
B–T	18
R–J	10
S–M	18

exiting square is now allocated to the entering basic square. Each donor square is decreased by this amount, and each "+" square on the path of the entering square is increased by this amount.

In our case we (1) allocate 10 units to $S–T$, (2) make $R–J$ an open square (having 0 allocation), (3) decrease each of the donors $B–T$ and $S–M$ by 10, and (4) increase $B–J$ and $R–M$ by 10. This procedure is summarized in Table 4.4.

The new "current solution" is shown in Fig. 4.9. Note that in step 2, the net cost increase for square $S–T$ was found to be −$20. Since $S–T$ entered at 10 units, the new feasible solution (Fig. 4.9) has an associated cost $20/ unit × 10 units = $200 *lower* than the cost of the solution shown in Fig. 4.5. Thus the new solution is *better*.

One other point you might wish to note: The exiting donor square is the donor square that would be driven to 0 *first* as the allocation to the entering square is increased.

This completes the first "iteration" of the transportation algorithm, Fig. 4.3, and brings us back to step 2 of the algorithm.

STEP 2. SECOND ITERATION. As before, we evaluate each open square of the current solution (Fig. 4.9) for the net cost increase. The results of this evaluation are summarized in Table 4.5.

Since not all evaluations are positive or 0, the current solution is not optimal and we must continue to step 3.

TABLE 4.4

		Square	Previous status	Previous value	New status	New value
Enter	→	S–T	Open (+)	0	Basic	10
		B–T	Basic (−)	18	Basic	8 (= 18 − 10)
		B–J	Basic (+)	2	Basic	12 (= 2 + 10)
Exit	→	R–J	Basic (−)	10	Open	0
		R–M	Basic (+)	1	Basic	11 (= 1 + 10)
		S–M	Basic (−)	18	Basic	8 (= 18 − 10)

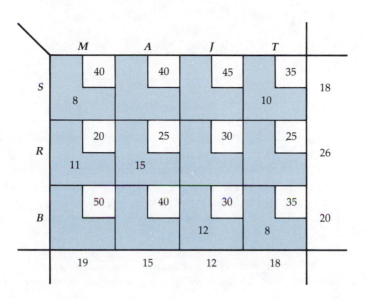

FIGURE 4.9
The result of the first iteration Whitny problem.

STEP 3. SECOND ITERATION. To determine the entering open square, we select the open square having the most negative net cost increase. Since $S{-}A$ and $B{-}A$ tie (with $-\$5$), we arbitrarily break the tie and decide to let $S{-}A$ be the entering square. (It would not be incorrect to let $B{-}A$ be the entering square.)

To determine the exiting basic square, we make the following list of the donors on the closed path of the entering variable $S{-}A$ (you may wish to trace out the closed path of $S{-}A$ in Fig. 4.9):

TABLE 4.5

Open square	Closed path	Net cost increase ($)	
$S{-}A$	$+SA - RA + RM - SM$	$40 - 25 + 20 - 40$	$= -5$
$S{-}J$	$+SJ - ST + BT - BJ$	$45 - 35 + 35 - 30$	$= +15$
$R{-}J$	$+RJ - RM + SM - ST + BT - BJ$	$30 - 20 + 40 - 35 + 35 - 30 = +20$	
$R{-}T$	$+RT - RM + SM - ST$	$25 - 20 + 40 - 35$	$= +10$
$B{-}M$	$+BM - SM + ST - BT$	$50 - 40 + 35 - 35$	$= +10$
$B{-}A$	$+BA - RA + RM - SM + ST - BT$	$40 - 25 + 20 - 40 + 35 - 35 = -5$	

Donor (on the path of S–A)	Allocated units
R–A	15
S–M	8

Since S–M has the minimum allocation, it is selected to be the exiting basic square.

To generate the new (and better) feasible solution, we let S–A enter as a basic square with an allocation of 8 units, increase R–M by 8, decrease R–A by 8, and make S–M an open square (having 0 allocation). The resulting feasible solution is given in Fig. 4.10. This solution has a cost that is $5/unit × 8 units = $40 less than the cost of the solution of Fig. 4.5.

This completes the second iteration of the transportation algorithm, Fig. 4.3, and again brings us back to step 2 of the algorithm.

STEP 2. THIRD ITERATION. We evaluate each open square in the current solution (Fig. 4.10) for the net cost increase and summarize the results in Table 4.6.

Since all net cost evaluations are positive or 0, the current solution (Fig. 4.10) is optimal and we STOP (the algorithm terminates).

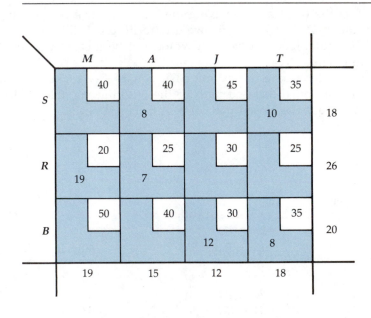

FIGURE 4.10   *The result of the second iteration Whitny problem.*

TABLE 4.6

Open square	Closed path	Net cost increase ($)	
S–M	+SM − SA + RA − RM	40 − 40 + 25 − 20	= +5
S–J	+SJ − ST + BT − BJ	45 − 35 + 35 − 30	= +15
R–J	+RJ − RA + SA − ST + BT − BJ	30 − 25 + 40 − 35 + 35 − 30 = +15	
R–T	+RT − RA + SA − ST	25 − 25 + 40 − 35	= +5
B–M	+BM − RM + RA − SA + ST − BT	50 − 20 + 25 − 40 + 35 − 35 = +15	
B–A	+BA − SA + ST − BT	40 − 40 + 35 − 35	= 0

The Whitny Solution

Using the results of the above iterations, we see that Whitny should send the following truckloads of gravel in order to minimize total weekly cost:

  8 from Stonefall to Albuq
10 from Stonefall to Torerel
19 from Rockgate to Mixer
  7 from Rockgate to Albuq
12 from Bedrock to Jackson
  8 from Bedrock to Torerel

The total (minimum) weekly cost to Whitny will be

$(8 \times 40) + (10 \times 35) + (19 \times 20) + (7 \times 25) + (12 \times 30) + (8 \times 35) = \$1,865$

You might note that this cost compares with the NW-corner solution cost of \$2,105. Thus we began with the NW-corner solution (step 1, Fig. 4.3), which was feasible (supplies and demands were met, and it had $r + c − 1$ $= 4 + 3 − 1 = 6$ allocations) but not optimal. Using the stepping-stone method, we then continued to improve the solution until we reached an optimal (minimum-cost) result (Fig. 4.10).

The Least Cost Method

We shall now illustrate another method for establishing an initial feasible solution, called the **least cost method.** This method requires more computational effort than the NW-corner rule. However, it typically provides a better starting solution, which will then require fewer iterations of the stepping-stone method.

Let us use the least cost method to establish a starting solution for the Whitny problem (refer to Fig. 4.4).

First, scan the table for the least cost square. The least cost ($20) occurs at square R–M. Now allocate as much to R–M as supply and demand constraints will allow. We see that we can allocate 19 units, which exhausts the demand in column M and results in the following table:

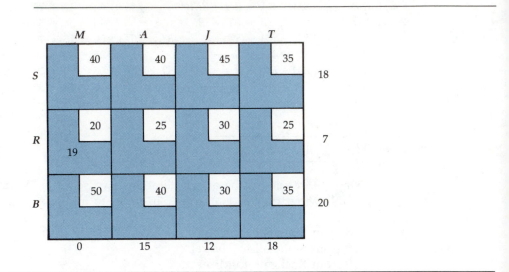

FIGURE 4.11

Now, with column M deleted, locate the least cost square. Squares R–A and R–T each contain the next least cost—$25. Breaking this tie arbitrarily, we will select R–A and allocate 7 units, resulting in the following table:

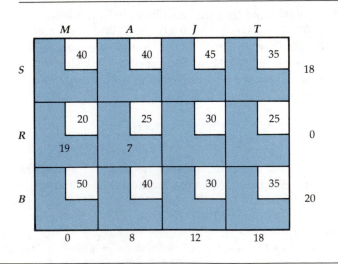

FIGURE 4.12

Now, column M and row R are deleted from consideration. Continuing in this manner, we allocate as follows:

12 units to $B-J$ (exhausting column J);
 8 units to $B-T$ (exhausting row B; also note that squares $S-T$ and $B-T$ tied, and we chose $B-T$ arbitrarily);
10 units to $S-T$ (exhausting column T);
 8 units to $S-A$ (exhausting column A and row S).

This procedure results in the following starting solution for the Whitny problem:

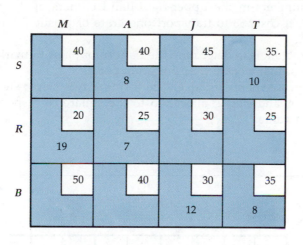

FIGURE 4.13

Now note the following:

1. The number of entries made is six, which equals $r + c - 1$. In the final step, if we had broken the tie at squares $S-T$ and $B-T$ by choosing $S-T$ instead of $B-T$, we would have ended up with only five entries. This problem is referred to as degeneracy and is easily dealt with. (See page 151.)
2. The least cost method actually gave us the optimal solution to the problem without further iterations of the stepping-stone method! This was merely accidental. The least cost method will not always perform so well, but it is typically much better than the NW-corner rule.

Normally, once an initial feasible solution is established using the least cost method, we then proceed as before with the stepping-stone method until an optimal solution is obtained.

Vogel's Approximation Method (VAM)

A third method for establishing an initial feasible solution is **Vogel's Approximation Method,** or **VAM.** VAM is a **heuristic;** that is, a method which produces results that are approximately optimal (see Chapter 18). In practice, VAM appears to produce the *optimal* solution in a large percentage of problems. We shall view VAM as a heuristic for the transportation problem.

Consider the following distribution problem facing Manufax, Inc., a manufacturer of plastic tubing. Manufax operates three plants and supplies four markets. Figure 4.14 shows the weekly production capacities (in crates) of each factory, the weekly market demands (in crates), and the cost (in $) of transporting a crate from each plant to each market. These costs are shown as the numbers in the upper-right-hand corners of the table squares. For example, it costs $8 to transport one crate of plastic tubing from plant 1 to market 2.

The problem is to determine the pattern of plant-to-market shipments that minimizes total weekly transportation costs.

VAM proceeds by iteratively performing two steps: step 1, calculation of rim values; and step 2, allocation to the square corresponding to the maximum rim value.

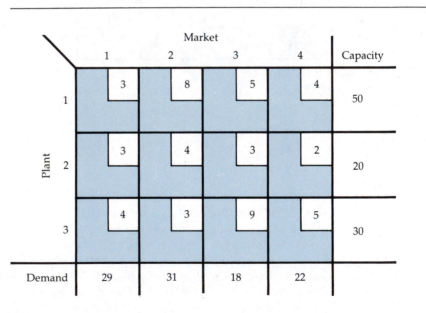

FIGURE 4.14

STEP 1. We first compute **rim values** for each row and column. The rim value for a given row (or column) is the difference between the two smallest costs in that row (or column).

For the Manufax problem, the rim values are computed as follows:

$$\begin{array}{ll} \text{Row 1} & 4 - 3 = 1 \\ \text{Row 2} & 3 - 2 = 1 \\ \text{Row 3} & 4 - 3 = 1 \end{array}$$

$$\begin{array}{ll} \text{Column 1} \quad 3 - 3 = 0 & \text{Column 3} \quad 5 - 3 = 2 \\ \text{Column 2} \quad 4 - 3 = 1 & \text{Column 4} \quad 4 - 2 = 2 \end{array}$$

Rim values can be interpreted as **minimum penalty costs.** For example, consider row 1. If we had complete choice, we would certainly like to ship all we could from plant 1 to market 1, since the unit shipping cost ($3) for this route is a minimum for row 1. Our second best choice would be to ship to market 4, since its shipping cost of $4 is the second-smallest row 1 cost. Thus the *minimum penalty cost* for not shipping to market 1 is $4 − $3 = $1 per crate. Of course, the penalty cost may be greater if we ship instead to market 2 or market 3.

STEP 2. Now select the largest rim value and allocate as many units of product as possible to the minimum-cost square in the corresponding row or column. The rationale behind this rule is that we would like first to make an allocation that would avoid incurring the largest penalty cost.

There is a tie for the maximum rim value, since columns 3 and 4 each have a rim value of 2. How should we break such ties? One way would be to break ties arbitrarily. Another way would be to follow the reasonable rule of thumb, which would select the tied rim value that has the lowest cost entry in its column (or row). Using this approach, we break the tie in favor of column 4, since the lowest cost in column 3 is $3 and the lowest cost in column 4 is $2. Thus we shall allocate as much as possible to the square in row 2, column 4. Since the supply (capacity) in row 2 is 20 and the demand in column 4 is 22, we can allocate 20 crates. The results of this first *iteration* (steps 1 and 2) are shown in Fig. 4.15. We have placed the rim values on the table, reduced the demand of column 4 by 20 (from 22 to 2), and have placed an "X" next to row 2 to indicate that this row will no longer participate in the algorithm.

ITERATION 2. We now must perform steps 1 and 2 above on the table of Fig. 4.15.

STEP 1. Compute the rim values as before, but this time do not use any costs that occur in rows or columns that have been deleted (X-ed out) from consideration.

These rim values, computed from Fig. 4.15, are as follows:

Row 1   no change (= 1)
Row 2   deleted
Row 3   no change (= 1)

Column 1   4 − 3 = 1   Column 3   9 − 5 = 4
Column 2   8 − 3 = 5   Column 4   5 − 5 = 1

STEP 2. The maximum rim value is 5, which corresponds to the figures given in column 2. The minimum-cost entry in column 2 (with row 2 deleted) is $3 (row 3, column 2), and we can allocate a maximum of 30 crates to that square.

The results of iteration 2 are shown in Fig. 4.16.

ITERATION 3. Note that since row 1 is the only row that is left, we have no choice concerning the remaining allocations. The results are shown in Fig. 4.17.

EVALUATING THE RESULT. How well did VAM perform? We note the following characteristics of VAM: (1) It is easy and fairly fast to perform and (2) it has rational intuitive appeal.

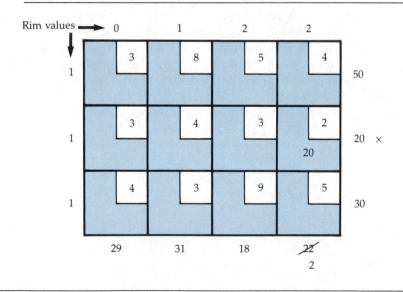

FIGURE 4.15   *Iteration 1, steps 2 and 3.*

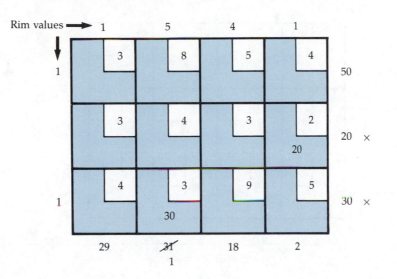

FIGURE 4.16   *Iteration 2.*

The cost of the VAM solution (see Fig. 4.17 below) is computed as follows:

$$(29)(3) + (1)(8) + (18)(5) + (2)(4) + (20)(2) + (30)(3) = \$323/\text{week}$$

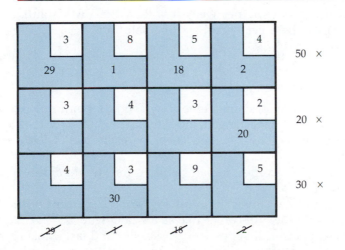

FIGURE 4.17   *Iteration 3.*

3 29	8	5 18	4 3
3	4 1	3	2 19
4	3 30	9	5

FIGURE 4.18

Using an optimal method, such as the stepping-stone method, we can derive the optimal shipping pattern shown in Fig. 4.18.

Thus the minimum attainable cost is

$$(29)(3) + (18)(5) + (3)(4) + (1)(4) + (19)(2) + (30)(3) = \$321/\text{week}$$

which is only $2 per week less than the VAM solution. Overall, VAM appears to be a very good starting solution.

VAM and the Stepping-Stone Algorithm

For the sake of completeness, we should point out that the primary use of VAM is in establishing an initial feasible solution for the stepping-stone method (see Fig. 4.3, step 1). Let us compare the use of VAM with the NW-corner rule.

The NW-corner initial solution for the Manufax problem is given in Fig. 4.19.

The cost of this solution is $507, or 157 percent of the VAM solution. We can view the NW-corner rule as a crude heuristic—it completely ignores costs, gives poor results, but is *extremely* easy and fast. Most management scientists would probably select VAM over the NW-corner rule, because VAM's additional computational cost seems to justify the large benefits realized.

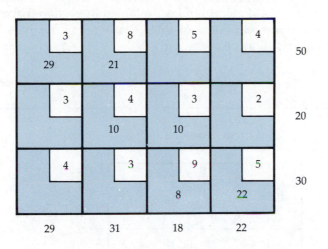

FIGURE 4.19

Problems

1. Consider the transportation problem given in Fig. 4.20.
   a. Construct the NW-corner solution.
   b. Compute the total cost of the NW-corner solution.
   c. Finally, using the stepping-stone method, find the minimum-cost solution.
2. How would the optimal solution to Problem 1 change if the costs from source 3 (row 3) were to change to those costs that are shown in Fig. 4.21?
3. Find the minimum-cost solution to the transportation problem given in Fig. 4.22.
4. We are given the transportation problem that is shown in Table 4.7, where costs are in $/unit shipped. Thus, for example, it costs $8 to ship one unit from factory 1 to market 1. Give the VAM distribution solution for this problem.

   Note: Before applying VAM, total capacity must equal total demand. In this case, capacity equals 250 and demand equals 225. To remedy this, include a dummy market that has 0 cost entries and a demand of 25 units in column 4.
5. *Maximization.* Suppose you are given the transportation problem shown in Table 4.8, where the entries indicate profit (in $) per unit shipped. The problem is to use VAM to determine a high-profit distribution plan. One

way to deal with profits is to convert them to negative costs and then apply the VAM algorithm, as explained in Section 3 above. You are asked to devise a modification of VAM that works directly with profits to solve this distribution problem.

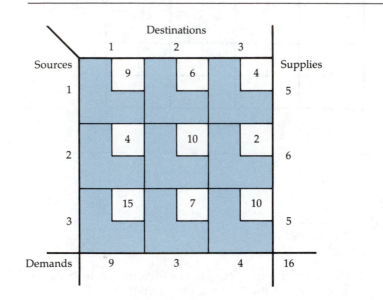

FIGURE 4.20

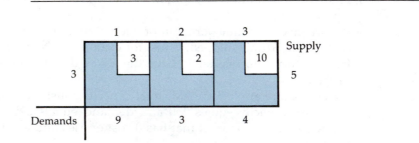

FIGURE 4.21

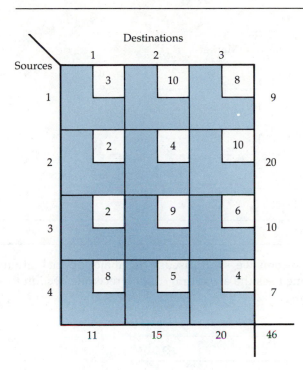

Destinations

	1	2	3	
Sources				
1	3	10	8	9
2	2	4	10	20
3	2	9	6	10
4	8	5	4	7
	11	15	20	46

FIGURE 4.22

TABLE 4.7

Factory				Capacity
1	8	5	10	80
2	15	20	5	70
3	10	15	7	60
4	10	19	20	40
Demand	100	50	75	

TABLE 4.8

	Market			
Factory	1	2	3	Capacity
1	10	5	3	100
2	20	8	15	50
3	12	15	7	75
Demand	75	75	75	225

4. SPECIAL SITUATIONS

In this section we shall discuss the major special situations that may arise when one uses the algorithm of the preceding section to solve transportation problems.

Demand Less Than Supply

According to step 1 of the algorithm (Fig. 4.3), total supply must equal total demand when setting up the transportation table. The next example shows what to do if total demand is less than total supply.

EXAMPLE 4.2: *When Demand Is Less Than Supply.* Amtex, Inc., operates three factories, each of which manufactures a common product that must be distributed to three markets ($M1$, $M2$, and $M3$). The monthly capacities of the three factories ($F1$, $F2$, and $F3$) are 100, 200, and 150 units of product, respectively, and the monthly market demands are 50, 250, and 75 units, respectively. The per-unit shipping costs from each factory to each market are given in Table 4.9 (in \$/unit of product). The problem is to set up the transportation table for Amtex.

TABLE 4.9

	Market		
Factory	$M1$	$M2$	$M3$
$F1$	10	15	11
$F2$	8	9	7
$F3$	6	12	14

Solution. Note that total supply equals 100 + 200 + 150 = 450 units per month and total demand equals 50 + 250 + 75 = 375 units per month. Since demand and supply are unequal, we cannot yet routinely construct the transportation table. To make demand equal supply, simply create a *dummy market* having a demand of 450 − 375 = 75 units per month. This dummy market does not physically exist; it is merely a mathematical device to make demand equal supply. The per-unit shipping cost from any of the three factories to the dummy market is $0. The reason for this is that such an allocation does not physically take place.

For example, suppose the optimal solution to the problem indicates that 10 units should be shipped from F1 to the dummy market per month. This would mean that F1 would not physically manufacture 10 units of its capacity of 100 per month. That is, F1 would have an excess capacity of 10 units per month.

The transportation table for this problem is shown in Fig. 4.23. (See Problem 1 at the end of this section.)   ▲

Supply Less Than Demand

When total supply is less than total demand, the problem is treated in a manner similar to the case in which total demand is less than total supply.

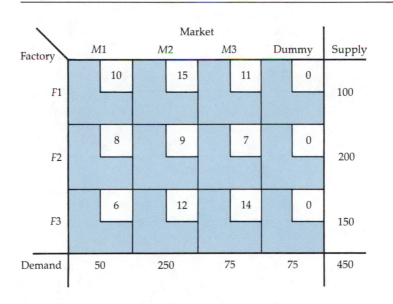

FIGURE 4.23

Simply create a dummy supply (such as a fictitious factory) having a zero cost row and a supply adequate to make total supply equal total demand. In the final solution to such a problem, some of the demands (for example, markets) will *not* be physically met.

Maximization Problems

It often happens that the objective in a given problem is to maximize rather than to minimize some measure of effectiveness—for example, to maximize profit. Such a problem can be handled directly by using the stepping-stone method to convert each profit to a negative cost.

EXAMPLE 4.3. *Profit Maximization.* Suppose that the objective in a given transportation problem is to maximize profit per week and that the transportation table is as shown in Fig. 4.24. Supply and demand are in units per week; numbers in the small upper right boxes represent dollars' profit per unit. Thus, for example, if 3 units are shipped from source 1 to destination 2, the weekly profit would be (3 units) × ($2/unit) = $6.

To determine the optimal solution, the stepping-stone method can be applied to the transportation problem shown in Fig. 4.25. (See Problem 2a at the end of this section.)   ▲

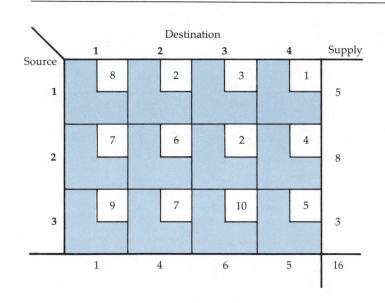

FIGURE 4.24

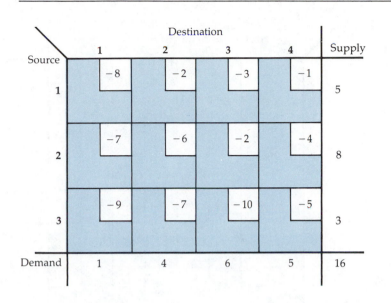

Destination

Source	1	2	3	4	Supply
1	−8	−2	−3	−1	5
2	−7	−6	−2	−4	8
3	−9	−7	−10	−5	3
Demand	1	4	6	5	16

FIGURE 4.25

A second (and more intuitive) method for solving maximization problems is to modify steps 2 and 3 of the stepping-stone algorithm as follows:

Step 2. Is the current solution optimal? To determine this, compute the net profit increase for each open square. If all such evaluations are zero or negative, the current solution is optimal. Otherwise, the solution is not optimal, and we must continue on to step 3.

Step 3. The only modification required here is in the criterion for determining the entering square. The open square having the *most positive* net profit increase is the entering open square. As before, ties are broken arbitrarily. (See Problem 2b at the end of this section.)

Degeneracy

A feasible solution is degenerate if it has less than $r + c - 1$ basic squares. The next two examples will illustrate (1) how degeneracy might occur, and (2) how to handle degeneracy if it does occur.

EXAMPLE 4.4. *Degeneracy in the NW-Corner Solution.* Suppose you are going to solve the transportation problem shown in Fig. 4.26. (It is not important whether it is a minimization or maximization problem.)

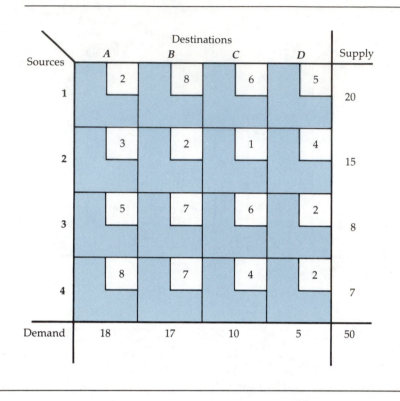

FIGURE 4.26

The NW-corner solution has the pattern shown in Fig. 4.27. (Check this.) In constructing this solution, the 15 units allocated to square 2–B *simultaneously* exhausted both the demand of column B, 17 units, and the supply of row 2, 15 units. The resulting solution has six basic squares; however, $r + c - 1 = 4 + 4 - 1 = 7$. Thus this initial solution is degenerate.

We mentioned that the reasons for requiring all basic feasible solutions to have exactly $r + c - 1$ basic squares is somewhat technical. However, one of the consequences of having fewer than $r + c - 1$ basic squares is that it may not be possible to evaluate open squares for net cost or profit increases. For example, closed paths do not exist in the above degenerate solution (Fig. 4.27) for the following open squares: 1–C, 1–D, 2–C, 2–D, 3–A, 3–B, 4–A, 4–B. (Check this.)

How do we repair the situation? Simply by placing a 0 allocation in either square 2–C or 3–B of Fig. 4.27 to form a "stair-step" pattern of basic squares, as shown in Fig. 4.28.

Now solve the problem as usual, treating the 0 as you would treat any other number in all calculations that arise in the stepping-stone algorithm. (See Problem 3 at the end of this section.) ▲

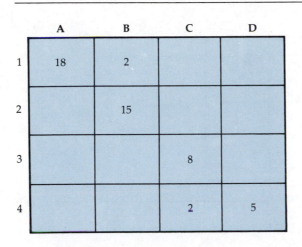

FIGURE 4.27

EXAMPLE 4.5. *Degeneracy While Executing the Stepping-stone Algorithm.* Degeneracy may also arise when an entering basic square comes into the solution at step 3 of the algorithm. Let us suppose you are solving a transportation problem, and during one of the iterations, you determine that square 3–B is the entering basic square at step 3 and the picture is as shown in Fig. 4.29. (The other rows and columns have been omitted from Fig. 4.29, as have the costs or profits.)

Which square is the exiting square? The closed path for 3–B is 3B − 3C + 4C − 4B, and the two donors are 3–C (with 5 units) and 4–B (with 5 units). Thus there is a tie for the exiting variable. We arbitrarily break the tie and select 3–C as the exiting square. So far we have done nothing incorrect. So 3–B enters with 5 units, 3–C exits, 4–C is increased to 8 + 5 = 13 units, and

18	2		
	15		
	0	8	
		2	5

OR

18	2		
	15	0	
		8	
		2	5

FIGURE 4.28

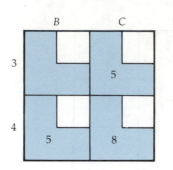

FIGURE 4.29

4–B is reduced by 5 units to $5 - 5 = 0$. Suppose the new picture is as shown in Fig. 4.30.

Now there is a problem. We entered *one* square (3–B) but took *two* squares out (3–C and 4–B). Thus there will now be one fewer than $r + c - 1$ basic squares.

The remedy for the problem is simple: We retain 4–B as a basic square (after all, it did not exit), giving it a 0 allocation (see Fig. 4.31).

Now proceed to solve the problem as usual.   ▲

Degeneracy in VAM. As with the NW-corner rule, degeneracy may occur in VAM if we delete both the row and the column when an allocation exhausts both the supply and the demand values simultaneously. To prevent degeneracy, we can arbitrarily select either the row or the column to delete, and then proceed as usual.   ▲

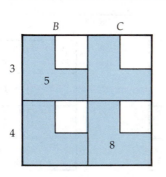

FIGURE 4.30

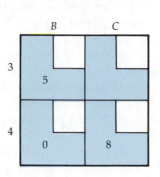

FIGURE 4.31

Multiple Optimal Solutions

Many transportation problems have more than one optimal solution. That is, there may be more than one allocation pattern (between sources and destinations) that yields the same minimum cost (or maximum profit).

Review the Whitny problem described in Example 4.1. We solved this problem in the text, and the optimal allocation was found to be that shown in Fig. 4.10, yielding a minimum cost of $1,865 per week. (See page 136.) Examine the net cost increase evaluations in Table 4.6. Note that the open square B–A has a 0 evaluation. This means that for every unit allocated to that square, the total cost will increase by 0 dollars. Thus, we can permit B–A to be an entering square in Fig. 4.10, and we will not increase the cost above the minimum $1,865. This would give management another alternative to consider for its production/distribution planning that would still result in the lowest weekly cost.

Problem 4 at the end of this section asks you to generate this alternative optimal solution.

Restricted Allocations

In some problems there may be nonquantitative considerations that prohibit certain allocations from being made. This may be the result of at least two possible factors:

1. Management may decree a *policy* of not using certain distribution routes or channels.
2. There may be physical constraints on the problem. For example, adequate truck or air routes may not exist between a certain factory and a given market.

EXAMPLE 4.6. *Restricted Allocation.* Consider the Whitny problem, Example 4.1, having the optimal solution as displayed in Fig. 4.10. Assume that Whitny's management is confronted with a new development—the roads between Stonefall and Torerel have become deteriorated, and the passenger-vehicle traffic has increased so much that it is difficult (if not impossible) to use the route for heavy truck traffic. Management decides to delete the route from consideration. With this restriction on the set of feasible solutions, determine the optimal production/distribution pattern for Whitny.

Solution. The question becomes: How can we make certain that the transportation algorithm does not make any allocations to square S–T of Fig. 4.4? Since we are minimizing costs, we can simply assign an "infinite" cost to square S–T, thus prohibiting such an allocation. We denote this cost by L; you may think of M as a very large number, such as 9,999. The transportation table for step 1 of Fig. 4.3 then becomes as shown in Fig. 4.32. Algebraically, M is treated like any other number in the calculations of the stepping-stone algorithm. For example $M - 5$ is larger than $M - 6$; also, $M - X$ is *always positive*, no matter what number X represents.

Problem 5 at the end of this section asks you to solve this modified version of the Whitny problem.

To prohibit an allocation in the case of maximization, simply assign an infinitely negative profit, $-M$, to the square. Recall that M is an arbitrarily large positive number.   ▲

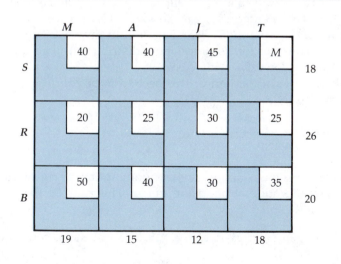

FIGURE 4.32

Problems

1. Solve the problem given in Fig. 4.23 (Example 4.2).
2. Solve the problem of Example 4.3 as follows:
    a. Minimize negative profit (see Fig. 4.25)
    b. Apply the modified stepping-stone algorithm for maximization problems (see step 3)
3. Solve the problem of Example 4.4 assuming the entries in Fig. 4.28 are costs.
4. For the Whitny problem (Example 4.1, Fig. 4.10), specify an alternate optimal (minimum-cost) production/distribution plan for the company's management to consider.
5. Solve the modified version of the Whitney problem (Example 4.6).
6. Does the transportation problem given in Fig. 4.20 on page 146 (Section 3, Problem 1) have multiple optimal solutions? If so, determine the other solutions.

5. APPLICATIONS

In this section we shall present a list of practical management applications of the transportation problem formulation and technique. We shall also present a description of a given problem within each area of application. Then the initial transportation table of step 1 (Fig. 4.3) will be formulated. You should check each of these formulations carefully to be certain you understand the details involved.

Production/Distribution Planning

We have already illustrated this application in the Whitny problem, Example 4.1. We should point out that the Whitny problem is a *production* problem as well as a product-distribution problem. The reason for this stems from the fact that the three stone quarries have different production costs. When production costs do not differ among production facilities, you can view the problem simply as a distribution problem.

Production/Inventory Planning

This area of application is generally included in the broader area of "Aggregate Production Planning," or "Master Scheduling."

EXAMPLE 4.7. Coronado Industries must schedule production of a 2,000-gallon water tank over the next four months. Demand for this tank is expected to be 20 units in January, 15 units in February, 19 units in March, and 24 units in April. Regular-time capacity is 17 units per month. By using over-time, an additional 5 units can be produced per month. A tank produced on regular time costs $400 to manufacture; on overtime the same tank costs $600 to manufacture. The holding cost to carry a tank in inventory from one month to the next is $50. Determine the optimal production/inventory plan for the next four months.

Solution. The objective is to plan production and inventory in order to min-imize the cost of meeting the forecasted demand over the four-month plan-ning horizon. The problem can be formulated and solved as a transportation problem in the following manner.

Each of the four months represents a destination with corresponding de-mands. There are eight possible sources of supply corresponding to regular-time and overtime production in each of the four months. Note that the total demand is $20 + 15 + 19 + 24 = 78$ units. The total supply is $4 \times (17 + 5) = 88$ units. Thus a dummy destination that has a demand of 10 units is required. The initial transportation table for this problem is given in Fig. 4.33, where Jan., Feb., Mar., and Apr. denote the four months; RT denotes regular time; and OT denotes overtime. Thus OT–Feb. represents the source "February overtime production."

Note the effect of the holding cost of $50 per tank per month. For example, a tank produced on regular time in February (RT–Feb. row) and sold in April costs $400 + (2 \text{ months} \times \$50/\text{month}) = \$500$.

Also, the Ms are used to prohibit certain allocations. For example, since it is physically impossible to satisfy January demand with February produc-tion (since we assume that backorders are not permitted), an infinite cost $M is placed in the (RT–Feb.)–Jan. and (OT–Feb.)–Jan. squares.   ▲

Variations of this basic problem can be found in the exercises at the end of this chapter.

Vendor Selection

The transportation algorithm can be used to determine solutions to vendor selection problems when vendors specify a limit on the quantities they are able to supply in the short run.

EXAMPLE 4.8. Greg's Slippery Wheel Pottery School uses three types of clay (C1, C2, and C3) for its pottery class instruction. Four wholesale vendors (V1, V2, V3, and V4) offer the clay. Each month Greg uses 1,500, 1,800, and 900 pounds of C1, C2, and C3, respectively. The vendors have indicated to Greg that they can supply the following monthly quantities of all three types of clay (in pounds):

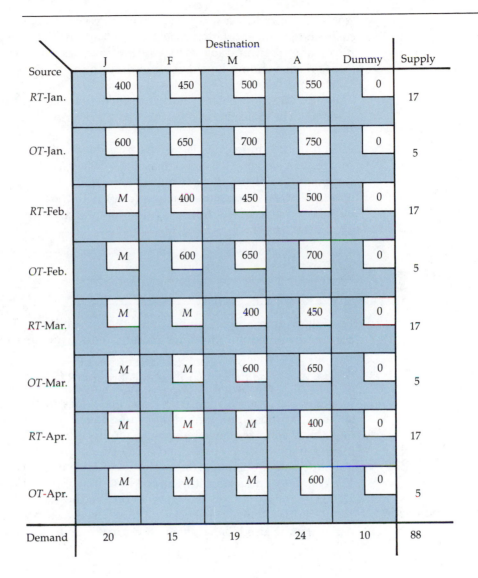

	Destination					
Source	J	F	M	A	Dummy	Supply
RT-Jan.	400	450	500	550	0	17
OT-Jan.	600	650	700	750	0	5
RT-Feb.	M	400	450	500	0	17
OT-Feb.	M	600	650	700	0	5
RT-Mar.	M	M	400	450	0	17
OT-Mar.	M	M	600	650	0	5
RT-Apr.	M	M	M	400	0	17
OT-Apr.	M	M	M	600	0	5
Demand	20	15	19	24	10	88

FIGURE 4.33   *Production/inventory planning.*

Vendor	V1	V2	V3	V4
Supply	1,000	800	1,500	1,200

Vendor prices for each type of clay vary due to variations in production costs and in transportation costs to ship the clay to Greg's workshop. These prices are given in Table 4.10 (in cents per pound). Greg must determine from which vendors he should purchase the various clays.

Solution. Greg's problem can be formulated and solved as a transportation problem. The objective is to minimize the monthly cost of purchasing the clay.

Each of the three clays is viewed as a destination, and each vendor as a source (or vice versa). Total demand is 1,500 + 1,800 + 900 = 4,200 pounds per month; total supply is 1,000 + 800 + 1,500 + 1,200 = 4,500 pounds per month. Thus a dummy destination (clay) with a demand of 300 pounds per month is needed. .The transportation table is given in Fig. 4.34. (Note the use of the M.) ▲

Scheduling Resource Requirements

The following example demonstrates the versatility of the transportation algorithm in scheduling resource requirements over time.

EXAMPLE 4.9. Setfirm Concrete Contractor has been awarded a contract to do part of the concrete work on a large university auditorium. Setfirm has scheduled a series of five large concrete pours in the upcoming week, to begin on Monday and go through to Friday. For these pours, Setfirm must use a new kind of concrete-forming method that requires special concrete-form panels. Setfirm currently does not own any of these panels and does not anticipate any immediate use for them once this special job is completed. The company anticipates it will need the following quantities of these panels: 100 on Monday, 130 on Tuesday, 80 on Wednesday, 150 on Thursday, and 140 on Friday. New panels can be purchased at a cost of $50 per panel. A panel that is used on a given day can be reused on the following day,

TABLE 4.10

Clay	Vendor			
	$V1$	$V2$	$V3$	$V4$
C1	25	28	30	22
C2	45	44	39	*
C3	60	62	57	52

*Does not supply C2.

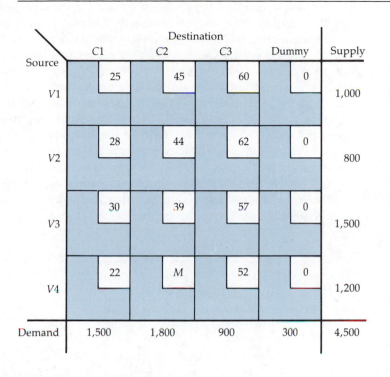

Source \ Destination	C1	C2	C3	Dummy	Supply
V1	25	45	60	0	1,000
V2	28	44	62	0	800
V3	30	39	57	0	1,500
V4	22	M	52	0	1,200
Demand	1,500	1,800	900	300	4,500

FIGURE 4.34   *Vendor selection.*

because the used panel can be removed as soon as the concrete has set. The cost of reusing a panel is estimated as follows:

Labor (for removing the panel from its form)	$13
Cleaning the panel (scrape and wash)	5
Reset special pins in the panel	2
	$20

Due to some labor-scheduling problems, only half of the panels used on Tuesday could be prepared for reuse on Wednesday; the other half could be ready by Thursday. Otherwise, panels used on a given day can be ready for reuse the following day.

In order to maximize profit for the job, Setfirm must decide how to supply the required panels at minimum cost for the week's work. Can you assist Setfirm?

Solution. As you might guess, Setfirm's problem can be formulated and solved as a transportation problem; however, the exact procedure may not yet be apparent to you. Perhaps you might wish to give this some thought before continuing.

The destinations are represented by each of the five days of the upcoming week, Monday, Tuesday, Wednesday, Thursday, and Friday. The sources of panel supply are of two general types: either brand-new panels (never used) or used panels (panels used on a previous day of the week). Setfirm could purchase as many as 600 panels (100 + 130 + 80 + 150 + 140). Of course it would not want to purchase more than this, since its total needs are only for this amount. Thus one *source* of supply is the *option* of purchasing up to 600 new panels before the week begins. This represents a possible source of supply for each of the five days of the upcoming week.

How can panels for Tuesday be supplied? In two ways: Either use brand-new panels (we already accounted for this option above) and/or reuse some of the panels from Monday. Since 100 panels are to be used on Monday, the source of reused panels for Tuesday has a supply of 100. Following similar reasoning, we can produce the transportation table shown in Fig. 4.35.

Source	Monday	Tuesday	Wednesday	Thursday	Friday	Dummy	Supply
(1) New Panels	50	50	50	50	50	0	600
(2) Reused from Monday	20	20	20	20	20	0	100
(3) Reused from Tuesday	M	M	20	20	20	0	65
(4) Reused from Tuesday	M	M	M	20	20	0	65
(5) Reused from Wednesday	M	M	M	20	20	0	80
(6) Reused from Thursday	M	M	M	M	20	0	150
Demand	100	130	80	150	140	460	1060

FIGURE 4.35   *Resource scheduling.*

Note the use of the dummy destination and the use of Ms. The panels reused from Tuesday have been separated into two groups, since half of them will be available on Wednesday ($1/2 \times 130 = 65$) and the other half on Thursday. Thus a large M is used in row (4) of the Wednesday column to show that 65 of the panels used on Tuesday cannot be reused until Thursday. ▲

Assignment Problems

Another major class of problems that can be modeled as transportation problems is assignment problems. Included in this class are the following applications: (1) personnel-to-job assignments, (2) contract awards to bidders, (3) assignment of salespeople to territories, and (4) strategic military assignments.

Since the next chapter is devoted to this class of problems, we shall omit further discussion of assignment problems at this time.

6. COMPUTER SOLUTION OF TRANSPORTATION PROBLEMS

Although transportation problems could be solved through standard linear-programming computer programs, it would be a tedious task and an inefficient use of such programs. A computer program which exploits the special structure of transportation programs would be more convenient, easier to use, and more efficient. In this section, we shall examine the use of PROC TRANS in SAS/OR, a program that implements the transportation algorithm. (See Section 8 of Chapter 3 for an introduction to SAS/OR.)

The Whitny Problem in SAS/OR PROC TRANS Format

One particular advantage in using the SAS/OR group of programs is that they share many common features. In this example, you will see programming statements similar to those for PROC LP in Chapter 3. In following chapters, you will see examples of the uses of other SAS/OR programs. As you study these examples, note the similarities in the manner in which data sets are named and entered, titles are specified, and variables are identified. In PROC TRANS, as in PROC LP, communication is through a group of keywords. These keywords are different from those of PROC LP because they are meant to identify the particular characteristics of transportation problems.

The PROC TRANS Program

```
1   TITLE 'WHITNY STONE AND GRAVEL';
2   DATA WHITNY;
```

```
3        INPUT MIXR ALBUQ JACK TOR SUP SORZ$;
4        CARDS;
5    19 15 12 18   .   .
6    40 40 45 35 18   STONEF
7    20 25 30 25 26   ROCKG
8    50 40 30 35 20   BEDRK
9    ;
10   PROC TRANS COST = WHITNY;
20        VAR MIXR ALBUQ JACK TOR;
30        ID SORZ;
40        SUPPLY SUP;
50   PROC PRINT;
```

The keywords in PROC TRANS are **DEMAND, SUPPLY,** and **COST,** the three sets of parameters of a transportation problem. The data are entered with the demands in the first data row (the two periods in that row mean that there are no values for **SUP** and for **SORZ**), followed by the cost coefficients, with the destinations as the columns and the sources (SORZ above) as the rows. With this format, the **DEMAND** keyword does not need to be used, since the program assumes that the demands are in the first row unless told otherwise. If demands are to be given in a data row other than the first, the entry **DEMAND=d** must be made in the PROC TRANS statement, where d is the number of the data line listing the demands. The other keywords must be shown. The **COST=WHITNY** entry in the PROC TRANS statement means that the cost coefficients are in the data set named **WHITNY.** The **SUPPLY SUP** statement means that the supply values are entered as the variable **SUP,** and the **ID SORZ** statement (optional) gives the names chosen for the supply sources. The statement PROC PRINT (which was not needed in PROC LP) is needed for printing the output of PROC TRANS. Minimization is assumed by PROC TRANS. If maximization is desired, the keyword **MAXIMIZE** has to be entered in the PROC TRANS statement.

Solution Output

The output of PROC TRANS is given in table format (see the WHITNY solution output below), with the destinations as columns and the sources as rows. The first row, labeled **DUAL,** gives the marginal cost of increasing the demand at each destination. The remaining rows show the optimal flow between each source and destination. The last column, also labeled **DUAL,** gives the marginal cost of increasing supply at each source (the negative value indicates cost reductions). The **DUAL** values, as in linear programming, can be used to evaluate the cost effects of marginal changes in the current problem (sensitivity analysis). For example, a one-unit increase in demand at **ALBUQ** would increase overall costs by $40. On the supply side, increasing the supply at **STONEF** by one unit would leave costs unchanged;

whereas increasing the supply at **ROCKG** by one unit would reduce overall costs by $15.

```
NOTE:   MINIMUM COST ROUTING = 1865.00

                    WHITNY STONE AND GRAVEL

OBS     SORZ        MIXR    ALBUQ    JACK     TOR     -DUAL-

 1      -DUAL-       35       40      30       35        .
 2      STONEF        0        8       0       10        0
 3      ROCKG        19        7       0        0      -15
 4      BEDRK         0        0      12        8        0
```

7. MODI—THE MODIFIED DISTRIBUTION METHOD (OPTIONAL)

In this section, we shall present another method for solving transportation problems, known as the **Modified Distribution Method,** or **MODI.** In essence, MODI is simply an algebraic version of the stepping-stone method already discussed. It is derived by examining the simplex solution of the transportation LP problem and exploiting special properties of the dual variables (see Section 7 of Chapter 3).

For our purposes, we shall only indicate how MODI works to solve transportation problems and present the mechanics of the method. So that MODI and the stepping-stone method may be compared, we shall illustrate the use of MODI in solving the Whitny problem, starting with the transportation table given in Fig. 4.4.

STEP 1. *Establish an Initial Feasible Solution.* We shall do this as before, using the NW-corner method, so our initial solution is the same as that given in Fig. 4.5.

STEP 2. *Is the Current Solution Optimal?* To answer this question, we must now introduce the algebra of MODI. For each row of the transportation table, we associate a variable u_i, and for each column a variable v_j. Since we have three rows and four columns, this produces the varibles u_1, u_2, u_3, and v_1, v_2, v_3, v_4, which are incorporated into the transportation table as shown in Fig. 4.36.

(Note that we have relabeled the rows 1, 2, 3, and the columns 1, 2, 3, 4.) The following is the key property which will help us determine the values of the variables u_i and v_j. Let c_{ij} be the unit cost associated with square (i, j) (the square in row i, column j). Thus, for example, $c_{11} = 40$, $c_{21} = 20$, $c_{31} = 50$, etc. If square (i, j) is a basic square, then

$$c_{ij} = u_i + v_j \tag{4–1}$$

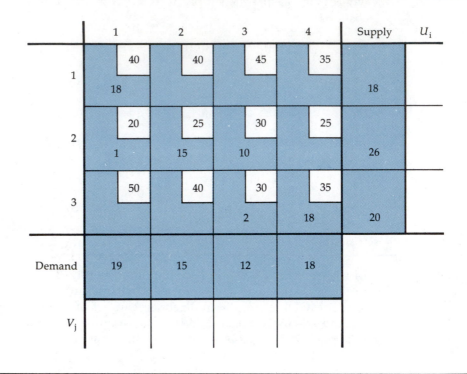

	1	2	3	4	Supply	u_i
1	40 18	40	45	35	18	
2	20 1	25 15	30 10	25	26	
3	50	40	30 2	35 18	20	
Demand	19	15	12	18		
v_j						

FIGURE 4.36

The only technical problem which arises is that there are only $(r + c - 1)$ = 6 basic squares, but $(r + c) = 7$ equations 4–1. To resolve this, we simply select any u_i or v_j, set it equal to zero, and then solve for the remaining values. We choose to select the row having the largest number of basic squares and set its u_i equal to zero.

Now, let's proceed to use EQ. 4–1 to solve for the u_i and v_j in Fig. 4.36.

Since row 2 has the largest number of basic squares (three), we shall set $u_2 = 0$. This starts the process of solving the other six equations [corresponding to the basic squares (1, 1), (2, 1), (2, 2), (2, 3), (3, 3), and (3, 4)] in the form of EQ. 4–1:

$$40 = c_{11} = u_1 + v_1$$
$$20 = c_{21} = u_2 + v_1$$
$$25 = c_{22} = u_2 + v_2$$
$$30 = c_{23} = u_2 + v_3$$
$$30 = c_{33} = u_3 + v_3$$
$$35 = c_{34} = u_3 + v_4$$

We can further calculate:

If $u_2 = 0$, then $v_1 = 20$ (from the second equation)
If $u_2 = 0$, then $v_2 = 25$ (from the third equation)
If $u_2 = 0$, then $v_3 = 30$ (from the fourth equation)
If $v_1 = 20$, then $u_1 = 20$ (from the first equation)
If $v_3 = 30$, then $u_3 = 0$ (from the fifth equation)
If $u_3 = 0$, then $v_4 = 35$ (from the sixth equation)

We can now record these results on the table, as in Figure 4.37.

Actually, the six equations drawn from EQ. 4–1 can be solved on Figure 4.36 in a very simple manner. We start with row 2 and set $u_2 = 0$ for the reasons discussed above. Now we identify the basic squares in row 2: (2, 1), (2, 2), (2, 3). Examining the costs c_{21}, c_{22}, and c_{33} (and keeping EQ. 4–1 in mind), we immediately see that $v_1 = 20$, $v_2 = 25$, and $v_3 = 30$, so we record these in Fig. 4.37. Next, knowing that $v_1 = 20$ and using basic square (1, 1), whose cost is 40, we can calculate $u_1 = 20$. Now we come down to the basic square (3, 3). We know that $v_3 = 30$, so $u_3 = 0$ (since $u_3 + v_3$ must equal c_{33},

	1	2	3	4	Supply	U_i
1	40	40	45	35		
	18				18	20
2	20	25	30	25		
	1	15	10		26	0
3	50	40	30	35		
			2	18	20	0
Demand	19	15	12	18		
V_j	20	25	30	35		

FIGURE 4.37

which equals 30). Finally, for the basic square (3, 4), we know that $u_3 = 0$ (as shown above), so v_4 must be 35, since $u_3 + v_4 = 35$.

Getting back to the question: Is the current solution optimal? We now calculate for each nonbasic square the value $c_{ij} - u_i - v_j$. If all of these values are nonnegative, the current solution is optimal and we STOP. If not, we move to step 3.

Let's evaluate the current solution. For each open square in Fig. 4.36, we calculate $c_{ij} - u_i - v_j$. These results are recorded in Fig. 4.38.

The allocations in basic squares are circled for clarity. As an example of these calculations, consider the open square (1, 2). There we have $c_{12} - u_1 - v_2 = 40 - 20 - 25 = -5$. You should check the rest of the calculations recorded in Fig. 4.38.

If you compare Fig. 4.41 with Table 4.2 (page 132), you will note that the open-square evaluations in the net-cost-increase column of Table 4.2 are the same as those of Fig. 4.38. This is what was meant in introducing MODI as an algebraic version of the stepping-stone method.

Since not all the $c_{ij} - u_i - v_j$ results are nonnegative, the current solution given in Fig. 4.38 is not optimal. We now move on to step 3.

	1	2	3	4	Supply	U_i
1	40 ⑱	40 −5	45 −5	35 −20	18	20
2	20 ①	25 ⑮	30 ⑩	25 −10	26	0
3	50 30	40 15	30 ②	35 ⑱	20	0
Demand	19	15	12	18		
V_j	20	25	30	35		

FIGURE 4.38

STEP 3. *Move to a Better Feasible Solution.* This step uses basically the same procedure as the stepping-stone method. The entering square is the one with the largest negative value of $c_{ij} - u_i - v_j$. In this case, open square (1, 4) enters, and basic square (2, 3) exits. Using the stepping-stone method, we generate a new feasible solution, as in Fig. 4.39.

We now return to step 2: Is the current solution optimal? Using Fig. 4.39, we find the u_i and v_j as before and then calculate the $c_{ij} - u_i - v_j$ equations for the open squares. The result is given in Fig. 4.40. (We set $u_1 = 0$ first.)

Since not all of the open-square values are nonnegative, the current solution is not optimal. Go to step 3.

STEP 3. *Second Iteration—Move to a Better Feasible Solution.* Using the rules discussed above, either (1, 2) or (3, 2) could enter. We arbitrarily choose (1, 2) to enter. Basic square (1, 1) then exits. The new feasible solution is given in Fig. 4.41.

STEP 2. *Third Iteration—Is the Current Solution Optimal?* In Fig. 4.41, we show the results of calculating the u_i and v_j (beginning with setting $u_2 = 0$)

	1	2	3	4	Supply	U_i
1	40	40	45	35		
	8			10	18	
2	20	25	30	25		
	11	15			26	
3	50	40	30	35		
			12	8	20	
Demand	19	15	12	18		
V_j						

FIGURE 4.39

FIGURE 4.40

	1	2	3	4	Supply	U_i
1	40 / (8)	40 / −5	45 / 15	35 / (10)	18	0
2	20 / (11)	25 / (15)	30 / 20	25 / 10	26	−20
3	50 / 10	40 / −5	30 / (12)	35 / (8)	20	0
Demand	19	15	12	18		
V_j	40	45	30	35		

FIGURE 4.40

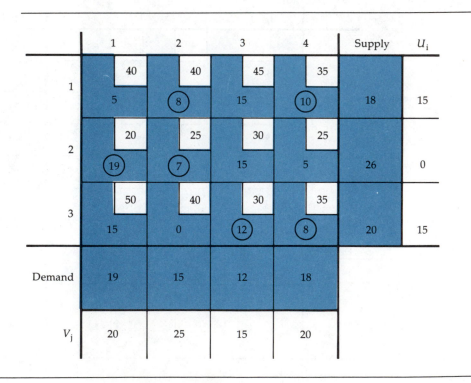

FIGURE 4.41

	1	2	3	4	Supply	U_i
1	40 / 5	40 / (8)	45 / 15	35 / (10)	18	15
2	20 / (19)	25 / (7)	30 / 15	25 / 5	26	0
3	50 / 15	40 / 0	30 / (12)	35 / (8)	20	15
Demand	19	15	12	18		
V_j	20	25	15	20		

FIGURE 4.41

170

and the $c_{ij} - u_i - v_j$ equations. Since all of these values are nonnegative, the solution shown is optimal.

Note: The sequence of MODI iterations corresponds to those of the stepping-stone method, Fig. 4.4 through Fig. 4.10.

8. CONCLUDING REMARKS

In this chapter we have studied the special class of linear programs called transportation problems. The transportation algorithm, an efficient and somewhat intuitive method, is used to solve such problems.

The basic steps of the transportation algorithm (Fig. 4.3) are listed below.

STEP 1. Start with an initial solution.

STEP 2. Test the solution to see whether you have found the optimal solution. This is done by evaluating each open square to determine whether the cost (or profit) could be decreased (or increased), using the stepping-stone method.

STEP 3. If the current solution is not optimal, move to a better solution: Enter the open square that decreases cost (or increases profit) at the greatest rate, and take out the minimum donor square. Now return to step 2 and test the new solution for optimality.

HOW GOOD IS THE NW-CORNER METHOD? To start step 1 of the transportation algorithm, we used the NW-corner rule and obtained an initial solution to the transportation problem.

The *advantages* of the NW-corner rule are as follows: (1) it is easy to perform; (2) it is fast; and (3) it requires very little arithmetic calculation.

The *disadvantage* of the NW-corner rule is that it completely ignores cost (or profit). Thus, for example, the NW-corner rule may allow an allocation to a square having a high unit cost (possibly to a square having a cost M). Because of this fact, using the NW-corner rule may not provide the best solution in terms of cost (or profit). It may take several iterations of the stepping-stone method to reach the optimal solution, especially for larger problems. (See Exercise 12 at the end of this chapter, for example.)

TERMINOLOGY

After studying this chapter you should be familiar with the following terms:

TERM	SECTION
basic square	3
degeneracy	3, 4
donor	3

EXERCISES

1. *Distribution.*   Jacks Hydrolics manufactures forklift trucks in two different plants, P1 and P2. It supplies three major markets (M1, M2, and M3) with its product. The plants (and yearly capacities), markets (and projected yearly demands), and unit shipping costs (dollars per unit) are given in Fig. 4.42. Determine the minimum-cost distribution plan for meeting market demand.

2. *Capacity Expansion.*   (Refer to Exercise 1 above.) The marketing and operations analysts at Jacks Hydrolics have forecasted that market demand in markets M1 and M2 will increase to 75 units and 225 units per year within the next three years. To meet this additional demand, Jacks is planning to build a new plant (P3) that will have a capacity of 300 units per year. The shipping costs to the three markets from P3 will be $75, $50, and $50 to M1, M2, and M3, respectively. Assuming that plant P3 is constructed, determine the minimum-cost distribution pattern, given the increased market demands.

3. *Plant Location: Capacity Planning.*   (Refer to Exercises 1 and 2 above.) Assume that market demand for the Jacks product in markets M1 and M2 is expected to increase to 75 units and 225 units per year, respectively, and that Jacks is planning to build a new plant, P3, that will have a capacity of 300 units per year. The possible locations for P3 have been narrowed down to two options, A and B. The relevant shipping costs are given in Table 4.11. Plant construction costs will be the same at either location A or location B. Determine the optimal location for P3, *based on distribution cost considerations.*

4. *Qualitative Factors in Plant Location.*   This exercise simply provides an opportunity to consider nonquantitative factors that might also enter into the plant-location problem presented in Exercise 3 above. Some of these

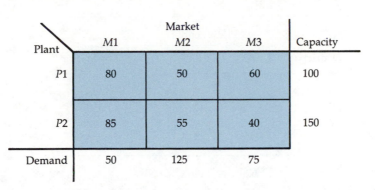

Plant \ Market	M1	M2	M3	Capacity
P1	80	50	60	100
P2	85	55	40	150
Demand	50	125	75	

FIGURE 4.42

factors are given in the list below and are intended to provide a basis for discussion:

a. Nearness to suppliers.

b. Nearness to subcontractors.

c. Operating costs: labor rates, utility/overhead costs, availability of skilled labor.

d. Social and cultural factors: climate, schools, housing market, recreation.

e. Political: taxes, local regulations such as zoning.

f. Proximity to technical training schools and universities for personnel development and recruiting.

5. *Capacity Expansion: Jacks Hydrolics.* Solve Exercise 2, assuming that Jacks has planned the capacity of P3 to be 400 units per year. What effects would the addition of P3 have on the existing plants?

6. *Assigning Students to Public Schools.* Rockville Public School system operates three high schools (H1, H2, and H3) to serve four school districts (D1, D2, D3, and D4). Table 4.12 gives the capacity of each high school (in students), the high school student population of each school district,

TABLE 4.11

Plants	Locations	Markets		
		M1	M2	M3
P3	A	75	50	50
P3	B	70	50	55

TABLE 4.12

| District | High school | | | Population |
	H1	H2	H3	
D1	1	2	2	200
D2	3	2	3	500
D3	2	1	2	400
D4	2	3	1	600
Capacity	500	600	600	

and the average distance between each high school and school district (in miles).

a. Determine the student-school assignment that minimizes the total student-miles traveled per day.

b. Solve part (a), assuming the population of D1 is 400 instead of 200. Such a computation would be of interest in the event that a population increase was expected for D1.

7. *Municipal Street Maintenance.* The city of Snobank operates three maintenance garages that house snow-removal equipment (trucks). The city is sectioned into three main areas (A1, A2, and A3) for snow-removal planning purposes. During a typical winter season, A1 requires the services of three snow-removal trucks per week to clear and maintain streets. The other two areas, A2 and A3, require the services of five trucks and four trucks per week, respectively. The three garages (G1, G2, and G3) have adequate resources to house and maintain six trucks, four trucks, and three trucks, respectively; these capacities are based on space, personnel, and mechanical maintenance facilities. The distances between each garage and city area are given in Table 4.13 (measured in kilometers from the garage to the geographic center of each area).

Based on the goal of minimizing total truck-kilometers, determine (a) how many trucks to place in each garage and (b) how to assign trucks to areas.

8. *Plant Layout: Storage-Bin Location.* Solarlite Manufacturing operates a factory that houses three work centers (C1, C2, and C3), each of which uses common solar-cell modules. The solar-cell modules are stored in four bins (B1, B2, B3, and B4). Table 4.14 gives the distances between each bin and work center (in feet), the number of modules used per day by each work center, and the capacity of each bin. Determine the bin-to-work-center allocation that minimizes the total "module-feet" traveled per day.

TABLE 4.13

Garage	Area		
	A1	A2	A3
G1	4	6	5
G2	7	9	6
G3	6	8	5

9. *Layout Planning.* (Refer to Exercise 8 above.) Solarlite is planning to relocate bin B1. The distance between the proposed new location and the existing work centers is 25 feet, 5 feet, and 10 feet, respectively. *Based on material-handling considerations,* would you support the proposed bin relocation?

10. *Production Scheduling and Inventory Control.* Greenwood Furniture is currently planning its production and inventory for the next four months. The forecasted demands in months 1, 2, 3, and 4 are 10, 20, 40, and 20 waterbeds, respectively. A waterbed manufactured on regular time costs $80 to build, and one manufactured on overtime costs $130 to build. In months 1, 2, and 3, production capacity is 20 units on regular time and 10 units on overtime. In month 4, regular-time capacity will be 25 units, and no overtime is currently planned. Units may be produced and stored in inventory for sale in a later month. The inventory carrying costs run $20 per bed stored from one month to the next.
    a. The task confronting Greenwood is to determine the minimum-cost production/inventory plan for the four-month horizon. Model this problem as a transportation problem.
    b. Solve the problem of part (a) above.

TABLE 4.14

Bin	Work center			Capacity
	C1	C2	C3	
B1	20	15	10	10
B2	25	20	5	20
B3	15	15	5	30
B4	20	15	10	15
Usage	30	20	25	

11. *Contract Awarding.* Weapons Design, Inc., requires certain quantities of various parts in order to manufacture a new missile system. These parts are labeled A, B, and C (they are top secret). Weapons Design will subcontract the manufacture of these parts out to some or all of five companies: the companies are numbered 1, 2, 3, 4, and 5. Weapons Design needs 1,000 parts A, 400 parts B, and 250 parts C. The five companies have submitted information concerning the number of parts each can provide and the corresponding costs, as shown in Table 4.15. From these data, we see that company 1 can supply a total of 490 parts (total of A, B, and C combined); it can supply A at $10 per part, B at $15 per part, and C at $20 per part.

    a. Model the problem of determining how contracts should be awarded as a transportation problem.

    b. Solve the problem of part (a) above.

12. *Coronado Industries.* Solve the production/inventory problem of Example 4.7.

13. *Greg's Slippery Wheel Pottery School.* Solve the vendor selection problem of Example 4.8.

14. *Setfirm Concrete Co.* Solve the resource-scheduling problem of Example 4.9.

15. *Distribution.* Rollermatic manufactures a special ball-bearing unit for automotive equipment. It operates three plants (1, 2, and 3) that supply four warehouses (A, B, C, and D). Plant capacities, warehouse demands, and unit shipping costs are given in Table 4.16. Determine the minimum-cost distribution plan.

16. *Distribution Planning with Restrictions.* Solve Exercise 15 above, assuming the following restrictions are to be observed (simultaneously):

    a. Rollermatic has already committed plant 2 to supplying warehouse C with *at least* 20 units per month.

    b. Due to insufficient supply routes, plant 3 cannot supply Warehouse A.

TABLE 4.15

Company	Parts ($/part)			Total no. of parts company can supply
	A	B	C	
1	10	15	20	490
2	11	13	23	530
3	9	10	31	320
4	13	8	30	150
5	15	10	25	650

17. *Modification of Distribution Planning with Restrictions.* How would you modify the transportation table shown in Table 4.16 if restriction (a) of Exercise 16 were replaced by the following restriction: Plant 2 is committed to supplying warehouse C with *exactly* 20 units per month. Solve this new problem.

18. *Municipal Snow Removal.* Taylorville is planning to locate six storage bins for salt to be used for snow and ice removal during the winter months. There are five major sections of town that must be served by the street department. The capacity of each storage bin and the monthly requirements for salt are given in Table 4.17 (in tons) along with the distances (in miles) between each bin location and section of town.

    a. Use VAM to determine a plan for serving each of the five sections of town.

    b. Is the VAM solution optimal? If not, use the stepping-stone method to derive an optimal bin-section allocation plan.

TABLE 4.16

Plant	Warehouse				Capacity (units/month)
	A	B	C	D	
1	1	2	1	3	100
2	4	2	1	4	200
3	3	3	2	2	150
Demand	100	175	75	100	

TABLE 4.17

Storage bin	Section of town					Capacity
	1	2	3	4	5	
1	2	3	4	1	5	10
2	1	3	1	1	2	15
3	2	1	2	1	5	18
4	4	3	1	6	2	12
5	5	5	4	3	1	13
6	3	2	2	1	2	9
Requirements	11	14	5	28	19	77

19. *Distribution Planning.* Natural Foods operates three warehouses to serve six markets. The warehouse capacities, market demands (truckloads per month), and cost per truckload of product shipped is given in Table 4.18 (in $/truckload).
   a. Use VAM to determine a plan for distributing the product to the markets.
   b. Is the VAM solution optimal? If not, derive an optimal distribution pattern.

20. *Facilities Planning.* (Refer to Exercise 19.) Based on a VAM analysis, how much should Natural Foods be willing to pay to expand the capacity of warehouse 3 from 8 to 20 truckloads of product?

   Note: To use VAM, since supply must equal demand, you must introduce a dummy market, having a demand of 12 truckloads per month and 0 shipping costs.

21. *Sales Territory Assignments.* Heavy Horse Feed must decide which of its five salespersons to assign to each of its five major rural sales territories. The estimated sales (in $000 per month) each salesperson could generate if assigned to each of the districts is given in Table 4.19.
   a. Use VAM to determine an assignment of salespersons to territories.

TABLE 4.18

| | Market | | | | | | |
Warehouse	1	2	3	4	5	6	Capacity
1	100	150	200	100	80	90	10
2	200	210	180	90	120	110	15
3	95	175	190	110	110	100	8
Demand	5	7	8	3	6	4	33

TABLE 4.19

| | District | | | | |
Salesperson	1	2	3	4	5
1	20	15	13	18	17
2	16	14	22	23	18
3	19	15	25	27	20
4	25	8	15	15	10
5	10	10	30	10	15

Note: View each salesperson as having a supply of one unit ("one person") and each territory as having a demand of one unit ("needs one person"). Modify VAM to handle maximization problems by computing rim values, using the largest and second largest figure in each row (column).

b. Is your solution optimal? If not, derive an optimal assignment pattern.

22. *Degeneracy in VAM.* Is the VAM solution to Problem 5 at the end of Section 3 (page 145) optimal? If not, use the stepping-stone method to obtain an optimal solution. *Beware of a technicality:* The VAM solution is degenerate; you should first repair this before proceeding with the stepping-stone method.

23. *Maximization—Industrial Distribution.* La Masa tortilla factory operates three plants (1, 2, and 3) that supply corn tortillas to four wholesale food distributors (A, B, C, and D). Plant capacities, distributor demands, and net profits per unit are given in Table 4.20. Determine the maximum-profit distribution plan.

24. *Maximization—Wholesale Distribution.* Nailrite, a large Midwestern manufacturer of pneumatic fastening devices and fasteners, owns three outlets in Los Angeles. These three outlets (1, 2, and 3) supply No. 16 nails (for use in their model N16 nailer) to four retailers in the greater Los Angeles area. Wholesale outlet capacities, retailer demands, and net profits per carton of nails are given in Table 4.21. For example, Nailrite will realize a net-profit of $10 for each carton of nails shipped from wholesale outlet 1 to retailer 1 (R1). Determine the maximum-profit distribution plan.

25. *Maximization—Industrial Distribution.* La Madera operates three sawmills. These sawmills, located at Pine Flats (PF), Pinon Ridge (PR), and Fir Valley (FV), supply white pine to four lumber yards located in the cities of Chaves (C), Marville (M), Pietown (P), and Deming (D). Manufacturing capacities, demands, and net profits (given in cents per board

TABLE 4.20

Plant	Distributors				Capacity (units/week)
	A	B	C	D	
1	10	9	10	8	200
2	7	9	10	7	400
3	8	8	9	9	300
Demand	200	350	150	200	

TABLE 4.21

| | Wholesale Outlet | | | Demand |
Retailer	1	2	3	(cartons/month)
R1	10	9	9	40
R2	8	9	8	100
R3	9	10	9	80
R4	9	8	10	120
Capacity (cartons)	100	120	120	

foot) are shown in Table 4.22. Determine the maximum-profit distribution plan for La Madera.

26. *Comparison of Initial Solutions.* Refer to the transportation table for Problem 8. Give *initial* solutions to this problem using each of the methods—NW-corner, least cost method, and VAM. Compare the resulting initial costs.

TABLE 4.22

| | Lumber Yards | | | | Capacity |
Sawmill	C	M	P	D	(board feet/month)
PF	60	60	55	65	36,000
PR	80	75	70	75	52,000
FV	50	60	70	65	40,000
Demand	38,000	30,000	24,000	36,000	

5 THE ASSIGNMENT PROBLEM

CONTENTS

1. INTRODUCTION

In Chapters 2,3, and 4 we discussed linear programming and transportation problems. The transportation problem was seen to be a special type of linear program. Because of this fact, special algorithms exist for solving transportation problems. In this chapter we shall study a special type of transportation problem called the **assignment problem.**

There are at least four ways to solve an assignment problem:

1. View it as a linear program and apply the simplex method to solve it.
2. View it as a transportation problem and apply the NW-corner rule and stepping-stone method to solve it.
3. Consider it as an assignment problem "in its own right" and apply the assignment method.
4. Solve the assignment problem by other specialized methods, such as dynamic programming or branch-and-bound.

In this chapter we shall discuss methods (2) and (3). Dynamic programming is discussed in Chapter 15 and branch-and-bound methods in Chapter 17.

2. THE ASSIGNMENT PROBLEM

In general an assignment problem is concerned with assigning n items to n other items on a one-to-one basis in such a way that some measure of effectiveness is optimized (that is, some cost is minimized, or some profit or benefit is maximized). The next example introduces a classic type of assignment problem.

EXAMPLE 5.1. *Job-Shop Work Assignments.* Ace Metalworks operates a small metalworking shop that has four machines. For convenience we will label the machines $M1$, $M2$, $M3$, and $M4$. The machines differ in their capacities to perform various machining operations. At the start of the week, Ace has four jobs to schedule in its shop. We will label these jobs $J1$, $J2$, $J3$, and $J4$. The cost of processing each of these jobs on the various machines is given in Table 5.1.

How should the job-machine assignments be made in order to minimize the total cost to complete the jobs? We shall solve this problem later in the chapter.   ▲

Solving the Assignment Problem by Using the Transportation Algorithm

It is possible to formulate the assignment problem as a transportation problem and then apply the stepping-stone method to the transportation algorithm to produce a solution. The next example illustrates how to formulate the appropriate transportation problem.

EXAMPLE 5.2. *Transportation Formulation of the Ace Metalworks Problem.* (Refer to Example 5.1 above.) To formulate the transportation problem, view each job as a source having a supply of one unit, and view each machine as a destination having a demand of one unit. Thus for the Ace Metalworks problem, we have the transportation table shown in Fig. 5.1.

TABLE 5.1

		Machine		
Job	$M1$	$M2$	$M3$	$M4$
$J1$	210	150	180	130
$J2$	140	160	200	190
$J3$	150	175	220	200
$J4$	200	115	160	190

Job	M1		M2		M3		M4		Supply
				Machine					
J1	210 1		150 0		180		130		1
J2	140		160 1		200 0		190		1
J3	150		175		220 1		200 0		1
J4	200		115		160		190 1		1
Demand	1		1		1		1		4

FIGURE 5.1

We have also indicated the NW-corner initial solution. Note that $r + c - 1 = 4 + 4 - 1 = 7$ and that degeneracy does seem to be a problem. We placed three zeros in the table to form a stair-step pattern. (There are several other ways to place these zeros; in fact, there are eight different patterns.) At the end of this section, you are asked to solve this problem by using the stepping-stone method. In working the problem, you will find that the presence of degeneracy causes the method to be somewhat inefficient, due in part to handling all the zeros. ▲

Problem

Solve the transportation problem of Example 5.2, using the stepping-stone method.

3. THE ASSIGNMENT METHOD

We now present the **assignment method** (also called the Hungarian method) for solving assignment problems. If you compare it with the transportation approach, you will find it to be much simpler and, perhaps, faster. To explain the method, we first shall demonstrate the solution of Example 5.1 step by step; we then shall give a summary of the general procedures to follow when using the assignment method.

APPLICATIONS

The following applications appear in this chapter in text, examples, or problems:

Assigning sales territories

Contract awarding

Crime prevention

Facilities layout for materials handling

Job-shop work assignments

Military combat effectiveness

Personnel job assignments

Production scheduling

Subcontractor selection

Television programming

EXAMPLE 5.3. *Solution of the Ace Metalworks Problem by the Assignment Method.* (Refer to Example 5.1 above.)

Step 1. Set Up the Cost Table. The first step requires that we set up a cost table showing the square array of possible assignments and costs. This array appears in Table 5.2.

Step 2. Reduce the Columns. For each column do the following:

a. Determine the minimum entry in the column.
b. Subtract this entry from each of the column entries.

TABLE 5.2

Job	M1	M2	M3	M4
J1	210	150	180	130
J2	140	160	200	190
J3	150	175	220	200
J4	200	115	160	190

(Machine columns: M1–M4)

For Ace Metalworks we have the following:

a. The minimum column entries are 140, 115, 160, and 130 for columns M1, M2, M3, and M4, respectively.
b. Reducing column M1, we get

$$210 - 140 = 70$$

$$140 - 140 = 0$$

$$150 - 140 = 10$$

$$200 - 140 = 60$$

This gives a new M1 column, as shown in Table 5.3(a). The other columns are reduced in the same manner.

Opportunity Cost Interpretation. We can think of the new columns in terms of opportunity costs. Consider column M1. If job J2 is assigned to machine M1, the cost of this assignment will be \$140. If, however, we assign J1 to M1, the cost will be \$210, for which we associate a \$70 opportunity cost over the J2–M1 assignment.

Step 3. Reduce the Rows. Using the table resulting from step 2, reduce the rows in the same way the columns were reduced. For Ace Metalworks, the minimum row entries in Table 5.3(a) are 0, 0, 10, and 0 for rows J1, J2, J3, and J4, respectively. Reducing row J1 gives the following new entries:

$$70 - 0 = 70$$

$$35 - 0 = 35$$

$$20 - 0 = 20$$

$$0 - 0 = 0$$

TABLE 5.3(a)

Job	Machine			
	M1	M2	M3	M4
J1	70	35	20	0
J2	0	45	40	60
J3	10	60	60	70
J4	60	0	0	60

TABLE 5.3(b)

Job	Machine			
	M1	M2	M3	M4
J1	70	35	20	0
J2	0	45	40	60
J3	0	50	50	60
J4	60	0	0	60

The other rows are reduced in a similar fashion to give the new table shown in Table 5.3(b).

Step 4. Can an Optimal Assignment Be Made? To determine whether an optimal assignment can be made, refer to the table resulting from step 3, cross out all zeros, using a minimum of horizontal and vertical lines. If the number of lines used equals the number of rows (or columns), an optimal assignment can be made. In this event, proceed to step 6 below; otherwise go to step 5 below.

For Ace Metalworks, crossing out the zeros in Table 5.3(b) and using the minimum number of horizontal and vertical lines gives Table 5.3(c). (This required only three lines; another correct way to cross out the zeros would be to use a vertical line for column M1, a vertical line for column M4, and a horizontal line for row J4.)

Since only three lines were required, an optimal assignment cannot yet be made; therefore, we must proceed to step 5.

Step 5. Further Reduction of the Cost Table. In this step we must further reduce the cost table of step 4. The procedure is as follows:

a. Determine the minimum entry that is not covered by a straight line in step 4.

TABLE 5.3(c)

Job	Machine			
	M1	M2	M3	M4
J1	70	35	20	0
J2	0	45	40	60
J3	0	50	50	60
J4	60	0	0	60

TABLE 5.4(a)

Job	Machine			
	M1	M2	M3	M4
J1	70 + 40 = 110	35	20	0
J2	0	5	0	20
J3	0	10	10	20
J4	60 + 40 = 100	0	0	60

TABLE 5.4(b)

Job	Machine			
	M1	M2	M3	M4
J1	110	35	20	0
J2	0	5	0	20
J3	0	10	10	20
J4	100	0	0	60

b. Reduce each entry that is not covered by a straight line by subtracting the minimum entry from it.

c. Add the minimum entry found in part (a) to each entry located at an intersection of two straight lines.

d. Return to step 4.

For Ace Metalworks, we have:

a. In Table 5.3(c) the minimum uncovered entry is 40.

b. The reduced table appears in Table 5.4(a).

c. Return to step 4.

Step 4. Second Iteration, Ace Metalworks. Drawing the minimum number of straight lines necessary to cross out the zeros in the table of Table 5.4(a) gives Table 5.4(b). Since the number of lines used (four) equals the number of rows (or columns), we proceed to step 6.

Step 6. Determine an Optimal Assignment. Let the number of rows be r. Then the objective of step 6 is to place r ones in the table in such a way that—

a. Each 1 is placed on a 0;
b. No more than one 1 is placed in each column or each row.

For Ace Metalworks, using the table of Table 5.4(b), perform step 6 to obtain the optimal assignment given in Table 5.5. The pattern of ones corresponds to the assignment J1 to M4, J2 to M3, J3 to M1, and J4 to M2, having a total cost of $130 + $200 +$150 + $115 = $595.   ▲

4. A SUMMARY OF THE GENERAL PROCEDURE

For ease of reference we now state, in algorithmic form, the general procedure to follow when solving an assignment problem.

The Assignment Method

STEP 1. SET UP THE INITIAL COST TABLE. This must be a *square* array, showing the cost of each possible assignment.

STEP 2. REDUCE THE COLUMNS. For each column subtract the minimum entry of the column from each entry of that column.

STEP 3. REDUCE THE ROWS. Using the table resulting from step 2, reduce each row in the same way that columns are reduced.

STEP 4. CAN AN OPTIMAL ASSIGNMENT BE MADE? In the table resulting from step 3, cross out all zeros, using the minimum number of horizontal and vertical lines. If the number of lines used equals the number of rows, then an optimal assignment can be determined. In this event, proceed to step 6, below; otherwise, go to step 5.

TABLE 5.5

Job	M1	M2	M3	M4
		Machine		
J1				1
J2			1	
J3	1			
J4		1		

STEP 5. FURTHER REDUCTION OF THE COST TABLE. Reduce the cost table resulting from step 4 as follows:

a. Determine the minimum entry that is not covered by a straight line.
b. Subtract this number from each entry that is not covered by a straight line.
c. Add this minimum number to each entry located at the intersection of two straight lines.

Now return to step 4.

STEP 6. DETERMINE AN OPTIMAL ASSIGNMENT. Place a 1 on each 0 of the final table so that there is exactly one 1 in each row and column. The placement of these ones indicates the optimal assignment. There may be more than one way to place the ones, in which case there are multiple optimal solutions to the problem.

Maximization Problems

If the objective is to maximize some measure of benefit (such as profit), convert each profit to a negative cost and apply the above algorithm. Thus, for example, if a given assignment gives a profit of $100, convert this to a cost of −$100. Then, by minimizing cost, the algorithm will produce the "most negative number," which, when made positive, will yield the "most positive profit."

Nonsquare Cost Array

Refer to the Ace Metalworks problem (Example 5.1), and suppose that the number of machines is three instead of four. In order to get a square cost array, simply add a fourth column (corresponding to a dummy machine) and assign 0 costs to each square of the fourth column. Then in the optimal solution to the problem, one job will not be processed—namely, the job that is assigned to the dummy machine.

Suppose, on the other hand, that only three jobs must be processed on four machines. Then to get a square cost array, add a fourth row (corresponding to a dummy job) and assign 0 costs to each square of the fourth row. Then in the optimal solution to the problem, one machine will be idle—namely, the machine to which the dummy job is assigned.

Restricted Assignments

Again using the Ace Metalworks problem (Example 5.1), suppose job 2 cannot be processed on machine 3. To incorporate this constraint, simply assign an infinite cost as the J2–M3 entry. It is common practice to denote this cost by M, and we think of M as an arbitrarily large number (much larger than all other entries in the cost table).

EXAMPLE 5.4. *A Comprehensive Modified Assignment Problem.* Suppose a machine shop has five machines and six jobs to do. Label the machines M1 through M5 and the jobs J1 through J6. Suppose M2 does not have the capacity to do J4. The cost of doing each job on each machine is given in Table 5.6. How should the job assignments be made in order to minimize costs?

Solution. We will formulate the problem as an assignment problem and ask you to solve it in Problem 1 at the end of this section.

The problem falls into the following category: nonsquare array (with six rows and five columns); restricted assignment (machine M2 cannot do job J4).

The cost table for step 1 of the assignment method is given in Table 5.7.   ▲

TABLE 5.6

| | | Machine | | | |
Job	M1	M2	M3	M4	M5
J1	20	30	10	14	21
J2	16	18	7	14	18
J3	19	27	15	16	19
J4	18	—	14	15	18
J5	20	20	21	18	15
J6	14	13	24	19	22

TABLE 5.7

| | | Machine | | | | |
Job	M1	M2	M3	M4	M5	M6
J1	20	30	10	14	21	0
J2	16	18	7	14	18	0
J3	19	27	15	16	19	0
J4	18	M	14	15	18	0
J5	20	20	21	18	15	0
J6	14	13	24	19	22	0

Problems

1. Solve the assignment problem of Example 5.4.
2. Solve the following assignment problem (minimize cost):

TABLE 5.8

	1	2	3
A	4	6	8
B	3	2	1
C	3	6	9

3. Solve the above assignment problem, assuming the numbers represent profits instead of costs; that is, find a maximum-profit assignment.

5. COMPUTER SOLUTION OF ASSIGNMENT PROBLEMS

A convenient program that implements the assignment algorithm is PROC ASSIGN, another of the SAS/OR group of programs. (See Section 8 in Chapter 3 for an introduction to SAS/OR.) PROC ASSIGN can handle nonstandard situations, such as nonsquare cost arrays, restricted assignments, and maximization problems. The example in this section shows the set-up and solution of the Ace Metalworks assignment problem.

The Ace Metalworks Problem in SAS/OR PROC ASSIGN Format

```
1    TITLE 'ACE METALWORKS';
2    DATA ACE;
3         INPUT JOB$ M1-M4;
4         CARDS;
5    JOB1 210 150 180 130
6    JOB2 140 160 200 190
7    JOB3 150 175 220 200
8    JOB4 200 115 160 190
9    ;
10   PROC ASSIGN DATA=ACE;
11        COST M1-M4;
12        ID JOB;
13   PROC PRINT;
```

This example shows an additional feature of SAS/OR (available for all PROCs) in the INPUT statement. Instead of listing all of the variable names, a range of names may be shown. To use this feature, the variables referenced must have the same name except for the last character, which is a sequence number. The entry $M1–M4$ above thus refers to $M1$, $M2$, $M3$, and $M4$.

The cost or profit data for PROC ASSIGN is arranged with the assignments as rows and the elements to be assigned as columns. If an assignment is restricted, the SAS missing value symbol (a period) is entered. The keyword **COST** followed by the column variable names is the only one required in PROC ASSIGN. If naming the assignments is desired, then the keyword **ID** followed by the variable labels (variable JOB, above, represents the labels) is required. PROC ASSIGN assumes minimization. If maximization is desired, the keyword **MAXIMUM** is entered on the PROC ASSIGN statement. The statement PROC PRINT is required to obtain a printout of the solution.

Solution Output

The solution output from PROC ASSIGN is a table showing the input data and the optimal assignment in the column labeled **ASSIGN.** The solution output for the Ace Metalworks problem is shown below.

```
NOTE:   MINIMUM COST ASSIGNMENT = 595.00


                        ACE METALWORKS


           A S S I G N M E N T   P R O C E D U R E



    OBS       JOB       M1      M2      M3      M4      -ASSIGN-

     1        JOB1      210     150     180     130        M4
     2        JOB2      140     160     200     190        M3
     3        JOB3      150     175     220     200        M1
     4        JOB4      200     115     160     190        M2
```

6. CONCLUDING REMARKS

The assignment method (or Hungarian method) is an easy and fairly efficient means of solving assignment problems. Both linear programming and the transportation method would be far less efficient. The reason for this derives from the presence of a large number of 0 entries in the transportation table. In fact, for an assignment problem having n rows and n columns, the number of rows plus columns minus 1 equals $n + n - 1 = 2n - 1$. But since assignments are made on a one-to-one basis, only n entries of the transportation table would contain ones, leaving $(2n - 1) - n = n - 1$ zeros. Check this for Problem 1 at the end of Section 2: $n = 4$, and the NW-corner solution required three zeros $(4 - 1)$. Many iterations of the transportation method might simply involve moving some of these zeros around. The assignment method avoids such inefficient calculations.

TERMINOLOGY

After studying this chapter you should be familiar with the following terms:

TERM	SECTION
assignment method	3
assignment problem	1,2
column reduction	3
Hungarian method	3
opportunity cost	3
row reduction	3

EXERCISES

1. *Machine-Job Assignment.* The Loosebolt Company must do three jobs on three machines. The cost of doing each job on each of the machines is given in Table 5.9. Determine the minimum-cost assignment, using the assignment method.

2. *Machine-Job Assignments.* Machine Master, Inc., must assign seven jobs to seven machines. Determine the minimum-cost job assignment, based on the cost data in Table 5.10, for doing each job on each machine.

3. *Personnel Job Assignments.* Jim's Bracket Manufacturing runs constant production of four products, using a work force of four people in its manufacturing facility. The net profits on the four products are $20, $15,

TABLE 5.9

	Machine		
Job	1	2	3
A	10	20	11
B	11	19	13
C	12	18	12

TABLE 5.10

				Machine			
Job	1	2	3	4	5	6	7
A	10	14	13	14	15	18	12
B	12	11	10	16	20	14	11
C	11	10	10	13	18	17	10
D	14	19	9	14	22	20	14
E	15	17	15	20	14	16	18
F	19	10	14	18	16	19	19
G	9	12	16	17	21	20	20

$16, and $10 per unit, respectively. The number of units of each of these products that each worker could produce per week if he or she worked exclusively on the given product is shown in Table 5.11. How would you make worker-product job assignments?

4. *Military Combat Effectiveness.* The Armed Forces Strategic Council is studying the combat effectiveness of four existing missile systems against five types of targets it has identified. Table 5.12 gives the effectiveness rating of each type of missile if deployed against each type of target. The ratings are based on a common unit measure of expected damage caused to a target. If each missile must be devoted to one and only one target, how should the assignments be made?

5. *Crime Prevention.* The city of Hyrisk must determine how to deploy four of its police patrol teams (each having two police officers) against its three highest crime sectors in the most effective manner. The teams differ in their abilities and the special equipment at their disposal. The police chief thought that an accurate measure of the crime level in each sector would be the average total dollar loss realized per week owing to crimes committed against property (theft, vandalism, and the like). Us-

TABLE 5.11

			Product	
Worker	1	2	3	4
Bob	9	18	9	21
Jane	12	15	9	18
Bill	15	21	6	24
Gomez	6	12	12	15

TABLE 5.12

Missile	Target				
	A	B	C	D	E
1	10	15	18	16	9
2	14	20	15	21	10
3	9	25	17	20	11
4	13	18	20	15	14

ing this criterion, Table 5.13 (based on historical records and judgmental factors) was set up to show the expected dollar loss that could be prevented if each of the four police teams were assigned to patrol each of the three city sectors (in $000/week). Determine the optimal team-sector assignments.

6. *Crime Prevention.* (Refer to Exercise 5 above.) It was brought to the attention of the police chief that the criterion of expected weekly dollar loss might not accurately reflect the real total harm caused to citizens for the following reasons:
   a. It ignores crimes against persons, such as rapes, beatings, murders, and even psychological damage that accompanies property loss crimes.
   b. It gives less weight to certain numerous crimes involving relatively small monetary losses, such as service station robberies, hold-ups of 24-hour convenience grocery stores, and robberies of pedestrians.
   It was argued that for many of the crimes listed in the above two categories, the total dollar loss is low (relative to major thefts, for example), even though the relative frequency of occurrence might be high. Thus a new effectiveness table, Table 5.14, was constructed, giving the expected *number of crimes* each police team could effectively prevent per week if assigned to each sector. Based on this table, determine the optimal team-sector assignments.

TABLE 5.13

Team	Sector		
	A	B	C
1	5	4	6
2	2	3	3
3	4	5	5
4	6	5	6

TABLE 5.14

	Sector		
Team	A	B	C
1	29	47	50
2	12	35	25
3	24	59	42
4	35	59	67

7. *Subcontractor Selection.* Bob's Woodworks is a one-man woodworking operation. In the first month of operation, Bob received custom orders for three different products. Although the net profits on the three orders potentially could be large, the set of orders would require the manufacture of four major subassemblies that Bob does not have the facilities to produce. Bob has contacted five other woodworking shops in the area and has received the bids shown in Table 5.15 for the four jobs from each of the five shops.
   a. If Bob is free to subcontract more than one job to a single shop, determine the minimum cost assignments.
   b. Bob may be constrained to subcontract no more than one job to a single shop. If this is the case, determine the minimum-cost assignments. This constraint may be due to any of the following factors or combination of factors:
      (1) Time constraints. Bob may need the subassemblies completed quickly, and this could be accomplished most effectively if they were spread out over four subcontractors for simultaneous processing.
      (2) The subcontractors may have short-run capacity constraints.
      (3) Qualitative considerations may encourage Bob to spread the work out over several contractors, thus maximizing the number of trade contacts made.

TABLE 5.15

	Subcontractor shop				
Job	1	2	3	4	5
1	$50	40	32	42	60
2	45	50	28	40	65
3	48	45	25	35	58
4	55	55	36	35	55

8. *Production Scheduling.*   After three months of operation, Bob's Wood-works (Exercise 7) receives an offer from a large retail furniture outlet to buy a full week's production of Bob's four top-selling products, a three-by-six-foot bookcase, a chest-of-drawers, a writing desk, and an occasional table. The retail outlet has indicated that it will purchase any quantity of the four products but makes the following stipulations:

a. Bob must include nonzero quantities of each of the four products.

b. Bob must devote one day to the manufacture of each product and make delivery of that product prior to 9:00 A.M. the following day.

The retailer's reason for setting these constraints is that it is planning a Super Sale Week and will be featuring each of Bob's products on one of the six sale days (Monday through Saturday). The current day is Thursday, and the sale is to begin next Monday. Bob must notify the retailer tomorrow, Friday, so that the advertising copy can be set for Saturday-Sunday newspaper editions.

Bob can work Sunday through Friday to turn out the production according to the above conditions. Besides direct production time, Bob must spend a certain amount of time on various days of the week purchasing materials, doing bookwork, receiving other customers, and making deliveries. Based on time available each day, Bob can manufacture the quantities shown in Table 5.16 of each of the four products on each of the six days of the week. To construct this table, Bob took various factors into account—set-up time, expected interruptions, production efficiency, and materials availability (included here are expected supplier deliveries). Net profit per unit on each of the four products is $20, $15, $25, and $7, respectively.

Determine how Bob should schedule his week's production in order to maximize his total net profit on the retailer's order.

9. *Contract Awarding.*   The government is planning to begin construction of four major bridges (B1, B2, B3, and B4) in the upcoming year. Four contractors have submitted bids on each of the four construction projects, as shown in Table 5.17. No single contractor is to be awarded more than one contract. Determine the minimum-cost contract assignments.

TABLE 5.16

Product	Day					
	S	M	T	W	T	F
Bookcase	8	7	5	5	8	6
Chest	5	4	3	4	3	5
Desk	6	6	4	5	3	4
Table	10	9	6	7	10	8

TABLE 5.17

	Contractor (bids in $ millions)			
Project	1	2	3	4
B1	9.5	7.0	4.5	8.0
B2	5.0	4.5	6.5	8.5
B3	7.0	5.0	6.5	7.0
B4	6.5	7.0	6.0	8.5

10. *Contract Awarding.* (Refer to Exercise 9 above.) Suppose the government receives a fifth bid on the projects from another contractor as follows: B1, 6.0; B2, 5.0; B3, 5; B4, 7.5. How would this change the optimal contract assignments?

11. *Contract Awarding.* (Refer to Exercise 9 above.) Suppose that contractor 3 does not submit a bid on B1. How would this change the optimal contract assignments?

12. Sally and Rod Jones have decided to do some extensive spring cleaning and home repairs during the first week of May. Although they will do much of the work themselves, they have decided to hire five independent residential repair services to do five jobs, each job requiring a full week to complete. These jobs and the bids of each service for each of the jobs are given in Table 5.18. How should Sally and Rod assign the jobs to the five services?

13. *Television Programming.* ACN Television Network is planning to schedule five television specials during a six-day week, Monday through Saturday. Based on projected market shares, Table 5.19 gives the expected number of television viewers (in millions) who will watch the specials if

TABLE 5.18

	Independent service				
Job	1	2	3	4	5
Landscaping yard	$ 900	700	800	850	1,000
Painting	700	600	800	750	650
Constructing patio	1,500	1,500	1,400	1,200	1,300
Fencing yard	400	450	400	500	550
Redoing plumbing	800	700	600	900	1,200

TABLE 5.19

Program	Day					
	M	T	W	T	F	S
1	20	20	10	8	30	25
2	15	30	15	10	25	15
3	8	7	5	6	10	20
4	9	8	3	7	7	10
5	12	15	15	20	10	13

they are aired on each of the six evenings. Based on these estimates, how should ACN schedule its specials?

14. *Facilities Layout for Materials Handling.* Miller Fox has just purchased five machines for his new job-shop operations. In studying his plant layout, he identifies five feasible locations for the machines. For each machine-location assignment there is an associated materials-handling requirement due to (a) receiving material shipments, (b) making trips to the tool and materials bins, and (c) meeting various storage demands. These materials-handling requirements are given in Table 5.20 (in pounds-feet per day). Determine how Fox should lay out his job shop in order to minimize materials-handling costs.

15. *Assigning Sales Territories.* The marketing manager of the Grocter and Pamble Company is studying past sales records and other performance evaluation data of the company's top five salespersons for industrial markets. Each salesperson must be assigned to one of the company's five major accounts during the next fiscal quarter. These five accounts represent potential sales of $1,000,000; $800,000; $600,000; $450,000; and $400,000, respectively, in the next three months. Table 5.21 (based on

TABLE 5.20

Machine	Location				
	1	2	3	4	5
1	200	500	300	250	600
2	300	600	400	250	400
3	350	200	175	100	150
4	500	800	550	650	750
5	600	700	650	400	500

TABLE 5.21

	Account				
Salesperson	1	2	3	4	5
1	0.10	0.20	0.40	0.40	0.30
2	0.15	0.30	0.80	0.20	0.50
3	0.20	0.25	0.85	0.30	0.60
4	0.15	0.30	0.50	0.40	0.70
5	0.30	0.50	0.60	0.70	0.45

past records and a few judgmental factors) gives the expected sales success probability for each salesperson if assigned to each of the five accounts. For example, if salesperson 1 is assigned to account 4, there is a 40 percent chance that he or she will be successful in winning the $450,000 sales. (*Note:* Grocter and Pamble is competing against two other companies.) How should the marketing manager assign each salesperson to each account?

II OPERATIONS MODELS

6 INVENTORY MODELS: PART I

CONTENTS

1. THE NATURE AND FUNCTION OF INVENTORIES

Inventories represent a significant asset to a business operation. In a manufacturing environment, inventories consist of raw materials, production supplies, work in process, finished goods, and replacement parts. Service organizations, such as hospitals, barber shops, and police departments, must maintain adequate inventories to perform customer services efficiently. Retailing operations must maintain inventories of finished goods to satisfy customer demand.

We define an **inventory** as the stock of any item kept to contribute to an organization's output. Inventory may be either a physical product or a service.

Functions of Inventories

Inventories may be classified by the functions they serve. Such functions include the following:

SIMPLIFYING THE COORDINATION OF OPERATIONS. Consider two work centers in a factory. Suppose an item must pass first through one work center, then through the second work center. Allowing an inventory of *work in process* material to accumulate in front of the second work center greatly simplifies coordinating the different rates of operation of the two work centers. Such an inventory acts as a *buffer* between the two centers. It ensures that the second work center has enough work to do and reduces the nonproductive idle time of that center. Scheduling work at one work center can be done to a greater degree *independently* of the other work center (see Fig. 6.1).

PRODUCTION SMOOTHING. Suppose a product has the following sales demand pattern: summer, 100 units; fall, 70 units; winter, 50 units; and spring, 90 units. Instead of varying work-force size and production rates from season to season, production can be maintained approximately constant by building inventory during the fall and winter months and by reducing this inventory in spring and summer. Cost savings may be realized by avoiding overtime, changing production rates, hiring and laying off workers, subcontracting, lost sales, training, interruption of supplies, and possible raw-material cost increases.

ECONOMIES OF SCALE. By allowing inventories to accumulate, larger quantities of materials may be purchased at quantity discounts. Also, the larger the orders for stock replenishment, the fewer are the number of orders placed per year. Since placing an order involves some fixed cost, a savings results. Also, from a production standpoint, allowing a stock of product to accumulate permits larger production lot sizes. This results in two cost savings: production set-up costs and production learning costs.

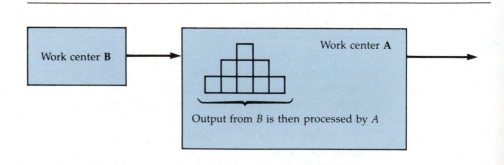

FIGURE 6.1   *Inventories simplify the coordination of operations.*

CUSTOMER SERVICE. By maintaining an inventory of finished goods, customer demand can be satisfied immediately from stock. In addition, buffer stocks are sometimes kept to guard against demand fluctuations during the period when a stock replenishment is on order from a supplier. This period is called the **lead time.** The lead time (or delivery time) itself may vary depending on the situation of the supplier. A buffer stock helps to satisfy customer demand during a varying lead time. Finally, a stock of inventory maintained in the distribution channels (in delivery to the warehouses or retail outlets) provides better customer service by guarding against an interruption of product supply.

2. THE ECONOMIC ORDER QUANTITY MODEL

In this section we shall introduce the basic **economic order quantity** (EOQ) inventory model. We must first define what is meant by a **stockkeeping unit** (SKU). Each item that is stocked in inventory is called a stockkeeping unit, for example:

APPLICATIONS

The following applications appear in this chapter in text, examples, or problems:

Agriculture

Control of high-volume items

Lot-size purchasing

Management of the maintenance function

Motel chain

Nightclub

Office supply

Public school

Public transportation

Purchasing department

Retailing
  Clothing
  Crafts
  Fabric shop
  Hardware
  Refrigerator sales
  Sporting goods
  Typewriter supply

Sensitivity analysis of costs

Service capacity expansion

Storage facility expansion

Vendor selection

Wholesale liquor

1. Suppose a retailer of pocket calculators stocks two makes of calculators. If the first make comes in two models and the second make comes in five models, the retailer would stock seven SKUs.
2. If a clothing retailer observes that customers will not generally substitute a blue sweater for a red sweater, then the two items should be stocked as two distinct SKUs.

Assumptions Underlying the Basic EOQ Model

One of the simplest mathematical inventory models and one of the first such models to appear in the inventory literature is the basic EOQ model. This simple model is the basis for many existing inventory systems.

The four assumptions underlying the EOQ model are:

1. Demand is deterministic and has a constant rate.
2. The lead time is zero.
3. Receipt of an order takes place instantaneously.
4. No backorders are permitted.

Each of these assumptions is explained below in detail.

ASSUMPTION 1—DETERMINISTIC DEMAND. If the demand for an SKU is known, we say that demand is *deterministic*. If the rate of demand does not change over time, then the demand rate is *constant*. Examples:

1. Suppose a firm has a contract to deliver 200 units of an item per month for fifteen months. Then demand for the item is deterministic at the constant rate of 200 units per month.
2. If a firm forecasts demand for the next four quarters to be 20 units each quarter, then demand is considered to be deterministic at the constant rate of 20 units per quarter. In this example, note that, strictly speaking, demand is not known for certain; only a forecast of demand is known. However, it is common practice to treat the forecasted figures as known quantities.
3. If demand for an SKU for the next four months is forecast to be 10, 12, 15, and 20 units, demand is again deterministic; however, it is *not* constant. In this chapter we shall not study the case of nonconstant demand. Methods for dealing with so-called time-varying demand can be found in Chapter 15, Section 4, and Chapter 18, Section 2. Inventory models that deal with such demand patterns are referred to as **dynamic demand** models.

4. If demand is expected to be 100, 103, 99, and 102 units for the next four months, then we have a case of nonconstant deterministic demand, as in the example above. However, when demand is *approximately* constant, we often use the average demand rate as a constant rate. In this example, average demand is (100 + 103 + 99 + 102)/4 = 101 units per month. Thus we treat the above demand pattern as a deterministic demand case having a constant rate of 101 units per month.

ASSUMPTION 2—LEAD TIME IS ZERO. **Lead time** is the time between deciding to place an order to replenish inventory and receiving the order from the supplier. Examples:

1. Suppose a retailer takes two days to prepare an order and mail it to the supplier. If it takes eight days for the supplier to fill the order and ship it to the retailer, lead time is ten days.
2. Consider the case of a merchant who uses certain office supplies in the conduct of business. Let us suppose the merchant orders the supplies from an office supply store nearby. Lead time may be very short, say, one hour, to replenish supplies. In such a case we might *assume* that lead time is zero.

Initially we shall assume that lead time is zero. Later, however, we shall relax this assumption (see Section 7).

ASSUMPTION 3—INSTANTANEOUS ORDER RECEIPT. When an order arrives at the place of business, we shall assume that the inventory level *instantly* rises by the size of the order. Examples:

1. A retailer of bicycles places an order for 150 bicycles. Ten days later the shipment arrives by truck at the retailer's place of business. Let us assume that the bicycles come off the truck assembled and ready to be placed on display. The receipt of this order is **instantaneous.**
2. Now take the same example as above, but let us assume that the bicycles come off the truck in boxes, unassembled, and that the retailer must assemble the bicycles at the rate of thirty per day. Order receipt in this case is *not* instantaneous. In fact, in addition to the lead time, it will take five days to receive the order in stock for retail sale.
3. In many cases, order receipt occurs so quickly that we often assume the receipt of the order is instantaneous. For example, a retailer of pocket calculators, upon receiving an order, requires some time to unpack boxes, inspect the calculators, and place them on display shelves. However, the time required is so short relative to the rate of demand for the calculators that we often assume the order is received in stock instantaneously.

In Section 2 of the next chapter we will relax this assumption.

ASSUMPTION 4—NO BACKORDERS. A **backorder** occurs when a customer places a demand for an item that cannot be satisfied from on-hand inventory. Example: Suppose a merchant has a current inventory of 7 units of a certain SKU and a customer orders 10 units of the SKU. If the customer will accept 7 units and will agree to wait for the remaining 3 units until the merchant restocks, then a backorder of 3 units has occurred.

In our basic EOQ model we assume that no backorders are allowed; that is, all customer demand must be satisfied from stock. In the next chapter we deal with the case of planned backorders.

Inventory Costs

In designing an inventory system, two costs are relevant—ordering costs and carrying (or holding) costs.

ORDERING COSTS. Each time an order is placed to replenish inventory, a fixed cost is incurred, independent of the size of the order placed. This cost is called the **ordering cost.**

The ordering cost consists of paperwork, typing, stationery, postage, telephone calls, and time spent receiving and inspecting the items. Each of these costs is a direct result of the decision to place an order.

CARRYING COSTS. Also called holding costs, **carrying costs** are the costs of maintaining an item in inventory.

Opportunity cost, or the cost of capital, is the largest component of carrying costs. This cost is usually set by management and depends on the firm's financial structure.

Other costs associated with carrying an inventory are insurance, taxes, pilferage, spoilage or damage, and product obsolescence.

The Inventory Problem: Resolving a Cost Trade-off

Ordering costs and carrying costs oppose each other: the greater the size of each order, the fewer the number of orders placed per year, and as a result, the lower the total ordering costs per year. However, a larger order entails a higher level of average inventory, and carrying costs will be high. Conversely, the greater the number of orders placed per year, the smaller is the size of each order, the less is the average inventory level, and the lower are the carrying costs.

There is a trade-off between the two costs, and this trade-off must be resolved when designing the optimal inventory policy. An **optimal policy** is a policy that results in minimizing the total annual average inventory cost (ordering cost plus carrying cost).

The problem of designing the optimal inventory policy can be stated as follows: Determine *when* to order and the *size* of each order in such a way that the total annual inventory cost (ordering cost plus carrying cost) is kept to a minimum.

3. GRAPH OF THE INVENTORY LEVEL OVER TIME

If the size of each order is Q units and demand occurs at the rate of D units per year, then a graph of the inventory level as a function of time appears as in Fig. 6.2. In that graph we place an order of Q units at time 0. Since delivery is instantaneous, inventory rises from 0 units to Q units. Demand is occurring at the rate of D units per year. Thus for each change of one year on the horizontal axis, the inventory falls by D units on the vertical axis; that is, the **slope** of the **sawtooth curve** is D. It also follows that the time required for the inventory level to reach 0 is Q/D years. (To see this, take a simple example: Suppose the demand rate is 2,000 units per year and the order size Q is 100 units. Then the time required to deplete the inventory is $Q/D = 100/2,000 = 0.05$ year, or 6/10 of a month.)

Thus at Q/D time units, inventory is 0. Since we are assuming that lead time is 0, we wait Q/D time units to place the next order, which we assume arrives instantly. When the order arrives, inventory instantly increases from 0 to Q units, and the process repeats.

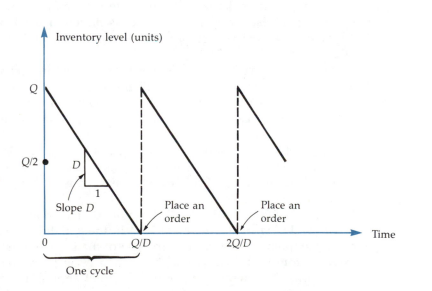

FIGURE 6.2   *Inventory level as a function of time.*

Finally, note in Fig. 6.2 that the **average inventory level** is $Q/2$ units. This is true, since inventory varies uniformly between 0 and Q units.

Our objective is to determine the optimal ("best") value of Q.

4. THE TOTAL COST EQUATION

We shall use the following notation:

TC = total annual inventory cost
TOC = total ordering cost/year
TCC = total carrying cost/year
D = demand rate (units/year)
F = fixed cost to place an order ($/order)
C = unit cost of the SKU ($/unit)
r = carrying cost rate ($/$product/year)
Q = the order size (units/order)
Q^* = the *optimal* order size (that is, the EOQ)
TC^* = the *minimum* total annual inventory cost

Since the total annual inventory cost is the sum of the total ordering cost and the total carrying cost, we can write the following equation:

$$TC = TOC + TCC \tag{6-1}$$

D is the constant, known demand rate for the SKU, measured in units of the item per year. Each time an order is placed, a fixed cost of F dollars is incurred. The cost of the product to the merchant is C dollars per unit of the item.

The cost to carry one dollar's worth of product in inventory for one year is r dollars. For example if $r = 0.25$ and the product cost $C = \$100$, then it would cost $rC = \$25$ to carry one unit of the item in inventory for one year.

Also, if the carrying cost rate on inventory is said to be 25 percent, we write this fact as $r = 0.25$, or $r = \$0.25/\$/year$.

The problem is to choose the optimal value of Q, denoted Q^*, to yield the minimum value of TC, denoted TC^*. This optimal Q value is called the **economic order quantity,** which we will also write as EOQ.

METHOD OF DERIVING EQ. (6-1). We now derive an algebraic expression for Eq. (6-1). In Figure 6.2 the **cycle length** (the length of time between placing orders) graphically includes one triangle of the sawtooth curve. The first cycle extends from 0 to Q/D years, the second cycle from Q/D to $2Q/D$ years, and so on. Our method of finding the total annual inventory cost will involve two steps:

Step 1. Find the total inventory cost *per cycle.*

Step 2. Multiply this result by the number of cycles per year.

This is summarized in Eq. (6.2):

$$\text{Total annual inventory cost} = \left(\begin{array}{c}\text{Total inventory}\\\text{cost per cycle}\end{array}\right) \times \left(\begin{array}{c}\text{Number of}\\\text{cycles per year}\end{array}\right) \qquad (6\text{-}2)$$

We now find expressions for the total ordering cost and carrying costs per cycle and the number of cycles per year. This will allow us to write an algebraic expression for Eq. (6–2).

1. *Total Ordering Cost per Cycle.* In one cycle, one order is placed; therefore the total ordering cost per cycle is simply F.
2. *Total Carrying Cost per Cycle.* In Fig. 6.2, during one cycle the inventory level falls uniformly from Q units to 0 units, implying an *average* inventory level of $Q/2$ units. The dollar value of this average inventory is $C(Q/2)$ dollars, and the carrying cost would be $Cr(Q/2)$ dollars *per year*. Since the number of years in one cycle is Q/D, the *total* carrying cost per cycle is $Cr(Q/2)(Q/D)$ dollars.
3. *Number of Cycles per Year.* The number of cycles per year equals the number of orders placed per year, which is D/Q. (For example, if demand D is 10,000 units per year and each order size is 500 units, then the number of orders per year must be $D/Q = 10{,}000/500 = 20$.)
4. *The Total Cost Equation.* We are finally ready to write an algebraic expression for Eq. (6–2). The total inventory cost per cycle is the sum of the total ordering cost per cycle and the total carrying cost per cycle, or $F + Cr(Q/2)(Q/D)$. The number of cycles per year was found to be D/Q. Multiplying these two quantities according to Eq. 6–2, and using the notation TC for total annual inventory cost, we obtain

$$TC = \left(F + Cr\left(\frac{Q}{2}\right)\left(\frac{Q}{D}\right)\right) \times \left(\frac{D}{Q}\right) \qquad (6\text{-}3)$$

$$= F\left(\frac{D}{Q}\right) + Cr\left(\frac{Q}{2}\right)$$

You should also note the correspondence between Eq. (6–3) and Eq. (6–1). We now have the following expressions for the total annual ordering cost (TOC) and total annual carrying cost (TCC):

$$TOC = F\left(\frac{D}{Q}\right) \qquad (6\text{-}4a)$$

$$TCC = Cr\left(\frac{Q}{2}\right) \qquad (6\text{-}4b)$$

Also, we have the following two useful expressions:

$$\text{Number of orders/year} = \frac{D}{Q} \qquad \text{(6–4c)}$$

$$\text{Cycle length} = \frac{Q}{D} \qquad \text{(6–4d)}$$

In Eq. (6–3), TC is the *objective function* and is a function of the order size Q. As we vary Q, the total annual cost TC will vary. We refer to Q as the *decision variable*. Our aim is to find the value of Q (denoted Q^* or EOQ) that *minimizes TC*.

Comment. If demand is D units per year and each unit costs C dollars, then we should incur an additional product cost of DC dollars per year. However, as you can see from Eq. (6–3), we have ignored this cost in the total cost equation. The reason for this is that the product cost is fixed at the constant value DC dollars and is *not affected by the inventory policy*. By changing the order size Q, we can change the total ordering cost $F(D/Q)$ and the total carrying cost $Cr(Q/2)$, but we cannot change the total product cost DC. Thus we choose to omit this latter term. Some authors *do include* this term. In any case, the resulting optimal value of Q is the same.

EXAMPLE 6.1. Wheels, Inc.—Tabular Solution of the EOQ Model. Wheels, Inc., retails Zephyr bicycles. Sales are running 100 per year. The cost to place an order with the Zephyr distributor is $4. Product cost to Wheels is $80 per bicycle, and the annual carrying cost rate is 0.10. Assume lead time is 0 and order receipt is instantaneous. Determine the EOQ.

Solution. First we identify the values of the various parameters: $D = 100$, $F = 4$, $C = 80$, and $r = 0.10$. Our approach will be to *search* over possible values of Q until we identify the value corresponding to the minimum total annual cost. In general, it is not clear what values of Q to examine. Where do we let Q start and end? Obviously we cannot possibly try all values. For example, how could we test each fractional value of Q *between* $Q = 1$ and $Q = 2$? In this example we choose to experiment somewhat by testing only whole number values of Q, from $Q = 1$ to $Q = 15$.

Let $Q = 1$, that is, suppose each order we place is for one bicycle. From Eq. (6–4a), the total annual ordering cost is

$$TOC = 4\left(\frac{100}{1}\right) = \$400$$

and from Eq. (6–4b), the total annual carrying cost is found to be

$$TCC = (80)(0.1)(1/2) = \$4$$

Then from Eq. (6–1), the total annual cost would be

$$TC = TOC + TCC = \$400 + \$4 = \$404$$

If you repeat this calculation for each value of Q from 2 to 15, you will obtain Table 6.1. (Check to see that the calculations are correct.) For this example, the total cost equation (6–3) takes the form

$$TC = 4\left(\frac{100}{Q}\right) + (80)(0.10)\left(\frac{Q}{2}\right) = \frac{400}{Q} + 4Q$$

In Table 6.1, the minimum total cost occurs at $Q = 10$. Thus the optimal order quantity is

$$EOQ = Q^* = 10$$

and the minimum total annual cost is

$$TC^* = \$80$$

(Actually, from the tabular analysis, we cannot be sure that $Q^* = 10$ is optimal. It could happen that $Q = 10.1$ might yield a lower value of TC. In this particular example, the EOQ does turn out to be 10 units per order, as will be shown mathematically in Example 6.4.)

TABLE 6.1   *Tabular Solution for Wheels, Inc.*

Q	Total annual ordering cost, TOC	Total annual carrying cost, TCC	Total annual cost, TC
1	$400.00	$ 4.00	$404.00
2	200.00	8.00	208.00
3	133.33	12.00	145.33
4	100.00	16.00	116.00
5	80.00	20.00	100.00
6	66.67	24.00	90.67
7	57.14	28.00	85.14
8	50.00	32.00	82.00
9	44.44	36.00	80.44
10	40.00	40.00	80.00 ←
11	36.36	44.00	80.36
12	33.33	48.00	81.33
13	30.77	52.00	82.77
14	28.57	56.00	84.57
15	26.67	60.00	86.67

Before concluding this example, note the logic behind calculating $TC^* = 80$. Since annual demand is 100 units and each order size is 10 units, $100/10 = 10$ orders will be placed each year at $4 per order, yielding $TOC = \$40$. Also, since inventory will vary from 0 to 10 units, average inventory is 5 units. Each unit costs $80, so $400 is tied up in average inventory at a rate of $0.10/\$/year, or $40 per year $(= TCC)$. The total annual cost TC is the sum of these two numbers, or $80.

Note also that at the EOQ, total ordering cost ($40), equals total carrying cost ($40). *This is not a coincidence.* It is a special property of the EOQ and always holds true.   ▲

EXAMPLE 6.2. *Wheels, Inc.—The Optimal Inventory Policy.* We continue Example 6.1 by making a precise statement of the optimal inventory policy for Wheels, Inc. In Section 2, we stated that it is necessary to specify both the order size and when to place each order. Since lead time is assumed to be 0 for Wheels, Inc., we can state: "When the inventory level reaches 0, place an order for 10 bicycles." thus

$$EOQ = Q^* = 10$$

$$TC^* = \$80/\text{year}$$

$$\text{Number of orders/year} = 10$$

$$\text{Cycle length} = 0.10 \text{ year}$$

Note that cycle length, which is the time between placing orders, equals $Q/D = 10/100 = 0.10$ year [see Eq. (6–4d)].

To conclude this example, let us look at a graph of inventory level over time, corresponding to Fig. 6.2.

We shall assume that Wheels, Inc., is open for business 250 days a year. Suppose the inventory level is 10 units. Since cycle length is 0.10 year, this would correspond to 25 days. This analysis is shown graphically in Fig. 6.3. (Compare to Fig. 6.2.)   ▲

EXAMPLE 6.3. *Wheels, Inc.—Graphical Analysis of the Total Cost Function.* In Example 6.1, we presented a tabular analysis of the inventory problem facing Wheels, Inc. Examine Table 6.1 above. The second column of Table 6.1 represents values of $TOC = FD/Q$. Since $F = 4$ and $D = 100$, $TOC = 400/Q$. In Fig. 6.4, we have graphed this function of Q. Column 3 of Table 6.1 represents values of $TCC = Cr(Q/2) = 4Q$ (since $C = 80$ and $r = 0.1$). The graph of TCC as a function of Q is a line having slope 4, and is also displayed in Fig. 6.4. The total annual cost, TC, column 4 of Table 6.1, is the sum of the two curves, TOC and TCC, and is shown as such in Fig. 6.4.

Note that the minimum total annual cost occurs at $Q^* = EOQ = 10$ units. Also observe that $Q = 10$ corresponds to the point at which ordering costs equal carrying costs; that is, at $Q = 10$ the TOC curve intersects the

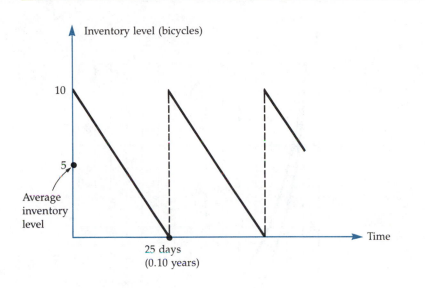

FIGURE 6.3   *Inventory level for Wheels, Inc.*

TCC curve. In Section 5 we shall show that this property always holds at the EOQ.

You should observe that the total cost curve is rather shallow around Q^* = 10. This means that the cost would not increase greatly if we were to order 8, 9, 11, or 12 units. This fact is also apparent from Table 6.1, column 4. We shall return to this observation in Section 6, which deals with sensitivity analysis.   ▲

Problems

1. Sally's Craft Shop sells a variety of craft and hobby supplies. One of her more expensive SKUs is an artist's easel. Her cost for the easel is $110; her retail price is $150. The supplier of the easel is located in the same town and can deliver within an hour. Demand for this easel is fairly uniform at the rate of six per month. The cost to place an order with her supplier is $5, and Sally figures that an approximate annual carrying cost rate is 12 percent.
   a. Identify the values of D, F, C, and r.
   b. Construct a table similar to Table 6.1 for values of Q ranging from one to ten.
   c. Specify the EOQ, *based on part (b)*.

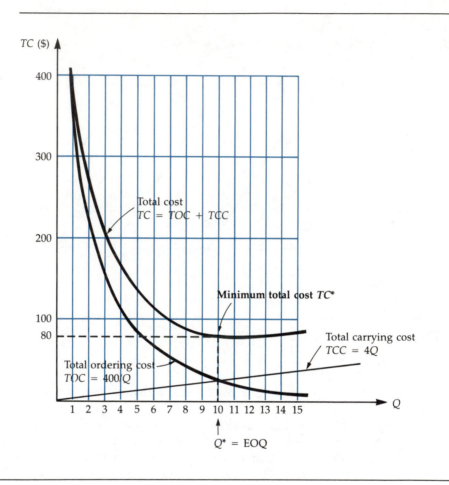

FIGURE 6.4

2. Assume Sally is open for business 300 days a year. Specify the optimal inventory policy, and display a graph corresponding to Fig. 6.3. Answer the following questions:
   a. How many orders should Sally place per year?
   b. What is her average inventory level of easels?
   c. What is the *cycle length* (that is, the length of time between placing successive orders)?
3. For Sally's inventory problem, construct a graph similar to Fig. 6.4.

5. COMPUTING THE EOQ MATHEMATICALLY

So far in this chapter we have employed tabular and graphical methods to compute the EOQ for Wheels, Inc. However, as shown in the appendix to this chapter, the EOQ can be easily computed mathematically, using the equation

$$EOQ = Q^* = \sqrt{\frac{2DF}{Cr}} \qquad (6\text{--}5)$$

Once Q^* is known, we can easily calculate other characteristics of the optimal inventory policy [see Eqs. (6–3) and (6–4a-d)].

1. *Minimum total annual cost:*

$$TC^* = F\left(\frac{D}{Q^*}\right) + Cr\left(\frac{Q^*}{2}\right) \qquad (6\text{--}6)$$

2. *Total annual ordering cost:*

$$TOC = F\left(\frac{D}{Q^*}\right) \qquad (6\text{--}7)$$

3. *Total annual carrying cost:*

$$TCC = Cr\left(\frac{Q^*}{2}\right) \qquad (6\text{--}8)$$

4. *Optimal number of orders per year (N^*):*

$$N^* = \frac{D}{Q^*} \qquad (6\text{--}9)$$

5. *Optimal cycle length (T^*):*

$$T^* = \frac{Q^*}{D} \qquad (6\text{--}10)$$

Ordering Costs = Carrying Costs

As shown mathematically in the chapter appendix, at the EOQ the total annual ordering costs equal the total annual carrying costs: $TOC = TCC$. This is a fairly intuitive notion. (Refer to Fig. 6.4.) At order quantities greater than Q^*, the average inventory is greater; therefore annual carrying costs exceed ordering costs. At smaller order quantities (less than Q^*), a greater number of orders must be placed each year, and total ordering costs exceed carrying costs. The EOQ is the order quantity that balances these two costs.

The EOQ as a Time Supply

As defined in Section 2, the **cycle length** is the length of time between placing successive orders. Thus we may also view the cycle length as *the EOQ
measured in time units*. This time supply is simply T^*, as given in Eq. (6–10)
above. In practice, T^* is often used as a reorder quantity in computerized
systems, driven by a forecasting system.

EXAMPLE 6.4. *Wheels, Inc.—Analytic Solution.* (Refer to Example 6.1.) For
Wheels, Inc., we have $D = 100$, $F = 4$, $C = 80$, $r = 0.10$. (In general, a good
first step in solving a problem is to identify the values of the parameters, or
variables, of the model, in our case D, F, C, and r.) From Eq. (6–5),

$$\text{EOQ} = Q^* = \sqrt{\frac{2DF}{Cr}} = \sqrt{\frac{2(100)(4)}{80(0.10)}} = 10 \text{ units}$$

After finding Q^* we can use Eq. (6–6) to calculate the minimum total
annual cost:

$$TC^* = \frac{FD}{Q^*} + Cr\left(\frac{Q^*}{2}\right) = \frac{4(100)}{10} + 80(0.10)\left(\frac{10}{2}\right) = \$80/\text{year}$$

We also have, from Eqs. (6–7) and (6–8), respectively, the total annual
ordering cost

$$TOC = \frac{4(100)}{10} = \$40$$

and the total annual carrying cost

$$TCC = 80(0.10)\left(\frac{10}{2}\right) = \$40$$

(Note that $TOC = TCC$.) Then, from Eqs. (6–9) and (6–10), respectively, we
can find the optimal number of orders per year

$$N^* = \frac{100}{10} = 10$$

and the optimal cycle length

$$T^* = \frac{10}{100} = 0.10 \text{ year}$$

Thus, assuming 250 days per year, the EOQ represents a time supply of

$T^* = 0.10 \times 250$ (days per year) $= 25$ days

which means that each time an order is placed, Wheels, Inc., orders a 25-day supply of bicycles.   ▲

Problems

1. Refer to Problem 1 of Section 4 (p. 215), Sally's Craft Shop. Compute the EOQ, using Eq. (6–5). Does your answer agree with your previous answer?
2. For Sally's Craft Shop, compute the annual inventory cost for the easel, using Eq. (6–6).
3. Suppose Sally projects that demand for easels will increase by a factor of four, from six to twenty-four per month, owing to the start of a new watercolor class at a local college. Should she now increase the size of her orders by a factor of four? Specify what her inventory policy should be; that is, specify the EOQ and when to order.
4. Davis Hardware stocks Superstick plastic roofing tar in one-gallon cans. Cost to Davis is $1.50 per can, and retail price is set at $2.10. Sales run fairly constant at the rate of 520 gallons per month (to local contractors and to individual homeowners). Due to limited shelf life as well as op-portunity-cost considerations, a carrying-cost rate of $.50 per can per year is applicable. A cost of $9 is incurred each time a stock-replenishment order is placed. Compute the EOQ and corresponding yearly costs, and identify both the ordering and carrying costs per year.
5. For Davis Hardware, compute the optimal number of orders to place per year.
6. Assume Davis Hardware remains open for business 350 days a year. Com-pute the optimal number of days of inventory to order at each stock re-plenishment.

6. SENSITIVITY ANALYSIS

Recall the equation for the total cost per year when the order quantity is Q units:

$$TC = F\left(\frac{D}{Q}\right) + Cr\left(\frac{Q}{2}\right)$$

In Example 6.3, we graphed TC as a function of Q for the special case of Wheels, Inc. (see Fig. 6.4). We noted that the total cost curve was somewhat shallow around Q^*, the EOQ. This property holds in general. In Fig. 6.5, we display a graph of TC as a function of Q in the general case. Note that the ordering cost is FD/Q and appears as the hyperbola; the holding cost is $Cr(Q/2)$ and is linear in Q. The total cost, TC, is the sum of these two costs.

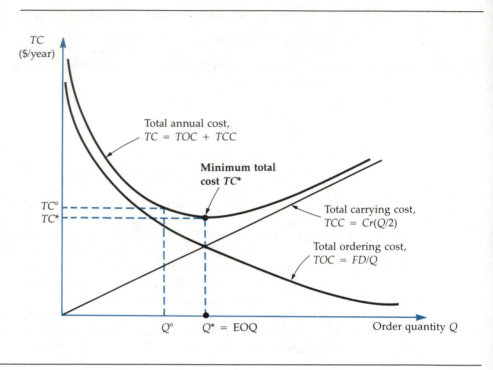

FIGURE 6.5

In Fig. 6.5, note that the total cost curve is rather shallow around its minimum point at Q^*, the EOQ. What practical significance does this have? The cost at Q^* is TC^* and is the minimum total cost obtainable. Consider a point close to Q^*, such as $Q°$ in that figure. With an order quantity of size $Q°$, total annual cost would be $TC°$, as shown. But from the graph it appears that $TC°$, although greater than TC^*, is not very much greater. This is illustrated in Example 6.5.

EXAMPLE 6.5. *Wheels, Inc.—Sensitivity Analysis.* In example 6.4, we computed the EOQ for Wheels, Inc., to be 10 units, and the total cost function was given by:

$$TC^* = TC(Q) = \frac{400}{Q} + 4Q$$

The minimum total annual cost was found to be $TC^* = TC(10) = \$80$. The values of TC for other order quantities, Q, were computed and recorded in Table 6.1. Suppose we use an order quantity of 8 units instead of 10. Then $Q^* = 10$, $TC^* = 80$, $Q° = 8$, $TC° = 82$, and the percentage cost increase incurred by using $Q°$ instead of Q^* is

$$\left(\frac{TC° - TC^*}{TC^*}\right) \times 100\% = \left(\frac{82 - 80}{80}\right) \times 100\% = 2.5\%$$

In other words, a 20 percent reduction in the order size (from 10 to 8 units) results in only a 2.5 percent annual cost increase.

To analyze a 20 percent order size increase, we have $Q° = 12$, $TC° = 81.33$, and

$$\left(\frac{TC° - TC^*}{TC^*}\right) \times 100\% = \left(\frac{81.33 - 80}{80}\right) \times 100\%$$

$$= 1.67\% \text{ annual cost increase}$$

Note that the total cost curve is "steeper" to the left of the EOQ than to the right. Thus it is better to overorder than to underorder by the same percentage (based on this analysis).   ▲

Mathematical Analysis. Suppose we let e denote the ratio of $Q° - Q^*$ to Q^*: $e = (Q° - Q^*)/Q^*$ = the ratio of the order quantity difference to the EOQ. It is possible to show mathematically that the corresponding relative percentage error in the total annual cost, denoted e_t, is

$$e_t = \left(\frac{TC° - TC^*}{TC^*}\right) \times 100\% = \left(\frac{1}{1 + e} + e - 1\right) \times 50\% \qquad (6\text{--}11)$$

Using this equation we can construct a graph as in Fig. 6.6. On the horizontal axis we have placed the relative percentage error in the order quantity (which is $e \times 100\%$), and vertically we plot e_t.

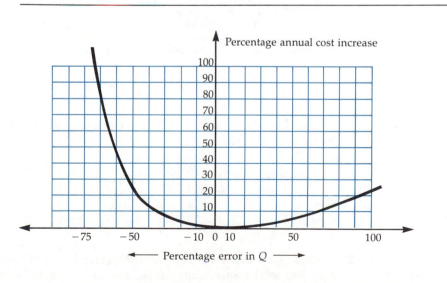

FIGURE 6.6   *Sensitivity of the total cost function, TC, to errors in the order quantity, Q.*

e(%)	e_t	e(%)	e_t
+ 5	0.12%	− 5	0.13%
10	0.45	−10	0.56
20	1.67	−20	2.50
25	2.50	−25	4.17
30	3.46	−30	6.43
40	5.71	−40	13.33
50	8.33	−50	25.00
75	16.07	−75	112.50
100	25.00	−90	405.00
200	66.67		
300	112.50		

EXAMPLE 6.6. Jane's Fabric Shoppe forecasts sales of a certain polyester cloth to be 1,500 yards for next year. The cost of the cloth to Jane is $2.50 per yard. To place an order requires one-half hour of paperwork and one long-distance telephone call, followed by postage incurred in payment of the invoice. The total of these costs is estimated to be $5.60. Based primarily on local bank lending rates, Jane estimates carrying costs to be 13 percent of the product price.

1. *Compute the EOQ, total annual cost, and inventory policy characteristics.* First, identify values of the inventory parameters: $D = 1,500$; $F = 5.60$; $C = 2.50$; $r = 0.13$. Then, using Eq. (6–5),

$$\text{EOQ} = Q^* = \sqrt{\frac{2(1,500)(5.60)}{2.50(0.13)}} = 227.36 \text{ units}$$

From Eq. (6–6), total annual inventory cost is

$$TC^* = \frac{5.60(1,500)}{227.36} + 2.50(0.13)\left(\frac{227.36}{2}\right) = \$73.89/\text{year}$$

From Eqs. (6–9) and (6–10), we can compute the following inventory policy characteristics:

$$\text{Cycle length} = T^* = \frac{Q^*}{D} = \frac{227.36}{1,500} = 0.15 \text{ year}$$

$$\text{Number of orders/year} = N^* = \frac{D}{Q^*} = \frac{1,500}{227.36} = 6.60$$

2. Suppose Jane implements an order quantity of 250 units per order. How does the total cost change? How are the other inventory policy characteristics affected?

For $Q = 250$, using the total cost Eq. (6–3), we compute the total annual inventory cost to be

$$TC = F\left(\frac{D}{Q}\right) + Cr\left(\frac{Q}{2}\right)$$

$$= (5.60)\left(\frac{1,500}{250}\right) + 2.50(0.13)\left(\frac{250}{2}\right)$$

$$= \$74.22/\text{year}$$

The cycle length is $Q/D = 250/1,500 = 1/6$ year, and the number of orders per year is 6.

The total annual cost has increased from \$73.89 to \$74.22, or by 0.45 percent. This is in response to a 9.96 percent increase in the order quantity, from 227.36 to 250 units. We calculated this result directly from the total cost equation. To demonstrate how Eq. (6–11) could have been used, we begin by calculating e:

$$Q° = 250$$

$$Q* = 227.36$$

and

$$e = \frac{Q° - Q*}{Q*}$$

$$= \frac{250 - 227.36}{227.36}$$

$$= 0.0996 \text{ (or a 9.96\% increase)}$$

Then

$$e_t = \left(\frac{1}{1 + 0.0996} + 0.0996 - 1\right)(50\%) = 0.45\%$$

This agrees with the previous approach. ▲

Managerial Implications

It is possible to show mathematically that the total cost, TC, is also relatively insensitive to small errors in the values of the parameters D, F, C, and r. The managerial implication of this fact is that it is perhaps not worth the time or effort to make highly refined estimates of D, F, C, and r as long as original estimates are "felt to be fairly accurate." The cost savings that might result would probably not be significant. Management could better spend time and money improving other aspects of the inventory system and procedures. Further implications of the sensitivity analysis presented in this section are given in Section 8.

Problems

1. Suppose demand per year is 2,500 units, product cost is $110, the fixed ordering cost is $16, and the carrying cost rate is 0.20:
   a. Compute the EOQ, Q^*.
   b. Compute the minimum total annual cost, TC^*.
   c. Round Q^* to the nearest whole number. Compute the percentage increase in total cost incurred by rounding the order quantity.
2. By what percentage would total annual cost increase if management were to order 50 percent above the EOQ?
3. Ordering too much compared to ordering too little:
   a. If a +10 percent error is made in the order quantity, how much higher (in percentage terms) will the total annual cost be? (This would correspond to ordering 10 percent above the EOQ.)
   b. If a −10 percent error is made in the order quantity, how much higher (in percentage terms) will the total annual cost be? (This would correspond to ordering 10 percent less than the EOQ.)

7. NONZERO LEAD TIME

In Section 2 one of the assumptions made in the basic EOQ model was that lead time is zero. A more realistic model is obtained by eliminating this assumption.

In the case of nonzero lead time, the computation of the optimal order quantity, Q^*, does not change. However, the time at which the order is placed does change. A **reorder point** must be calculated. The following example illustrates these concepts.

EXAMPLE 6.7. *Nonzero Lead Time.* A merchant retails a product having an annual demand of 5,000 units per year (assume 250 days per year). The cost of the product to the merchant is $12 per unit. Fixed ordering costs run $13 per order, and the supplier requires 10 days to make delivery of an order. The carrying-cost rate is 9 percent. Compute the optimal inventory policy.

Solution. The EOQ is calculated as usual. We have $D = 5,000$, $C = 12$, $F = 13$, $r = 0.09$, and lead time $= 10$ *days*. Thus

$$EOQ = Q^* = \sqrt{\frac{2(5,000)(13)}{12(0.09)}} = 346.9 \text{ units}$$

Demand *per day* is 5,000/250 = 20 units. Since lead time is 10 days, the *reorder point* equals 10 days × (20 units per day) = 200 units. That is, when the inventory level reaches 200 units, the merchant must place an order for 346.9 units. It then takes 10 days for this order to arrive, at which time the inventory level exactly equals 0. This is illustrated graphically in Fig. 6.7. ▲

Thus in the case of nonzero lead time, the answer to the question "What is the optimal order quantity?" does not change. [Use Eq. (6–5) as usual.] However, the answer to the question *"When* should the order be placed?" is given by the reorder point. If we express both the lead time and the demand rate in the *same* time units (days or years) then

Reorder point = (lead time) × (demand)   (6–12)

The optimal policy specifies that when the inventory level reaches the reorder point, an order should be placed for Q^* units. The reorder point "triggers" an order placement.

Problem

1. Janet's Poundem Typewriter Company sells 50 Model P–2 typewriters per month. Janet's cost per P–2 unit is $200; the fixed ordering cost is $11 per order, and Janet uses a 13 percent carrying cost rate. Her distributor for

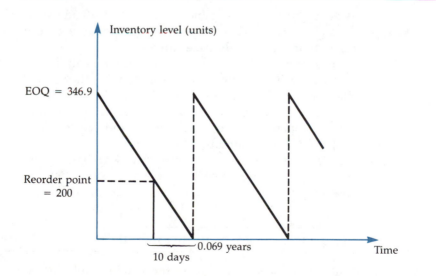

FIGURE 6.7   *Nonzero lead time.*

P–2 units is located two days away by truck. It takes Janet one day to prepare an order. (It actually takes only a few hours for order preparation, but
by the time Janet has completed the task, the post office has already shipped
out the day's mail. Thus effectively it takes one day for Janet to get an order
in the mail.) The post office takes one day to deliver mail from Janet to her
distributor. The distributor takes three days to fill an order, and then the
order is shipped back to Janet by truck. Janet's company is open for business
350 days per year.

a. Compute the EOQ.
b. Compute the total annual ordering cost.
c. Compute the total annual carrying cost.
d. Compute the total annual inventory cost.
e. Specify the optimal inventory policy for Janet's company.
f. Construct a graph similar to Fig. 6.7. Show all details.

8. PRACTICAL CONSIDERATIONS IN COMPUTING EOQ

In practice, there may be constraints on desirable or feasible order quantities.
In this section we shall discuss some of these. Each case will be illustrated
by an example.

When the Order Quantity Must Be in Discrete Units

Although it may be possible to order, say, 10.5 bushels of produce, it is not
possible to order 10.5 typewriters. In the latter case we say that the order
quantity must be in **discrete units.**

To determine the optimal *discrete* order quantity, first calculate the EOQ
as usual, using Eq. (6–5). If the EOQ is a whole number, you have solved
the problem. Otherwise, round Q^* up to the nearest whole number and compute the total cost, Eq. (6–6); then round Q^* down and compute the total
cost. Compare the two values of TC and select the discrete order quantity
that yields the minimum value of TC.

Note: From Section 6, "Sensitivity Analysis," you should observe that
rounding up or down will make a very small percentage difference in the
total cost.

When the Order Quantity Must Be in Lot Sizes

Often a supplier will provide the product only in whole-number lot sizes.
For example, oranges may be available only in lots of a dozen crates, heavy
appliances may be delivered a truckload at a time, office supplies such as
paper clips may be packaged in lots of ten boxes per package, and beer may

only be supplied in lots of 4 six-packs to the case. The procedure for computing the optimal order quantity is very similar to the algorithm given above, the only difference being that if the EOQ, as calculated from Eq. (6–5), is not a whole-number lot size, the EOQ is rounded up and then down to the nearest whole-number lot size, and the corresponding values of the total cost are compared.

EXAMPLE 6.8. Bob's Refrigerator Sales must determine how many basic model refrigerators to order from its distributor. Sales run 150 units per year, wholesale cost to Bob is $375 per refrigerator, fixed order cost is $10, and carrying charges run 12 percent on an annual basis.

1. Determine the EOQ.
2. Determine the optimal discrete order quantity.
3. Assume that Bob's supplier will ship refrigerators only in lots of three at a time. Determine the optimal order quantity.

Solution

1. We have $D = 150$, $C = 375$, $F = 10$, and $r = 0.12$. Using Eq. (6–5), we calculate the EOQ to be 8.16 refrigerators.
2. If we round down, we get $Q = 8$; then using Eq. (6–6), the total annual cost would be

$$TC(8) = 10\left(\frac{150}{8}\right) + 375(0.12)\left(\frac{8}{2}\right) = \$367.50$$

If we round the EOQ up to 9, the total cost would be

$$TC(9) = 10\left(\frac{150}{9}\right) + 375(0.12)\left(\frac{9}{2}\right) = \$369.17$$

Thus, since $TC(8) < TC(9)$, we would use a discrete order quantity of eight refrigerators. Bob's total cost function is given by $TC = 1,500/Q + (22.5)Q$ and is graphed in Fig. 6.8.
3. Since the EOQ $= 8.16$ is not a multiple of 3, we must round the EOQ down to 6 up to 9 and then compare the resulting total costs:

$$TC(6) = \frac{10(150)}{6} + 375(0.12)\left(\frac{6}{2}\right) = \$385.00$$

$$TC(9) = \frac{10(150)}{9} + 375(0.12)\left(\frac{9}{2}\right) = \$369.17$$

Since $TC(9) < TC(6)$, we would use $Q = 9$ as the optimal order quantity. ▲

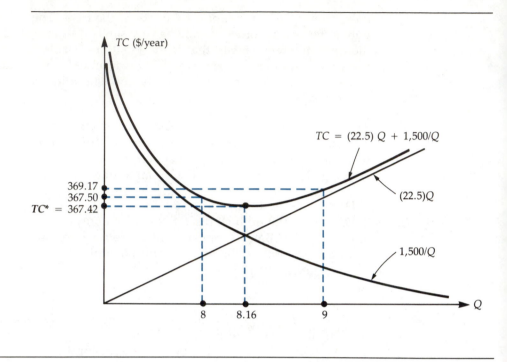

FIGURE 6.8   *The total cost function for Bob's Refrigerator Sales.*

When a Minimum-Order Quantity Is Specified by the Supplier

Often a supplier will stipulate that a minimum quantity must be ordered each time a shipment is made. For example, a wholesale food distributor is not likely to fill an order for two $0.90 packages of fig cookies. In some instances a minimum-order quantity may be imposed by the requirement of filling a semitrailer truck load, or train boxcar load.

To find the best order quantity in this case, first compute the EOQ, using Eq. (6–5). If the EOQ is greater than or equal to the minimum-order quantity specified by the supplier, we then may use the EOQ as the order quantity; otherwise, we must order the minimum quantity specified by the supplier.

EXAMPLE 6.9. Once again we will use Bob's Refrigerator Sales, Example 6.8. Recall that $Q^* = 8.16$. Suppose Bob's supplier says that she will not ship less than seven refrigerators at a time. Letting Q_m denote the minimum order quantity, $Q_m = 7$, and since $Q_m < Q^*$, the optimal order quantity is the EOQ, 8.16 units (appropriately rounded, as in Example 6.8). On the other hand, suppose she tells Bob that her company will not make shipments of less than ten refrigerators at a time. In this case $Q_m = 10$, and since $Q_m > Q^*$, the optimal policy for Bob is to order 10 units at a time. To fully understand this decision rule, you should study Fig. 6.8. When $Q_m = 7$, it is possible to order the EOQ of 8.16, which corresponds to the absolute minimum total cost. When $Q_m = 10$, we must then incur a larger total cost (compared to the total cost at 8.16 units) by ordering at least 10 units. However, *it is the best we can do, given that the order size must be at least 10 units*. Another way to put this is that 10 units is the closest order size to the EOQ of 8.16 units, given that we *must* order 10 or more units.   ▲

When an Upper Limit Is Given on the Time Supply

In the case of perishable goods such as food, it may not be desirable to order more than so many days' supply. In the electronic pocket-calculator industry, technology application is changing rather quickly. Models are being improved in short time spans. Thus a retailer of such products might be wise not to order more than, say, a six-month supply of solid-state calculators, because of the possibility of product obsolescence.

In other cases, owing to future uncertainties in product cost and demand, it simply may not be desirable to place orders for large time supplies. For example, a bookstore owner may be hesitant to order a two-year supply of a book that sells only one copy every two months.

An Algorithm for Computing the Optimal Order Quantity, Given a Time Limit on Supply

Step 1. Let T_m denote the maximum allowable time supply for a given order. In Section 5, Eq. (6–10), we gave an expression for the optimal time supply corresponding to the EOQ, denoted by T^*.

Step 2. If T^* is less than or equal to the maximum allowable time supply, T_m, then use Q^* as the optimal order quantity. Otherwise, go to step 3.

Step 3. If T^* exceeds the maximum allowable time supply, T_m, then order the quantity corresponding to T_m. To do this, set $T_m = Q/D$ and solve for Q: $Q = DT_m$. Then use this value of Q as the optimal order quantity.

EXAMPLE 6.10. Refer to Example 6.8, Bob's Refrigerator Sales. Let us assume that Bob sets a policy of not ordering more than a two-month supply of refrigerators.

Step 1. Compute the EOQ, Q^*. This was done in Example 6.8 and found to be 8.16. Thus $T^* = Q^*/D = 8.16/150 = 0.054$ *year*. We convert this to months to get $T^* = 0.054(12) = 0.65$ month.

Step 2. Since $T_m = 2$ months and since T^* is less than T_m, we can use $Q^* = 8.16$ as the optimal order quantity.

Now assume that Bob changes his policy and decides not to order over a half-month supply at a time. Then we proceed as follows:

Step 1. Same as above.

Step 2. $T_m = 0.50$ month, and since $T^* > T_m$, we proceed to step 3.

Step 3. Since $T^* > T_m$, we use the order quantity corresponding to T_m, which is computed first by converting T_m to years (the same units as D) and setting $Q = DT_m = 150(0.50/12) = 6.25$ units. (The optimal order quantity is taken to be 6.25 units, which is then rounded *down* to 6 units so as not to exceed the half-month time supply constraint.)   ▲

Problem

1.   Refer to Example 6.8, Bob's Refrigerator Sales. Suppose Bob's supplier specifies that she will ship only in multiples of three and requires a minimum order of $4,000. Determine the optimal order quantity and annual inventory costs (ordering cost plus carrying cost).

9. THE ABC INVENTORY CLASSIFICATION

In practice, it is often economically infeasible to incur the expense of controlling all inventory SKUs as suggested by the methods presented in this chapter. In fact, it is often unnecessary to do so, especially for slower moving and/or less expensive items.

The ABC inventory classification is a method of dividing the stock of all SKUs into three categories, based on total dollar volume. In practice it has been observed that often only 20 percent of all SKUs account for 80 percent or more of the total dollar volume. (These percentages will vary, of course, depending on the particular operation, but the principle is the same.) Thus, for control purposes, it may be necessary to direct our attention primarily to only a small percentage of the SKUs. Less stringent control measures may be used for slower-moving items.

The top 5 to 25 percent of the SKUs ranked by total dollar volume may be put into class *A*, the next 50 percent into class *B*, and the remaining SKUs into class *C*. Again, these are rules of thumb and may be set according to managerial judgment. In fact, management may decide simply to place a certain SKU into class *A* for control purposes even though the item does not carry a large dollar sales volume. (An example of this would be a new product that is to be observed carefully.)

Class A items then are subject to high management control, class B items to moderate control, and class C items to a lower level of control. Typically, class C items are less expensive items, and higher safety stocks may be maintained as a buffer against unexpected high-demand fluctuations.

EXAMPLE 6.11. *Ranking SKUs by Value.* In Table 6.2, we have listed the SKUs of Ace Boxem. For each SKU, the annual demand, D, appears in column 2, and the unit product cost is given in column 3. Column 4 contains the total dollar volume for each item. In Table 6.3, we have ranked the SKU by *value* and have indicated a possible classification into classes A, B, and C. Note that we have chosen to include 26.67 percent of the SKUs in class A (items 3, 15, 7, and 4), which accounts for 80.5 percent of the total dollar value ($620,837). We have included the next 40 percent of the SKUs in class B (items 1, 6, 12, 5, 2, and 11), and the remaining SKUs in class C.

Note that item 3, a low-volume, high-value item, appears in class A and that item 7, a high-volume, low-value item, also appears in class A. A distribution-by-value curve can be constructed from Table 6.3, as shown in Fig. 6.9.   ▲

TABLE 6.2   *SKUs for Ace Boxem*

Item	Annual demand (units/year)	Unit cost $1	Total dollar volume ($/year)
1	10,000	2.25	22,500
2	25,000	0.50	12,500
3	7,000	35.50	248,500
4	12,000	2.05	24,600
5	11,000	1.18	12,980
6	10,000	1.50	15,000
7	75,000	1.05	78,750
8	8,500	0.25	2,125
9	8,750	0.80	7,000
10	500	10.00	5,000
11	11,200	1.10	12,320
12	10,500	1.40	14,700
13	40,000	0.20	8,000
14	15,750	0.55	8,662
15	52,000	2.85	148,200

TABLE 6.3   *Distribution-by-Value Ranking for Ace Boxem*

Item	Total dollar value ($/year)	Cumulative percentage of dollar volume		Cumulative percentage of SKUs	
3	248,500	40.0		1/15 = 6.67%	
15	148,200	63.9	A	2/15 = 13.33	A
7	78,750	76.6		3/15 = 20.00	
4	24,600	80.5		4/15 = 26.67	
1	22,500	84.1		5/15 = 33.33	
6	15,000	86.6		6/15 = 40.00	
12	14,700	88.9	B	7/15 = 46.67	B
5	12,980	91.0		8/15 = 53.33	
2	12,500	93.0		9/15 = 60.00	
11	12,320	95.0		10/15 = 66.67	
14	8,662	96.4		11/15 = 73.33	
13	8,000	97.7		12/15 = 80.00	
9	7,000	98.8	C	13/15 = 86.67	C
10	5,000	99.6		14/15 = 93.33	
8	2,125	100.0		15/15 = 100.00	
Total:	620,837				

10. QUANTITY DISCOUNTS

In practice it is common for a vendor (or supplier) to offer a quantity discount on items purchased in larger quantities. This gives the buyer the opportunity to purchase items at a lower unit cost. Additionally, when larger quantities are purchased, fewer orders per year are required. On the other hand, larger purchases might push carrying costs higher, owing to larger average inventory levels.

The EOQ formula, Eq. (6–5), cannot be used simply to calculate the optimal order quantity, since the unit cost, C, is not fixed but depends on the quantity purchased. However, it is easy to adapt the basic EOQ method to the quantity discount situation.

An **all-units quantity discount** schedule presents a sequence of price breaks applicable to all units within each range of the schedule. The following example will illustrate this type of schedule, together with a method for calculating the EOQ.

EXAMPLE 6.12. *An All-Units Quantity Discount Algorithm.* Suppose demand for a product is 700 units per year, fixed-order cost is $15, and the carrying-cost rate is $0.09/$/year. The unit product-cost is given in the all-units dis-

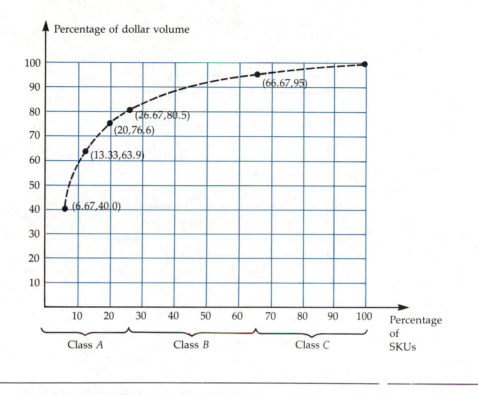

FIGURE 6.9   *Distribution-by-value curve for Ace Boxem.*

count schedule, Table 6.4. To illustrate the use of the schedule, suppose we assume an order quantity of 260 units. Since 260 falls in the third range ($250 \leq 260 < 300$), a unit product price of $4 applies, and total annual product cost would be ($4/unit)(700 units/year) = $2,800/year. Fig. 6.10 is a graph of unit product-cost versus order quantity.

We have $D = 700$, $F = 15$, $r = 0.09$. The value of C depends on the range of the order quantity. We now define $C_1 = 5.75$, $C_2 = 5.00$, $C_3 = 4.00$,

TABLE 6.4   *All-Units Quantity Discount*

Quantity ordered	Cost per unit
$0 \leq Q < 150$	$5.75
$150 \leq Q < 250$	5.00
$250 \leq Q < 300$	4.00
$300 \leq Q$	3.50

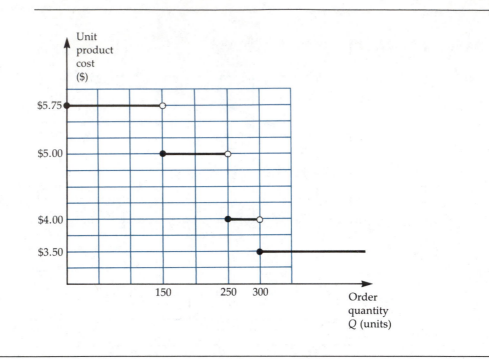

FIGURE 6.10   *Graph of all-units discount schedule of Table 6.4.*

$C_4 = 3.50$, and write the total cost function for Q in the ith range, where $i = 1, 2, 3, 4$:

$$TC = F\left(\frac{D}{Q}\right) + C_i r\left(\frac{Q}{2}\right) + DC_i \qquad (6\text{--}12)$$

To demonstrate the meaning and use of Eq. (6–12), suppose an order quantity of 260 units per order is used. Then $Q = 260$, and since Q falls in the third range, $i = 3$ and $C_i = C_3 = 4.00$. So

$$TC = 15\left(\frac{700}{260}\right) + 4.00(0.09)\left(\frac{260}{2}\right) + 700(4.00)$$

$$= \$2{,}887.18/\text{year}$$

A graph of TC as a function of Q appears in Fig. 6.11. We have labeled the regions from left to right as 1, 2, 3, 4.

Always begin with the region farthest to the right; in our case this is region 4. *For region 4,* calculate the minimum point on the TC curve. To do this, first use Eq. (6–5) with $C = C_4 = 3.50$ to find the *unconstrained* minimum, denoted Q_4^*:

$$Q_4^* = \sqrt{\frac{2(700)(15)}{3.50(0.09)}} = 258.20 \text{ units}$$

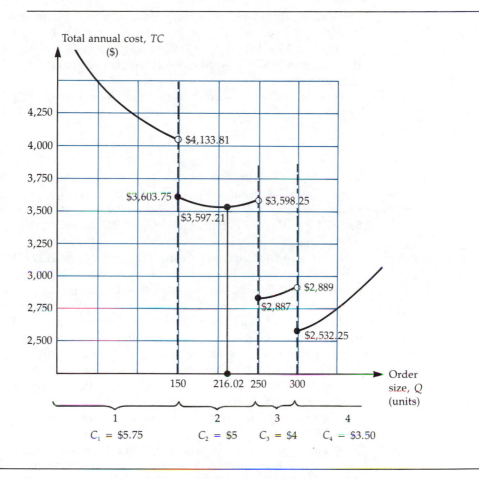

FIGURE 6.11   *The graph of TC for the quantity discount problem.*

But note that 258.20 does *not* belong to region 4. In such a case we need to calculate TC when $Q = 300$, which will then be the lowest point on the TC curve for region 4. When $Q = 300$, using Eq. (6–12) with $C_4 = 3.50$, we obtain

$$TC_4 = 15\left(\frac{700}{300}\right) + 3.50(0.09)\left(\frac{300}{2}\right) + 700(3.50)$$

$$= \$2,532.25/\text{year}$$

Now we store $Q_4 = 300$ and $TC_4 = \$2,532.25$ for future reference.

We now repeat the above process for region 3. Using Eq. (6–5) with $C = C_3 = 4.00$, we obtain

$$Q_3^* = \sqrt{\frac{2(700)(15)}{4(0.09)}} = 241.52 \text{ units}$$

Once again, this value is *not* included in region 3. Examining the graph shown in Fig. 6.11, we see that the lowest point on the *TC* curve *in region 3* must be at $Q = 250$. When $Q = 250$, using Eq. (6–12) with $C_3 = 4.00$, we obtain $TC_3 = \$2,887.00$. Again, we store $Q_3 = 250$ and $TC_3 = \$2,887.00$ for future reference.

Next we examine region 2. Using Eq. (6–5) with $C = C_2 = 5.00$, we obtain

$$Q_2^* = \sqrt{\frac{2(700)(15)}{5(0.09)}} = 216.02 \text{ units}$$

This time we obtain a result that *is* contained within the corresponding interval. Thus the minimum point on the *TC* curve *in region 2* must be at 216.02 units. Using $Q = 216.02$ and $C_2 = 5.00$ in Eq. (6–12), we compute $TC_2 = \$3,597.21$ per year. Again, store $Q_2 = 216.02$ and $TC_2 = \$3,597.21$ for future reference.

Do we need to continue to the region(s) lying to the left of region 2 (in this case region 1)? The answer is "no." Note that when $C = 5.75$, every point on the *TC* curve lies *above* every point on the *TC* curve when $C = 5.00$. Thus we can do no better, in terms of the total cost, by considering region 1.

The results of the above analysis are summarized in Table 6.5. Examining that table, we see that the *global minimum* of the *TC* curve occurs at 300 units, which has a total annual cost of \$2,532.25. The economic order quantity is 300 units. The number of orders per year is $D/Q^* = 700/300 = 2.33$, and the cycle length is $Q^*/D = 0.43$ year. Also note the cost breakdown: ordering cost equals $15(700/300) = \$35$ per year; carrying cost equals $3.50(0.09)(300/2) = \$47.25$ per year; and product cost equals $700(3.50) = \$2,450$ per year. ▲

By studying this example in light of Fig. 6.11, you should be able to solve similar EOQ problems when an all-units quantity discount exists. We shall now summarize the general quantity discount algorithm for ease of reference.

The Quantity Discount Algorithm

STEP 1. Start with an all-units quantity discount schedule, as shown in Table 6.4. Number the regions from top to bottom as 1, 2, . . . , n, and let C_i be

TABLE 6.5   *Quantity Discounts*

Region	Minimum cost	Order quantity
4	\$2,532.25	300
3	\$2,887.00	250
2	\$3,597.21	216.02

the corresponding unit cost for region i. Also, given the values of F, D, and r, write down an equation for TC corresponding to Eq. (6–12).

STEP 2. Begin with the region farthest to the right—n. Using $C = C_n$ in the basic EOQ formula Eq. (6–5), calculate Q_n^*. If Q_n^* lies in region n, calculate TC at Q_n^* and go to step 3 below. Otherwise evaluate TC at the *left end point of region n* and store the results (Q_n^*, TC_n) in a table such as Table 6.5. Now repeat this process for regions $n - 1$, $n - 2$, and so on, until finding an EOQ, Q_n^*, that is *contained within its region*.

STEP 3. Compare the TC values obtained in the above process to identify the minimum-cost order quantity.

   Note: If you study the above algorithm, you will see that it is not really necessary to construct a graph such as Fig. 6.11. All that is necessary is to perform the arithmetic of the steps of the algorithm. Also, if the supplier specifies a minimum order quantity, m, we need only set the *left* end point of region 1 equal to m.

Problems

1. Shatsky's Wholesale Liquors experiences a demand of 5,000 cases per year for Old Parrot Whiskey. Shatsky's supplier (distributor) offers the following all-units discount schedule for order sizes: $144 per case for orders less than 250 cases; $138 per case for orders of 250 cases up to 499 cases; and $130 per case for orders of 500 cases or more. The fixed ordering cost is $10, and the carrying-cost rate is 0.25.
   a. What would be the total cost for an order size of 110 cases? Of size 270 cases? Of 502 cases?
   b. Graph the total cost function ($/year) as a function of order size.
   c. *From the graph* determine the *approximate* optimum order size.

2. Refer to Shatsky's Wholesale Liquors above. Following the algorithm of Section 10, compute the economic order quantity and the minimum total annual cost.
   a. Calculate the length of time (in days) between placing successive orders. Assume 360 days per year.
   b. How many orders should Shatsky place per year?

3. John's Specialty Shoppe sells three hundred four-by-eight-inch-square candles per month. Ordering cost is $10, and carrying costs are 12 percent of inventory value. John's supplier offers discounts on lot-size purchases. For an order size of 50, unit cost is $5; for an order size of 100, unit cost is $4; and for an order size of 150, unit cost is $3.50. Determine the optimal inventory policy (also specify the minimum total monthly cost, the number of orders per month, and the time supply of each order).

Note: This is *not* an all-units quantity discount problem. John has only three choices for the order quantity—50, 100, or 150 units per order. Thus to solve this type of problem, you should simply evaluate the total cost function, Eq. (6–12), at each of the three combinations (50, $5), (100, $4), and (150, $3.50) and select the order quantity corresponding to the minimum total cost.

11. CONCLUDING REMARKS

In this chapter we have studied the basic EOQ inventory model. This model provides the basis for more advanced inventory models in management science.

Determining an optimal inventory policy amounts to specifying answers to "How much to order?" and "When should orders be placed?"

The relevant equations for the basic model are given in Section 5, Eqs. (6–5) through (6–10).

The total cost curve (Fig. 6.5) exhibits two interesting properties:

1. At the economic order quantity (EOQ or Q^*), where the total annual cost reaches a minimum, the total annual ordering and carrying costs are equal.
2. The total cost curve is very shallow near its minimum point (where $Q =$ EOQ). This fact has significant managerial implications in terms of sensitivity analysis (Section 6). Fig. 6.6 summarizes the sensitivity of the total cost to the order quantity. In general, relatively large deviations from the EOQ result in small cost increases. For example, Fig. 6.6 shows that ordering *50 percent more* than the EOQ results in only an 8.33 percent cost increase above the EOQ cost.

The answer to the question "When should orders be placed?" is given by the reorder point, Eq. (6–12).

Other Topics

Sections 8, 9, and 10 addressed a few of the more realistic problems of inventory analysis; in addition, the next chapter is devoted to several other topics related to the basic EOQ method.

The interested student should consult the references to this chapter given in Appendix A at the end of this text. We particularly recommend *Decision Systems for Inventory Management and Production Planning,* by Peterson and Silver. This book is easily read, contains a comprehensive coverage of topics, and maintains a realistic management focus.

TERMINOLOGY

After studying this chapter you should be familiar with the following terms:

TERM	SECTION
ABC classification	9
backorder	2
carrying cost	2, 4, 5
cycle length	4, 5
deterministic demand	2
EOQ	2, 4, 5
holding cost	2
inventory	1
lead time	1, 2
number of orders per year	4, 5
optimal inventory policy	2
ordering cost	2, 4, 5
quantity discount	10
reorder point	7
sensitivity analysis	6
SKU	2
total inventory cost	2, 4, 5

EXERCISES

1. *Managing Office Supplies.* National Computing Machinery annually uses 200 boxes of mimeograph paper, which it purchases at a cost of $12 per box. The cost to place an order with the office supply vendor is $20 (including telephone calls, clerical work, managerial time, and paperwork). Carrying costs are estimated to be 12 percent. It takes 14 working days from the time the ordering process is initiated to receipt of an order. National is open for business 250 days per year.
   a. Determine the EOQ.
   b. Specify the optimal inventory policy (include the reorder point).
   c. Compute the minimum total annual inventory cost. Break the cost down into its two components.
   d. Graph the inventory level as a function of time; show the lead time and the reorder point.
   e. How many days' supply does each order represent?

2. *Sensitivity Analysis.* (National Computing, Exercise 1 above.) Suppose the unit product price increases from $12 to $16 a box. How does this

affect the optimal inventory policy? Answer parts (a)–(d) of Exercise 1. In response to the 33-1/3 percent product cost increase, by what percentage does the total annual cost, TC, increase?

3. *Agriculture.* Superbiff Cattle Ranch uses 1,000 bags of cattle feed annually at a unit cost of $7 per bag. Each time the feed is purchased, Superbiff sends two ranch hands into town to bring back a large feed supply. The total cost to prepare paperwork, telephone the feed supplier, and send the workers into town for a load of feed is $80. The lead time is two days (one day for purchase order preparation and one day for transportation both ways). Superbiff's carrying cost is 20 percent.
   a. Compute the EOQ.
   b. What is the reorder point (assume a 365-day/year operation)?
   c. Compute the minimum total annual inventory cost.
   d. How many days' supply does each order represent?

4. *Lot-Size Purchasing.* (Superbiff Cattle Ranch, Exercise 3 above.)
   a. Suppose the feed supplier will sell the feed at $7 per bag only if purchases are made in lots of 20 bags at a time. In other words, order quantities must be in multiples of 20 bags. Determine the EOQ, minimum total annual cost, and reorder point.
   b. Now assume that if purchases are made in multiples of 50 bags at a time, the unit cost will be reduced to $6.20. Determine the optimal inventory policy.

5. *Purchasing Department Management.* Steelforme, Inc., uses 1,500 tons of steel annually in its fabrication operations. Steelforme's carrying cost is 25 percent, and the cost to place an order with its steel supplier is $100 (most of this cost is for purchasing department clerical work in order preparation coordinated with production supervisors). The product cost varies, depending on the order size, according to the all-units discount schedule shown in Table 6.6. Lead time is 20 days, since shipment takes place from a warehouse 700 miles away. Steelforme operates 250 days a year.
   a. Determine the optimal inventory policy.
   b. Compute the annual inventory cost (include the product cost).
   c. How many days' supply does each order represent?

TABLE 6.6

Order quantity Q (tons)	Cost ($/ton)
$0 \leq Q < 250$	$400
$250 \leq Q < 500$	380
$500 \leq Q < 1{,}000$	360
$1{,}000 \leq Q$	355

TABLE 6.7

Vendor	Unit cost ($/ounce)	Ordering cost ($)	Terms of sale
1	6.10	30	The minimum order quantity is 1,600 ounces.
2	6.30	25	Purchases must be made in lots of 200 ounces.
3	5.90	27	The minimum order quantity is 1,800 ounces.

6. *Vendor Selection.* Sandia Trading Company (an Indian-owned operation) employs several silversmiths to handcraft silver and turquoise jewelry. It uses 16,000 ounces of sterling silver annually. Sandia's carrying cost is 10 percent. Three vendors (metal dealers) have offered to supply the silver. The unit product costs, terms of sale, and associated fixed ordering costs vary according to the vendor chosen, as shown in Table 6.7.
   a. From which vendor should Sandia purchase its silver?
   b. Specify the optimal inventory policy, assuming a lead time of 5 days and that Sandia operates 250 days per year.

7. *Retail Clothing.* Highstep Fashions retails several categories of quality clothing items and apparel. Its product data are given in Table 6.8. (These categories are broadly defined, and costs shown are averages over all

TABLE 6.8

Item	Average unit cost	Annual sales (units)
Men's shirts	$ 18	3,500
Ladies' shirts	22	4,500
Fashion boots	125	600
Jewelry	25	500
Leather belts	12	1,400
Purses	15	500
Lingerie	35	750
Men's suits	300	600
Men's slacks	32	1,800
Ladies' slacks	27	4,200
Ladies' hats	9	300
Umbrellas	10	250
Billfolds	11	400

item types in each class. For example, the average piece of jewelry sold costs $25 per unit to stock and may be a necklace, a ring, or a bracelet.)

a. Determine an ABC classification for the items. Category *A* should contain 80 percent of the total dollar value.

b. Construct a distribution-by-value curve.

8. *Control of High-Volume Items.*   (Highstep Fashions, Exercise 7 above.) Determine the EOQs for the category *A* items, assuming a fixed ordering cost of $50 and a carrying cost rate of 25 percent.

9. *Expansion of Storage Facilities.*   Lucy's Woodshop uses 1,600 planks of red oak annually. The planks measure (nominally) $3/4'' \times 10'' \times 14'$ and are kept in a storage bin Lucy has constructed in her shop storage area. The capacity of the bin is 150 planks. Each plank costs $17.50. The fixed cost to place an order is $50, which includes $5 for order preparation, $4 for Lucy's time to straighten up the bin (removing scraps and some sorting), $3 for gasoline for her truck (since she picks up the wood herself), and $38 for her time in transporting the wood. Her carrying cost runs 12 percent of product cost (comprised mainly of fire insurance and capital costs).

a. Determine the optimal order quantity, given the 150-plank storage constraint. Compute the annual inventory costs.

b. If Lucy can expand the storage bin to hold 300 planks at a cost of $50 in time and materials (primarily two-by-fours), would you recommend she do so? Specify clearly the costs of the two alternatives ("expand" or "don't expand"). Note: The $50 is a one-time cost.

10. *Nightclub Management.*   Uptown Easy Lounge stocks a special higher-priced scotch, Revas Chegal, which it purchases for $12 a bottle. Annual usage requires, on the average, 150 bottles of the scotch. Ordering costs run $10 per order, and carrying costs amount to 20 percent of product cost. The management of Uptown Easy Lounge does not wish to stock more than a two-month supply of any item behind the bar. Determine the EOQ and minimum total annual inventory costs. Would you object to management's two-month supply policy?

11. *Public Transportation Management.*   The city of Endicott operates a shuttlebus service for its senior citizens and for the handicapped who are not able to drive their own vehicles. It currently operates 20 buses that are maintained by city repair garages. The 20 buses use an average of 100 new tires each year, which are purchased at a cost of $65 each. It costs $8 a year to carry a tire in inventory and $40 to place an order to replenish inventory. Determine the EOQ and resulting annual inventory cost.

12. *Service Capacity Expansion.*   (Refer to Exercise 11 above.) The city of Endicott is planning to expand its shuttle bus service to include other areas of the city as well as nearby rural areas. It is estimated that 15 additional

TABLE 6.9

Order size Q (bars)	Cost/bar of soap
$0 \leq Q < 20{,}000$	$0.30
$20{,}000 \leq Q < 50{,}000$	0.20
$50{,}000 \leq Q$	0.17

buses will be needed. The manager of the city repair facility would like to estimate the space requirements for storing the additional inventory of tires. Each tire requires 6 cubic feet of space. She estimates that the 15 new vehicles will use 75 tires annually (based on the current 20:100 ratio). Determine the additional space that will be required if the service expansion project gets the "go ahead" from City Hall.

13. *Motel Chain Management.* Motel 66 is a nationwide chain of motels offering economy rates. Every year it must purchase 70,000 bars of hand soap to distribute to its franchises. The supplier of the soap offers the quantity discounts shown in Table 6.9. The fixed cost to place an order is $150, and the carrying-cost rate is 25 percent.
    a. Determine the EOQ.
    b. Compute the total annual inventory cost; specify values of the three cost components (ordering, carrying, and product costs).

14. *Vendor Selection.* (See Motel 66, Exercise 13 above.) Suppose another supplier offers the product cost discount schedule shown in Table 6.10. If the fixed cost to place an order with this vendor is $160, from which vendor should Motel 66 purchase the bars of soap?

15. *Public School Management.* Kantrite Public School System annually uses 1,200 fairly expensive plastic rulers for its mathematics and art courses. This demand occurs at a fairly uniform rate throughout the year. The rulers cost one dollar each, the cost to carry a ruler in inventory for one year is 10 percent of product cost, and the fixed cost to place an order is $15.

TABLE 6.10

Order size Q (bars)	Cost/bar of soap
$0 \leq Q < 15{,}000$	$0.32
$15{,}000 \leq Q < 25{,}000$	0.28
$25{,}000 \leq Q < 35{,}000$	0.22
$35{,}000 \leq Q$	0.21

   a. Determine the EOQ.
   b. Assume demand doubles to 2,400 rulers annually. Compute the EOQ.
   c. Assume a demand level of 2,400 rulers annually. Another vendor approaches the purchasing department with an offer to supply the rulers at a cost of $0.85 each if the school will order at least 800 rulers at a time *and* if the order size is in multiples of 100. Should the purchasing department switch to this vendor or continue according to the policy computed in part (b) above?

16. *Management of the Maintenance Function.* Euclid University's maintenance department keeps an inventory of fluorescent light bulbs that are used as replacement bulbs at the fairly uniform annual rate of 2,000 bulbs. The cost of the bulbs is $2, and the carrying cost rate on the inventory averages 20 percent of product cost. The fixed cost to place an order is $40. The existing storeroom for the bulbs has a capacity of 300 bulbs.
   a. Determine the EOQ and total annual cost.
   b. The maintenance supervisor indicates that the storage capacity could be doubled by expanding the storage area and that the annual cost of maintaining the additional space would only be about $40. Evaluate the supervisor's suggestion from an inventory management perspective.

CHAPTER APPENDIX

Section 6. Computing the EOQ Mathematically

We will derive Eq. (6–5) and also show that, at the EOQ, total ordering cost equals total carrying cost.

   For ease of reference, we reproduce the total cost function, *TC*, from Eq. (6–3):

$$TC = F\left(\frac{D}{Q}\right) + Cr\left(\frac{Q}{2}\right) \qquad (6\text{--}13)$$

Proof of Eq. (6–5)

Using calculus, we can minimize the *TC* function with respect to Q by finding the value of Q at which the first derivative is 0 and then testing the second derivative to see that it is nonnegative. You may recall this procedure in calculus as the so-called "first and second derivative tests." We may rewrite Eq. (6–13) as $TC = FDQ^{-1} + Cr(Q/2)$. Then, setting the first derivative equal to 0 gives the following series of computations:

$$\frac{d(TC)}{dQ} = FD(-Q^{-2}) + \frac{Cr}{2} = 0$$

$$-FDQ^{-2} = -\frac{Cr}{2}$$

$$\frac{FD}{Q^2} = \frac{Cr}{2} \qquad\qquad (6-14)$$

$$\frac{Q^2}{FD} = \frac{2}{Cr}$$

$$Q^2 = \frac{2FD}{Cr}$$

$$Q^* = \sqrt{\frac{2FD}{Cr}} \qquad\qquad (6-15)$$

Eq. (6–15) is precisely Eq. (6–5). It remains to test to see if the second derivative is nonnegative at Q^*:

$$\frac{d^2(TC)}{dQ^2} = \frac{2FD}{Q^3} > 0 \text{ when } Q = Q^*$$

Thus Q^* is indeed the point at which TC is minimized.

Proof That at the EOQ, TOC = TCC

Study the proof of Eq. (6–5) given above. In the derivation there, we produced Eq. (6–14) as an intermediate step. Q^* must satisfy Eq. (6–14), and thus

$$\frac{FD}{(Q^*)^2} = \frac{Cr}{2}$$

Multiplying both sides by Q^* gives

$$\frac{FD}{Q^*} = Cr\left(\frac{Q^*}{2}\right)$$

[See Eq. 6–4(a) and 6–4(b).]
or

$$TOC = TCC \text{ when } Q = Q^* = EOQ$$

This completes the proof.   ▲

7 INVENTORY MODELS: PART II

CONTENTS

1. INTRODUCTION

In this chapter we shall first discuss two extensions of the basic EOQ model, which was presented in the previous chapter. The first model treated will be a production lot-size model that can be employed to determine optimal ordering policies when the product is being manufactured in-house. In addition, we shall study a backorder model that allows the decision maker to *plan* to have shortages that are to be backordered; that is, sales are not lost. In both of these models you will notice close similarities to the basic EOQ model, and the two models will be compared with the basic model.

In Section 4, we shall discuss one means of dealing with demand uncertainty in the basic EOQ model (which applies as well to the production lot-size model). This technique focuses on the use of "buffer stocks" and has found widespread application in practice.

Finally, in Section 5, we shall study a simple inventory model in which it is assumed that demand is not known for certain and is treated as a random variable. The analysis of the optimal policy for this model has an intuitive interpretation in terms of marginal economic analysis.

246

2. THE PRODUCTION MODEL

In the basic EOQ model (see Section 2 of Chapter 6), we assume that receipt of an order takes place instantly; that is, when an order of size Q arrives, we assume that the inventory level instantly increases by Q units. In this section we relax that assumption. The following example will demonstrate the application of such a model.

Prototype Production Example

A manufacturing plant produces an item that must pass through two departments for processing. Department A, which performs final assembly operations on the finished product, uses a certain component item in the assembly operation that is produced by department B. The stock replenishment procedure can be described as follows (see Fig. 7.1):

1. The lead time L, or the setup time for department B, is given. This is the time required for department A to prepare and place a production order and for department B to set up and prepare to begin production of the item.
2. Prior to reaching a zero inventory level, department A places an order

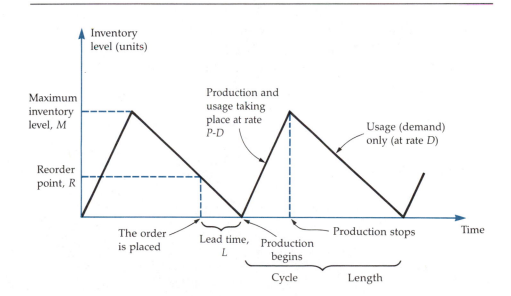

FIGURE 7.1   *The production inventory model.*

with department B for Q units. Then, department B begins to manufacture product components and delivers the components to department A.

3. Thus the inventory at department A does not instantly increase by Q units, the order quantity. As the units are manufactured at department B they are sent to department A, where they are used. The production rate at department B is P units per year, and the demand rate at department A (or the rate at which department A uses the components produced by department B) is D units per year. We assume that P is greater than D; that is, we assume that capacity at department B is sufficient to meet the production requirements of department A. Then inventory will increase at department A at the net rate of $P - D$ units per year until the production run at department B is complete. After that time, production is terminated at department B, and the *work-in-process* inventory at department A is depleted at the rate of D units per year.   ▲

Assumptions and Notation

We make the following assumptions for the production model:

1. Demand is deterministic at a constant rate.

APPLICATIONS

The following applications appear in this chapter in text, examples, or problems:

Analysis of subcontracting options

Customer-service planning

Dealing with shipping schedule uncertainties

Fad-products inventories
   Sporting goods

Inventories for major sales promotions
   University bookstore

Inventories subject to spoilage
   Blood bank
   Fresh produce

"Newsboy problem"

Procurement planning

Production planning
   Custom auto manufacture

Purchasing discontinued products

Retailing
   Fashion clothing
   Hardware store management

2. Lead time is not restricted. It may be either 0 or some specified positive value. As in the basic EOQ model, the consideration of lead time does not affect the economic order quantity or the minimum total cost; it only affects *when* to order—that is, the reorder point.
3. No backorders are permitted.

The meaning of D, F, C, r, Q, $Q^* =$ EOQ, TC, TC^*, and L are the same as defined in Section 4 of Chapter 6. In addition, we define P to be the production rate (the rate at which units of product are delivered). P is measured in the same units as the demand rate D—namely, in units per year. We assume that P is greater than D. In a given problem you must be careful to express D, P, and the lead time, L, in time units appropriate to the needs of the problem. Examples in this section will illustrate this.

Derivation of the Total Cost Equation

As in the basic EOQ model, we express the total cost per year (TC) as the sum of the total ordering cost per year (TOC) and the total carrying cost per year (TCC): $TC = TOC + TCC$.

The expression for the total ordering cost per year is the same as before. The number of orders placed per year is D/Q, and the cost per order is F; thus $TOC = F(D/Q)$.

To find an expression for the total carrying cost per year, we write $TCC = Cr \times$ (average inventory). We then need an expression for average inventory. This is equal to half the maximum inventory level, M. The order quantity is Q. The length of the production run is Q/P years. In this length of time the number of units used by department A is $(Q/P)D$ units. Thus the maximum inventory level $M = Q - (Q/P)D = Q(1 - D/P)$ units. (Refer to Fig. 7.1 to help you understand this line of reasoning.) Finally, we can write $TCC = Cr \times$ (average inventory) $= Cr(M/2) = Cr(Q/2)(1 - D/P)$. We can now write the following equations:

$$\text{Annual ordering cost} = TOC = F\left(\frac{D}{Q}\right) \qquad (7\text{--}1)$$

$$\text{Annual carrying cost} = TCC = Cr\left(\frac{Q}{2}\right)\left(1 - \frac{D}{P}\right) \tag{7-2}$$

$$\text{Total annual cost} = \quad TC = TOC + TCC$$

$$TC = F\left(\frac{D}{Q}\right) + Cr\left(\frac{Q}{2}\right)\left(1 - \frac{D}{P}\right) \tag{7-3}$$

The Economic Order Quantity for the Production Model

In Eq. (7–3) the **decision variable** is the order quantity Q. We want to select Q to yield the minimum total annual cost. As usual, we denote the optimal order quantity by $Q^* = \text{EOQ} = $ optimum production lot size, and denote the minimum total annual cost by TC^*. Using a proof similar to that in the appendix to Chapter 6, we can show that

$$Q^* = \sqrt{\frac{2FD}{Cr(1 - D/P)}} \tag{7-4}$$

Also, at Q^*, the total ordering cost equals the total carrying cost. See Fig. 7.2 for a graph of the TC curve, Eq. 7–3, as a function of Q. As in the basic EOQ model, the total cost curve is rather shallow around the EOQ. Thus the total annual cost is fairly insensitive to changes in the order quantity near Q^*.

You will notice that the treatment given here closely parallels the discussion of the basic EOQ model.

Other Useful Relationships for the Production Model

Using Eq. (7–4), we can calculate two more related quantities of interest:

$$\text{Optimal cycle length} = \frac{Q^*}{D} \tag{7-5}$$

$$\text{Optimal number of orders (or production runs)/year} = \frac{D}{Q^*} \tag{7-6}$$

Also, the optimum length of a production run is given by:

$$\text{Length of production run} = \frac{Q^*}{P} \tag{7-7}$$

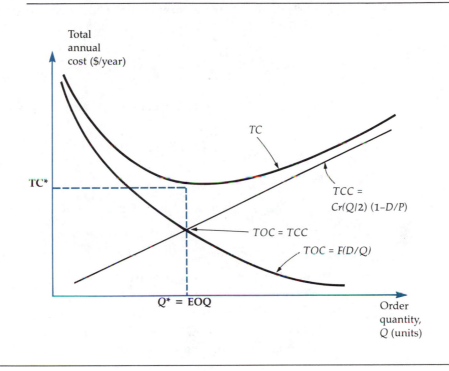

FIGURE 7.2   *The total cost curve for the production model.*

EXAMPLE 7.1. *Use of the Production Model Equations.* In the prototype example presented above, suppose annual usage of the component by department *A* is 2,000 units per year. Department *B* is able to manufacture these components at the rate of 4,500 units per year. Component cost is $5.50 per unit, and inventory carrying costs run $0.40/$/year. The cost for department *A* to prepare and place an order and for department *B* to set up for a production run totals $125 per order. The time required for department *A* to place such an order and for department *B* to begin production is three days. The plant operates 300 days a year. Calculate the optimal inventory policy for the plant.

Solution. The *first step* is to identify the values of the various parameters that appear in the above production model equations:

D = 2,000 units/year
P = 4,500 units/year
F = 125 $/production run
C = 5.50 $/unit
r = 0.40 $/$/year
L = 3 days = 3/300 = 0.01 year

The *next step* is to calculate the optimal production lot size (or the EOQ). Using Eq. (7–4), this becomes

$$Q^* = \sqrt{\frac{2(125)(2,000)}{5.50(0.40)(1 - 2,000/4,500)}} = 639.60 \text{ units}$$

The resulting minimum total annual cost given by Eq. (7–3) is

$$TC^* = 125\left(\frac{2,000}{639.60}\right) + 5.50(0.40)\left(\frac{639.60}{2}\right)\left(1 - \frac{2,000}{4,500}\right)$$

$$= \$781.74 \text{ per year}$$

Demand *per day* is 2,000/300, or 6.67 units. Since lead time is 3 days, the reorder point is

$$\text{Reorder point } R = (\text{Lead time } L) \times (\text{Demand rate } D)$$

$$= (3 \text{ days}) \times (6.67 \text{ units/day})$$

$$= 20 \text{ units}$$

The *optimal inventory policy* can be stated as follows: When the inventory level falls to 20 units, place a production order for 639.60 units.

OTHER QUANTITIES OF INTEREST. Management may be interested in other characteristics of the optimal inventory policy. We now list these and demonstrate how to calculate them.

1. The optimal cycle length (time between placing production orders) is calculated from Eq. (7–5):

$$\text{Cycle length} = \frac{Q^*}{D} = \frac{639.60}{2,000} \text{ years}$$

$$= 0.32 \text{ year}$$

$$= (0.32 \text{ year})(300 \text{ days/year})$$

$$= 96 \text{ days}$$

2. The optimal number of production runs per year, see Eq. (7–6), is

$$\text{Number of production runs/year} = \frac{D}{Q^*}$$

$$= \frac{2,000}{639.60}$$

$$= 3.13$$

Thus in one year, three production runs of size 639.60 units are completed and an additional 0.13 order is completed.

3. The optimum length of a production run, Eq. (7–7), is

$$\frac{Q^*}{P} = \frac{639.60}{4,500} \text{ years}$$

$$= 0.14 \text{ year}$$

$$= (0.14 \text{ year})(300 \text{ days per year})$$

$$= 42 \text{ days}$$

4. The total annual set-up cost, Eq. (7–1), is

$$F\left(\frac{D}{Q^*}\right) = \$125 \left(\frac{2,000}{639.60}\right)$$

$$= \$390.87$$

5. The total annual carrying cost, Eq. (7–2), is

$$Cr\left(\frac{Q^*}{2}\right)\left(1 - \frac{D}{P}\right) = 5.50(0.40)\left(\frac{639.60}{2}\right)\left(1 - \frac{2,000}{4,500}\right)$$

$$= \$390.87$$

Note that, at the EOQ, total annual set-up (ordering) cost equals total annual carrying cost.

6. The maximum inventory level is

$$M = Q^*\left(1 - \frac{D}{P}\right)$$

$$= (639.60)\left(1 - \frac{2,000}{4,500}\right)$$

$$= 355.33 \text{ units} \qquad \blacktriangle$$

Relationship Between the Production Model and the Basic EOQ Model

Let Q^*_{EOQ} and Q^*_{PROD} denote the EOQ for the basic EOQ model and the production model, respectively. Using Eq. (7–4), we find that as $P \to + \infty$ (that is, as P gets larger), $D/P \to 0$, so $1 - D/P \to 1$, and $Q^*_{PROD} \to Q^*_{EOQ}$.

Equivalently, if P is large relative to D, Q^*_{PROD} is approximately equal to Q^*_{EOQ}. The basic EOQ model can be thought of as an instance of the production model, where the production rate P is infinite. (See Problem 3 below.)

This justifies using the basic model in place of the production model in many practical situations. For example, an office supply retailer who receives a shipment of twenty boxes of office supplies sent by truck must wait for the boxes to be unloaded. If $D = 100$ per year and $P = 5,000$ per year (that is, the truck driver can unload 5,000 boxes per year), then properly we should use the production model equation to calculate the economic order quantity. However, since P is much larger than D, the basic EOQ equation can be used to give approximately the same result. In fact, as you may already be thinking, one does not even view the above example as an instance of the production model. See Problem 1 below for a numerical calculation related to this example.

Problems

1. For the production model, let $F = \$10$, $C = \$25$, $r = 0.10$. Calculate the EOQ for each of the following pairs of values, using both the production model equation *and* the basic EOQ model equation. Compare the results.
   a. $D = 100$, $P = 200$
   b. $D = 100$, $P = 1,000$
   c. $D = 100$, $P = 5,000$
   d. $D = 100$, $P = 10,000$
2. For the prototype production model, calculate the optimal production policy and the other quantities of interest, using the following parameter values: $D = 250$, $P = 400$, $F = 50$, $C = 25$, $r = 0.25$, $L = 4$ days (use a 250-day year). How would your analysis change if $D = 500$ and $P = 800$ (twice the given levels above)?
3. Explain in algebraic terms, using Eq. (7–4), why Q^*_{PROD} gets close to Q^*_{EOQ} as P gets larger relative to D.

3. A BACKORDER MODEL

We assumed in Section 2 of Chapter 6 that no backorders were permitted in the basic EOQ model. In this section we will study an inventory model in which we permit planned backorders.

The Nature of Backorders

Recall what is meant by a backorder. A *backorder* occurs when a customer's demand cannot be satisfied from inventory on hand *and* when the customer agrees to wait for the delivery of the next order; that is, the sale is not lost.

A merchant selling a high cost item might find it advantageous to *plan* for backorders. Examples of this can be found in the retailing of high-quality furniture, new cars, expensive wood- or metal-working tools, rare collectibles (coins, stamps, antiques), and higher-priced books on specialized topics. In these cases, where it would be expensive to place frequent orders to restock such items, it might be desirable to permit some backorders to occur.

In some businesses, backorders may seldom or never occur because of lost sales. An example of this is a grocery store.

Assumptions and Notation

The assumptions we make here are the same as for the basic EOQ model in Chapter 6 except that we do allow backorders to occur. For each unit of item backordered, the merchant incurs a cost of b dollars per year.

The cost b is comprised of two component costs. A backorder necessitates additional paperwork, clerical work, and customer follow-up. These factors constitute one cost component. The second cost component, the cost of customer goodwill, may be difficult to measure in practice. Management might employ any of a number of guidelines to set a value on goodwill, including the following: (1) using managerial judgment; (2) setting the cost b subjectively as a *policy* variable; and (3) devising some crude quantitative measure for the cost of goodwill.

As an example of the third guideline, assume that a merchant observes that 10 percent of all backorders result in lost sales of a product that costs $15 and retails for $20. Thus there is a 0.10 probability that the sale of a backordered unit will be lost, resulting in a loss of $5 profit. The *expected* loss on a backordered unit then is (0.10)($5), or $0.50. If we further assume that the dissatisfied customer will never return, then in a rough sense we might say that approximately $0.50 in sales have been lost on an annual basis. We would then include $0.50 in the computation of b. Note that this procedure is meant to serve only as an example of the type of thinking that might enter into estimating b. This method is the author's concoction and may be criticized on the basis that it mixes the issue of lost sales with the notion of backorders.

We denote the maximum inventory level by M. The parameters D, F, C, r, Q, Q^*, TC, TC^*, L, and R are defined as in Chapter 6.

Advantages and Disadvantages of Allowing Backorders

The main *advantage* to the merchant of allowing backorders is that the cycle length can be increased; that is, the total number of orders per year can be decreased. As a result, less-frequent ordering is required.

The *disadvantage* of backordering is the cost b to the merchant.

The Total Cost Equation and Optimal EOQ Policy

We have graphed the inventory level as a function of time in Fig. 7.3. At time 0 on the horizontal axis, the inventory is at its maximum level, M. An order for Q units is placed at the reorder point, R (L time units prior to expecting an order to arrive). The time required for the inventory to fall to zero is M/D years, so at M/D years backorders begin to occur because demands cannot be met from on-hand inventory. Thus an inventory level of -1 corresponds to one unit on backorder. Eventually the inventory level reaches its maximum backorder position of $-m$ units; the cycle length is then seen to be Q/D years. At the instant the inventory level hits $-m$ units, the previously placed order of size Q arrives and the inventory level rises by Q units from $-m$ to M. Note that the first m units of the order are used to satisfy customers who have backorders outstanding.

To derive an expression for the total annual cost, the method of Eq. (6–2) in Chapter 6 can be used as in the case of the basic EOQ model. Order

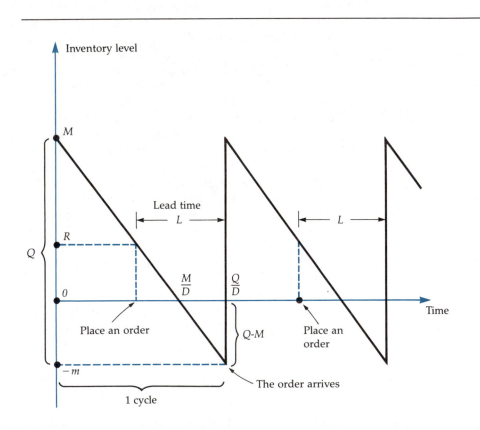

FIGURE 7.3   *The inventory level for the backorder model.*

costs per cycle are F, as before. Carrying costs per cycle are Cr (Average inventory level)(Inventory depletion time). Since the inventory level starts at M units and drops to zero at a constant rate, the average inventory level is $M/2$. The depletion time is M/D (see Fig. 7.3), so carrying costs per cycle are $Cr(M/2)(M/D) = CrM^2/2D$. Similarly, backorder costs are b (Average backorder level)(Backorder period). Backorders start at zero and reach a maximum of $Q - M$ at a constant rate, so the average backorder level is $(Q - M)/2$. The period over which backorders exist is (Cycle length) $-$ (Inventory depletion time), or $Q/D - M/D = (Q - M)/D$. Backorder costs per cycle are then $b[(Q - M)/2][(Q - M)/D] = b(Q - M)^2/2D$. Multiplying each of the per-cycle cost components by the number of cycles per year, D/Q, we get the Total Annual Cost, Eq. 7–8:

1. The *total annual cost* is given by

$$TC = F\left(\frac{D}{Q}\right) + \frac{CrM^2}{2Q} + \frac{b(Q - M)^2}{2Q} \tag{7-8}$$

$$= \text{Total annual} \atop \text{ordering cost} + \text{Total annual} \atop \text{carrying costs} + \text{Total annual} \atop \text{penalty costs}$$

In this equation, Q and M are the *decision variables*. By specifying Q, we have the order quantity. Q and M together tell us the maximum backorder to permit: $m = Q - M$.

2. *Optimal Policy.* In Eq. (7–8) we seek the optimal values of the decision variables Q and M. Denote these by Q^* and M^*. It can be shown mathematically that

$$Q^* = \sqrt{\frac{2DF}{Cr}} \sqrt{\frac{b + Cr}{b}} \tag{7-9}$$

$$M^* = \sqrt{\frac{2DF}{Cr}} \sqrt{\frac{b}{b + Cr}} \tag{7-10}$$

The minimum total annual cost TC^*, can be found by substituting Q^* and M^* back into Eq. (7–8).

3. Optimal cycle length $= Q^*/D$.
4. Optimal number of orders per year $= D/Q^*$.
5. The maximum number of units backordered $= Q^* - M^*$.
6. The fraction of time a shortage does *not* exist equals $(M^*/D)/(Q^*/D) = b/(b + Cr)$.

EXAMPLE 7.2. *Use of the Backorder Model Equations.* Suppose annual demand is 500 units, fixed ordering cost is $15, product cost is $600, carrying cost rate is $0.25/$/year, and cost per backorder is estimated to be $12/unit backordered/year. The number of business days per year is assumed to be

250, and the lead time on orders placed is five days. Find the optimal inventory policy.

Solution. First identify the values of the model parameters. We see that D = 500 units/year, F = $15/order, C = $600/unit, r = $0.25/$/year, b = $12/unit/year, and L = 5 days. Using Eqs. (7–9) and (7–10), we calculate

$$Q^* = \sqrt{\frac{2(500)(15)}{600(0.25)}} \sqrt{\frac{12 + 600(0.25)}{12}}$$

$$= \sqrt{100} \sqrt{13.5}$$

$$= 10(3.674)$$

$$= 36.74 \text{ units}$$

and

$$M^* = \sqrt{\frac{2(500)(15)}{600(0.25)}} \sqrt{\frac{12}{12 + 600(0.25)}}$$

$$= \sqrt{100} \sqrt{0.0741}$$

$$= 10(0.2722)$$

$$= 2.72 \text{ units}$$

Since demand per year is 500 units, demand per day is 500 (units per day)/250(days per year), or 2 units per day. Lead time is given as five days, so the lead time use is:

$L \times D$ = (5 days) $\times$ (2 units per day) = 10 units

Thus, place an order before reaching the maximum backorder position: order when the inventory position is $-34.02 + 10 = -24.02$ (see Fig. 7.4).
    The cycle length is Q^*/D, or

$$\text{Cycle length} = Q^*/D = \frac{36.74}{500} = 0.073 \text{ year} = 18.25 \text{ days}$$

and the optimal number of orders per year, N^*, is

$$N^* = \frac{D}{Q^*} = \frac{500}{36.74} = 13.61$$

The maximum number of units backordered is $Q^* - M^* = 36.74 - 2.72 = 34.02$, and the fraction of time a shortage does not exist is

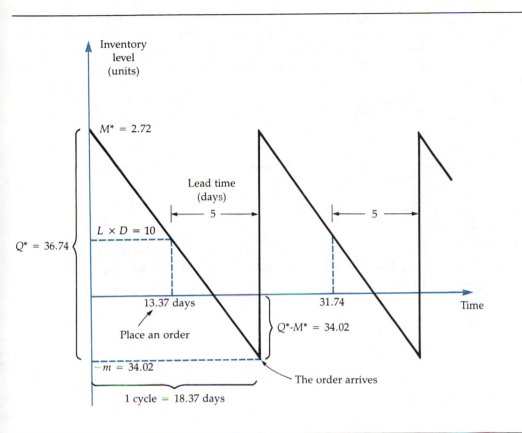

FIGURE 7.4   *Inventory policy for Example 7.2.*

$$\frac{b}{b + Cr} = \frac{12}{12 + 600(0.25)} = 0.074$$

That is, 7.4 percent of demands are met from inventory on hand and 92.6 percent are backordered.

Finally, the minimum total annual inventory cost can be found by substituting Q^* and M^* into Eq. (7–8), as follows:

$$TC^* = F\left(\frac{D}{Q}\right) + \frac{CrM^2}{2Q} + \frac{b(Q - M)^2}{2Q}$$

$$= 15\left(\frac{500}{36.74}\right) + \frac{600(0.25)(2.72)^2}{2(36.74)} + \frac{12(36.74 - 2.72)^2}{2(36.74)}$$

$$= 204.14 + 15.10 + 189.01$$

$$= \$408.25/\text{year}$$

Note from the computation of TC^* that we broke the calculations down into the three relevant costs: (1) ordering cost is \$204.14 per year, carrying cost is \$15.10 per year, and backorder cost is \$189.01 per year.

The results of this example are shown graphically in Fig. 7.4.   ▲

Relationships Between the Backorder Model and the Basic EOQ Model

From Chapter 6, Eq. 6–5 for the optimal order quantity for the basic EOQ model is

$$Q^*_{EOQ} = \sqrt{\frac{2DF}{Cr}}$$

Examining the optimal order quantity for the backorder model, Eq. (7–9), we see that

$$Q^*_B = Q^*_{EOQ} \sqrt{\frac{b + Cr}{b}} \tag{7–11}$$

where the subscript B denotes "backorder model." If we assign a very high backorder cost to b—that is, if we let $b \to +\infty$ (read "b approaches infinity")—then

$$\frac{b + Cr}{b} = \frac{b}{b} + \frac{Cr}{b} = 1 + \frac{Cr}{b} \to 1 + 0 = 1$$

Thus from Eq. (7–11), as $b \to +\infty$, $Q^*_B \to Q^*_{EOQ}$. In words, as b gets very large, the optimal order quantity for the backorder model gets close to the optimal order quantity for the basic EOQ model.

In a sense, then, you can think of the basic EOQ model as a model that imposes an *infinite* cost to backorders; therefore no backorders will ever occur.

4. SAFETY STOCKS FOR PROBABILISTIC DEMAND

Thus far in this chapter, as in the previous chapter, we have assumed that the demand rate is deterministic. However, it is often the case that demand is not constant but, instead, is random. Models that deal with random demand are referred to as *probabilistic demand models*. In this section we present a model of this type that has found widespread practical application. We shall continue to assume that demand is deterministic (or can be approximated as such) *except during the lead time*. During the lead time, we shall assume that demand is a random variable. The reason for concentrating on the nature of demand during the lead time is that the greatest risk of a stock-out exists during this time interval. Orders will then be lost or backordered. In either case, both the merchant and the customer will experience some inconvenience and cost.

A graphical illustration of a stockout is shown in Fig. 7.5. At point P, an order is placed. (This corresponds to the reorder point, R, and the lead time allowance, L.) Before the order arrives, a stockout occurs and the inventory becomes negative (corresponding to backorders). Demand during lead time has exceeded the reorder point R. Note that up to the reorder point R, demand—although shown as being random—is *approximately* uniform at rate D.

To avoid a stockout during lead time, a fixed quantity of product is maintained in inventory to absorb possible demand fluctuations. This inventory classification is referred to as *safety* (or *buffer*) *stock*. The advantage of carrying a safety stock is that some or all stockouts can be avoided. The disadvantage is the additional carrying cost. If the safety-stock level is Q_s units, then, on the average, the additional annual carrying cost will be CrQ_s dollars. We are faced with the problem of determining the appropriate trade-off between risking a stockout and incurring additional carrying costs.

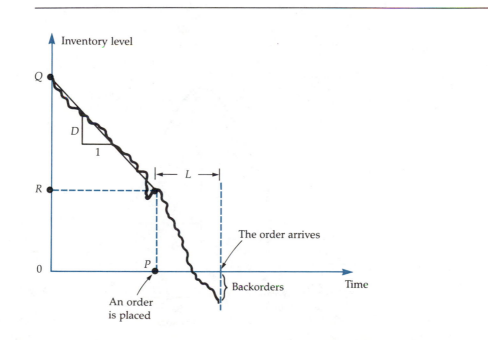

FIGURE 7.5   *A stockout during lead time.*

Case 1—Random Demand Rate, Constant Lead Time

We first assume that the lead time can be constant but that demand *during lead time* is a random variable. (This case is illustrated in Fig. 7.5.) Our objective is to determine the appropriate safety stock level to guard against stockouts. The success of the technique depends in large part upon a managerial assessment of the desired *customer-service level*. If it is desired to meet 95 percent of customer demand during lead time, the service level is said to be 95 percent.

Assume that demand during lead time is a random variable having mean μ and standard deviation σ. To meet a service level s (where $0 < s < 1$ corresponds to a percentage service level, as in the above example where $s = 0.95$), we simply find the point d that satisfies the relation

Probability{lead time demand $\leq d$} = s

(or $\geq s$ if rounding occurs in calculations or table lookups). Then the reorder point equals d.

In practice, a common probability density, the normal density, is used to model lead time demand, especially for faster moving items. This case is illustrated in Fig. 7.6. The method is outlined as follows: Let demand during lead time be a random variable, D_L, with a normal probability density having

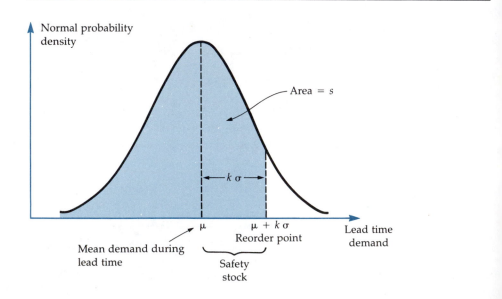

FIGURE 7.6   *Normal probability density for lead time demands.*

mean μ and standard deviation σ. To establish a service level s, proceed as follows:

1. Find the number, k, of standard deviations that s lies to the right of the mean μ.
2. Set the desired safety-stock level equal to $k\sigma$.
3. The reorder point then equals $\mu + k\sigma$.

EXAMPLE 7.3. *Computing Safety Stock When Lead Time Demand Is Variable.* Ace Boxem is a distributor for packaging materials. One of its SKUs, a 3.1-cubic-foot cardboard box, has an annual sales demand of 25,000 boxes. The cost runs $1.50 per box to Ace, ordering cost is estimated at $50, lead time is 10 days (use 250 days per year), and carrying cost is 10 percent of product cost. Demand is approximately uniform throughout the cycle, and during the lead time of 10 days, demand fluctuations suggest that lead time demand follows a normal probability density having a mean of 1,000 boxes and a standard deviation of 100. Compute the optimal inventory policy for a customer service level of 95 percent.

Solution. Notationally, we have $D = 25,000$, $C = 1.50$, $F = 50$, $L = 10$ days, $r = 0.10$, $\mu = 1,000$, $\sigma = 100$, $s = 0.95$. First, from Eq. (6–5), the EOQ is found to be

$$Q^* = \sqrt{\frac{2(25,000)(50)}{1.50(0.10)}} = 4,082.5 \approx 4,082$$

and from Eq. (6–3) we have

$$TC = 50\left(\frac{25,000}{4,082}\right) + (1.50)(0.10)\left(\frac{4,082}{2}\right) = \$612.37 \text{ per year}$$

To find the required safety-stock level, use the Table of Normal Probabilities in Appendix K to see that $k = 1.64$ standard deviations to the right of the mean. Thus

Safety stock = $k\sigma$ = 1.64(100) = 164 boxes

and

Reorder point = $\mu + k\sigma$ = 1,000 + 164 = 1,164 boxes

(Now examine Fig. 7.6 using these computed values for Ace.)

The optimal inventory policy specifies ordering 4,082 boxes when the inventory level falls to 1,164. The mean demand during lead time is 1,000 boxes, and 95 percent of the time 1,164 boxes will be sufficient to cover lead time demand variability. The safety stock equals 164 boxes, which costs $CrQ_s = 1.50(0.10)(164) = \$24.60$ per year to carry.   ▲

EXAMPLE 7.4. *The Cost of Providing Customer Service.* You may have noticed that so far we have not considered the *cost* of providing the desired service level. Mathematical methods that deal with the appropriate service level/service cost trade-off do exist but are beyond the scope of this textbook. However, you can get some idea of the costs involved simply by experimenting with different service levels.

In Example 7.3 above, a safety stock of 164 boxes was required for a 95 percent service level. The carrying cost on this level of safety stock for one year amounts to (164 boxes)($1.50/box)($0.10/$/year) = $24.60.

For a service level of 70 percent, $s = 0.70$, $k = 0.52$, safety stock equals $k\sigma$ = (0.52)(100) = 52 boxes, and the carrying cost is (52 boxes)($1.50/box)($0.10/$/year) = $7.80 per year.

For a service level of 99.9 percent, $k = 3.09$, safety stock equals 309 boxes, and carrying cost equals $46.35.

Based on such calculations, you could then *subjectively* determine the appropriate service level/service cost trade-off. (See Fig. 7.7 for a graph of these calculations.)   ▲

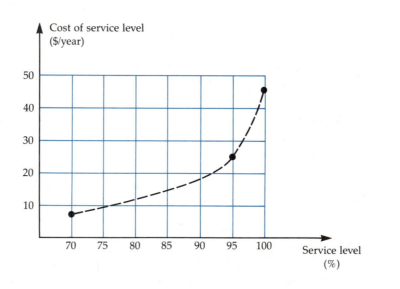

FIGURE 7.7   *The cost of providing customer service.*

Case 2—Constant Demand Rate, Random Lead Time

So far we have assumed that *demand* during lead time is a random variable with a known probability density; however, it may also happen that the *lead time* itself is a random variable. This might be the case due to variations in the workload of the supplier or to variations in the rates of packaging and shipping. The methods used to deal with this situation are very similar to those already discussed, as illustrated in the following example.

EXAMPLE 7.5. *Computing Safety Stock When Lead Time Is Variable.* Bookworm Bookstore regularly stocks a popular collegiate dictionary. Demand for the dictionary is fairly uniform, at the rate of three per day (on a 300-day/year basis), and the wholesale cost to Bookworm is $17.50 per copy. Carrying charges run 11 percent of product cost, and the fixed ordering cost is estimated to be $10. Lead time appears to fluctuate. An examination of historical (inventory) records indicates that lead time can be approximated by a normal probability density having a mean of 12 days and a standard deviation of 2 days. Determine the optimal inventory policy for a 97 percent service level.

Solution. We compute the EOQ from Eq. (6–5) to be

$$Q^* = \sqrt{\frac{2(900)(10)}{17.50(0.11)}} = 96.7 \text{ books} \approx 97 \text{ books}$$

and from Eq. (6–3) we have

$$TC = 10\left(\frac{900}{97}\right) + (17.50)(0.11)\left(\frac{97}{2}\right)$$

$$= \$186.15/\text{year}$$

The time between placing orders is $32\frac{1}{3}$ days. (Check this.)

For a 97 percent service level, $k = 1.88$ standard deviations (to the right of the mean), so safety stock equals $k\sigma$ times the *demand per day*, or (1.88)(2 days)(3 books per day) = 11.28 books. The average lead time is 12 days, so the reorder point is

(12 days)(3 books per day) + safety stock = 36 + 11.28 ≈ 47 books

The additional carrying cost of the safety stock is (11.28 books)($17.50/book)($0.11/$/year) = $21.71 per year (*in addition* to the *TC* calculated above).

The optimal policy calls for placing an order for 97 books when the inventory level falls to 47 books. The *average* lead time is 12 days, during which 36 books will be sold. The extra 11 books (47 − 36) are sufficient to cover lead time variability 97 percent of the time.   ▲

Case 3—Both Lead Time and Demand During Lead Time Are Random

The other case to consider is when *both* the lead time and demand during lead time are random. In this case the method of calculating safety stock is similar to the two cases already studied except that the relevant equations are somewhat more complex. For the details of how to handle this third case, you may consult the book by Peterson and Silver (see the references to this chapter in Appendix A).

Problems

1. Suppose demand averages 10 units per day (for a 250-day year). Lead time is 5 days, and demand during lead time has a normal probability density with a mean of 50 units and a standard deviation of 10 units. Product cost is $12, fixed ordering cost is $25, and the carrying-cost rate is 20 percent.
   a. Determine the EOQ.
   b. Find the safety-stock level for a 95 percent service level.
   c. What is the annual cost of carrying this safety stock?
   d. Calculate the reorder point.
   e. Specify the optimal inventory policy. (Include the total annual cost.)
2. Assume annual demand for a product is 1,000 units (for a 250-day year). Product cost is $20, fixed ordering cost is $30, and the carrying cost rate is 25 percent. Lead time has a normal probability density with a mean of 12 days and a standard deviation of 3 days. Answer parts (a)–(e) of Problem 1 above for this problem.

5. SINGLE-PERIOD MODELS: THE NEWSBOY PROBLEM

In the inventory models considered above, we have assumed that the merchant operates an ongoing process. We now consider a probabilistic inventory model that deals with a single time period. The merchant must stock an inventory of items *prior to the start* of the time period (day, week, month, or year). Demand during the time period is a random variable; therefore, the merchant does not know for certain how many units of product should be stocked. The merchant must pay a unit purchase cost for each item stocked. Then under these circumstances a "penalty cost" is incurred for each unit the merchant falls short of demand during the period; but if, instead, units are left over at the end of the period, a "holding cost" is incurred. The problem is to determine the optimal beginning stock level. Later we shall state this problem more specifically, but first we shall list a few practical applications of the single-period model.

Applications

The applications that follow can be treated as single-period inventory problems:

1. *The Classic "Newsboy Problem."* In this case the paper carrier must decide how many copies of a newspaper to have in stock for a given day.
2. *Retail Clothing Outlet.* The owner/manager of a retail clothing store must decide how many units of a certain stylish, or fashionable, clothing item should be stocked prior to the selling season; leftover inventory will be out of style next season.
3. *Fad Items.* Many retailers of consumer products are faced with the decision of how much stock to carry of various fad items. This is true for retailers who stock modern jewelry items, certain items of clothing such as faddish hats, T-shirts, belt buckles, toys, and so forth.
4. *Goods Subject to Spoilage.* Items in this category include bread and pastries, fresh fruits and vegetables, certain chemicals, and cafeteria meals.
5. *High-Technology Products.* Inventory decisions must be made with regard to products, which are quickly made obsolete by changing technology. Items in this category might include pocket calculators, videotape equipment (recently threatened by video discs, and in the future, the use of digital recording methods may quickly replace video discs), telephone equipment, and many of the popular consumer items currently utilizing microprocessor technology.
6. *Seasonal Items.* Items that fall into this category include swim suits, Christmas items, lawnmowers, air conditioners, seasonal clothing, and sports equipment.

Before proceeding to the development of the single-period model, we shall make the following remarks concerning the six application categories listed above. First, the categories may overlap. Second, in some cases the categories may include instances which do not strictly fit the single-period model. For example, what appears to be a fad may remain for some length of time (note the case of the "Frisbee" toy flying saucer). Also, not all high-technology products are superseded in a short length of time by better products. Third, the decision makers mentioned above may include manufacturers as well as retailers. Fourth, in many instances, especially where longer time periods are involved, the merchant has a chance to reorder before the period ends. This option will not be incorporated in the simple model discussed in this introductory treatment. Finally, many single-period inventory problems are recurring and must be solved period after period; however, the inventory left over at the end of a period *cannot be carried without penalty* to the next period. For example, donuts may be carried over to the next day, but in order to sell, they must be marked down as "day old." This is the distinguishing feature of single-period models.

Costs

The three cost components are as follows:

1. The *unit product cost, c,* is simply the cost the merchant must incur to acquire one unit of the product. Cost *c* is expressed as "$ per unit" (stocked at the start of the period).
2. The *penalty cost, p,* is measured in the "$ per unit" that the merchant is short at the *end of the period.* The penalty cost may include any of the following components:
   a. The cost of having to provide the item by purchasing it or by manufacturing it at a higher cost either in-house or at an outside source
   b. Lost revenue
   c. The cost of expediting (assuming the product can be obtained and delivered within the period), which would include special manufacturing set-ups, special shipping/freight arrangements, additional sales personnel effort, and so on
   d. The cost of losing customer goodwill (averaged on a per-unit basis due to lost sales)
   We will make the assumption that $p > c$. This is a reasonable assumption because the penalty cost, p, should be at least as large as the revenue lost from the sale of one unit of product, and since revenue is greater than unit cost, p will be greater than the unit cost c.
3. The *holding cost, h,* is measured in the "$ per unit" that the merchant must incur for each item left over at the *end of the period.* This cost may include any of the following components:
   a. Holding costs on inventory held during the period
   b. Additional *net* costs of disposing of the item at the end of the period, which would include the item cost, plus disposal costs, less salvage value

Note: In this basic single-period model there is no fixed cost to place an order. The single-period model that does incorporate a fixed ordering cost is considerably more complex mathematically.

Analysis of the Model

To make the problem at hand precise, let us briefly state the situation facing the decision maker.

The Problem. Prior to the start of the period, the decision maker must stock Q units of inventory of a given item at a unit cost of c dollars each. The demand during the period, denoted D, is a random variable having a known (or estimated) probability density. If the single-period demand, D, exceeds the inventory, Q, a penalty cost (p dollars) is incurred for each unit of unsatisfied demand. If Q exceeds D, a holding cost (h dollars) is incurred for each unit held at the end of the period. The problem is to determine the optimal beginning inventory, denoted Q^*, that minimizes total expected costs for the single period.

We now employ an intuitive **marginal analysis** line of reasoning to derive an expression that can be solved for the value of Q^*. This nonrigorous proof will assume that D *is a continuous random variable*. We will then point out how to treat the discrete demand case.

Marginal Analysis. Suppose the decision maker elects to purchase units 1, 2, 3, . . . , $Q - 1$ on a unit-by-unit basis and is trying to decide whether or not to stock the Qth unit. If he decides to stock the Qth unit, the expected purchase cost plus the holding cost on the Qth unit would be the product cost, c, plus the expected holding cost on the Qth unit. The expected holding cost on the Qth unit is h times the probability that demand is less than or equal to Q. Thus if he decides to stock the Qth unit, the expected purchase cost plus the holding cost would be $c + hP\{D \leq Q\}$. On the other hand, he can expect to *avoid* a penalty cost, p, with probability $1 - P\{D \leq Q\}$; that is, the expected penalty cost saved is $p(1 - P\{D \leq Q\})$.

If the expected purchase cost plus the holding cost is greater than the expected penalty cost saved, he *would not* stock the Qth unit; if it is less than the expected penalty cost saved, he *would* stock the Qth unit. Thus, as long as the expected purchase cost plus holding cost is less than the expected savings in penalty costs, he would continue to stock units until the two costs became equal; then he would stop adding units to inventory.

We see from this analysis that Q^* satisfies the equality $c + hP\{D \leq Q^*\} = p(1 - P\{D \leq Q^*\})$, which can be simplified as follows:

$$c + hP\{D \leq Q^*\} = p - pP\{D \leq Q^*\}$$

$$hP\{D \leq Q^*\} + pP\{D \leq Q^*\} = p - c$$

$$P\{D \leq Q^*\}(p + h) = p - c$$

$$P\{D \leq Q^*\} = \frac{p - c}{p + h} \tag{7-12}$$

Discrete Demand. In the problems we will examine, the demand D will be a discrete random variable. In this case the optimal beginning inventory Q^* must satisfy the following:

$$P\{D \leq Q^* - 1\} \geq \frac{p - c}{p + h} \leq P\{D \leq Q^*\} \tag{7-13}$$

You should note that, if demand is discrete, there may not be a value Q^* that satisfies Eq. (7–12) exactly: this is the reason for having to use Eq. (7–13) instead. The proof behind Eq. (7–13) is somewhat technical and can

TABLE 7.1

Demand D equals number of bushels	Number of weeks this demand occurred
1	6
2	10
3	18
4	9
5	8

be found in the text by Taha, which is listed in the references to this chapter in Appendix A. For our purposes, it is only important that you know how to use Eq. (7–13).

EXAMPLE 7.6. Fruitcake's Fresh Produce stocks a weekly supply of green onions. The unit cost of the onions is $2.00 a bushel. Onions left over at the end of the week must be sold for $0.50 a bushel; also holding costs run $0.75 for each bushel of onions left over at the end of the week (including carrying costs, cooling, and maintaining an appealing product display). The selling price of a bushel of onions is $3.50, and if a shortage occurs this revenue is lost. Historical sales records indicate demand levels as shown in Table 7.1. How many bushels of onions should Fruitcake's Fresh Produce stock at the beginning of each week?

Solution. First we note that c = $2.00, p = $3.50 and h = $0.75 − $0.50 = $0.25 (net holding cost per bushel after salvage value). The total number of weeks observed is 6 + 10 + 18 + 9 + 8 = 51; therefore, if we divide the entries in the table by 51, we derive the table of frequency probabilities and cumulative probabilities shown in Table 7.2. The value $(p - c)/(p + h)$ in Eq. (7–13) becomes ($3.50 − $2.00)/($3.50 + $0.25) = 0.40. The *first* Q satisfying Eq. (7–13) is $Q = Q^* = 3$.

TABLE 7.2

Number of bushels	Probability of occurrence	Cumulative probability
1	6/51 = 0.118	0.118
2	10/51 = 0.196	0.314
3	18/51 = 0.353	0.667
4	9/51 = 0.176	0.843
5	8/51 = 0.157	1.000

$$P\{D \le 3 - 1\} = 0.314$$

$$P\{D \le 3\} = 0.667$$

so,

$$P\{D \le 3 - 1\} \le \frac{p - c}{p + h} \le P\{D \le 3\}$$

Thus Fruitcake's Fresh Produce should stock 3 bushels of onions at the beginning of each week.   ▲

EXAMPLE 7.7. *The Normal Density.* The normal probability density is, of course, a continuous density. However, in practice, only discrete values of the normal distribution are tabulated as in the Table of Normal Probabilities, Appendix K. Thus Eq. (7–13) can be used when single-period demand is assumed to be normally distributed. As an example, Newsclip News Agency has observed that demand for the daily morning paper is approximately normally distributed, having a mean of 50 papers per day and a standard deviation of 12 papers. It pays $0.10 for each copy and sells the paper for $0.25. The penalty cost for being short is taken to be the lost revenue. Holding costs run $0.02 per copy to cover the expense of maintaining a store display for the papers. Papers left over at the end of the day can be sold to a recycling plant for an average of $0.001 each. Determine the optimal number of newspapers to stock each morning.

Solution. We have $c = \$0.10$, $p = \$0.25$, and $h = \$0.02 - \$0.001 = \$0.019$. Therefore

$$\frac{p - c}{p + h} = \frac{.25 - .10}{.25 + .019} = 0.5576$$

From the Table of Normal Probabilities (Appendix K), the value 0.15 corresponds to 0.15 standard deviations above the mean and has a cumulative probability value of 0.5596. The value 0.15 is the *first* normal value to satisfy

$$P\{D \le Z\} \ge 0.5576 = \frac{p - c}{p + h}$$

Therefore, $Q^* = 0.15$ standard deviations above the mean $= \mu + 0.15\sigma = 50 + 0.15(12) = 51.8 \approx 52$ papers per day.   ▲

Problems

1. Solve the inventory problem of Example 7.6 (Fruitcake's Fresh Produce), assuming that the demand data change as shown in Table 7.3.

TABLE 7.3

Demand D	Number of weeks observed
10	18
11	15
12	8
13	6
14	4

2. How would the optimal ordering policy change for Example 7.7 if demand is normally distributed with a mean of 50 and a standard deviation of 16?

3. Solve Example 7.7 if the recycling value of a newspaper increases from $0.001 to $0.005. Interpret your results.

4. Solve Example 7.6, assuming that Fruitcake's Fresh Produce has an initial inventory of 2 bushels of fresh green onions.

6. CONCLUDING REMARKS

In this chapter we have studied several extensions of the basic EOQ model (Chapter 6). There is almost no end to the number of such extensions that have appeared in management science literature. The value of studying the more elementary models found in this chapter and in Chapter 6 is that most advanced models and practical inventory systems are based on simpler models and concepts.

An example of a popular inventory model is the (s, S) model. This model is a more advanced version of the single-period model discussed in Section 5. In this version of the one-period model, it is assumed that the merchant must pay a *fixed ordering cost* (at the start of the period) in addition to the variable product cost, c. This fixed ordering cost is the same sort of cost discussed at length in the previous chapter (denoted F). As in Section 5, demand is assumed to be probabilistic, there is a holding cost, h, and a penalty cost, p. In this case, it can be shown that an (s, S) policy is optimal. This means that it is possible to calculate two numbers, denoted s and S, such that if the initial inventory level is less than s, the merchant should order enough stock to bring the inventory level up to S units; if the initial inventory is greater than or equal to s, then no stock replenishment should take place.

As an example of another extension of the more elementary models, it is possible to devise a model that combines the production and backorder models of Sections 2 and 3.

For these and other inventory models, the interested reader should consult the references to Chapters 6 and 7 listed in Appendix A.

A Summary of the Models

It is important that you clearly understand the differences between the various models discussed in this chapter.

PRODUCTION MODEL. In the basic EOQ model, we assumed that receipt of an order took place instantly; that is, when an order arrived, the inventory level instantly increased from 0 to Q^* units, where Q^* is the EOQ. The production model allows for noninstantaneous delivery of items to the inventory stock. Specifically, we made the assumption that items are delivered to inventory at the rate of P units per year. The EOQ is now thought of as the optimum *production lot size* and is given by Eq. (7–4). The total annual cost is given by Eq. (7–3).

BACKORDER MODEL. In the basic EOQ model, we assumed that no backorders were allowed; that is, the inventory level was not allowed to be "negative," which would represent items promised to people but not yet delivered. The backorder model in Section 3 extended the basic EOQ model to account for backorders. The advantage of allowing backorders is that less ordering is required, thus saving the fixed order cost F; the disadvantage is the backorder cost h ($/unit backordered/year). The total cost for this model is given by Eq. (7–8).

In order to specify the optimal inventory policy, we must calculate two numbers: Q^* and M^*, using Eqs. (7–9) and (7–10), respectively. The difference $m = Q^* - M^*$ tells us the maximum backorder level that will occur; that is, when m units are on backorder, a stock replenishment of Q^* units should take place.

SAFETY-STOCK MODEL. The basic EOQ model (Chapter 6) assumes that the demand rate is constant. The safety-stock model in Section 4 assumes that the demand rate is fairly constant except during the lead time. During the lead time, we made the assumption that demand has a normal probability density. In this model the problem is to determine the reorder point based on maintaining a given customer service level. The reorder point is based not only on lead time but also on carrying a safety (or buffer) stock. (See Case 1 in Section 4.) In Case 2 we considered the situation where the demand rate is constant throughout the cycle but the lead time itself may vary. Specifically, lead time is assumed to have a normal probability density. The problem (as in Case 1) is to determine the reorder point based on a customer service level.

SINGLE-PERIOD MODEL. The single-period model in Section 5 considers the situation where (1) the inventory decision is to be made for one period, and (2) the demand during the entire period is a random variable. Equations (7–12) and (7–13) indicate the nature of the optimal inventory policy: first find

Q^*; then if the initial inventory level is 0, bring it up to Q^* units at the start of the period.

TERMINOLOGY

After studying this chapter you should be familiar with the following terms:

TERM	SECTION
backorder	3
buffer stock	4
customer-service level	4
probabilistic demand	4
production lot size	2
production model	2
safety stock	4
single-period model	5
stockout	4

EXERCISES

1. *Production Planning.* Custom Caddy, Inc., specializes in converting standard Cadillac sedans to convertibles. To attach the convertible top unit to the modified body, a special part, E26–40, is required. Custom Caddy has the facilities to manufacture 500 of these parts per year. Its annual requirements for the part average 300 units. Production costs run $250 per part, and carrying costs are estimated to be 15 percent. The cost to set up for a production run is $350. It takes three days to set up for production. Assume a 300-working-day year.
   a. Determine the optimal production policy (how many units to produce and when to produce them).
   b. Compute the annual inventory costs.
   c. What is the length of each production run?
   d. How many days' supply does each production lot represent?
   e. What will be the maximum inventory level?

2. *Procurement Planning—Analysis of Subcontracting Options.* (See Custom Caddy, Inc., Exercise 1 above.) Custom Caddy is considering subcontracting the production of part E26–40. Two job shops are being considered.

   Shop A charges $260 per part, requires a 14-day lead time, and will produce the part only in multiples of five units; the fixed cost to place an order with Shop A would be $20.

Shop B charges $240 per part, requires a 10-day lead time, and will not accept an order for less than 25 units; the fixed cost to place an order with Shop *B* would be $25.

Should Custom Caddy, Inc., continue to manufacture part E26–40 in-house, subcontract to Shop *A*, or subcontract to Shop *B*?

3. *Sales versus Production and Inventory Management.* Blic, Inc., manufactures several lines of writing and drawing pens, and is currently introducing a new model called the "Apple." Blic has the capacity to manufacture 10,000 Apples a year at a unit cost of $1.50 each. The set-up cost for a production run is $500, and the carrying cost rate on inventory is 25 percent.
   a. The sales manager indicates a first-year sales forecast of 1,800 Apples. Based on this figure, compute the optimal production lot size and the total inventory cost.
   b. In the first year of introduction, the company did indeed sell about 1,800 Apples. The sales manager's forecast for second-year sales is 7,200 Apples, four times first-year sales. This sales forecast is thought to be fairly accurate. The sales manager scrambles to the production manager and says to her, "You can now increase average inventory levels fourfold over last year. Our sales will push four times last year's level." What inventory policy should the production manager plan to pursue during the second year? Comment on the cost of the sales manager's "suggestion."

4. *Hardware Store Management.* Messrs. Gyoka and Igurashi own and operate the only hardware store in a small midwestern town. In their store, Messrs. Gyoka and Igurashi maintain a display of brand-name power tools, many of which are relatively inexpensive hand tools. However, they do carry a 10-inch, 1-1/2-hp table saw that costs $450 to stock. Sales of this saw average 90 per year. The fixed cost to place an order with the supplier is $50, and the carrying cost rate is 25 percent. Lead time on orders is 10 days, and the hardware store is open for business 270 days a year.
   a. Currently no backorders are planned—all demand is to be met from stock on hand. Compute the optimal inventory policy, specifying clearly how much to order, when to order, ordering costs, carrying costs, total costs, number of orders per year, time between placing orders, and average inventory level.
   b. Mr. Gyoka believes that the store could save money by maintaining a lower inventory of table saws. Also, he would like to cut down on the ordering costs. He estimates that they could backorder the table saws without losing customers—they are the only supplier in the area, people know and like the management, and the lead time of ten days offers fairly fast service. Backordering, which requires extra clerical work to maintain a file of customers and then to telephone them when their saw arrives, would cost an average of $5 per saw per year. Mr.

Igurashi likes the idea of planning backorders, but he would like to combine the idea with the following promotional gimmick: For each day a customer has to wait for a backordered unit to arrive, a $0.50 credit will be given; this credit can then be applied toward the purchase of any item in the store. Since the store is open 270 days a year, this would add $135 to the yearly backorder cost: ($0.50)(270) = $135. Compute the optimal inventory policy. Clearly specify each of the factors listed in part (a) above, in addition to the percentage of time no backorders will exist.

c. To examine the effects of Mr. Igurashi's idea, solve part (b) above *without* the $0.50 per day promotional consideration. Tabulate your results as before and compare parts (a), (b), and (c).

5. *Retail Management.*   Digital Stereo Systems stocks a certain digital playback device that costs $700 to stock and has annual sales of 250 units. The cost to place an order is $100, carrying cost rate is 15 percent, and the backorder cost is $15 per unit per year.

   a. Compute the optimal inventory policy, specifying the maximum inventory level, the percentage of sales that can be met from stock on hand, and the maximum number of units on backorder.

   b. Repeat the calculations of part (a) if demand increases to 1,000 units per year.

6. *Wholesale Liquor Warehousing.*   John Doe owns a wholesale liquor warehouse that serves several nearby small towns. The sale of Roocs beer averages 3,500 cases per year (based on a 250-day business year). Demand for Roocs beer during the 8-day replenishment lead time is approximately normally distributed, with a mean of 112 cases and a standard deviation of 20 cases. The cost to stock Roocs beer is $4 per case, ordering costs are $50 per order, and the carrying cost rate is 20 percent. Determine the optimal inventory policy for a 95 percent customer-service level. What is the annual cost of maintaining the safety stock?

7. *Sensitivity to Demand Variability.*   (See John Doe's wholesale liquor warehousing problem in Exercise 6 above.) For John Doe's problem, compute the annual cost of maintaining a 95 percent safety stock of Roocs beer for each of the following values of the standard deviation of lead time demand: 5, 10, 20, 30, 40, 50, 60. Graph your results (put standard deviation on the horizontal axis and cost of the safety stock on the vertical axis).

8. *Cost of Providing Customer Service.*   (Refer again to Exercise 6 above, where $\mu = 112$, $\sigma = 20$, $C = \$4$/case, and $r = 0.20$.) Construct a graph similar to Fig. 7.7, showing service level versus cost of service level.

9. *Determining Customer-Service Level.*   Tom Run operates a small coin and stamp shop. His primary business is selling and buying rare coins and stamps; however, he does stock a comprehensive coin catalogue that costs

him $20 a copy. His carrying costs run rather high, around 30 percent per year, due to rather high opportunity costs. The lead time to replenish the stock of this book is 15 days; lead-time demand is assumed to be normally distributed, with a mean of 15 copies and a standard deviation of 3. Tom says he is willing to maintain a buffer stock during lead time, provided he does not have to tie up over $25 a year in safety stock costs. Given this information, what sort of customer service will Tom be able to provide?

10. *Vendor Selection—Analysis of Shipping Schedule Uncertainties.* Jamie Robinson's Plumbing and Heating stocks a certain forced air, up-flow gas heating unit for residential installation. The company would like to maintain a 95 percent customer-service level on the furnaces, which sell at a fairly constant rate of two per day (on a 250-day/year basis). Two vendors offer the unit: Vendor *A* can sell the unit to Robinson for $450 each and indicates that the shipping time will fluctuate. After some discussion, analysis, and making a few reasonable assumptions, it is determined that vendor *A*'s lead time can be approximated by a normal probability density having a mean of 15 days and a standard deviation of 4 days. Vendor *B*'s price for the same furnace is $475, and lead time would be normally distributed, with a mean of 13 days and a standard deviation of 4 days. If Robinson's carrying rate is 20 percent:
a. Determine from which vendor he should order.
b. Specify the nature of his inventory policy.

11. *Seasonal Items.* A major producer of Texicone antifreeze is planning its production for the upcoming winter season. The cost to produce the antifreeze is $4 per gallon, and the product is wholesaled to Texicone dealers for $6.50 per gallon. For each gallon short of demand, the producer will lose the revenue of $6.50. For each gallon left over at the end of the season, a holding cost of $1.70 is incurred to carry the product over to the next winter season. One production run is made each summer. The demand for the product is a random variable having a normal distribution with mean 20,000 gallons and standard deviation of 4,000 gallons.
a. Determine the optimal beginning inventory at the start of this season.
b. If the producer currently has an inventory of 5,000 gallons (carried over from last winter), how many gallons must be produced this summer?

12. *Blood Bank Inventories.* Hampshire Blood Bank, operated by General Hospital, obtains blood supplies from a regional main blood bank cooperative at a unit cost of $30 per pint at the start of each three-week period. Blood that is not used during that period is subject to spoilage and has no residual value. Holding cost per pint of blood left over at the end of the period is $6. If Hampshire Blood Bank runs short of supplies prior to the end of the period, it can obtain additional supplies at a cost of $35 a pint from neighboring banks or by special shipment from the main

TABLE 7.4

Demand	Probability
10	0.05
11	0.15
12	0.20
13	0.25
14	0.15
15	0.15
16	0.05

cooperative. Assume demand is normally distributed, with a mean of 120 pints and a standard deviation of 50 pints (per three-week period). Using the one-period model of Section 5, determine the optimal beginning inventory to stock.

13. *Fad Items.*   Jan's Sporting Goods is planning to place an order for a faddish straw, military-looking helmet that people in her town are currently wearing to midnight beach parties at the local county reservoir. There is only one month of this summer's swimming season remaining. Jan must purchase the hats at a cost of $4 each and can retail them for $9. Thus for each hat short of demand, she will lose $9 in revenue. Hats left over at the end of the one-month season must be discounted and sold for $2 each. Jan's estimate of the demand distribution is summarized in Table 7.4.
    a. Determine how many hats she should order. (*Hint:* The holding cost h may be negative.)
    b. How would her ordering decision change if she thought that leftover hats could be sold at cost ($4 each)?
    c. If she follows the policy specified in part (a), what will be her expected one-period profit? (*Hint:* For each demand level, calculate the profit or loss Jan will realize; then sum these results, weighting each by the corresponding demand probability.)

14. *The Use of Class Ranges.*   The University Bookstore maintains a stock of electronic pocket calculators to sell to students. The manager of the bookstore is currently preparing a large order in anticipation of students arriving at the beginning of the fall semester. The calculators cost the bookstore $30 and are retailed at $50. For each unit of unsatisfied demand, the bookstore will lose the $50 sale to other nearby competitors. However, calculators left over at the end of the fall rush are expected to remain unsold for an average of four months, during which time the carrying costs will be $5 per calculator. The demand density is given in the *class range* table on page 279 (Table 7.5).
    To illustrate the meaning of such a table, consider the first range $0 \leq D \leq 20$. This range contains 0.10 probability, and this probability is

TABLE 7.5

Demand D	Probability of class range
$0 \leq D \leq 20$	0.10
$21 \leq D \leq 30$	0.15
$31 \leq D \leq 40$	0.30
$41 \leq D \leq 50$	0.25
$51 \leq D \leq 60$	0.20

uniformly spread across the values of the range. Thus, for example, $P\{D \leq 10\} = (11/21)(0.10) = 0.0524$. Note that we used 21 because there are 21 values in the range $(0, 1, 2, \ldots, 19, 20)$ and the event $D \leq 10$ includes 11 of those values; thus the event $D \leq 10$ contains 11/21 of the total probability for that range. As another example, check that $P\{D \leq 22\} = 0.10 + (2/10)(0.15) = 0.13$. Determine how many calculators the bookstore manager should stock prior to the fall rush.

15. *Goods Subject to Spoilage.* Joanne Bieglespiker sells fresh apples as a city street vendor in Manhattan. She purchases each day's supply of apples from a large grower at a price of $10 a bushel and sells the apples individually for what amounts to a bushel price of $20. Apples left over at the end of the day can be sold at certain stores for $9 a bushel. Shortages represent lost revenue. The historical demand density is given in Table 7.6.
   a. Determine how many bushels Joanne should stock daily.
   b. Assume that local stores will no longer purchase left over apples from Joanne, so she decides to donate them to the Good Shepherd Shelter. Joanne estimates that it will cost her one dollar a bushel to transport the apples to the Shelter. Determine her optimal starting inventory for each day.

TABLE 7.6

Demand D	Probability
1	0.08
2	0.12
3	0.20
4	0.40
5	0.20

16. *Purchasing Discontinued Products.*   Zappo Drug Store has a chance to purchase a batch of a certain Model T digital watch, manufactured by Taxess Instruments. The company indicates to Zappo management that the Model T watch will be discontinued in 30 days, and a newer and better model will replace it. Zappo can buy the watches for $7 each and retail them at $12. Shortages would represent lost revenue, and watches left over at the end of the period would be sold for $3 each; however, the inventory holding costs plus additional advertising costs in the left-over watches will amount to $5. The marketing manager's analysis is given as follows:

Demand D	Probability
$0 \le D \le 25$	0.15
$26 \le D \le 50$	0.40
$51 \le D \le 80$	0.45

(See Exercise 14 for the interpretation of class range probabilities.) Determine the optimal order quantity for Zappo's purchase.

8   QUEUING MODELS

CONTENTS

1. INTRODUCTION

Whenever customers line up at a service facility, a queuing system exists. You may find yourself entering several such systems during a typical day. Some examples you may recognize include the following:

1. Lines forming in front of a water cooler
2. Cars lined up at a stoplight

281

3. People lined up in front of a checker at a grocery store, bookstore, or other place of business
4. Lines that form at a fast-food chain counter or at the drive-up service window
5. Cars lined up in various directions waiting for instructions from a police officer directing traffic at an intersection
6. Students waiting to see an academic counselor
7. Students waiting for the assistance of a programming consultant at a computer center

In this chapter we shall discuss a branch of management science that concerns itself with the general phenomenon of "customers lining up for service." We shall define precise terminology for describing such situations, recognize various structural models, and study certain mathematical quantities of interest that help quantify characteristics of such models. This mathematical framework will also assist us in designing system facilities. An example of this is the problem of determining the number of bank tellers to hire to reduce customer waiting time to acceptable levels.

2. THE STRUCTURE OF QUEUING SYSTEMS

Figure 8.1 shows the general structure of a queuing model. Customers arrive at a queuing system that consists of two components: (1) the line, or queue, that forms, and (2) the service facility. Customers line up in the queue to wait for service. Each customer, in turn, enters the service facility, receives service, and then departs from the system.

EXAMPLE 8.1 *A Gas Station.* Suppose a gas station consists of three pumps and a driveway, as shown in Fig. 8.2. In this *model* of a gas station, we assume that the gas pumps are identical (all pump regular gas). The queuing system consists of the driveway where the queue forms and the three gas pumps (which represent the service facility). Also, *as a modeling assumption,* we suppose in Fig. 8.2 that all arriving cars line up in a single line in front of the service facility. When a pump becomes available, the car at the head of the line moves to that pump for service (first come, first served, denoted FCFS).

You may not agree with the way we have chosen to model a gas station, and herein lies the key to the successful application of queuing concepts. Deciding *how to model* a queuing system is very important. In the case of a gas station, you might think it would be more realistic that arriving cars not form a single queue but instead form a queue in front of each of the pumps. Also, perhaps the pumps are not identical in their service capacity— that is, one pump is for regular gas, one for unleaded gas, and one for premium gas. ▲

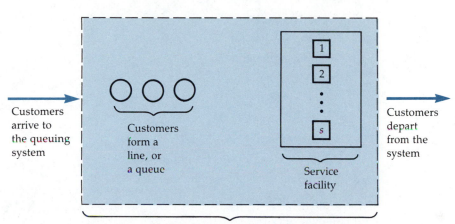

FIGURE 8.1   *Queuing-system structure.*

APPLICATIONS

The following applications appear in this chapter in text, examples, or problems:

Bank drive-up teller service

Bank facilities

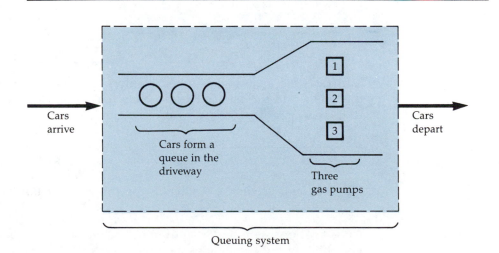

FIGURE 8.2   *A gas station.*

Computer center facilities

Computer printer facilities

Equipment selection

Facilities expansion

Fast-food chain

Freight unloading

Gas station model

Hospital emergency facilities

Machine-shop storage for in-process inventory

Maintenance facility for city vehicles

Medical clinic services/design

Medical services

Parking lot design

Police vehicle maintenance

Recreational facilities planning

Repair facilities

Selecting materials-handling equipment

Self-service car wash

Student registration center

Supermarket design/operation

Telephone switchboard operation

Toll gate operation

Tool-crib operation

Truck weigh station

In Table 8.1 we list some other queuing systems and identify the items in the queue and the service facility. Note that, in some cases, the servers go to the customer (fire department operation, for example).

Steps in Queuing Analysis

The general procedure to follow in working with queuing techniques can be described as follows:

STEP 1. The system under study must be viewed as a queuing system. Do you think of a gas station as a queuing system?

STEP 2. Choose an appropriate queuing model to represent the system. In the case of our gas station, at least three models come to mind: (a) three

TABLE 8.1   *Examples of Queuing Systems*

System	The queue or waiting line	Service facility
Airport	Planes in a holding pattern waiting to land	Landing strips
Bank	People	Tellers
Bridge	Vehicles	Toll booth
Car wash	Cars	Car-wash bays
Cargo loading/unloading	Ships Trucks Railroad cars	Docks or unloading facilities
City fire department	Buildings on fire	Fire trucks
Computer system	Computer programs being run	CPUs, printers, etc.
Court scheduling	Cases to be considered (docket)	Courts
Emergency medical aid	People	Ambulances
The game of golf	Golfers	Golf course
Job shop	Jobs to be processed or worked	Machines
Library	Books to be shelved	Librarian assistants
Office	Letters, memos, and other communications	Secretary or secretarial pool
Office telephone system	Callers on hold	Switchboard
Ski slope	Skiers	Ski slopes Chair lifts
Student registration	Students	Registration center

regular pumps with one queue in front of them, (b) three regular pumps with a separate queue in front of each, and (c) one regular pump, one unleaded pump, and one premium pump, with separate queues in front of each. In many cases, the practical situation will help decide the appropriate model to choose.

STEP 3. Use mathematical formulas or simulation methods (Chapter 12) to analyze the queuing model.

Through the use of examples and exercises, we hope to give you some practice in performing the analysis required for step 1. The following discussion will identify precisely the factors that characterize a queuing model. This terminology will give you a framework for conducting step 2. We shall then present the quantities useful in describing the behavior of a queuing system. In the remainder of the chapter, we give formulas and tables for these quantities and show how they are used to analyze several queuing models.

Components of a Queuing System

Look again at the general structure of a queuing system shown in Fig. 8.1. A queuing system consists of the following components:

THE INPUT POPULATION. How many potential customers can enter the queuing system? Suppose that ten machines are serviced by a single mechanic working in a factory. As the machines break down, they enter a queue of machines waiting to be repaired by the mechanic. Suppose that ten machines are working. Then one breaks down and enters repair, leaving nine working machines. The arrival rate of machines at the repair facility will now differ from the rate that existed when ten machines were working; that is, the number of potential customers has changed from ten to nine. Once a machine is repaired, it reenters the population of potential customers. This is an example of a **finite input population.** (The number of machines is finite.)

In practice, virtually every queuing system has a finite input population; however, the population of potential customers is often so large that it can be considered infinite. In the case of our gas station, if the number of cars in the city is 20,000, we can safely consider this population to be "infinite" relative to the three-pump service capacity.

THE INPUT OR ARRIVAL DISTRIBUTION. It is necessary to describe the distribution of customers entering the system. Do they arrive every five minutes (a **constant arrival distribution**), or is the arrival pattern random? There are two ways of expressing this arrival pattern: We can describe it in terms of the number of arrivals to the system per unit of time or, equivalently, we can describe it in terms of the time between successive arrivals (an **interarrival time distribution).**

THE SERVICE DISCIPLINE. The service discipline refers to the order in which arriving customers are served. FCFS refers to a *first come, first served* discipline, and LCFS refers to a *last come, first served* discipline. Customers may also be served in random order. (Did you ever enter a crowded delicatessen that did not use a number tag system for selecting the next customer?) Another discipline is called "priority." In an emergency room of a hospital, for example, a person arriving with a broken leg will have priority over a person with a minor bruise.

THE SERVICE FACILITY. The service facility is classified according to the number of servers available. A **single-channel** system consists of a single server with customers forming a single queue, as shown in Fig. 8.3.

The model of the gas station shown in Fig. 8.2 is an example of a **multiple-channel** system (having three channels). A multiple-channel system consists of a single queue in front of two or more parallel servers. A customer can be served by any one of the servers and then depart from the system.

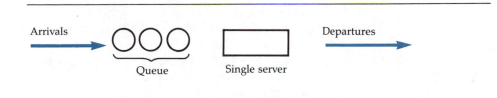

Arrivals   Queue   Single server   Departures

FIGURE 8.3

THE SERVICE DISTRIBUTION. This is generally specified in one of two ways: (1) How many customers can be served per unit time? or (2) How long does it take to serve a given customer? In either case, a probability distribution is used to describe the service rate.

SYSTEM CAPACITY. The system capacity equals the maximum number of customers allowed in the system (those in the queue plus those being served). The capacity may be finite (as in the case of a doctor's office that has a very small waiting room and only three examination rooms) or infinite (as in the case where cars are lined up on a highway in front of a toll booth).

OTHER SYSTEM CHARACTERISTICS. In practical queuing systems, customers may not enter the queue if there are already too many customers waiting; instead, they may **balk.** (Have you ever balked at a supermarket when the parking lot was completely full?)

Another situation involves customers who, after entering a queue, later decide to leave before receiving service. This is called **reneging.** (Have you ever reneged at a supermarket after joining the end of a waiting line of several customers, each of whom has a full cart of groceries?)

In the case of the supermarket, have you ever left a long waiting line in front of one checker to enter a shorter line in front of another checker? In such a case, **switching** has occurred.

Steady-State Queuing Statistics

In studying a queuing system, we are interested in characterizing and quantifying its behavior in a long-run-average sense. A queuing system that is allowed to operate for a long time is said to reach a **steady-state** condition. This is a mathematical notion that is somewhat difficult to define in a basic text such as this. However, for our purposes here, it is accurate for you to think of steady-state behavior in the following terms: *In the long run, and on the average, what can we expect to observe in the behavior of the system?*

Notation

The following notation and steady-state statistics will be used to describe the queuing systems we shall study:

n = number of customers in the system

p_n = (steady-state) probability that there are exactly n customers in the system

λ = average number of customers (arrivals) per unit time

μ = average number of customers a server can service per unit time

ρ = the traffic intensity (to be defined later)

L = the expected (average) number of customers in the system

L_q = the expected number of customers waiting in the queue

W = the expected time a customer will spend in the system (waiting and being served)

W_q = the expected time a customer will spend waiting in the queue

(In the above list, λ is the Greek letter "lambda," μ is the Green letter "mu," and ρ is the Greek letter "rho." In queuing studies, these symbols are standard.)

We hope you have not gotten lost or lost interest because of all these definitions and notation. In the next section we shall present our first queuing model along with a numerical example. You will then begin to develop a better feeling for the above concepts and statistics.

3. A SINGLE–CHANNEL MODEL

One of the simplest queuing models is referred to as the single-channel exponential model and is written in shorthand notation as the "$(M/M/1)$ system." The components of this model are the following:

1. The input population is infinite—that is, there are an infinite number of potential customers (arrivals).
2. The input (or arrival) distribution is Poisson distributed with rate λ. This means that the number of customers (arrivals) in one unit of time is a random variable that has a Poisson probability density. The average arrival rate per unit time is λ customers. (Equivalently, the time between successive customers arriving is a random variable having an exponential probability density with mean $1/\lambda$.) See Appendix F, Section 5, for a detailed discussion of these densities. In the notation "$(M/M/1)$," the first M means that the arrival pattern is Poisson. The meaning behind the use of M will be explained below.
3. The service discipline is first come, first served (FCFS).
4. The service facility consists of a single channel. The one in $(M/M/1)$ means "one channel."
5. The service distribution is also Poisson. The mean number of customers served per unit of time by a busy server is μ. (Equivalently, service time per customer is a random variable having an exponential probability density with a mean of $1/\mu$.) In the notation $(M/M/1)$, the second M means that the service rate is Poisson. We assume that $\lambda < \mu$: the average number

of customers (arrivals) per unit of time is less than the average number of customers who could be served by the system per unit time.
6. System capacity is assumed to be infinite.
7. Balking and reneging are not allowed.

Comment

Management scientists have found that use of the Poisson (or equivalently, the exponential) probability densities is justified in many situations. The use of these densities is very common in queuing theory because they greatly simplify the mathematical analysis. You might keep the following points in mind concerning the Poisson probability density. The Poisson probability density is a good tool to use for determining the number of events that will take place when:

1. The occurrence of an event is random, and the chance of an event happening in any unit time is constant. Thus the chance of an event (such as a customer arrival) in the first hour is the same as the chance of an event occurring in the second hour.
2. The occurrence of an event in one time period is independent of whether an event occurred in the previous time period. Thus the chance that an event (such as a customer arrival) occurs in the second hour does not depend on whether one occurred in the first hour.
3. There will be at most one event occurring in a small interval of time.

Queuing systems that have Poisson arrivals and service distributions are known as **Markov Processes;** thus the use of the "M" notation in (M/M/1), for example. A. A. Markov was a Russian mathematician who worked with such special processes around the early 1900s.

Steady-State Equations for the (M/M/1) System

The following equations can be shown to hold for the (M/M/1) system:

$$\rho = \frac{\lambda}{\mu} \tag{8-1a}$$

$$p_n = \rho^n(1 - \rho) \tag{8-1b}$$

$$L = \frac{\lambda}{\mu - \lambda} = \frac{\rho}{1 - \rho} \tag{8-1c}$$

$$L_q = \frac{\lambda^2}{\mu(\mu - \lambda)} = \frac{\rho^2}{1 - \rho} \tag{8-1d}$$

$$W = \frac{1}{\mu - \lambda} \tag{8–1e}$$

$$W_q = \frac{\lambda}{\mu(\mu - \lambda)} \tag{8–1f}$$

Traffic Intensity

The **traffic intensity** is denoted by ρ and is given by Eq. (8–1a). Traffic intensity equals the proportion of time that the server will be *busy* serving customers who arrive; it is sometimes referred to as the **utilization factor** of the queuing system. Since we have assumed that $\lambda < \mu$, we have that $\rho < 1$.

Idle Time

What proportion of time will the server be idle? If ρ equals the busy time, then $1 - \rho$ equals the idle time. This can also be seen from Eq. (8–1b). The server is idle when there are no customers in the system. The probability of there being no customers in the system is p_0, which from Eq. (8–1b) is

$$p_0 = \rho^0(1 - \rho) = 1(1 - \rho) = 1 - \rho$$

Mean Service Time

If the average number of customers served per unit time is μ, then the mean (or average) service time per customer is $1/\mu$ time units. For example, if $\mu = 10$ customers per hour, then mean service time is $1/\mu = 0.10$ hour (per customer).

We now present the numerical example we promised in Section 2.

EXAMPLE 8.2. *A Simple (M/M/1) Gas Station.* Joe's Service Station operates a single gas pump (see Figure 8.4). Cars arrive according to a Poisson distribution at an average rate of fifteen cars per hour. Joe can service cars at the rate of twenty cars per hour on the average, with service time per car following an exponential probability distribution. Assuming we model Joe's Service Station as an (M/M/1) queuing system, compute the steady-state statistics for the system.

Solution. We have $\lambda = 15$ and $\mu = 20$. Thus

$$\rho = \frac{\lambda}{\mu} = \frac{15}{20} = 0.75$$

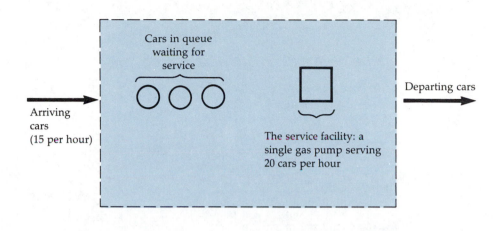

FIGURE 8.4

Joe's Gas Station as an (M/M/1) queuing system.

and we see that Joe will be busy servicing cars 75 percent of the time. (This leaves an idle time of $1 - \rho = 0.25$, or 25 percent, for Joe to do paperwork, maintenance, and so on.) From Eq. (8–1c)

$$L = \frac{\lambda}{\mu - \lambda} = \frac{15}{20 - 15} = 3$$

so on the average Joe can expect to find three cars at his station. From Eq. (8–1d)

$$L_q = \frac{\lambda^2}{\mu(\mu - \lambda)} = \frac{(15)^2}{20(20 - 15)} = 2.25$$

so on the average 2.25 cars will be waiting in line for service. (If you are wondering why L_q does not equal $L - 1$, see the discussion of key relationships in Section 5.) From Eqs. (8–1e) and (8–1f)

$$W = \frac{1}{\mu - \lambda} = \frac{1}{20 - 15} = 0.20 \text{ hour}$$

and

$$W_q = \frac{\lambda}{\mu(\mu - \lambda)} = \frac{15}{20(20 - 15)} = 0.15 \text{ hour}$$

On the average, a car spends 0.20 hour in the system (or 12 minutes) and 0.15 hour waiting for service (9 minutes).

To demonstrate the use of Eq. (8–1b), suppose we ask "What is the probability that there are four cars or less in the system?" This equals the sum

$$p_0 + p_1 + p_2 + p_3 + p_4$$

Note that from Eq. (8–1b)

$$p_n = \rho^n(1 - \rho)$$

$$= (0.75)^n (1 - 0.75)$$

$$= (0.75)^n (0.25)$$

Thus we have

n	$p_n = (0.75)^n(0.25)$
0	$[(0.75)^0](0.25) = 0.250$
1	$[(0.75)^1](0.25) = 0.188$
2	$[(0.75)^2](0.25) = 0.141$
3	$[(0.75)^3](0.25) = 0.105$
4	$[(0.75)^4](0.25) = \underline{0.079}$
	$\Sigma = 0.763$

There is a 76.3 percent chance of finding four or fewer cars lined up at the service station. ▲

Problems

1. *Maintenance Facility for City Vehicles.* The city of Craksmith maintains a central repair garage for its refuse-removal trucks. The number of trucks requiring repair seems to follow a random pattern, following a Poisson density, at the mean rate of five per day. The maintenance time on a truck is exponentially distributed, having a mean of 1/7-day per truck needing repair.
   a. What percentage of time is the repair facility busy repairing trucks?
   b. On the average, how many trucks are idle because they need repair?
   c. How long can a truck driver expect to wait before his or her truck enters the maintenance facility to be repaired?
   d. If a truck is in need of repair, how long on the average will the truck be out of service?
2. *Facilities Design.* Refer to Problem 1 above. The city engineer of Craksmith is planning to set aside an area of land near the repair facility to park trucks *waiting to be repaired.* If each truck requires 250 square feet of space, *on the average* how much space would be required?
3. Suppose an $(M/M/1)$ queuing system has the following arrival and service rates: $\lambda = 5$ customers/hour, $\mu = 10$ customers/hour.
   a. Draw a diagram of the queuing system (see Fig. 8.1). Label all parts of the system.
   b. What percentage of the time is the server busy?

c. Compute L, L_q, W, W_q, and the mean service time per customer.
d. Suppose it is observed that λ has increased to nine customers per hour and the service rate has not changed. Answer parts (b) and (c).

4. SENSITIVITY TO THE TRAFFIC INTENSITY

In the discussion of the basic $(M/M/1)$ system, we defined the traffic intensity by

$$\rho = \frac{\lambda}{\mu}$$

and stated that ρ equals the proportion of busy time for the system. Further, we required that λ be less than μ:

$$\lambda < \mu$$

This last condition is required for steady-state conditions to occur. If $\lambda \geq \mu$ the number of customers in the system will increase without limit; that is, L will be infinite.

Let us see if this sort of behavior is evident in the $(M/M/1)$ equations. Specifically, let us rewrite the expression for L (Eq. 8–1c) in terms of the traffic intensity ρ:

$$L = \frac{\lambda}{\mu - \lambda}$$

$$= \frac{\dfrac{\lambda}{\mu}}{\dfrac{\mu - \lambda}{\mu}} \quad \text{(divide numerator and denominator by } \mu\text{)}$$

$$= \frac{\dfrac{\lambda}{\mu}}{1 - \dfrac{\lambda}{\mu}} \quad \text{(simplify the denominator)}$$

$$= \frac{\rho}{1 - \rho} \quad \text{(use the definition of } \rho\text{)}$$

In Fig. 8.5 we graph L as a function of ρ. If $\rho = 0$, $L = 0$. As ρ gets close to one, note that L approaches infinity (gets larger). (Try a few examples: if $\rho = 1/2$, $L = 1$; if $\rho = 3/4$, $L = 3$; if $\rho = 99/100$, $L = 99$; if $\rho = 0.9999$, $L = 9999$; and so on.) Note that letting ρ get close to one is equivalent to letting

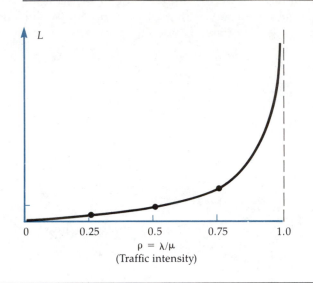

FIGURE 8.5

Sensitivity of L to the traffic intensity.

λ get close to μ. If you have taken a calculus course, you can summarize this discussion in terms of limits:

$$\lim_{\rho \to 1} L = +\infty$$

read "the limit of L as ρ approaches one is infinite."

Problems

1. Suppose a gas station is modeled as an $(M/M/1)$ queuing system with a service rate $\mu = 20$ cars per hour. Let λ take on the values 1, 5, 10, 15, 16, 17, 19, and 19.9 cars per hour. For each λ compute the expected number of cars in the system, L. Summarize your results by constructing a table, using the following headings:

λ	μ	ρ(busy time)	$L = \dfrac{\rho}{1-\rho}$

2. In Problem 1 above, construct a graph of L versus ρ as in Fig. 8.5. At a minimum, plot the ρ values computed in your table.

5. KEY RELATIONSHIPS

In every Poisson queuing system, certain relationships will always hold between L, L_q, W, and W_q. These are as follows:

$$L = \lambda W \tag{8-2}$$

$$L_q = \lambda W_q \tag{8-3}$$

$$W = W_q + \frac{1}{\mu} \tag{8-4}$$

You should check that each of these holds for the $(M/M/1)$ system. For example, consider Eq. (8-2). If we multiply Eq. (8-1e) by λ, we get

$$\lambda W = \lambda \left(\frac{1}{\mu - \lambda} \right) = \frac{\lambda}{\mu - \lambda} = L$$

which is Eq. (8-2).

What use do these relationships serve? If we know the value of any *one* of the four parameters, L, L_q, W, or W_q, we can solve for the other three using the key relationships.

EXAMPLE 8.3. *Use of the Key Relationships.* Suppose that we have an $(M/M/1)$ system in which $\lambda = 15$ and $\mu = 20$ (such as in Example 8.2). From Eq. (8-1e), we compute W as follows:

$$W = \frac{1}{\mu - \lambda} = \frac{1}{20 - 15} = 0.20$$

We could calculate L, L_q, and W_q using Eqs. (8-1c), (8-1d), and (8-1f) as we did in Example 8.2. Instead, we shall demonstrate the use of the key relationships.

Since we know W, we can use Eq. (8-4) to find W_q:

$$W_q = W - \frac{1}{\mu} = 0.20 - \frac{1}{20} = 0.15$$

Now that we know W_q, we can use Eq. (8-4) to find L_q:

$$L_q = \lambda W_q = 15(0.15) = 2.25$$

Finally, we can use Eq. (8-3) to find L:

$$L = \lambda W = 15(0.20) = 3$$ ▲

The Relationship Between L and L_q

If we put Eq. (8–4) into Eq. (8–2) for W, we get

$$L = \lambda W = \lambda \left(W_q + \frac{1}{\mu} \right) = \lambda W_q + \frac{\lambda}{\mu} = L_q + \rho \tag{8–5}$$

since $\lambda W_q = L_q$ and $\lambda/\mu = \rho$.

You might have thought that L should equal L_q plus one, not L_q plus ρ. The catch is that we are dealing with mathematical expectations. We can explain Eq. (8–5) more directly as follows:

L = The expected number of customers in the system

$$= \left(\begin{array}{c} \text{The expected number of} \\ \text{customers in the queue} \end{array} \right) + \left(\begin{array}{c} \text{The } \textit{expected} \text{ number of} \\ \text{customers in service} \end{array} \right) \tag{8–6}$$

Now, the expected number of customers *in service* is written as:

$$\left(\begin{array}{c} \text{Probability that} \\ \text{the system is busy} \end{array} \right) (1 \text{ customer}) + \left(\begin{array}{c} \text{Probability that} \\ \text{the system is idle} \end{array} \right) (0 \text{ customers})$$

$$= \rho(1) + (1 - \rho)(0) = \rho$$

Thus Eq. (8–6) becomes

$$L = L_q + \rho$$

which agrees with Eq. (8–5).

Problems

1. In an $(M/M/1)$ queuing model, results of a computer output analysis indicate that $L = 0.5$. Can you find the values of the other statistics (L_q, W, and W_q), assuming $\lambda = 5$ and $\mu = 15$?
2. If you are told that $L = 4$, can you compute ρ, the proportion of time the system is busy? (*Hint:* Use the results of Section 4.)

6. MULTIPLE-CHANNEL MODEL

A basic multiple-channel queuing model is the $(M/M/s)$ system. The only difference in the model components between the $(M/M/s)$ and the $(M/M/1)$ systems is that the $(M/M/s)$ system may have more than one service channel. In fact, the letter s stands for the number of parallel service channels.

EXAMPLE 8.4. An emergency room of a hospital contains a separate three-room section for patients (arrivals) with minor injuries. Each of these three rooms is staffed by one doctor assisted by one nurse. On the average, a doctor-nurse team can treat five people per hour. Records indicate that patients with minor injuries arrive at an average rate of ten per hour. Some brief statistical analysis indicates that arrivals and service completions are Poisson distributed.

Model Analysis

We can model the emergency room as an $(M/M/3)$ queuing system, as illustrated in Fig. 8.6. The patient arrivals are Poisson distributed. Patients wait in the waiting room until their turn comes for treatment. As soon as a doctor-nurse team becomes idle, the patient at the head of the line moves to that doctor-nurse team for treatment. *Each* doctor-nurse team is capable of treating five patients per hour.

Note that in practice the queue may not actually consist of a *line* of patients. Waiting patients may be seated at random in a waiting room with

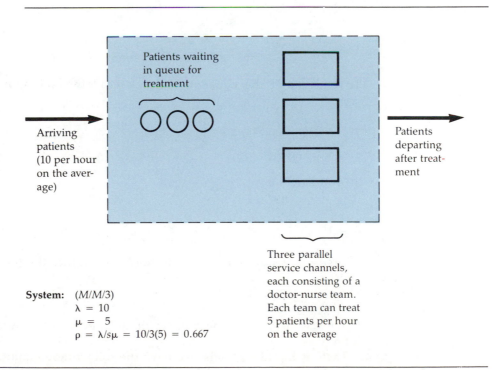

Patients waiting in queue for treatment

Arriving patients (10 per hour on the average)

Patients departing after treatment

Three parallel service channels, each consisting of a doctor-nurse team. Each team can treat 5 patients per hour on the average

System: $(M/M/3)$
$\lambda = 10$
$\mu = 5$
$\rho = \lambda/s\mu = 10/3(5) = 0.667$

FIGURE 8.6   *Emergency room model.*

a nurse-receptionist keeping a record of the order in which the patients arrived.

In Problem 1 of this section you are asked to analyze this queuing model.   ▲

Steady-State Equations for the ($M/M/s$) System

The notation is the same as it was before, except for the following two modifications:

μ = Average service rate *per service channel*   (8–7)

$$\rho = \frac{\lambda}{\mu s}$$

For example, in Example 8.4,

$\lambda = 10$

$\mu = 5$

$s = 3$

$$\rho = \frac{10}{(5)(3)} = 0.667$$

To understand the equations below, recall the definition of the factorial sign, "!":

$7! = (7)(6)(5)(4)(3)(2)(1) = 5,040$

$5! = (5)(4)(3)(2)(1) = 120$

$3! = (3)(2)(1) = 6$

$1! = 1$

$0! = 1$

First, for steady-state results to hold, we require the following condition:

$\lambda < s\mu$ (or $\rho < 1$)   (8–8)

Otherwise, if $\lambda \geq s\mu$, the number of customers in the system will grow to infinity.

Then, if Eq. (8–8) holds, we have the following equations for the ($M/M/s$) system:

$$p_0 = \left\{ \sum_{n=0}^{s-1} \frac{\left(\dfrac{\lambda}{\mu}\right)^n}{n!} + \frac{\left(\dfrac{\lambda}{\mu}\right)^s}{s!\left(1 - \dfrac{\lambda}{s\mu}\right)} \right\} \qquad (8\text{--}9a)$$

$$p_n = \begin{cases} \dfrac{\left(\dfrac{\lambda}{\mu}\right)^n}{n!}(p_0) & \text{if } 0 \le n \le s \qquad (8\text{--}9b) \\[6mm] \dfrac{\left(\dfrac{\lambda}{\mu}\right)^n}{s!\,s^{n-s}}(p_0) & \text{if } n \ge s \end{cases}$$

$$L_q = \frac{p_0\left(\dfrac{\lambda}{\mu}\right)^s \rho}{s!(1 - \rho)^2} \qquad (8\text{--}9c)$$

$$W_q = \frac{L_q}{\lambda} \qquad (8\text{--}9d)$$

$$W = W_q + \frac{1}{\mu} \qquad (8\text{--}9e)$$

$$L = \lambda W = L_q + \frac{\lambda}{\mu} \qquad (8\text{--}9f)$$

Equations (8–9b) and (8–9c) require the value of p_0 (the probability that the system is idle, that is, it has no customers). Since the formula for p_0 is somewhat complex, we have tabulated values of this statistic in Appendix L.

You should recognize Eqs. (8–9d), (8–9e), and (8–9f) to be the key relationships of Section 5. Thus, using λ, μ, and s, look up the value of p_0 in Appendix L, use this value in Eq. (8–9c) to get L_q, then use Eqs. (8–9d), (8–9e), and (8–9f) to get W_q, W, and L.

EXAMPLE 8.5. A self-service car wash has five identical bays. Arriving cars form a single queue in front of these bays. When a bay becomes empty, the car at the head of the line moves to that bay. Cars arrive according to a Poisson process at an average rate of twenty per hour. The time required to wash a car is random, following an exponential density with a mean of ten minutes. Compute the steady-state statistics L, L_q, W, W_q, and p_0 for this system.

Solution. The car wash can be modeled as an $(M/M/5)$ queuing system. It is clear that $\lambda = 20$. To find μ, note that the mean service time is $1/\mu$; but this equals 10 minutes or 1/6 hour. Thus

$$\frac{1}{\mu} = \frac{1}{6} \text{ hour/car}$$

$\mu = 6 \text{ cars/hour}$

We check to see that $\rho = \lambda/(\mu s) = 20/30$ is less than one.

Using these values and $s = 5$, we find the value of p_0 in Appendix L to be $p_0 = 0.0311$. From Eq. (8–9c)

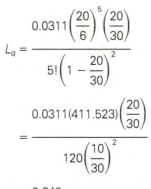

$$L_q = \frac{0.0311\left(\frac{20}{6}\right)^5\left(\frac{20}{30}\right)}{5!\left(1 - \frac{20}{30}\right)^2}$$

$$= \frac{0.0311(411.523)\left(\frac{20}{30}\right)}{120\left(\frac{10}{30}\right)^2}$$

$$= 0.640$$

so

$$W_q = \frac{L_q}{\lambda} = \frac{0.640}{20} = 0.032 \text{ hour}$$

$$W = W_q + \frac{1}{\mu} = 0.032 + \frac{1}{6} = 0.199 \text{ hour}$$

$$L = \lambda W = 20(0.199) = 3.98$$

▲

Problems

1. *Hospital Emergency Services.* For the hospital emergency room, Example 8.4:
   a. Find the value of ρ.
   b. Determine the percentage of time the three-room emergency ward has no patients.
   c. Find the value of L_q.
   d. Compute the values of L, W, and W_q.
   e. Why might the value of W_q have more relevance than the value of W in this example?
2. *Student Registration.* Students arriving at a student registration center of a

university must have their registration materials processed by an operator seated at a computer terminal. The system design calls for four operators to be on duty, each operator performing an identical service. Students arrive according to a Poisson process at an average rate of 100 per hour. Each operator can process 40 student registrants per hour with service time per student being exponentially distributed.

  a. What percentage of time are there no students in the registration center?
  b. How long does the average student spend in the registration center?
  c. On the average, how long is the line of students waiting to register?
  d. Once a student arrives at the center, how long on the average can he or she expect to stand in line waiting to see a computer terminal operator?
  e. If the *waiting area* inside the center building will comfortably accommodate five students, what percentage of time will there be students lined up *outside* the building?

7. FACILITIES-DESIGN APPLICATIONS

Thus far we have given sets of steady-state equations for the two queuing models $(M/M/1)$ and $(M/M/s)$. We can use these mathematical models to assist in the design of service facilities, as illustrated in the examples of this section.

EXAMPLE 8.6. *Planning In-Process Storage for a Machine Shop.* Consider a machine operating in a plant. This machine is designed to perform various operations on arriving jobs. The time to process a job is a random variable having an exponential probability density with a mean of five minutes. Job arrivals follow a Poisson process with a mean rate of seven per hour. Jobs waiting to be processed are placed in a storage area in front of the machine. If this area fills up, the newly arriving jobs must be placed in an aisle next to a wall. The production manager is currently planning the capacity of the storage area. Each waiting machine would occupy 9 square feet of space. How much floor space should be planned for the storage area if it is to be adequate at least 80 percent of the time?

Solution. An $(M/M/1)$ model is appropriate for this system. The mean rate is $\lambda = 7$, and since the mean service time is 5/60 hour, we can find μ as follows:

$$\text{Mean service time} = \frac{1}{\mu} = \frac{5}{60} \text{ hour/job}$$

$$\mu = 12 \text{ jobs/hour}$$

Next, we compute the probabilities of the system state, that is, the values of p_n. We cumulate the p_n until we reach at least 0.80. Recall that p_n is given by Eq. (8–1b):

$$p_n = \rho^n(1 - \rho)$$

$$= \left(\frac{7}{12}\right)^n \left(1 - \frac{7}{12}\right)$$

$$= \left(\frac{7}{12}\right)^n \left(\frac{5}{12}\right)$$

Thus we construct Table 8.2.

If the storage area is 9 square feet, it will be adequate 80.2 percent of the time, since 80.2 percent of the time there are two jobs or less in the system, one of which will occupy the storage area.   ▲

EXAMPLE 8.7. *Planning the Number of Bank Tellers to Hire.* The First National Bank of Boonesville has decided to operate its lobby service according to an *(M/M/s)* model. Customers arrive at the bank at an average rate of forty per hour. Each bank teller can serve ten people per hour on the average. How many bank tellers should be hired so that the average time a customer spends waiting in the queue does not exceed 0.75 minute?

Solution. Since 0.75 minute equals 0.0125 hour, we want to find the *first s* such that $W_q \leq 0.0125$ hour.

We have that $\lambda = 40$, $\mu = 10$. Since $\lambda/(s\mu)$ must be less than one, we must hire at least five tellers. So $s \geq 5$.

We next construct Table 8.3 by increasing s until W_q is less than 0.0125. For each s, use Appendix L to find p_0, then use Eq. (8–9c) to get L_q, and finally use Eq. (8–9d) to compute W_q.

Thus the bank must hire at least seven tellers in order that W_q not exceed 0.0125 hour.   ▲

Problems

1. *Determining the requirements for providing medical service.* Refer to the emergency room example in Section 6 (Example 8.4). For treatment of minor

TABLE 8.2

n	p_n	Cumulative sum of the p_n
0	0.417	0.417
1	0.243	0.660
2	0.142	0.802

TABLE 8.3

s	p_0	L_q	W_q
5	0.0130	2.219	0.0555
6	0.0163	0.556	0.0140
7	0.0180	0.182	0.0046

injuries, the doctors have decided that a patient should not have to wait longer than four minutes. What is the minimum number of doctor-nurse teams necessary to provide this level of medical treatment?

2. *Providing customer service at a fast-food chain.* A fast-food chain outlet provides a drive-up window for the convenience of its customers. Based on some observations, it is assumed that cars enter the drive-up lane at a Poisson rate of fifteen per hour. If n workers are assigned to work as a *team* at the drive-up window, an average of $8n$ cars can be served per hour, with service time per car being exponentially distributed. The manager of the food chain believes that a customer should not wait longer than four minutes to be served. What is the minimum number of workers that should be assigned to the drive-up window team?

8. COST-MINIMIZATION MODELS

In some queuing applications it is possible to design systems that minimize costs per unit of time for system operation. In general we can use the following cost equation:

$$TC = SC + WC \qquad\qquad (8\text{--}10)$$

where TC is the total cost per hour, SC is the service cost per hour, and WC is the waiting cost per hour.

The expression for SC will depend upon the particular application. However, for our purposes here, we can write down a general algebraic expression for WC. Suppose the cost of having one customer wait one hour (in the queue or in service) is c_w. On the average a customer spends W hours in the system, so the average waiting cost per customer is Wc_w. But since λ customers arrive per hour to the system, in steady-state, we use the key relationship $L = \lambda W$, Eq. (8–2), to obtain the total waiting cost per hour:

$$WC = \lambda(Wc_w) = (\lambda W)c_w = Lc_w \qquad\qquad (8\text{--}11)$$

EXAMPLE 8.8. *Freight Unloading.* Workfor Metals purchases metals to be recycled from several sources. These metals consist of steel bars and sheets, aluminum shapes, and iron plates. Truckload shipments of scrap metals arrive at Workfor in a more or less random pattern at an average rate of one truckload per day. These trucks are owned and operated by Workfor Metals. Each shipment must be unloaded by a crew of workers. A combination of unloading operations is used: simple dumping, use of a crane or forklift, and direct manual labor. A crew of n workers can unload $0.8n$ trucks per day.

For each day that a truck is detained in unloading, a cost of $300 is incurred (due to lost productive use of the truck and hourly wages of the truck driver and his or her assistant). Each worker in the unloading crew is paid $105 per day.

Determine the optimal number of crew members to hire, assuming that arrival and service rates are Poisson.

Solution. We model the system as an $(M/M/1)$ queue with $\lambda = 1$ truck per day. The service rate $\mu = 0.8n$, where $n =$ the number of crew members.

Note: We have designed the system as a single-channel model. The reason for this is that the *entire* crew works to unload each truck as it arrives. If each worker worked alone unloading separate trucks, we would have an $(M/M/s)$ system with $s =$ the number of workers. Of course, μ would then refer to the number of trucks a worker could unload per day working alone.

The problem is to determine the value of n that minimizes the total cost per day.

If n workers are on the crew, the service cost is given by

$$SC = 105n \quad (\$/\text{day for wages})$$

The waiting cost is given by Eq. (8–11). We know that

$$c_w = 300 \quad (\$/\text{day/truck})$$

and we can determine L by using Eq. (8–1c) with $\lambda = 1$ and $\mu = 0.8n$:

$$L = \frac{\lambda}{\mu - \lambda} = \frac{1}{0.8n - 1}$$

Thus the total cost equation, Eq. (8–10), becomes

$$TC = 105n + \frac{300}{0.8n - 1}$$

In this equation the total cost per day, TC, is a function of the *decision* variable n. We must choose n to minimize TC.

Recall the condition necessary for steady-state: $\lambda < \mu$. Thus we must choose n to be at least 2. For $n = 2$

$$TC = 105(2) + \frac{300}{0.8(2) - 1} = \$710/\text{day}$$

For $n = 3$

$$TC = 105(3) + \frac{300}{0.8(3) - 1} = \$529/\text{day}$$

For $n = 4$

$$TC = 105(4) + \frac{300}{0.8(4) - 1} = \$556/\text{day}$$

Thus $n = 3$ is optimal, and our decision is to hire three crew members (see Fig. 8.7). In Problem 1 of this section, you are asked to calculate the steady-state operating characteristics of this system. ▲

The Trade-off Between Service Cost and Waiting Cost

Recall from Eq. (8–10) that the general expression for the total cost per unit time to operate a queuing system is $TC = SC + WC$. We demonstrated the use of this equation in Example 8.8 (Freight Unloading). The total cost in that case was

$$TC = 105n + \frac{300}{0.8n - 1}$$

The variable n is a measure of the level of service provided. As n is increased, the service cost, $105n$, increases and the waiting cost $300/(0.8n - 1)$ decreases, as you would expect. These two cost components and their sum, TC, are shown in Fig. 8.8. The optimal trade-off point occurs at $n = 3$.

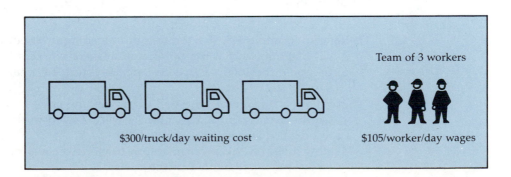

Team of 3 workers

$300/truck/day waiting cost $105/worker/day wages

FIGURE 8.7

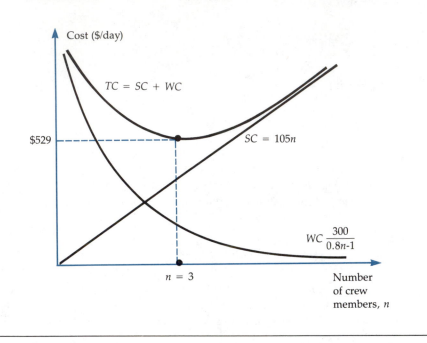

Cost ($/day)

TC = SC + WC

SC = 105n

$529

WC $\dfrac{300}{0.8n-1}$

n = 3

Number
of crew
members, n

FIGURE 8.8   *The service cost/waiting cost trade-off.*

In general, this sort of trade-off between the two cost components will hold in other queuing problems: the greater the level of service provided the higher the service cost and the lower the waiting cost. The problem of minimizing total cost involves determining the optimal trade-off between the two costs.

Problems

1. Refer to Example 8.8. For the freight unloading problem presented there, it was determined that the optimal number of workers to hire was three.
   a. Compute the total service cost per day and the total waiting cost per day.
   b. What percentage of time will the unloading crew be idle?
   c. On the average how many trucks will be idled in the system (waiting to be unloaded or being unloaded)?
   d. How long, on the average, can a truck driver expect to rest while his or her truck is detained in the system?
2. Robert Quigly is organizing a small business to perform home repairs for individual homeowners. Quigly estimates that calls from homeowners will

arrive randomly at an average rate of three per day. To attract customers, Quigly has advertised that he will give a $5 per day discount for each day a customer is made to wait for work to *begin* on his or her home. A team of n workers can perform $2n$ jobs per day on the average. Quigly plans to pay each of his workers $20 per day. How many workers should he hire?

Hint: The method of solving this problem is the same as presented in the text, except that the waiting cost is based on L_q rather than on L: $WC = L_q c_w$.

3. For Problem 2 above, construct a graph of the total daily cost function versus the number of team members. (See Fig. 8.8 as an example.)
4. Solve Problems 2 and 3, assuming the discount is $14 per day and workers' wages are $15 per day.

9. NON-POISSON SERVICE RATES: A USEFUL MODEL

In the $(M/M/1)$ and $(M/M/s)$ systems we made the assumption that the service rate (customers served per unit time) has a Poisson probability density. This is equivalent to assuming that the *time* to serve a customer has an exponential probability density.

The assumption that customer arrivals are Poisson distributed is generally a reasonable assumption, since the Poisson probability density is ideal for modeling random arrivals. However, often we would like to have more flexibility concerning the probability density of service times. For example, suppose the time to service a customer is constant (such as five minutes per customer), or suppose service time follows a normal probability density. Are such systems easy to analyze mathematically? Fortunately, the answer is "yes."

The queuing system we wish to discuss is usually referred to as the "$(M/G/1)$ system." The M stands for Poisson arrivals, the G means general service time, and the one means the system has one channel.

Suppose the time required to serve a customer has mean $1/\mu$ and variance σ^2, and assume that $\rho = \lambda/\mu < 1$. Then the following steady-state equations can be used:

$$p_0 = 1 - \rho \quad \text{(idle time)} \qquad (8\text{-}12a)$$

$$L_q = \frac{\lambda^2 \sigma^2 + \rho^2}{2(1 - \rho)} \qquad (8\text{-}12b)$$

$$W_q = \frac{L_q}{\lambda} \qquad (8\text{-}12c)$$

$$W = W_q + \frac{1}{\mu} \qquad (8\text{-}12d)$$

and

$$L = \lambda W \tag{8–12e}$$

$$L = L_q + \rho \tag{8–12f}$$

Which of these equations do you recognize as being a key relationship discussed in Section 5? Equation (8–12b) is the Pollaczek-Khintchine formula (which you should feel free to call the P-K formula).

EXAMPLE 8.9. *Normal Service Rate Density.* Consider an $(M/G/1)$ system in which arrivals occur according to a Poisson process at a rate of five per hour. The time it takes to service a customer is normally distributed with a mean of ten minutes and a standard deviation of two minutes. Determine the steady-state statistics of this system.

Solution. The mean service time is 1/6 hour per customer. We check that the steady-state assumption holds:

$$\rho = \frac{\lambda}{\mu} = \frac{5}{6} = 0.833 < 1$$

The proportion of time the server is idle is calculated from Eq. (8–12a) to be

$$p_0 = 1 - \rho = 0.167$$

and equals the probability that there are no customers in the system.

The other quantities of interest are easily computed from the above equations (with $\mu = 6$ and $\sigma = 2/60$ hours):

$$L_q = \frac{(5)^2 (2/60)^2 + (0.833)^2}{2(1 - 0.833)} = 2.167$$

$$W_q = \frac{2.167}{5} = 0.433$$

$$W = 0.433 + 1/6 = 0.600$$

$$L = 5(0.600) = 3.000$$

Note that since the standard deviation is 2, the variance is $(2)^2 = 4$. ▲

EXAMPLE 8.10. *An Empirical Distribution of Service Time.* Arrivals at AAA Transmission Repair are observed to be random at the Poisson rate of 1.5 per day. The time required to repair transmissions varies, and a frequency distribution of this time is given in Table 8.4. The frequencies are converted

TABLE 8.4   *An Empirical Service-Time Distribution*

(1) Service time (days)	(2) Number of times observed	(3) Probability	(4) (1) × (3)	(5) (1) minus the mean	(6) $(5)^2$	(7) (2) × (6)
0.25	100	0.274	0.068	−0.242	0.058564	5.85640
0.50	200	0.548	0.274	0.008	0.000064	0.01280
0.75	40	0.110	0.082	0.258	0.066564	2.66256
1.00	25	0.068	0.068	0.508	0.258064	6.45160
	$\Sigma = 365$	$\Sigma = 1.000$	$\Sigma = 0.492$		$\Sigma = 0.383256$	$\Sigma = 14.98336$

to probabilities by dividing by the total number of observations (365). The mean service time is computed by summing the products of each service time multiplied by its probability and is given in Table 8.4 as 0.492 day. The variance is also estimated by summing the weighted squares of the deviations from the mean and dividing by 365. (If you are "statistically conscientious," you would divide by the number of degrees of freedom, 365 − 1 = 364, instead of by 365.)

Thus the mean service time and its variance are

$$\frac{1}{\mu} = 0.492 \text{ day}$$

$$\sigma^2 = 14.98336/365 = 0.041 \text{ day}$$

Queuing Analysis

We model the system as an $(M/G/1)$

$$\lambda = 1.5 \text{ cars/day}$$

$$\mu = \frac{1}{0.492} = 2.03 \text{ cars/day}$$

and check to see that the steady-state condition holds:

$$\rho = \frac{\lambda}{\mu} = \frac{1.5}{2.03} < 1$$

In Problem 1 at the end of this section you are asked to verify the following:

$$p_0 = 0.261$$

$$L_q = 5.358 \text{ (cars)}$$

$$W_q = 3.572 \text{ (days)}$$

$$W = 4.064 \text{ (days)}$$

$$L = 6.096 \text{ (cars)}$$ ▲

Problems

1. *An Empirical Distribution of Service Time.* Verify the calculations of p_0, L_q, W_q, W, and L shown in Example 8.10 above.
2. *Constant Service Times.* Suppose service time is a constant—that is, assume it takes exactly $1/\mu$ time units to service each and every customer.
   a. What is the variance in this case?
   b. Write a simplified expression for L_q, Eq. (8–12b), using the variance of part (a).
   c. Give three practical examples of systems where the service time is a constant.
3. *A Comparison of Service-Time Distributions.* In this problem you are asked to compare three different systems:

SYSTEM A: (*M/M/1*). Let $\lambda = 5$ and $\mu = 6$. From Appendix F we know that the variance of this exponential service time is $(1/\mu)^2 = (1/6)^2 = 1/36$.

SYSTEM B: (*M/G/1*). Let $\lambda = 5$ and $\mu = 6$. Also, assume the service time variance is 1/36, which is the same as that for the (*M/M/1*) system above.

SYSTEM C: (*M/G/1*). Let $\lambda = 5$, $\mu = 6$. Also assume the variance is 0; thus the service time is the constant 1/6.
   Fill in Table 8.5.

10. DIFFERENT TYPES OF CUSTOMER CLASSES

Thus far we have assumed that the customers (arrivals) were identical with respect to their service needs. However, in practice, it is common for cus-

TABLE 8.5

	λ	μ	ρ	p_0	L	L_q	W	W_q
System A								
System B								
System C								

tomers to require different types of service. In such situations we say that there exist **heterogeneous** (different) customer classes. Many such systems are easily handled, as the next example demonstrates.

EXAMPLE 8.11. *Different Customer Classes in a Supermarket.* Supershopper Supermarket operates two types of checkout lanes: an express lane (for customers purchasing eight items or less) and a regular lane. The person at the express lane cash register can check out fifteen customers per hour, and a person working at the regular checkout lane can service eleven customers per hour on the average. The average arrival rate of customers at the checkout area is fifteen per hour. Sixty percent of these have over eight grocery items. Assume the arrival and service rates are Poisson distributed, and analyze the steady-state system behavior.

Solution. From the data of the problem, 60 percent or nine customers arrive at the regular lane per hour and six customers arrive at the express lane per hour. It is a fact, from probability theory, that these separate arrival rates are also Poisson distributed. (You may be thinking "Isn't that obvious?" and we agree that it would seem so.) Thus as in Figure 8.9, we can view the system as two separate $(M/M/1)$ systems:

1. Regular lane system: $\lambda = 9$, $\mu = 11$.
2. Express lane system: $\lambda = 6$, $\mu = 15$.

Using the basic $(M/M/1)$ equations of Section 3, Eqs. (8–1a)–(8–1f), we have constructed Table 8.6.

From that table we see that, on the average, there will be 5.167 customers in the system with 3.949 customers lined up waiting to check out. The two

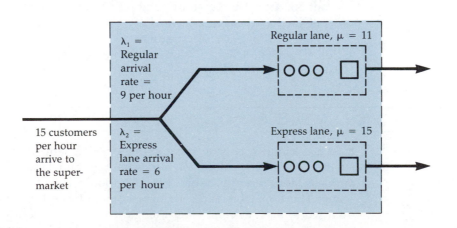

FIGURE 8.9   *Different customer classes at Supershopper Supermarket.*

TABLE 8.6   *Supershopper Supermarket Analysis*

	λ	μ	ρ	p_0	L	L_q	W (in hours)	W_q (in hours)
Regular lane	9	11	0.818	0.182	4.500	3.682	0.500	0.409
Express lane	6	15	0.400	0.600	0.667	0.267	0.111	0.044
				Σ	5.167	3.949		

systems are considered independent, so the probability that the system is empty is the product of the respective values of p_0. The proportion of time that there are no customers at the checkout area is

(p_0 for regular lane) × (p_0 for express lane) = 0.182(0.600) = 0.109

As a final note related to facilities design, you will notice the long waiting period (0.5 hour) in the regular lane subsystem. Thus Supershopper should consider the following options: (1) hire a faster checker for this lane; (2) provide more help for this checker (such as a bagger); or (3) add a second regular lane checkout register.   ▲

Problems

1. For the Supershopper problem (Example 8.11), construct a diagram similar to Fig. 8.9 and a table similar to Table 8.6 using the following additional assumption:
   Supershopper management decides to add a second regular lane checkout counter. The person operating the new register works at the same rate as the other regular checker. Also assume that half the regular customers go to one of the regular checkers and half go to the other.
2. Solve Problem 1 above, assuming that the two regular checkers are arranged in an (M/M/2) system.

11. SELF-SERVICE FACILITIES

It is becoming increasingly common for merchants to provide self-service facilities for their customers. Supermarkets and large drug stores are examples. More recently, large discount food retailers have appeared on the scene. These retailers allow their customers to perform all or most of their own work, such as removing a single can of food from an unpacked case, pricing the can, and bagging their own groceries. The same sort of structure exists in large discount liquor warehouses.

Other examples of self-service systems include:

- Golf courses
- Self-service car washes
- Self-service gas stations
- Vending-machine areas in cafeterias
- Parking lots
- Mailboxes on street corners
- Post office boxes
- Hardware stores

Some of these self-service systems can be designed as $(M/M/s)$ queuing models. For example, in the case of the self-service car wash, s = the number of wash bays and μ = the average number of cars passing through each bay per unit of time. However, what about larger systems such as a supermarket?

In a supermarket a customer enters the store and, once he or she obtains a cart, proceeds to place groceries in the cart without delay. This aspect of self-service is carried on throughout the store with essentially no waiting involved. (Of course, two people may reach at the same time for a box of cereal, but the delay caused by such an incident is negligible.) What we are getting at here is that, *essentially*, the number of servers is *infinite*. The reason for this observation is that no waiting time occurs or, viewed another way, no queue forms. Another point to emphasize is that we are looking only at that subsystem of the supermarket, which consists of people shopping through aisles of food items. What happens at the checkout counter(s) is quite another matter. This brings us to our next queuing system.

The $(M/M/\infty)$ Model

In the notation "$(M/M/\infty)$" the two Ms have the same meaning as before. The "∞" means "infinitely many servers" (or "no waiting is necessary").

The steady-state results for this system are

$$\rho = \frac{\lambda}{\mu} \qquad\qquad (8\text{--}13a)$$

(and we do *not* require that ρ be less than one),

$$p_n = \frac{e^{-\rho}\rho^n}{n!} \quad n = 0, 1, 2, 3, \ldots \qquad\qquad (8\text{--}13b)$$

$$L = \rho \qquad\qquad (8\text{--}13c)$$

$$W = \frac{1}{\mu} \qquad\qquad (8\text{--}13d)$$

$$L_q = 0 \tag{8–13e}$$

$$W_q = 0 \tag{8–13f}$$

(Recall that $e = 2.71828$.)

EXAMPLE 8.12. *A Self-Service System.* Supershopper Supermarket has fifteen customers entering per hour on the average. Each customer spends an exponentially distributed amount of time shopping before approaching the checkout counters. The average time spent shopping is twenty minutes.

1. On the average how many customers can be found shopping in the aisles?
2. What is the average length of time a customer spends shopping in the aisles?
3. Find the probability of there being six or more customers shopping in the aisles.

Solution. We have $\lambda = 15$, $\mu = 3$ (since $1/\mu = 20/60$).

1. $L = \rho = \lambda/\mu = 15/3 = 5$ means that five people can be found shopping in the aisles on the average.
2. $W = 1/\mu = 1/3$ hour (or 20 minutes) is the length of time spent in the system.
3. The required probability can be found by computing one minus the probability of five or fewer customers. We determine the probability of n customers in the system as follows:

$$p_n = \frac{e^{-\rho}\rho^n}{n!} = \frac{e^{-5}5^n}{n!}$$

We then construct Table 8.7 to find $p_0 + p_1 + p_2 + p_3 + p_4 + p_5$. The number e^{-5} is found (either by using a pocket calculator or by referring to Appendix J) to be 0.00674.

Thus the answer to part (3) is $1 - 0.61615 = 0.38385$.   ▲

Problem

1. Cars arrive in a large parking area serving a shopping center at the average rate of 100 per hour. The average time a customer spends in the shopping center is thirty minutes. Assuming the interarrival time and shopping time are exponentially distributed: (a) On the average how many cars are in the parking lot? (b) What is the probability that the parking lot is empty?

TABLE 8.7

n	p_n	
0	0.00674	$\left(\dfrac{(0.00674)(5^0)}{0!}\right)$
1	0.03370	$\left(\dfrac{(0.00674)(5^1)}{1!}\right)$
2	0.08425	
3	0.14042	
4	0.17552	
5	0.17552	
Σ	0.61615	

12. QUEUING NETWORKS

In many practical situations, a system may be composed of a combination of the $(M/M/1)$ and $(M/M/s)$ models. The Supershopper Supermarket problem in Sections 10 and 11 is an example of a $(M/M/\infty)$ system (people shopping in the aisles) followed by a checkout system [two or more $(M/M/s)$ systems]. We can even divide the checkout system into three separate systems: (1) the groceries are priced out at the cash register, (2) they are bagged, and (3) they are taken to the customer's car. Such systems are called *queuing networks*.

A **series system** consists of one subsystem followed by another; that is, a customer must go through one subsystem and then through the succeeding subsystem(s).

A **parallel system** involves two or more subsystems arranged so that a customer must only go through one of the subsystems.

These concepts are illustrated in Fig. 8.10. In that figure, a subsystem (enclosed in a dashed box) may be an $(M/M/1)$ or an $(M/M/s)$ system.

Examples of series systems include:

- A doctor's office in which a patient is first seen by a nurse and then by the doctor
- A job shop in which a part is processed first on one machine and then passes to the next machine for further machining
- The supermarket: waiting for a cart, followed by shopping for the groceries, followed by the checkout system
- A ski slope: waiting for a chair lift, followed by a wait for open space on the slope
- Student registration, where a student must go from one table to the next

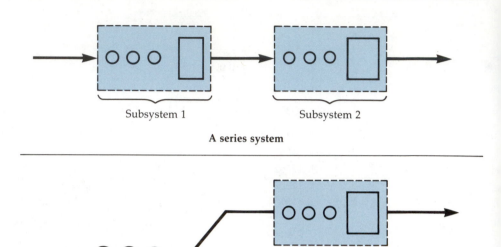

Subsystem 1   Subsystem 2

A series system

A parallel system

FIGURE 8.10   *Queuing networks.*

In analyzing Poisson systems in series, the following major result of operations research can be used:

The output rate of a system equals its input rate in steady-state. This output rate becomes the input rate for the system which follows.

Although this may sound confusing at first, an example will show that the idea is very simple. Consider a series system that consists of an $(M/M/1)$ followed by an $(M/M/1)$, as shown in Fig. 8.11. Let us assume that customers arrive at system 1 at the rate of $\lambda_1 = 10$ people per hour and that the server at system 1 works at the rate of $\mu_1 = 20$ people per hour. Then the major result stated above says that, in the long run, the average number of customers coming *out* of system 1 = $\lambda_1 = 10$ people per hour. Since these same people must then enter system 2, the arrival rate at system 2 = $\lambda_2 = 10$ people per hour. (Note that the value of $\mu_1 = 20$ has nothing to do with this.)

The major result goes on to state something more:

The subsystems of such a *network* may be treated independently of one another.

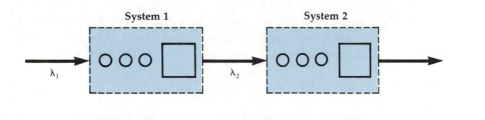

System 1   System 2

FIGURE 8.11

The example presented below will tie all of this together for you.

EXAMPLE 8.13. *Student Registration System.* The student registration system of a local college consists of the following three phases:

1. The student must first go to table 1 for a preliminary checking of registration status.
2. The student then goes to any of tables, 2, 3, or 4 to pay tuition.
3. The student then goes to table 5 for final checking, and departs.

The students arrive at a Poisson rate of thirty per hour. The person at table 1 can service students at a Poisson rate of forty students per hour, each of the workers at tables 2, 3, and 4 can service twenty students per hour, and the person working at table 5 can service fifty students per hour.

A diagram of this registration system is given in Fig. 8.12. The system consists of three models in series: $(M/M/1)$, followed by $(M/M/3)$, followed by $(M/M/1)$.

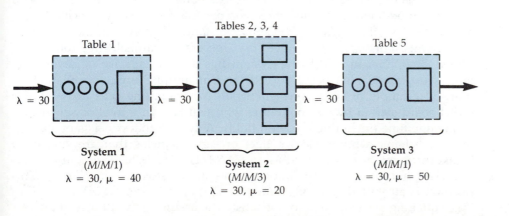

FIGURE 8.12   *Student registration center.*

Using the major results stated in the text, we can deduce the following: For the $(M/M/1)$ at table 1, $\lambda = 30$, $\mu = 40$; for the $(M/M/3)$ at tables 2, 3, and 4, $\lambda = 30$, $\mu = 20$; and for the $(M/M/1)$ at table 5, $\lambda = 30$, $\mu = 50$.

Since the three systems are to be treated independently, the total number of students in the registration center is as follows:

L (at system 1) + L (at system 2) + L (at system 3)

Also, the probability that there are no students in the center equals the product of the p_0's for the three systems. In Exercise 24 at the end of this chapter, you are asked to compute these steady-state quantities.   ▲

13. CONCLUDING REMARKS

In this chapter you studied various basic queuing models:

- $(M/M/1)$—single-channel
- $(M/M/s)$—multiple-channel
- $(M/G/1)$—single-channel, non-Poisson service rates
- Poisson queuing systems having heterogeneous customer types
- $(M/M/\infty)$—self-service facilities
- Networks of Poisson systems

Other Topics

Steady-state equations are also available for queuing systems that have finite capacities (such as a medical clinic) and for systems in which the population of arrivals is finite (see Section 2). There is a notation used to represent such systems. In addition to the first three components $(M/M/s)$, we include three more. For example, $(M/M/2)$: $(FCFS/7/\infty)$ stands for a system that has Poisson arrivals; Poisson service rates, two servers in parallel; first come, first served discipline, in which the system has a total capacity of seven customers (in queue plus being served) and an infinite input population. A practical example of such a system would be telephone calls arriving at a switchboard staffed by two operators who will handle a total of seven calls at any one time (including those on hold). A system that consists of a single repair mechanic who services a fleet of eight vehicles that are subject to breakdowns might be modeled as an $(M/M/1)$: $(FCFS/8/8)$, where the second eight indicates the population of potential customers (machines). This notation is attributed to D. G. Kendall (1953) and A. Lee (1966).

For queuing systems that do not satisfy the assumption of Poisson arrivals and service rates, the analysis becomes much more complex. A widely used technique for such systems is computer simulation (Chapter 12).

A field that has recently attracted much interest is **queuing optimization,** in which the objective centers on either optimizing the behavior of the queue over time or minimizing the cost of system operation over time. Section 8 of this chapter is a brief introduction to some of the more basic aspects of queuing optimization.

TERMINOLOGY

After studying this chapter you should be familiar with the following terms:

TERM	SECTION
balking	2
constant arrival distribution	2
empirical service-time distribution	9
facilities design	7
FCFS	2
finite input population	2
heterogeneous customer classes	10
idle time	3
input (arrival) distribution	2
input population	2
interarrival time distribution	2
key relationships	5
LCFS	2
Markov processes	3
$(M/G/1)$—non-Poisson service rates	9
$(M/M/1)$	3
$(M/M/s)$	6
$(M/M/\infty)$	11
multiple-channel system	2
parallel system	12
priority discipline	2
queue	2
queuing networks	12
queuing optimization	13
reneging	2
self-service facilities	11
series system	12
service discipline	2
service distribution	2

service facility	2
single-channel system	2
steady-state (statistics)	2
switching	2
system capacity	2
traffic intensity (utilization factor)	3

User Beware

At times there has been some criticism concerning the use and benefits of queuing theory when applied to management problems. It is generally true in mathematics and the sciences that a model is only of value to the extent that the real-world situation satisfies its assumptions. The same is true here. Before applying a queuing model, it is first *essential* to have an adequate knowledge of the assumptions involved and to check that the assumptions are satisfied by the problem being analyzed. If the assumptions are not adequately satisfied, another approach may provide a better solution to the problem.

List of Examples

Several numerical examples were presented to illustrate the concepts and computations involved in analyzing queuing systems. You may wish to refer back to these as you work to solve the exercises in this chapter. For ease of reference we list some useful examples below:

Example	Page	Concepts illustrated
8.2	290	$(M/M/1)$ calculations
8.3	295	Use of the key relationships
8.5	299	$(M/M/5)$ calculations
8.6	301	Facilities design, $(M/M/1)$, planning for adequate storage space
8.7	302	Facilities design, $(M/M/s)$, planning the number of servers to hire
8.8	303	Cost minimization, $(M/M/1)$, optimal size of work crew
8.9	308	Non-Poisson service rate (normal service times)
8.10	308	Non-Poisson service rate (an empirical distribution of service time)
8.11	311	Different customer classes
8.12	314	$(M/M/\infty)$ calculations, self-service facility

EXERCISES

1. *Computer Printer Terminal.* A computer system has a single printer attached to print out the computer-program output of the users. The operating system software sends an average of twenty requests per hour to the printer. The printer is capable of printing out thirty-five jobs per hour on the average. Assume that the job arrival rate and printer rate are Poisson distributed.
   a. On the average how many jobs are in the output queue waiting to be printed out?
   b. How many jobs are in the "printer output system" on the average?
   c. How long can a user expect to wait to have his or her job printed out once job execution is complete?
   d. Once a job enters the output queue, how long does it take before printing begins on the job?
   e. What percentage of time will the printer be busy outputting jobs?

2. *Facilities Expansion.* (Refer to Exercise 1 above.) Assume that a second printer is added to the system and that jobs are printed on a first come, first served basis (FCFS). Answer questions (a)–(e) of Exercise 1, assuming that the two printers are identical.

3. *Auto Repair Facilities.* Campbell's Auto Repair has two repair bays, each manned by one mechanic. The mechanics work at the same rate, each capable of servicing two cars per hour on the average. Cars arrive at Campbell's at an average rate of three per hour. Assume that arrival and service rates are Poisson and compute the following (use a FCFS service discipline):
   a. p_0
   b. L
   c. L_q
   d. W
   e. W_q

4. *(M/M/1) Compared to (M/M/s).* Refer to Campbell's Auto Repair, Exercise 3 above. The two mechanics, Suzanne and James, are concerned about the work load that seems to build up in the queue. Working together on each car, they feel that the average number of cars waiting to be repaired could be reduced. Their combined service rate as a team would be four cars per hour on the average.
   a. Compare this system to the existing system by computing p_0, L, L_q, W, and W_q.
   b. Can the queue length be reduced as claimed by Suzanne and James?

5. *Toll Gate Operation.* A toll gate at the Oilgate Bridge on Interstate I–671 is staffed by one attendant. The time it takes him to collect the toll

from a car is *exactly* thirty seconds. Cars arrive at the toll booth at a Poisson rate of seventy-five cars per hour.

a. What percentage of the time is the attendant free to read magazines?

b. On the average how many cars are lined up on the highway waiting to approach the toll booth?

c. What is the expected number of cars tied up at the bridge due to the toll gate bottleneck?

d. What is the average length of time a traveler can expect to wait before paying the toll?

e. How long on the average is a car detained on the highway due to the toll gate operation?

6. *Estimating* λ *and* μ.   Once it is felt that the Poisson density reasonably describes arrival and service rates, it is necessary to *observe* the queuing system to estimate these rates. Statisticians have provided the following (somewhat obvious) method for doing this. (A) To estimate λ, decide beforehand how many arrivals you are going to observe, say N. Let T be the time it takes for N arrivals to occur. Then an estimate of λ is N/T (arrivals per unit time). (B) To estimate μ, decide beforehand how many completed services you are going to observe, say M. Let B be the sum of all the busy periods during the time you are counting service completions. Then an estimate of μ is M/B. (If you are statistically inclined, you will probably recognize these as "unbiased maximum-likelihood estimators.")

Let us suppose you observe a local bank's drive-up teller window. You decide beforehand that you will wait until you have counted ten cars pulling up to the window and ten cars *fully completing* service. In two hours (8:00 A.M.–10:00 A.M.), a total of ten cars had arrived at the drive-up window. You made the observations shown in Table 8.8 about the teller at the window. (For example, the teller was idle from 9:40 to 10:10

TABLE 8.8

Time	Teller status	Total service completions
8:00– 8:15	Idle	0 customers
8:15– 8:30	Busy	2 customers
8:30– 8:50	Idle	2 customers
8:50– 9:00	Busy	3 customers
9:00– 9:20	Idle	3 customers
9:20– 9:40	Busy	6 customers
9:40–10:10	Idle	6 customers
10:10–10:30	Busy	8 customers
10:30–10:35	Idle	8 customers
10:35–10:45	Busy	10 customers

A.M. and then was busy during the next twenty minutes from 10:10 to 10:30. At 9:40, he had served a total of six customers. By 10:30, the total was eight.)

a. Estimate λ and μ.

b. Assuming an $(M/M/1)$ model for this system, compute L, L_q, W, W_q. What proportion of time is the teller idle in the long run?

7. *Telephone Switchboard Operations.* Telephone calls arrive at a large switchboard at the Poisson rate of twenty per hour. The calls are transferred to an office that can handle twenty-five callers per hour (assume that this service time is exponentially distributed). The office can handle only one caller at a time; if it is busy, arriving calls are put on hold.

This model might also be applicable to U.S. government services, such as income tax advice, that are provided toll free to U.S. citizens.

Assume that *no limit* is placed on the number of calls that can be put on hold.

a. What percentage of time is the office busy?

b. On the average, how many callers are on hold?

c. On the average, how long can a caller expect to spend on the telephone when calling this office?

d. What is the average length of time a caller must wait on hold?

8. *Telephone Switchboard Operation—Facilities Redesign.* Let us consider Excercise 7 again. Suppose the office handling the calls is reorganized so that it can handle two calls at a time, with mean service time per call the same as before. Answer parts (a)–(d) of Exercise 7.

9. *Customer-Service Analysis.* In Exercise 8, suppose the office management feels that, in order to provide good customer service, a caller should not have to wait longer than twenty seconds on hold. How many telephone operators should be hired to work in the office answering calls?

10. *Tool-Crib Operation.* A manufacturing facility operates a central tool crib for its machinists. The crib operates like an $(M/M/s)$ system. Arrivals occur at an average rate of thirty machinists requiring tools per hour. Each worker behind the tool counter can service the requests of fifteen machinists per hour on the average and is paid an hourly wage of $8.50. The machinists' wages run $15.75 per hour on the average.

a. How may tool-crib attendants should be hired?

b. For the system resulting from your analysis of part (a), determine the following: How many machinists are idle (at the tool crib) on the average? How long can a machinist expect to spend at the tool crib?

11. *Medical Clinic Services.* Patients arrive at a medical clinic at a Poisson rate of ten per hour. The small clinic is staffed by one doctor, assisted by several nurses. Patients wait in the waiting room until the doctor can see them (on a FCFS basis). The time the doctor spends with a patient has an exponential probability density with a mean of five minutes.

a. How many patients are in the clinic on the average?
b. How long must a patient wait before seeing the doctor?
c. How long can a patient expect to spend in the clinic?
d. On the average how many patients are in the waiting room?

12. *Medical Clinic Design.* (Refer to Exercise 11 above.) For the medical clinic in Exercise 11 above, the staff is planning to purchase new furniture for the waiting room. How much seating capacity must be purchased if the waiting area is to be adequate at least:
a. 50 percent of the time?
b. 75 percent of the time?
c. 95 percent of the time?
d. 99 percent of the time?
e. Graph these results by plotting these percentages on the horizontal axis and the required number of seats on the vertical axis. If we assume that the cost of the furniture is proportional to the number of seats required, this graph will illustrate *the cost of providing patient conveniences.*

13. *Computer Center Facilities.* Students arrive at the university's computer center at a Poisson rate of twenty per hour. The center has six on-line terminals for student use. The time a student spends at a terminal appears to follow an exponential probability density with a mean of 0.20 hour (12 minutes).
a. On the average, how many students are at the computing center?
b. How many students are waiting to use a terminal?
c. How long can a student expect to spend at the center?
d. What is the average waiting time for a student before having access to a terminal?
e. What percentage of time is the center busy?

14. *Computer Center Facilities.* (Refer to Exercise 13.) Students arriving at the computer center can wait at a small table in the center (which will seat four students), or if the table is full they can go to a nearby student lounge, or they can wait in the hall. What percentage of time will the waiting area inside the computer center be sufficient to accommodate the waiting students?

15. *Police Vehicle Maintenance.* The city of Padouaka operates a large fleet of police squad cars. When a car breaks down due to a minor malfunction, it is sent to a single-garage repair facility, where it is repaired by a crew of mechanics. The crew foreman, Joanne, must put in a request to hire her team mechanics. If n mechanics work on a single car together, repair time for minor repairs is approximately *constant* at $20/n$ minutes. Disabled squad cars arrive at the repair facility at the Poisson rate of five cars per hour. The police chief tells Joanne that on the average he does not want a squad car to be out of commission for longer than fifteen minutes.

a. What is the minimum number of mechanics Joanne should hire?

b. On the average, how many squad cars are out of commission?

16. Solve Joanne's facility design problem (Exercise 15 above) under the assumption that the repair time of $20/n$ minutes is a mean *exponential* time. Answer both parts (a) and (b) of the problem.

17. *Selecting Material-Handling Equipment.* The Manufacturing Supervisor of Hardpresd Industries must decide between three makes of forklift trucks to use on the plant floor. The truck will be used to move raw materials from raw-materials storage bins to work centers in a section of the plant. Requests from these work centers occur according to a Poisson process at a mean rate of eight per hour. The time to move raw materials is exponentially distributed. The service rates per hour for each of the trucks under consideration are given in Table 8.9 along with estimated costs per hour (operating costs plus depreciation). For each hour a work center is idle waiting for raw materials, an average cost of $100 is incurred (wages plus lost productivity).

   Which truck would you purchase based on queuing analysis? (Be sure to specify clearly the queuing model you are using.)

18. In Exercise 17, would your purchase choice change if the Manufacturing Supervisor felt that the service times of the forklift trucks were (more or less) constant times? That is, truck 1 can service work centers at the *constant rate* of ten jobs per hour, truck 2 at fifteen per hour, and truck 3 at eighteen per hour. (What would be the total cost per hour of using each of the trucks?)

19. *Parking Lot Capacity.* One hundred cars per hour arrive at a large parking lot at an airport. The time spent by a car averages 1/2 hour and is exponentially distributed. Assume the arrival rate is Poisson.

    a. What is the probability that the parking lot is empty?

    b. On the average, how many cars are in the parking lot?

20. *Recreational Facilities Planning.* Campers arrive at the Brown County State Park at a Poisson rate of 100 per month. The time spent in the park by a camper varies according to an exponential distribution with a mean of 0.10 month. Since the park is very large, campers have no problem

TABLE 8.9

Truck	Service rate (jobs/hour)	Cost ($/hour)
1	10	30
2	15	50
3	18	40

finding a campsite. However, the state recreation officials have a policy of maintaining a certain level of forest-ranger work force for the convenience and safety of the campers. The current policy is to have one ranger per ten campers.

a. How many campers are using the park on the average?

b. What percentage of the time is the park empty?

c. How many forest rangers should the state employ at Brown County State Park?

21. *Truck Weigh Station.*   The state operates a weigh station for trucks traveling on the highway. Every truck must pull off the highway, enter the weigh station, and undergo state inspection procedures before continuing on. Trucks arrive at this station at a Poisson rate of seven per hour. The time to inspect/weigh a truck varies, having an exponential probability density with a mean of seven minutes.

a. How many trucks are detained at the station on the average?

b. How long can a truck driver expect to be detained?

c. How many trucks are lined up in front of the station on the average?

d. How long on the average does a truck driver have to wait in line for the truck to be inspected?

22. *Equipment Selection for the Highway Weigh Station.*   (Refer to Exercise 21 above.) The truck drivers traveling the route passing the weigh station have complained of long waiting times at the inspection point. The major phase of the inspection procedure consists of weighing-in the truck. The state highway commissioner has decided to look into ways of reducing the average time a trucker must spend at the weigh station to twenty-five minutes or less. The commissioner is considering the purchase of a new digital, solid-state, weighing scale that should reduce the weighing time. Three manufacturers' products are available: model 1 costs $10,000 and could check ten trucks per hour, model 2 costs $12,000 and would have an average service time of 5-1/2 minutes, and model 3 costs $8,500 and would have an average service time of 6-1/2 minutes.

a. Determine which model to purchase.

b. For the decision made in part (a), determine system operating characteristics p_0, L, L_q, W, and W_q.

23. *Bank Lobby Operations.*   Customers arrive at the lobby of the Commercial Bank at a Poisson rate of twenty per hour. On the average, twenty-five percent of these customers go to a teller who handles bank money orders, CDs, bonds, and travelers checks. This teller can service forty customers per hour on the average. Ten percent of the customers go to the business deposits window, whose teller can service an average of thirty customers per hour. The remaining customers require regular banking services from a teller who works at an average rate of fifty customers per hour. Assume all service rates are Poisson.

    a. Draw a diagram of the bank's lobby and identify the queuing systems involved.

    b. On the average, how many customers are in the lobby?

    c. What is the probability that the lobby is busy servicing customers?

24. *Student Registration System.*   Refer to Example 8.13 (p. 317) and compute the following:

    a. The expected total number of students in the registration center.

    b. The probability that there are no students in the center.

    c. The probability that there are more than two students in the center.

    d. How long a student can expect to spend in the system.

9 PROJECT MANAGEMENT: CPM AND PERT

1. INTRODUCTION

Controlling large projects requires careful coordination and planning of the many activities involved. Examples of such projects include:

- Political campaigns
- Personnel training
- Design of academic programs
- Construction projects
- Research and development
- New-product development
- Surgical operations
- Planned maintenance of machines and buildings
- Start-up of a new business

328

- Advertising/promotion campaigns
- Development and implementation of computer programs
- Computer installation
- Congressional investigation

In this chapter we discuss two techniques that have been successfully applied to project management: CPM and PERT. CPM (Critical-Path Method) was developed in 1957 by E. I. du Pont de Nemours & Company for the control of construction projects. PERT (Program Evaluation and Review Technique) was developed in 1958 for the U.S. Navy's Polaris Missile Program by the consulting firm of Booz, Allen, and Hamilton.

Phases of Project Management

Generally, successful project management involves the following three phases:

1. *Planning*. This phase involves identifying the main activities to be performed, time estimates of these activities, and precedence relationships between them. In CPM and PERT, this phase will result in the construction of a project network.
2. *Scheduling*. From the planning phase a time chart is made, showing the scheduling of resources (people, machines, and money). It may happen that significant irregularities will arise in the level of resource requirements; for example, the work force size may fluctuate widely from week to week. *Resource leveling* may become an important task in the scheduling phase.
3. *Control*. This phase involves issuing progress reports, updating the network in response to changes that occur (regenerating the network in part or in its entirety), and shifting or increasing resources to shorten project duration.

2. CRITICAL-PATH METHOD (CPM)

To illustrate the planning aspects of CPM, we shall study a small business in the initial stages of start-up. For illustration purposes, we have greatly simplified the typical problems faced in business start-up.

EXAMPLE 9.1. *Small-Business Start-up.* Copyfast is a newly organized copying and printing business that is about to open a retail store, and in the next several weeks, many activities must be performed. These activities are listed in Table 9.1. To each activity we assign a label that will be used later as a convenient reference in certain network calculations. To understand the table, look at activity *I*, "Set up and test office equipment." This activity will require three days to complete and must first be *immediately* preceded by

TABLE 9.1   *Small Business Start-up Activities: Copyfast*

(1) Activity symbol	(2) Activity	(3) Time required (days)	(4) Immediate predecessors
A	Meet with lawyer	4	—
B	Meet with CPA	3	A
C	Secure lease	5	A
D	Have natural gas hooked up	1	C,B
E	Purchase office equipment	3	C,B
F	Have electric service hooked up	1	C,B
G	Get state gross receipts number	1	B
H	Get local license	1	G
I	Set up and test office equipment	3	E,F
J	City fire/safety inspection	2	D,I

activities *E* and *F*; that is, the equipment must be purchased and the electrical service must be connected to the premises. From Table 9.1, a **CPM network** is constructed, as shown in Fig. 9.1.

The network consists of *nodes* and *branches*. The nodes are the circles (numbered from 1 to 9); the branches represent the activities. Note the use of two

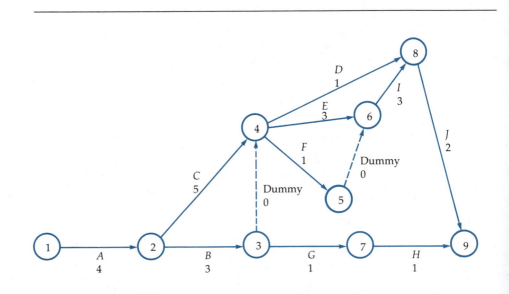

FIGURE 9.1   *CPM network for Copyfast.*

dummy activities, one connecting nodes 3 and 4 and the other connecting nodes 5 and 6. As a rule, in constructing a project network, it is not permitted to have two nodes directly connected by more than one activity. Thus the connections illustrated in Fig. 9.2 would *not* be permitted.

APPLICATIONS

The following applications appear in this chapter in text, examples, or problems:

Advertising/promotion campaigns

Cash planning

Computer system installation

Construction projects

New product development

Planned maintenance of machines and buildings

Political campaign management

Research and development

Start-up of a new business

To get around this restriction, a dummy activity is used, as shown in Fig. 9.3. A dummy activity requires 0 time and 0 resources (money, people). Thus in Fig. 9.1, nodes 3 and 4 are "essentially" the same node.

A node represents an **event.** Thus node 8 represents the event that is the completion of activities *D* and *I*.

This example is used below to demonstrate the calculation of the critical path. ▲

Graphical Analysis

Study Fig. 9.1. What sequence of activities will be critical to successfully completing the project on time? You will note that the *path A–C–E–I–J* is the

---

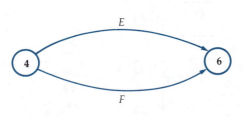

FIGURE 9.2

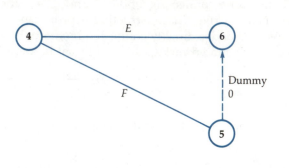

FIGURE 9.3

longest path from the initial node 1 to the terminal node 9, requiring 17 days to complete. The other paths are of shorter duration, as shown in Table 9.2.

All seven paths must be completed before the project is complete. Thus you can see that the path *A–C–E–I–J* is the **critical path** of the network: It takes the greatest time to complete. Once all activities on the critical path are completed, the project will be complete, assuming that the noncritical activities (*B, D, F, G, H*) are completed on time.

In larger networks it becomes difficult to find the critical path by visually inspecting the network to locate the longest path from start to finish. Also, information other than identifying the critical path is often needed. Such a method is illustrated next in Fig. 9.4.

Computing the ES and EF Times

The **earliest start** time (ES) for an activity is the earliest time the activity could begin, assuming all preceding activities are completed as soon as possible.

The **earliest finish** time (EF) for an activity equals the earliest start time for the activity *plus* the duration time for the activity.

TABLE 9.2

	Days
A–C–D–J	12
A–C–F–Dummy–I–J	15
A–B–Dummy–D–J	10
A–B–Dummy–E–I–J	15
A–B–Dummy–F–Dummy–I–J	13
A–B–G–H	9

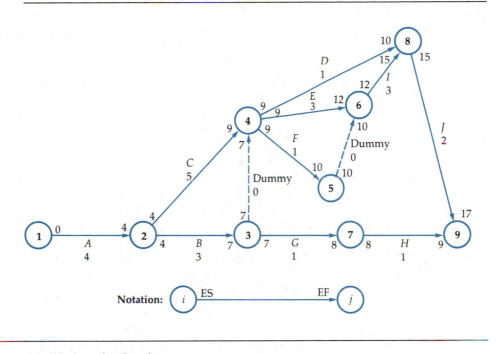

FIGURE 9.4   *ES, EF times for Copyfast.*

The ES and EF times for the Copyfast method are computed in a **forward pass** through the network, beginning with the initial node 1. Starting at node 1, we assign 0 as the ES time for activity A. Since the duration time of A is four days, the earliest time A could be finished is day 4, so EF = 4 for A. Now let us look at activity C. It cannot start until A is finished. Since EF = 4 for A, the earliest time C could start is day 4. Since its duration time is five days, the earliest time C could be finished is day 9, so EF = 9 for activity C. Continuing in this manner, we obtain the results shown in Fig. 9.4 and summarized in Table 9.3, columns 3 and 4. Notice what happens when two or more activities lead into a single node. For example, look at node 8. The EF time for activity D is 10 days and for activity I is 15 days. Activity J leads out of node 8 and cannot begin until *both* D and I are complete. Thus the ES time for J is the maximum of the EF times of D and I as follows:

$$ES_J = \max(EF_D, EF_I) = \max(10, 15) = 15$$

Computing the LS and LF Times

The **late start** time (LS) for an activity is the latest time an activity can begin without causing a delay in the project completion time.

TABLE 9.3   *Copyfast Network Summary*

(1)	(2)	(3)	(4)	(5)	(6)	(7)	(8) On critical path
Activity	Duration	ES	EF	LS	LF	Slack*	
A	4	0	4	0	4	0	*
B	3	4	7	6	9	2	
C	5	4	9	4	9	0	*
D	1	9	10	14	15	5	
E	3	9	12	9	12	0	*
F	1	9	10	11	12	2	
G	1	7	8	15	16	8	
H	1	8	9	16	17	8	
I	3	12	15	12	15	0	*
J	2	15	17	15	17	0	*

*Slack (7) = LS − ES = LF − EF

The **late finish** time (LF) for an activity is the latest time the activity can be completed without causing a delay in the project completion time.

The LS and LF times for the Copyfast network are computed in a **backward pass** through the network, beginning with the terminal node 9 and working to the left. The results are shown on the network of Fig. 9.5 and summarized in Table 9.3, columns 5 and 6.

The backward pass proceeds as follows: We begin with the terminal node 9 and set LF time for J equal to the EF time for $J = 17$. Also, LF time for H = 17 (otherwise, the project would be delayed beyond its earliest possible completion time of 17). Then the LS time for J equals (LF for J) − (duration of J) = 17 − 2 = 15. If J is begun later than day 15, the project will not be completed on time (day 17). The late start time for H equals its late finish time minus its duration: LS for H = (LF for H) − (duration of H) = 17 − 1 = 16. If H starts after day 16, the project completion time will be delayed beyond its earliest finish time (day 17). For activity D, the latest time it can finish equals the latest time that J is allowed to start. So (LF for D) = (LS for J) = 15. The LS time for D equals its LF time minus its duration, or (LS for D) = 15 − 1 = 14. We continue through the network in this way, working backwards from node 9 toward node 1, computing first the LF time and then the LS time for each activity.

Note what happens when two or more activities lead out of a node. For example, look at node 2. The LS times for B and C are 6 and 4, respectively. Thus the latest time we can finish activity A is day 4; otherwise, we will delay the start of C beyond its latest start time (and then cause a chain reaction that will delay the completion of the project beyond day 17). We com-

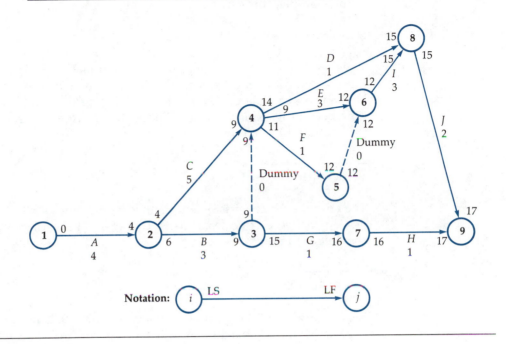

FIGURE 9.5   *LS, LF times for Copyfast.*

pute the LF time of *A* as follows:

$$LF_A = \min(LS_B, LS_C) = \min(6, 4) = 4$$

Slack Times

The **slack time** for an activity is the amount of time we can delay the start of the activity beyond its ES time without delaying the completion of the project beyond its earliest finish time. Thus slack time can be thought of as "float," or "slack," allowed in starting an activity.

The slack time for an activity can be computed in the following two ways:

Slack time = LS − ES

or

Slack time = LF − EF

The slack times for the activities of the Copyfast project are computed from the data of Table 9.3 and are shown in column 7.

For example, for activity B,

Slack time for $B = LS_B - ES_B = 6 - 4 = 2$

Thus we can start B as early as day 4 (ES) or as late as day 6 (LS). The slack time of two days means that we have up to two days to start activity B beyond the ES time of day 4 without delaying the total project completion time beyond its earliest finish. (Check that you get the same answer using the formula LF $-$ EF.)

The Critical Path

The critical path consists of all activities having zero slack time. For the case of Copyfast, the critical path is $A–C–E–I–J$. The earliest project finish (or completion) time is 17 days.

Comments

1. We did not list the dummy activities in Table 9.3. In general you may if you wish include the dummy activities explicitly in the table. For the dummy connecting node 5 to node 6, ES = 10, EF = 10, LS = 12, LF = 12, and slack time = 2, which agrees with the slack time for activity F, immediately preceding.
2. A word of caution is in order concerning the meaning of slack time. As an illustration, consider the path $A–B–G–H$. The length of time on this path is 9 days (4 + 3 + 1 + 1), which is 8 days short of the critical path time of 17 days. From Table 9.3, the *individual* slack times of the activities $A, B, G,$ and H are

A	0 days
B	2
G	8
H	8
Total	18 days

Thus we cannot delay each of the activities by their slack times (resulting in a delay of 18 days) without exceeding the project completion time. The *total* delay allowed along the path $A–B–G–H$ cannot exceed 8 days. In a sense, this 8 days of slack is *shared* by all four activities.

On Notation

You may find it convenient to compute and record both the forward pass and the backward pass on the same network diagram. For example, instead of using two separate diagrams such as Fig. 9.4 and Fig. 9.5, you would use one diagram with the following notational convention:

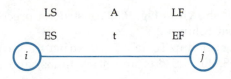

where t is the duration of time of activity A. As an example, for activity D in the Copyfast problem, we would have:

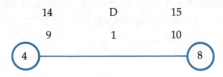

Problems

1. Construct the network for the project described by Table 9.4.
2. For the network of Problem 1 above, compute the ES, EF, LS, LF, and slack times for each activity. Identify the critical path.
3. Construct the project network corresponding to these specifications:

   Activities A and B are the first activities of the project and can begin immediately and simultaneously. Activity C can begin only after both A and B are completed. (C is the terminal activity.)

4. Construct the project network corresponding to the specifications that follow on page 338:

TABLE 9.4

Activity	Duration (weeks)	Immediate predecessors
A	10	None
B	3.5	A
C	1	A
D	2	B
E	2.5	C

Activities A and B can begin immediately and simultaneously. C cannot begin until both A and B are completed. Activity D can begin after only B is completed. (C and D are terminal activities.)

5. From the network shown in Fig. 9.6, construct a precedence table similar to Table 9.1. (Omit column 2.)
6. For the project specified in Table 9.5, construct the project network; compute the times ES, EF, LS, LF, and slack times; and identify the critical path.

3. COST/TIME TRADE-OFFS: A CRASHING ALGORITHM

In this section we examine how a project's duration may be shortened by increasing the amount of money spent on the project. In Table 9.6, we spec-

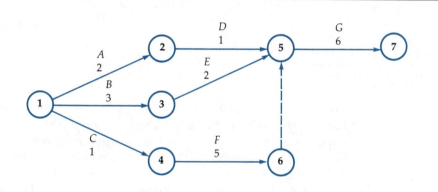

FIGURE 9.6   *(Time is shown in five-day work weeks.)*

TABLE 9.5

Activity	Duration (days)	Immediate predecessors
A	5	None
B	2	A
C	3	A
D	1	A
E	6	B, C, D
F	3	E
G	2	C
H	5	F, G

TABLE 9.6

(1) Activity	(2) Immediate predecessors	(3) Normal time*	(4) Normal cost†	(5) Crash time*	(6) Crash cost†	(7) Cost to crash per week†
A	None	2	3	1	5	2
B	None	3	4	2	5	1
C	A	3	2	2	6	4
D	A	1	1	0.5	3	4
E	B	2	5	1	8	3
F	C	4	3	2	4	0.5
G	D, E	1	2	1	2	∞

*In weeks
†In $000

ify the activities of a certain project. Columns 1 and 2 are self-explanatory. The **normal time** and **normal cost** for an activity are the time and cost incurred if the activity is executed at a normal rate. The **crash time** and **crash cost** for an activity are the time and cost incurred if the activity is executed as fast as possible. These four quantities are given in columns 3, 4, 5, and 6, respectively.

For example, activity B can be performed at a normal rate in three weeks at a total cost of $4,000. If we are willing to spend $5,000, activity B can be performed in just two weeks. The cost to *compress* activity B is calculated as follows:

$$\left| \frac{\text{Crash cost} - \text{normal cost}}{\text{Crash time} - \text{normal time}} \right| = \left| \frac{5,000 - 4,000}{2 - 3} \right|$$

$$= \left| \frac{1,000}{-1} \right| = |-1,000|$$

$$= \$1,000/\text{week}$$

Thus activity B can be compressed, at a cost of $1,000 per week, down to a minimum of two weeks. The pair (two weeks, $5,000) is termed the **crash point** for B, and (three weeks, $4,000) is the **normal point** for B. These notions are illustrated graphically for activity B in Fig. 9.7. In computing the cost to crash in this way, we are *assuming* that this cost is linear as a function of time. Also note that the cost to crash per week is given in column 7 of Table 9.6 for each activity.

Since activity G cannot be crashed below its normal time of one week, we assign an infinite crashing cost to it in column 7 of the table.

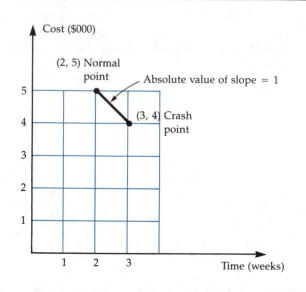

FIGURE 9.7   *Activity B of Table 9.6.*

The Normal Schedule

The **normal schedule** is the network that results from using normal times and normal costs for each activity. For our example, the normal schedule appears in Fig. 9.8. Thus if we use normal times and costs, the project will be completed in nine weeks at a cost of $20,000 (obtained by summing all

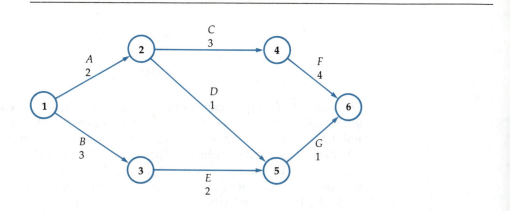

FIGURE 9.8   *The normal schedule.*

the normal costs of column 4, Table 9.6. The critical path is A–C–F. In finding the critical path, it is generally necessary to go through all the computations of ES, EF, LS, and LF. However, in this small example, you can graphically identify the critcal path as the longest path connecting the initial node 1 and the terminal node 6.

The Crash Schedule

The **crash schedule** is the network that results from using crash times and crash costs for each activity. For our example, the crash schedule is given in Fig. 9.9 and results in a project completion time of five weeks and a total project cost of $33,000 (obtained by summing column 6 of Table 9.6). The critical path is A–C–F.

Our Objective in Crashing

We have seen that the project can be completed in anywhere from five to nine weeks at a cost ranging from $20,000 to $33,000. Is it possible to achieve a project completion time of five weeks at a cost lower than $33,000? Generally, the answer is "yes." The resulting schedule is called the **minimum-cost crash schedule.** The process of obtaining such a schedule from the normal schedule is called **crashing.**

A Crashing Algorithm

We shall use the following algorithm in crashing the normal schedule of Fig 9.8:

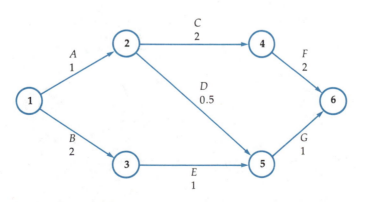

FIGURE 9.9   *The crash schedule.*

STEP 1. Set up the normal schedule and calculate the cost to crash each activity.

STEP 2. Shorten the project completion time by one time unit at the lowest cost possible. This is done by crashing the activity on the critical path having the smallest cost-to-crash slope. If there are two or more critical paths, it may be necessary to crash more than one critical activity.

    If at step 2 the project duration cannot be shortened because the critical activities are at their crash points, then STOP—you have the minimum-cost crash schedule. (See Problem 1 at the end of this section.)

STEP 3. Construct a new critical path using the newly created activity times, and then repeat step 2.

    Let us go through this algorithm with our current example.

    For step 1, we set up the normal schedule in Fig. 9.8 and the cost to crash each activity in column 7 of Table 9.6.

    For step 2, the critical path is A–C–F. The cost (in $000) to crash each of these by one week is $2 for A, $4 for C, and $0.5 for F (see column 7, Table 9.6). Thus we choose to crash F by one week—from four weeks to three weeks.

    For step 3, our new network is as shown in Fig. 9.10. Note that only the activity time for F is changed. The critical path shown darkened is A–C–F at eight weeks.

    We now repeat step 2 on the new network. The critical path is A–C–F, the costs (in $000) to crash are $2 for A, $4 for C, and $0.5 for F. So we crash F by one week. For step 3 this gives the new network shown in Fig. 9.11. The asterisk next to F indicates that F is at its crash point of two weeks and cannot be crashed further.

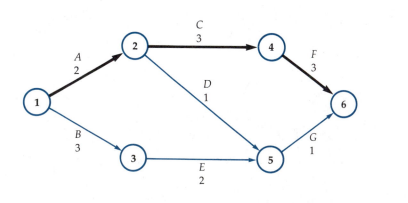

FIGURE 9.10

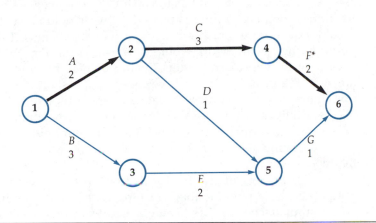

FIGURE 9.11

Perform step 2 on the new network: The critical path is *A–C–F*. The costs (in $000) to crash the critical activities that are *not at their crash points* are $2 for *A* and $4 for *C*. Thus we choose to crash *A* by one week from two to one week. For step 3, this gives the new network shown in Fig. 9.12. Note that *A*, *F*, and *G* are at their crash points and that two paths become critical at six weeks: *A–C–F* and *B–E–G*.

Next, perform step 2 on this new network. The critical paths are *A–C–F* and *B–E–G*. The costs (in $000) to crash the critical activities that are not at their crash points are $4 per week for *C*, $1 per week for *B*, and $3 per week for *E*. Now observe that in order to shorten the project completion time by one week we must shorten *both* critical paths by one week. On the path

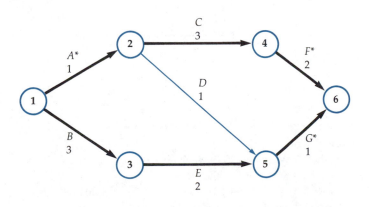

FIGURE 9.12

A–C–F we have no choice but to crash C by one week (since A and F are at their crash points). On the path B–E–G, we would crash B by one week (E would cost more to crash and G is at its crash point). In step 3 of the algorithm, the new network would be as shown in Fig. 9.13.

Once again we return to step 2 with our new network: The critical paths are A–C–F and B–E–G at five weeks each. To shorten the project completion time by one week we must shorten both paths by one week. *But* all the activities of path A–C–F are at their crash points, so A–C–F cannot be shortened further. Thus we STOP: the minimum-cost crash schedule has been found. (Do you see why it would do no good to crash activity E by one week?)

What is the cost of the final schedule? The cost equals the cost of the normal schedule plus the total crashing costs, as shown in Table 9.7.

The normal schedule has been crashed from nine weeks to five weeks at an additional cost of only $8,000, compared to the crash schedule difference of $13,000. (From Fig. 9.9 the cost of the crash schedule is $33,000, or $13,000 more than the normal schedule cost of $20,000.) If you compare the final

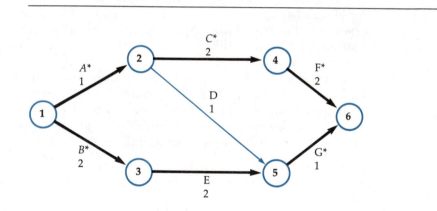

FIGURE 9.13

TABLE 9.7

Normal schedule cost	$20,000
F crashed 2 weeks at $500/week	1,000
A crashed 1 week at $2,000/week	2,000
C crashed 1 week at $4,000/week	4,000
B crashed 1 week at $1,000/week	1,000
Total minimum-crash schedule cost	$28,000

network arrived at above with the crash schedule of Fig. 9.9, you will see where the cost savings come from.

A flowchart representation of the crashing algorithm appears in Fig. 9.14.   ▲

Problems

1. You should be careful to crash only one unit at a time in step 2 of the crashing algorithm. You *may* crash the minimum-cost critical activity by more than one time unit as long as another path does not become critical in the process. Suppose you are given the network shown in Fig. 9.15. Assume that the costs to crash are $5 per week for *A*, $3 per week for *C*, $2 per week for *B*, and $4 per week for *D*. Also, the crash point for *C* is two weeks. None of the activities has reached its crash point. In step 2 of the crashing algorithm you would choose *C* to crash. What is the maximum amount by which you would crash *C*?

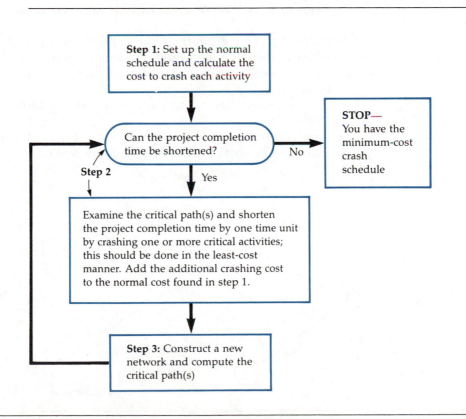

Step 1: Set up the normal schedule and calculate the cost to crash each activity

Can the project completion time be shortened?

Step 2

No

Yes

STOP—
You have the minimum-cost crash schedule

Examine the critical path(s) and shorten the project completion time by one time unit by crashing one or more critical activities; this should be done in the least-cost manner. Add the additional crashing cost to the normal cost found in step 1.

Step 3: Construct a new network and compute the critical path(s)

FIGURE 9.14   *The crashing algorithm*

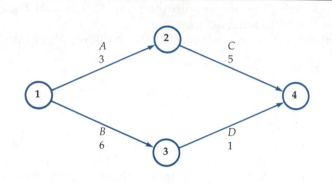

FIGURE 9.15

2. For critical paths having common activities:
   a. Suppose you are given the network shown in Fig. 9.16. Assume that none of the activities are at their crash points. The costs to crash are given in Table 9.8. Which activity would you choose to crash by one week?
   b. Suppose you are given the same network as in part (a) above, with the following modification of the cost to crash schedule: Cost to crash G is $375 per week. Which activity (or activities) would you choose to crash by one week?
3. Suppose a project has the specifications given in Table 9.9 (time is given in weeks).
   a. Construct the normal CPM schedule.
   b. Compute the costs to crash each activity by one week.

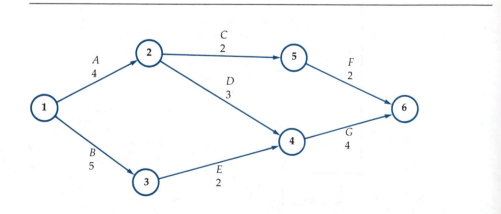

FIGURE 9.16

TABLE 9.8

Activity	Cost to crash ($/week)
A	500
B	300
C	100
D	100
E	250
F	125
G	50

TABLE 9.9

Activity	Immediate predecessors	Normal time	Normal cost ($)	Crash time	Crash cost
A	None	5	100	4	200
B	A	3	300	2	350
C	A	2	200	1	325
D	B,C	2	250	1	300
E	C	1	400	1	400
F	D	4	500	2	900
G	E	4	150	2	350

c. Construct the crash schedule.
d. Following the crashing algorithm, find the minimum-cost crash schedule.
e. Compare the cost of the crash schedule, part (c), to the minimum-crash cost, part (d).

4. DIRECT AND INDIRECT COST ANALYSIS

In the crashing algorithm of Section 3, the costs we referred to were **direct costs,** such as costs of labor, materials, equipment, overtime labor, and time-saving methods. The shorter the time duration of an activity, the higher are these costs. In practice we must also consider another class of costs, **indirect costs,** such as overhead, supervision, clerical, contractual penalties for late work, interest charges on funds used, and facilities. In general, these costs tend to increase as the duration of the project increases.

In Fig. 9.17, we show a typical graph of these two opposing cost curves. To generate such a curve, we could start with the normal schedule (at the

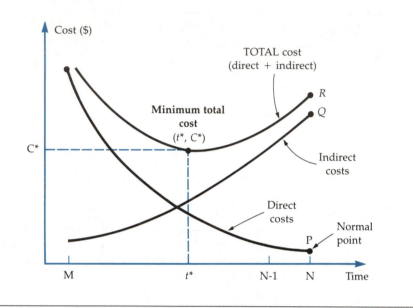

FIGURE 9.17   *Minimizing total project completion cost.*

right of the graph, labeled the normal point). We would calculate the direct costs to get point P, the indirect project costs to get point Q, and then add P and Q to get the total project cost, point R.

Using the crashing algorithm, we would decrease project completion time by one time unit, moving from N to $N-1$ on the horizontal (time) axis. At $N-1$, we would calculate direct, indirect, and total costs as before. We would continue this procedure moving to the left on the time axis until reaching the crash point M.

The minimum total project cost would be at (t^*, C^*), as shown on the graph.

5. TIME-CHART SCHEDULING OF RESOURCES

Once a CPM network is constructed and the critical path calculated, resources needed to complete the project activities must be scheduled over time. These resources may include people, money, machines, or equipment. Our goal is to construct a graph of resource requirements over time. We demonstrate these basic notions in the next example.

EXAMPLE 9.2. *Time-Chart Scheduling of Personnel for Copyfast.* Refer to Example 9.1, Copyfast, together with the network shown in Fig. 9.1 and the calculation of ES, EF, LS, and LF for each activity given in Table 9.3. We display these activities over time in Fig. 9.18.

Along the top line, we have placed the activities of the critical path, using solid-line segments. Below this we have represented each noncritical activity by a solid-line segment connecting the activity's ES time with its LF time. Activity *B*, for example, has a segment connecting its ES time of 4 to its LF time of 9; its duration time of 3 days is shown in parentheses: "*B*(3)."

Suppose the personnel requirements for each activity are as shown in Table 9.10. These are given in Fig. 9.18. Thus *A* is shown to require 3 people.

Our task is to schedule the activities and people over time. To do this, we use Fig. 9.18 *and* the precedence relationships of the network shown in Fig. 9.1. The need for the precedence relationships can be seen by observing that even though the solid line for *B* overlaps the solid line for *G* (in Fig. 9.18), we must be careful to schedule *G after B*.

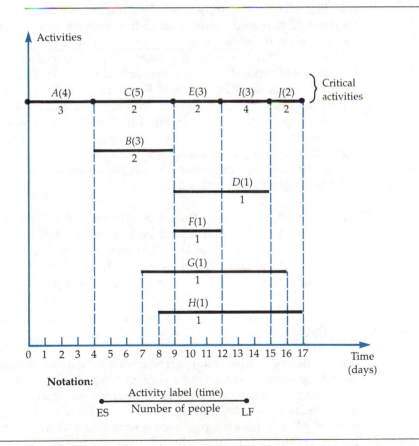

FIGURE 9.18   *Time-chart scheduling of personnel for Copyfast.*

TABLE 9.10

Activity	People needed
A	3
B	2
C	2
D	1
E	2
F	1
G	1
H	1
I	4
J	2

In Fig. 9.19(a), we show the scheduling of all activities to begin at their ES times (this would correspond to the network of Fig. 9.4). The personnel requirements are given as a function of time in Fig. 9.19(b).

In Fig. 9.20(a), we show the scheduling of all activities to begin at their LS times (corresponding to the network of Fig. 9.5). The corresponding personnel requirements are given in Fig. 9.20(b).

By comparing the two figures, you can see the effect of scheduling on resource requirements. Bear in mind that intermediate schedules can also be constructed.

Another fact is easily seen from such an analysis. The critical activities dictate the absolute minimum resource requirements. In the present example, they are given as follows:

From day 0 to day 4, at least 3 people are needed for A
From day 4 to day 9, at least 2 people are needed for C
From day 9 to day 12, at least 2 people are needed for E
From day 12 to day 15, at least 4 people are needed for I
From day 15 to day 17, at least 2 people are needed for J   ▲

6. RESOURCE LEVELING

It often happens that resource requirements corresponding to a given time chart may be impossible, inconvenient, and/or costly to meet.

For example, suppose we have a time-chart and resource schedule as shown in Fig. 9.20(b) (constructed using LS times for Copyfast). If the work force consists of only four people, such a schedule will not be feasible, since five people are called for during the fifteenth day of the project. By shifting starting times, a schedule such as Fig. 9.19 may be obtained.

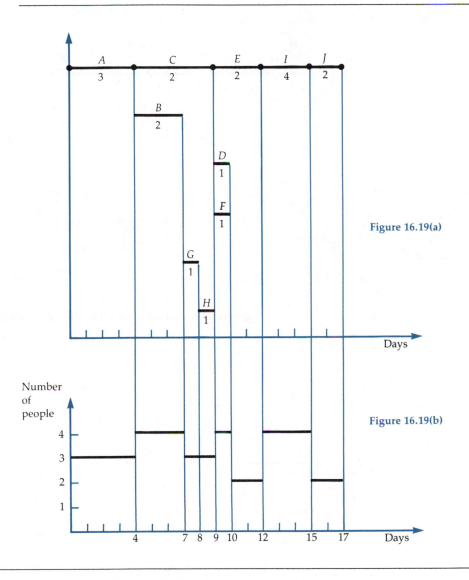

Figure 16.19(a)

Figure 16.19(b)

FIGURE 9.19   *Scheduling according to ES times for Copyfast.*

Resource leveling may also be necessitated by the presence of hiring and firing costs and by the goal of maintaining employee morale and job security. In addition, idle time may be reduced. For example, in Fig. 9.19 four people are required during the tenth day and only two people are needed on days 11 and 12. Thus two people will be idle on these days. In certain projects it may be possible to shift activity times to decrease such idle time, assuming that the idled people are qualified to do other jobs. In our example, suppose

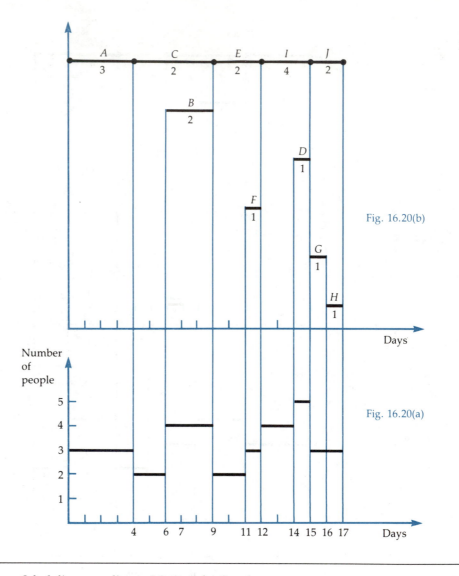

Fig. 16.20(b)

Fig. 16.20(a)

FIGURE 9.20   *Scheduling according to LS times for Copyfast.*

we schedule activity *F* to begin at the start of day 11. The resulting schedule is shown in Fig. 9.21. The idle time is reduced by one person-day. (One person will be idle during the eleventh day and two people will be idle during the twelfth day, compared to two people idle on days 11 and 12 in Fig. 9.19.)

In larger projects, the benefits derived from such resource leveling may be even greater. Procedures employing various "rules of thumb" to shift activity start times have been devised for practical applications. Such rule-of-thumb

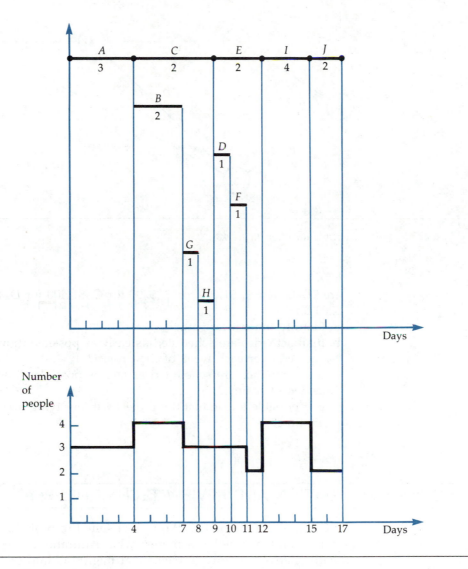

FIGURE 9.21   *Resource leveling.*

procedures are referred to as "resource-leveling **heuristics.**" A good heuristic is an approximate method based on rule-of-thumb reasoning that is easy to apply and gives nearly optimal results.

Problem

1. Suppose a project consists of the six activities shown in the following project network (Fig. 9.22). Assume the funds required for each activity

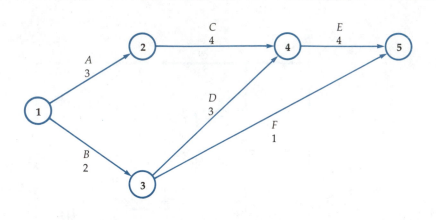

FIGURE 9.22   *Activity duration in weeks.*

are $1,200 for A, $1,000 for B, $700 for C, $1,400 for D, $2,100 for E, and $200 for F.

a. Identify the critical path.
b. If all activities are scheduled as early as possible, how much money is required over each week of the project?
c. If all activities are scheduled as late as possible, how much money is needed over time?
d. Is it possible to conduct the project without tying up over $2,100 at any one time?

7. PROGRAM EVALUATION AND REVIEW TECHNIQUE: PERT

The Critical-Path Method (CPM) is well suited to projects that are repetitive in nature and/or involve activities whose duration times can be estimated with relative certainty. Projects that might fall into this category include running political campaigns (according to election schedules), training personnel, designing academic programs, managing construction projects, planning maintenance functions, and preparing advertising and promotion campaigns.

Other projects may, in practice, have activities whose duration times may not be known with much degree of certainty. Such projects might include certain research and development projects, new product development, surgical operations, development and implementation of computer programs, and installation of a new computer system.

A method that is designed to treat activity duration times as random variables is called **Program Evaluation and Review Technique** (PERT).

Activity Times in PERT

Each activity's duration time is considered to be a random variable (you may wish to review "Probability Densities," Appendix F). PERT assumes that this random variable has a beta probability density. The following method is used to calculate an estimate of the mean and standard deviation of each activity.

For a given activity, management is asked to specify three estimates: the **optimistic time** (if everything goes extremely well), the **pessimistic time** (if everything goes badly), and the **most likely time** (if progress occurs at a normal rate). In practice, a rule of thumb is that the optimistic time is chosen when there is only a one percent chance that the activity will be completed in less time. The pessimistic time is used when there is only a one percent chance that the activity will require more time to complete.

The following notation for these three estimates is commonly used:

a = the optimistic time

b = the pessimistic time

m = the most likely time

Once values for these parameters are given, the mean activity duration is computed as

$$\text{Mean} = \frac{a + b + 4m}{6} \tag{9-1}$$

In this expression, a and b are each given a weight of one and the most likely time is given a weight of 4. Since the total number of weights is 6 (1 + 1 + 4), we divide by 6 to get a weighted average.

Since the difference, $b - a$, is assumed to include about 98 percent of the total probability, we set $b - a$ equal to 6 standard deviations. Thus one standard deviation is given by

$$1 \text{ standard deviation} = \frac{b - a}{6} \tag{9-2}$$

As an example, assume management supplies the following estimates for a given activity: a = 2 weeks, b = 6 weeks, and m = 3 weeks. Then the mean (or expected) activity time is

$$\frac{a + b + 4m}{6} = \frac{2 + 6 + 4(3)}{6} = 3.3 \text{ weeks}$$

and the standard deviation is computed as follows on page 356:

$$\frac{b - a}{6} = \frac{6 - 2}{6} = 0.67 \text{ week}$$

The probability density of the duration time for the activity is represented by the following beta density (Fig. 9.23). The mode is 3 and the mean is 3.3. Note that the density is not symmetric about the mean.

An Outline of the PERT Method

Step 1. For each activity, specify a, b, and m, then calculate its mean and standard deviation, using Eqs. (9–1) and (9–2).

Step 2. Using the mean activity times in step 1, construct a PERT network as in CPM. Compute the ES, EF, LS, LF times and critical path as usual.

Step 3. The critical-path time is also considered to be a random variable having a normal probability density. Its mean equals the sum of the means of the activities on the critical path. The variance of the critical-path time equals the sum of the variances of the activities on the critical path.

Step 4. From step 3, probability calculations can be made concerning project completion time.

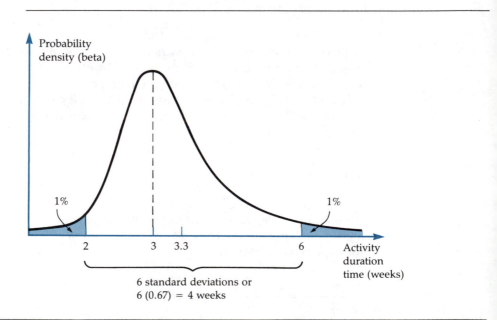

FIGURE 9.23

EXAMPLE 9.3. *PERT Calculations.* The activity specifications for a project are given in Table 9.11, columns 1–5.

Step 1. In columns 6 and 7, we compute the mean and standard deviation of each activity duration time, using Eqs. (9–1) and (9–2).

Step 2. Using the mean activity times from column 6, we construct the PERT network and calculate the ES, EF, LS, LF times for each activity. (See Fig. 9.24.) The critical path is seen to be A–C–F–G.

Step 3. The critical-path time is a normal random variable. The mean expected project completion time is 25.2 weeks. The variance of the project completion time is the sum of the variances of the activities on the critical path and equals (see column 7):

$$(0.67)^2 + (0.83)^2 + (0.50)^2 + (0.83)^2 = 2.0767$$

Since the standard deviation is the square root of the variance, we have

SD of critical-path time = $\sqrt{2.0767}$ = 1.44

The normal density of the critical-path time can now be displayed as shown in Fig. 9.25.

Step 4. Various probabilities of interest may now be calculated—such as, what is the probability the project will be completed in 27 weeks or less?

Solution. The computation that follows on page 358 shows that 27 weeks is 1.25 standard deviations to the right of the mean:

TABLE 9.11   *Activities for a PERT Network Project (Example 9.3)*

(1) Activity	(2) Immediate predecessors	(3) a	(4) b	(5) m	(6) Mean, $\dfrac{a + b + 4m}{6}$	(7) Standard deviation, $\dfrac{b - a}{6}$
A	None	2	6	3	3.3	0.67
B	A	1	1	1	1.0	0.00
C	A	4	9	8	7.5	0.83
D	A	3	5	4	4.0	0.33
E	B	2	10	3	4.0	1.33
F	C	6	9	7	7.2	0.50
G	D, E, F	5	10	7	7.2	0.83

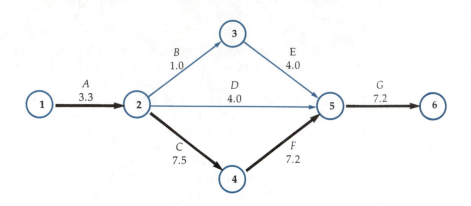

Activity	ES	EF	LS	LF	Slack	Critical path
A	0	3.3	0	3.3	0.0	*
B	3.3	4.3	13.0	14.0	9.7	
C	3.3	10.8	3.3	10.8	0.0	*
D	3.3	7.3	14.0	18.0	10.7	
E	4.3	8.3	14.0	18.0	9.7	
F	10.8	18.0	10.8	18.0	0.0	*
G	18.0	25.2	18.0	25.2	0.0	*

FIGURE 9.24   *Network for Table 9.11.*

$$\text{Number of SDs} = \frac{27 - 25.2}{1.44} = 1.25$$

From Appendix K the required probability is seen to be 0.89. Thus there is an 89 percent chance of completing the project within 27 weeks.   ▲

Comments

1. The properties of the critical-path time in step 3 are based on the assumption that the activities on the critical path are independent. Thus their sum is approximately normal by the central limit theorem. The variance of a sum of independent random variables equals the sum of the variances. (See Appendix F, Section 6.)
2. There has been some criticism concerning the use of the beta distribution as a model for the activity times. As you can see from the discussion above, the beta distribution is certainly convenient and easy to use, in addition

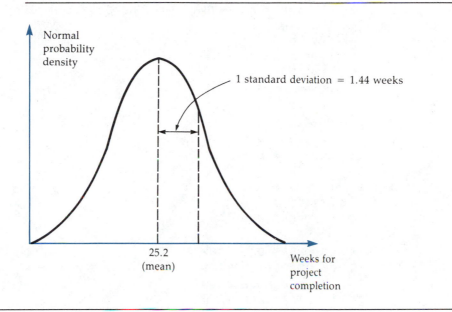

Normal probability density

1 standard deviation = 1.44 weeks

25.2
(mean)

Weeks for project completion

FIGURE 9.25

to having some intuitive appeal. A classic discussion of this issue is presented in: F. Grubbs, "Attempts to Validate Certain PERT Statistics or 'Picking on PERT,'" *Operations Research* 10 (1962): pp. 912–915. PERT is subject to some other criticisms that are beyond the scope of this text.

Problem

1. In Example 9.3, suppose the time estimates for activity G were changed to $a = 5$, $b = 13$, and $m = 7$. What is the probability that the project will be completed in 27 weeks or less?

8. COMPUTER SOLUTION OF CPM PROBLEMS

In this section, you will see how to set up scheduling problems for solution using PROC CPM in SAS/OR. (See Section 8 in Chapter 3 for an introduction to SAS/OR.) You will also see how to produce charts using PROC TIMEPLOT and how to sort data using PROC SORT.

The Copyfast Problem in SAS/OR PROC CPM Format

```
1   TITLE1 'COPYFAST STARTUP SCHEDULE';
2   DATA COPYF;
```

```
3        INPUT ACT$ TIME TAIL HEAD;
4        CARDS;
5   LAWYER 4 1 2
6   CPACCT 3 2 3
7   LEASES 5 2 4
8   DUMMY1 0 3 4
9   NATGAS 1 4 8
10  BUYOEQ 3 4 6
11  ELECTR 1 4 5
12  DUMMY2 0 5 6
13  GROSSR 1 3 7
14  LICENS 1 7 9
15  TESTOE 3 6 8
16  INSPEC 2 8 9
17  ;
18  PROC CPM DATA=COPYF;
19      DURATION TIME;
20      HEADNODE HEAD;
21      TAILNODE TAIL;
22      ID ACT;
```

The data for this procedure is set up with the activities (**ACT**) as rows, and the activity times (**TIME** in the INPUT statement), starting node symbols (**TAIL**), and ending node symbols (**HEAD**) as columns. The symbols used for these variables are identified for PROC CPM using the **DURATION, HEADNODE,** and **TAILNODE** keywords followed by the appropriate variable name. The **ID** keyword is used to identify the activity names (optional), here identified by the variable **ACT.**

Solution Output

The standard output from PROC CPM is a table showing the following: the names of the activities; the input values; and the early start, early finish, late start, late finish, total float (T_FLOAT—the difference between late start and early start times), and free float (F_FLOAT—the difference between the early finish time of an activity and the early start time of the activity's immediate successor) times. Optionally, a Gantt chart can be printed by using PROC TIMEPLOT in SAS/OR. Adding the following lines to the program above produces a Gantt chart in addition to the ES, LS, EF, and LF times.

```
23  TITLE2 'GANTT CHART'
24  PROC SORT; BY E_START;
25  PROC TIMEPLOT DATA=COPYF;
26      CLASS ACT;
27      PLOT E_START='+' L_START='L' E_FINISH='E'
28      L_FINISH='+'/OVERLAY HILOC;
```

This program produces a Gantt chart ordered in early start sequence (by PROC SORT).

Both versions of the solution output for the Copyfast problem are shown below. Lines starting and ending with a '@' in the Gantt chart represent critical activities.

```
                    COPYFAST  STARTUP  SCHEDULE

        ACT     TAIL HEAD TIME  ES   EF   LS   LF  T_FLOAT  F_FLOAT

        LAWYER   1    2    4    0    4    0    4      0        0
        CPACCT   2    3    3    4    7    6    9      2        0
        LEASES   2    4    5    4    9    4    9      0        0
        DUMMY1   3    4    0    7    7    9    9      2        0
        NATGAS   4    8    1    9   10   14   15      5        5
        BUYOEQ   4    6    3    9   12    9   12      0        0
        ELECTR   4    5    1    9   10   11   12      2        0
        DUMMY2   5    6    0   10   10   12   12      2        2
        GROSSR   3    7    1    7    8   15   16      8        0
        LICENS   7    9    1    8    9   16   17      8        8
        TESTOE   6    8    3   12   15   12   15      0        0
        INSPEC   8    9    2   15   17   15   17      0        0


   ACT      ES  LS  EF  LF   MIN                                    MAX
                             0                                      17
                             *----------------------------------------*
   LAWYER    0   0   4   4   @-------@                               I
   CPACCT    4   6   7   9   I       +---L-E---+                     I
   LEASES    4   4   9   9   I       @---------@                     I
   DUMMY1    7   9   7   9   I               @---@                   I
   GROSSR    7  15   8  16   I                   +-E------------L--+I
   LICENS    8  16   9  17   I                     +-E------------L-+
   NATGAS    9  14  10  15   I                       +-E-------L-+   I
   BUYOEQ    9   9  12  12   I                   @-----@             I
   ELECTR    9  11  10  12   I                     +-E-L-+           I
   DUMMY2   10  12  10  12   I                     @---@             I
   TESTOE   12  12  15  15   I                           @-----@     I
   INSPEC   15  15  17  17   I                                 @---@
                             *----------------------------------------*
```

9. CONCLUDING REMARKS

We have discussed two project management techniques, CPM and PERT. CPM is most suited to projects that are repetitive in nature or in which there is little uncertainty in activity duration times. CPM is widely used in the construction industry. PERT incorporates uncertainty in activity durations into the critical-path method.

Criticisms

Criticisms of the methods presented in this chapter may be applied in the following areas:

1. In Section 3, cost/time trade-offs may not be linear.
2. PERT assumes that activities on the critical path are independent.
3. The beta distribution may not be an accurate method of modeling activity times.
4. Suppose the number of activities on the critical path is not large. If so, the use of the central limit theorem may not be justifiable.
5. The method of determining the critical path in PERT is questionable. For example, suppose the longest path has a mean of twenty weeks and standard deviation of two weeks, but another path has a mean of eighteen weeks and standard deviation of six weeks. We could consider the second path to be critical because of its high degree of completion time uncertainty.
6. The time estimates a, b, and m are difficult to obtain in practice.

Advantages of Using CPM and PERT

On the positive side, CPM and PERT require management to conduct **activity analysis;** that is, well-defined activities must be identified, and consideration must be given to the duration times and precedence relationships. This process in itself can be a valuable and informative aspect of the planning phase.

The CPM/PERT system offers an organized method for project planning, scheduling, and control. The benefits derived from its use must be weighed against the costs involved. A primary cost, especially for larger projects, is the cost involved with data processing, computing, and implementation of an information system needed to support a CPM/PERT system.

Variations of CPM/PERT

Several variations of CPM and PERT have been devised to meet special project needs. Two of these are **GERT** and **PERT/COST.**

GERT (Graphical Evaluation and Review Technique) was developed to deal with uncertainty in project networks.

PERT/COST was developed to deal specifically with costs as they occur in project network analysis for planning and control.

TERMINOLOGY

After studying this chapter you should be familiar with the following terms:

TERM	SECTION
activity	2
branch	2
CPM	2
crash cost	3
crash point	3
crash schedule	3
crashing	3
crash time	3
critical path	2
direct costs	4
dummy activity	2
earliest finish time (EF)	2
earliest start time (ES)	2
event	2
GERT	9
indirect costs	4
late finish time (LF)	2
late start time (LS)	2
minimum-cost crash schedule	3
most likely time	7
node	2
normal cost	3
normal point	3
normal schedule	3
optimistic time	7
PERT	7
PERT/COST	9
resource leveling	6
resource scheduling	5
slack time	2

EXERCISES

1. For each activity of the CPM network shown in Fig. 9.26, calculate the ES, EF, LS, LF, and slack, and identify the critical path(s).

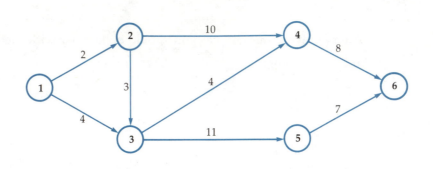

FIGURE 9.26

2. For each activity of the CPM network shown in Fig. 9.27, calculate the ES, EF, LS, LF, and slack, and identify the critical path(s).

3. For the network shown in Fig. 9.27, specify for each activity all the immediately preceding activities; that is, construct an activity precedence table.

4. Given the data shown in Table 9.12:
   a. Construct the CPM network.
   b. For each activity, compute the ES, EF, LS, LF, and slack.
   c. Identify the critical path(s).

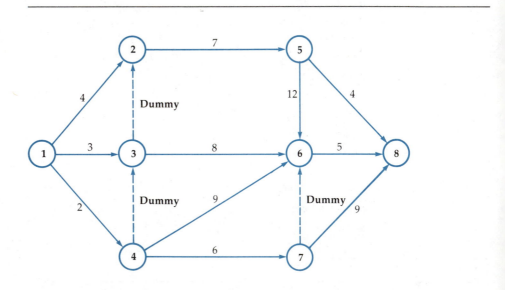

FIGURE 9.27

TABLE 9.12

Activity	Immediate predecessors	Activity duration (weeks)	Number of people required
A	None	2	4
B	None	3	3
C	A	5	1
D	A, B	3	2
E	C, D	6	2
F	C	1	2

5. For the CPM project in Exercise 4, assume that all noncritical activities are scheduled as early as possible. Construct a time chart showing the number of people working (on the vertical axis) versus the time in weeks (on the horizontal axis).

6. Refer to Exercise 5 above.
   a. Repeat Exercise 5, with the noncritical activities scheduled as late as possible.
   b. Regardless of attempts to bring about resource leveling, what will be the absolute minimum number of people required during each week of the project?

7. Given the information in Table 9.13:
   a. Construct the CPM network.
   b. Using normal times and costs, compute the critical path and total project cost.

TABLE 9.13

Activity	Immediate predecessors	Time in weeks Normal time	Time in weeks Crash time	Normal cost	Crash cost
A	None	10	9	10	16
B	None	13	10	6	10
C	A	15	13	4	5
D	B	8	7	9	13
E	A	10	10	8	8
F	D, E	8	7	6	12
G	C, F	20	19	7	15
H	D, E	9	6	7	9

c. Using crash times and costs for each activity, compute the critical path and total project cost.

d. Starting with the normal schedule of part (b), specify the first activity you would crash in order to shorten the project completion time by one week.

e. Following the crashing algorithm (Fig. 9.14), find the minimum cost crash schedule.

8. *Cash Planning.* Consider the CPM project network shown in Fig. 9.28 (activity duration times are shown in weeks). Suppose the cash required for each of the activities shown in the figure is given by Table 9.14.

a. Graph the cash needed each week (that is, plot cash required vertically and time horizontally), assuming that all noncritical activities are started as soon as possible (that is, at their ES times).

b. Graph cumulative cash required for part (a) above; that is, for each

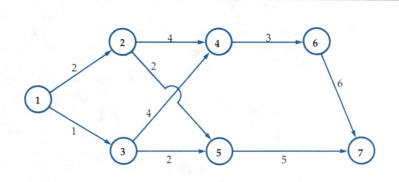

FIGURE 9.28

TABLE 9.14

Activity	Cash required
1–2	$ 8,000
1–3	15,000
2–4	4,000
2–5	20,000
3–4	6,000
3–5	2,000
4–6	9,000
5–7	12,000
6–7	10,000

week compute (and plot vertically) the total amount of cash spent on the project up to and including the current week.

c. Repeat parts (a) and (b), assuming that all noncritical activities are started as late as possible (that is, at their LS times).

9. *Research and Development.* Chemcom, Inc., is planning to develop a new chemical process. They have identified the following activities:

  A. Test method 1 for the process
  B. Test method 2 for the process
  C. Select the best method and refine the process
  D. Complete initial preparation of production facilities
  E. Train personnel
  F. Develop final procedures manual
  G. Run tests on the refined process
  H. Adjust the production method
  I. Set up complete production system
  J. Run final tests

These activities, their precedence relationships, and PERT time estimates are given in Table 9.15 (in weeks).

a. Develop a project network and determine the expected project completion time.

b. What is the probability that the project completion time will be ten percent under the expected time? Ten percent over? Twenty percent over? Fifty percent over?

10. A project has the specifications shown in Table 9.16.
   a. Construct the project network.
   b. For each activity, compute the mean and variance of the activity time.

TABLE 9.15

Activity	Immediate predecessors	a	b	m
A	None	10	20	15
B	None	8	15	10
C	A, B	3	8	5
D	None	10	13	12
E	D	2	3	2
F	D	2	4	3
G	C, E	1	2	1
H	F, G	1	3	2
I	F	2	7	4
J	H, I	1	1	1

TABLE 9.16

Activity	Immediate predecessors	a	b	m
A	None	2	9	6
B	A	7	7	7
C	A	1	6	2
D	C	1	4	3
E	B	4	6	5
F	D, E	2	9	6
G	B	3	7	4

c. Construct a table showing the ES, EF, LS, LF, and slack for each activity, and specify the critical path(s).

d. What is the probability that the project will be completed in twenty weeks or less? In twenty-five weeks or less?

11. *New-Product Development.* Quikcalc is working on the development of a new model pocket calculator. It has identified various major activities involved in the product development project, as listed in Table 9.17.

Construct the project network, compute all ES, EF, LS, LF, and slack times, and identify the critical path(s).

12. *Political-Campaign Management.* Millie Carelli is planning to run for state senator and has identified the activities required to prepare for the primary elections, as shown in Table 9.18.

TABLE 9.17

Activity label	Description	Immediate predecessors	Time duration (weeks)
A	Consumer research	None	4
B	Market analysis	A	2
C	Economic analysis	None	2
D	Feasibility analysis	B, C	3
E	Analysis of alternative designs and selection of the best design	D	7
F	Address marketing considerations	D	4
G	Manufacturing process selection	E	3
H	Set product price	F, G	2
I	Quality-control/maintenance policy	E	2

TABLE 9.18

Activity label	Description	Immediate predecessors	Time (days)	Campaign workers needed
A	Contact prospective campaign workers	None	7	1
B	Meet with local labor groups	C, F	2	2
C	Prepare campaign literature	A	4	3
D	Establish travel itinerary	None	4	2
E	Plan fundraising dinner at state capital	D	1	3
F	Attend first meeting with party leaders	D	3	2
G	Plan second major fundraising dinner	B, E	1	2
H	Contact voter groups	D	5	6
I	Attend second meeting with party leaders	E, H	1	2
J	Make trip to the city of Bigtown	I	1	2
K	Design and implement major radio advertising campaign	B, E	3	3
L	Set plans for the major push before election day	J, K	3	5

a. Construct the project network.

b. For each activity, compute the ES, EF, LS, LF, and slack, and specify the critical path.

c. Construct a worker requirement chart as a function of time, assuming all activities are started as soon as possible. (This is a conservative measure decided upon by Ms. Carelli to hedge against the possibility that something might not go as planned.)

13. *Installing a Computer System.* A simplified model of a computer system installation project is given by the list of activities in Table 9.19.

a. Construct a CPM network.

b. Compute the ES, LS, EF, LF, and slack, and identify the critical path(s).

14. *Installation of a Computer System—Uncertainties.* Refer to Exercise 13 above. It was felt that there was considerable uncertainty in the duration times of the various tasks involved in the computer system installation. The PERT estimates shown in Table 9.20 were obtained.

a. Calculate the expected project completion time.

b. What is the probability that the project will be completed within twenty weeks?

TABLE 9.19

Activity	Description	Immediate predecessors	Duration (weeks)
A	Prepare physical facilities (building, electrical, air-conditioning, etc.)	None	6
B	Train system and application programmers	None	8
C	Install the computer hardware	A	4
D	Prepare test data	B	2
E	Prepare existing company files and records for data entry	B	3
F	Test software and debug	C, D	5
G	Train clerical personnel	E	2
H	Implement system	F, G	4

TABLE 9.20

Activity	a	b	m
A	4	7	5
B	6	10	8
C	4	4	4
D	1	3	2
E	2	4	2
F	3	7	4
G	2	2	2
H	3	6	4

TABLE 9.21

Range (weeks)	Probability	Cumulative probability
Less than 15		
Between 15 and 18		
Between 18 and 21		
Between 21 and 24		
Longer than 24		

15. *PERT Analysis: Project Completion Time Distribution.* Refer to Exercise 14 above. Calculate the probability that the project will be completed in each time range listed in Table 9.21.

16. *Planning the Maintenance Function.* University plant maintenance is planning to check out the heating system of the university's main

TABLE 9.22

Activity	Description	Immediate predecessors	Duration (days)
A	Check electrical service to furnace	None	2.0
B	Change filters	None	1.0
C	Check ducts	None	3.0
D	Oil motor bearings	B	0.5
E	Check motor belts	D	0.5
F	Clean vents	C	0.5
G	Check electrical wiring to thermostats	A	2.0
H	Test motor	A, E, F	0.5
I	Test thermostats	G, H	0.5
J	Check building insulation and windows for heat leaks	F	2.0

TABLE 9.23

Activity	Description	Immediate predecessors	Duration (days)
A	Excavate and set forms	None	5
B	Order custom doors	None	8
C	Install exterior plumbing and electrical	None	7
D	Pour concrete foundation	A	3
E	Construct frame	B, C, D	8
F	Prepare exterior for stucco	E	3
G	Install solar system on roof	E	5
H	Install interior plumbing and heating	B, C, D, G	5
I	Install insulation	H	2
J	Install sheet rock	I	4
K	Finish interior	J	10
L	Stucco exterior	F	3
M	Complete landscaping	K, L	5

library. The activities chart shown in Table 9.22 has been constructed. Develop a CPM network, and determine the critical path.

17. *Construction Projects.*   The major steps used by Solarcom Construction Co. in building its Model S1S home are shown in Table 9.23.

Construct a CPM network, and determine the critical activities and project duration.

APPENDIX TO SECTION TWO:
TIME-SERIES FORECASTING

CONTENTS

1. INTRODUCTION

We shall use the term **forecasting** interchangeably with the term **prediction.** A forecast is a prediction, estimate, or determination of some future value based on a certain set of factors.

The value being forecasted may be sales (in units of product or in terms of revenue), interest rates, housing starts, the availability of funds, GNP, oil supplies, coal supplies, energy requirements, technological status (such as the status of solid-state circuitry applications), and so on.

The factors on which a forecast is based might be any of the following:

past data, judgment or opinion, management consensus, internal company data, external data, or a perceived pattern related to time (such as seasonal variations).

In this chapter we shall give a brief overview of some basic forecasting methods.

2. CLASSIFICATION OF FORECASTING METHODS

Different schemes may be employed for classifying forecasting methods. Possible criteria for this classification are listed as follows:

- *By use:* To what use or purpose will the result of the forecast be put?
- *By method:* Is the forecasting technique qualitative (judgmental) or quantitative? If it is quantitative, what are its basic mathematical or statistical properties?
- *By time horizon:* How far ahead must the forecast be made?

In this text we shall classify the various forecasting methods by the time horizon to which they apply. Authors will differ in their definitions of the major categories of forecasts; however, the definitions given below are fairly typical.

SHORT-TERM FORECASTS. Short-term forecasts cover one day to one year and are used primarily for short-run control, such as adjustment of production rates, employment, purchasing, scheduling (labor and other resource inputs), and sales forecasts.

The methods employed are time-series smoothing, regression, decomposition, graphical techniques, and judgment. *Decomposition* is a process of breaking a past pattern of data down into four components: (1) seasonal factors, (2) a broad general trend (upward or downward), (3) business cycle effects, and (4) random variations. Time-series smoothing and regression will be discussed later in this chapter.

INTERMEDIATE-TERM FORECASTS. This category of forecasts covers forecasts made for periods ranging from one season to one or two years and are used for planning operating budgets, cash flow, production schedules, and sales. Methods employed include time series, regression, judgment, decomposition, and econometric models. Econometric models attempt to relate several variables to other variables over time by means of a system of interrelated mathematical equations.

LONG-TERM FORECASTS. Long-term forecasts are made for periods ranging from two to five years or more. Such forecasts are used for broad planning in areas such as general policy, facilities expansion, research and development of new products or technologies, and general trends in the market and society.

The methods employed to make such forecasts include technological forecasting, econometric models, qualitative-judgmental decisions, and other techniques. One technique employed is called the **Delphi method,** which involves a panel of executives and other experts individually making judgments, predictions, and analyses. Under various arrangements, the group then moves incrementally (step by step) toward a general consensus.

There is not space in a basic textbook for a detailed discussion of the wide variety of technological forecasting methods. However, the following short list gives you some idea of the types of applications that might be subject to technological forecasting:

1. What percentage of electrical power will be generated ten years from now by using solar methods?
2. How long will it take to send a manned mission to Jupiter?
3. What will be the pattern of discoveries for successful cancer cures and treatments?
4. What (if anything) will replace the internal-combustion-powered automobile? When?

APPLICATIONS

The following applications appear in this chapter in text, examples, or problems:

Agricultural imports

Commodity prices

Forecast responsiveness

Gold prices

Maintenance expenses

Sales forecasting
  Hardware
  Bakery
  Department store

Seasonal smoothing

Tracking signals

Quantitative versus Qualitative Forecasts

Qualitative (or technological) **forecasting** involves management judgment, consensus, drawing analogies with other known developments, brainstorming, writing "scenarios" of the possible events that might occur, and more recent techniques such as "catastrophe theory," a field of study geared to the development of mathematical models that can be used to predict major events, turning points, or changes in various phenomena.

Qualitative methods are useful when past data does not exist or (if they do exist) when one cannot assume that the data will continue to follow a pattern. These methods also apply when the forecast concerns unlikely or unexpected future events. For example, what will come after integrated-circuit technology for pocket-calculator application?

Quantitative forecasting can be used if (1) past data are available and (2) the past data can be fitted into a pattern that can be expected to continue into the future. Even in the case where no past data are available (such as in the case of a new business), quantitative forecasting methods can be used if it can be assumed that the data generated (such as sales) will follow some sort of pattern.

There are two main types of quantitative forecasting models: (1) causal models and (2) time-series models.

A **causal model** attempts to relate some quantity (such as sales) to other factors (such as time, GNP, personal income, and population).

A **time-series model** attempts to relate some quantity (such as sales) strictly to *time*.

We shall expand upon some of these points later in this chapter as various techniques are demonstrated. This chapter introduces just a few basic forecasting techniques that are widely used. Although we discuss some of the simpler methods, most of the more sophisticated mathematical models are based on these simpler techniques.

Definition of Time Series

A **time series** is simply a sequence of variables related to sequential time periods. For example, suppose we refer to the months of January through December as months 1 through 12. Let X_i be the sales of a company in the ith month; thus X_2 = sales during February (month 2). Then the sequence of variables X_1, X_2, X_3, X_4, X_5, X_6, X_7, X_8, X_9, X_{10}, X_{11}, X_{12} is a time series "indexed" or "related" to a monthly time period.

A Constant Time Series

A **constant time series** has the form

$$X_t = C + E$$

where X_t denotes the value in period t, C is a constant, and E is a random error component that represents "noise" and has an average value of 0.

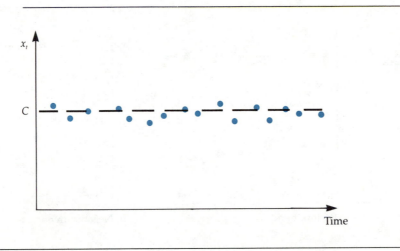

FIGURE 1   *Constant time series.*

In Fig. 1, we present a graphic example of a constant time series. Note that, *on the average*, X_t has the constant value, C. However, X_t may vary somewhat because of some random influences in the environment; the random variable, E, takes these random factors into account.

A Time Series with Trend

A time series exhibits a linear **trend** if it has the form

$$X_t = a + bt + E$$

where a and b are constants and E is a random error and has an average value of 0. Fig. 2(a) shows a trend having positive slope ($b > 0$), and Fig. 2(b) illustrates a negative trend ($b < 0$). When $b = 0$, we have the special case of a constant time series whose average is the constant a.

Notation

As above, we shall denote a time series by X_1, X_2, X_3, ... We are interested in forecasting future values of various time series, so we let F_1 denote the forecast for X_1. Thus, for example, suppose we observe sales for three months: $X_1 = 20$, $X_2 = 30$, and $X_3 = 15$ (units of product); then, F_4 will denote the sales forecast for the fourth month, based on the first three months.

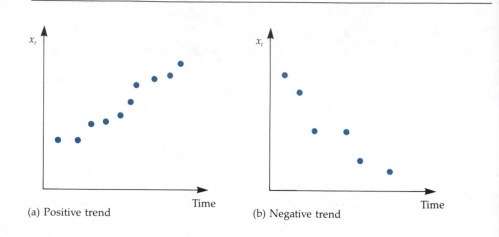

(a) Positive trend   (b) Negative trend

Time series with trend.

3. MOVING AVERAGE SYSTEM

A simple **moving average forecasting system** uses the average of a number of periods of past data to forecast future values. In order to implement a moving average system, the number of past periods used in the average must be specified. We shall denote this parameter by N. The moving average system discussed is designed for constant time series. However, if only a slow trend is present, the system may still be used. The following example illustrates the method.

EXAMPLE 1. *A Moving Average Forecasting System.* Hole-in-One Bakery has observed the following sales pattern for donuts in the past six weeks:

Week	1	2	3	4	5	6
Sales (dozens)	50	55	48	49	51	53

If Hole-in-One uses a three-week moving average forecasting system, what would be the sales forecast for the seventh week?

Solution. Here $N = 3$. To forecast week 7 with a three-week moving average system, simply calculate the average of the last three weeks and use this figure as a forecast for week 7. Notationally,

$$F_7 = \frac{X_4 + X_5 + X_6}{3}$$

$$= \frac{49 + 51 + 53}{3}$$

$$= 51$$

How would a three-week moving average system have performed on *past data?*

Solution. Since three weeks are needed to make a forecast, the first week for which we can compute a forecast is week 4. The results follow:

Week	1	2	3	4	5	6	7
Actual sales	50	55	48	49	51	53	?
Forecast				51	51	49	51

Note how we interpret such a past forecast. Imagine that you are currently in week 3 and you have observed sales of 50, 55, and 48 for the first three weeks. Based on this information, your forecast for week 4 would be as follows:

$$F_4 = \frac{50 + 55 + 48}{3} = 51$$

Then in week 4 you observed *actual sales* to be 49, so your forecast for week 5 would be

$$F_5 = \frac{55 + 48 + 49}{3} = 50.7 \qquad \blacktriangle$$

The Effect of *N*

The parameter N determines how fast the forecast responds to changes in the data. The larger the value of N, the slower the forecast will respond to changes in the underlying time series.

EXAMPLE 2. *Forecast Response.* In this example we shall illustrate the effect of the parameter N on forecast response to (1) actual changes in the data and (2) random disturbance.

Part A. Response to Actual Changes in the Data. Suppose past sales have been recorded as follows:

Week	1	2	3	4	5	6	7	8	9
Sales	20	21	20	22	25	26	25	27	?

Forecasts using a two-week and a five-week moving average (MA) system are given below (that is, we compare the two systems $N = 2$ and $N = 5$):

Week	1	2	3	4	5	6	7	8	9
Sales	20	21	20	22	25	26	25	27	?
2-week MA			20.5	20.5	21	23.5	25.5	25.5	26
5-week MA						21.6	22.8	23.6	25

Note the differences in how the two forecasting systems respond. If you study the actual sales data, you will notice that there seems to be a change in the average sales level at week 5. The sales jump from 22 in week 4 to 25 in week 5 and remain above 25 in weeks 5 through 8. The two-week system responds rather quickly in week 6 and by week 7 has "caught up" with the new sales pattern. The five-week system forecasts 21.6 for week 6, which is more "representative" of the old sales pattern in weeks 1 to 4. It is not until week 9 that the five-week forecasting system catches up to the new sales level that began in the fifth week.

We can say that the larger N is, the slower the forecasting system responds to *actual changes* in the level of sales.

Part B. Response to Random Disturbances. Let us repeat the analysis of Part A, using a different time series of sales data. The new data are presented below along with the two- and five-week forecasts:

Week	1	2	3	4	5	6	7	8	9
Sales	20	21	20	22	27	21	19	20	?
2-week MA			20.5	20.5	21	24.5	24	20	19.5
5-week MA						22	22.2	21.8	21.8

Study the (actual) sales data. The average sales figure for the eight weeks is

$$\frac{20 + 21 + 20 + 22 + 27 + 21 + 19 + 20}{8} = 21.25$$

and the time series (sales) appears to be fairly constant *except* for a "wild" jump in week 5 to a sales of 27. The two-week moving average responded to this random jump by forecasting 24.5 and 24 for weeks 6 and 7, respectively. However, the five-week moving average system displays more stability and continues to give forecasts closer to the eight-week average of 21.25.

We can say that the larger N is, the more *stable* the forecasts will be; that is, the system is less likely to respond to random influences that are not representative of a basic, underlying constant pattern. ▲

The Issue of Responsiveness

As Example 2 illustrates, the larger the value of N, the slower the forecasts respond to *actual* changes in the time series. However, for large values of

N, the forecasting system is more stable and will not respond inappropriately to exceptional random data fluctuations.

So, you may ask, how does one decide to use a large N or a small N? There is no simple answer to this. One method, based on the concept of MAD (mean absolute deviation) will be discussed in the next section. At this point, two facts should be noted:

1. There is nothing that dictates that you must continue to use the same value of N if you sense that the actual data (time series) is changing. In Example 2, Part A, if you had been using a five-week moving average system up to week 8, you could switch to a more responsive system (smaller N) after observing the increase in the sales level that begins in week 5. Your decision to use a smaller value of N would be especially appropriate if you suspect that *another* change in the sales pattern might occur, say, in week 9 or 10.
2. There are more advanced techniques (beyond the scope of our discussion here), called **adaptive methods,** that *automatically adjust the forecasting system in response to changes in the time series.*

The Concept of Lag

A three-week moving average system uses data from the past three weeks to forecast the next week, as shown below (the *current* week is 12; we are forecasting for week 13):

Week	10	11	12	13
Sales	8	7	10	?
Forecast				8.33

The forecast for week 13 uses three past data points: 8, 7, 10. The sales figure of 8 is *two* weeks old (relative to week 12), the sales figure of 7 is one week old, and the sales figure of 10 is zero weeks old (since we have just observed it). The average age of the three data points is

$$\frac{2 + 1 + 0}{3} = 1 \text{ week}$$

That is, the *average age of past data* used by a three-week moving average forecasting system is one week. We say that the system *lags* the data by one week, or that the *lag* is one week, or that the system is "centered" one week in the past. In our example, the forecast uses weeks 10, 11, and 12; therefore the forecast is "centered" on week 11.

In general, the *lag* of an N period moving average forecasting system can be calculated as follows:

$$\frac{N - 1}{2} \text{ periods}$$

Weighted Moving Averages

In the case of an N-period moving average system, each past data point is given the same weight of $1/N$. For $N = 3$, for example, each past data point is given an equal weight of $1/3$.

A **weighted moving average system** assigns different weights to the past data points. For example, if it is felt that the most recent period is more representative of what to expect in the future, more weight could be given to this period. The next example illustrates how to use a weighted moving average forecasting system.

EXAMPLE 3. *Weighted Moving Average System.* A three-week weighted moving average system is to be employed to forecast sales for Slowyear Tire Company. The past three data points are to be given weights of 1, 2, and 3 (from past to present). Sales for April, May, and June were 2,000, 1,800, and 2,200, respectively. What would be the sales forecast for July?

Solution.

$$F_{July} = \frac{1(2,000) + 2(1,800) + 3(2,200)}{6} = 2033.3$$

Note that since a total of six weights were used ($1 + 2 + 3$), we use 6 as the denominator. We can also view the weights as 1/6, 2/6, and 3/6 (which add up to one).   ▲

Computational Requirements

One of the disadvantages of a moving average system is the amount of storage required. An N period moving average requires that we store N periods of past data. If N is large, say 50 or 100, this can be an inconvenience (in terms of keeping records) and/or a technical disadvantage (in terms of computer storage requirements and data entry).

Problems

1. On a graph, plot the results of Example 2, Part A. Label the horizontal axis weeks 1–9, and plot the actual sales, the two-week moving average forecast, and the five-week moving average forecast on the vertical axis.
2. What is the lag of a two-period moving average forecast? Of a five-period moving average forecast?

3. Sales of Sturdi-Trailers for the past ten months are given below:

Month	1	2	3	4	5	6	7	8	9	10	11
Sales	20	22	21	19	23	23	24	26	23	20	?

   a. How would a three-month moving average system have performed using this data? (Start the first forecast at period 4.)
   b. Repeat part (a), using a six-month moving average system. What is the lag of this system?
   c. Using a six-month moving average system, what would your forecast be for months 11, 12, and 13, based on your *current perspective* in week 10?

4. Given the following data:

Week	1	2	3	4	5	6	7	8	9	10
Sales	3	5	7	9	11	13	15	17	19	21

   a. Determine whether this time series follows a constant or a trend model.
   b. Use a three-week and a five-week moving average system on these past data. (Start the three-week system at week 4 and the five-week system at week 6.)
   c. Plot the results of part (b) on a graph. (Label the weeks on the horizontal axis, and place the actual sales and the two forecasting systems on the vertical axis.)
   d. Compute the lag for each system. Given a choice of the two systems, which would you select?

5. Use a weighted three-week moving average system on the data given in Problem 4 above:
   a. Use weights of 1, 1, and 2.
   b. Use weights of 1, 2, and 3.
   c. Plot the results on a graph. Which system seems to "track" the data more closely?

4. MEAN ABSOLUTE DEVIATION (MAD)

The **mean absolute deviation** (commonly referred to as MAD) is a device that measures how close a forecast is to the actual data.

   If we denote the forecast for the ith period as F_i and the actual data by X_i, then the **forecast error,** denoted e_i, is simply

$e_i = X_i - F_i$

The **absolute forecast error** is the absolute value of e_i, or $|e_i|$. Suppose we have n data points and n forecasts. The MAD is simply the sum of the n absolute forecast errors divided by n. The next example will make this clear.

TABLE 1   *Computing MAD*

Week	Actual data	3-week MA forecast	Forecast error $e_i = X_i - F_i$	Absolute error $\|e_i\|$
1	20			
2	22			
3	18			
4	19	20.00	−1.00	1.00
5	23	19.67	3.33	3.33
6	23	20.00	3.00	3.00
7	21	21.67	−0.67	0.67
8	20	22.33	−2.33	2.33
9	19	21.33	−2.33	2.33
10	23	20.00	3.00	3.00
11	25	20.67	4.33	4.33

$$\Sigma|e_i| = 19.99$$
$$\text{MAD} = \Sigma|e_i| \div 8 = 2.50$$

EXAMPLE 4. *Computing MAD.* In Table 1, we have used a three-week moving average system on a set of past data. Also shown are the forecast errors, e_i, the absolute forecast errors, and the MAD. You should carefully check these calculations. Note that eight periods were used (weeks 4–11).   ▲

Selecting a Moving Average System

One method of selecting a moving average system is to try various moving average systems on past data and then select the system having the minimum MAD value. The rationale behind this is clear: the smaller the value of the MAD, the closer the forecast is to the actual data.

Problem 1 at the end of this section asks you to apply this criterion.

Problems

1. Refer to the data given in Table 1.
   a. Compute the MAD for a four-week moving average forecasting system.
   b. Since the four-week moving average system does not start until week 5, recompute the MAD for the three-week moving average system, starting with week 5.

      c. Now compare the two systems on the basis of the MAD values. Which system seems to give better forecasts?

      d. Using the system chosen in part c above, forecast week 12.

2. Suppose you use a moving average system on a set of past data and find that the forecast errors, $e_i = X_i - F_i$, are consistently *positive*. What would this tell you?

5. SINGLE EXPONENTIAL SMOOTHING

Another forecasting system that is useful for the constant model ($X_t = C + E$) is **single exponential smoothing.** Again, letting F_t denote the forecast for period t and X_t denote the actual data in period t, the exponential smoothing model can be written as follows:

$$F_t = \alpha X_{t-1} + (1 - \alpha)F_{t-1} \qquad (1)$$

where α is a number, called the **smoothing parameter,** between 0 and 1: $0 \le \alpha \le 1$. Just as it was necessary to specify the parameter N for a moving average system, it is necessary to specify the parameter α for an exponential smoothing system.

    Let us look at Eq. (1) to get some idea of how it works and the rationale behind it. Suppose we have chosen α to be 0.25. Then Eq. (1) would become

$$F_t = (0.25)X_{t-1} + (0.75)F_{t-1}$$

Now imagine that we are in period $t - 1$ (the current time period). Our forecast for this period *was* F_{t-1} and the *actual* data turned out to be X_{t-1}. Then the above equation tells us that, to get a forecast for the *next* period (t), we compute a weighted average of the current data, X_{t-1}, and our past forecast, F_{t-1}. The weights are 0.25 and 0.75, respectively. The next example illustrates how an exponential smoothing system works.

EXAMPLE 5. *Exponential Smoothing.* This example illustrates an exponential smoothing system for $\alpha = 0.25$. Suppose the sales for a company over the past five weeks are observed to be the following:

Week	1	2	3	4	5	6
Sales	10	12	15	13	12	?

We wish to examine how our forecasting system would have performed on this time series of sales data. We shall start the forecast with week 2. Then Eq. (1) becomes

$$F_2 = 0.25X_1 + 0.75F_1$$

(Note that we are substituting $t = 2$ to forecast for week 2.)

Now X_1 equals sales for week 1, so $X_1 = 10$. But what about F_1, our forecast for week 1? We do not yet have a value for F_1. In practice, to get the forecasting equation started, F_1 can be chosen in any of the following ways:

1. Use the first actual data point as the first forecast. (In our case, we could take F_1 to be X_1, or $F_1 = 10$.)
2. Use the average of past data observed (historically) prior to the start of the current record. (In our case, if the company had past data *prior* to week 1 listed above, we could use the average of these data as a forecast for week 1.)
3. Use an intelligent guess or an otherwise reasonable and acceptable figure for F_1.

For this example, we shall use the first method. Thus we set $F_1 = X_1 = 10$. Then the forecast for week 2 is computed as follows:

$$F_2 = 0.25X_1 + 0.75F_1 = 0.25(10) + 0.75(10) = 10$$

The forecast for week 3 would be

$$F_3 = 0.25X_2 + 0.75F_2 = 0.25(12) + 0.75(10) = 10.5$$

And for weeks 4, 5, and 6 we would have the following forecasts:

$$F_4 = 0.25X_3 + 0.75F_3 = 0.25(15) + 0.75(10.5) = 11.62$$

$$F_5 = 0.25(13) + 0.75(11.62) = 11.96$$

$$F_6 = 0.25(12) + 0.75(11.96) = 11.97$$

Notes. We make the following observations concerning the above example.

1. How we start the forecasting system with F_{t-1} is not too important. As time passes (say in fifty weeks) the effect of this starting value will soon disappear, or "wash out."
2. Note the *dynamic nature of the forecasting process.* In the present example we have forecasted sales for week 6 to be 11.97. Suppose that in week 6 actual sales are observed to be 14. Then we combine these two figures to forecast sales for week 7 as follows:

$$F_7 = 0.25(14) + 0.75(11.97) = 12.48$$

We then observe actual sales for week 7, and the process continues. The dynamic nature of the forecasting process applies in the same manner as do the moving average systems.
3. *From your perspective in week 5* (after observing sales of 10, 12, 15, 13, and 12), what would be your forecast for the next *three* weeks? The answer to

this is quite clear. You would forecast 11.97 units each for weeks 6, 7, and 8, for a cumulative sales figure of 35.91 (11.97 + 11.97 + 11.97). However, as discussed in Note 2 above, your forecasts for weeks 7 and 8 will change, depending on actual sales observed in weeks 6 and 7. However, for *planning purposes in week 5*, you would prepare for total sales of 35.91 units over the next three weeks.   ▲

Selecting the Smoothing Parameter α

The following factors can be taken into account in selecting the value of the smoothing parameter:

1. *Responsiveness.* The higher the value of α, the faster the system responds to current data (and to changes in the basic level of the data). Look at the extreme cases. Suppose $\alpha = 1$. Then $F_t = X_{t-1}$—that is, the forecast for the next period *coincides* with this period's data. No weight is given to the previous forecast. If $\alpha = 0$, then $F_t = F_{t-1}$, and the forecast never changes (it always agrees with the previous forecast). No weight is given to new data. Intermediate values of α result in intermediate weighting schemes. If α is large, the forecasting system will give a lot of weight to new data (that is, to X_{t-1}) and the forecasting system will respond quickly to *actual* changes in the basic level of data. However, for large α, the system will also respond "inappropriately" to large random fluctuations in the data. See Problems 1 and 2 at the end of this section.
2. *MAD.* Given a set of past data, one method of selecting the value of α to use for future forecasts would be to try several α values on the past data and then select the value that gives the minimum MAD. See Problem 3 at the end of this section.
3. In more advanced textbooks on forecasting, **adaptive smoothing methods** are discussed. These methods allow you to start with a certain value of α. The forecasting system then *automatically* adjusts the α value according to new data values as they are observed. In a sense, α "adapts" to the time series data.
4. It can be shown mathematically that the lag for an exponential smoothing system is

$$\text{lag} = \frac{1 - \alpha}{\alpha} \tag{2}$$

Thus, for example, if $\alpha = 0.25$, the lag is

$$\frac{1 - 0.25}{0.25} = 3 \text{ periods}$$

This means that the average age of past data incorporated into a forecast would be three periods; or the forecast would be "centered" three periods in the past.

5. Select a value of α which would correspond to an "equivalent" moving average system. See Exercise 4 at the end of this chapter for a discussion of this system.

Computational Requirements

One of the main advantages of an exponential smoothing forecasting system is that it requires only two data points to be stored—namely, X_{t-1} (the last period's data) and F_{t-1} (the forecast for last period).

Problems

1. Fill in the following table, using two exponential smoothing systems, $\alpha = 0.1$ and $\alpha = 0.6$. Note that we have arbitrarily set the forecast for month 1 to be 12 units.

Month	1	2	3	4	5	6	7	8
Actual sales	12	11	12	14	15	17	16	?
Forecast $\alpha = 0.1$	12							
Forecast $\alpha = 0.6$	12							

Which system responds more accurately to the increasing sales level that seems to begin in period 4?

2. Repeat Problem 1, using the data given below:

Month	1	2	3	4	5	6	7	8
Actual sales	12	11	12	10	19	10	11	?
Forecast $\alpha = 0.1$	12							
Forecast $\alpha = 0.6$	12							

Sales in month 5 appear to be a random exception to the generally stable sales pattern. Which forecasting system is more stable?

3. For Problem 1 above, compute the MAD for each system. On the basis of MAD, which system would you choose to use for making future forecasts?

4. Compare the value of MAD for the two systems in Problem 2 above.

6. DOUBLE EXPONENTIAL SMOOTHING

Exponential smoothing systems exist for forecasting time-series data following a trend model

$$X_t = a + bt + E$$

In this section we shall briefly describe one such system. An outline of the method follows.

First it is necessary to select a smoothing parameter α. This may be done by trial and error, by judgment, or by using the MAD as a selection criterion as described in the previous section.

The system operates by the following steps:

STEP 1. Compute

$$S_t = \alpha X_{t-1} + (1 - \alpha)S_{t-1} \tag{3}$$

STEP 2. Compute

$$S'_t = \alpha S_t + (1 - \alpha)S'_{t-1} \tag{4}$$

STEP 3. Compute

$$a_t = S_t + (S_t - S'_t) \tag{5}$$

STEP 4. Compute

$$b_t = \left(\frac{\alpha}{1 - \alpha}\right)(S_t - S'_t) \tag{6}$$

STEP 5. Let the current period be denoted t. Then the forecast for period $t + k$, denoted F_{t+k}, is

$$F_{t+k} = a_t + b_t k \tag{7}$$

EXAMPLE 6. *Double Exponential Smoothing.* In Table 2, we present a time series of sales data and past forecasts using the double exponential smoothing system. The value $\alpha = 0.30$ was employed.

The actual data are X_t, and Eqs. (3) through (7) were used to compute the entries in the columns. Note that we began by setting $S_1 = S'_1 = X_1 = 10$.

The S_t column gives the single exponential smoothed forecast, as discussed in the previous section. The last column, headed $F_{t+1} = a_t + (1)b_t$, gives the doubly smoothed forecast according to Eq. (7). As you can see, the doubly smoothed forecast more closely follows the time series X_t than does the singly smoothed forecast S_t.

The average change in the X_t column is two units, which represents an approximate slope of 2. The b_t column gives current estimates of the trend (or slope). You will notice that b_t appears to be moving upward toward the value of 2.

In general, it takes any smoothing system some time to begin to forecast accurately. In Table 2, we have shown only 14 weeks of data. In a realistic application, we would continue to operate the forecasting system for sev-

TABLE 2   *Double Exponential Smoothing* ($\alpha = 0.3$).

Week	X_t	S_t	S_t'	a_t	b_t	$F_t = a_t + (1)b_t$
1	10	10.00	10.00	10.00	0.00	
2	12	10.00	10.00	10.00	0.00	10.00
3	13	10.60	10.18	11.02	0.18	10.00
4	15	11.32	10.52	12.12	0.34	11.20
5	18	12.42	11.09	13.75	0.57	12.46
6	20	14.09	12.00	16.18	0.90	14.32
7	21	15.86	13.16	18.56	1.16	17.08
8	23	17.40	14.43	20.37	1.27	19.72
9	26	19.08	15.82	22.34	1.40	22.64
10	28	21.16	17.42	24.90	1.60	23.74
11	28	23.21	19.16	27.26	1.74	26.50
12	30	24.65	20.81	28.49	1.64	29.00
13	33	26.26	22.44	30.08	1.64	30.13
14	36	28.28	24.19	32.37	1.75	31.72
15	?					34.12

eral periods into the future. The initial effects of setting $S_1 = S_1' = X_1 = 10$ would disappear, and b_t would more strongly reflect slope consistency. Note that the quantity S' is used in computing the slope b_t; that is, S' is introduced into the basic model to detect any trend (slope) that might be present in the data.   ▲

---

7. A TIME-SERIES REGRESSION MODEL

In this section we shall present a basic regression model that is useful in time-series forecasting problems. The model presented is referred to as **simple linear regression.**

Suppose we are given pàst data points, $X_1, X_2, \ldots, X_n$, corresponding to time periods 1 through n. We could then plot these values on a graph, placing the time periods $1, 2, \ldots, n$ on the horizontal axis and plotting the values of the data points vertically. We might then try to "fit" a straight line through these points. This line would not pass exactly through every point (unless the data points followed a perfectly straight line, which is not very likely); that is, the line would deviate from the data points. The line that fits closest to the data points (that is, the line that minimizes the sum of the squared deviations) is called the **linear regression line.**

The equation of this regression line is

$$F_t = a + bt, \quad t = 1, 2, \ldots, n \tag{8}$$

where the slope b is computed by

$$b = \frac{\Sigma t X_t - n \bar{t} \bar{X}}{\Sigma t^2 - n(\bar{t})^2} \tag{9}$$

and the intercept a is given by

$$a = \bar{X} - b\bar{t} \tag{10}$$

In these equations,

$$\bar{t} = \frac{n+1}{2} \tag{11}$$

and $\bar{X}$ = the average of the Xs, or

$$\bar{X} = \frac{\Sigma X_t}{n} \tag{12}$$

and the sums run from $t = 1$ to $t = n$.

The **standard error of the estimate** is

$$\sigma = \sqrt{\frac{\Sigma(X_t - F_t)^2}{n-2}} \tag{13}$$

As a rule of thumb, 68 percent of the data points (the Xs) should fall within a distance of σ from the regression line; 95 percent should fall within 2σ of the line. Thus, σ measures how well the line fits the points. The smaller the value of σ, the closer the Xs are to the regression line.

The next example should help make all of this clear to you.

EXAMPLE 7. *Time-Series Regression.* Hardly's Hardware Store has recorded its yearly gross sales for the past seven years (in \$000) as 20, 22, 27, 25, 30, 32, and 35. Hardly observes an upward trend in his sales and would like to quantify the pattern formally. In particular, he would like an estimate of gross sales for each of the next two years. Can you assist him?

Solution. In the above notation, we have the time variable t going from 1 to 7, with $X_1 = 20$, $X_2 = 22$, $X_3 = 27$, $X_4 = 25$, $X_5 = 30$, $X_6 = 32$, and $X_7 = 35$; also $n = 7$. Table 3 organizes the calculations for Eqs. (9) through (12). From Table 3, the regression line is seen to be

$$F_t = a + bt \tag{14}$$

$$F_t = 17.56 + 2.43t$$

TABLE 3

(1) t	(2) X_t	(1) × (2) tX_t	(1)^2 t^2
1	20	20	1
2	22	44	4
3	27	81	9
4	25	100	16
5	30	150	25
6	32	192	36
7	35	245	49
Σ	191	832	140

$$\bar{t} = \frac{(n + 1)}{2} = 4 \qquad \text{Eq. (11)}$$

$$\bar{X} = \frac{\Sigma X_t}{n} = \frac{191}{7} = 27.28 \qquad \text{Eq. (12)}$$

$$b = \frac{\Sigma tX_t - n\bar{t}\bar{X}}{\Sigma t^2 - n(\bar{t})^2} = \frac{832 - 7(4)(27.28)}{140 - 7(4)^2} = 2.43 \qquad \text{Eq. (9)}$$

$$a = \bar{X} - b\bar{t} = 27.28 - (2.43)(4) = 17.56 \qquad \text{Eq. (10)}$$

In Table 4, we organize the calculations for the standard error of the estimate. For example, if $t = 2$, then $F_2 = 17.56 + 2.43(2) = 22.42$—that is, the column headed F_t is calculated from Eq. (14). The standard error of the estimate is seen to be 1.43.

TABLE 4

t	X_t	F_t	$X_t - F_t$	$(X_t - F_t)^2$
1	20	19.99	0.01	0.00
2	22	22.42	−0.42	0.18
3	27	24.85	2.15	4.62
4	25	27.28	−2.28	5.20
5	30	29.71	0.29	0.08
6	32	32.14	−0.14	0.02
7	35	34.57	0.43	0.18
				Σ 10.28

$$\sigma = \sqrt{\frac{\Sigma(X_t - F_t)^2}{n - 2}} = \sqrt{\frac{10.28}{7 - 2}} = 1.43$$

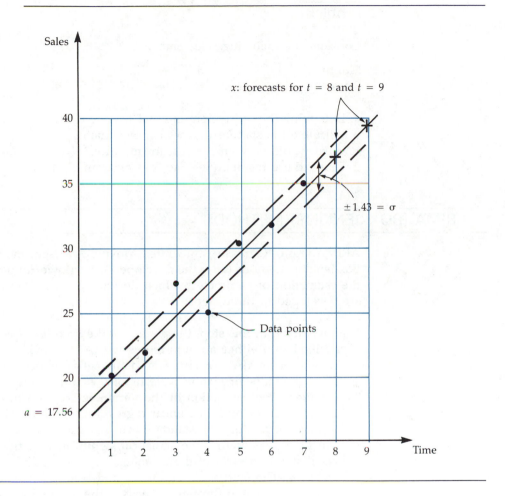

FIGURE 3

To forecast for the next two years, we calculate the following:

$$F_8 = 17.56 + 2.43(8) = 37$$

$$F_9 = 17.56 + 2.43(9) = 39.43$$

That is, sales in the next two years are forecast to total $76,430 [(37 + 39.32) × $1,000].

The results of this example are summarized in Fig. 3.   ▲

Problem

Consider the following sales data:

Month	1	2	3	4	5
Sales	10	12	15	14	16

a. Determine the regression line that fits the data.
b. Calculate the standard error of the estimate.
c. What would be your forecast for month 6?
d. Graph these results. (See Fig. 3 as an example.)

8. ARIMA (BOX-JENKINS) METHODS

ARIMA (Auto-Regressive Integrated Moving Average) methods, also called Box-Jenkins methods (after the developers), are powerful new techniques for the estimation of parameters which describe a time series. ARIMA models are developed in three steps:

1. *Identification.* In this step, the pattern of the time series is investigated and classified into either an auto-regressive (AR), moving average (MA), or combined (ARIMA) pattern. The identification is done through the analysis of the auto-correlation patterns of the time series.
2. *Estimation.* The estimation of the parameters of the model specified are accomplished through nonlinear regression methods. The results include the parameter estimates, standard errors of the parameters estimated, test statistics for evaluating the statistical significance of the results, and the overall standard error of the estimate.
3. *Evaluation.* The statistical soundness and completeness of the model estimated is evaluated through analysis of the residual errors. If the residual errors are auto-correlated, this indicates the presence of additional parameters to be estimated, and the model-building process returns to identification. If the residual errors are normally distributed and random, then as much information as possible has been extracted from the time series, and the model estimated is statistically sound.

9. MONITORING FORECAST PERFORMANCE: TRACKING SIGNALS

Various methods exist for monitoring how well a forecasting system is performing over time. Obviously, if the system fails to give acceptably accurate forecasts, we would want to reexamine the forecasting model. One device employed for this purpose is a tracking signal. In this section we shall present one such method that is applicable to single exponential smoothing systems.

Recall our previous notation:

$e_i = X_i - F_i$ = forecast error

MAD = mean absolute deviation

In addition, let us define S to be the simple algebraic sum of the forecast errors as follows:

$S = \Sigma e_i$

The **tracking signal** T for a single exponential smoothing system is defined by

$$T = \left| \frac{S}{MAD} \right| \tag{15}$$

If it is desired that the forecast errors be contained within k standard deviations, then T must satisfy

$$T = \left| \frac{S}{MAD} \right| < k(1.25) \sqrt{\frac{1}{2\alpha}} \tag{16}$$

Thus for a 95 percent confidence level, k equals approximately 2 (from cumulative normal tables). If we give a value to k and to α, and if at some point T exceeds the right-hand side of Eq. (16), then this would signal that the forecasting system is not performing according to the confidence level set by the value of k.

The mathematical details behind Eq. (16) are beyond the scope of this discussion. However, it is not necessary to understand the proof behind Eq. (16) in order to apply the tracking signal method successfully.

EXAMPLE 8. *Monitoring Forecast Performance.* Suppose we have an exponential smoothing system with $\alpha = 0.2$ and we set a 95 percent confidence level on the tracking signal, T. Thus 95 percent of the time we would expect inequality, Eq. (16) to hold—if it fails to be satisfied, this will give us a reason to reexamine our forecasting system.

Let us first compute the right-hand side of Eq. (16) as follows:

$$k(1.25) \sqrt{\frac{1}{2\alpha}} = 2(1.25) \sqrt{\frac{1}{2(0.2)}} = 3.95$$

We now present a sequence of events that we assume will occur with regard to the sales of a given company:

1. Suppose we forecast that sales in January will be 10 units, but actual sales turn out to be 9 units. Then

$$e_1 = X_1 - F_1 = 9 - 10 = -1$$

$$S = e_1 = -1$$

$$\text{MAD} = \left|\frac{e_1}{1}\right| = |-1|/1 = 1$$

$$T = \left|\frac{S}{\text{MAD}}\right| = \left|\frac{-1}{1}\right| = 1$$

Since $T = 1 < 3.95$, we conclude that the forecasting system is operating acceptably. Note that we are labeling January as month 1.

2. Our forecast for February is

$$F_2 = \alpha X_1 + (1 - \alpha)F_1 = 0.2(9) + 0.8(10) = 9.8$$

Suppose *actual* sales for February turn out to be 12. Then

$$e_2 = X_2 - F_2 = 12 - 9.8 = 2.2$$

$$S = e_1 + e_2 = -1 + 2.2 = 1.2$$

$$\text{MAD} = \frac{|e_1| + |e_2|}{2} = \frac{1 + 2.2}{2} = 1.6$$

$$T = \left|\frac{S}{\text{MAD}}\right| = \left|\frac{1.2}{1.6}\right| = 0.75$$

Since $T = 0.75 < 3.95$, the system seems to be operating acceptably.

3. March's forecast would be

$$F_3 = \alpha X_2 + (1 - \alpha)F_2 = 0.2(12) + 0.8(9.8) = 10.24$$

Suppose actual sales for March turn out to be 15. Then

$$e_3 = X_3 - F_3 = 15 - 10.24 = 4.76$$

$$S = e_1 + e_2 + e_3 = -1 + 2.2 + 4.76 = 5.96$$

$$\text{MAD} = \frac{|e_1| + |e_2| + |e_3|}{3} = \frac{1 + 2.2 + 4.76}{3} = 2.65$$

$$T = \left|\frac{S}{\text{MAD}}\right| = \left|\frac{5.96}{2.65}\right| = 2.25$$

Again, since $T = 2.25 < 3.95$, we can assume that our forecasting system is performing acceptably.

Now suppose the process continues through the month of June, as shown by the data displayed in Table 5. Notice that in June the tracking signal equals 4.05, which exceeds the 95 percent confidence limit of 3.95. What action should be taken? In practice, the following options would be considered:

1. Reexamine the value of α. Should α be increased? Decreased?
2. Reexamine the choice of forecasting system. Is the exponential system really appropriate in the first place? Perhaps a regression model or a model that accounts for seasonal variation should be considered. Or could we combine the exponential system (with $\alpha = 0.2$ or with a changed α value) with more management judgment?
3. Are we being too "hard" on the system? Instead of insisting on a 95 percent confidence limit for forecast errors, would a higher confidence limit (such as 99.7 percent, $k = 3$) be acceptable?
4. Perhaps we should give the system another chance. In this case we could set S back to 0 and continue. If T again violates the 95 percent confidence limit, *then* we might consider one of the above three alternatives.   ▲

Problem

Let $\alpha = 0.10$ and $k = 2$ (95 percent confidence limit for forecast error). Suppose your forecast for week 1 is 20 and the weekly sales are as given below:

Week	1	2	3	4	5	6	7
Sales	18	23	25	26	22	29	24

Compute the tracking signal for each week. Is the forecasting system acceptable?

TABLE 5   *(Refer to Example 8)*

Time period t	Actual X_t	Forecast F_t	Error $e_t = X_t - F_t$	Sum of errors S	MAD	Tracking signal $T = |S/\text{MAD}|$
1 (Jan)	9	10.00	−1.00	−1.00	1.00	1.00
2 (Feb)	12	9.80	2.20	1.20	1.60	0.75
3 (Mar)	15	10.24	4.76	5.96	2.65	2.25
4 (Apr)	15	11.19	3.81	9.77	2.94	3.32
5 (May)	10	11.95	−1.95	7.82	2.74	2.85
6 (June)	16	11.56	4.44	12.26	3.03	4.05

10. SELECTING A FORECASTING SYSTEM

In this section we shall give a basic framework for deciding upon a forecasting system. The following sequence of steps offers such an approach.

STEP 1. Are the criteria satisfied for a quantitative forecasting system? If not, explore the qualitative methods (managerial, judgmental, technological). If so, proceed to step 2 below.

STEP 2. Attempt to discern a pattern for the past data. Is it a constant model? Is a trend present? What about seasonal variation?

STEP 3. Select a forecasting model and a system appropriate to the pattern. For a constant model, consider moving averages or exponential smoothing. For a trend model, double exponential smoothing or linear regression, as well as other specialized trend models, might be appropriate. Methods also exist for time series that follow a seasonal variation. In making a selection of a system, we must consider the following factors: accuracy, management acceptance, simplicity, cost, time, and computer requirements for implementing the system.

STEP 4. Fit the model selected to the data. For example, if we decide that an exponential smoothing model is appropriate, we must select a value for the smoothing parameter.

STEP 5. What role should judgment play in using the system? Should controls, such as a tracking signal, be established to monitor the performance of the system?

11. CONCLUDING REMARKS

The intent of this chapter is to give you a brief overview of forecasting methods that have found popular application. It should be pointed out that the study of forecasting methods has been rather active in recent years. The statistical and computational aspects of forecasting techniques have enjoyed various advances. The value of studying the simple models of this chapter lies in the fact that most of the more sophisticated models are conceptually based on such simple notions as smoothing, averaging, or best-fit estimating. The interested student should consult the references listed for this chapter in Appendix A.

TERMINOLOGY

After studying this chapter you should be familiar with the following terms:

TERM	SECTION
absolute forecast error	4
adaptive methods	3
ARIMA	8
causal model	2
constant time series	2
decomposition	2
Delphi method	2
double exponential smoothing	6
forecast error	4
forecasting	1
intermediate-term forecasts	2
lag	3
linear regression line	7
long-term forecasts	2
MAD	4
moving averages	3
prediction	1
qualitative forecasting	2
quantitative forecasting	2
short-term forecasts	2
simple linear regression	7
single exponential smoothing	5
smoothing parameter	5
time series model	2
tracking signal	9
weighted moving average system	3

EXERCISES

1. *Retail Sales—Moving Averages.*   Stears Department Stores has recorded retail sales (in $ million) for the past five months to be:

Month	1	2	3	4	5
Sales	2.3	2.0	2.2	2.3	2.4

     a. Using a three-month moving average system, forecast sales for month 6.

     b. How would the three-month system have performed on months 3, 4, and 5?

     c. Graph the past data points and the results of part (b).

2. *Retail Sales—Single Exponential Smoothing.* For the Stears sales record given in Exercise 1, use a single exponential smoothing system to forecast sales in month 6. Let $\alpha = 0.20$, and let F_5 equal the *average* sales for months 1 through 5.

3. *Retail Sales—Single Exponential Smoothing.* For Exercise 1, how would a single exponential smoothing system with $\alpha = 0.20$ have performed on months 2 through 6?

     a. First, let $F_1 = 2.3$.

     b. Repeat the forecasts with F_1 equal to the average sales level for months 1 through 5.

4. *Equivalent Systems—Moving Average versus Smoothing.* If the lag for an exponential system equals the lag for a moving average system, we might say that the two systems are *equivalent*. This does not mean that the two systems will yield the same forecasts. It simply means that the average age of past data used by the two systems in deriving a forecast is the same.

     If we equate the lags for the two systems, we get

$$\frac{N-1}{2} = \frac{1-\alpha}{\alpha}$$

     a. If $\alpha = 0.1$, what is the equivalent moving average parameter N?

     b. If $N = 5$, find the equivalent exponential smoothing parameter α.

     c. Consider the following time series data:

Week	1	2	3	4	5	6	7
Sales	10	13	14	12	14	15	?

First, use an exponential smoothing system to forecast weeks 4 through 7, using $\alpha = 0.5$. Start the forecast at week 4:

$$F_4 = \alpha X_3 + (1 - \alpha)F_3$$

For F_3, use the average of weeks 1, 2, and 3.

Second, compute past forecasts, using the equivalent moving average system.

Do the two forecasting systems yield the same forecasts?

5. *Selecting the Smoothing Parameter.* Timeout Watch Sales has observed the following sales for one of its digital watches over the past 12 months (starting in February): 25, 28, 30, 27, 26, 25, 31, 31, 28, 29, 40, and 34.

a. What is the average monthly sales figure?
b. Timeout would like to implement a formal forecasting system and has called upon you as a consultant. Since the sales pattern seems fairly constant (except for the month of December, which had sales of 40), you decide to see how various exponential systems would perform on the above sales record. Using a February forecast of 25 units, compute the next eleven forecasts, setting $\alpha = 0.1$, $\alpha = 0.2$, and $\alpha = 0.3$. Compute the MAD for each system (starting with March to compute the forecast errors). On the basis of the MAD, which system would you select?

6. *Maintenance Expense.* The public school system of Claysville has incurred the following maintenance expenses (in $000) over the past fifteen months, according to Building and Grounds records:

Month	1	2	3	4	5	6	7	8
Expense	2	2	3	1	3	3	1.5	1

Month	9	10	11	12	13	14	15
Expense	2	2.5	2.7	2	3.1	1.9	2.2

The B & G plant manager would like to have a forecast of the school system's maintenance expenses for next month (month 16). After studying the monthly expense records above:
a. Compute a forecast for next month's expenses, using a five-month moving average system.
b. Compute the forecast, using a ten-month moving average system.
c. Compute the forecast, using single exponential smoothing. Let $\alpha = 0.2$ and F_1 equal the average expense incurred in months 1 through 15.
d. Fit a regression line to the data. Does there seem to be a trend? (This would be reflected in the value of the slope b.)

7. *Agricultural Imports.* Imports of coffee to this country (in millions of tons) have followed the pattern below:

Year	1	2	3	4	5	6
Imports	3	3.5	4.5	6	8.2	9.5

a. Use a single exponential smoothing system, setting $\alpha = 0.3$ and $F_1 = 3$, to forecast years 1 through 7.
b. Compute the MAD for years 2–6 in part (a).
c. Repeat parts (a) and (b), using $\alpha = 0.7$.

8. Repeat Exercise 7 above, using a three-year moving average system for part (a) and a two-year system for part (c). In the first case, compute the MAD for years 4, 5, 6; in the second case, compute the MAD for years 3 through 6.

9. *Agricultural Imports: Use of Trend Systems.* Using the data from Exercise 7 above:

a. Fit a linear regression line to the data. Describe the trend. Compute the standard error of estimate, MAD, and project a forecast for year 7.

b. Use double exponential smoothing, letting $\alpha = 0.7$, $S_1 = S_1' = 3$. Compute the MAD for years 2 through 6. What is your forecast for year 7?

10. *Seasonal Smoothing.* Sales for Slip Snowmobiles have followed the pattern below, where F = fall, W = winter, S_g = spring, S = summer, and sales are in $000:

Season	F	W	S_g	S	F	W	S_g	S	F	W	S_g	S
Sales	10	30	5	1	11	35	6	2	9	32	7	1

a. Compute sales forecasts on the past data, using a single exponential smoothing system with $\alpha = 0.10$ and F_1 = sales for the first Fall season = 10. Compute the MAD.

b. Repeat part (a) with $\alpha = 0.8$.

c. Graph the past data and the results of the two forecasts
(As noted in this chapter, there are specialized forecasting systems that are far more reliable for seasonal patterns.)

11. *Gold Prices: A Regression Model.* The average price of gold per troy ounce over the past six years has been recorded as follows:

Year	1	2	3	4	5	6
Price ($)	150	145	160	180	220	260

a. Fit a linear regression line to these data.

b. Compute the standard error of estimate.

c. Forecast gold price for year 7, based on the regression model.

d. Compute the MAD for years 2 through 6.

12. *Gold Prices—An Exponential Smoothing Model.* In Exercise 11 above, use a single exponential smoothing forecasting system with $\alpha = 0.6$ and F_1 = 150 to forecast years 2 through 7. Compute the MAD for years 2 through 6. Does the system seem to perform adequately?

13. *Trend Model for Gold Prices.* In Exercise 11 above, use a double exponential smoothing system with $\alpha = 0.6$ and $S_1 = S_1' = 150$ to forecast years 2 through 7, *and compute the MAD.*

14. *Patient Admissions.* Patient admissions to General Hospital (in 000s) have been recorded as follows:

Year	1	2	3	4	5	6	7	8	9
Number of patients	3.2	3.3	3.6	3.8	4.1	3.9	4.0	4.3	4.6

a. Graph these data. Is a trend present? Estimate the slope of this trend by drawing a freehand line through the data points.

b. Fit a linear regression line to the data. Note the slope coefficient. Compute the MAD for years 2 through 9, using past data.

c. Compute the MAD for a single exponential smoothing system for years 2 through 9, using $\alpha = 0.2$. Use $F_1 = 3.2$.

d. Repeat part (c), using $\alpha = 0.7$.

e. Repeat part (c), using a double exponential smoothing system with $\alpha = 0.2$ and $S_1 = S'_1 = 3.2$.

f. Repeat part (e), using $\alpha = 0.7$ and $S_1 = S'_1 = 3.2$.

g. Based on the values of MAD, select the best system of the five tested, and forecast year 10 admissions.

15. *Commodity Prices: Tracking Signal Analysis.* Prices of copper (in cents per pound) have been recorded as follows:

Month	1	2	3	4	5	6	7	8
Price	50	60	50	90	65	70	70	85

a. Use a single exponential system to compute past forecasts for months 2 through 8. Let $\alpha = 0.2$ and $F_1 = 67.5$ (average of the eight-month data).

b. Compute the values of the tracking signal for months 2 through 8, using a 95 percent confidence level.

c. Repeat parts (a) and (b), using $\alpha = 0.7$.

16. *Selecting the Smoothing Parameter.* This exercise applies to students with computer programming experience (either with a programmable pocket calculator or a higher-level programming language supported by a larger computing system).

Write a computer program that is designed to select the best value of α for an exponential smoothing system based on minimizing the MAD.

Inputs to the program might include the following:

a. A set of past data (and the number of such data points).

b. An initial forecast for the first period.

c. A starting value of α (A) and an ending value of α (B).

d. The increment by which α is to be increased (D).

The computer program should then start α at A. Compute the MAD, then increase α to $A + D$ and compute the MAD, and so on, until α reaches B. (For example, α might be increased from 0.05 to 0.3 in increments of 0.1; this would correspond to the input values $A = 0.05$; $B = 0.3$, and $D = 0.1$.)

The program *output* would then include:

a. The value(s) of α yielding the minimum MAD.

b. The value of this MAD.

c. A forecast for the next period using the selected α value.

III | PROBABILISTIC MODELS

10 DECISION THEORY

CONTENTS

1. INTRODUCTION

Organizations and individuals are faced almost daily with the problems of having to make decisions. The decision-making process is made difficult by the presence of uncertainty concerning the surrounding environment. For example, a company in the process of formulating an advertising strategy is uncertain not only of its competitors' responses but also of the market demand for its product. Yet a decision must be made on product pricing, the choice of markets, the advertising media, and the size of the advertising budget. Prior to these decisions, the same company must decide on the scale

of its productive facilities. What machines should be purchased to manufacture the product? Should the company start out on a small production scale and later expand, or should it remain small? Should it start out
with a large production capacity on the premise that the market demand
will be great?

In this chapter we shall present the basic concepts of decision theory and
illustrate various methods that have been employed to solve management
decision problems.

2. A FRAMEWORK FOR DECISION MODELS

In this section we shall present the basic definitions needed to understand
the various decision models that you will study in this chapter. Example 10.1
is introduced to illustrate the basic notions and will be used later in the chapter to demonstrate the decision models.

Problem Identification

When faced with a decision-making situation, you must identify two components of the problem:

1. *Decision Alternatives.* Make a list of the possible courses of action or decisions that are available to you and that you wish to include as *feasible*
   courses of action. We shall use the terms "action," "decision," and "decision alternative" to mean the same thing.
2. *Events.* Make a list of all possible events that might occur after your decision is made. The list should include all possibilities relevant to the situation; furthermore, the events should be mutually exclusive.

Payoff Tables

After you have identified the decision alternatives and the events, associate
with each pair (decision, event) a "payoff," which is the reward obtained if
the particular decision is made and the event occurs. This information should
then be structured into a table, called the **payoff table,** as in Table 10.1. It
is important to note that the payoff is determined jointly by the action and
the event that is observed, as shown in Fig. 10.1.

EXAMPLE 10.1. Blockwood Designs, Inc., is a newly organized light manufacturer of furniture products. The president, James Block, must decide what
type of truck to purchase for use in the company's operations. The truck is
needed to pick up raw-material supplies, to make deliveries, and to transport
product samples to commercial exhibits during the coming year. Block is

TABLE 10.1 · *A Payoff Table*

Decision alternatives (actions)	Events		
	e_1	e_2	e_3
a_1	r_{11}	r_{12}	r_{13}
a_2	r_{21}	r_{22}	r_{23}
a_3	r_{31}	r_{32}	r_{33}
a_4	r_{41}	r_{42}	r_{43}

hesitant to tie up a lot of money in a large-capacity truck if demand is slow to take off in the initial year. On the other hand, if demand is great, the company's capacity to meet the demand will be lessened if a small truck must be relied upon to perform the above functions.

Block has identified three alternatives for the truck purchase: (1) a small commercial import, (2) a standard-size pickup, and (3) a large flatbed truck. It is expected that first-year sales will fall into one of four categories: $0–$20,000; $20,000–$40,000; $40,000–$60,000; and above $60,000. After meeting with the company's production manager and marketing manager, Block determined the payoff table shown in Table 10.2. Note that (1) the decision alternatives are the three choices of truck types and (2) there are four events corresponding to the four possible ranges for first-year sales, denoted by 1, 2, 3, and 4, respectively.

APPLICATIONS

The following applications appear in this chapter in text, examples, or problems.

Advertising strategy (against a competitor)

Analysis of marketing research

Car buying

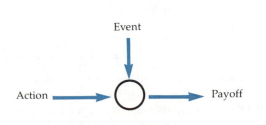

FIGURE 10.1

TABLE 10.2   *Payoff Table for Blockwood (payoffs in $000 profit for first year)*

	Sales (events)			
Truck type (actions)	(Low) 1	2	3	(High) 4
Import	20	10	15	25
Standard	15	25	12	20
Flatbed	−20	−5	30	40

Energy research

Equipment selection

Facilities expansion

Facilities location

Horse-track betting

Inventory management

Joint-venture analysis (oil drilling)

Make or buy decisions

Medical care

Military strategy: military preparedness

Municipal street planning

Oil drilling

Personnel selection

Quality control

Real estate investment

Reconnaissance effectiveness/planning

Resort facility planning

Selection of a marketing consulting firm

The value of market research information

Value of information

We shall refer back to this example throughout this chapter and present alternative criteria for deciding which truck Blockwood should purchase. You might note that the two negative entries correspond to losses. For example, if Blockwood decides to go with the flatbed truck and sales turn out to be in range 1 ($0–$20,000), the company will lose $20,000; if sales fall into the second range ($20,000–$40,000), $5,000 will be lost.   ▲

Loss Tables

A payoff table may always be converted to a **loss table.** To make this conversion, consider each column of the payoff table separately. For each column identify the largest entry in the column, then subtract each entry in the column from the largest entry to convert each payoff to a loss. These losses correspond to "regrets," or "opportunity losses," for not choosing the action corresponding to the highest payoff. The next example will illustrate this.

EXAMPLE 10.2. *Loss Table for Blockwood.* We shall convert the payoff table for Blockwood (Table 10.2) to a loss table, as follows:

1. Start with column 1. The highest entry in that column is 20, so we subtract each entry in column 1 from 20 to obtain the corresponding loss. The three losses are calculated to be $20 - 20 = 0$; $20 - 15 = 5$; and $20 - (-20) = 40$. Thus column 1 entries become 0, 5, and 40. Note the meaning of these losses: If event 1 occurs and if we had purchased the import, we would have chosen the best act possible *given that event 1 occurs;* that is, our regret, or opportunity loss, would be 0. If we had purchased the standard truck, the payoff would be $15,000, which is $5,000 less than the best possible payoff; our regret, or opportunity loss, then would be $5,000. Similarly, the opportunity loss for purchasing the flatbed truck would be $40,000.
2. Repeat the above conversion procedure on Table 10.2, columns 2, 3, and 4, as follows:

Column 2	Column 3	Column 4
$25 - 10 = 15$	$30 - 15 = 15$	$40 - 25 = 15$
$25 - 25 = 0$	$30 - 12 = 18$	$40 - 20 = 20$
$25 - (-5) = 30$	$30 - 30 = 0$	$40 - 40 = 0$

The resulting loss table is shown in Table 10.3.

▲

TABLE 10.3

Loss Table for Blockwood (in $000)

	1	2	3	4
T1	0	15	15	15
T2	5	0	18	20
T3	40	30	0	0

Note that although payoffs may be positive, 0, or negative, losses are always nonnegative (either 0 or positive).

We see, then, that the first step in solving decision-making problems is to produce a payoff table that lists (1) all feasible decision alternatives we wish to consider, and (2) all possible events that may occur following our decision.

Decision Trees

Another method of representing a decision problem is a graphical device called a **decision tree.** Such a tree reads from left to right in the order in which decisions and events occur. Two types of nodes are used in such a tree: **decision nodes** and **event nodes.** A decision node represents a point in time at which the decision maker selects a decision alternative. An event node marks the occurrence of one of the various events that may occur after a decision is made. In this text we shall graphically denote decision nodes as squares and event nodes as circles. A **branch** drawn from a decision node represents a course of action chosen at that decision node. A branch drawn from an event node represents an event that can occur at that event node. The next example illustrates these notions.

EXAMPLE 10.3. *A Decision Tree for Blockwood.* In Fig. 10.2 we have displayed a decision tree representing the problem facing Blockwood Designs. Node 1, represented by a square, is a decision node that denotes the point at which Blockwood must select one of the three decision alternatives. These three decision alternatives are represented as branches leaving node 1. Suppose the import is selected. Node 2, represented by a circle, is an event node. Once the import truck is purchased, four events may occur (1, 2, 3, or 4), corresponding to the four possible sales levels. These four events are shown in Fig. 10.2 as four branches leaving node 2. Similarly, nodes 3 and 4 are event nodes having the same interpretation. The numbers at the tips of the branches indicate the payoffs that may be realized for each action-event combination. For example, if we select action "purchase the standard truck" at decision node 1, this puts us at event node 3. Then if sales fall into range 2, a payoff of 25 (or $25,000) is realized.   ▲

The *advantages* of decision trees are:

1. They offer an intuitive means of viewing the problem.
2. They are convenient to work with.
3. They force the analyst to think through the problem in chronological order.

The main *disadvantage* of the use of decision trees is that they may become too large (and cumbersome to use) in more complex decision problems.

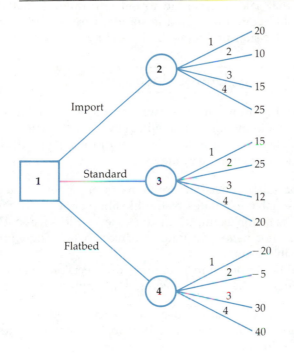

FIGURE 10.2   *Decision tree for Blockwood.*

3. CLASSIFYING DECISION PROBLEMS

A convenient means of classifying the types of decision problems faced by management is to determine the degree of information one has concerning the likelihood of the occurrence of various events. In this text we recognize two basic categories of problems: (1) decision making under certainty, and (2) decision making under uncertainty.

Decision Making Under Certainty

In this class of problems, the decision maker (by some means) knows for certain which event will occur. In the context of the types of problems presented in this chapter, decision making under certainty is reduced to the trivial task of selecting the action yielding the highest payoff once we know what event to expect. For example, referring to Example 10.1, if the management of Blockwood Designs feels certain that first-year sales will be in range 1 ($0–$20,000), it would purchase the small import truck; if management feels that sales are certain to fall into range 2 ($20,000–$40,000), the decision would be to purchase the standard truck; and so on. As you might guess, such decision problems rarely occur.

Decision Making Under Uncertainty

Decision making under uncertainty refers to problems in which the decision maker does not know for certain which event will occur. There are two types of such problems—probabilistic and nonprobabilistic decision problems— each of which is defined as follows:

1. **Nonprobabilistic decision problems** occur when management does not have reasonable estimates of the likelihoods of the occurrence of various events. Thus, for example, in the case of Blockwood Designs, management may not have adequate information to assign probabilities to the four possible events.
2. In **probabilistic decision problems** the decision maker is able to assign probabilities to the various events that may occur.

In Section 4, we shall discuss the primary methods used to solve nonprobabilistic decision problems. Probabilistic decision problems are presented in Section 5.

4. NONPROBABILISTIC DECISION RULES

In this section we shall demonstrate three decision rules for nonprobabilistic decision problems, using Blockwood Designs, Inc. (Example 10.1). Thus, in this section we assume that the management of Blockwood is unable to assess reliably the probabilities of occurrence of the four events (the four sales levels—1, 2, 3, 4).

Maximin

The **maximin rule** can be stated as follows:

STEP 1. For each decision alternative (or action), identify the minimum payoff that can occur.

STEP 2. Select the decision alternative having the largest of the minimum payoffs identified in step 1. Ties are broken arbitrarily.
   This rule *max*imizes the *min*imum possible payoff, thus the term *maximin*. Maximin is a conservative, or pessimistic, decision rule. Note the rationale behind step 1: For each decision alternative we assume that the *worst* event will occur. In step 2, we maximize these pessimistic outcomes.

EXAMPLE 10.4. *The Maximin Rule: Blockwood Designs.* For Blockwood Designs we apply the maximin rule as follows:

Step 1. Identify the minimum payoff for each decision alternative. The minimum payoff if the import is purchased is 10. The minimum payoff if the standard truck is purchased is 12. The minimum payoff if the flatbed is purchased is −20.

Step 2. Select the decision alternative with the largest minimum payoff. The maximum of the above payoffs is 12, corresponding to the decision to purchase the standard truck. Thus, using the maximin rule, Blockwood should decide to buy a standard-size pickup truck.

Note the sequence of events: Blockwood first purchases the standard pickup. Then during the upcoming year any one of the four sales levels may be realized and Blockwood may gain $15,000, $25,000, $12,000, or $20,000, respectively. Blockwood will gain at least $12,000, whereas either of the other two alternatives *could* lead to a gain of less than $12,000.   ▲

Maximax

The **maximax rule** is stated as follows:

STEP 1. For each decision alternative (or action), identify the *maximum* possible payoff.

STEP 2. Select the decision alternative having the largest of the payoffs identified in step 1. Ties are broken arbitrarily.

This rule *max*imizes the *max*imum possible payoff, which justifies the term *maximax*. Maximax is considered a risky or optimistic decision rule. In step 1, we optimistically assume that for each decision alternative the best event will occur. In step 2 we maximize these optimistic outcomes.

EXAMPLE 10.5. *The Maximax Rule: Blockwood Designs.* For Blockwood Designs we apply the maximax rule as follows:

Step 1. Identify the maximum payoff for each decision alternative. The maximum payoff if the import is purchased is 25. The maximum payoff if the standard truck is purchased is 25. The maximum payoff if the flatbed is purchased is 40.

Step 2. Select the decision alternative with the largest payoff. The maximum of these payoffs is 40, corresponding to the decision to purchase the flatbed. Thus, using the maximax rule, Blockwood should purchase the flatbed truck. Note that by doing so, Blockwood could realize a first-year profit of $40,000, but if sales are in range 1, there is the risk of losing $20,000.

Minimax

This rule is sometimes called the "minimax regret rule." For this rule it is necessary to work from the loss table. The **minimax rule** is:

STEP 1. For each decision alternative (or action), identify the *maximum* possible *loss*.

STEP 2. Select the decision alternative having the smallest of the losses identified in step 1. Ties are broken arbitrarily.
   This rule is considered to be neither pessimistic nor optimistic. See Problem 3 at the end of this section for an illustration of this fact. ▲

EXAMPLE 10.6. *The Minimax Rule: Blockwood Designs.* (Refer to the loss table, Table 10.3.) For Blockwood Designs we apply the minimax rule as follows:

Step 1. Identify the maximum possible loss for each decision alternative. The maximum loss if the import is purchased is 15. The maximum loss if the standard truck is purchased is 20. The maximum loss if the flatbed is purchased is 40.

Step 2. Select the decision alternative having the smallest loss. The minimum of these losses is 15, corresponding to the purchase of the import. Thus, using the minimax rule, Blockwood should decide to purchase the import truck. ▲

Problems

1. Use the maximin rule on the following payoff tables. Would you abide by the maximin decision?

a.	s_1	s_2
a_1	$100	100
a_2	50,000	0

b.	s_1	s_2
a_1	$-10	50,000
a_2	0	0

2. Would you feel comfortable with the maximax rule on the following payoff tables?

a.	s_1	s_2
a_1	$-5,000	5,000
a_2	4,000	4,000

b.	s_1	s_2
a_1	$5,000	5,000
a_2	5,001	0

TABLE 10.4

	s_1	s_2	s_3	s_4
a_1	$46	38	38	38
a_2	40	40	40	40
a_3	50	41	31	5

3. You are given the payoff table shown in Table 10.4
   a. Construct the loss table for this decision problem.
   b. What is the maximin decision?
   c. What is the maximax decision?
   d. What is the minimax decision?
   e. Can you interpret the reasonableness of these results using the notions of risk, optimism, and pessimism?

5. PROBABILISTIC DECISION PROBLEMS

When the decision maker is able to assign probabilities to the various events, it is then possible to employ a probabilistic decision rule called the **Bayes criterion.** The Bayes criterion selects the decision alternative having the maximum expected payoff. If the decision maker is working with a loss table, the Bayes criterion selects the decision alternative having the minimum expected loss. The decision obtained by maximizing expected payoff will be the *same* as the decision that minimizes expected loss, so it does not matter whether one works with a payoff or a loss table.

The **Bayes decision rule** (maximizing expected payoffs) is implemented as follows:

STEP 1. For each decision alternative, compute the expected payoff. This is done by weighting each payoff in the row corresponding to the decision alternative by the probability of the corresponding event and then summing these terms.

STEP 2. Select the decision alternative having the maximum expected payoff. This decision is called a **Bayes decision.** Ties are broken arbitrarily.

Notationally, we shall let R denote payoff (reward) and L denote loss. Also, the expected payoff if we choose action a will be written $ER(a)$.

EXAMPLE 10.7. *The Bayes Criterion.* Suppose you are given the payoff table shown in Table 10.5. You are also told that the probabilities of occurrence for the three events, s_1, s_2, and s_3, are 0.2, 0.7, and 0.1, respectively. (We shall often write this as follows: $P(s_1) = 0.2$, $P(s_2) = 0.7$, and $P(s_3) = 0.1$, where the P denotes "probability.")

TABLE 10.5

	s_1	s_2	s_3
a_1	10	15	13
a_2	7	20	15
a_3	8	20	10

a. Determine the Bayes decision using the maximum expected payoff rule.

Solution. The expected payoff if we select aciton a_1 is computed as follows:

$ER(a_1) = (0.20)(10) + (0.70)(15) + (0.10)(13) = 13.8$

For actions a_2 and a_3, we have

$ER(a_2) = (0.20)(7) + (0.70)(20) + (0.10)(15) = 16.9$

$ER(a_3) = (0.20)(8) + (0.70)(20) + (0.10)(10) = 16.6$

The action that maximizes the expected payoff is a_2. Thus the Bayes decision is a_2.

b. Determine the Bayes decision using the minimum expected loss rule.

Solution. The loss table is given in Table 10.6. The expected losses are computed in the same manner as expected payoffs:

$EL(a_1) = (0.20)(0) + (0.70)(5) + (0.10)(2) = 3.7$

$EL(a_2) = (0.20)(3) + (0.70)(0) + (0.10)(0) = 0.6$

$EL(a_3) = (0.20)(2) + (0.70)(0) + (0.10)(5) = 0.9$

TABLE 10.6

	s_1	s_2	s_3
a_1	0	5	2
a_2	3	0	0
a_3	2	0	5

The action that minimizes the expected loss (the Bayes action) is seen to be a_2.

The two methods (maximizing ER and minimizing EL) give the same Bayes decision, and as we stated, this will always be the case.   ▲

EXAMPLE 10.8. *The Bayes Criterion: Blockwood Designs, Inc.* Let us suppose that James Block, president of Blockwood Designs, calls a meeting of the company officers concerning the truck purchase that must soon be made. Blockwood's marketing manager has been conducting a market analysis on possible first-year sales, and based on this analysis, she supplies what she feels are the probabilities for the following four sales levels:

$P(1) = 0.20$, $P(2) = 0.35$, $P(3) = 0.30$, $P(4) = 0.15$

After some discussion, Block indicates that basically he considers these probabilities reasonable, although he thinks the probability of sales falling into range 2 should be somewhat higher—say, 0.40 instead of 0.35—and that the probability of sales falling into range 4 should be 0.10 instead of 0.15.

The problem is to determine the Bayes decision.

Solution. Blockwood management has decided to calculate the Bayes decision in two ways: (1) using the probability estimates of the marketing manager (based on research), and (2) using Block's estimates (based on research, subjectively modified).

CASE 1. The expected payoffs using the marketing manager's estimates are as follows:

$ER(\text{import})$ $= (0.20)(20)$ $+ (0.35)(10)$ $+ (0.30)(15)$ $+ (0.15)(25) = 15.75$

$ER(\text{standard}) = (0.20)(15)$ $+ (0.35)(25)$ $+ (0.30)(12)$ $+ (0.15)(20) = 18.35$

$ER(\text{flatbed})$ $= (0.20)(-20) + (0.35)(-5)$ $+ (0.30)(30)$ $+ (0.15)(40) =$ 9.25

The Bayes decision is to purchase the standard truck.

CASE 2. The expected payoffs, using Block's estimates, are as follows:

$ER(\text{import})$ $= (0.20)(20)$ $+ (0.40)(10)$ $+ (0.30)(15)$ $+ (0.10)(25) = 15.00$

$ER(\text{standard}) = (0.20)(15)$ $+ (0.40)(25)$ $+ (0.30)(12)$ $+ (0.10)(20) = 18.60$

$ER(\text{flatbed})$ $= (0.20)(-20) + (0.40)(-5)$ $+ (0.30)(30)$ $+ (0.10)(40) =$ 7.00

The Bayes decision again is to purchase the standard truck.

CONCLUSION. It is clear that the Bayes decision *for this particular problem* is fairly insensitive to the slight disagreement between the two probability estimates. In either case, the Bayes decision is the same, so Blockwood decides to purchase the standard truck. If there had been a disagreement, it would be necessary for management either to decide the issue based on more discussion or to conduct more marketing research to refine the probability estimates further.   ▲

The Probabilities for the Events

The probabilities for the events used in calculating the Bayes decision come from the following sources:

1. *Sample information* (such as the marketing research in Example 10.8). A study or research analysis of the environment is used to assess the probability of occurrence of each possible event.
2. *Historical records* may be available to indicate the likelihood of occurrence for each event. For example, suppose that for inventory-ordering purposes a company must determine the sales level for the upcoming month. If the company has been in business for several years, historical records may indicate the probabilities of occurrence for various sales levels.
3. *Subjective probabilities.* Probabilities may be subjectively assessed, based on judgment, sample information, and historical records.

Whichever method is used to determine the probabilities, when there is significant doubt or disagreement it is a good idea to perform a *sensitivity analysis* to see how the Bayes decision is affected. An example of this was given in Example 10.4. The general procedure simply involves trying different sets of probabilities for the possible events and determining whether the Bayes decision changes in response to the different probability distributions.

See Exercise 6 at the end of this chapter for another probabilistic decision rule.

Decision-Tree Analysis

It is possible to work directly with the decision tree to determine a Bayes decision. Recall that each branch of a decision tree that leaves an event node (circular node) represents an event that can occur at that point. On each such branch we place the probabilities of occurrence for that event. We then go through a procedure of *folding* the tree back to determine the Bayes decision. This procedure is outlined below:

Start at the right of the tree. Using the payoffs written next to each tip node and the probabilities assigned to each event branch, calculate the expected payoff and write this number next to each event node. After all event nodes following a decision node are evaluated, assign to the decision node the maximum of the event node values. Continue this process, working from right to left, until arriving at the leftmost node. The tree can then be read from left to right for the Bayes decision.

EXAMPLE 10.9. *Using Decision Trees to Determine the Bayes Decision: Blockwood Designs.* Figure 10.3 illustrates the decision-tree analysis for the Blockwood problem, showing the results of the folding procedure. Note that the outcome probabilities 0.20, 0.35, 0.30, and 0.15 are those of the marketing manager (Example 10.8) and are written next to each event branch. Then the expected payoffs for each of the three event nodes, 2, 3, and 4, are calculated and placed next to the particular event node. (These numbers are 15.75, 18.35, and 9.25.) Since all the event nodes following the decision node 1 have been evaluated, we can evaluate the decision node 1 by assigning to it the maximum of the event node values—namely, 18.35. Note that we have also placed a slash mark on the "standard" branch to indicate which decision resulted in the payoff of 18.35—namely, the Bayes decision.

The tree can now be read from left to right (following the slash marks at each decision node). Starting at node 1, we see that the *expected* payoff is 18.35 and the slash mark indicates that the Bayes decision is to purchase the standard truck. If this decision is followed, the expected payoff (shown at event node 3) is 18.35, which corresponds to four uncertain events 1, 2, 3, and 4, having respective probabilities 0.20, 0.35, 0.30, and 0.15. The *actual* payoff may be $15,000, $25,000, $12,000, or $20,000, according to these probabilities. ▲

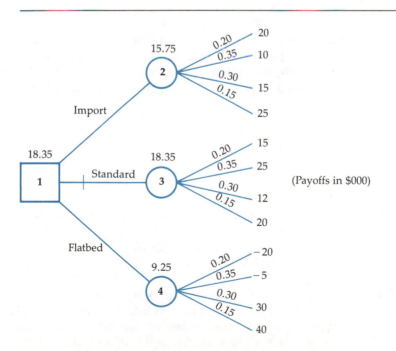

(Payoffs in $000)

FIGURE 10.3   *Folding back the decision tree for Blockwood Designs.*

6. EXPECTED VALUE OF PERFECT INFORMATION (EVPI)

Given a probabilistic decision problem, what would it be worth to the decision maker to have access to an information source that would indicate for certain which of the events will occur? Such an information source would offer *perfect information* to the decision maker. The expected value of such information is referred to as the **expected value of perfect information** (EVPI). In the next example we shall illustrate the calculation of EVPI. Following this we shall outline the general procedure.

EXAMPLE 10.10. *EVPI: Blockwood Designs.* Given the current state of information, the marketing manager's estimates of the probabilities for the four (sales) outcomes are 0.20, 0.35, 0.30, and 0.15. Thus there is a 0.20 probability that a perfect information source would reveal to Blockwood that sales will fall into range 1. If this happens, the best decision alternative would be to purchase the import giving a profit of 20. If the source reveals that sales will be in ranges 2, 3, or 4, the best decisions would give profits of 25, 30, and 40, respectively. Thus the *expected profit,* calculated from a perfect information source, would be (0.20)(20) + (0.35)(25) + (0.30)(30) + (0.15)(40) = 27.75 (or $27,750). Without such perfect information, the Bayes decision yields an expected profit of 18.35 ($18,350). Thus

EVPI = 27.75 − 18.35 = 9.4   (or $9,400)

In general, to calculate EVPI, we use the following steps:

Step 1. For each event identify the best possible payoff given that it is known for certain the outcome will occur. Weight each of these payoffs by the probability of the respective events and sum these products. This sum equals the **expected payoff given perfect information** (EPPI). We might write this sum as

$$\text{EPPI} = \sum (\text{Best payoff given event } i) P(i)$$

where the sum is taken over all events, i.

Step 2. Let EVPI denote the expected value of perfect information. Then

$$\text{EVPI} = \text{EPPI} - \left(\begin{array}{l} \text{The expected payoff using the} \\ \text{Bayes decision} \end{array} \right)$$

The EVPI is a theoretical notion; it would be a rare situation for a decision maker to have access to a perfect information source. *The primary use of EVPI is to determine the maximum amount a decision maker should be willing to pay for additional information (imperfect information) that could be employed to refine further the probability estimates of the various events.*

Thus, for example, in the case of Blockwood Designs, the company should pay *no more* than \$9,400 (EVPI) for additional marketing research or other information needed to estimate more accurately the probabilities of the four possible sales levels. This includes the value of additional management effort in studying the problem. ▲

EXAMPLE 10.11. Given the payoff table shown in Table 10.7, calculate the decisions according to each of the decision rules: maximin, maximax, and minimax regret. Also, given $P(s_1) = 0.6$ and $P(s_2) = 0.4$, calculate the Bayes decision, expected payoff, EPPI, and EVPI; display a decision tree.

Solution.

1. Maximin: The minimum payoffs for the three actions are 10, 12, and 7. The maximum of these is 12, corresponding to a_2. Thus the maximin decision is a_2.
2. Maximax: The maximum payoffs for the three actions are 15, 14, and 25. The maximum of these is 25; thus, the maximax decision is a_3.
3. Minimax: The loss table is given in Table 10.8. The maximum losses for the three actions are 10, 11, and 5. The minimum of these is 5; thus, the minimax decision is a_3.
4. Bayes decision: The expected payoffs for each of the three actions are as follows:

$$ER(a_1) = (0.6)(10) + (0.4)(15) = 12.0$$

$$ER(a_2) = (0.6)(12) + (0.4)(14) = 12.8$$

$$ER(a_3) = (0.6)(7) \ + (0.4)(25) = 14.2$$

The maximum of these is 14.2, so the Bayes decision is a_3, and the expected payoff is 14.2.
5. EVPI: First, EPPI is calculated:

$$EPPI = (0.6)(12) + (0.4)(25) = 17.2$$

So EVPI = EPPI − 14.2 = 17.2 − 14.2 = 3.0

TABLE 10.7

	s_1	s_2
a_1	10	15
a_2	12	14
a_3	7	25

TABLE 10.8

	s_1	s_2
a_1	2	10
a_2	0	11
a_3	5	0

6. Decision tree: The decision tree for part (4) is given in Fig. 10.4. The tree has been folded from right to left. You should go through this folding procedure. First, evaluate event nodes 2, 3, and 4; then, evaluate the decision node 1.

An alternative method for calculating EVPI is given in Problem 2 at the end of this section. ▲

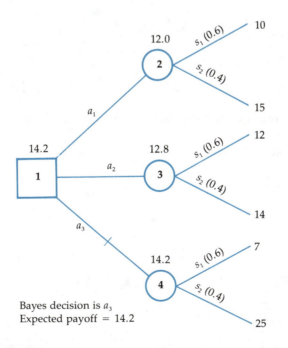

Bayes decision is a_3
Expected payoff = 14.2

FIGURE 10.4   *Example 10.11.*

Problems

1. For the payoff table given in Table 10.9, calculate (a) the Bayes decision and the expected payoff with the Bayes decision, and (b) the EVPI.
2. For the payoff table in Problem 1 above:
   a. Find the corresponding loss table.
   b. Compute the minimum expected loss, and note that this equals the EVPI. This is not a coincidence! *The equality always holds.* We can state this as a rule: The EVPI equals the expected *loss,* using the Bayes decision.

7. THE CONCEPT OF UTILITY

Suppose someone offers you the following bet. A fair coin is flipped. If it comes up heads, you win $1; if it comes up tails, you lose $1. Would you take this bet? The payoff table for this decision problem is shown below.

	Events	
Actions	Heads	Tails
Take bet	1	−1
Don't bet	0	0

Of course, $P(\text{Heads}) = 1/2 = P(\text{Tails})$. The expected payoffs for the two actions are

$$ER(\text{Take bet}) = \left(\frac{1}{2}\right)(\$1) + \left(\frac{1}{2}\right)(\$-1) = \$0$$

$$ER(\text{Don't bet}) = \left(\frac{1}{2}\right)(\$0) + \left(\frac{1}{2}\right)(\$0) \quad = \$0$$

TABLE 10.9

	s_1	s_2	s_3	s_4	
a_1	20	20	14	15	$p(s_1) = 0.5$
a_2	21	18	14	16	$p(s_2) = 0.2$
a_3	18	20	15	15	$p(s_3) = 0.2$
a_4	19	16	17	20	$p(s_4) = 0.1$

Thus according to the Bayes criterion you should be *indifferent,* whether you bet or not. The *value* of winning $1 should be the same to you as the value of losing $1. If you are *not* indifferent and if you would *prefer* to bet, then you are a **risk taker.** If you definitely *prefer* not to bet, you are a **risk avoider.** But note that if you believe in the Bayes criterion of maximizing monetary payoffs, you *should* be indifferent to this fair bet.

Let us take another example. Suppose you are offered the same game except that you will win $300 on heads and lose $300 on tails. Once again:

$$ER(\text{Take bet}) = \left(\frac{1}{2}\right)(\$300) + \left(\frac{1}{2}\right)(\$-300) = \$0$$

$$ER(\text{Don't bet}) = \left(\frac{1}{2}\right)(\$0) \quad + \left(\frac{1}{2}\right)(\$0) \qquad = \$0$$

So you should be indifferent, according to the Bayes criterion applied to the stated *monetary* payoffs. Would *you* be indifferent? If you would prefer to bet, you are a *risk taker;* the risk of losing $300 does not deter you. If you would prefer not to bet, you are a *risk avoider.* If you are indifferent, you are neither a risk taker nor a risk avoider, and you can be said to abide by the Bayes criterion for monetary rewards.

For a third example, suppose you are offered a chance to play the same game, but this time you will win $100 if heads turn up and lose $75 if tails turn up. The payoff table and expected payoffs for each action are as follows:

Actions	Event		ER(a)	
	Heads	Tails		
Take bet	$100	$-75	$12.5	[= 1/2(100) + (1/2)(-75)]
Don't bet	$0	$0	$0	[= 1/2(0) + (1/2)(0)]

Would *you* take the bet? According to the Bayes criterion, you *should,* since the expected monetary payoff of betting ($12.50) is greater than the expected payoff of not betting (zero). If you would not take the bet, apparently the possible loss of $75 means more to you than a purely monetary loss; perhaps your personal financial situation could not easily absorb a reduction of $75 cash. Try this same example using a gain of $1,000 on heads and a loss of $750 on tails. Now how do you feel about taking the bet on the toss of a fair coin having an expected payoff of 1/2($1,000) + 1/2(-$750) = $125?

Let us try one more example. You are given a choice of two bets. In each bet a fair coin is tossed.

- *Bet A.* If heads appears, you win $10,000. If tails appears, you also win $10,000. Thus the expected payoff of this bet is $ER = 1/2(\$10,000) + 1/2(\$10,000) = \$10,000$.
- *Bet B.* If heads appears, you win $40,000. If tails appears, you win nothing. The expected payoff of this bet is $ER = 1/2(\$40,000) + 1/2(0) = \$20,000$.

Which bet would you choose? According to the Bayes criterion, you should select bet B. However, many (if not most) people would prefer bet A to bet B, since bet A offers a certain chance to gain $10,000. In bet B there is a 50 percent chance that you may end up with nothing, even though you might gain $40,000.

In these examples, each person would have his or her own response to the various betting opportunities. There are two factors (although not unrelated) that enter into the fact that the Bayes criterion does not always lead to the most preferred decision *when applied to monetary rewards.*

The first factor is *risk.* Different decision makers deal with risk in different ways. We have given examples of risk aversion and risk taking. In each case, behavior under conditions of risk differs from that prescribed by the Bayes criterion.

The second factor is the notion of *value.* Can the value of payoffs in decision problems be measured proportionately in monetary terms? For example, does a monetary payoff of $10 have 10 times the "value" of a monetary payoff of one dollar? To some decision makers the answer is yes, to others (risk takers) $10 has more value than 10 times the "value" of one dollar, and to others (risk averters) it has less value.

Utility theory is a branch of decision theory that deals with the issue of measuring the "value" of payoffs to decision makers. Instead of the Bayes criterion being the maximization of expected monetary rewards, the Bayes criterion becomes the maximization of expected **utility**.

In Fig. 10.5, we display a particular utility function, U, *for a risk-averse decision maker*. Utility is measured as a number. Furthermore, it measures preferences. For example, since $1,000 is preferred to $500, $U(1,000) > U(500)$. Also, since distance A, $U(1,000) - U(0)$, is less than distance B, $U(0) - U(-1,000)$, the decision maker places more value (or *utility*) on losing $1,000 than on winning $1,000. Such a decision maker would not take a bet to gain or lose $1,000 based on the toss of a fair coin. To see why, we construct the following payoff table:

	Event	
Action	Heads	Tails
Take bet	$U(1,000) = 0.65$	$U(-1,000) = 0.25$
Don't bet	$U(0) = 0.5$	$U(0) = 0.5$

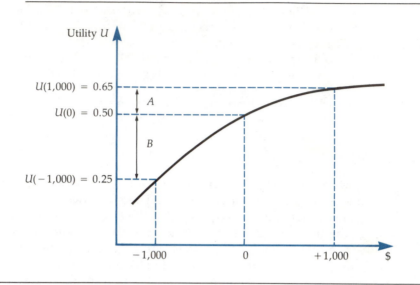

Utility U

$U(1,000) = 0.65$

$U(0) = 0.50$

A

B

$U(-1,000) = 0.25$

$-1,000$ 0 $+1,000$ $\$$

FIGURE 10.5   *A risk-averse utility function.*

Then the expected utilities are

$$EU(\text{Take the bet}) = \left(\frac{1}{2}\right)(0.65) + \left(\frac{1}{2}\right)(0.25) = 0.45$$

$$EU(\text{Don't bet}) = \left(\frac{1}{2}\right)(0.50) + \left(\frac{1}{2}\right)(0.50) = 0.50$$

The Bayes decision (*based on maximizing expected utility*) is "Don't bet." *The decision maker is averse to the risk of losing $1,000.*

Figures 10.6(a) and (b) show utility functions for decision makers who are risk takers and who are neither risk takers nor risk averse. The utility function of Fig. 10.6(b) is *linear. It can be proved that for linear utility functions, maximizing expected monetary payoffs yields the same decisions as maximizing expected utility.* If the range of possible payoffs in a decision problem is not too large, it is often fairly accurate to approximate nonlinear utility functions, such as in Figs. 10.5 and 10.6(a), by linear functions and simply use the Bayes criterion applied to monetary payoffs.

We have given you only a brief overview of the concepts of utility from a decision maker's viewpoint. A utility function simply measures the relative *preferences* of a decision maker and, as a built-in feature, takes into consideration the effects of *risk*. There are two very important issues we shall not discuss in this introductory text. The first concerns some of the mathematical foundations of utility theory, and the second deals with how one actually goes about computing utilities, for example, what procedure does one follow

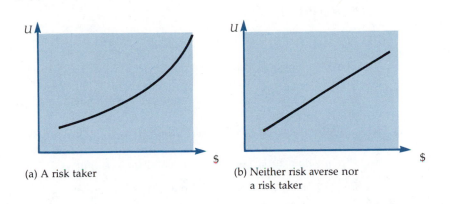

(a) A risk taker

(b) Neither risk averse nor
a risk taker

FIGURE 10.6

to derive a utility function such as that in Fig. 10.5? Interested readers might wish to consult some of the references given at the end of this text.

8. SEQUENTIAL DECISION-MAKING

The decision models presented so far in this chapter have dealt with decision problems that are one-time problems. We have not considered the case in which the decision maker has the option of following one decision with a second decision.

A **sequential decision problem** is one in which the decision maker must initially select a decision alternative; once the outcome following that decision is observed, an opportunity again exists to select another decision alternative (possibly from a different set of decisions than the initial set of alternatives). Thus *over time* the decision maker sequentially makes decisions and observes outcomes from those decisions. The criterion for making decisions is maximization of expected payoffs. We shall illustrate this class of problems in the next example.

EXAMPLE 10.12. *Facilities Expansion: Sequential Decision Making.* Plastipan manufactures plastic housewares and is considering expanding its product line to include plastic food-storage containers to be used in home kitchens. Initially it can purchase one of two machines to manufacture the containers, M1 and M2, requiring investments of $15,000 and $35,000, respectively. Of course, M1 has less productive capacity than M2 does.

The demand for the containers for the first year is projected to be low, moderate, or high, with respective probabilities of 0.3, 0.5, and 0.2. If demand during year 1 is low, the demand during year 2 will be low with probability 0.8 and high with probability 0.2. Note that these are *conditional probabilities:*

P(year 2 demand is low | year 1 demand is low) = 0.8

P(year 2 demand is high | year 1 demand is low) = 0.2

In these expressions, the P means "probability" and the vertical bar, |, is read "given that."

The remaining conditional demand probabilities for year 2 are as follows:

P(year 2 demand is low | year 1 demand is moderate) = 0.3

P(year 2 demand is high | year 1 demand is moderate) = 0.7

P(year 2 demand is low | year 1 demand is high)   = 0.1

P(year 2 demand is high | year 1 demand is high)   = 0.9

Management also identifies the following alternative courses of action (decision alternatives) for year 2:

1. If $M1$ is purchased in year 1 and if demand is low, Plastipan will continue to employ $M1$ the second year.
2. If $M1$ is purchased in year 1 and if demand is moderate or high during year 1, Plastipan will consider two decision alternatives at the end of year 1. It either will continue to operate with $M1$ or will expand by purchasing new equipment to supplement $M1$ capacity; this expansion would require an additional $13,000.
3. If $M2$ is purchased in year 1 and demand is low for year 1, the option will exist to close down some of the production capacity of $M2$, which would require an outlay of $5,000 for modifications. This would then cut down on operating, maintenance, and management costs of employing the large $M2$ facility.
4. If $M2$ is purchased in year 1 and demand is moderate during year 1, Plastipan management has decided it would continue to operate $M2$ during year 2 without modifications. If demand in year 1 is high, it will then consider the options of making no changes or expanding slightly (at a cost of $5,000).

These alternatives are displayed in the form of a decision tree (see Fig. 10.7). In addition, payoffs are given at the tip nodes of the tree (to the right). All of the information displayed on the tree is derived from managerial judgment, market research, and production factors. All monetary amounts shown are in thousands of dollars ($000).

Reading the Tree—(Fig. 10.7). To illustrate how this tree is to be read, let us take a specific example of one possible route through the tree. Starting

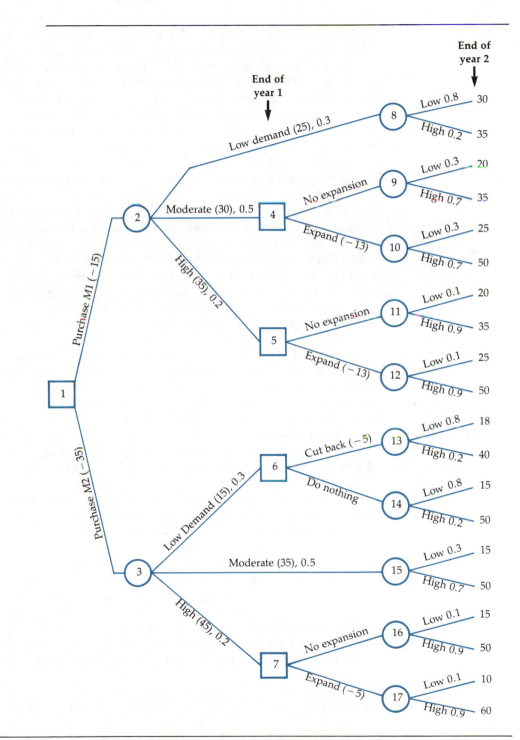

FIGURE 10.7 *Facilities planning for Plastipan.*

with decision node 1, suppose it is decided to purchase facility *M*2; the cost of this decision alternative is shown as −$35 (corresponding to a $35,000 cash outlay). This puts us at event node 3. Suppose first-year demand turns out to be high. The chance of this happening is 0.2, as shown on the event branch connecting nodes 3 and 7. Also shown on that branch is the $45 (or $45,000) Plastipan can expect to earn during the first year *if* demand is high and *given* the purchase of *M*2. Now we are at decision node 7 and at the end of year 1. We have two decision alternatives to consider: to expand or not to expand facilities. Suppose we choose to expand. This corresponds to the decision branch connecting nodes 7 and 17. We see that the expansion will cost $5 (or $5,000). We are now at event node 17. Two things can happen in year 2: With probability 0.1, demand will be low; with probability 0.9, demand will be high. Let us assume that demand for year 2 turns out to be low. The 10 at the tip of the event branch labeled "Low 0.1" coming out of node 17 indicates that profits for year 2 will be only $10 ($10,000). This low profit figure is due in part to the low demand and in part to the fact that, owing to the larger expanded facilities (at node 7), operating costs will be high. Thus we examined the sequence of nodes 1, 3, 7, and 17 and then the low-demand event branch. We made two decisions. At node 1 we decided on facility *M*2, and at node 7 we decided to expand.

The problem is to determine what sequence of decisions to follow. The means of solving this problem are precisely the same as those we employed to fold back the decision tree for Blockwood (see Fig. 10.3). The only difference here is that the tree is larger. In Fig. 10.8, we show the results of folding back the tree shown in Fig. 10.7. The Bayes decision at each decision node (nodes 1, 4, 5, 6, and 7) is marked with a slash on the appropriate decision branch. These calculations will be explained shortly.

From Fig. 10.8, we see that the optimal policy is the following:

- At decision node 1 the Bayes decision is to purchase *M*1 (as indicated by the slash on the upper branch). The expected profit over the two-year horizon is $45.95, or $45,950 (indicated above node 1).
- At event node 2 three things could happen:
  a. If demand is low, no further decisions are required.
  b. If demand is moderate, we make the decision at decision node 4 (*not to* expand). The expected value of this decision starting at the beginning of year 2 is $30.5 (or $30,500), which appears above node 4.
  c. If demand is high, we make the decision at decision node 5 to expand facilities (at a cost of $13,000). Starting at node 5, the expected profit from the Bayes decision to expand is $34.5, shown above node 5.

Calculations for Fig. 10.8—Folding Back the Tree

STEP 1. Evelute nodes 8–17. The procedure for evaluating these nodes is the same, and we shall demonstrate it on node 8. Starting with event node 8,

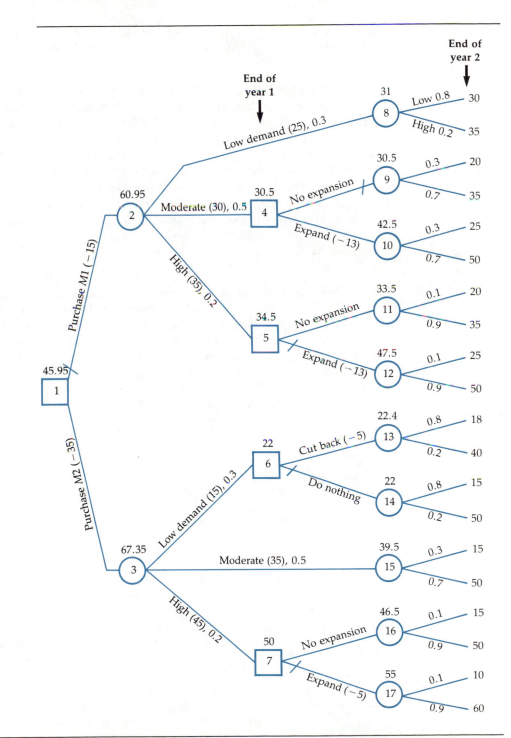

End of year 1

End of year 2

Purchase M1 (−15)

Purchase M2 (−35)

45.95
①

60.95
②

Low demand (25), 0.3

Moderate (30), 0.5

High (35), 0.2

30.5
④ No expansion

Expand (−13)

34.5
⑤ No expansion

Expand (−13)

31
⑧

Low 0.8   30

High 0.2   35

30.5
⑨   0.3   20

0.7   35

42.5
⑩   0.3   25

0.7   50

33.5
⑪   0.1   20

0.9   35

47.5
⑫   0.1   25

0.9   50

67.35
③

Low demand (15), 0.3

Moderate (35), 0.5

High (45), 0.2

22
⑥ Cut back (−5)

Do nothing

50
⑦ No expansion

Expand (−5)

22.4
⑬   0.8   18

0.2   40

22
⑭   0.8   15

0.2   50

39.5
⑮   0.3   15

0.7   50

46.5
⑯   0.1   15

0.9   50

55
⑰   0.1   10

0.9   60

FIGURE 10.8   *Folding back the tree of Fig. 10.7.*

the expected profit for year 2 is $(0.8)(30) + (0.2)(35) = \$31.0$. You should check the calculations for the other event nodes listed above.

STEP 2. Evaluate decision nodes 4–7. For node 4 (at the end of year 1), we have two choices: "No expansion" and "Expand." If we select "No expansion," our expected payoff will be the payoff at event node 9, or $30.5. If we select "Expand," our payoff will be $42.5 *minus* the cost of expansion, $13, or $42.5 − 13 = \$29.5$. Since the expected payoff for the "No expansion" alternative, $30.5, is greater than the expected payoff for the "Expand" alternative, $29.5, the Bayes decision at node 4 is "No expansion." We then place a slash mark on the "No expansion" branch and place $30.5 above node 4. You should now check your understanding by computing nodes 5, 6, and 7; that is, find the Bayes decisions and expected payoffs at these decision nodes.

STEP 3. Evaluate event nodes 2 and 3. We shall evaluate node 2 and leave node 3 for you to check. At node 2, three possible demand levels may occur in year 1—low, moderate, and high, having probabilities 0.3, 0.5, and 0.2, respectively. If the demand is low, the expected payoff equals the immediate $25 for year 1 (shown on the low demand branch) *plus* the expected payoff of $31 for year 2 (shown above node 8). If demand for year 1 is moderate, the expected payoff is $30 *plus* $30.5 (shown above node 4). If demand is high in year 1, the expected payoff is $35 *plus* $34.5 (shown above node 5). Thus the expected payoff at node 2 is

$$(0.3)(25 + 31) + (0.5)(30 + 30.5) + (0.2)(35 + 34.5)$$

$$= (0.3)(56) + (0.5)(60.5) + (0.2)(69.5) = \$60.95$$

(shown above node 2). Now use the same sort of reasoning to evaluate node 3.

STEP 4. Evaluate node 1. At node 1 we have two decision alternatives: $M1$, costing $15, and $M2$, costing $35. If we choose $M1$, our expected two-year profit will be $60.95 (at node 2) *minus* $15 (the cost of $M1$), or $45.95. If we choose $M2$, the expected two-year profit will be $67.35 (above node 3) *minus* $35 (the cost of $M2$), or $32.35. The Bayes decision selects the larger of these, $45.95, corresponding to the purchase of $M1$. We place a slash on the $M1$ branch and place 45.95 above node 1.

Thus the optimal policy is initially to start out small with $M1$. If demand during year 1 is low to moderate, no further expansion is called for. If demand is high for year 1, we should then expand facilities. Note the time-sequential nature of this decision-making process.   ▲

Problems

1. *Sensitivity Analysis.* Find the optimal sequence of decisions for the problem given in Fig. 10.7 if the cost of expansion at node 4 is decreased from $13,000 to $5,000 and the cost of machine $M2$ is $29,000 instead of $35,000.
2. Modify the decision tree in Fig. 10.7 to include the following: Initially (at node 1) a third machine, $M3$, is available, costing $25,000. First-year profits for low, moderate, and high demand would be $20,000, $37,000, and $40,000, respectively, if $M3$ is used. At the end of year 1, the option exists to expand capacity at a cost of $10,000 or to continue with $M3$. Second-year profits are given as follows ($000):

	Demand, year 2	
Decision at end of year	Low	High
Don't expand	19	38
Expand	26	53

3. Determine the optimal policy for the decision problem of Problem 2 above.

9. POSTERIOR ANALYSIS

Prior to selecting a decision alternative in a given decision problem, management may have the option of obtaining new information that could be used to refine the probability estimates of the events, thus, it is hoped, leading to a better decision. The information obtainable may be sample data, market research, data collected by electronic testing or surveillance, or the advice of a paid expert (consultant). Such information is often referred to as **sample** information. Once obtained, sample information is used to *revise* the set of probabilities of the events.

Bayes' Theorem

The original probabilities of the various events are called **prior probabilities.** They exist prior to the use of sample information. Once the sample information is obtained, the prior probabilities and the sample information are used to determine revised probabilities, called **posterior probabilities.** Posterior probabilities are calculated *after* the sample information is obtained. To calculate posterior probabilities, a formula called Bayes' theorem is used (see

Appendix E). Bayes' theorem can be written as follows:

$$P(A|B) = \frac{P(A)P(B|A)}{P(B)} \qquad (10\text{--}1)$$

For our applications the event A will correspond to an event s_i, B will correspond to sample information O_j, $P(A|B) = P(s_i|O_j)$ is, then, the *posterior probability* of an event s_i given the sample outcome O_j. On the right side of Eq. (10–1), $P(A) = P(s_i)$ is the *prior probability* of event s_i (before having the information O_j), $P(B|A) = P(O_j|s_i)$ is called a **likelihood probability,** and $P(B) = P(O_j)$ is called a **predictive probability.** An example will best illustrate these concepts.

EXAMPLE 10.13. Suppose Blockwood Designs, Inc. (Example 10.1) acquires the services of a market-research consulting firm, Adrite, Inc. Adrite will conduct a market study that will result in one of two outcomes: (1) O_1 will be a favorable indication of the market for Blockwood products, and (2) O_2 will be an unfavorable indication. In this case, O_1 and O_2 are referred to as the **sample outcomes.**

We question Adrite concerning the accuracy of its marketing research techniques, and it supplies us with the following eight *likelihood probabilities:*

$$P(O_1|s_i), i = 1, 2, 3, 4$$

and $P(O_2|s_i), i = 1, 2, 3, 4$

The values of these conditional probabilities are given in Table 10.10. These probabilities were arrived at from considerable Adrite experience, using historical market-research records in Adrite's files; the statisticians at Adrite had primary input to the evaluation of these probabilities.

As an example of the meaning of the conditional likelihood probabilities, Table 10.10 shows that $P(O_2|s_1) = 0.95$. This tells us that, *given* that the *true* state of nature is s_1 (sales *will fall* in the low range \$0–\$20,000), there is a 0.95 probability that the results of Adrite's analysis will indicate an unfavorable market (O_2). Note the confidence Adrite has in the entry $P(O_1|s_1) =$

TABLE 10.10   *Likelihood Probabilities: Table of $P(O_j|S_i)$; $j = 1, 2$; $i = 1, 2, 3, 4$*

	Sales			
	(Low) s_1	s_2	s_3	(High) s_4
Favorable indication, O_1	0.05	0.30	0.70	0.90
Unfavorable indication, O_2	0.95	0.70	0.30	0.10

0.05. This says that if, indeed, the *true* state of nature is s_1, there is only a 0.05 probability that the marketing analysis will indicate a favorable market. The other six entries can be similarly interpreted. Note that $P(O_1|s_i) + P(O_2|s_i) = 1$ for each $i = 1, 2, 3, 4$.

Part 1. Assume Adrite's market research results in sample outcome O_1. Compute the *posterior probabilities* of the states of nature (that is, "revise" the prior probabilities in light of the sample outcome O_1).

Solution. We must use Bayes' theorem, Eq. (10–1). The likelihood probabilities $P(B|A)$ were given in Table 10.10. The prior probabilities are the marketing manager's estimates given in Example 10.8, as follows:

$$P(s_1) = 0.20, \ P(s_2) = 0.35, \ P(s_3) = 0.30, \ P(s_4) = 0.15$$

It remains to compute the denominator of Eq. (10–1), $P(B)$, where B is the sample outcome O_1. As mentioned above, $P(O_1)$ is called a *predictive probability*. (The rationale behind this terminology will become apparent in the next section.)

Note that the four events, s_1, s_2, s_3, and s_4, are mutually exclusive (they do not "overlap" or "intersect" each other) and exhaustive (they include all possible sales ranges that can occur). You may recall the following fundamental theorem of probability:

$$P(O_1) = P(O_1 \cap s_1) + P(O_1 \cap s_2) + P(O_1 \cap s_3) + P(O_1 \cap s_4)$$

The intersection symbol, $\cap$, is read "and." Also recall the general relation $P(A \cap B) = P(B)P(A|B)$, read "the probability of A and B equals the probability of B times the probability of A given B." For $P(O_1)$, this gives

$$P(O_1) = P(s_1)P(O_1|s_1) + P(s_2)P(O_1|s_2) + P(s_3)P(O_1|s_3) + P(s_4)P(O_1|s_4)$$

For the terms $P(s_1)$, we will substitute the Blockwood marketing manager's estimates given in Example 10.8. The values of $P(O_1|s_i)$ are given in Table 10.10. This gives

$$P(O_1) = (0.20)(0.05) + (0.35)(0.30) + (0.30)(0.70) + (0.15)(0.90)$$

$$= 0.46$$

Note: A general formula for the predictive probabilities is

$$P(O_j) = \sum_{all \ i} P(s_i)P(O_j|s_i) \qquad (10\text{–}2)$$

We are now ready to calculate the posterior probabilities of the events s_1,

s_2, s_3, and s_4 using Bayes' theorem. For s_1 we have

$$P(s_1|O_1) = \frac{P(s_1)P(O_1|s_1)}{P(O_1)}$$

Note that the numerator is the product of the prior probability $P(s_1)$ and the likelihood probability $P(O_1|s_1)$. The denominator is the predictive probability $P(O_1)$. The calculation becomes

$$P(s_1|O_1) = \frac{(0.20)(0.05)}{0.46} = 0.022$$

The other posterior probabilities are calculated in a similar manner. The general formula is

$$P(s_i|O_j) = \frac{P(s_i)P(O_j|s_i)}{P(O_j)}, \text{ for } i = 1, 2, 3, 4 \tag{10–3}$$

$$\text{and } j = 1, 2.$$

Thus we obtain the following results:

$$P(s_2|O_1) = \frac{P(s_2)P(O_1|s_2)}{P(O_1)} = \frac{(0.35)(0.30)}{0.46} = 0.228$$

$$P(s_3|O_1) = \frac{P(s_3)P(O_1|s_3)}{P(O_1)} = \frac{(0.30)(0.70)}{0.46} = 0.457$$

$$P(s_4|O_1) = \frac{P(s_4)P(O_1|s_4)}{P(O_1)} = \frac{(0.15)(0.90)}{0.46} = 0.293$$

Note that $P(s_1|O_1) + P(s_2|O_1) + P(s_3|O_1) + P(s_4|O_1) = 1$ as it should. (Given that O_1 occurs, one of the outcomes s_1, s_2, s_3, or s_4 *must* occur.)

Observe the nature of the results obtained. The outcome O_1 indicates that a favorable market exists. Comparing the prior and posterior probabilities of the events (the four sales ranges), we see that

The probability of s_1 *decreased* from 0.20 to 0.022

The probability of s_2 *decreased* from 0.35 to 0.228

The probability of s_3 *increased* from 0.30 to 0.457

The probability of s_4 *increased* from 0.15 to 0.293

Part 2. Now let us assume that Adrite's market research results in sample outcome O_2. The posterior probabilities are calculated in the same manner as before.

First we calculate the predictive probability $P(O_2)$ from Eq. (10–2) as follows:

$$P(O_2) = P(s_1)P(O_2|s_1) + P(s_2)P(O_2|s_2) + P(s_3)P(O_2|s_3) + P(s_4)P(O_2|s_4)$$

$$= (0.20)(0.95) + (0.35 (0.70) + (0.30)(0.30) + (0.15)(0.10)$$

$$= 0.54$$

After calculating $P(O_1)$, we could have found $P(O_2)$ more easily by using the fact that $P(O_2) = 1 - P(O_1) = 1 - 0.46 = 0.54$. This does serve to check our calculations.

Next, Bayes' theorem, Eq. (10–3), is used to find the posterior probabilities as follows:

$$P(s_1|O_2) = \frac{P(s_1)P(O_2|s_1)}{P(O_2)} = \frac{(0.20)(0.95)}{0.54} = 0.352$$

$$P(s_2|O_2) = \frac{P(s_2)P(O_2|s_2)}{P(O_2)} = \frac{(0.35)(0.70)}{0.54} = 0.454$$

$$P(s_3|O_2) = \frac{P(s_3)P(O_2|s_3)}{P(O_2)} = \frac{(0.30)(0.30)}{0.54} = 0.167$$

$$P(s_4|O_2) = \frac{P(s_4)P(O_2|s_4)}{P(O_2)} = \frac{(0.15)(0.10)}{0.54} = 0.028$$

(These probabilities add up to 1.001 owing to round-off errors. They should add up to 1.000; however, the difference is slight.)

As in Part 1, above, you should compare the prior and posterior probabilities, given the "unfavorable" sample outcome O_2, and interpret the results.   ▲

Bayes' Decision

Recall the general situation: We start with a payoff table and are given prior probabilities of the events. Before making a decision, we obtain some additional information (*sample information*) concerning the events. We then revise the prior probabilities using Bayes' theorem to calculate posterior probabilities of the events based on the sample outcome obtained. Now the next step in posterior decision analysis is to employ the Bayes criterion, *using the posterior probabilities* to select a decision alternative.

EXAMPLE 10.14. In Example 10.13, we calculated the posterior probabilities for each of the sample outcomes, O_1 and O_2, from Adrite's marketing analysis.

1. Determine the Bayes decision if the sample outcome is O_1.

Solution. The decision tree for this problem is given in Fig. 10.9. Note that the posterior probabilities are used for the event branches from nodes 2, 3, and 4. The results of folding back the tree are also shown. Thus if the sample outcome is "favorable," the Bayes decision is to purchase the large flatbed truck. The expected payoff is $23.85 ($23,850).

2. Determine the Bayes decision if the sample outcome is O_2.

Solution. The solution to this problem, shown in Fig. 10.10, indicates that if the sample outcome is "unfavorable," the Bayes decision is to purchase the standard-size pickup. The expected payoff from the decision is $19,194.   ▲

Example 10.14 demonstrates that both the Bayes decision *and* the expected payoffs can be greatly affected by the sample outcomes in posterior analysis.

The procedure for conducting posterior analysis is summarized below.

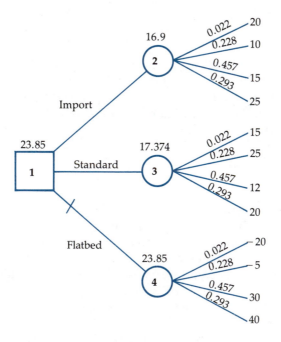

FIGURE 10.9   *Example 10.14, Part 1.*

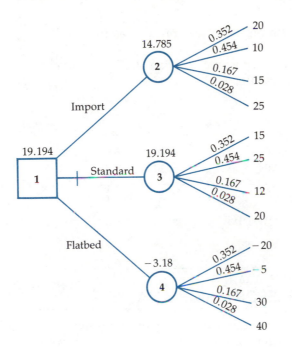

FIGURE 10.10   *Example 10.14, Part 2.*

Summary: Posterior Analysis

STEP 1. Obtain conditional sample outcome probabilities. (In our example, these probabilities are shown in Table 10.10.)

STEP 2. Obtain the sample outcome. (In our example, Blockwood Designs hires Adrite to conduct a market analysis and obtains either sample outcome O_1, "a favorable market," or O_2, "an unfavorable market.")

STEP 3. Calculate the posterior probabilities of the events. This requires the use of Bayes' theorem, Eq. (10–3). The numerator is the prior probability times the likelihood; the denominator is the predictive probability, Eq. (10–2). (Example 10.13 illustrates the use of Bayes' theorem.)

STEP 4. Use the posterior probabilities calculated in step 3 to determine the Bayes decision. (Example 10.14.)

Problems

Refer to Example 10.13 and proceed as follows:

1. Calculate the posterior probabilities if the likelihood table were changed to the following:

	s_1	s_2	s_3	s_4
O_1	0.10	0.25	0.80	0.95
O_2	0.90	0.75	0.20	0.05

2. Determine the Bayes decision and expected payoff for each of the two outcomes.

10. EXPECTED VALUE OF SAMPLE INFORMATION (EVSI)—PREPOSTERIOR ANALYSIS

In Section 6 we found that the largest amount management should pay for sample information can be determined by computing the EVPI. In Section 9 we studied *posterior analysis,* which tells us what to do *after* obtaining additional information (sample information) concerning the events. In this section we study **preposterior analysis,** which tells us whether it would pay us to purchase sample information. This will involve computing the expected value of "imperfect" information, or the **expected value of sample information** (EVSI) as it is referred to in management science literature.

For illustration purposes, suppose Blockwood Designs, Inc., must pay $950 to acquire the services of Adrite. Should Adrite's services be purchased? (Note that in the previous section we *assumed* that Adrite's services were *already* obtained, so we ignored the cost involved.) To answer this question we shall carry out a five-step EVSI analysis.

STEP 1. Obtain conditional sample outcome probabilities. For our situation, Adrite has provided us with Table 10.10.

STEP 2. Calculate the predictive probabilities of all possible sample outcomes.

In our case we must calculate $P(O_1)$ and $P(O_2)$. This was accomplished in Example 10.13. The results were $P(O_1) = 0.46$ and $P(O_2) = 0.54$. Note the meaning of the predictive probabilities: "$P(O_1) = 0.46$" means that *prior* to conducting the Adrite analysis, and based on our *current* best estimates of the probabilities $P(s_i)$ (the prior probabilities), we would *predict* with probability 0.46 that Adrite's results will be O_1. Similarly, we would expect that with a 0.54 probability, the results will be O_2.

STEP 3. Compute the posterior probabilities of the events, given every possible sample outcome.

In our case (see Example 10.13), we computed the eight (conditional) posterior probabilities as follows:

$P(s_i|O_1)$, $i = 1, 2, 3, 4$ (Part 1, Example 10.14)

$P(s_i|O_2)$, $i = 1, 2, 3, 4$ (Part 2, Example 10.14)

STEP 4. Place the results of steps 2 and 3 in a decision tree and proceed to fold the tree back from right to left in the usual manner.

The decision tree for our example is given in Fig. 10.11. Note that the two possible sample outcomes, O_1 and O_2, are represented as branches out of node 1; the respective predictive probabilities are given on these two branches. Note also that the decision tree shown in Fig. 10.11 simply combines the decision trees of Figs. 10.9 and 10.10.

STEP 5. Compute EVSI, using the following equation:

$$\text{EVSI} = \left(\begin{array}{c}\text{Expected payoff with}\\\text{sample information}\end{array}\right) - \left(\begin{array}{c}\text{Expected payoff without}\\\text{sample information}\end{array}\right)$$

$$= 21.34 - 18.35 \text{ (see Figs. 10.3 and 10.11)}$$

$$= 2.99, \text{ or } \$2,990 \text{ (since all payoffs are expressed in \$000)}$$

Conclusion. For the present problem the expected gain using sample information (that is, Adrite's analysis) is $2,990 over the expected payoff without sample information. Since this is greater than the cost of the sample information (the $950 Adrite fee), we *would* purchase the additional information. We define the **expected net gain of sampling** (ENGS) to be $2,990 − 950 = $2,040. We conclude that the Adrite analysis will refine our prior probability estimates enough to justify paying $950 for the information. In Problem 1 at the end of this section, you are asked to repeat the EVSI analysis, using information offered by a different set of likelihood probabilities $P(O_j|s_i)$.

Preposterior Analysis

The entire procedure outlined in this section is referred to as **preposterior analysis.** If we *actually* were to purchase additional sample information (for example, to employ Adrite), we would then obtain sample information O_1 or O_2 and use this information to calculate the posterior probabilities of the events, using the formula given in step 3, below. These posterior probabilities would then be entered on a decision tree (see Figs. 10.9 and 10.10), the tree folded back, and the Bayes decision identified.

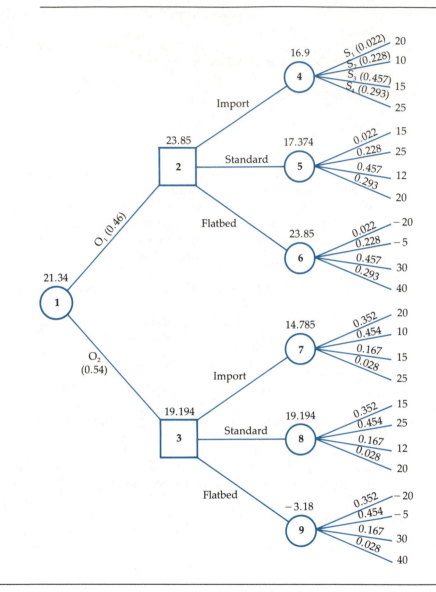

FIGURE 10.11

But we do not actually obtain the sample information in steps 1–6, below. Instead we perform a hypothetical analysis to project what could be expected to happen *if* we were to obtain sample information and *if* we then computed corresponding posterior probabilities. Thus we refer to this type of analysis as *preposterior* analysis.

Summary—Preposterior Analysis

To evaluate whether additional sample information should be purchased, proceed according to the following steps:

STEP 1. Obtain conditional sample outcome probabilities. These take the form

$$P(\text{sample outcome} \mid \text{the true event}) = P(O_j|s_i)$$

for all possible sample outcomes O_j and events s_i. These probabilities are termed **conditional likelihood probabilities.**

STEP 2. Compute the probabilities of the occurrence of each possible sample outcome, $P(O_j)$. These probabilities are termed **predictive probabilities.** The formula to use is Eq. (10–2):

$$P(O_j) = \sum_{\text{all } i} P(s_i)P(O_j|s_i)$$

where the $P(s_i)$ are the *prior probabilities* of the events and the $P(O_j|s_i)$ are the likelihoods from step 1. The prior probabilities are the current event probabilities, based on our best information to date.

STEP 3. Calculate the *posterior probabilities* of the events using Bayes' theorem, Eq. (10–3),

$$P(s_i|O_j) = \frac{P(s_i)P(O_j|s_i)}{P(O_j)}$$

for each event s_i and possible sample outcome O_j.

STEP 4. Using the predictive and posterior probabilities (steps 2 and 3), fold back the decision tree from right to left in the usual manner. The evaluation of node 1 (the leftmost node) gives the *expected payoff with sample information* (EPSI).

STEP 5. Compute the expected value of sample information, using

$$\text{EVSI} = \left(\begin{array}{c}\text{Expected payoff with}\\\text{sample information}\end{array}\right) - \left(\begin{array}{c}\text{Expected payoff without}\\\text{sample information}\end{array}\right)$$

STEP 6. Compute the *expected net gain of sampling* (ENGS) as follows:

$$\text{ENGS} = \text{EVSI} - (\text{Cost of sampling: CS})$$

If ENGS > 0, the sample information should be purchased; otherwise, it is not worthwhile (on an expected net gain basis) to obtain the sample information.

Problems

1. Suppose Blockwood Designs, Inc., is approached by a second market research consulting firm that offers to conduct a market study to determine next year's sales. This second firm's fee is $900, and the likehood probabilities are given below:

	s_1	s_2	s_3	s_4
O_1	0.05	0.10	0.75	0.95
O_2	0.95	0.90	0.25	0.05

(This corresponds to Table 10.10.) Should Blockwood employ the services of this firm?

2. Assume that Blockwood does employ the services of Adrite and that Adrite's analysis indicates an unfavorable market; that is, the outcome of the sample information is O_2. Given these conditions, compute the Bayes decision and the expected payoff for the upcoming year. Subtract Adrite's fee from this payoff. Is the result greater or less than the expected payoff without sample information? (See Fig. 10.3.) Answer the same question if Adrite's outcome were O_1.

11. CONCLUDING REMARKS

We have discussed several methods that are available to assist management in making decisions under various conditions. These methods fall into two general categories.

1. Nonprobabilistic problems, in which the probabilities of the events are not specified. Methods available for decision making are maximax (risky, optimistic), maximin (conservative, pessimistic), and minimax (loss).
2. Probabilistic problems, in which probabilities of the events are specified. Method for decision making is the Bayes criterion (maximize expected payoff or minimize expected loss).

The nonprobabilistic case was first treated by Von Neumann and Morgenstern (1947). The original reference for Bayes' theorem is Bayes (1763).

Other Topics

The interested reader may wish to consult the references in this chapter for additional topics in decision theory.

The assessment and interpretation of *subjective probabilities* is a topic of central importance in probabilistic decision problems, as is the notion of *utility* and the construction of actual utility functions. The foundations of utility theory were established in the classic work of Von Neumann and Morgenstern (1947). We especially recommend the book by Robert L. Winkler, *An Introduction to Bayesian Inference and Decision,* as a very readable introduction to these and other decision theory topics.

TERMINOLOGY

After studying this chapter you should be familiar with the following terms:

TERM	SECTION
Bayes decision rule	5
Bayes' theorem	9
decision tree	2
branch	2
cost of sampling	10
decision nodes	2
ENGS	10
EPPI	6
EPSI	10
event nodes	2
EVPI	6
EVSI	10
likelihood probability	10
loss table	2
maximax rule	4
maximin rule	4
minimax rule	4
nonprobabilistic decision problems	3
payoff table	2
posterior analysis	9
posterior probabilities	9
predictive probability	9
preposterior analysis	10
prior probabilities	9

EXERCISES

Note: It is suggested that you get into the practice of using decision trees by constructing a decision tree for each problem you attempt to solve in this exercise set.

1. *Buying a Car.* You are considering purchasing one of three cars. At the end of four years you will sell whichever car you decide to buy. Your maintenance and operating expenses over the four years will depend on the price of gasoline and the pollution control requirements set by the city and state. You identify four possibilities: (a) moderate gas prices and few government regulations; (b) moderate gas prices and more stringent regulations; (c) higher gas prices and moderate regulations; (d) higher gas prices and stringent regulations.

   Your estimates of total net operating costs (after selling the car) over the four-year period for each car are given in Table 10.11 (in $).
   a. Specify the minimax decision.
   b. Specify the maximax decision.
   c. Specify the maximin decision.
   d. Suppose your estimates of the event probabilities are $P(a) = 0.30$, $P(b) = 0.35$, $P(c) = 0.30$, and $P(d) = 0.05$. Specify the Bayes decision.
   e. Compute the EVPI. (*Hint:* You may construct a table of negative payoffs, or you may work directly with costs.)

2. *Advertising Strategy.* Dino's Dinettes retails dinette sets for residential homes. Dino's has been in business for a short length of time and com-

TABLE 10.11

	a	b	c	d
Car 1	5,000	5,000	7,000	9,000
Car 2	4,000	6,000	6,200	7,000
Car 3	6,500	6,500	6,600	6,700

petes against a large, well-established firm, Discount Dinette Center (DDC). Although Dino's products are of higher quality than those of DDC and lower in price on many items, Dino's has had some difficulty gaining its market share, owing to the heavy advertising regularly used by DDC, a strategy that Dino's has not yet been able to afford. Dino's is planning to counterattack by placing some advertising this week to show its lower prices and is considering three levels of advertising effort: major, moderate, and minor. Of course, DDC's advertising plans are not known to Dino's, but based on past data, Dino's assesses the various probabilities of DDC's advertising efforts to be $P(\text{major}) = 0.30$, $P(\text{moderate}) = 0.45$, $P(\text{minor}) = 0.25$. The payoff table for Dino's is shown in Table 10.12 (in $000 additional sales generated by advertising):

a. Determine the maximin decision.
b. Determine the maximax decision.
c. Determine the minimax decision.
d. Determine the Bayes decision.
e. Compute the EVPI.
f. Which criterion, (a), (b), (c), or (d), would *you* abide by?

3. *Military Strategy.*   The Armed Forces, by direction of the Pentagon, are simulating war games for a special project on military preparedness. The scenario setup is as follows: Country A is about to launch either a light, medium, or heavy attack on a region occupied by an enemy. The enemy concentration may be rated 0, 1, 2, or 3, from light to heavy, as measured by personnel, materiel, and armaments present in the target region. The payoff table for County A, as measured in "damage units," is given in Table 10.13. For example, a medium-level attack against a dense target (level 3) would score 45 damage units, whereas a heavy attack would score 60.

a. Determine the maximin strategy.
b. Determine the maximax strategy.
c. Determine the minimax strategy.

4. *Sensitivity Analysis—Military Strategy.*   (Refer to Exercise 3 above.) Compute the Bayes decision for each of the following sets of probabilities of the enemy concentration level in Table 10.14.

TABLE 10.12

Dino's	DDC		
	Major	Moderate	Minor
Major	3	5	6
Moderate	1	4	7
Minor	0	3	8

TABLE 10.13

Country A attack	Enemy concentration			
	0	1	2	3
Light	10	20	30	50
Medium	20	30	35	45
Heavy	15	25	40	60

TABLE 10.14

	$P(0)$	$P(1)$	$P(2)$	$P(3)$
Case 1	0.10	0.20	0.30	0.40
Case 2	0.15	0.35	0.35	0.15
Case 3	0.05	0.10	0.60	0.25
Case 4	0.40	0.30	0.20	0.10
Case 5	0.45	0.05	0.05	0.45

5. *Reconnaissance Effectiveness Planning.* (Refer to Exercise 3 above on military strategy.) Assume the probability density of the enemy concentration level is given by $P(0) = 0.05$, $P(1) = 0.10$, $P(2) = 0.60$, $P(3) = 0.25$.
   a. Compute the Bayes decision and expected payoff.
   b. Compute the EVPI.
   c. Suppose a reconnaissance mission can be conducted that returns information O_1 or O_2. The likelihood probabilities are given in Table 10.15. (Thus O_1 indicates a light concentration, and O_2 indicates a heavy concentration.) If the reconnaissance mission is conducted and outcome O_1 results, compute a posterior decision strategy.
   d. Now let us assume that the reconnaissance mission has not yet been conducted but is in the planning stage. If the damage (cost) incurred

TABLE 10.15

	s_1	s_2	s_3	s_4
	0	1	2	3
O_1	0.90	0.75	0.35	0.20
O_2	0.10	0.25	0.65	0.80

by the reconnaissance mission is expected to be 0.50 damage units, should Country A plan to go ahead with the reconnaissance effort? (Conduct a *preposterior analysis;* note that the "cost of sampling" equals 0.50.) This exercise demonstrates the value of preposterior analysis to the planning function.

6. *Aspiration Level.* In some decision problems, management may wish to maximize the probability of achieving a certain level of performance or profits. A probabilistic decision rule applicable to such an objective is the *aspiration level criterion.* Suppose management wishes to maximize the probability of earning at least $A in profits. The aspiration level rule can be stated as follows:
   - *Step 1.* For each action, compute the probability of receiving a payoff of at least $A.
   - *Step 2.* Select the action that maximizes the probabilities computed in step 1.

   In the payoff table given in Table 10.16, suppose $P(s_1) = 0.1$, $P(s_2) = 0.4$, $P(s_3) = 0.45$, $P(s_4) = 0.05$. Also you are told that management would like to maximize the probability of earning at least $50. Use the aspiration level rule to determine which action to take.

7. *Aspiration Level.* Suppose Blockwood's management (Example 10.1) wishes to maximize the probability of realizing a payoff of at least $15,000. Which action should it select? (Use the marketing manager's assessed probabilities given in Example 10.8.)

8. *Energy Research.* The government is planning to launch an extensive energy project to explore alternative energy sources. It has put together three major policy alternatives—a_1, a_2, and a_3—that differ with respect to the relative emphasis placed on each energy alternative (gasohol, coal, solar, nuclear, shale oil, oil exploration, common market possibilities, conservation, and tar sands). Four scenarios of the future state of the world have been identified and defined according to the following parameters: oil import prices, political and military factors, projected energy needs, the existence and abundance of raw materials, and tech-

TABLE 10.16

	s_1	s_2	s_3	s_4
a_1	10	60	55	40
a_2	40	50	30	56
a_3	58	52	40	51

TABLE 10.17

Government policy	State of the world			
	s_1	s_2	s_3	s_4
a_1	3	4	2	3
a_2	1	5	6	2
a_3	4	3	1	5

nological factors. The payoff table is shown in Table 10.17 (expressed in terms of millions of barrels of oil equivalent gained per day by the year 2000).

a. Determine the maximin policy.
b. Determine the maximax policy.
c. Determine the minimax policy.
d. Suppose the government considers each state of the world to be equally likely. Determine the Bayes decision.
e. Now suppose the government funds university and government research that suggests the following probabilities of the future state of the world: $P(s_1) = 0.20$, $P(s_2) = 0.30$, $P(s_3) = 0.35$, $P(s_4) = 0.15$. Determine the Bayes decision.
f. Compute the EVPI for part (e).

9. *Oil Drilling.* Lukistrike Oil Co. is studying the possibility of drilling an oil well in Nomansland. The payoff table is given below (in $000 net profit).

a. Determine the maximin decision.
b. Determine the maximax decision.
c. Determine the minimax decision.
d. Suppose $P(\text{Oil}) = 0.20$ and $P(\text{No oil}) = 0.80$. Determine the Bayes decision, expected payoff, and EVPI.
e. *Sensitivity Analysis.* Let $P(\text{Oil}) = p$. What is the minimum value of the probability, p, that would result in the Bayes decision to drill?

	Oil	No oil
Drill	300	−150
Don't drill	0	0

10. *Oil Drilling: Joint Ventures.* Suppose Lukistrike Oil Co. is studying the possibility of drilling an oil well. It has the following four options to take concerning drilling interests:

TABLE 10.18

	Oil	No oil
100% interest	300	−150
50% interest	160	−50
25% interest	75	−40
Sell the well	32	32

a. Drill with 100 percent interest.
b. Drill with 50 percent interest with another oil company.
c. Drill with 25 percent interest with another oil company.
d. Sell the rights to a competitor.

The payoff table is given in Table 10.18 (in $000). (Drilling with a partner not only shares losses but also decreases drilling cost by pooling expertise and knowledge.)

a. If $P(\text{Oil}) = 0.4$, $P(\text{No oil}) = 0.6$, determine the Bayes decision.
b. Compute the EVPI.
c. *Posterior Analysis.* Suppose Lukistrike has a geological testing firm conduct tests to determine the presence of oil. The tests result in one of three outcomes, O_1, O_2, or O_3, where O_1 is a favorable indication of oil, O_3 is unfavorable, and O_2 is somewhere in between. The likelihood table is shown in Table 10.19. If the lab tests result in O_2, determine the Bayes decision based on the revised probabilities.

TABLE 10.19

	Oil	No oil	
O_1	0.75	0.05	[Gives the probabilities
O_2	0.20	0.15	$P(O_i|\text{Oil})$ and
O_3	0.05	0.80	$P(O_i|\text{No oil})$, $i = 1, 2, 3$]

11. *Oil Drilling: Preposterior Analysis.* (Refer to Exercise 10.) Let us assume that Lukistrike has not yet employed the geological testing firm to conduct tests. Suppose that the testing firm's fee is $15,000. Should Lukistrike have the tests conducted? (Specify the EPSI, CS, and ENGS. Display a complete decision tree showing the results of folding the tree back.)

12. *Inventory Management.* Blumburg's Department Store will hold a one-month suit sale. The suits can be purchased in lots of twenty-five each, and the wholesale cost per suit is a function of the number of suits ordered, as shown on the next page.

Number of suits ordered	25	50	75	100
Cost per suit ($)	80	75	70	65

Each suit left over at the end of the month will be sold at a clearance sale for half the retail sales price of $140. If a shortage arises during the month, suits will be backordered at a cost of $85. The possible sales levels are 25, 50, 75, and 100, having probabilities of 0.20, 0.30, 0.40, and 0.10, respectively.

a. Construct a payoff table for this decision problem.

b. Construct a decision tree to represent the problem.

c. Fold back the decision tree to determine the optimal inventory ordering decision.

d. *Marketing Analysis.* Suppose Blumburg's could purchase the services of a marketing consultant who would conduct a survey that could be summarized by one of two outcomes: O_1 (a favorable market exists for the sale) or O_2 (an unfavorable market exists). The likelihoods, estimated by Blumburg's from past experience with this consultant, are given in Table 10.20. What is the maximum amount Blumburg's should pay for the consultant's services? (*Hint:* Conduct a preposterior analysis.)

13. *Personnel Selection.* The personnel manager of a small manufacturing firm has been recruiting in an effort to hire an employee to work under the production supervisor. The production supervisor indicates that the person hired will be placed in one of three positions, and he estimates that there is a 20 percent chance of placement in job 1, a 65 percent chance of placement in job 2, and a 15 percent chance of placement in job 3. Although the actual placement decision will not be made for one week, due to uncertainties in the production schedule, the production supervisor prefers to hire the person as soon as possible, not only to expedite the recruiting but also to save time in reference checks, medical checkups, and payroll processing that must be accomplished on new employees.

TABLE 10.20

$P(O_j|s_i)$	Sales (states of nature)			
	$s_1 = 25$	$s_2 = 50$	$s_3 = 75$	$s_4 = 100$
O_1	0.05	0.50	0.70	0.85
O_2	0.95	0.50	0.30	0.15

TABLE 10.21

Prospective employee	Job		
	1	2	3
1	1.0	2.0	1.5
2	2.0	2.0	1.0
3	1.0	3.0	0.5
4	3.0	1.0	2.0

The personnel manager has four candidates in mind and has rated each one in terms of the output each could produce if placed in each of the three positions (in $000), as shown in Table 10.21. Determine the Bayes decision for this problem.

14. *Medical Care.* A doctor must diagnose the condition of one of her patients. She is certain that the condition is not life threatening, so there is no risk to the patient's life. However, in diagnosing the condition the doctor would like to minimize the cost to the patient. There are three tests she could conduct on her patient. The doctor has narrowed the range of possibilities down to three disease conditions and indicates her professional judgmental probability assessments of the three conditions as 40 percent, 25 percent, and 35 percent that the disease is type 1, type 2, and type 3, respectively. The cost (in $) to the patient for diagnosis and treatment is given in the table of possibilities shown in Table 10.22, depending on the test employed. Answer the following by dealing directly with *costs* (the problem can also be solved by constructing a table of negative payoffs):
   a. Determine the Bayes decision (the test which minimizes the expected cost).
   b. Compute the EVPI.

TABLE 10.22

Test	Disease condition		
	1	2	3
1	500	300	400
2	600	500	300
3	300	550	450

c. Suppose the doctor first administers a special blood test that could be used to refine her probability estimates. The cost of the blood test is $50, and it would indicate one of two results—O_1 or O_2. The likelihood probabilities are given in the following table:

		Disease condition		
	$s_1 = 1$	$s_2 = 2$	$s_3 = 3$	
O_1	0.80	0.05	0.40	$P(O_1|s_i),\ i = 1, 2, 3$
O_2	0.20	0.95	0.60	$P(O_2|s_i),\ i = 1, 2, 3$

Should the doctor administer the blood test prior to selecting one of the three major tests?

15. *Facilities Location.*   A company is planning to locate a large nightclub in the city of Yorkville and is considering three locations (L1, L2, and L3). The company's annual profits will depend on the city's future policies concerning expanding its mass-transit system. Each of the locations will be affected differently by the city's policies. Four general possibilities have been identified for future city policies. The payoff table (in $000 profit per year) is shown in Table 10.23.
a. Determine the maximin decision.
b. Determine the maximax decision.
c. Determine the minimax decision.
d. Assume that it is equally likely that the city will adopt each of the four policies. Determine the Bayes decision. Compute the EVPI.
e. *Posterior Analysis.*   Now suppose the company president obtains some inside information (at no cost) from a friend of his who works in the mayor's office. Let us denote this information by *I*. The company president quantifies his faith in this source of information by estimating (subjectively and based on personal knowledge of his friend's

TABLE 10.23

	City policies			
Location	1	2	3	4
L1	100	50	60	30
L2	20	50	80	40
L3	40	60	30	65

reliability) the following conditional likelihood probabilities:

$P(I|\text{Policy 1}) = 0.20$ $P(I|\text{Policy 2}) = 0.50$

$P(I|\text{Policy 3}) = 0.60$ $P(I|\text{Policy 4}) = 0.10$

Revise the prior probabilities of part (d) above and determine the posterior Bayes decision.

16. *To Make or Buy.* Soundisc Stereo Components requires a certain integrated circuit board in one of its new amplifiers. Soundisc can either (1) manufacture the circuit board in-house by acquiring the production facilities and setting up a production system in its existing plant, or (2) purchase the circuit from an electronics manufacturer. Sales of the amplifier will fall into one of four ranges, from low (I) to high (IV). The payoff table (in $000 profit per year) is shown below:

	Sales			
	I	II	III	IV
Make the circuit	−10	20	50	150
Buy the circuit	5	30	40	120

a. If the prior probability density is given by $P(I) = 0.10$, $P(II) = 0.20$, $P(III) = 0.60$, and $P(IV) = 0.10$, construct a decision tree for this problem and determine the Bayes decision.

b. Compute the EVPI.

c. A marketing-research study can be purchased for $1,500 that will result in one of two outcomes, O_1, or O_2, with conditional likelihood probabilities given by:

	I	II	III	IV
O_1	0.05	0.25	0.80	0.90
O_2	0.95	0.75	0.20	0.10

Should Soundisc purchase this study?

17. *Municipal Street Planning.* The city of Spencer is planning to construct a street that will run through the city perpendicular to the main east-west street. The city planners have to make a choice between a modern, wide (four-lane) street that would cost $2 million or a lesser-quality, narrower street that would cost $1 million. We shall denote these two alternatives as $W1$ and $N1$. After four years, depending on whether the

traffic on the street turns out to be light or heavy (*L1* or *H1*), the city will have the option of widening the street. The probabilities of these traffic conditions are estimated by city planners and economists to be $P(L1) = 0.25$ and $P(H1) = 0.75$. If alternative *W1* is selected, maintenance expenses during the first four years will be $5,000 or $75,000, depending on whether the traffic is light or heavy. If *N1* is selected, these costs are expected to be $30,000 and $150,000, respectively.

Suppose street *W1* is built. Then at the end of four years, if traffic has been light, no further work is required. If traffic has been heavy, either a minor or a major repair must be made at costs of $150,000 or $200,000, respectively.

If street *N1* is built, then at the end of four years, if traffic has been light, either a minor or major repair must be made at costs of $50,000 or $100,000, respectively. If traffic has been heavy, a major repair (which includes widening the road) must be made at a cost of $900,000.

Traffic during the next six years (following years 1–4) will be classified as light or heavy (*L2* or *H2*). The probabilities of these two events, conditional on the traffic condition in years 1–4, are given as follows:

$$P(L2|L1) = 0.75 \qquad P(L2|H1) = 0.10$$

$$P(H2|L1) = 0.25 \qquad P(H2|H1) = 0.90$$

Maintenance costs over years 5–10 will depend on which street was built in year 1, what type of repair was made at the end of year 4, and the amount of traffic during years 5–10, as given in Table 10.24.

TABLE 10.24

Street year 1	Repair year 4	Traffic years 5–10	Maintenance years 5–10
		L2	200,000
W1	None	H2	250,000
		L2	150,000
	Minor	H2	175,000
		L2	125,000
	Major	H2	100,000
		L2	200,000
N1	Minor	H2	250,000
		L2	175,000
	Major	H2	150,000

TABLE 10.25

		Demand	
Plan	Low	Medium	High
1	80	85	90
2	75	95	100
3	70	85	150
4	40	75	250

a. Construct a decision tree for this problem. (Work directly with costs; you need not convert costs to negative profits.)
b. Fold back the decision tree to determine the optimal sequential strategy for the city of Spencer.
c. Do you see the value of using a decision tree?

18. *Resort Facility Planning.* Pleasure, Inc., is planning to build a recreational resort in northern Iowa. Four plans are being considered, depending on the size of the resort and the number of sporting and recreational facilities to be included. These plans range from a less expensive, smaller resort (plan 1) to an expensive, full-service resort (plan 4). Demand for the resort's services is expected to be low, medium, or high, with probabilities 0.20, 0.45, and 0.35, respectively. The payoff table (in $000 profit per year) is shown in Table 10.25.
  a. Determine the Bayes decision for this problem and the expected annual profit.
  b. Compute the EVPI.
  c. Suppose Pleasure, Inc., conducts a market-research study and obtains an analysis which we will denote by I. The conditional likelihoods of I are as follows: $P(I|Low) = 0.10$, $P(I|Medium) = 0.50$, and $P(I|High) = 0.40$. Determine the posterior Bayes decision.
  d. If Pleasure, Inc., paid $15,000 for the report, did they pay too much? *Hint*: Compare the expected payoff in part (a) to that of part (c).

19. *Quality Control.* Blockwood Designs, Inc., regularly purchases 5,000 board feet (bd. ft.) of walnut lumber for use in its cabinet-making operations. Its policy in the past has been to telephone the lumber supplier and have the walnut delivered. Thus the *supplier* selects the boards, and Blockwood is obligated to accept the shipment. Of course Blockwood expects a certain amount of defective wood in each shipment; in fact, past records indicate the following defective rates:

Percentage of time	10	15	45	15	10	5
Percentage of 5,000 bd. ft. defective	0	1	2	3	4	5

Blockwood estimates that each defective board foot costs an average of one dollar in waste, sorting out, planing, or cutting costs.

The other option Blockwood has is to send two employees to the supplier to select the lumber. This would cost Blockwood $25. In addition, the supplier would reduce its wholesale discount by $20 to cover the cost of the inconvenience of sorting out the lumber. Furthermore, Blockwood would still end up with one percent defective wood 95 percent of the time (and with 0 percent defective wood 5 percent of the time).

a. Construct a decision tree for this problem. (Work directly with costs.)

b. Determine the Bayes decision and expected cost due to defectives.

20. *Horsetrack Betting.* Shifty Lamar is about to place a bet on the third race of the day at Waterfall Downs. He has designed three betting strategies, each of which involves a combination of horses and positions (win, place, show). There are four possible outcomes of the race that will determine his payoff, as shown in Table 10.26 (in $ net payoff). (Thus s_4 represents all outcomes that would not pay. The negative amounts indicate the size of each bet.)

a. Determine the Bayes decision if Shifty assesses the probabilities to be $P(s_1) = 0.20$, $P(s_2) = 0.15$, $P(s_3) = 0.25$, and $P(s_4) = 0.40$.

b. Just before Shifty places the bet, a young lady claims she has inside information on the race (since her friend is one of the owners). She says that if Shifty will first pay her $65, she will then tell him which of the four outcomes will occur. Assuming that Shifty believes in her predictive ability, should he purchase this information?

TABLE 10.26

Bet	Race results			
	s_1	s_2	s_3	s_4
1	100	200	50	−25
2	200	150	125	−40
3	150	350	40	−30

21. *Real Estate Investment.*   A large real estate development company, Real-rip, Inc., is considering the purchase of one of three "packages" put together by its director of marketing. Each package contains a different combination of land acreage by type of land, zoning, and geographic location. The value of the investment will depend on which of four population growth/mobility patterns occurs in the next few years. The pay-off table is given in Table 10.27 (in $ million).

   a. Determine the Bayes decision, given the following probability density: $P(s_1) = 0.20$, $P(s_2) = 0.25$, $P(s_3) = 0.45$, and $P(s_4) = 0.10$.

   b. Compute the EVPI.

   c. Suppose the marketing director spends $100,000 on a market study and obtains some information, which we denote by I. The conditional likelihood probabilities of I are as follows: $P(I|s_1) = 0.10$, $P(I|s_2) = 0.30$, $P(I|s_3) = 0.35$, $P(I|s_4) = 0.25$. Determine the posterior Bayes decision. Was the $100,000 well spent?

22. *Who Made the Cookies?*   John Smith has a cook, Bert, and a butler, Suzanne, to help with the house while his wife, Patricia, works as an apprentice carpenter. John is to entertain some of Patricia's guests this evening. She called this morning to inform John of his duty to provide the drinks, a good dinner, and a magician for entertainment.

   After consulting with the butler, John has decided to serve cookies for dessert. The cook, Bert, indicates that he already has too much to do in the way of preparation of the dinner. He tells John that there is only a 30 percent chance that he will have time to bake the cookies. John accepts that response, but as a hedge he consults the butler, Suzanne, who says that she will bake the cookies if Bert is too busy to bake them.

   A note about cookies in the Smith house: When Bert bakes cookies, 20 percent of them turn out very large (about 17 cm. in diameter) and the rest are of normal size (about 10 cm. in diameter). When Suzanne bakes cookies, 30 percent turn out very large and 70 percent are of normal size.

   The evening arrives. After dinner Bert serves the cookies; Patricia tastes a cookie and says, "Oh, how delicious, John! Did you make these yourself?"

TABLE 10.27

| Package | Population pattern | | | |
	s_1	s_2	s_3	s_4
1	1.5	3.5	2.0	1.0
2	2.5	1.7	2.1	4.8
3	0.9	2.5	3.6	1.9

John's response: John quickly counts that nineteen cookies were served and that six of those were extraordinarily large. Not knowing exactly who baked the cookies that afternoon, John immediately does a Bayesian probabilistic update of his prior probability distribution to obtain the posterior distribution, and responds, "No dear, there is a _____ percent chance that the cook did it, and a _____ percent chance that the butler did it."

11 MARKOV CHAINS

CONTENTS

Many management problems can be modeled by using Markov chains. A Markov chain is a probabilistic device that is useful for representing systems that change over time. In this chapter we shall present an introduction to Markov chains and illustrate their use in analyzing several practical problems.

Note: This chapter requires the use of matrix algebra. You may wish to consult Appendix D for a review of matrices.

1. A BRAND-SWITCHING MODEL

National Brands, a large retail-grocery chain, has been studying the brand-switching behavior of its customers in the purchase of two major brands of breakfast cereal, which we shall refer to as brand A and brand B. The marketing staff of National Brands has collected data over the past year to support the following buyer behavior patterns: There is a 0.7 probability that a buyer of brand A in one week will purchase brand A again in the following week and a 0.3 probability that the customer will switch to brand B. A customer who purchased brand B in one week will again purchase brand B the following week with a probability of 0.6 and will switch to brand *A* with a probability of 0.4.

National Brands would like to use the results of this marketing research to deduce some generalizations concerning buyer behavior in the future.

Defining a Markov Chain

TIME. Let us focus our attention on a single consumer and observe the consumer's brand switching over time. We shall measure time in weeks and arbitrarily designate the start of our observations as time 0. Thus we view the future as a time axis (see Fig. 11.1). At the start of each week, the consumer makes a purchase of either cereal brand *A* or brand *B*.

STATES. How would you describe the buying behavior of this consumer at any given time? It is clear that you would only need to indicate which cereal brand the consumer is purchasing during the given week. In other words, during any given week we can say that the consumer is either a brand *A* buyer or a brand *B* buyer. We refer to brands *A* and *B* as **states** of the system. The state tells us all we need to know to describe the consumer's behavior at any given time.

TRANSITIONS. When the consumer moves from a state during one week to a state in the following week, we say that a **transition** has occured; sometimes we will use the expression "state transition." A **transition diagram** is useful for visualizing state transitions, especially when there is a large number of states.

The state transition diagram for our problem is given in Fig. 11.2. Each state is represented by a *node* (or a circle), and each possible transition is represented by an arrow between two states. The state transition diagram in Fig. 11.2 tells us the following:

- There is a probability of 0.7 that a brand *A* customer this week will be a brand *A* customer next week.
- There is a probability of 0.3 that a brand *A* customer this week will be a brand *B* customer next week.

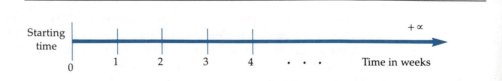

FIGURE 11.1

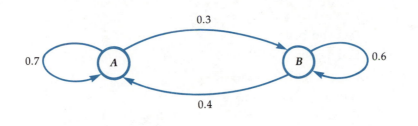

FIGURE 11.2

- There is a probability of 0.6 that a brand *B* customer this week will be a brand *B* customer next week.
- There is a probability of 0.4 that a brand *B* customer this week will be a brand *A* customer next week.

TRANSITION MATRIX. We can represent the transitions of a process more concisely by using a transition matrix, *P*, which simply contains all the transition probabilities, as follows:

State next week

$$P = \begin{bmatrix} 0.7 & 0.3 \\ 0.4 & 0.6 \end{bmatrix} = \left\{ \begin{array}{l} \text{State this} \\ \text{week} \end{array} \begin{array}{c} A \\ B \end{array} \begin{bmatrix} A & B \\ 0.7 & 0.3 \\ 0.4 & 0.6 \end{bmatrix} \right\}$$

Note that all row sums equal one; this is the case because, for example, for row 1, a purchaser of brand *A* this week *must* either be a purchaser of brand *A* or brand *B* next week. Thus the two events, "*A* → *A*" and "*A* → *B*," include all possibilities *given state A* and therefore must have probabilities that sum to one. This also applies to row 2. (We use an arrow, →, to denote transition.)

APPLICATIONS

The following applications appear in this chapter in text, examples, or problems:

Accounts receivable analysis

Advertising strategy

Brand-share projections

Brand-switching models

Car rental agency

Committee decisions

Crime analysis

Demand patterns

Equipment/facilities utilization

Equipment selection

Gambler's ruin

Gambling device

Inventory planning

Machine maintenance

Management credit policies

Manufacturing processes

Population mobility

Sales planning

Stock market prices

THE MARKOV PROPERTY. Suppose our consumer initially (at time 0) is a buyer of brand A and in weeks 1, 2, 3, 4, and 5 purchases brands A, B, B, A, and B, respectively. Then what is the probability that in week 6 the consumer will purchase brand B? From our description of the problem, this probability (0.6) equals the probability that the consumer purchases brand B given that the previous purchase was brand B. The important point to note is that this probability depends only on the current state of the system (in week 5) and not on the past. In a sense, the system "forgets" the past; the current state tells us all we need to know in order to compute probabilities of future states.

A process that possesses this "lack of memory" is called a **Markov process.** A **Markov chain** is simply a Markov process in which state transitions can take place only at discrete points in time (in contrast to a more general Markov process in which state transitions could occur continuously at any instant). Since we have assumed that brand switching can only occur at discrete times (weeks 1, 2, 3, and so on), the brand-switching process we have described is a Markov chain.

2. N-STEP TRANSITIONS

Suppose our consumer is a brand A buyer at time 0. We might be interested in the probabilities of the consumer's future buyer behavior. To illustrate, let us calculate a few such probabilities.

ONE-STEP TRANSITIONS. Given state A, what is the probability that the next state is A? This involves what is called a **one-step transition**. Transition matrix P gives a probability of 0.7. What is the probability that the next state is B given the current state is A? This one-step transition probability, also given in the "P-matrix" (as it is sometimes called), equals 0.3.

TWO-STEP TRANSITIONS. Given that the current state is A, what is the probability that the state will be A in week 2? This is a **two-step transition,** since it involves a transition from the state at time 0 to a state at time 1 and then another transition to a state at time 2. The question becomes, How could we get from state A to state A in two steps?

One way would be to go from A at time 0 to A at time 1 and then again to A at time 2. The probability of this possibility is

$$P(A \text{ at time } 1 | A \text{ at time } 0) \cdot P(A \text{ at time } 2 | A \text{ at time } 1) = (0.70)(0.70) = 0.49$$

The above expressions are conditional probabilities. For example, $P(A$ at time $1|A$ at time 0) is read "the probability that the state is A at time 1 *given that* (|) the state is A at time 0." We can represent this possibility as follows:

State at time 0		State at time 1		State at time 2
A	$\rightarrow$	A	$\rightarrow$	A

The other possibility would be to switch from A to B at week 1, and then switch from B to A at week 2, or "$A \rightarrow B \rightarrow A$." The probability of this occurring is

$$P(B \text{ at time } 1 | A \text{ at time } 0) \cdot P(A \text{ at time } 2 | B \text{ at time } 1) = (0.30)(0.40) = 0.12$$

The numbers 0.30 and 0.40 come from the transition matrix P.

Thus the *two-step probability* of going from state A to state A is the sum of the probabilities of the two possibilities, or $0.49 + 0.12 = 0.61$.

There are three other two-step probabilities: $A \rightarrow B$, $B \rightarrow A$, and $B \rightarrow B$. These probabilities are represented in Fig. 11.3, using tree diagrams that show all possibilities for two-step transitions. Each of these can occur in exactly two ways as shown by the eight tip nodes (including the two-step transition $A \rightarrow A$, which we have already analyzed). Table 11.1 summarizes the results shown in the tree diagrams and gives the final calculation of the two-step transition probabilities. Study each of these illustrations, carefully checking all computations.

Since a two-step transition consists of 2 one-step transitions, could we hope to learn anything about two-step transitions by multiplying the one-step

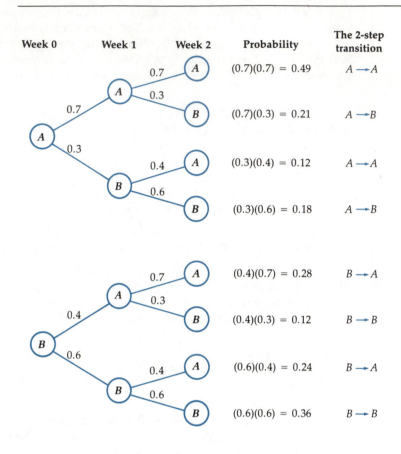

Week 0	Week 1	Week 2	Probability	The 2-step transition
		A	(0.7)(0.7) = 0.49	A → A
		B	(0.7)(0.3) = 0.21	A → B
		A	(0.3)(0.4) = 0.12	A → A
		B	(0.3)(0.6) = 0.18	A → B
		A	(0.4)(0.7) = 0.28	B → A
		B	(0.4)(0.3) = 0.12	B → B
		A	(0.6)(0.4) = 0.24	B → A
		B	(0.6)(0.6) = 0.36	B → B

FIGURE 11.3

transition matrix P by itself? We would have

$$P \cdot P = \begin{bmatrix} 0.7 & 0.3 \\ 0.4 & 0.6 \end{bmatrix} \begin{bmatrix} 0.7 & 0.3 \\ 0.4 & 0.6 \end{bmatrix}$$

$$= \begin{bmatrix} (0.7)(0.7) + (0.3)(0.4) & (0.7)(0.3) + (0.3)(0.6) \\ (0.4)(0.7) + (0.6)(0.4) & (0.4)(0.3) + (0.6)(0.6) \end{bmatrix} \tag{11-1}$$

$$= \begin{bmatrix} 0.61 & 0.39 \\ 0.52 & 0.48 \end{bmatrix} \tag{11-2}$$

We call the matrix in Eq. (11–2) the two-step transition matrix and denote it by P^2. As you can see, the four entries of the matrix in Eg. (11–1) are exactly the same terms that were computed in column 3 of Table 11.1. The

TABLE 11.1   *Two-Step Transitions: Brand Switching*

(1) Two-step transition	(2) Possibilities/ probabilities	(3) Probability of the two-step transition	(4) Totals
$A \rightarrow A$	$A \rightarrow A \rightarrow A$ (0.7)(0.7) $A \rightarrow B \rightarrow A$ (0.3)(0.4)	(0.7)(0.7) + (0.3)(0.4) = 0.49 + 0.12	= 0.61
$A \rightarrow B$	$A \rightarrow A \rightarrow B$ (0.7)(0.3) $A \rightarrow B \rightarrow B$ (0.3)(0.6)	(0.7)(0.3) + (0.3)(0.6) = 0.21 + 0.18	= 0.39 $\Sigma = 1.00$
$B \rightarrow A$	$B \rightarrow A \rightarrow A$ (0.4)(0.7) $B \rightarrow B \rightarrow A$ (0.6)(0.4)	(0.4)(0.7) + (0.6)(0.4) = 0.28 + 0.24	= 0.52
$B \rightarrow B$	$B \rightarrow A \rightarrow B$ (0.4)(0.3) $B \rightarrow B \rightarrow B$ (0.6)(0.6)	(0.4)(0.3) + (0.6)(0.6) = 0.12 + 0.36	= 0.48 $\Sigma = 1.00$

resulting simplified calculations shown in Eq. (11–2) are those given in column 4 of Table 11.1. Since starting in A, the system must either go to A or B in two steps, the row sum for row 1 of P^2 is one (0.61 + 0.39); similarly, row 2 sums to one (0.52 + 0.48). The matrix P^2 is to be read as follows:

$$\begin{array}{cc} & \text{State in 2 weeks} \\ \text{State this week} & \begin{array}{c} \\ A \\ B \end{array} \begin{array}{cc} A & B \\ \left[\begin{array}{cc} 0.61 & 0.39 \\ 0.52 & 0.48 \end{array}\right] \end{array} \end{array}$$

THREE-STEP TRANSITIONS. We can now generalize the above discussion to compute *three-step probabilities*. Let us first begin by calculating $P \cdot P \cdot P$, or P^3 as follows:

$$P^3 = P \cdot P \cdot P = (P \cdot P)P = P^2 \cdot P \qquad (11\text{–}3)$$

So

$$P^3 = \begin{bmatrix} 0.61 & 0.39 \\ 0.52 & 0.48 \end{bmatrix} \begin{bmatrix} 0.7 & 0.3 \\ 0.4 & 0.6 \end{bmatrix}$$

$$\begin{bmatrix} (0.61)(0.7) + (0.39)(0.4) & (0.61)(0.3) + (0.39)(0.6) \\ (0.52)(0.7) + (0.48)(0.4) & (0.52)(0.3) + (0.48)(0.6) \end{bmatrix}$$

$$P^3 = \begin{bmatrix} 0.583 & 0.417 \\ 0.556 & 0.444 \end{bmatrix} \qquad (11\text{–}4)$$

Let us check to see if P^3 gives us the three-step transition probabilities. We will check the entry 0.583 and leave the other three for you to check in Problem 1 at the end of this section.

What is the probability of our consumer being a brand A buyer in week 3, given that he or she is a brand A consumer at week 0? There are two ways this could happen: (a) a two-step transition from A to A, followed by a one-step transition in week 3 to A, or (2) a two-step transition from A to B, followed by a one-step transition to A. Do you see why we wrote P^3 as $P^2 \cdot P$ in Eq. (11–3)? We now have

Event	Probability
$A \xrightarrow{\text{two steps}} A \xrightarrow{\text{one step}} A$	$(0.61)(0.7) +$
$A \xrightarrow{\text{two steps}} B \xrightarrow{\text{one step}} A$	$(0.39)(0.4) = 0.427 + 0.156$
	$= 0.583$

This agrees with the row 1, column 1 entry of P^3. Compare the terms of this calculation to the row 1, column 1 entries of the matrix preceding Eq. (11–4).

Note that once again the row sums of the resulting matrix (P^3) equal one.

N-STEP TRANSITIONS. In general, the N-step transition probabilities are given by the entries of the matrix P^N (P multiplied N times by itself).

Use of the N-Step Transition Matrix

Let us now assume that the transition matrix P applies to the buying behavior of the typical National Brands consumer. If we denote the initial brand shares by s_1 and s_2 of brands A and B, respectively, then after N weeks (N transitions) the brand shares will be

$$[s_1 \quad s_2] \cdot P^N \tag{11–5}$$

where we have a row vector with entries s_1 and s_2 multiplied by the N-step transition matrix P^N. The following two examples illustrate the use of Eq. (11–5).

EXAMPLE 11.1. *Brand-Share Projections.* Assume that the marketing analysts at National Brands estimate the initial market shares of brands A and B to be 30 percent and 70 percent, respectively. What will the brand shares be in three weeks (that is, at the start of week 3)?

Solution. We will write s_1 and s_2 as decimals 0.30 and 0.70, respectively. The answer to the question is given by Eq. (11–5) for $N = 3$ [see Eq. (11–4)] as follows:

$$[s_1 \quad s_2]P^3 = [0.30 \quad 0.70]\begin{bmatrix} 0.583 & 0.417 \\ 0.556 & 0.444 \end{bmatrix}$$

$$= \left[\big((0.30)(0.583) + (0.70)(0.556)\big)\big((0.30)(0.417) + (0.70)(0.444)\big) \right]$$

$$= \begin{bmatrix} 0.564 & 0.436 \end{bmatrix}$$

or 56.4 percent and 43.6 percent, respectively. Do you see the rationale behind the calculations? For example, let us take the resulting brand A share, 0.564. Initially, the proportion of brand A consumers is given as 0.30; of these, the proportion 0.583 will also be brand A consumers in three weeks. This gives the term (0.30)(0.583). Initially, the proportion of brand B consumers is given as 0.70, and of these, the proportion 0.556 will be brand A consumers in three weeks, giving the term (0.70)(0.556). We then add the two contributing terms to get the total brand A market share as 0.564. You should similarly interpret the calculation of 0.436.   ▲

EXAMPLE 11.2. *Sales and Inventory Planning.* Assume that National Brands has a total of 4,500 customers who regularly purchase cereal brands A and B and that the initial brand shares are 0.30 and 0.70, respectively. Each consumer purchases, on the average, one 283-gram (10-ounce) box of cereal per week. A box of brand A costs \$0.70, and a box of brand B costs \$0.67. For planning purposes, project the inventory requirements and sales for week 3.

Solution. Inventory Planning: From the market-share analysis in Example 11.1, the market shares of brands A and B will be 0.564 and 0.436, respectively. On a unit product basis, these yield the following inventory requirements:

Brand A = (0.564)(4500) = 2,538 boxes

Brand B = (0.436)(4500) = 1,962 boxes

Sales Planning: Projected sales volume is calculated easily, as follows:

Brand A = (2,538 boxes)(\$0.70) = \$1,776.60

Brand B = (1,962 boxes)(\$0.67) = $\underline{\$1,314.54}$

Total = \$3,091.14   ▲

Problems

1. Verify that the matrix P^3, Eq. (11–4), does give the three-step probabilities $A \rightarrow B$, $B \rightarrow A$, and $B \rightarrow B$.

2. For the P matrix governing the one-step transitions for National Brands products A and B:
   a. Compute the four-step transition matrix P^4.
   b. If the initial brand shares are 0.30 and 0.70 for A and B, respectively, calculate the expected brand shares for week 4.
3. Assume the brand-switching matrix for two products, C and D, is

$$P = \begin{array}{c} C \\ D \end{array} \begin{bmatrix} \overset{C}{0.50} & \overset{D}{0.50} \\ 0.10 & 0.90 \end{bmatrix}$$

   a. Compute P^2, P^3, and P^4.
   b. Compute expected brand shares for weeks 2, 3, and 4 if initial brand shares probabilities are 0.45 and 0.55 for products C and D, respectively.
   c. If the market consists of 2,000 consumers, and each unit of product C sells for $15 and each unit of product D sells for $10, forecast *total* (cumulative) sales volume over the weeks 2, 3, and 4.

3. STEADY-STATE PROBABILITIES

Let us look again at the transition matrix P for National Brands products A and B. In Section 2, we computed the two- and three-step transition matrices by calculating the matrices P, P^2, and P^3. If we continue to calculate some other powers of P, we get the following:

$$P^4 = \begin{bmatrix} 0.575 & 0.425 \\ 0.567 & 0.433 \end{bmatrix} \qquad P^5 = \begin{bmatrix} 0.573 & 0.427 \\ 0.570 & 0.430 \end{bmatrix}$$

$$P^6 = \begin{bmatrix} 0.572 & 0.428 \\ 0.571 & 0.429 \end{bmatrix} \qquad P^7 = \begin{bmatrix} 0.572 & 0.428 \\ 0.571 & 0.429 \end{bmatrix}$$

We have rounded all calculations to three decimal places. Note that the entries in the two rows seem to be approaching the same values. In fact, if we were to make more precise calculations (say, to ten decimal places), we would see that

$$P^8 = \begin{bmatrix} 0.571457 & 0.428543 \\ 0.571391 & 0.428609 \end{bmatrix}$$

and, continuing, would give

$$P^{15} = \begin{bmatrix} 0.5714286 & 0.4285714 \\ 0.5714286 & 0.4285714 \end{bmatrix}$$

(accurate to seven places). It is possible to show that the limit of the P^Ns, as N approaches infinity, equals the matrix

$$P^\infty = \begin{bmatrix} 4/7 & 3/7 \\ 4/7 & 3/7 \end{bmatrix}$$

where $4/7 = 0.5714286714$ and $3/7 = 0.4285714286$.

In the context of our brand-switching model, this result tells us two things: (1) Whether or not the consumer is initially a brand A buyer or a brand B buyer, we can expect in the long run that the proportion of time the consumer purchases brand A will be 4/7 (as shown in column 1 of the P^∞ matrix); and (2) the proportion of time the consumer purchases brand B will be 3/7 (as shown in column 2).

The row vector [4/7 3/7] is called the vector of **steady-state probabilities,** which we often denote by the Greek letter pi:

$$\pi = \begin{bmatrix} \pi_A & \pi_B \end{bmatrix} = \begin{bmatrix} \dfrac{4}{7} & \dfrac{3}{7} \end{bmatrix}$$

where $\pi_A = 4/7$ and $\pi_B = 3/7$.

In general, the vector of *steady-state probabilities* for a Markov chain gives the expected long-run proportion of time the system will spend in each state.

EXAMPLE 11.3. *Brand-Share Analysis.* Given the data in this chapter on National Brands, what is the expected brand share of each of the products A and B in the long run?

Solution. The answer is given simply by π. Note that this is true regardless of the initial market shares. Recall that if the initial market shares are s_1 and s_2, then the expected market share in N weeks (N transitions) is given by

$$[s_1 \quad s_2] \cdot P^N$$

[See Eq. (11–5).] Letting N approach infinity, we obtain the steady-state market shares

$$\begin{bmatrix} s_1 & s_2 \end{bmatrix} P^\infty = \begin{bmatrix} s_1 & s_2 \end{bmatrix} \begin{bmatrix} 4/7 & 3/7 \\ 4/7 & 3/7 \end{bmatrix}$$

$$= [s_1(4/7) + s_2(4/7) \quad s_1(3/7) + s_2(3/7)]$$

$$= [(4/7)(s_1 + s_2) \quad (3/7)(s_1 + s_2)]$$

$$= [4/7 \quad 3/7] \text{ (since } s_1 + s_2 = 1)$$

$$= \pi$$

This proof *did not* depend on what values we chose for s_1 and s_2. For *every* pair s_1 and s_2, we obtain the same steady-state market shares 4/7 and 3/7. ▲

Assumptions and Interpretations

You should note the assumptions we have made in this section as well as in the preceding section—namely, that we have a Markov chain. Specifically, due to the Markov property, the transition matrix P does not change from week to week. If consumer research suggests a different transition matrix, we should recalculate the steady-state probability vector π and revise our planning and marketing strategies accordingly.

Care must be taken in interpreting the steady-state probabilities. We found that as N gets large, P^N becomes almost constant, with entries equal to those of P^∞. In fact, P^{15} is very close to P^∞. Does this mean, for example, that in week 15 if a consumer is a buyer of brand A, he or she will purchase brand A next week with a probability of 4/7 and will purchase brand B with a probability of 3/7? Not at all. In week 15, our consumer will still behave according to the *original* transition matrix P.

So what *does* P^∞ or π mean? For our example the entries of π mean the following: From our viewpoint, *at time 0* we can expect (in a probabilistic sense) that in the long run our typical consumer will purchase brand A 4/7 of the time and brand B 3/7 of the time. Thus brand A will capture 4/7 of all sales, and brand B will capture 3/7 of all sales over time.

Mean Return Times

Given a particular state of the system, the **mean return time** is defined as the expected (or average) length of time before the system returns to that state. For the Markov chains we will study in this chapter, the mean return time for a given state equals the reciprocal of the steady-state probability of the state.

For example, if a National Brands consumer purchases brand A during a given week, the average length of time before he or she will again purchase brand A is given by

$$\frac{1}{(4/7)} = 1.75 \text{ weeks}$$

Computing Steady-State Probabilities

The probability that the system is in state 1 at time $N + 1$ equals the probability that the state is one at time N and that it stays in state 1 at time N

+ 1 *plus* the probability that the state is two at time N and that it switches to state 1 at time $N + 1$, or

$$P_1(N + 1) = P_1(N)p_{11} + P_2(N)p_{21}$$

Now, if we let N approach infinity, $P_1(N)$ approaches π_1 and $P_2(N)$ approaches π_2 by definition of the steady-state probabilities. Thus the above equation becomes

$$\pi_1 = \pi_1 p_{11} + \pi_2 p_{21} \qquad (11\text{–}6)$$

Similarly, we can reason that the equation for π_2 is

$$\pi_2 = \pi_1 p_{12} + \pi_2 p_{22} \qquad (11\text{–}7)$$

We must also require that

$$\pi_1 + \pi_2 = 1 \qquad (11\text{–}8)$$

Taken together, Eqs. (11–6) and (11–7) can be written in *matrix form* as

$$[\pi_1 \quad \pi_2] = [\pi_1 \quad \pi_2]\begin{bmatrix} p_{11} & p_{12} \\ p_{21} & p_{22} \end{bmatrix} \qquad (11\text{–}9)$$

$$\text{or } \pi = \pi P \qquad (11\text{–}10)$$

METHOD OF SOLVING THE EQUATIONS.

Step 1. One of the equations—that is, Eq. (11–6) or Eq. (11–7)—is redundant, so we shall discard one of them, say, Eq. (11–6).

Step 2. Solve Eq. (11–8) for π_1 in terms of π_2. Substitute this π_1 into Eq. (11–7) and solve for π_2.

Step 3. Now set $\pi_1 = 1 - \pi_2$.

EXAMPLE 11.4. *Computing Steady-State Probabilities.* For National Brands, Eqs. (11–6), (11–7), and (11–8) become

$$\pi_A = \pi_A(0.7) + \pi_B(0.4)$$

$$\pi_B = \pi_A(0.3) + \pi_B(0.6)$$

$$\pi_A + \pi_B = 1$$

Step 1. We discard the first of these equations.

Step 2. We solve the third equation for $\pi_A = 1 - \pi_B$ and substitute into the second equation to find π_B as follows:

$$\pi_B = (1 - \pi_B)(0.3) + \pi_B(0.6)$$

$$= 0.3 - \pi_B(0.3) + \pi_B(0.6)$$

$$0.7\pi_B = 0.3$$

$$\pi_B = 3/7$$

Step 3. Then $\pi_A = 1 - \pi_B = 1 - 3/7 = 4/7$. Thus

$$\pi = [\pi_A \quad \pi_B] = [4/7 \quad 3/7]$$

Problems

1. Refer to Problem 3 of Section 2. For the P matrix given there, calculate the steady-state probabilities. If the initial brand-share probabilities are 0.45 and 0.55 for products C and D, respectively, what are the long-run average brand shares?
2. Suppose that whether or not a secretary makes a single-character typing error depends only on whether he has made an error on the previous key stroke. Specifically, if he correctly types a character, he will type the next character correctly 95 percent of the time. If he makes an error, he will again make an error on the next key stroke 3 percent of the time. In typing a lengthy job, what proportion of the characters will be incorrectly typed, on the average?

4. DECISION-MAKING APPLICATIONS: ADVERTISING STRATEGY

In this section we shall illustrate the use of steady-state probabilities in determining advertising strategy. We shall continue with the National Brands example. The manufacturers of brand A cereal are planning to launch an advertising strategy that, in the long run, is designed to increase the brand loyalty of brand A by increasing the probability of the one-step transition $A \rightarrow A$ from a probability of 0.7 to 0.85. The weekly cost of the promotional efforts is expected to be $200. The current market consists of 4,500 consumers, each purchasing one box of cereal per week. The profit per box of brand A cereal is $0.18 to the manufacturer. Analyze the profitability of the proposed campaign.

Analysis

The new transition matrix and corresponding set of steady-state equations are given below:

$$P = \begin{bmatrix} 0.85 & 0.15 \\ 0.40 & 0.60 \end{bmatrix} \qquad \begin{aligned} \pi_A &= \pi_A(0.85) + \pi_B(0.40) \\ \pi_B &= \pi_A(0.15) + \pi_B(0.60) \\ \pi_A + \pi_B &= 1 \end{aligned}$$

Solving the three equations (as in Section 3 above) for the steady-state probability vector yields $\pi = [\pi_A \quad \pi_B] = [8/11 \quad 3/11]$. The expected weekly profit for brand A would be

(8/11) (4,500 boxes/week)($0.18/box) = $589.09

Without the advertising campaign, $\pi_A = 4/7$ (calculated in Example 11.4) and the expected weekly profit is

(4/7) (4,500 boxes/week)($0.18/box) = $462.86

The gain in profit would be $589.09 − $462.86 = $126.23, which is not enough to justify the $200 weekly promotional expense.

The problems at the end of this section present an alternate advertising strategy for your analysis.

Problems

1. In the context of the example given in this section, suppose the brand A manufacturer has designed an alternate promotional strategy that would cost $125 weekly and have the intended effect of attracting customers away from brand B. Specifically, the one-step transition probability $B \to A$ is expected to increase from 0.4 to 0.55 (in the original transition matrix). Perform a profitability analysis on the proposed strategy.
2. In Problem 1 above, what would your conclusion be if the transition probability $B \to A$ could be increased from 0.40 to 0.55 *and* the transition probability of $A \to A$ could be increased from 0.70 to 0.80 at a total promotional outlay of $110 per week?

5. ACCOUNTS RECEIVABLE ANALYSIS

In this section we shall present what has come to be (along with brand-share analysis) a classic application of Markov chains—the analysis of accounts receivable. In the process of studying this application we shall also encounter a different type of Markov chain.

Johnson's Hardware classifies its accounts receivable into two categories: 0–30 day accounts and 31–60 day accounts. Johnson's employs the "total balance" method of aging the accounts, which places a customer's *entire* balance into a single category. As an example, Suzy Chargesse has the following balance with Johnson's: On July 27 she charged $15 worth of merchandise; on August 28 she charged $23 worth; and on September 21 she charged $18 worth. The current date is September 24. The three purchases are fifty-nine days old, twenty-seven days old, and three days old, respectively. By the total balance method, the entire balance of $56 would be aged by the oldest purchase (59 days) and would be placed in the 31–60 day category. If Suzy pays off the $15 charged on July 27, her balance of $41 would be placed in the 0–30 day account (according to the twenty-seven-day-old purchase of August 28). However, in four days this $41 would be moved to the 31–60 day category, since the August 28 purchase would then be thirty-one days old.

The accounting personnel at Johnson's have analyzed historical records of customer accounts and have determined the following transition matrix:

States

		1 (Paid)	2 (Bad debt)	3 (0–30)	4 (31–60)
	1	1	0	0	0
$P =$	2	0	1	0	0
	3	0.35	0	0.25	0.40
	4	0.50	0.20	0.20	0.10

The transitions are assumed to occur at one-week intervals, and we imagine a single dollar in accounts receivable moving from state to state. For example, a dollar in the 0–30 day category this week (state 3) has a 0.35 probability of being paid off next week; it has a 0 probability of becoming a bad debt next week; it will remain in the 0–30 day category with a probability of 0.25; and it will move to the 31–60 day category with a probability of 0.40.

This defines a four-state Markov chain; however, it differs from those we have studied so far in that there are two so-called **absorbing states** (also called *trapping states*), states 1 and 2. Once a dollar makes a transition to either of these states (becomes paid off or becomes a bad debt), it remains in that state forever. The probabilities in rows 1 and 2 of the matrix P indicate this:

P(1 next week|1 this week) = 1, and P(2 next week|2 this week) = 1

The question of interest to Johnson's management is: "If a dollar is in either states 3 or 4, what are the probabilities that it ends up in state 1 (paid) or state 2 (bad debt)?"

The matrix P given above is in a special standard form. We define four submatrices I, O, Q_1, and Q as follows:

$$I = \begin{bmatrix} 1 & 0 \\ 0 & 1 \end{bmatrix} \qquad O = \begin{bmatrix} 0 & 0 \\ 0 & 0 \end{bmatrix}$$

$$Q_1 = \begin{bmatrix} 0.35 & 0 \\ 0.50 & 0.20 \end{bmatrix} \qquad Q = \begin{bmatrix} 0.25 & 0.40 \\ 0.20 & 0.10 \end{bmatrix}$$

Then we can "partition" the P matrix as follows:

$$P = \begin{bmatrix} I & O \\ Q_1 & Q \end{bmatrix}$$

States 3 and 4 are called **transient states** for the following reason: If a dollar is in one of these states, sooner or later it will leave the state, making a transition to either state 1 or 2, and never again return to either state 3 or 4. We see then that matrix I describes the transitions of the absorbing states; Q_1 describes transitions between the transient states and the absorbing states; and Q describes transitions from transient states to transient states.

Calculating the Fundamental Matrix

The **fundamental matrix** S will be the primary tool used to calculate the probabilities of interest for the accounts receivable problem. S is defined to be

$$S = (I - Q)^{-1} \qquad\qquad (11\text{--}11)$$

The superscript -1 indicates matrix inversion. To calculate S for our problem, we proceed as follows:

STEP 1. Calculate $I - Q$ as follows:

$$I - Q = \begin{bmatrix} 1 & 0 \\ 0 & 1 \end{bmatrix} - \begin{bmatrix} 0.25 & 0.40 \\ 0.20 & 0.10 \end{bmatrix}$$

$$= \begin{bmatrix} 1 - 0.25 & 0 - 0.40 \\ 0 - 0.20 & 1 - 0.10 \end{bmatrix} = \begin{bmatrix} 0.75 & -0.40 \\ -0.20 & 0.90 \end{bmatrix}$$

STEP 2. Invert the matrix $I - Q$, using Eq. (D–5) in Appendix D, as follows:

$$S = (I - Q)^{-1} = \begin{bmatrix} 0.90/0.595 & -(-0.40/0.595) \\ -(-0.20/0.595) & 0.75/0.595 \end{bmatrix}$$

$$= \begin{bmatrix} 1.513 & 0.672 \\ 0.336 & 1.260 \end{bmatrix}$$

Use of the Fundamental Matrix

Suppose i is a transient state and j is an absorbing state. Define $F(i, j)$ to be the probability that the system will eventually end up in state j, given that it starts in state i. We are interested in the probabilities $F(3, 1)$, $F(3, 2)$, $F(4, 1)$, and $F(4, 2)$. The matrix of these values can be computed by using the fundamental matrix S and the submatrix Q_1 as follows:

$$\begin{bmatrix} F(3, 1) & F(3, 2) \\ F(4, 1) & F(4, 2) \end{bmatrix} = SQ_1 \qquad\qquad (11\text{–}12)$$

For our problem this becomes

$$SQ_1 = \begin{bmatrix} 1.513 & 0.672 \\ 0.336 & 1.260 \end{bmatrix}\begin{bmatrix} 0.35 & 0 \\ 0.50 & 0.20 \end{bmatrix} = \begin{bmatrix} 0.866 & 0.134 \\ 0.748 & 0.252 \end{bmatrix}$$

Thus from Eq. (11–12), $F(3, 1) = 0.866$, and $F(3, 2) = 0.134$. (These two probabilities add to one as they *must*. Do you see why?) Also, $F(4, 1) = 0.748$, and $F(4, 2) = 0.252$ (and these last two values also add to one).

Application: Estimating Bad Debts

Johnson's Hardware currently has $7,000 of its accounts receivable in the 0–30 day category and $5,200 in the 31–60 day category. How much of this $12,200 will be paid and how much will become bad debts?

Solution. The answers to these two questions are given by the two entries of the row vector $[7,000 \quad 5,200]SQ_1$, or

$$[7,000 \quad 5,200]\begin{bmatrix} 0.866 & 0.134 \\ 0.748 & 0.252 \end{bmatrix} = [9,951.60 \quad 2,248.40]$$

Thus $9,951.60 will eventually be paid (state 1), and $2,248.40 will become bad debts (state 2). The accounting personnel may now use the figure $2,248.40 to set up an "Allowance for Bad Debts Account."

Application: Analysis of Management Credit Policies

The rate of bad debts for Johnson's Hardware is seen to be $2,248.40/12,200 = 0.184$, or about 18.4 percent on current accounts. The credit manager has a plan for a new credit-granting policy that she estimates will result in the following ("better") transition matrix:

$$P = \left[\begin{array}{cc|cc} 1 & 0 & 0 & 0 \\ 0 & 1 & 0 & 0 \\ \hline 0.45 & 0 & 0.30 & 0.25 \\ 0.60 & 0.20 & 0.15 & 0.05 \end{array}\right] = \left[\begin{array}{c|c} I & O \\ \hline Q_1 & Q \end{array}\right]$$

Analyze the expected effects of such a policy.

Solution. We first calculate the fundamental matrix S as follows:

$$S = (I - Q)^{-1} = \left\{\begin{bmatrix} 1 & 0 \\ 0 & 1 \end{bmatrix} - \begin{bmatrix} 0.30 & 0.25 \\ 0.15 & 0.05 \end{bmatrix}\right\}^{-1}$$

$$= \begin{bmatrix} 0.70 & -0.25 \\ -0.15 & 0.95 \end{bmatrix}^{-1} = \begin{bmatrix} 1.514 & 0.398 \\ 0.239 & 1.116 \end{bmatrix}$$

Next, compute

$$[7,000 \quad 5,200]SQ_1 = [7,000 \quad 5,200]\begin{bmatrix} 1.514 & 0.398 \\ 0.239 & 1.116 \end{bmatrix}\begin{bmatrix} 0.45 & 0 \\ 0.60 & 0.20 \end{bmatrix}$$

$$= [7,000 \quad 5,200]\begin{bmatrix} 0.920 & 0.080 \\ 0.777 & 0.223 \end{bmatrix}$$

$$= [10,480.40 \quad 1,719.60]$$

The bad debts percentage would be $1,719.60/12,200 = 0.141$, or about 14.1 percent. This is a 23.4 percent decrease from the current level of an 18.4 percent bad debts rate.

The credit manager has two general options available for changing the credit policy: (1) She could implement her proposed policy after weighing the costs involved in doing so against the expected savings to be accrued from a decrease in bad debts expense, or (2) she could reexamine the current transition matrix in light of her experience in credit management and see if some other policy might be feasible (resulting in changes in the entries of Q_1 and Q) and, thus, more cost-effective than the proposed policy discussed above.

Problems

1. In the Johnson's Hardware example, explain why $F(3, 1) + F(3, 2)$ must equal one. Also why $F(4, 1) + F(4, 2) = 1$.
2. For the Johnson's Hardware problem, analyze the effectiveness of a new

credit policy for reducing bad debts, which would modify Q_1 and Q to assume the following values:

$$Q_1 = \begin{bmatrix} 0.60 & 0 \\ 0.50 & 0.15 \end{bmatrix} \qquad Q = \begin{bmatrix} 0.30 & 0.10 \\ 0.30 & 0.05 \end{bmatrix}$$

Compare this policy to the two policies analyzed in this section.

6. CONCLUDING REMARKS

Markov chains are useful for modeling processes that change over time and that satisfy two basic properties:

THE MARKOV PROPERTY. In order to predict future states of the process, it is sufficient to know only what the current state is and not previous (past) states.

STATIONARY TRANSITIONS. The one-step transition matrix does not change over time; that is, the P matrix contains the one-step transition probabilities for state changes at any time t to $t + 1$. In the early 1900s, the Russian mathematician A. A. Markov first developed the material described in this chapter. Since then, Markov chains have been applied as models for various physical processes and for certain management problems.

Other Topics

This chapter presented fairly basic concepts of Markov chains. The material through Section 4 applies to what are called *ergodic* Markov chains. There are several questions we left unanswered. For example, if the current state is state 1, what is the average number of transitions until state 2 is *first* visited? This is an example of a **first-passage** time.

Continuous Markov processes are processes that obey the Markov property in which state transitions can occur at any instant in time and not just at discrete points in time.

Markov decision processes are Markov processes in which, after each state transition, the decision maker is allowed to take a course of action that changes the P matrix for the next transition time period.

These and other topics are of a more advanced nature. The interested reader may wish to consult some of the references to this chapter in Appendix A.

TERMINOLOGY

After studying this chapter you should be familiar with the following terms:

EXERCISES

1. *Brand-Share Analysis.* Suppose the weekly brand-switching probabilities for two products, A and B, are given by the transition matrix below:

$$
\begin{array}{cc}
 & \begin{array}{cc} A & B \end{array} \\
\begin{array}{c} A \\ B \end{array} & \begin{bmatrix} 0.55 & 0.45 \\ 0.20 & 0.80 \end{bmatrix}
\end{array}
$$

a. If a consumer is a brand A buyer, what is the probability that he or she will be a brand A buyer next week? In two weeks? In three weeks?
b. If the brand shares of products A and B are currently 40 percent and 60 percent, respectively, compute the expected brand shares next week. In two weeks. In three weeks.

2. *Advertising Strategy.*
a. For the transition matrix given in Exercise 1 above, compute the expected long-run market shares of the two products.
b. *Mean Recurrence Times.* If a consumer purchases brand A this week, what is the expected length of time before the consumer again purchases brand A? Answer the same question for a brand B buyer.

c. Assume the net profit on each unit of product B is $10. The manufacturer of product B is planning a promotional strategy designed to lure customers away from product A. The planned effect of the strategy would be to reduce the probability of the one-week transition A → A from 0.55 to 0.35. The promotional costs would run $15,000 per week to maintain effectiveness. Currently, the market consists of 6,000 potential buyers of the two products. Analyze the expected profitability of the project. If the project is carried out and is successful, what would be the expected length of time before a brand B consumer again purchases brand B? Compare to the mean recurrence time computed in part (b) above.

3. *Brand-Share Analysis: A Second-Order Process.* Assume you know the current state of a system. If the probability of the next state of the system depends on both the current state *and* the previous state, the process is called a **second-order process.** Thus a second-order process remembers one period back into the past. In some cases (as with Markov chains), it is possible to "convert" a second-order process to a first-order process.

   As an example, let us consider a brand-switching model for two products, A and B, and this time assume that a consumer's purchase next week depends on the consumer's purchases this week and the previous week. Specifically, the purchase probabilities are given in Table 11.2. (The probabilities of next purchasing product B are simply one minus these probabilities.)

   a. Define states appropriately so that the above process can be represented by a Markov chain.
   b. Compute the steady-state probabilities for the states of the system.

4. *Car Rental Agency.* Real Cheap Car Rental Agency operates agencies in two cities, city 1 and city 2. The fractions of the number of cars rented in one city and returned in the same city or to the other city are given

TABLE 11.2

Purchase in previous week	Purchase this week	Probability of purchasing A next week
A	A	0.70
A	B	0.45
B	A	0.55
B	B	0.20

in the following transition matrix:

City at which
car is returned

		1	2	
City at which	1	0.65	0.35	(one-day
car is rented	2	0.60	0.40	transitions)

a. If a car is rented in city 1, what is the probability that the car is returned in one day to city 1? In two days? In three days?
b. If the company owns 500 cars, in the long run how many, on the average, will be in each city?
c. If a car at city 2 is rented, what is the expected length of time before that car will again end up in city 2?

5. *Car Rental Agency: A Three-State Model.* Suppose Real Cheap Car Rental (Exercise 4 above) opens an agency in a third city, city 3, and adds 100 cars to its inventory. Answer the questions for this modified model of parts (a)–(c) of Exercise 4 if the transition matrix is estimated to be the following:

City

		1	2	3
	1	0.60	0.20	0.20
City	2	0.40	0.10	0.50
	3	0.25	0.10	0.65

6. *Crime Analysis.* A study has revealed several patterns concerning the behavior of juvenile offenders in Crowsville. A juvenile offender is either in the custody of a halfway house supervised by resident social workers, is on probationary status, or is free. The results of the study can be summarized by the following transition matrix for a typical juvenile offender (the transition-time period is one month):

	Halfway	Probation	Free
Halfway	0.6	0.4	0
Probation	0.3	0.4	0.3
Free	0.1	0.1	0.8

a. For a typical juvenile offender, what proportion of time can he or she expect to spend in the halfway house?
b. For a juvenile offender in the halfway house this month, what is the mean number of months before the juvenile returns to the halfway house?
c. If there are approximately 900 juveniles on record as having engaged in criminal activities, what is the expected number of juveniles in each of the three categories?

7. *A Gambling Device.* Suppose a gambling device is rigged so that a player who wins on a given trial will win on the next trial with a probability

of 0.4 and will lose with a probability of 0.6. If the player loses on a given trial, he or she will win or lose on the next trial with probabilities of 0.7 and 0.3, respectively.

a. Design a Markov chain model for this process; specify the transition matrix.

b. If a player wins on a given trial, what is the probability that the player will win on each of the next three trials? (Three wins in a row.)

c. In the long run, what proportion of time will the player win? Lose? Is this a fair game?

d. If the player wins on a given trial, on the average how many games will he or she play before winning again?

e. If the player receives one dollar for each trial on which he or she wins, and pays 50¢ for each loss, what is the player's expected gain (or loss) per trial?

8. *Manufacturing Processes.* A pottery maker specializes in the manufacture of intricately designed, handcrafted flower pots and has hired three apprentices to work in his shop to manufacture the pots. Each pot is considered to be in one of four categories during any given day: finished (and ready for shipment); damaged beyond rework capability; in the process of manufacture; or being reworked (to correct defects which occur during the in-process stage). The transition matrix describing the status of a typical flower pot is given in Table 11.3 (the transition time period is one day).

a. If a flower pot is in process, what is the probability that it will eventually be finished? That it will be damaged beyond repair?

b. Answer the same question for a flower pot that is being reworked.

c. If there are currently ten flower pots in process and three flower pots in rework, and if each finished flower pot yields a $75 profit and each damaged pot results in a $20 loss, what is the expected net profit on the current work?

9. *Analysis of Committee Decisions.* The School of Business of a local university makes curriculum decisions by first sending a proposal to the curriculum committee (CC), which considers the matter and may either

TABLE 11.3

	Finished	Damaged	In process	Rework
Finished	1	0	0	0
Damaged	0	1	0	0
In process	0.4	0.25	0.20	0.15
Rework	0.5	0.30	0	0.20

adopt the proposal as official school policy or send the proposal to the policy committee (PC) for recommendations and further study. The policy committee may adopt the proposal as official policy, reject the proposal (in which case it will not again be considered), or send the proposal back to the curriculum committee. Historically, the pattern of movement of curriculum-related proposals can be summarized by the transition matrix that describes the status of a typical proposal from week to week in Table 11.4.

Currently, there are fifteen proposals before the Curriculum Committee and eight proposals before the Policy Committee. How many of the twenty-three proposals can be expected eventually to be adopted? To be rejected?

10. *Gambler's Ruin.* The "gambler's ruin" problem is a classic problem in probability; the current exercise presents a simplified version of this application of Markov chains. Consider a gambler who, at each trial of a game, can either win $100 with a probability of 0.6 or can lose $100 with a probability of 0.4. The game continues until the gambler either goes broke or accumulates $300.

   a. Model the game as a Markov chain, assuming the gambler starts with either $0, $100, $200, or $300. Of course, if he or she starts with $0, the game is over, since the gambler is broke; if the gambler starts with $300, the game is also over.

   b. Compute the probability of "going broke" and the probability of "winning the game (with $300)," if the gambler starts the game with $100. With $200.

11. *Demand Patterns.* Ace Auto Sales, a used-car dealer, has observed that sales during the first half of the year (January–June) tend to be related to sales during the second half (July–December). If sales are under 200 cars during the first half, there is a probability of 0.65 that sales during the second half will be under 200 cars. If sales during the first half are over 200, there is a probability of 0.75 that sales in the second half will exceed 200 cars. In the long run, what percentage of the time will sales be over 200 cars?

TABLE 11.4

	Adopted	Rejected	In CC	In PC
Adopted	1	0	0	0
Rejected	0	1	0	0
In CC	0.2	0.6	0.1	0.1
In PC	0.1	0.7	0.15	0.05

TABLE 11.5

	In adjustment	Out of adjustment
In adjustment	0.70	0.30
Out of adjustment	1	0

12. *Stock Market Prices: A Simplified Markov Model.*   Suppose it is observed that if the closing price per share of a certain stock A is $105 on a given day, it will lose $5 by closing time on the next day 40 percent of the time. If the closing price per share is $100, there is a 55 percent chance that the closing price per share the next day will be up $5 to $105.
    a. Give the transition matrix for a Markov chain representing the stock price movements.
    b. What is the long-run expected price per share of the stock?

13. *Machine Maintenance.*   A machine can be in one of two states: "in adjustment" or "out of adjustment." If it is in adjustment, the machine earns revenue at the rate of $200 per day. If the machine is out of adjustment at the start of a day, it is repaired at a cost of $100, which then places it in adjustment. The repair time requires a full day, during which no revenue is earned. The transition matrix is given in Table 11.5. (Do you see why the probabilities in row 2 are 1 and 0?)
    a. What fraction of time in the long run can the machine be expected to be in adjustment? Out of adjustment?
    b. Compute the expected long-run daily revenue earned by the machine.

14. *Equipment Selection.*   (Refer to Exercise 13 above.) Clipco, Inc., a manufacturer of paper clips and other fasteners, must select one of two machines to employ in its operations. The revenue, operating characteristics, and repair costs for the two machines are given in Table 11.6. Which machine should Clipco purchase?

15. *Population Mobility.*   A southwest state has been sectioned into three geographic regions for population study purposes. The study has pro-

TABLE 11.6

Machine 1: The data are given in Exercise 13 above.
Machine 2: Daily revenue (in adjustment) = $225; repair cost (when out of adjustment) = $90; and operating characteristics are as follows:

	In adjustment	Out of adjustment
In adjustment	0.75	0.25
Out of adjustment	1	0

TABLE 11.7

		Region		
		I	II	III
Region	I	0.70	0.20	0.10
	II	0.30	0.60	0.10
	III	0.05	0.05	0.90

duced the transition matrix describing interregion yearly changes as shown in Table 11.7. For example, of the people living in region I at the start of a year, 70 percent will remain in region I at the end of the year, 20 percent will move to region II, and 10 percent to region III.

a. If the current population distribution is 40 percent, 35 percent, and 25 percent in regions I, II, and III, respectively, determine the population distribution in two, three, and four years.

b. If the trend continues, what will be the expected long-run population distribution?

16. *Equipment/Facilities Utilization.* James Dom, director of a university computing center, has been collecting data on student usage of a new CRT terminal that is accessible twenty-four hours a day. If the terminal is busy during a given minute, there is a 70 percent chance it will remain busy during the next minute. If the terminal is idle during a given minute, it will become busy in the succeeding minute 40 percent of the time. In the long run, determine how many hours per day the terminal can be expected to be busy.

17. *Accounts Receivable.* Gambles Department Store has constructed (through historical records) the transition matrix shown in Table 11.8 for its accounts receivable categories (refer to Section 5 of this chapter). If the current accounts contain $10,000 in the 0–30 day category and $7,000 in the 31–60 day category, determine the expected bad debts allowance on the $17,000.

TABLE 11.8

	Paid	Bad debt	0–30	31–60
Paid	1	0	0	0
Bad Debt	0	1	0	0
0–30	0.95	0	0.03	0.02
31–60	0.50	0.30	0	0.20

12 SIMULATION

CONTENTS

1. INTRODUCTION

Simulation is a procedure of developing a model of a process and then experimenting systematically with the model in order to learn more about the process over time. The components describing the process as well as variables under the control of the decision maker may be systematically varied in a simulation experiment to ascertain how the process behaves. In a sense, simulation is the management scientist's technique for conducting "laboratory experiments."

Uses of Simulation

Typically, simulation is used to analyze complex systems or processes for which either mathematical models do not exist or existing mathematical models are difficult (if not practically impossible) to solve. It is a common occurrence in management science for a researcher to derive complex equations that presumably will solve the problem at hand but then to find that the resultant equations have no simple solutions. Even in these cases, most such equations are derived after assuming away all the realistic problems that might occur in practice. Examples of these occurrences frequently can be found in complex inventory and queuing models.

It should be noted that simulation is used to study processes involving probabilistic elements; that is, processes which depend upon probabilistic aspects of its components. As an example, consider the problem of planning expansion of a public school system over time. Decisions must be made concerning where new schools should be built, how to staff the schools (student-teacher ratios), and so on. The nature of the school system involves such components, yet these components depend probabilistically on population and demographic aspects as well as on political factors. It would be difficult, if not impossible, to construct a solvable mathematical model of such a complex system, but by using simulation, various future scenarios can be tested against different planning policies to analyze the overall school system performance.

Advantages of Using Simulation

The advantages of using simulation to study a given problem include the following:

1. Complex systems can be analyzed with relative ease.
2. Once a simulation model is constructed and implemented on a computer, it is easy to experiment with the model to ascertain its behavior under different assumptions; it is easy to answer "What if . . .?" questions.
3. For many systems it would be expensive and time consuming, if not practically impossible, to observe and study the actual system over time; thus experimenting with the system would be out of the question. Examples of these kinds of systems would include analyzing various engineering designs of a product (such as an automobile); analyzing various strategic offensive and defensive scenarios in the event of a war; studying the performance characteristics of a space vehicle; analyzing the effects of population trends on school systems or on future energy needs; experimenting with different scheduling and operations procedures in a manufacturing plant; and analyzing governmental policy decisions on the national economy.
4. Using simulation it is possible to obtain approximate solutions to complex mathematical models which cannot easily be solved from a practical standpoint.
5. The results of developing a simulation model can be analyzed to discern whether any systematic patterns exist in the system's behavior. Detecting such patterns can then lead to formulating theoretical conjectures that the analyst can then proceed to verify mathematically. Thus the analyst can hope to gain theoretical insight into the nature of the system.

Disadvantages of Using Simulation

Using simulation involves certain disadvantages that must be weighed against its advantages. Some of the disadvantages are these:

1. Solutions obtained from a simulation are only approximate.
2. It is expensive to implement large-scale simulation models. The expense includes the model design process, collecting data about the real process (if relevant), writing and debugging computer programs, **validating** the model (asking if the model yields reasonable results), and running the computer program on a computer system.
3. In more complex simulations, it is necessary to employ specialized statistical techniques to ensure accuracy of the simulation results.

APPLICATIONS

The following applications appear in this chapter in text, examples, or problems:

Card games

Coin toss

Fire department location

Gambling

Inventory planning

Job processing times: assembly-line operations

Machine maintenance

Military planning

New-product development

Queuing simulation: service facilities

Rate-of-return distributions

Vendor selection

---

2. MACHINE MAINTENANCE: A SIMULATION ANALYSIS

To demonstrate the nature and use of a simulation model, we shall analyze alternative maintenance/replacement policies for a machine that contains two major components, C1 and C2, essential to the operation of the machine. If either of these two components fails, the machine must be shut down and the failed component must be replaced. The replacement costs of the two components are $20 and $30, respectively. In addition, it takes one day to replace C1 and three days to replace C2. If both components are replaced at the same time, the replacement time is only two days. For each day the machine is shut down for repairs, a cost of $50 is incurred owing to lost production. To complicate the matter even more, the lifetimes of the two components (when new) are random variables. Let $L1$ and $L2$ denote these lifetime random variables. Their probability densities are given in Table 12.1.

TABLE 12.1

$L1$	Probability	$L2$	Probability
10 days	0.20	15 days	0.35
25 days	0.50	20 days	0.65
30 days	0.30		

These probabilities were computed from historical records on component failures. For example, 20 percent of all $C1$ components failed in ten days, 50 percent failed in twenty-five days, and 30 percent failed in thirty days.

Two replacement policies are being considered—policy 1: replace each component when it fails, and policy 2: replace both components when either of them fails.

The problem is to determine which policy should be employed to minimize the total average cost per day in the long run.

Solution

This type of problem, which could be solved analytically with a mathematical model, would require some detailed mathematical analysis. However, to demonstrate the simulation technique, we shall simulate the operation of the machine over time, under each of the two policies, and select the minimum-cost policy.

Determining Component Lifetimes

In order to simulate the operation of the machine, we need a method of determining the component lifetimes, $L1$ and $L2$, consistent with their probability densities. For example, we need a device that would select a value of $L1$ (component $C1$ lifetime) equal to ten days 20 percent of the time, twenty-five days 50 percent of the time, and thirty days 30 percent of the time. To construct such a device, we use the Table of Random Numbers in Appendix G. This table displays twenty-four lines of 10 five-digit random numbers each. The digits are arranged in groups of five simply for ease of reading the table. Each of the ten digits—0, 1, 2, 3, 4, 5, 6, 7, 8, 9—appears with equal probability at each occurrence—namely, 0.10. The numbers in the table are considered to be purely random (more will be said about this in Section 3).

To see how to use such a table as a device for determining component lifetimes, suppose we select the first two digits of each five-digit number, starting in line 1 and going from left to right. In order to determine values of $L1$, whenever the two-digit random number falls into the range 00 to 19 we shall set $L1 = 10$ days; if the two-digit random number falls into the range 20 to 69, we shall set $L1 = 25$ days; and if it falls into the range 70 to 99, we shall set $L1 = 30$ days. To see why this scheme will work, note that the sequence of numbers—00, 01, 02, ... , 99—includes 100 numbers. Range 1, from 00 to 19, includes 20 numbers; range 2, from 20 to 69, includes 50 numbers; and range 3, from 70 to 99, includes 30 numbers. Each two-digit random number selected from the Table of Random Numbers in Appendix G has an equal probability of being selected, that is, 1/100 or 0.01. Therefore, 20 percent of the time the random number we select will fall into range 1, 50 percent of the time it will fall into range 2, and 30 percent of the time it will fall into range 3, thus determining component C1 lifetimes consistent with the probability density of $L1$.

Similarly, we can devise a scheme for determining values of $L2$. The device we shall use to determine component lifetimes is summarized in Table 12.2.

Policy 1 Simulation

Let us label the current time as day 0 and imagine that we start the machine at this time. When will it first fail? To answer this question, we first determine the component lifetimes. Using the scheme in Table 12.2, we select a random number to determine $L1$ as the first two digits of the first number of row 1: 00980; thus the two-digit number selected is 00. Since this falls into the range 00 to 19, $L1 = 10$ days. Selecting a second two-digit random num-

TABLE 12.2	*Random Number Generation for Policy 1*

Device for determining component lifetimes

Step 1: Select a two-digit random number from the table in Appendix G. (In the course of the simulation we start with line 1 and select the first two digits of each five-digit number, working from left to right.)

Step 2: Determine the component lifetime $L1$ or $L2$ according to the following:

$L1$		$L2$	
Range of random number	Value of $L1$	Range of random number	Value of $L2$
00 to 19	10	00 to 34	15
20 to 69	25	35 to 99	20
70 to 99	30		

ber (using 50494), we get 50, which falls into the range 35 to 99, so $L2 = 20$ days. Thus the machine will first fail due to a C1 failure in ten days. At that time: (1) a replacement cost of $20 is incurred, (2) the machine will be shut down for one day to make this replacement (from the start of day 11 to the start of day 12), and (3) a cost of $50 is incurred owing to lost production. So the cost incurred equals $70.

At this point in the simulation we must generate a component lifetime for the new C1 component. Since the next two-digit random number is 72, $L1 = 30$ days. Also, *within our simulation model* we must schedule the next machine failure. The old C2 component had a lifetime of twenty days and has been in operation for ten days. Thus the existing C2 component has ten days left before it will fail. Since the new C1 component has thirty days left, the next machine failure will be caused by a C2 failure at the end of day 21, which is equal to the start of day 12 plus ten days of C2 operation.

The results of the simulation thus far are summarized in Table 12.3. The first column, labeled "Time," gives the status of the simulator's **clock.** Column 2, labeled "R1," will record the random numbers selected to determine values for $L1$, which are then entered in column 3. Similarly, columns 4 and 5 record the determination of C2 lifetimes. Column 6 tells us which event occurs at the end of the day listed in column 1, and the cost due to this event is recorded in column 7. The day of the next scheduled *machine failure*

TABLE 12.3   *Replacement Policy 1*

(1) Time (end of day)	(2) R1	(3) L1	(4) R2	(5) L2	(6) Event	(7) Cost	(8) C1	(9) C2
							Next scheduled failure (at end of day)	
0	00	10	50	20	Nothing	$ 0	10	
10	72	30			C1 fails	70		21
21			66	20	C2 fails	180	44	44
44	63	25	70	20	C1 and C2 fail	150		66
66			70	20	C2 fails	180	74	
74	05	10			C1 fails	70	85	
85	22	25			C1 fails	70		91
91			42	20	C2 fails	180	114	114
114	62	25	56	20	C1 and C2 fail	150		136
136					C2 fails	180		
					Total cost in 136 days	$1,230		

is indicated in column 8, if it will be due to a C1 failure, or in column 9, if it is due to a C2 failure.

We then continue the above process. At the end of day 21, C2 fails. The cost is $30 (replacement) plus $150 (three days lost production), or $180. We *generate* the next lifetime of the new C2 component, using the next two-digit random number (66) to get $L2 = 20$ days. At the end of day 11, the new C1 component shows a lifetime of thirty days. The machine was then in operation for ten days (through the end of day 21). Thus the remaining lifetime of C1 is twenty days ($30 - 10$). Since the lifetime of the new C2 component is also twenty days, the next machine failure will be caused by a simultaneous failure of both C1 and C2 at the end of day 44. The number 44 is determined as follows: The machine failed at the end of day 21, it was inoperative for three days (the time required after a C2 failure), and the next failure will occur in twenty days: $21 + 3 + 20 = 44$. The diagram in Fig. 12.1 is helpful to visualize this sequence of events.

In summary form, the calculation is as follows:

Current time: end of day 21

Remaining life of C1: 20 days (C1 is 10 days old)

Remaining life of C2: 20 days (C2 is new)

Next failure caused by: C1 + C2 in 20 days

Time of next failure: end of day 44 (= 21 + 3 + 20)

As Table 12.3 shows, we have simulated 136 days of operation. The average cost per day equals the sum of column 7 divided by 136:

Policy 1, average cost/day = $9.04

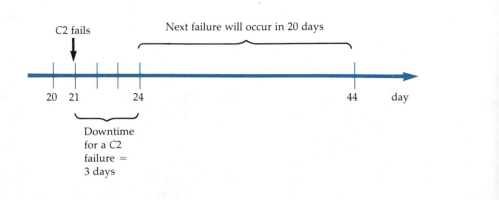

FIGURE 12.1

Policy 2 Simulation

We now repeat the simulation of the machine operation, this time using replacement policy 2. Thus when the machine fails, whether due to a C1 failure or a C2 failure, *both* components will be replaced by new ones. The total cost of each machine failure will be $20 (for C1 replacement) plus $30 (for C2 replacement) plus $100 for lost production (two days at $50 per day), or a total cost of $150. To conduct the simulation, we will use the same format to record the results. In addition, we will use the same sequence of random numbers (starting at the first entry of line 1 of the Table of Random Numbers).

The results of this simulation are summarized in Table 12.4. Check carefully each line of that table to make certain you understand how the simulation works when using policy 2.

The average cost per day using policy 2 equals the sum of column 7 divided by the total number of days simulated, 149. Thus average cost per day of policy 2 is $8.05.

We see then that, based on the simulation, policy 2 would be implemented because it has a lower average daily cost than policy 1, as follows:

Policy 1 cost:	$9.04/day
Policy 2 cost:	8.05/day
Policy 2 advantage:	$0.99/day

TABLE 12.4   *Replacement Policy 2*

(1) Time (end of day)	(2) R1	(3) L1	(4) R2	(5) L2	(6) Event	(7) Cost	Next scheduled failure (at end of day)	
							(8) C1	(9) C2
0	00	10	50	20	Nothing	$ 0	10	
10	72	30	66	20	C1 fails	150		32
32	63	25	70	20	C2 fails	150		54
54	70	30	05	15	C2 fails	150		71
71	22	25	42	20	C2 fails	150		93
93	62	25	56	20	C2 fails	150		115
115	27	25	55	20	C2 fails	150		137
137	14	10	96	20	C2 fails	150	149	
149					C1 fails	150		
					Total cost in 149 days	$1,200		

3. COMPUTER SIMULATION

In practice, simulations are conducted by using a computer. As you observed in the simulation of the machine repair problem in Section 2, the process of simulating a system manually (as in Tables 12.3 and 12.4) can be very time-consuming and certainly subject to calculation errors. Furthermore, there are certain distinct advantages in computerizing a simulation, as we will note later in this section.

The management scientist has two general options open for computerizing a simulation experiment. First, a special-purpose programming language, specifically designed for simulation modeling, can be used. Examples of such simulation languages include GPSS, GASP, and SIMSCRIPT. The second option would be to write the simulation program, using a general-purpose programming language such as FORTRAN, PL–1, PASCAL, or BASIC.

Flowchart for the Machine-Repair Simulation

We now present a flowchart to simulate the machine operation, using policy 1. It would be a simple task to write a single computer program that could be used to test both policies 1 and 2; however, to keep the illustration clear we will assume that separate computer programs are written to test the two policies.

The flowchart of a computer program for testing policy 1 is shown in Fig. 12.2. The flowchart is written in general form and omits the details which would be required by the particular programming language chosen. The boxes of the flowchart are labeled from 1 to 8. The corresponding computer program is designed to simulate 1,000 days of machine operation and proceeds as follows:

1. In box ① the program variables are **initialized.** This corresponds to determining the first line of Table 12.3. In particular, a variable called "CLOCK" is used to keep track of the current day, and as the simulation program executes, CLOCK takes on values corresponding to column 1 of Table 12.3.
2. In box ② a check is made to determine whether 1,000 days of simulated machine operation has taken place: if so, box ⑧ is executed and the average cost per day is computed and printed out; if not, box ③ is executed.
3. Box ③ indicates that the machine has failed at the end of the day as indicated by the value of CLOCK. It is then determined whether the failure was caused by a failure in C1, a failure in C2, or a failure of both. If C1 has failed, the operations indicated in box ④ are executed; if C2 has failed, box ⑥ is executed; and if both have failed, box ⑤ is executed.
4. After one of boxes 4, 5, or 6 is executed, box ⑦ is executed: The value of CLOCK is advanced to the time of the next failure (as determined in either box 4, 5, or 6).

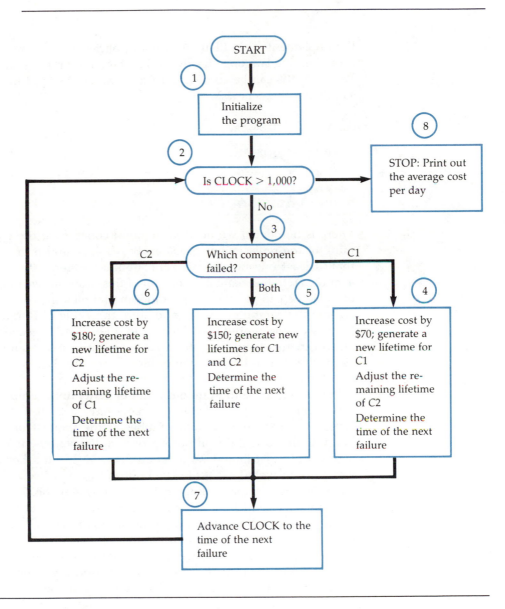

FIGURE 12.2   *Policy 1 simulation.*

5. The program then returns to box ② to see whether 1,000 days of operation have been simulated, and the process continues until box ⑧ is finally
   executed.

   In Exercise 1 at the end of this chapter, you are asked to construct a similar
flowchart for simulating the effect of replacement policy 2.

Results

We implemented simulations of both policies 1 and 2 on an IBM 3081 in the programming language BASIC and obtained the results shown in Table 12.5. These results can be compared to the results obtained by using the manual simulation in Section 2:

Policy 1 cost: $9.04/day

Policy 2 cost: $8.05/day

Pseudo-Random Numbers

There is one detail we need to mention concerning the computer programming of the replacement problem. Boxes 4, 5, and 6 in Fig. 12.2 all require that at least one new component lifetime be generated ($L1$, $L1$ and $L2$, or simply $L2$). In the manual simulation of this problem, we employed the scheme of Table 12.1 to generate these random lifetimes. It would be possible when writing the computer program to store the Table of Random Numbers (Appendix G) in computer memory and then use the scheme of Table 12.2. However, this would require a large amount of computer memory as well as much manual data entry in order to enter the Table of Random Numbers into the computer.

In practice, a **pseudo-random-number generator** is employed in simulation programming. Most computer systems have a built-in function that is designed to produce a random number at the request of the computer program. In the case of the author's program, the statement $Y = $ RND produced a uniformly distributed random number, Y, located between 0 (inclusive) and 1 (exclusive): $0 \le Y < 1$. The built-in function RND is based on a mathematical formula that is known to produce, statistically, numbers between zero and one, which *for all practical purposes* appear to be randomly distributed. However, since the random numbers are based on a specific formula, they are called **pseudo-random numbers** (instead of "purely" random numbers). As a matter of fact, we used the RND function, suitably modified, to produce the table of Appendix G. Now suppose you have a number Y, *chosen at random*, between 0 and 1. How could you use it to determine whether

TABLE 12.5

Policy	Number of days simulated	Total cost	Average cost	Computer time
1	1,030	$10,160.10	$9.87	0.12 second
2	1,030	8,373.90	8.13	0.12 second

$L1$ equals 10, 25, or 30? The answer is simple:

If $0.00 \leq Y < 0.20$, let $L1 = 10$

If $0.20 \leq Y < 0.70$, let $L1 = 25$

If $0.70 \leq Y < 1.00$, let $L1 = 30$

Similarly, the scheme for determining $L2$ is

If $0.00 \leq Y < 0.35$, let $L2 = 15$

If $0.35 \leq Y < 1.00$, let $L2 = 20$

Advantages of the Computer Simulation

There are several advantages of the computer simulation of the machine-repair problem over the manual simulation presented in Tables 12.3 and 12.4.

1. The computer simulation is much faster and less subject to errors. Imagine simulating policy 1 for 1,000 days of machine operation: If each line of Table 12.3 takes two minutes to compute and double-check for accuracy, and if it takes 100 such lines of the table to reach 1,000 simulated days, it would take over thirty-three hours to get results for policy 1 alone. Add about thirty-three hours to obtain results for policy 2, and you have a full week's work.
2. The computer simulation is more flexible. It would be a very simple programming task to make the probability densities of $L1$ and $L2$ changeable at the manager's option. This would be useful if (a) there was some uncertainty about the probabilities or (b) different vendors were being considered as the supplier of component $C1$ (and/or $C2$). Each vendor's product might exhibit different failure properties.
3. A wide range of more realistic possibilities can easily be incorporated and handled by the computer simulation. For example, instead of a fixed replacement time of one day for component $C1$, this time could be modeled as a random variable. Perhaps 10 percent of the time it takes one-half day to replace $C1$, 60 percent of the time it takes one day, and 30 percent of the time it takes two days. Similar modeling assumptions could easily be made for $C2$ replacement time and for the joint replacement time. A replacement problem with these features would be virtually impossible to solve mathematically without the use of simulation.

The Machine-Repair Simulation in SIMSCRIPT II.5

SIMSCRIPT II.5 is a powerful discrete-event simulation language with a large variety of statements implemented through a free-form, English-like syntax.

Discrete-event simulation models a system over time through the changes in the state variables of the system at discrete points in time. Programs may be written in SIMSCRIPT II.5 with either an **event orientation,** which concentrates on the changes taking place (in the state variables) as each event occurs, and in which time is not explicitly accounted for, or a **process orientation,** which concentrates on an item as it flows through the system, and in which time is explicitly taken into account.

Policies 1 and 2 of the machine-repair problem are simulated using an event orientation. The program structure consists of three parts: the **PREAMBLE,** in which modeling elements are declared; the **MAIN,** in which the model is initialized and the simulation clock is started (here the clock merely counts the number of time periods simulated); and the **EVENT** section, in which a routine is included for every event simulated. In the SIMSCRIPT II.5 program below, the PREAMBLE and the MAIN sections are self explanatory. They merely list, define, and set initial values for the state variables. Notice that variable names can be quite long (up to 80 characters, including the periods), and that periods can be included to facilitate reading (FAILED.TIME.COMP1 is easier to read than FAILEDTIMECOMP1). The EVENT section is the heart of the simulation. Here, the first part simulates the failure of each component by using a random-number generator to simulate the failure distributions (the **ALWAYS** is the ending point of **IF** statements). The second part determines which component failed first by comparing the two FAILED.TIME's generated. The smaller of the values indicates a failure of that component, and the proper cost and time values are up-dated. The routine then returns to the beginning of the event (**START.WORKING**). When the time specified has been reached (here **SIM.TIME** is 400 days), the event **REPORT** is performed. This event is merely the definition of the contents and the format of the output.

```
    "SIMULATION CHANGING FAILING COMPONENT-POLICY1

PREAMBLE
    EVENT NOTICES INCLUDE START.WORKING AND REPORT
    DEFINE FAILED.TIME.COMP1, FAILED.TIME.COMP2 AS INTEGER
      VARIABLES
    DEFINE TIME.NEXT, TOT.COST AS INTEGER VARIABLES
    DEFINE REPL.COST.COMP1, REPL.COST.COMP2 AS INTEGER
      VARIABLES
    DEFINE DAY.DOWN.COST, REPL.TIME.COMP1 AS INTEGER
      VARIABLES
    DEFINE REPL.TIME.COMP2, SIM.TIME AS INTEGER VARIABLES
    DEFINE RD AS A VARIABLE
END
MAIN
    LET SIM.TIME = 400
    LET REPL.COST.COMP1 = 20
```

```
    LET REPL.COST.COMP2 = 30
    LET REPL.TIME.COMP1 = 1
    LET REPL.TIME.COMP2 = 3
    LET DAY.DOWN.COST = 50
    SCHEDULE A REPORT IN SIM.TIME DAYS
    SCHEDULE A START.WORKING NOW
    START SIMULATION
END
EVENT START.WORKING
"COMMENT-GENERATE FAILURE DISTRIBUTION WHEN NECESSARY
    IF FAILED.TIME.COMP1 = 0
       LET RD = RANDOM.F(2)
       IF RD < .2
          LET FAILED.TIME.COMP1 = 10
       ELSE
          IF RD > .7
             LET FAILED.TIME.COMP1 = 30
          ELSE
             LET FAILED.TIME.COMP1 = 25
          ALWAYS
       ALWAYS
    ALWAYS
    IF FAILED.TIME.COMP2 = 0
       LET RD = RANDOM.F(1)
       IF RD < .35
          LET FAILED.TIME.COMP2 = 15
       ELSE
          LET FAILED.TIME.COMP2 = 20
       ALWAYS
    ALWAYS
"COMMENT-COMPUTE NEXT START AND COST DEPENDING ON
  COMP. FAILED
    IF FAILED.TIME.COMP1 > FAILED.TIME.COMP2
       LET TIME.NEXT = FAILED.TIME.COMP2 + REPL.TIME.COMP2
       LET FAILED.TIME.COMP1 = FAILED.TIME.COMP1 -
         FAILED.TIME.COMP2
       LET FAILED.TIME.COMP2 = 0
       LET TOT.COST = TOT.COST + REPL.COST.COMP2
       LET TOT.COST = TOT.COST + REPL.TIME.COMP2 *
         DAY.DOWN.COST
    ELSE
       LET TIME.NEXT = FAILED.TIME.COMP1 + REPL.TIME.COMP1
       LET FAILED.TIME.COMP2 = FAILED.TIME.COMP2 -
         FAILED.TIME.COMP1
       LET FAILED.TIME.COMP1 = 0
       LET TOT.COST = TOT.COST + REPL.COST.COMP1
```

```
                    LET TOT.COST = TOT.COST + REPL.TIME.COMP1 *
               DAY.DOWN.COST
        ALWAYS
"COMMENT-SCHEDULE NEXT EVENT
        SCHEDULE A START.WORKING IN TIME.NEXT DAYS
    END
    EVENT REPORT
        LET DAY.COST = TOT.COST / SIM.TIME
        PRINT 4 LINES WITH TOT.COST, DAY.COST THUS

            TOTAL COST FOR POLICY 1 = $*********
            DAILY COST FOR POLICY 1 = $ ***.** /DAY


        STOP
    END


    RESULT POLICY 1:

            TOTAL COST FOR POLICY 1 = $3570
            DAILY COST FOR POLICY 1 = $    8.93 /DAY


        "SIMULATION CHANGING BOTH COMPONENTS-POLICY 2

    PREAMBLE
        EVENT NOTICES INCLUDE START.WORKING AND REPORT
        DEFINE FAILED.TIME.COMP1, FAILED.TIME.COMP2 AS INTEGER
            VARIABLES
        DEFINE TIME.NEXT, TOT.COST AS INTEGER VARIABLES
        DEFINE REPL.COST.COMP1, REPL.COST.COMP2 AS INTEGER
            VARIABLES
        DEFINE DAY.DOWN.COST, REPL.TIME.BOTH AS INTEGER
            VARIABLES
        DEFINE SIM.TIME AS INTEGER VARIABLES
        DEFINE RD AS A VARIABLE
    END
    MAIN
        LET SIM.TIME = 400
        LET REPL.COST.COMP1 = 20
        LET REPL.COST.COMP2 = 30
        LET REPL.TIME.BOTH = 2
        LET DAY.DOWN.COST = 50
        SCHEDULE A REPORT IN SIM.TIME DAYS
        SCHEDULE A START.WORKING NOW
        START SIMULATION
    END
    EVENT START.WORKING
```

```
"COMMENT-GENERATE FAILURE DISTRIBUTION
    LET RD = RANDOM.F(2)
    IF RD < .2
        LET FAILED.TIME.COMP1 = 10
    ELSE
        IF RD > .7
            LET FAILED.TIME.COMP1 = 30
        ELSE
            LET FAILED.TIME.COMP1 = 25
        ALWAYS
    ALWAYS
    LET RD = RANDOM.F(1)
    IF RD < .35
        LET FAILED.TIME.COMP2 = 15
    ELSE
        LET FAILED.TIME.COMP2 = 20
    ALWAYS
"COMMENT-COMPUTE TIME TO NEXT START
    IF FAILED.TIME.COMP1 > FAILED.TIME.COMP2
        LET TIME.NEXT = FAILED.TIME.COMP2 + REPL.TIME.BOTH
    ELSE
        LET TIME.NEXT = FAILED.TIME.COMP1 + REPL.TIME.BOTH
    ALWAYS
"COMMENT-COMPUTE COSTS
    LET TOT.COST = TOT.COST + REPL.COST.COMP1 +
        REPL.COST.COMP2
    LET TOT.COST = TOT.COST + REPL.TIME.BOTH *
        DAY.DOWN.COST
"COMMENT-SCHEDULE NEXT EVENT
    SCHEDULE A START.WORKING IN TIME.NEXT DAYS
END
EVENT REPORT
    LET DAY.COST = TOT.COST / SIM.TIME
    PRINT 4 LINES WITH TOT.COST, DAY.COST THUS

        TOTAL COST FOR POLICY 2 = $*********
        DAILY COST FOR POLICY 2 = $ ***.** /DAY


    STOP
END


RESULT POLICY 2:

        TOTAL COST FOR POLICY 2 = $3150
        DAILY COST FOR POLICY 2 = $   7.88 /DAY
```

4. CONCLUDING REMARKS

Without going into technical details, we shall present the following list of some of the major issues in simulation modeling.

1. *Start-up Conditions.* How should the simulation model be initialized? In the machine-repair example initialization amounted to starting with line 1 of Table 12.3 or 12.4. In more complex simulations, it may not be apparent how to start the simulation.

2. *Steady-State.* How long does it take for the simulation to achieve a steady-state condition? That is, after starting the system, how long does it take before the simulation begins to represent the behavior of the actual system? Steady-state is an equilibrium condition. The possibly erratic effects caused by system start-up disappear as the system attains steady-state condition.

3. *Length of Run.* How long should the simulation be run in order to obtain reasonable results? In the machine-repair simulation, is a 1,000-day simulation run sufficient to estimate the average cost per day? Is it more than sufficient?

4. *Variance Reduction.* Because of the large number of random variables used to model a real-world system in a given simulation, there may be tremendous variability in the numerical results obtained from trial to trial. For example, in the machine-repair simulation, we obtained estimates of the mean cost per day for the two policies. But how reliable are these estimates? Are the variances large or small? Imagine the variability that would be encountered in the modified machine-repair problem where the replacement times are allowed to be random variables. Techniques for reducing the variance of results obtained in a simulation are called **Monte Carlo** methods.

5. *Validation.* Once a computer program for a simulation is written and debugged, how can the analyst determine whether the simulation is producing reasonable results, that is, results truly representative of the real system being studied? What is at issue here (in the view of management) is the credibility of the simulation. When past data exist on the actual system's performance, the simulation program can be run to determine whether it would have given approximately the same results. When comparison with the actual system is not possible, expert analysis must be relied upon to judge whether the simulation is producing reasonable results.

6. *Experimental Design.* One typical issue that arises in experimental design is illustrated by the following situation. Suppose a model of a complex system involves ten decision (or policy) variables under the control of the manager. Suppose each variable has five possible values. Then, assuming independence of the policy combinations, there are 5^{10} or 9,765,625 different experiments that must be conducted, using the simulation program. If each experiment requires fifteen minutes of computer time (not a very

large figure for complex simulations), it would take 2,441,406.25 *hours* of computer time (*or about 279 years*) to test all possible policies. The analyst must employ judgment and specialized techniques to deal with such "combinatorial" problems.

TERMINOLOGY

After studying this chapter you should be familiar with the following terms:

TERM	SECTION
event orientation	3
Monte Carlo methods	4
process orientation	3
pseudo-random-number generator	3
simulation	1
simulation clock	2, 3
start-up conditions	4
steady-state	4
validation	1, 4
variance reduction	4

EXERCISES

1. *Computer Simulation.* For the machine-repair problem, construct a flowchart (along the lines of Figure 12.2) for a computer program that would simulate the machine operation under policy 2.

2. *Coin Toss.* Consider the experiment of flipping a coin twenty times. Each time, note whether "heads" or "tails" appears.
   a. Simulate this experiment, using the last digit of each five-digit number, starting with line 8 of the Table of Random Numbers. Let "heads" be the event that one of the digits 0, 1, 2, 3, or 4 appears, and let 5, 6, 7, 8, or 9 represent "tails." Construct a table with the following headings to record your results: Column 1, Experiment number (1–20); Column 2, Result (heads or tails); Column 3, Total number of heads obtained so far; and Column 4, Proportion of heads obtained so far. Based on your experiment, estimate the probability of heads.
   b. Can you devise other schemes for using the random number table to model the toss of a coin?

3. *Vendor Selection.* Refer to the machine-repair problem described in Section 2. Suppose a vendor offers a machine whose components have the failure characteristics shown in Table 12.6. Component 1 costs $22, and

TABLE 12.6

	Component C1		Component C2
Days	Lifetime probability	Days	Lifetime probability
10	0.30	5	0.10
20	0.70	10	0.25
		15	0.50
		25	0.15

C2 costs $29. Replacement time on C1 is two days, on C2 is one day, and, if C1 and C2 are replaced at the same time, the replacement time is two days. Use the first two digits of the five-digit numbers, starting with line 1 of the Table of Random Numbers, to simulate 125 days of machine operation under (a) policy 1, (b) policy 2. Then answer part (c): Which machine would you purchase—the one described in the text or the one offered by this vendor?

4. *Inventory Planning.* Benny's Bakery has recorded the following daily sales of fresh bread over the past 100 days:

Sales (loaves)	20	30	40	50
Number of days	10	60	25	5

Each loaf costs $0.50 to bake and sells for $0.75. Loaves left over at the end of the day sell for $0.30 the next day as "day-old" bread. There is no penalty cost for being short (that is, if customer demand exceeds supply).

a. Construct a simulation model to determine whether to prepare 20, 30, 40, or 50 loaves of bread each morning in order to maximize daily profit. Simulate fifteen days of operation to evaluate each policy, using the last two digits of the five-digit numbers in column 1 of the Table of Random Numbers, Appendix G.

b. If sales are known to range from twenty to fifty loaves per day, how would you modify your simulation model to represent more realistically the actual bakery sales? By what factor would this version exceed that of part (a) in terms of computing time?

5. *Job Processing Times—Assembly-Line Operations.* A product must go through three phases of operations on an assembly line. The time spent at each of the three work stations is a random variable. The probabil-

TABLE 12.7

| | Station 1 | | Station 2 | | Station 3 |
Time	Probability	Time	Probability	Time	Probability
3	0.40	5	0.10	1	0.65
4	0.30	6	0.90	2	0.35
5	0.30				

ity densities of these times are given in Table 12.7 (time is measured in minutes).

Simulate the processing of ten jobs through the three work centers to estimate the average total processing time per job. (Use the second and third digits of the first three 5-digit numbers of rows 1–10 of the Table of Random Numbers.)

6. *The Effect of Sample Size.*   Continue the simulation of Exercise 5 on ten more jobs, using lines 11–20 of the Table of Random Numbers. Construct a table with the following headings—*Job number, Processing time for the current job,* and *Average total processing time per job*—based on the jobs simulated to this point. Compare to the theoretical answer of 11.15 minutes per job.

7. *Simulating Interdependencies.*   Suppose a product must be processed through two work centers. In work center A, the processing time is one hour 80 percent of the time and two hours 20 percent of the time. The processing time in work center B depends upon the processing time required in work center A. If the product takes one hour in work center A, the time it takes in work center B will be one hour, two hours, or three hours, with respective probabilities 0.60, 0.30, and 0.10. If the product takes two hours in work center A, the processing time in work center B will be two hours or three hours, with respective probabilities 0.60 and 0.40.

Simulate the flow of ten jobs through work centers $A \rightarrow B$. Estimate the expected processing time for a job through system. Use the last two digits of the numbers in rows 10 and 11 of the Table of Random Numbers.

8. *New-Product Development.*   The initial capital investment required to manufacture a proposed new product will be $1 million. There are several variable factors that could affect final product-development costs before the product is suitable for marketing. The product-development costs will be either $2 million or $3 million, with respective probabilities of 0.70 and 0.30. Total sales of the product are expected to be $2 mil-

lion, $4 million, or $6 million, with probabilities 0.25, 0.40, and 0.35, respectively.

Conduct fifteen simulation trials to estimate expected net profit from the product. Use the first two digits of the five-digit numbers in lines 17, 18, and 19 of the Table of Random Numbers.

9. *Sensitivity Analysis.* Repeat Exercise 8, assuming the sales levels are taken to be $2 million, $4 million, and $6 million, with respective probabilities of 0.10, 0.50, and 0.40.

10. *Rate-of-Return Distributions.* Often management is not interested simply in the expected profit or expected rate of return on a given project but is also concerned about the *distribution* of possible returns. Conduct thirty trials of the simulation experiment in Exercise 8. For each trial, compute the rate of return. For example, if development costs are $2 million and sales are $4 million, compute the (simple) rate of return as follows: Investment = $1 million (initial) + $2 million (developmental) = $3 million; sales = $4 million; net profit = $4 million − $3 million = $1 million; rate of return = $1 million/$3 million or 33-1/3 percent. Using the output of your simulation, construct a curve by plotting the rate of return horizontally and the probability vertically. Indicate the expected rate of return. Use the last two digits of the numbers starting with line 1 in the Table of Random Numbers.

11. *Military Planning.* A military mission requires three operations, A, B, and C. A and B can be conducted simultaneously; C cannot begin until both A and B are complete. The probability densities of the operation completion times (in days) are given in Table 12.8.

Conduct a simulation to estimate expected mission completion time. Conduct twenty simulation trials using the last two digits of the numbers in columns 3, 4, and 5 of the Table of Random Numbers. What is the probability that the project will be completed in five days or less?

12. *Queuing Simulation—Service Facility Analysis.* This problem applies to single-server queuing systems, such as a gas station with a single pump, a doctor treating patients, or a checker at a drug store. (See Chapter 8.)

TABLE 12.8

	A		B		C	
Time	Probability	Time	Probability	Time	Probability	
1	0.60	1	0.20	3	0.25	
2	0.40	2	0.70	4	0.75	
		3	0.10			

Suppose a single server provides a service to arriving customers on a first come, first served basis (FCFS). The service times and the time between successive arrivals (interarrival times) are random variables having the probability densities shown in Table 12.9 (times are in minutes).

Simulate ten customer arrivals to determine the expected number of customers in the system (in the queue waiting for service or being served) at any given time. Use the first two digits of the five-digit numbers starting with line 1 of the Table of Random Numbers.

Hint: Let T be the total simulated time of the queuing simulation (in minutes). Let $S(i)$ be the total number of minutes during which there were i customers in the system. Then the expected number of customers in the system, L, can be estimated by

$$L = \frac{\Sigma\, iS(i)}{T}$$

Does this formula make sense to you?

13. *Gambling.* The game of craps is played as follows: A pair of dice is rolled. If a 7 or 11 appears on the first roll, you win; if a 2, 3, or 12 appears, you lose; if 4, 5, 6, 8, 9, or 10 appears, designate the particular number as your "point," which we denote by N. In this latter case you continue to roll the dice. If a 7 appears before the number N appears, you lose the game; if your point N appears before a 7, you win the game. Use simulation to determine the probability of your winning this game. Use the following process to model the roll of the dice: Use the single digits starting in line 1 of the Table of Random Numbers. Imagine rolling the two dice separately. To determine the value of the first die, examine the digits sequentially until reaching one of the numbers—1, 2, 3, 4, 5, 6. Then continue scanning single digits to determine the roll of the second die. Add the two values obtained. For example, the first six digits are 0, 0, 9, 8, 0, 5. So on the first roll, die 1 equals 5; the sequence of digits continues: 0, 4. So die 2 equals 4. Thus the first roll of the dice equals 5 + 4, or 9. Simulate ten games.

TABLE 12.9

Service times		Interarrival time	
Time	Probability	Time	Probability
1	0.65	1	0.20
2	0.35	2	0.70
		3	0.10

TABLE 12.10

Location	Subdivision		
	A	B	C
1	10	5	7
2	6	8	9

14. *Card Games.* Consider a deck of fifty-two cards: thirteen values, each having four suits. How could you use the Table of Random Numbers to simulate dealing a hand of five cards?

15. *Fire Department Location.* A city is planning to locate a new fire station to serve three new city subdivisions. Two locations are being considered as possibilities for the new fire station. The travel times between each location and subdivision are given in Table 12.10 (in minutes). During a given week the probabilities of a fire occurring in each of the subdivisions is 0.30, 0.45, and 0.25, respectively.

    For each location, simulate ten weeks to determine an average travel time to fire occurrences (total travel time in ten weeks divided by total number of fires in ten weeks). Use consecutive pairs of digits, starting with line 1 of the Table of Random Numbers.

IV ADVANCED TOPICS

13 GOAL PROGRAMMING

1. INTRODUCTION

In chapters 2 and 3 we saw that linear programming is an extremely useful technique for formulating and solving a wide range of management problems. A major component of any linear program is the objective function, expressing a *single criterion* that must be maximized or minimized, such as cost, profit, person-exposures to advertising, and so on.

However, it may not always be appropriate or feasible for management to state explicitly a single criterion that is to be optimized in a given problem. Examples might include the following:

1. *Conflicting objectives.* Management may want to attain conflicting objectives, such as "minimize cost and maximize customer service." Typically the greater the level of customer service, the greater will be the cost of providing the service.
2. *Objectives having different dimensions.* An example of a pair of objectives that are measured in different units would be "maximize profit and maximize market share."
3. *Objectives that are difficult to quantify.* The objective of maximizing the level of customer service would fall into the category of being difficult to quantify.

Goal programming (GP) is a recent extension of linear programming in which management objectives are treated as goals to be attained as closely as possible within the practical constraints of the problem. Each goal, instead of being part of the objective function, is expressed as a constraint. The objective function contains variables that measure the amount by which goal achievements deviate from target values set by management. The objective of the goal program is to minimize these deviations. In the following section we shall present an example to illustrate the goal programming method.

2. GOAL PROGRAMMING: A PRODUCT MIX PROBLEM

Pramco Manufacturing currently manufactures a single product, an open, tube-frame dune buggy for sporting enthusiasts. Due to increasing gasoline prices, there appears to be a promising national market for moped motorbikes. Although sales of the dune buggy have been extremely strong, the Pramco management, in consultation with its engineering staff, has decided to commit some of the company's resources to the manufacture of a moped model as a second product.

The profit on each dune buggy is $260, and projected profit per moped is estimated to be $160. Each of these products must go through two major fabrication and assembly centers in the company's plant. Center A (fabrication) has a monthly capacity of 192 hours, and center B (assembly) has a capacity of 240 hours. Each dune buggy requires 3 hours in fabrication and 2 hours in assembly; each moped requires 1.75 hours in fabrication and 2.5 hours in assembly.

LP Solution

Assuming the single objective of Pramco is to maximize profits, the following linear program will determine the optimal product mix:

Let x_1 = number of dune buggies manufactured per month.

    x_2 = number of mopeds manufactured per month.

Maximize $Z = 260x_1 + 160x_2$

Subject to:

(1) $3x_1 + 1.75x_2 \leq 192$

(2) $2x_1 + 2.5x_2 \leq 240$

(3) $x_1, \quad x_2 \geq 0$

The solution to this LP is easily found to be:

$x_1^* = 15$ (dune buggies)

$x_2^* = 84$ (mopeds)

$Z^* = \$17,340$ profit per month

After examining the above LP solution, it was the general feeling of management that such a low output of their standard dune-buggy product clearly would not be desirable. In addition, the marketing manager expressed some uncertainty over the precise sales potential of the new moped product, and the production manager indicated that there would be some time and risk involved in working some of the engineering bugs out of the moped. Of course, in the long run, Pramco can expand its capacity to manufacture both products at desired levels, but for the first year it is constrained to experiment with the product, using existing facilities.

After some discussion it was finally decided to establish a goal of producing a total of 110 units of output per month (dune buggies and mopeds combined). Furthermore, an effort was to be made to produce at least 75 dune buggies and 50 mopeds per month.

APPLICATIONS

The following applications appear in this chapter in text, examples, or problems:

Community health care

Employee problems: work-force smoothing

Employee scheduling

Media mix

Medical clinic location

Military spending

Portfolio selection

Product mix

Public parks planning

Goal Programming Formulation

We illustrate the goal programming technique by formulating a goal program to solve the Pramco product mix problem stated above. We shall then indicate the general procedure underlying goal programming formulation.

First, our goal program should incorporate constraints (1) and (2) of the LP.

Second, we must express the fact that the target goal for total production is 110 units. To accomplish this, define d_1^+ to be the overachievement of this goal and d_1^- to be the underachievement of the goal. Since the total production is simply $x_1 + x_2$, we can write the constraint as follows:

(3) $x_1 + x_2 - d_1^+ + d_1^- = 110$

It may not be possible to hit the target of 110 exactly, and this is the reason for including the terms d_1^+ and d_1^-. If the goal is overachieved, d_1^+ will be positive and d_1^- will be 0. For example, suppose a total of 120 units are produced, so $x_1 + x_2 = 120$. Then $d_1^+ = 10$, $d_1^- = 0$ and $x_1 + x_2 - d_1^+ + d_1^- = 120 - 10 + 0 = 110$. Similarly, if the goal is underachieved, d_1^+ will be zero and d_1^- will be positive, and equal to the difference $110 - (x_1 + x_2)$. In either case constraint (3) will be satisfied with equality. The variables d_1^+ and d_1^- are called **deviation variables.**

We can use the same method to express the other two goals:

(4) $x_1 - d_2^+ + d_2^- = 75$

(5) $x_2 - d_3^+ + d_3^- = 50$

The only remaining task is to determine the objective function. In a goal program the objective function involves only the deviation variables, and the criterion is minimization. In our example, management has expressed the goal of achieving a total target production of 110 units. Thus in the solution to the problem, we would like the deviation variables d_1^+ and d_1^- both to be 0. Thus the term $d_1^+ + d_1^-$ will appear in the objective function.

Furthermore, management would like to minimize the underachievement of producing 75 dune buggies. The deviation variable that measures underachievement of this target goal is d_2^-, so it too will appear in the objective function. Similarly, d_3^- should be placed in the objective function. Thus the objective function is to minimize $d_1^+ + d_1^- + d_2^- + d_3^-$. The complete goal program is stated as follows:

Minimize $Z = d_1^+ + d_1^- + d_2^- + d_3^-$
Subject to:

(1)	$3x_1 + 1.75x_2$		$\leq$	192
(2)	$2x_1 + 2.5x_2$		$\leq$	240
(3)	$x_1 + x_2 - d_1^+ + d_1^-$		$=$	110
(4)	$x_1 + d_2^+ + d_2^-$		$=$	75
(5)	$x_2 - d_3^+ + d_3^-$		$=$	50
(6)	$x_1, \quad x_2, \quad d_i^+ \quad d_i^-, (i = 1,2,3)$		$\geq$	0

Using a canned LP (based on the simplex method), the solution to this goal program is easily found to be

$Z^* = 65.333$
$x_1^* = 34.833$, $x_2^* = 50.000$
$d_1^+ = 0$, $d_1^- = 25.167$
$d_2^+ = 0$, $d_2^- = 40.167$
$d_3^+ = 0$, $d_3^- = 0$

Thus the total production goal of 110 units is underachieved by 25.167 units, the dune buggy production goal of 75 units is underachieved by 40.167

units, and the moped production goal of 50 mopeds per month is fully achieved. Also the total profit of this product mix is ($260)(34.833) + ($160)(50) = $17,056, or $283.42 per month below the LP solution. Although yielding slightly less dollar profit per month, the GP solution *more closely satisfies management's stated goals*, which take into account a wider range of factors than the single LP criterion of maximizing profit.

Goal Program Formulation

We now summarize the steps involved in formulating a goal program:

STEP 1. State goals explicitly with target values.

STEP 2. Express each goal as an *equality* constraint that includes two deviation variables, d_i^+ and d_i^-, where d_i^+ measures the amount by which the goal is overachieved and d_i^- measures the amount by which the goal is underachieved.

STEP 3. Express the objective function in minimization form, involving *only* deviation variables (and not the original decision variables). Write down all the problem constraints, including the practical constraints of the problem (such as resource limitations) as well as the goal constraints.

3. GOAL TRADE-OFFS: THE USE OF DIFFERENTIAL WEIGHTS

In addition to specifying goals, management may express its judgment concerning the relative importance of the stated goals by assigning weights to the goals. These weights can then be used as coefficients for the deviation variables in the objective function. The next example illustrates this technique.

EXAMPLE 13.1 *Media Mix.* Adcom Market Analysis, Inc., is planning an advertising program for the coming year to promote a new product for one of its clients. Three media are being considered. The cost per ad placed in each of the media and their reach (in terms of person-exposures) are given in Table 13.1. For example, each ad in medium 1 costs $15 and reaches 110 people, 70 of whom are under 25 years of age. The client provides Adcom with the following information:

• Its advertising budget is $300 weekly.
• Goal 1 is to reach 2,500 persons per week.
• Goal 2 is to minimize the underachievement of reaching 2,000 persons per week under twenty-five years of age. This demographic segment is a particularly desirable target market for the client's new product.

TABLE 13.1

Media	Cost/ad	Person-exposures	
		Under 25 years old	25 years and older
1	$15	70	40
2	11	40	25
3	18	60	100

- Goal 3 is to minimize the amount of money spent in excess of $250 per week on media 2 and 3 combined. The reason given for this is twofold. First, media 2 and 3 have proven effective in the past, so no effort will be made to put an absolute ceiling on these two media. On the other hand, medium 1 has not yet been tried by the company. In fact there is some doubt concerning the relatively high expected effectiveness of 70 person-exposures (under age 25). Yet management does not want to commit all its budget to the other two media because it would like to leave some room for testing medium 1.
- Finally, the client company indicates that goal 1 is three times as important as goal 3 and one-and-a-half times as important as goal 2.

Formulate a GP to determine a satisfactory media mix.

Solution. Define the decision variables as follows: Let x_1, x_2, and x_3 be the number of ads placed per week in media 1, 2, and 3, respectively. Let d_1^+, d_2^+, and d_3^+ be the overachievement of goals 1, 2, and 3, respectively, and let d_1^-, d_2^-, and d_3^- be the underachievement of the three goals. Using the importance weightings expressed by the client company as differential weights, we can write the following goal program:

Minimize $Z = 3d_1^+ + 3d_1^- + 2d_2^- + d_3^+$

Subject to:

(1)	$15x_1 + 11x_2 + 18x_3$	$\leq$	300
(2)	$110x_1 + 65x_2 + 160x_3 - d_1^+ + d_1^-$	$=$	$2{,}500$
(3)	$70x_1 + 40x_2 + 60x_3 - d_2^+ + d_2^-$	$=$	$2{,}000$
(4)	$11x_2 + 18x_3 - d_3^+ + d_3^-$	$=$	250
(5)	$x_1, \quad x_2, \quad x_3, \quad d_i^+, \quad d_i^-, (i = 1,2,3),$	$\geq$	0

Note in particular the weights of the deviation variables in the objective function.

The following solution was obtained by using a canned LP (simplex) program:

$$x_1^* = 7.14286, \quad x_2^* = 0, \quad x_3^* = 10.71429$$
$$d_1^+ = 0, \qquad\qquad d_1^- = 0$$
$$d_2^+ = 0, \qquad\qquad d_2^- = 857.14286$$
$$d_3^+ = 0, \qquad\qquad d_3^- = 57.14286$$

Thus goal 1 is met exactly, goal 2 is underachieved by 857.14286, and goal 3 (minimizing expenditures in excess of $250 per month for media 2 and 3) is met satisfactorily, since the value of d_3^- indicates that this expenditure is actually $57.14 *short* of $250. ▲

4. PRIORITY LEVELS

In the previous section we illustrated the use of weighting factors on the deviation variables of the objective function. It is important to note that the use of such weights only helps to quantify the *relative trade-offs* between the various goals. In examining the solution to Example 13.1 (the Adcom problem), we see that although goal 1 is met exactly, goal 2 is not met as closely as goal 3.

By using **priority factors** it is possible to ensure that higher priority goals will be met as much as possible before lower priority goals are met. When a lower priority goal is considered, it will not be met at the expense of re-laxing a higher priority goal.

The priority factors are denoted typically by P_1, P_2, P_3, and so on, where P_1 represents the highest priority, P_2 the second highest, and so on. For example, consider the objective function: minimize $Z = P_1 d_2^- + P_2 d_1^+ + P_3 d_3^+ + P_3 d_3^-$. The P_is are not assigned any specific numerical values; they simply indicate an *ordinal* ordering of the goals. In this example the term $P_1 d_2^-$ indicates that minimizing the underachievement of goal 2 has the highest priority, and efforts will first be directed toward this goal; *then* the goal program will work to minimize the overachievement of goal 1, as indicated by the term $P_2 d_1^+$; and *finally*, the goal program will work toward meeting the target for goal 3 exactly, as indicated by the term $P_3 d_3^+ + P_3 d_3^- = P_3(d_3^+ + d_3^-)$—a third-priority term.

We shall illustrate how priority factors operate to satisfy goals by presenting a graphical solution of a simple product mix problem.

EXAMPLE 13.2 *Priority Factors.* Innex Corporation manufactures two products, *A* and *B*. Product *A* requires five hours on machine 1 and two hours on machine 2; product *B* requires two hours on machine 1 and four hours on machine 2. The weekly capacities of machines 1 and 2 are fifty hours and forty-eight hours, respectively. Management has established the following goals in order of priority:

1. Minimize underachievement of a total production of ten units (of products A and B combined) per week.
2. Minimize underachievement of producing eight units of product A weekly.
3. Minimize underachievement of producing thirteen units of product B weekly.

Find the product mix that most closely achieves these goals.

Solution. The GP is stated as follows:

Let x_1 = number of units of A produced weekly
     x_2 = number of units of B produced weekly
Minimize $Z = P_1 d_1^- + P_2 d_2^- + P_3 d_3^-$
Subject to:

(1)	$5x_1 + 2x_2$	≤ 50
(2)	$2x_1 + 4x_2$	≤ 48
(3)	$x_1 + x_2 - d_1^+ + d_1^-$	$= 10$
(4)	$x_1 - d_2^+ + d_2^-$	$= 8$
(5)	$- x_2 - d_3^+ + d_3^-$	$= 13$
(6)	$x_1, + x_2, d_i^+, + d_i^+, (i = 1,2,3) \geq 0$	

These constraints are shown graphically in Fig. 13.1. The underachievement (d_i^-) and overachievement (d_i^+) of each of the three goals are indicated by arrows attached to each constraint line. For example, for constraint (4) the vertical line $x_1 = 8$ is graphed. Any point lying to the left of this line (as indicated by the arrow labeled d_2^-) underachieves this goal. Any point to the right of the line (the arrow labeled d_2^+) overachieves this goal.

To solve this GP, proceed as follows:

1. First, graph the region of feasible solutions, using constraints (1) and (2). This step is shown in Fig. 13.2.
2. Use constraint (3), goal 1, to reduce further the feasible region. We selected this constraint first among the three goals due to the P_1 priority level assigned to its deviation variable d_1^- in the objective function. Minimizing d_1^- would place us on or above the constraint (3) line (see Fig. 13.1) and would reduce the feasible region to that shown in Fig. 13.3.
3. Since d_2^- has the second highest priority level in the objective function, we use constraint (4) to reduce the region obtained in Fig. 13.3. This pushes us to the line $x_1 = 8$, which cuts through the shaded region.
4. Finally, dealing with the third priority goal of minimizing d_3^-, we are pushed upward along the line $x_1 = 8$ toward the line $x_2 = 13$. The optimal GP solution is point X, Fig. 13.4. The coordinates of X are easily found by

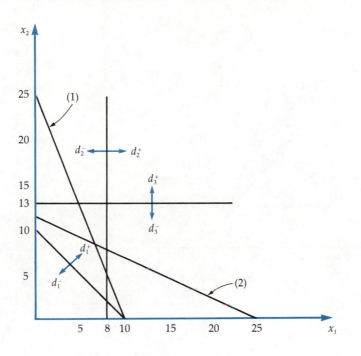

FIGURE 13.1

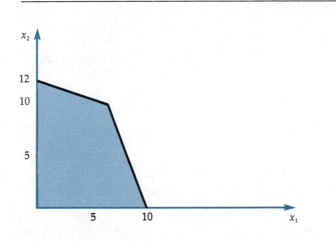

FIGURE 13.2

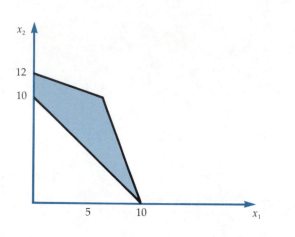

FIGURE 13.3

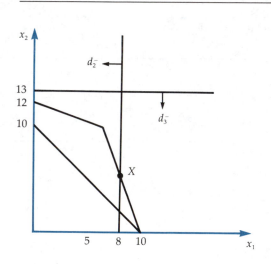

FIGURE 13.4

solving the following set of constraint equations:

(1) $5x_1 + 2x_2 = 50$

(2) $x_1 \quad = 8$

   This gives $x_1 = 8$ and $x_2 = 5$. Also check that $d_1^- = 0$, $d_1^+ = 3$, $d_2^- = 0$, $d_2^+ = 0$, $d_3^- = 8$, and $d_3^+ = 0$.   ▲

5. CONCLUDING REMARKS

The foundations of goal programming were developed by Sang Lee (see the references for this chapter in Appendix A). Goal programming is a useful technique for solving linear programming problems, where the objective consists of achieving a set of goals as opposed to the single criterion of minimizing cost or maximizing profit.

Computation

A goal program consisting of two decision variables that involve two or more priority levels can be solved graphically, as demonstrated in Example 13.2. More general goal programs are solved by using simplex-based computer programs. Such programs are based on the simplex method and are modified to account for priority levels.

Goal programming has been extended to handle decision variables that are restricted to take on only whole-number values (that is, integer values). So-called "integer goal programming" is discussed at length in the book *Goal Programming and Extensions* by James P. Ignizio (see references in Appendix *A*).

TERMINOLOGY

After studying this chapter you should be familiar with the following terms:

TERM	SECTION
differential weights	3
deviation variables	2
goal programming (GP)	1
priority factors	4
priority levels	4

EXERCISES

In some of the following problems you are asked to formulate a GP that could be used to solve for an optimal solution; do not solve the GP unless the problem calls for a graphical solution.

1. *Product Mix.* Kataco, Inc., manufactures three products, *A*, *B*, and *C*. The processing times (in hours per unit) of each of these products on machines *M*1 and *M*2 are given below, along with the machine capacities (hours per week):

Machines	Products			Capacity
	A	B	C	
M1	5	3	4	60
M2	2	6	1	60

Kataco's goals (in order of priority) are as follows:
a. Hit a total production target of sixty units of product per week.
b. Minimize overproduction of product A above seven units, since this seems to be the maximum sales potential for product A.
c. Orders for product C are estimated at sixteen units; minimize underachievement of this target.
d. Minimize underutilization of the capacities of the two machines below fifty hours.
Formulate a GP to determine the desired product mix.

2. *Medical Clinic Location.* A new medical clinic is to be located in an urban area to serve three major sections of town. A map of these sections, showing rectangular coordinates of their centers, is given in Fig. 13.5. If the medical clinic is located at (3,1), its distance to center C, for example, would be $(5 - 3) + (2 - 1) = 3$ miles, this being the *rectilinear distance—* that is, the distance that must be traveled following east-west and north-south streets.

Formulate a GP to determine the location (x,y) of the medical clinic that minimizes total distance to the three sections of town.

3. *Media Mix.* Goldies Fashions is planning an advertising program to promote its fall fashions. It is planning to use three media; these media

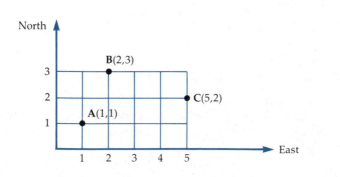

FIGURE 13.5

TABLE 13.2

Media	Cost per ad ($)	Person-exposures per ad
Newspaper	500	2,000
Radio	750	4,000
Television	2,000	13,000

are listed in Table 13.2 along with cost per ad and expected person-exposures in Goldies's target market.

Goldies's goals are the following:
a. Minimize expenditures over $10,000.
b. Minimize expenditures on television over $4,000.
c. Minimize underachievement of reaching less than 50,000 people.
d. Avoid spending less than $1,500 on newspaper advertising.
e. Maintain an expenditure ratio of radio to newspaper advertising of at least 2:1.
(1) Assuming these goals have equal priority, formulate a GP to determine the optimal media mix.
(2) Assuming these goals have equal priority, formulate a GP that would give three times as much weight to goal c as to any other goal.
(3) Formulate a GP that would give priorities to the goals in the following order (from highest to lowest): c, b, e, d, a.

4. *Portfolio Selection.* George Slipfot has $5,000 to invest in stock *A* (priced at $15 per share), stock *B* ($10 per share), and bonds ($50 per bond). These three investments yield 10 percent, 14 percent, and 9 percent, respectively. George has six equally important goals:
a. Earn at least $600 per year in returns.
b. Minimize the overachievement of putting more than $1,200 in bonds.
c. Invest at least $1,200 in stock *B*, preferably more.
d. Invest in stocks *A* and *B* in a 3:2 ratio (for every dollar invested in stock *B*, he would like to invest $1.50 in stock *A* as a hedge against the riskier stock *B*).
e. Since the bonds are considered safe, George would like to maximize the overachievement of putting more than $900 in bonds.
f. Minimize the underachievement of investing less than $5,000.
Formulate a GP for the problem of selecting the best portfolio.

5. *Employee Problems: Work-Force Smoothing.* Intal, Inc., manufactures two products, *A* and *B*. Profit on product *A* is $200 per unit, and profit on product *B* is $250 per unit. Each unit of product *A* requires 2 labor-hours in department 1 and 4 labor-hours in department 2; product *B* requires 3 labor-hours in department 1 and 1.5 labor-hours in department 2. The

regular-time capacities of the two departments are 600 and 450 labor-hours, respectively.

a. Solve an LP to determine the profit-maximizing product mix.

b. The workers in department 2 are requesting that management increase their work time. After some analysis, management sets the following equally important goals:

(1) Minimize underachievement of a profit goal of $45,000.

(2) Minimize underachievement of a 550 labor-hour utilization in department 2.

(3) Maintain the 600 labor-hour utilization of department 1.

   Formulate a GP to determine the optimal product mix.

6. *Priorities in Work-Force Smoothing.*   Refer to Exercise 5 above. Suppose management orders the goals from highest to lowest priority as (2), (1), (3). Formulate a GP and solve graphically to determine the optimal product mix. Compare the resulting profit to the LP solution, Exercise 5(a).

7. *Military Spending.*   The Department of Defense is currently planning the development of two types of ICBMs (intercontinental ballistic missiles). Model 1 would cost $2 million each, and model 2 would cost $1.5 million each. After studying budget spending, long-range goals, and recent military planning on the part of other nonallied countries, the following goals were set (in order of priority):

a. Minimize underproduction of model 1 below five units.

b. Minimize underproduction of model 2 below seven units.

c. Minimize spending in excess of $19 million.

Formulate and solve graphically a GP to determine how many missiles of each model to develop.

8. Solve a modification of Exercise 7 above by inserting the following goal between goals (a) and (b) in order of priority: Minimize underproduction of a total of thirteen missiles.

9. *Community Health Care.*   The city of Dixon must determine how many patients to refer to each of its two city medical clinics. Clinic *A* is a newer clinic and operates fifty-two hours a week (including four hours on Saturday); this clinic requires an average of 1.5 hours to treat each patient referred to it (including paperwork processing). (Assume that only one patient at a time can be treated at each clinic.) Clinic *B* is open only forty-eight hours a week and requires 2 hours to handle each patient. The community incurs a cost of $10 for each patient referred to the clinics. The following goals, in order of priority, were set by the public-health officials:

a. Minimize the underachievement of treating 100 people per week.

b. Meet the fifty-two-hour capacity of clinic *A* (which is almost its limit).

c. Meet the forty-eight-hour capacity of clinic *B*. This has lower priority than meeting the capacity at clinic *A*, since clinic *B* could be pushed to operate longer hours.

d. Try to keep spending below $800 per week as much as possible. Formulate and solve a GP to determine how many patients should be assigned to each clinic.

10. *Community Health Care.* Formulate and solve a GP to determine the number of patients to be assigned to each of two medical clinics, given the following data: The number of doctor-hours available at clinic *A* is 160 per week (5 doctors × 32 hours per week each) and the number of clerical person-hours is 96 (2 receptionists × 48 hours a week each). Each patient assigned to clinic *A* requires one-half hour of a doctor's time and one hour of a receptionist's time (for processing paperwork and government forms). Each patient assigned to clinic *A* costs the community $17 per visit. The corresponding data for clinic *B* are as follows: 128 doctor-hours, 120 clerical-hours, 1/2 hour required of a doctor's time per patient, 3/4 hour of clerical work required (clinic *B* has begun to implement a minicomputer system to handle some of the paperwork), and cost to the community for each patient assigned to clinic *B* is $20.

In addition to being practically constrained by the available doctor and clerical hours, the health officials have set the following goals in order of priority:

a. Serve at least 200 patients per week.
b. Attempt to spend no more than $4,220 per week on the two clinics.
c. Equalize the number of patients assigned to the two clinics.

11. *Public Parks Planning.* Durango is planning to locate a public park to meet the recreational needs of four northeast neighborhoods. A map of these neighborhoods, showing their coordinates (in miles), is given in Fig. 13.6.

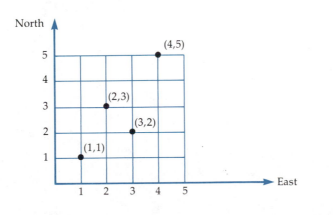

FIGURE 13.6

Formulate a GP to determine the location (x,y) of the park nearest the four neighborhoods.

12. *Employee Scheduling.* Brooks Booles Bookstore is open from 8:00 A.M. to 8:00 P.M., with employees reporting to work at 8:00 A.M., 12:00 M. (noon), and 4:00 P.M. Part-time employees work only four-hour shifts, whereas full-time employees work eight-hour shifts. The hourly wage rates for part-time and full-time employees is $2.50 and $3.40, respectively. In addition, the other costs of employing a full-time person average $5 per eight-hour shift. Brooks Booles must determine how many part-time and how many full-time employees should report to work at the start of each shift. The employee schedule should satisfy the following goals in order of priority:

a. If possible, the total daily payroll should not exceed $115.

b. Three goals, each on second priority: Exactly two, three, and five employees should be on duty for shifts 8:00 A.M.–12:00 M. (noon), 12:00 M. (noon)–4:00 P.M., and 4:00 P.M.–8:00 P.M., respectively.

c. There should be at least twice as many full-time employees as part-time employees, to ensure stability and continuity in the store's operations (bookkeeping, inventory, number of assistant manager candidates, and so on).

d. To further public relations with the local university and school, at least three workers should be part time, since part-time help is typically recruited from the local school populations.

Formulate a GP to determine the optimal employee schedule.

14 INTEGER PROGRAMMING

CONTENTS

1. INTRODUCTORY CONCEPTS

In chapters 2 and 3, we discussed the topic of linear programming and made note of the divisibility assumption placed on the decision variables: It is possible for the solution of an LP to be noninteger. For example, the solution to a product mix problem may indicate that a company should produce 10.2 bicycles per day. An economic interpretation of such a result is that the company should *complete* production on ten bicycles per day and start production on an eleventh bicycle, completing 20 percent of the work required to finish the eleventh unit. There are several linear programming problems in which such an interpretation may not be feasible or desirable, as the examples in this chapter will illustrate.

The primary objectives of this chapter are: (1) to help you develop an appreciation for the difficulty in dealing with LPs when some or all decision variables are restricted to be integers, and (2) to train you in the skill of using integer variables for formulating special, realistic management science problems. There will be virtually no emphasis placed on the details of special-purpose solution methods for integer programs. You will learn how to formulate certain problems as integer programs, which could then be solved using canned integer computer programs.

Types of Integer Programs

An **integer linear program** or **integer program** (IP) is simply a linear program in which some or all of the decision variables are required to be integers.

If *all* the decision variables are restricted to integers, the problem is called a **pure integer program.** If only some of the variables are restricted to integers, the problem is a **mixed integer program** (MIP). If it is stipulated that an integer variable can only take on the values 0 or 1, such a variable is called a **binary variable,** or a **0–1 variable.** If all variables of a pure integer program are specified as 0–1 variables, the problem is a **0–1 integer program** (or binary integer program).

Solving Integer Programs

Integer programs are solved in practice by the use of canned computer programs. There are currently several commercial programs available, each of which is based on a special solution approach. Generally speaking, each such program is designed to handle a certain class of problems and is limited (far more than LP codes) in the size of program that can be solved efficiently. Much research and work is being done to develop better solution methods and computer programs for solving IPs.

Cutting-plane methods constitute one such class of solution procedures. Essentially these methods involve successively cutting away parts of the feasible linear programming solution space until only *integer* corner points remain. This procedure is conducted in such a way that the cutting-plane algorithm progresses toward the optimal integer solution. Cutting-plane methods have not had a good performance record in terms of efficiently solving IPs, and partly because of this, much work has been directed toward other methods, called **enumerative methods.**

An enumerative method is one that attempts to enumerate all possible integer solutions "intelligently." The methods are cleverly designed so that it is not necessary to actually list all possibilities but rather only the most promising ones until the optimal solution is reached. The term "branch-and-bound" refers to a general problem-solving method that can be applied to solve integer programs following the enumerative philosophy (Chapter 17).

Dynamic programming can also be used to solve certain IPs (Chapter 15). Some IPs have enough special structure so that specialized solution methods have been designed to produce efficiently an optimal solution. Two such types of problems are transportation problems (Chapter 4) and assignment problems (Chapter 5).

For solving two-variable problems, a simple graphical method can be used (Section 2 below). For larger problems, when the values of the decision variables are large, it is common practice to solve an LP and then simply round the result to an integer solution. However, there are difficulties associated with this approach, as demonstrated in the next section.

2. GRAPHICAL SOLUTION OF THE TWO-VARIABLE INTEGER PROGRAM

Waveco, Inc., manufactures two types of surfboards, model A and model B, having unit profits of \$60 and \$85, respectively. Two machines are required to manufacture these products. Model A requires nine hours on machine 1 and four hours on machine 2; model B requires three hours and six hours on machines 1 and 2, respectively. Due to major maintenance requirements

---

---

this week, machine 1 will only be available for twenty-seven hours and machine 2 will only be available for twenty-three hours. How many units of each of the two products should Waveco manufacture? This is a simple product-mix problem. The LP for this problem is given as follows:

Let x_1 = number of model A boards to make this week
  x_2 = number of B boards to make this week
Maximize $Z = 60x_1 + 85x_2$ (\$ profit this week)
Subject to:
(1) $9x_1 + 3x_2 \leq 27$ (machine-hours, machine 1)

(2) $4x_1 + 6x_2 \le 23$ (machine-hours, machine 2)
(3) $x_1, \quad x_2 \ge 0$ (nonnegativity)

This LP is solved graphically in Fig. 14.1. The solution is seen to be $x_1^* = 2.21$, $x_2^* = 2.36$, and $Z^* = \$332.20$.

The Effects of Rounding

Suppose it is specified that x_1 and x_2 must be positive integers. To see what happens if we attempt to round the LP solutions, we must consider four possibilities: (1) round x_1 up to 3 and x_2 up to 3, (2) round x_1 up to 3 and x_2 down to 2, (3) round x_1 down to 2 and x_2 up to 3, and (4) round x_1 down to 2 and x_2 down to 2.

The first combination (3, 3) violates both constraints (1) and (2) and therefore is *infeasible*. The second combination (3, 2) is also infeasible since it violates both constraints (1) and (2). The third possibility (2, 3) violates constraint (2) and therefore is infeasible. The last possibility (2, 2) is feasible and would yield a profit of $Z = 60(2) + 85(2) = \$290$.

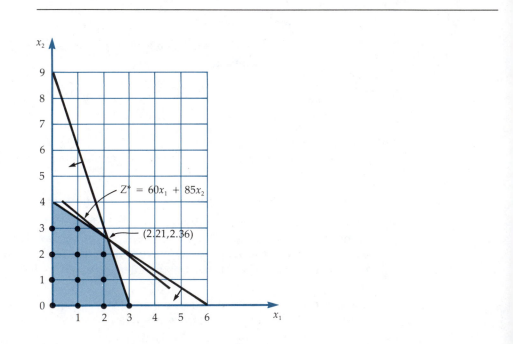

FIGURE 14.1

A Graphical Solution

In Fig. 14.1 we have marked each *feasible integer solution* by a heavy dot. Just as for a graphical LP, we move the Z line parallel to itself until it touches the northeast-most integer feasible solution, which is easily seen to be the point (1, 3) or $x_1^* = 1$, $x_2^* = 3$, and for which $Z^* = 60(1) + 85(3) = \$315$ (see Fig. 14.2).

Summary Observations

We first solved an LP that ignored the requirement that the optimal solution be integer valued. This yielded a maximum profit of $332.20.

Next we placed an additional constraint on the LP that made the problem an IP; namely, that x_1 and x_2 must be integers. To solve the IP we attempted to round the solutions obtained for the LP. In doing so we encountered three difficulties:

1. *Combinatorially*, we had to examine four possibilities. If the problem had involved ten decision variables, we would have had to consider as many as $2^{10} = 1{,}024$ possibilities, and for 20 decision variables, $2^{20} = 1{,}048{,}576$ possibilities.
2. *Infeasibility*. When LP solutions are rounded up or down to integer values, the resulting solution may not be a feasible solution to the problem. In our example three out of the four possibilities turned out to be infeasible.

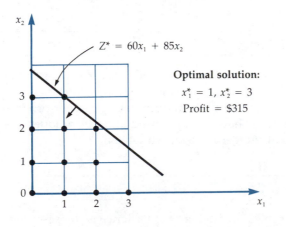

FIGURE 14.2   *Feasible integer solutions are represented by the heavy dots.*

Determining whether a possible solution is feasible requires checking to see whether *each* constraint is satisfied.

3. *Nonoptimality.* If an LP solution is rounded to an integer solution, and if the result is feasible, it still may not (in fact, *probably* will not) be optimal. For our example, the rounded solution (2, 2) gives a $290 profit, compared to the *optimal IP solution* (1, 3), which gives a $315 profit. Also note that the optimal solution $x_1^* = 1$ *could not have been obtained* by rounding the LP solution.

It is because of these difficulties that the special IP solution methods mentioned in Section 1 have been developed. (In Chapter 17, we solve the above problem using the branch-and-bound method.)

If an integer program is solved by rounding the solution to an LP, the result may be **infeasible** *or* **nonoptimal.**

Problems

We are given the following information on a problem: A furniture manufacturer makes two styles of dining tables. The manufacturer does not expect to sell more than three tables of style *A* or more than four tables of style *B* per week. This places upper limits on the production of tables *A* and *B*. In addition, each unit of table *A* requires five labor-hours and table *B* requires six labor-hours to produce. The profit on table *A* is $150, and the profit on table *B* is $225. The weekly labor-hour capacity is thirty hours.

1. Formulate the above problem as a linear program and determine the optimal product mix and weekly profit. Use the graphical solution method.
2. Round your solution in Problem 1 to a "best" integer solution.
3. Using the graphical method, solve the problem as an integer program.

3. APPLICATIONS: IP FORMULATION

In this section we shall present some classic problems that can be formulated and solved as integer programs. Our objective here is to give you an opportunity to develop skills in formulating integer programs and, specifically, to learn some of the standard formulation techniques that are made possible by the use of integer decision variables.

Cargo Loading—The Knapsack Problem

A classic problem in management science is the so-called **knapsack problem.** One version of this problem addresses the question of which items a hiker

FIGURE 14.3   *Cargo loading—a profit objective with weight and volume constraints.*

should include in his or her backpack in order to maximize the total "value" of the items to the hiker (in terms of survival value and comfort value). The hiker is limited by the amount of space in the pack and/or by the amount of weight that he or she can comfortably carry.

A practical management science version of the knapsack problem is the cargo-loading problem illustrated in the following example and in Fig. 14.3.

Littleton Trucking Co. must select which of four items to load in a semi-trailer truck to haul across country. The weight and volume capacities of the truck are 6 tons and 3,000 cubic feet, respectively. The weights, space requirements, and profits of each of the four products are given in Table 14.1.

Formulate an IP for the problem of determining which products to include in the shipment. The program we formulate will be a 0–1 IP. Define four decision variables by $x_i = 0$ if product i is *not* included in the shipment and

TABLE 14.1

	Product			
	1	2	3	4
Weight (tons)	2	2.2	1.1	2.5
Volume (cubic feet)	1,400	1,200	900	1,300
Profit ($)	2,900	3,500	2,000	3,700

$x_i = 1$ if product i is included. Then the IP is easily stated as follows:

Maximize $Z = 2{,}900x_1 + 3{,}500x_2 + 2{,}000x_3 + 3{,}700x_4$ ($ profit for the load)
Subject to:
(1) $2x_1 + 2.2x_2 + 1.1x_3 + 2.5x_4 \leq 6$ (weight)
(2) $1{,}400x_1 + 1{,}200x_2 + 900x_3 + 1{,}300x_4 \leq 3{,}000$ (volume)
(3) $x_1, \quad x_2, \quad x_3, \quad x_4 = 0 \text{ or } 1$

INTERDEPENDENCIES. Now suppose that if product 2 is included, it is required that product 3 also be included. That is, if $x_2 = 1$, then x_3 must also equal 1. (However, it is not required that product 2 be included if product 3 is included.) The following fourth constraint must then be included in the original IP:

$x_2 \leq x_3$ (or $x_2 - x_3 \leq 0$)

Thus if $x_2 = 1$, x_3 cannot be 0; therefore, x_3 must equal 1. However, it is possible for x_3 to equal 1 and x_2 to equal 0.

If products 2 and 3 must accompany *each other*, then we would have to include the constraint

$x_2 = x_3$ (or $x_2 - x_3 = 0$)

Then products 2 and 3 may both be excluded ($x_2 = x_3 = 0$) or both be included ($x_2 = x_3 = 1$).

"k-out-of-m" Constraints

It is easy in the 0–1 cargo-loading IP to handle the case where k out of m products must be included. For example, suppose it is stipulated that of products 1, 3, and 4, two must be included. The following constraint will force *exactly* two of the corresponding decision variables to equal 1:

$x_1 + x_3 + x_4 = 2$

(This is a "2-out-of-3" constraint.)

If a given problem requires that *at least* k out of m must hold, the above equality constraint is replaced by "$\geq$"; if the condition is stated as "at most k out of m" must hold, the constraint becomes "$\leq$."

EITHER-OR. Suppose it is stated that either product 1 or product 4 must be included in the shipment, but not both. This is a special case of "k-out-of-m"—namely, "1-out-of-2":

$x_1 + x_4 = 1$

This will force x_1 to be 1 and x_4 to be 0, or vice versa.

Warehouse Location

Tecktrex, Inc., a manufacturer of refrigerators, ships its product to three markets, M1, M2, and M3. In order to improve its operations, the company is planning to build two warehouses. Three sites are being considered for warehouse location. Warehouse construction costs (capital investment), capacity, and operating costs will vary, depending on the site selected. These variables are shown in Table 14.2.

The shipping costs between sites and markets are given in Table 14.3 (in dollars per refrigerator).

The monthly market demands are 500, 700, and 800 refrigerators, respectively, at M1, M2, and M3.

Which sites should be selected for warehouse location?

Solution. Let us first examine the constraints. It seems natural to begin by defining some decision variables that will indicate which sites are selected for warehouse location. This requires three 0–1 variables:

$$x_i = \begin{cases} 0 & \text{if site } i \text{ is } not \text{ selected} \\ 1 & \text{if site } i \text{ is selected} \end{cases} \quad (i = 1, 2, 3)$$

Since only two warehouses are to be built, our first constraint is

(1) $\qquad x_1 + x_2 + x_3 = 2$

Next we must ensure that, if a warehouse is built at a given site, the planned warehouse capacity is not exceeded. We must first define decision variables that will tell us how many refrigerators are to be shipped from each site to each market. Thus let Y_{ij} equal the number of refrigerators shipped per month from the warehouse located at site i to market j. This defines nine more decision variables, since $i = 1, 2, 3$ and $j = 1, 2, 3$.

The warehouse capacity constraints can then be written as follows:

(2) $\qquad Y_{11} + Y_{12} + Y_{13} \leq 1{,}000 x_1 \quad \text{(site 1)}$

(3) $\qquad Y_{21} + Y_{22} + Y_{23} \leq 900 x_2 \quad \text{(site 2)}$

(4) $\qquad Y_{31} + Y_{32} + Y_{33} \leq 1{,}500 x_3 \quad \text{(site 3)}$

TABLE 14.2

Site	Capital outlay for warehouse construction	Capacity (refrigerators)	Operating cost ($/ refrigerator/month)
1	$ 900,000	1,000	60
2	750,000	900	50
3	1,250,000	1,500	56

TABLE 14.3

		Market	
Site	M1	M2	M3
1	25	20	10
2	15	30	8
3	10	15	13

To see how these constraints work, consider constraint (1). The left side equals the total number of refrigerators shipped *from* site 1 to M1, M2, and M3. If a warehouse is built at site 1, then in the optimal IP solution, x_1 will equal 1, so contraint (1) becomes $Y_{11} + Y_{12} + Y_{13} \leq 1{,}000$. This will ensure that, whatever the optimal values of Y_{11}, Y_{12}, and Y_{13} are, their sum will not exceed the stated capacity of 1,000. On the other hand, if site 1 is not selected as a warehouse location, x_1 will equal 0 in the optimal IP solution and constraint (1) becomes $Y_{11} + Y_{12} + Y_{13} \leq 0$. Since the Y_{ij}s are nonnegative, this will *force* Y_{11}, Y_{12}, and Y_{13} to be 0. After all, products cannot be shipped from a warehouse that does not exist.

Since the demand of each market must be met, we need the following three monthly demand constraints:

(5) $Y_{11} + Y_{21} + Y_{31} = 500$ (M1)

(6) $Y_{12} + Y_{22} + Y_{32} = 700$ (M2)

(7) $Y_{13} + Y_{23} + Y_{33} = 800$ (M3)

The remaining task is to formulate the objective function, Z. It is clear that the criterion is to minimize total costs, so we must derive an algebraic expression for the total cost, Z, in terms of the decision variables. There are three cost categories involved: capital outlays for warehouse construction, operating costs, and shipping costs.

Consider site 1. The term $\$900{,}000x_1$ accounts for the capital outlay for warehouse construction at that site. If a warehouse is constructed at site 1, $x_1 = 1$, and the capital outlay would be $\$900{,}000(1) = \$900{,}000$; otherwise, $x_1 = 0$, and the capital outlay would be 0. This is an example of a **fixed-charge**, or **set-up, cost.**

The operating cost at site 1 is a variable cost and equals $60Y_{11} + 60Y_{12} + 60Y_{13}$, since the operating cost of a warehouse built at site 1 is $60 per refrigerator.

The other variable cost associated with site 1 is shipping cost, which can be expressed as $25Y_{11} + 20Y_{12} + 10Y_{13}$.

Refer to the discussion of constraint (1) above. We noted that if site 1 is *not* selected, then $x_1 = 0$, so the capital outlay $\$900{,}000x_1$ will also be 0; furthermore, if $x_1 = 0$, this would *force* $Y_{11} = Y_{12} = Y_{13} = 0$, so neither of the two variable costs (operating or shipping) will be incurred. Only when $x_1 = 1$ will the above three costs associated with site 1 be incurred.

To complete the expression for Z, we must include the three cost components for sites 2 and 3. Doing so gives the following objective function for the IP (check this):

$$\text{Minimize } Z = \$900,000x_1 +$$
$$\left.\begin{array}{l} 60Y_{11} + 60Y_{12} + 60Y_{13} + \\ 25Y_{11} + 20Y_{12} + 10Y_{13} + \end{array}\right\} \text{site 1}$$

$$\left.\begin{array}{l} \$750,000x_2 + \\ 50Y_{21} + 50Y_{22} + 50Y_{23} + \\ 15Y_{21} + 30Y_{22} + 8Y_{23} + \end{array}\right\} \text{site 2}$$

$$\left.\begin{array}{l} \$1,250,000x_3 + \\ 56Y_{31} + 56Y_{32} + 56Y_{33} + \\ 10Y_{31} + 15Y_{32} + 13Y_{33} \end{array}\right\} \text{site 3}$$

The complete formulation of the IP consists of:

1. The definition of the 0–1 decision variables $x_1, x_2, x_3 = 0$ or 1
2. The definition of the decision variables Y_{ij}, $i = 1, 2, 3$, $j = 1, 2, 3$, $Y_{ij} \geq 0$
3. Constraints (1) through (7)
4. The objective function, Z

The optimal solution of the IP will specify which two of the three variables x_1, x_2, and x_3 are equal to 1 (the remaining one being 0), and the optimal values of the Y_{ij}s. As a technical note, it is not *necessary* to specify that the Y_{ij}s must be integers, since it can be proved that in the optimal solution to the problem these variables will always turn out to be integers. Thus the above IP is a mixed integer program (MIP).

Machine Selection for a Product Mix Problem

Boltco, Inc., is planning monthly production of two major products, bolt B6A and fastener F7A. Profits per box of these two products are $30 and $20, respectively. It is desired that a whole number of boxes of each of these products be scheduled for production this month. Each of the products must be processed on machine 1, which has a monthly capacity of 300 hours. Product B6A requires 2 hours of time on machine 1, and product F7A requires 1.5 hours on machine 1.

In addition, each product must be processed on *either* machine 2 or machine 3 (but not on both). The monthly capacities are 200 hours and 350 hours for machines 2 and 3, respectively. Product B6A would require either 1.9 hours per box on machine 2 or 1.7 hours per box on machine 3. Product F7A would require either 1.7 hours per box on machine 2 or 1.8 hours per box on machine 3. The production manager will permit only one machine, either machine 2 or machine 3, to be operative during the month.

Determine the optimal product mix.

Solution. First, it is clear that we must define the decision variables x_1 and x_2:

Let x_1 = number of boxes of bolt B6A to be manufactured
   x_2 = number of boxes of fastener F7A to be manufactured
The IP can then be written as follows:
Maximize $Z = 30x_1 + 20x_2$ ($ profit this month)
Subject to:
(1) $2x_1 + 1.5x_2 \leq 300$ (machine-hour capacity, machine 1) and if machine 2 is used
   (a) $1.9x_1 + 1.7x_2 \leq 200$ (machine-hour capacity, machine 2)
      and if machine 3 is used instead of machine 2, constraint (a) would be replaced by
   (b) $1.7x_1 + 1.8x_2 \leq 350$ (machine-hour capacity, machine 3)

Finally, we require that $x_1 \geq 0$, $x_2 \geq 0$, and that both x_1 and x_2 are integers.

We are saying in effect that either constraint (a) or constraint (b) must hold, but not both. In order to handle this *mechanically* (for input to a canned computer program designed to solve IPs), the following "trick" is used. Let M denote a *very large* number. For our problem we might set $M = 100,000$ as part of a computer input. Define a 0–1 variable Y to be 0 if machine 2 is selected for use this month, and 1 if machine 3 is selected for use. Then instead of the single constraint, "either (a) or (b)," we use the following *two* constraints:

(2) $1.9x_1 + 1.7x_2 \leq 200 + MY$

(3) $1.7x_1 + 1.8x_2 \leq 350 + M(1 - Y)$

To see why this trick works to select exactly one of the machines 2 or 3, suppose $Y = 0$ in the solution to the IP. Then, the right side of (2) equals 200, indicating that machine 2 has a capacity of not more than 200 machine-hours. This will place realistic, practical limitations on x_1 and x_2. When $Y = 0$, the right side of (3) equals $350 + M$, a very large number, so large in fact that constraint (3) will have no limiting effect on x_1 and x_2. This means that if x_1 and x_2 are integers satisfying constraints (1) and (2), they will automatically satisfy (3). We say that constraint (3) becomes inactive when $Y = 0$. Similarly, $Y = 1$ corresponds to the selection of machine 3 instead of machine 2.

In summary, the IP consists of the definitions of the decision variables x_1, x_2, and Y, the objective function Z, constraints (1), (2), (3) together with the integer requirements on x_1 and x_2, and the requirement that Y is a 0–1 variable.

4. CONCLUDING REMARKS

In this chapter we have presented a brief introduction to integer programming. An integer program is a linear program in which some or all of the decision variables are restricted to integers. Integer programs are classified as pure integer or mixed integer.

One method of solving integer programs is to solve the associated linear program and then round the resulting solution to integer values. However this may result in a solution that is infeasible or nonoptimal. A two-variable IP can be solved graphically as in Section 2. If the IP contains more than two variables, other solution methods must be used, such as cutting-plane techniques or branch-and-bound methods (Chapter 17).

Section 3 demonstrates the great degree of flexibility that integer variables (0–1 variables) provide in formulating different types of management problems. Binary variables can be used to model (1) knapsack problems, (2) interdependencies, (3) "k out of m" choices, (4) "either-or" choices, and (5) fixed-charge, or set-up, costs.

Students interested in pursuing the study of integer programming further should consult Chapter 17 of this text as well as the references for this chapter in Appendix A.

TERMINOLOGY

After studying this chapter you should be familiar with the following terms:

TERM	SECTION
binary variable	1
cutting-plane methods	1
"either-or" constraints	3
enumerative methods	1
fixed-charge cost	3
integer linear program	1
integer program	1
knapsack problems	3
"k-out-of-m" constraints	3
mixed integer program (MIP)	1
pure integer program	1
set-up cost	3
0–1 integer program	1
0–1 variable	1

EXERCISES

1. *Capital Budgeting.* World Ventures, Inc., has $2 million to invest among seven projects. The initial capital outlays and expected profits (in current dollars) of the seven projects are given in the following table (outlays and profits are expressed in $ million):

Project	1	2	3	4	5	6	7
Outlay	0.5	0.2	0.7	0.4	0.6	1.1	0.3
Profit	2.5	1.5	5.5	3.0	4.5	7.0	2.4

   Formulate an IP to determine in which projects to invest.

2. *Capital Budgeting.* (Refer to Exercise 1 above.) Taking into consideration certain qualitative factors such as risk and management objectives, reformulate the World Ventures problem incorporating the following constraints:
   a. Either project 2 or project 4 must be selected but not both.
   b. At least two projects must be selected from the group 1, 2, 5, and 6.
   c. If project 7 is selected, project 1 must also be included.

3. *Sales-Display Design.* Superlook Cosmetics, a national cosmetics producer, must determine which of its ten top products to place on display in Marcel's Fashion Wear Shop. Marcel has made available a one × three × two-foot display area for Superlook's products. The profit per unit of the ten products and the space requirements are given in the table below. The space requirements are expressed in cubic feet and include additional surrounding space desirable for an attractive visual effect.

Product	1	2	3	4	5	6	7	8	9	10
Profit	$3	2	1	4	9	7	6	3	2	8
Space	0.5	0.6	0.4	1.0	1.2	1.7	1.5	0.4	0.3	2.1

   Formulate an IP to determine which products to include in the display in order to maximize the total profit potential of the displayed products.

4. *Sales Display.* (Refer to Exercise 3 above.) Reformulate the IP for the Superlook Cosmetics problem, incorporating the following considerations: Products 3 and 8 are matching cologne products for males and females. Either they must both be included or they must both be excluded. Product 9 nicely complements Product 1, so if Product 1 is included, Product 9 should be included. (Product 9 is a powder, and Product 1 is a bath soap.) Products 2, 4, 6, 8, and 10 are new products, and at least two of these should be displayed. Products 1 and 4 are similar, so it is not necessary to display both of them.

5. *Product Mix.* Abcom manufactures two products, A and B. Each product must be processed on two machines, M1 and M2. Product A requires 2 hours on M1 and 3 hours on M2; product B requires 1.7 hours on M1 and 3.1 hours on M2. Weekly capacities of M1 and M2 are 70 hours and

60 hours, respectively. Unit profits on *A* and *B* are $90 and $110, respectively. Formulate an IP to determine the optimal product mix. Solve graphically.

6. *Personal Investment Decisions.* Kristina has $1,200 to put into five investments: a rare coin priced at $500, a troy ounce of gold priced at $280, a block of uranium stock priced at $400, a bond priced at $250, and a share of stock priced at $200. The expected three-year returns (net of capital gains taxes, initial outlay, and transaction costs) of these investments are $110, $95, $120, $80, and $75, respectively.

   a. Formulate an IP to determine which investments to make.

   b. Solve the IP by trial and error (or "complete enumeration"). To do this, make a table listing all thirty-two possibilities (portfolios). Indicate which ones are feasible and compute the expected return for each feasible portfolio.

7. *Advertising—Media Selection.* The National Cancer Institute is planning an advertising campaign to raise funds for cancer research. It has $200,000 available for a one-month campaign. In addition it has access to 4,000 person-hours of volunteer-worker support (20 days × 2 hours per day × 100 people). Four advertising alternatives are being considered: television, radio, magazine, and direct mail. Each of these alternatives would reach different numbers of people, have different costs, and require different volunteer-worker support, as shown in Table 14.4.

   Formulate an IP to determine which media to utilize in order to maximize the total number of person-exposures to the fund-raising campaign.

8. *Health Care Facilities Location.* A western state is planning to design a system of medical clinics to serve ten small communities that currently have inadequate medical services. Five sites have been identified as potential locations for medical clinics. The map below (Fig. 14.4) shows these five sites (represented by the squares) and the ten communities. The branches indicate which communities could be adequately served by medical clinics located at the various sites. (The adequacy of medical service is determined by the population of the community, the distances

TABLE 14.4

Medium	Cost ($)	Worker person-hours	Person-exposures per medium
Television	70,000	1,000	8,000,000
Radio	60,000	1,500	3,000,000
Magazine	80,000	1,900	4,000,000
Direct mail	50,000	2,500	5,000,000

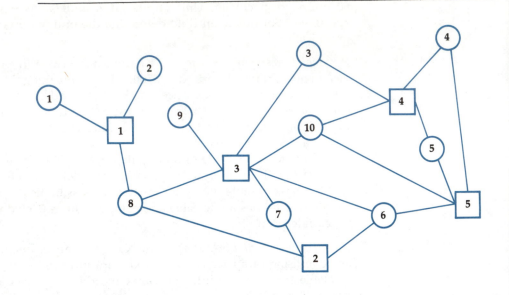

FIGURE 14.4

involved, and the quality of available transportation that connects the community to the site.) For example, community 8 could be adequately served by clinics located at sites 1, 2, and 3. Formulate an IP to determine the minimum number of clinics required to ensure that each community is served by *at least* one clinic. Can you solve this problem by trial and error?

9. *Service/Support Facility Location.*   Refer to Exercise 8 above. The application of the type of IP formulation given there is useful for locating other types of service/support facilities. Listed below are some areas of potential applications:

Military	Government services
Emergency services	Private enterprise
Political campaigning	Communications

State specific location/support/service problems in each of these general categories. (Think in terms of the network representation—nodes and branches—exemplified by the application of Exercise 8 above.)

10. *Capital Budgeting—A Multiperiod Model.*   TIA, Inc., is planning to invest $1 million this year and $750,000 next year in some highly experimental research and development projects. TIA has identified a list of five potential projects. These projects, their expected five-year net re-

TABLE 14.5

	Projects (in $ million)				
	1	2	3	4	5
Return	5	10	7	4	6
Outlay 1	0.50	0.30	0.40	0.10	0.25
Outlay 2	0.30	0.15	0.25	0.10	0.20

turns, and their required capital outlays in years 1 and 2, are given in Table 14.5.

a. Formulate an IP to determine which projects should be undertaken.

b. Modify the IP formulation in part (a) above to account for the stipulation that either project 1 or 4 must be selected.

11. *Equipment Selection—Medical Care.* A medical laboratory conducts a large number of blood tests of two special types, which we shall refer to as test 1 and test 2. Each of these tests must pass through two processes, $P1$ and $P2$. Two machines ($M1$ and $M2$) can be purchased to accomplish $P1$, and two machines ($M3$ and $M4$) can be purchased to accomplish $P2$. (It is only necessary to use one machine, either $M1$ or $M2$, for $P1$; and only one machine, either $M3$ or $M4$, for $P2$.) The processing times of each test on each of the machines is given below (in hours):

	Process $P1$		Process $P2$	
	$M1$	$M2$	$M3$	$M4$
Test 1	0.5	0.2	0.4	0.3
Test 2	0.6	0.3	0.5	0.2

The weekly machine-hour capacities of machines $M1$, $M2$, $M3$, and $M4$ are 140, 120, 150, and 110, respectively. Formulate an IP to determine which machines to purchase ($M1$ or $M2$?/$M3$ or $M4$?) in order to maximize the total number of tests that are conducted weekly.

12. *Plant Location.* Electro-Tronics, Inc., is planning to locate two manufacturing plants and has identified four potential plant sites. Electro-Tronics serves three markets, $M1$, $M2$, and $M3$. The construction costs, production costs ($/unit of product), shipping costs ($/unit of product), plant capacities at each site (units per month), and market demands (units per month) are given in Table 14.6.

TABLE 14.6

Site	Construction costs ($)	Production costs	Shipping costs			Plant capacity
			M1	M2	M3	
1	500,000	18	3	5	4	5,000
2	750,000	15	4	4	5	8,000
3	600,000	14	5	3	2	7,000
4	800,000	13	6	6	8	9,500
		Demand:	10,000	5,000	8,000	

Formulate an IP to determine which two sites should be selected for plant location and the corresponding optimal market distribution pattern. Note that this problem would apply to the case where the markets are replaced by warehouses. In this case the shipping costs would also include warehousing costs.

13. *Military Planning.* The Armed Forces are constructing alternative scenarios as part of their defense-preparedness planning. One particular scenario involves planning the sequences of counteroffensive actions that should be taken in response to a specified enemy attack. These reactions to the enemy attack are to be conducted in three phases. Various plans are available for each phase. These phases, the feasible plans for each phase, the cost of each plan (in dollars for military weapons, equipment, and supplies), and the expected damage caused to the enemy forces (in predefined "damage units") are given in Table 14.7, below:

TABLE 14.7

Phase	Action	Cost ($ million)	Damage
1	A	50	6
	B	40	3
	C	45	5
2	D	20	4
	E	25	5
3	F	35	4
	G	40	6
	H	60	8
	I	50	7

One action must be chosen for phase 1, one action for phase 2, and up to two actions can be combined for phase 3; however, if action F is used, action G (which is not compatible with action F) *cannot* be employed.

Formulate an IP to determine the maximum damage that can be produced, using a $120 million weapons budget.

15 DYNAMIC PROGRAMMING

1. INTRODUCTION

Dynamic programming is a general technique for solving problems involving a set of interrelated decisions in which the goal is to optimize overall effectiveness. This method is used to break larger problems down into smaller subproblems. The smaller problems are solved sequentially until the solution of the original problem is reached. In the process of solving the smaller subproblems, the decision maker uses the solutions to other subproblems already obtained at the previous stage. Thus the subproblems do not have to be solved "from scratch" but are solved by using previously solved subproblems.

Unfortunately, there is no single rule or procedure to follow in formulating a problem as a dynamic program. It is fair to say that every dynamic program is distinct; this makes it difficult both to teach and to learn dynamic programming. In fact, even the notation commonly used is a little difficult to get used to. However, all dynamic programs do share certain general properties that can be written in specific terms. Also, after a little practice you will be able to formulate dynamic programs with little difficulty.

In this chapter we shall proceed as follows: In Section 2, we shall present a fairly standard problem and then solve the problem, using the reasoning and method of dynamic programming; in the process, we shall refrain from using any of the notation or equations of dynamic programming. In Section 3, we shall introduce the general notions, definitions, and notation of dynamic programming, and indicate how it applies to the example problem. Then, in Sections 4 and 5, we shall illustrate the method of dynamic programming for other problems.

2. THE SHORTEST–PATH PROBLEM

Nancy and Jim Wheeler own and operate an independent trucking company. Recently they contracted to deliver a product for a local manufacturer, based in Caberville, to the city of Pinbolle. A map showing Caberville and Pinbolle is given in Fig. 15.1. The diagram shown is referred to as a **network.** The circles are **nodes** and represent cities. Node 1 represents Caberville, and node 9 represents Pinbolle. The line segments connecting the nodes are called **branches** and represent travel routes between the cities. The arrows indicate the direction of travel. The distances along these routes are given by the numbers placed on the branches. The problem is to determine the travel route from node 1 to node 9 having a minimum total distance. A **path** connecting two nodes in a network is a sequence of branches starting at one

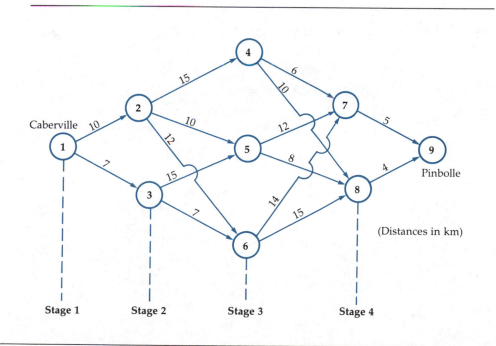

FIGURE 15.1   *The shortest-path problem.*

node and terminating at the second node. Thus our problem is to find the **shortest path,** starting at the initial node (node 1) and ending at the terminal node (node 9). There are two immediate approaches that you may be thinking will solve this problem:

1. A "myopic" approach—that is, simply selecting the shortest route at each node going from left to right. If we do this we get the route 1–3–6–7–9 having a total length of $7 + 7 + 14 + 5 = 33$. But, as we shall see, the optimal solution to the problem has a travel distance of 32. Thus the myopic approach will not work. Can you provide logical reasons why the myopic procedure fails for shortest-path problems?
2. An enumeration approach—that is, simply listing all possible routes as shown in Table 15.1 and then selecting the shortest one. This is not a very appealing method. Imagine a more realistic network, having, say, twenty nodes. Also, we had to calculate the subroute 5–7–9 *twice* (in routes 1–2–5–7–9 and 1–3–5–7–9). The same is true for the subroutes 5–8–9, 6–7–9, and 6–8–9. It would be nice to avoid these duplicate calculations.

APPLICATIONS

The following applications appear in this chapter in text, examples, or problems:

Activity planning

Advertising mix

Automobile replacement

Cargo loading

Cutting stock problems

TABLE 15.1

Route	Distance
1–2–4–7–9	36
1–2–4–8–9	39
1–2–5–7–9	37
1–2–5–8–9	32 ← Optimal
1–2–6–7–9	41
1–2–6–8–9	41
1–3–5–7–9	39
1–3–5–8–9	34
1–3–6–7–9	33
1–3–6–8–9	33

Discounted dynamic programming
Equipment replacement
Inventory planning
Investment planning
Job shop planning
Knapsack problem
Mining operations
Oil pipeline layout
Personnel assignments
Police patrol assignments
Procurement planning
Product distribution
Production planning
Resource allocation
Shortest-path problem: travel routes
Transporting raw materials
Wagner-Whitin inventory model

Another very important point to note is this: *Starting at node 5,* the shortest route to node 9 is 5–8–9, having a distance of twelve. You will note that 5–8–9 is part of the optimal route, 1–2–5–8–9. Thus once we find ourselves at node 5, the shortest-path *subproblem* of getting to node 9 is solved by 5–8–9; however, our enumeration process completely ignores this useful fact. For example, we evaluated the route 1–3–5–7–9. In doing so, we took a *nonoptimal* route from 5 to 9. You will see that the dynamic programming method will not make these mistakes.

The Dynamic Programming Solution

You will note in Fig. 15.1 that we have organized the nodes into **stages.** The stage 4 nodes are one branch away from the destination, node 9; the stage 3 nodes are two branches away from node 9; the stage 2 nodes are three branches away; and the stage 1 node, node 1, is four branches away from node 9. We shall solve the shortest-path problem by solving stages 4, 3, 2, and 1 *in that order*. Each of these steps will be viewed as a shortest-path *subproblem*. The nodes at each stage will be referred to as **states.** For example, the two states at stage 2 are nodes 2 and 3. The possible choices we can make in each state will be called *decisions*. Thus in state 2 (node 2) there are three possible decisions corresponding to selecting branch 2–4, 2–5, or 2–6. We shall denote these three decisions by the destination node selected; that is, selecting branch 2–4 corresponds to the decision "4," selecting 2–5 corresponds to decision "5," and selecting 2–6 corresponds to decision "6." The dynamic programming solution proceeds as follows:

Stage 4. We begin with stage 4 and solve two shortest-path subproblems. By starting with stage 4, we are solving the problem in a backward direction, working toward stage 1.

At stage 4, suppose we are in state 7. The subproblem we wish to solve is: *Starting* at node 7, what decision should we make in order to minimize the length of the path to node 9? Of course the solution is clear because we have only one choice—namely, to take branch 7–9. Similarly, the shortest path from node 8 to node 9 has a length of 4 km, and the optimal decision in state 8 is to take branch 8–9.

We summarize this analysis at stage 4 in Table 15.2.

Stage 3. We now move back to stage 3 and solve three shortest-path subproblems: *Starting* in states 4, 5, or 6, what is the shortest path to node 9?

Starting in state 4, we have two available decisions. If the decision is to take branch 4–7, the immediate distance is 6 km. The *minimum* path from node 7 to node 9 is given in the *above table for stage* 4 as 5 km. Adding these distances gives 11 km and represents the best we can do *if* we are at node 4 and *if* we select branch 4–7. Similarly, if we select branch 4–8, the total distance to node 9 is 10 km plus the *minimum* distance from node 8 to node 9 (4 km), for a total of 14 km. The optimal decision in stage 3 if the state is 4 would be to select branch 4–7, or "go to node 7."

Starting in state 5, the two decision alternatives are either branch 5–7, which has a total distance of $12 + 5 = 17$ km, or branch 5–8, which has a total distance of $8 + 4 = 12$ km. Thus the optimal decision would be to take branch 5–8, or "go to node 8."

Starting in state 6, the two choices are 6–7 with a distance of $14 + 5 = 19$ or 6–8 with a distance of $15 + 4 = 19$. Thus either choice is optimal.

Note that to solve the subproblems at stage 3, we used the solutions to the subproblems at stage 4. Table 15.3 summarizes the results. The two *decisions* "7" and "8" mean "go to node 7" and "go to node 8," respectively.

TABLE 15.2   *Stage 4*

State	Decisions	Optimal decision	Minimum path length to node 9 (km)
	9		
7	5	9	5
8	4	9	4

TABLE 15.3   *Stage 3*

State	Decisions		Optimal decision	Minimum path length to node 9 (km)
	7	8		
4	11	14	7	11
5	17	12	8	12
6	19	19	7 or 8	19

Stage 2. We move back to stage 2 and solve two shortest-path subproblems.

Starting in state 2, we shall solve the shortest-path problem of getting to node 9. We have three immediate decision alternatives: go to nodes 4, 5, or 6. If the decision is node 4, the total distance to node 9 would be

(Distance from 2 to 4) + (Shortest distance from 4 to 9)

The distance from node 2 to node 4 is found on branch 2–4 to be 15 km. The shortest distance from 4 to 9 is itself a shortest-path problem that we have already solved in stage 3. Looking at the table for the stage 3 results (Table 15.3), we see that, when the state is 4, the minimum path length to node 9 is 11 km. Adding these two numbers gives $15 + 11 = 26$ km. Similarly, if the decision is to go from node 2 to node 5, the total distance would be $10 + 12 = 22$ km. (The distance from 2 to 5 is 10 km, and from Table 15.3, the minimum distance from node 5 to node 9 is 12 km.) Finally, if we go from node 2 to node 6, the total distance would be $12 + 19 = 31$ km. Thus if we find ourselves in state 2 (that is, at node 2), the best decision to make is to go to node 5.

Still working at stage 2, we must now solve the shortest-path problem *starting* at node 3. There are two decision alternatives. If we go to node 5, the total distance would be $15 + 12 = 27$ km; if we decide to go to node 6 from node 3, the total distance would be $7 + 19 = 26$ km. Thus *starting* in state 3, the best decision would be to go to node 6.

Table 15.4 on page 556 summarizes these calculations.

Stage 1. Finally, we move back to stage 1 and solve the shortest-path problem of how best to travel from node 1 to node 9, the *original* problem facing Nancy and Jim Wheeler. The procedure used at this stage is the same as that used at the other stages.

Starting in state 1, we have two decision alternatives. If we go to node 2, the distance is 10 km (from 1 to 2) plus the shortest path from 2 to 9. The subproblem of getting from 2 to 9 was solved at stage 2 above, and from Table 15.4 we see that the shortest distance from 2 to 9 is 22 km. Thus the

TABLE 15.4   *Stage 2*

| | Decisions | | | Optimal | Minimum path length to |
State	4	5	6	decision	node 9 (km)
2	26	22	31	5	22
3	—	27	26	6	26

TABLE 15.5   *Stage 1*

| | Decisions | | Optimal | Minimum path length to |
State	2	3	decision	node 9 (km)
1	32	33	2	32

best distance traveled, if we go from node 1 to node 2, would be 10 + 22 = 32 km. Similarly, if we decide to go from node 1 to node 3, the best total distance to node 9 would be 7 + 26 = 33. Thus starting at node 1, we would first decide to go to node 2. These results are summarized in Table 15.5.

Reading the Optimal Solution from the Tables. We have now solved the Wheeler problem: the minimum distance from node 1 to node 9 is 32 km, as shown in Table 15.5. Tables 15.2 to 15.5 also indicate the route to take (in the "optimal decision" column): First go to node 2.

Now, *starting* at node 2, what do we do? This question is answered in Table 15.4. Node 2 corresponds to state 2 (in dynamic programming terminology), so we look at the first line of the table. The "optimal decision column" indicates that when in state 2 we should next go to node 5.

Starting at node 5, Table 15.3 indicates the optimal decision for state 5 is to go to node 8.

Then, *starting* at node 8, Table 15.2 indicates the optimal decision for state 8 is to go to node 9 (the only choice).

Thus the optimal travel route is 1–2–5–8–9, with a path length of 32 km (see Fig. 15.2).

3. GENERAL DYNAMIC PROGRAMMING CONCEPTS AND NOTATION

In general, dynamic programming is useful for solving problems involving **interrelated decisions.** In the shortest-path problem, if we make the decision

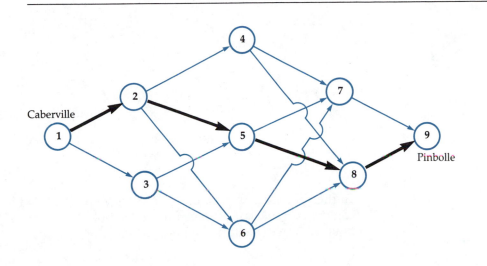

FIGURE 15.2   *Shortest path 1–2–5–8–9, 32 km.*

to take branch 1–3 at node 1, this will affect subsequent decisions that we
make; for example, we could not then take branch 4–8 to get to node 8.

Stages

To formulate the dynamic program for a given problem, we first identify
stages of the decision process. Let us say we have n stages and label them
1, 2, 3, ... , $n - 1$, n. Stages may correspond to geometric stages (as in the
shortest-path problem, where stages were identified by the distance away
from node 9 as measured by the number of branches to node 9); stages may
be related to time periods; or may be determined by some other criterion
that depends in a particular way on the specific problem. If the notion of
stages seems somewhat vague to you, you are doing fine. Identifying how
to divide a problem into stages is more an art than a science, and only practice will help you understand this notion more clearly. In the meantime,
simply refer back to the shortest-path problem of Section 2.

States

A set of *states* must be identified at each stage. A *state* describes the status
of the system being analyzed and contains all the information necessary to
make decisions.

TABLE 15.6

Stages	States: current location (node)
4	7, 8
3	4, 5, 6
2	2, 3
1	1

In the shortest-path problem, the states were identified as shown in Table 15.6. The current state at stage i will be denoted by s_i. Thus if we are at node 5 at stage 3, we would write $s_3 = 5$.

Decisions

We denote a *decision* at stage i by d_i. For example, at stage 3, if the state is 5, d_3 may equal 7 or 8 ("go to node 7" or "go to node 8"). Typically, the set of available decisions will depend on the state. For example, at stage 2 in the shortest-path problem, if the state is 2, d_2 may equal 4, 5, or 6; however, if the state is 3, d_2 may equal either 5 or 6.

Return Functions

The measure of effectiveness will be denoted by a function, f, which may be cost, profit, distance (as in the shortest-path problem), or some other measure. The function f is called the **return function.**

The return function, using decision d_i in state s_i at stage i and *then proceeding optimally at stage $i + 1$*, will be written $f_i(s_i, d_i)$. An optimal decision at stage i in state s_i will be written d_i^*, and is the decision that minimizes or maximizes $f_i(s_i, d_i)$. The optimal value of f_i will then be written $f_i^*(s_i)$. Thus for the shortest-path problem, we write

$$f_i^*(s_i) = \min f_i(s_i, d_i)$$

where f_i^* is called the **optimal return function.**

For example, at stage 2 of the shortest path problem, if the state is 2, we would write $i = 2$, $s_i = 2$, and

$$f_2^*(2) = \min_{d_2} f_2(2, d_2)$$

$$= \min \{f_2(2,4),\ f_2(2,5),\ f_2(2,6)\}$$

$$= \min \{26, 22, 31\} \text{(corresponding to } d_2 = 4, 5, \text{ or } 6)$$

$$= 22, \text{ with } d_2^* = 5$$

In words this says that if the state is 2 at stage 2, the *optimal return* (that is, minimum path length from node 2 to node 9) equals 22 and is obtained using the (optimal) decision $d_2^* = 5$ ("go to node 5"). Note that $f_2(2, d_2)$ equals the path length from node 2 to node 9 if decision d_2 is made at node 2, and then the optimal decision is made at node d_2 of stage 3. Similarly, if the state is 3 at stage 2,

$$f_2^*(3) = \min_{d_2} f_2(3, d_2)$$

$$= \min \{f_2(3,5), \ f_2(3,6)\}$$

$$= \min \{27, 26\}$$

$$= 26, \text{ with } d_2^* = 6$$

Recursions

A **recursion** is an equation that expresses a function in terms of itself. For example, in the shortest-path problem we view f^* as a function—the optimal return "operator." In the example above for state 2 at stage 2, we wrote

$$f_2^*(2) = \min_{d_2} f_2(2, d_2)$$

Note that $f_2(2, d_2)$ is composed of two parts, the immediate distance from node 2 to node d_2, *plus* the shortest distance from node d_2 to node 9. Let us define $D(2, d_2)$ to be the immediate distance from node 2 to node d_2. Then we can write

$$f_2^*(2) = \min_{d_2} f_2(2, d_2)$$

$$= \min_{d_2} \{D(2, d_2) + f_3^*(d_2)\}$$

Ignoring the subscripts, we have defined f^* in terms of itself, since f^* appears on both sides of the equal sign. Thus the above equation is a recursion. The general recursion for the shortest-path problem is

$$f_i^*(s_i) = \min_{d_i} \{D(s_i, d_i) + f_{i+1}^*(d_i)\} \tag{15–1}$$

where $i = 1, 2, \text{ or } 3$. Every dynamic program can be expressed by a recursion involving an optimal return function f^*.

Principle of Optimality: Optimal Policies

A general principle that applies to dynamic programs is the **principle of optimality.** This principle states that the optimal decisions for stage i are independent of the decisions employed at stage $i - 1$ *given* the current state at stage i. For example, in the shortest-path problem the optimal decision, given state 5 at stage 3, does not depend on the decisions we make at stage 2. Or to put it yet another way, the best way to get from node 5 to node 9, *once we find ourselves at node 5,* does not depend on how we got to node 5.

An **optimal policy** is a rule that states which decisions should be made at each stage in order to minimize or maximize f_1^*. The optimal policy for the shortest-path problem can be stated as follows:

Stage 1   Given state 1, $d_1^* = 2$ ("go to node 2").

Stage 2   Given state 2, $d_2^* = 5$ ("go to node 5").

Stage 3   Given state 5, $d_3^* = 8$ ("go to node 8").

Stage 4   Given state 8, $d_4^* = 9$ ("go to node 9").

This policy will minimize the length of the path from node 1 to node 9—that is, will yield the result $f_1^*(1)$.

Application to the Shortest-Path Problem

How did we use the principle of optimality in solving the dynamic programming recursion, Eq. (15–1), for the shortest-path problem? Let us describe the solution method in terms of the definitions and notations introduced in this section.

We proceeded "backwards," solving subproblems at stages 4, 3, 2, and 1, in that order. To solve stage 3 subproblems, we used the results obtained at stage 4; to solve stage 2 subproblems, we used stage 3 results; finally, to solve stage 1 subproblems, we used stage 2 results. The goal is to find $f_1^*(1)$, the minimum path length from node 1 to node 9.

Stage 4. If we define f_5^* to be identically 0, and use the fact that the only possible decision in stage 4 is $d_4 = 9$, Eq. 15–1 becomes

$$f_4^*(7) = \min_{d_4} D(7, d_4) = \min D(7, 9) = 5$$

$$f_4^*(8) = \min_{d_4} D(8, d_4) = \min D(8, 9) = 4$$

See Table 15.7(a). Compare to Table 15.2, Section 2.

Stage 3. We must solve three shortest-path subproblems: Find the shortest paths from nodes 4, 5, and 6 to node 9; that is, compute $f_3^*(4)$, $f_3^*(5)$, and

TABLE 15.7(a)   *The Shortest-Path Problem:*
                   Stage 4

s_4	$f_4(s_4, d_4)$ d_4 9	d_4^*	$f_4^*(s_4)$
7	5	9	5
8	4	9	4

$f_3^*(6)$ and find the corresponding optimal decisions $d_3^*(4)$, $d_3^*(5)$, and $d_3^*(6)$. The *principle of optimality* states that we can solve these problems independent of the solutions to stage 2 subproblems; that is, the shortest paths from nodes 4, 5, or 6 to node 9 do not depend on what we did in stage 2 to get to these nodes. This principle obviously applies to the shortest-path problem. Thus Eq. (15–1) becomes

$$f_3^*(s_3) = \min_{d_3} \{D(s_3, d_3) + f_4^*(d_3)\}$$

For state 4, $s_3 = 4$, and we have

$$f_3^*(4) = \min \begin{cases} D(4, 7) + f_4^*(7) & d_3 = 7 \\ D(4, 8) + f_4^*(8) & d_3 = 8 \end{cases}$$

$$= \min \begin{cases} 6 + 5 \ (= 11) & d_3 = 7 \\ 10 + 4 \ (= 14) & d_3 = 8 \end{cases}$$

$$= 11 \text{ with } d_3^* = 7$$

The values of $f_4^*(7)$ and $f_4^*(8)$ were obtained from Table 15.7(a). Note how we are using the solutions to the previous stage to solve the problem at the current stage. These results are summarized for $s_3 = 4$ in the first line of Table 15.7(b). Similarly, if $s_3 = 5$, we have

$$f_3^*(5) = \min \begin{cases} D(5, 7) + f_4^*(7) & d_3 = 7 \\ D(5, 8) + f_4^*(8) & d_3 = 8 \end{cases}$$

$$= \min \begin{cases} 12 + 5 \ (= 17) & d_3 = 7 \\ 8 + 4 \ (= 12) & d_3 = 8 \end{cases}$$

$$= 12 \text{ with } d_3^* = 8 \text{ [see line 2, Table 15.7(b)]}$$

Finally, if $s_3 = 6$, then

$$f_3^*(6) = \min \begin{cases} D(6, 7) + f_4^*(7) & d_3 = 7 \\ D(6, 8) + f_4^*(8) & d_3 = 8 \end{cases}$$

TABLE 15.7(b)   *Stage 3*

s_3	$f_3(s_3, d_3)$		d_3^*	$d_3^*(s_3)$
	d_3			
	7	8		
4	11	14	7	11
5	17	12	8	12
6	19	19	7 or 8	19

$$= \min \begin{cases} 14 + 5 \,(= 19) & d_3 = 7 \\ 15 + 4 \,(= 19) & d_3 = 8 \end{cases}$$

$$= 19 \text{ with } d_3^* = 7 \text{ or } 8 \text{ (a tie) [see line 3, Table 15.7(b)]}$$

Stage 2. We now solve two shortest-path subproblems at stage 2: Find $f_2^*(2)$ and $f_2^*(3)$ and corresponding optimal decisions $d_2^*(2)$ and $d_2^*(3)$. In doing so, we use the results of stage 3 for the values of f_3^* in Table 15.7(b). Also, from the principle of optimality, we are not concerned with *how we get to* nodes 2 or 3 from stage 1.

For state 2, Eq. (15–1) becomes

$$f_2^*(2) = \min \begin{cases} D(2, 4) + f_3^*(4) & d_2 = 4 \\ D(2, 5) + f_3^*(5) & d_2 = 5 \\ D(2, 6) + f_3^*(6) & d_2 = 6 \end{cases}$$

$$= \min \begin{cases} 15 + 11 \,(= 26) & d_2 = 4 \\ 10 + 12 \,(= 22) & d_2 = 5 \\ 12 + 19 \,(= 31) & d_2 = 6 \end{cases}$$

$$= 22 \text{ with } d_2^* = 5 \text{ [see line 1, Table 15.7(c)]}$$

TABLE 15.7(c)   *Stage 2*

s_2	$f_2(s_2, d_2)$			d_2^*	$f_2^*(s_2)$
	d_2				
	4	5	6		
2	26	22	31	5	22
3	—	27	26	6	26

For state 3, we have

$$f_2^*(3) = \min \begin{cases} D(3, 5) + f_3^*(5) & d_2 = 5 \\ D(3, 6) + f_3^*(6) & d_2 = 6 \end{cases}$$

$$= \min \begin{cases} 15 + 12 \, (= 27) & d_2 = 5 \\ 7 + 19 \, (= 26) & d_2 = 6 \end{cases}$$

$$= 26 \text{ with } d_2^* = 6 \text{ [see line 2, Table 15.7(c)]}$$

Stage 1. We now solve the shortest-path problem at stage 1: Find $f_1^*(1)$ and the corresponding optimal decision, $d_1^*(1)$. Note that this will then solve the original shortest-path problem, since $f_1^*(1)$ equals (by definition) the minimum path length from node 1 to node 9. At this stage, we use the results at stage 2 for the values of f_2^* in Table 15.7(c).

We have from Eq. (15–1)

$$f_1^*(1) = \min \begin{cases} D(1, 2) + f_2^*(2) & d_1 = 2 \\ D(1, 3) + f_2^*(3) & d_1 = 3 \end{cases}$$

$$= \min \begin{cases} 10 + 22 \, (= 32) & d_1 = 2 \\ 7 + 26 \, (= 33) & d_1 = 3 \end{cases}$$

$$= 32 \text{ with } d_1^* = 2 \text{ [see Table 15.7(d)]}$$

The Optimal Policy. Thus the minimum path length from node 1 to node 9 is 32 km, and the optimal policy is read from Table 15.7(a–d): Go from node 1 to node 2, then to node 5, then to node 8, and finally to node 9.

The Nature of Stage Transitions

The nature or "dynamics" of stage transitions can be represented by the diagram in Figure 15.3. At stage i, we are *given* state s_i as an *input*. A decision d_i is made. Then two things occur. First, we incur an immediate cost $C(s_i, d_i)$, which depends both on state s_i and decision d_i. Second, as a result of

TABLE 15.7(d)

s_1	$f_1(s_1, d_1)$		d_1^*	$f_1^*(s_1)$
	d_1			
	2	3		
1	32	33	2	32

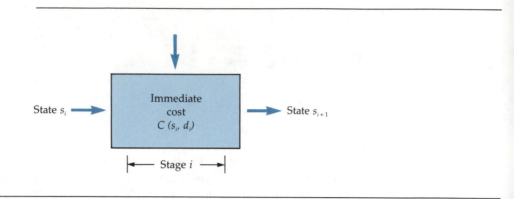

FIGURE 15.3

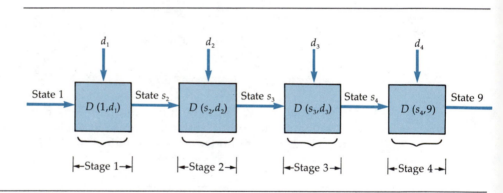

FIGURE 15.4   *A dynamic representation of the shortest-path problem.*

the decision d_i given state s_i, the system moves to a new state s_{i+1}, which is an *output* of stage i and becomes an input to stage $i + 1$.

A dynamic state diagram for the shortest-path problem is given in Fig. 15.4. The objective of that problem is to select the sequence of decisions, d_1, d_2, d_3, and d_4, to minimize the sum of the distances $D(s_i, d_i)$.

A Summary of the Dynamic Programming Method

The dynamic programming method is based on the principle of optimality. In order to formulate a problem as a dynamic program, the following steps are required.

1. Identify stages of the decision process and states of the system at each stage. The states should be defined in such a way that they contain sufficient information about the system so that the principle of optimality can be applied to solve the problem by working backward through the stages.
2. Define the objective function of the problem (minimize distance, minimize cost, maximize profit, and so on). This will define the return functions $f_i(s_i, d_i)$ and $f_i^*(s_i)$. Write a recursion involving the f_i^*.
3. Solve the recursion, starting with f_n^* and solving for $f_n^*, f_{n-1}^*, \ldots, f_2^*$, and f_1^* (for an n stage problem). The solution to the problem is then given by f_1^*. Tables such as those used for the shortest-path problem (Table 15.7) are useful in solving the recursion.

At this point we suggest that you review Sections 2 and 3. Make certain you understand the process of deriving the recursion, Eq. (15–1), for the dynamic program that solves the shortest path problem.

4. RESOURCE ALLOCATION PROBLEMS

Many management science problems can be viewed as resource allocation problems. That is, there is a fixed amount of resource(s) available to allocate among several activities or projects. The objective is to allocate the limited resources to the activities in order to optimize an overall measure of effectiveness. A list of such problems is presented below. The dynamic programs for these problems are very similar to each other in form.

1. THE KNAPSACK PROBLEM. This is a classic problem in operations research. A basic form of the problem can be stated as follows: A hiker carries a pack having a limited space (volume) capacity in which she or he will pack certain hiking or camping items. Each item has associated with it a "value" to the hiker. The problem is to determine how many units of each item to carry in the pack in order to maximize total value. Here the limited resource is space, that is, the number of cubic centimeters in the pack. Many resource allocation problems can be viewed as special cases or variations of the knapsack problem.
2. INVESTMENT PLANNING. Given a list of securities (stocks, bonds, and other investment alternatives) and a fixed budget for investment, how should the budget be allocated in order to maximize yearly return or net present value? The limited resource is the amount of money in the budget.
3. PERSONNEL ASSIGNMENTS. Suppose there are n people available for assignment to m projects. How many people should be assigned to each project in order to maximize the total profit from the projects? The limited resource is the group of people available for assignment. The return from each project depends on how many people are assigned to it. This return may be an expected return (in a probabilistic sense). Research and development problems (assigning technical personnel to research projects), sales

territory problems (assigning salespeople to territories), and political campaign problems (assigning campaign workers to political regions such as states or precincts) are examples of problems that fall into this category.

4. ADVERTISING EFFECTIVENESS. How should an advertising budget be allocated to several media to maximize the number of persons exposed to a product in a given time span? Again, the limited resource is the amount of money in the budget.

5. PRODUCT DISTRIBUTION. Suppose a company has n units of product to distribute to m markets to be sold. The sales potentials of the m markets differ from each other. How should the company distribute (allocate) its product to the markets in order to maximize total profit on the lot of n units? The limited resource in this example is the finite quantity of n items to be sold.

6. CUTTING STOCK PROBLEMS. Suppose a lumber company stocks precut lengths of 10-in. pine boards in its home improvement center. The company purchases the boards in lengths of 16 ft. and 20 ft. and cuts lengths of 3 ft., 4 ft., 6 ft., 8 ft., and 12 ft. that sell for various prices (not necessarily in the same direct proportion to length). How should the 16-ft. and 20-ft. boards be cut for store display in order to maximize total profit per 16-ft. and 20-ft. board? For a 16-ft. (20-ft.) board, the "limited resource" is the 16 ft. (20 ft.) of board; this resource is to be "allocated" to the five products.

Investment Planning

To illustrate the dynamic programming formulation of resource allocation problems, suppose you have $1,000 to invest in bonds, rare coins, and antiques. Investments in these categories must be made in multiples of $200, $250, and $320, respectively. The average annual return on each such purchase would be $20 per bond, $35 per lot of rare coins, and $56 per antique purchase. How should you invest the $1,000 to maximize average annual return?

Solution. We formulate the problem as a three-stage dynamic program. At stage 3, we decide how many $320 antique purchases to make; at stage 2, we decide how many $250 lots of rare coins to purchase; and at stage 1, we decide how many bonds to purchase. The state s_i is defined as the amount of money left for investment at the beginning of stage i.

Define $f_i(s_i, d_i)$ to be the total return earned from stage i to stage 3 if we begin stage i with s_i dollars, purchase d_i investments at stage i, and then proceed to invest optimally at stage $i + 1$. The optimal decision at stage i is d_i^* and $f_i^*(s_i)$ equals the maximum return from stage i to stage 3 starting with s_i dollars. We define f_4^* to be 0. Our goal is to compute $f_1^*(1,000)$. We shall define the recursions as we proceed to examine each stage, starting with stage 3.

Stage 3. If we begin each stage 3 with s_3 dollars, how much should be invested in antiques to maximize our yearly return? Since stage 3 is the last stage of the dynamic program, we would invest as much as possible in antiques. Since each antique purchase costs \$320, we need to consider the following ranges of the stage variables s_3: $0 \leq s_3 < 320$; $320 \leq s_3 < 640$; $640 \leq s_3 < 960$; and $960 \leq s_3 \leq 1{,}000$. Corresponding to these four ranges, the feasible values for the decision d_3 are: 0 for the first range; 0 or 1 for the second range; 0, 1, or 2 for the third range; and 0, 1, 2, or 3 for the fourth range.

Table 15.8 presents the results of computing f_3 and f_3^*. Here we have $f_3(s_3, d_3) = \$56 d_3 + f_4^*(s_3 - 320 d_3)$. The first term, $56 d_3$, is the return from purchasing d_3 lots of antiques. Since each lot costs \$320, this would cost $320 d_3$ dollars, leaving $s_3 - 320 d_3$ dollars to spend. But since stage 3 is the last stage, there is nothing left in which to invest the remaining $s_3 - 320 d_3$ dollars. This is why we defined f_4^* to be 0. Thus $f_3(s_3, d_3) = 56 d_3$.

The optimal return function is

$$f_3^*(s_3) = \max \{f_3(s_3, d_3): \text{all feasible } d_3\}$$

$$= \max \{56 d_3: \text{all feasible } d_3\}$$

The sets of feasible decisions d_3 were defined above for various ranges of s_3. We note that the integer d_3 must satisfy $0 \leq d_3 \leq s_3/320$.

Stage 2. If we begin stage 2 with s_2 dollars, how much should be invested in rare coins to maximize our yearly return over stages 2 and 3?

Here we have $f_2(s_2, d_2) = 35 d_2 + f_3^*(s_2 - 250 d_2)$, where $35 d_2$ is the return on the purchase of d_2 lots of rare coins. Starting with s_2 dollars, this would leave $s_2 - 250 d_2$ dollars to invest in antiques. Thus $f_3^*(s_2 - 250 d_2)$ represents the optimal return from antique purchases at stage 3, starting with $s_2 - 250 d_2$ dollars. This is shown in Table 15.8(a).

TABLE 15.8(a)   *Stage 3   Antiques*

| | $f_3(s_3, d_3)$ | | | | | |
| | d_3 | | | | | |
s_3	0	1	2	3	d_3^*	$f_3^*(s_3)$
$0 \leq s_3 < 320$	0				0	0
$320 \leq s_3 < 640$	0	56			1	56
$640 \leq s_3 < 960$	0	56	112		2	112
$960 \leq s_3 \leq 1{,}000$	0	56	112	168	3	168

The optimal return function is

$f_2^*(s_2) = \max \{35d_2 + f_3^*(s_2 - 250d_2): \text{all feasible } d_2\}$

The integer d_2 must satisfy $0 \le d_2 \le s_2/250$. Table 15.8(b) displays the results of calculating f_2 and f_2^* for all possible state values s_2. To demonstrate how the above recursive equations are used to compute the entries for that table, let us calculate the entries for the row $s_2 = 800$. If we have \$800 to invest in rare coins, and each lot of rare coins costs \$250, the feasible values of the decision variable d_2 (number of lots) are 0, 1, 2, and 3. Thus

$f_2^*(s_2) = \max \{35d_2 + f_3^*(s_2 - 250d_2): \text{all feasible } d_2\}$

$f_2^*(800) = \max \{35d_2 + f_3^*(800 - 250d_2): d_2 = 0, 1, 2, 3\}$

Also recall that the expression inside the braces equals $f_2(800, d_2)$:

$f_2(800, d_2) = 35d_2 + f_3^*(800 - 250d_2)$

If $d_2 = 0$, $f_2(800, 0) = 35(0) + f_3^*(800) = 0 + 112 = 112$. The value of $f_3^*(800)$ is found in Table 15.8(a).

If $d_2 = 1$, $f_2(800, 1) = 35(1) + f_3^*(550) = 35 + 56 = 91$.

If $d_2 = 2$, $f_2(800, 2) = 35(2) + f_3^*(300) = 70 + 0 = 70$.

If $d_2 = 3$, $f_2(800, 3) = 35(3) + f_3^*(50) = 105 + 0 = 105$.

TABLE 15.8(b)   *Stage 2   Rare Coins*

| | $f_2(s_2, d_2)$ | | | | | | |
| | d_2 | | | | | | |
s_2	0	1	2	3	4	d_2^*	$f_2^*(s_2)$
0	0					0	0
100	0					0	0
200	0					0	0
300	0	35				1	35
400	56	35				0	56
500	56	35	70			2	70
600	56	91	70			1	91
700	112	91	70			0	112
800	112	91	70	105		0	112
900	112	147	126	105		1	147
1,000	168	147	126	105	140	0	168

Thus

$$f_2^*(800) = \max \begin{cases} 112 & d_2 = 0 \\ 91 & d_2 = 1 \\ 70 & d_2 = 2 \\ 105 & d_2 = 3 \end{cases}$$

$$= 112 \text{ with } d_2^* = 0$$

The meaning of this calculation is as follows: If we end up at the start of stage 2 with $800, we should invest $0 in rare coins and carry the $800 to stage 3 (antique investment). The other lines of Table 15.8(b) are computed in a similar manner, using the results of the stage 3 calculations in Table 15.8(a).

Stage 1. Our problem here is to compute $f_1^*(1,000)$—that is, the maximum yearly return over stages 1, 2, and 3 (the three investment alternatives) if we have $1,000 to invest. Thus s_1 takes on the single value 1,000. Since stage 1 investment consists of bonds priced at $200 each, d_1 may equal 0, 1, 2, 3, 4, or 5. We have the following recursion for stage 1:

$$f_1^*(1,000) = \max \{f_1(1,000, d_1): \text{all feasible } d_1\}$$

$$= \max \{20d_1 + f_2^*(1,000 - 200d_1): d_1 = 0, 1, 2, 3, 4, 5\}$$

If $d_1 = 0$ (purchase 0 bonds), then

$$f_1(1,000, 0) = 20(0) + f_2^*(1,000) = 0 + 168 = 168$$

where $f_2^*(1,000)$ is found in Table 15.8(b).

If $d_1 = 1$, $f_1(1,000, 1) = 20(1) + f_2^*(800) = 20 + 112 = 132$.

If $d_1 = 2$, $f_1(1,000, 2) = 20(2) + f_2^*(600) = 40 + 91 = 131$.

If $d_1 = 3$, $f_1(1,000, 3) = 20(3) + f_2^*(400) = 60 + 56 = 116$.

If $d_1 = 4$, $f_1(1,000, 4) = 20(4) + f_2^*(200) = 80 + 0 = 80$.

If $d_1 = 5$, $f_1(1,000, 5) = 20(5) + f_2^*(0) = 100 + 0 = 100$.

Therefore

$$f_1^*(1,000) = \max \begin{cases} 168 & d_1 = 0 \\ 132 & d_1 = 1 \\ 131 & d_1 = 2 \\ 116 & d_1 = 3 \\ 80 & d_1 = 4 \\ 100 & d_1 = 5 \end{cases}$$

$$= 168 \text{ with } d_1^* = 0$$

These results appear in Table 15.8(c).

TABLE 15.8(c)   *Stage 1   Bonds*

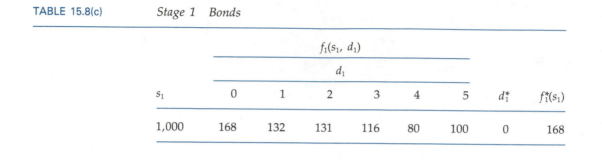

	$f_1(s_1, d_1)$							
	d_1							
s_1	0	1	2	3	4	5	d_1^*	$f_1^*(s_1)$
1,000	168	132	131	116	80	100	0	168

The Optimal Policy. The optimal policy is read from Tables 15.8(c), (b), and (a), in that order.

Starting with $1,000, the results of stage 1 indicate that for $s_1 = 1,000$, $d_1^* = 0$, and $f_1^*(1,000) = 168$. Thus we can earn $168 annual return by using the optimal policy. Since $d_1^* = 0$, we purchase 0 bonds. Then $s_2 = 1,000 - 200(0) = 1,000$. Table 15.8(b) indicates that if $s_2 = 1,000$ dollars, $d_2^* = 0$; that is, we should purchase 0 lots of rare coins. Then $s_3 = s_2 - 250d_2^* = 1,000 - 250(0) = 1,000$. Table 15.8(a) indicates that if $s_3 = 1,000$, we should make three antique purchases. This leaves $1,000 - 320(3) = 40$ dollars not invested. In summary, the optimal policy for this investment planning problem is: purchase no bonds; purchase no rare coins; purchase three lots of antiques; and retain $40 cash. This investment policy will produce an annual return of $168.

Problems

1. Modify the problem of this section to include a fourth investment alternative priced at $100 and yielding an annual return of $14.
2. *Sensitivity analysis.* For the problem solved in this section, would your investment strategy change if you only had $900 to invest? [*Hint:* You *do not need* to completely re-solve the problem. The answer can be found in Table 15.8(c).] This illustrates a general property of dynamic programs—it is often very simple to perform sensitivity analysis.
3. For the problem solved in this section, would your investment strategy change if the return on bonds was $36 instead of $20? [*Hint:* Simply *recalculate* Table 15.8(c).]

5. THE DYNAMIC INVENTORY PROBLEM

Management science literature contains a large variety of production/inventory problems solvable by dynamic programming. In this section we shall present a well-known version called the Wagner-Whitin model.

The Wagner-Whitin Model

We shall consider a finite time horizon over which we have forecasted demand to be varying. Such a demand pattern is termed **dynamic demand.** For example, suppose we forecast demand for the months of January through June to be 20, 30, 60, 50, 20, and 15 units each month, respectively. This would be a case of dynamic demand over a six-month time horizon: demand varies from month to month.

The problem is to determine how many units to produce (or purchase) each month in order to minimize total production (or procurement) plus inventory costs. Inventory costs consist of two components: (1) a fixed ordering cost, and (2) a holding cost. Each time an order is placed to replenish inventory, a fixed ordering cost is incurred. Holding cost is expressed in "$ per unit of product per period" and is incurred for each unit *carried over from one period to the next.* (See Chapter 6 for concepts of inventory theory.)

The following fairly intuitive special property, which will greatly simplify the dynamic program for this problem, was proved by Wagner and Whitin:

> A stock replenishment (an *order*) will be made at the beginning of a period only if the ending inventory of the previous period is 0. Thus orders will be placed only when the inventory is 0, and then the size of the order will be sufficient to cover a whole number of months' demand.

For example, if the inventory at the end of March is 0 (in the example above), then at the start of April an order could be placed to cover April demand only, April and May demand, or April, May, and June demand; that is, the order size could be 50, 70, or 85 units, respectively. Do you see why this special property simplifies the decision process? In the present case, for example, at the start of April we do not have to consider all the other possible order sizes, such as 51, 52, 53, ... , 84 units, but only three—50, 70, and 85. Note that we assume that orders are placed at the *beginning* of a period and arrive instantly (or in time for the demand). The Wagner-Whitin model can be adapted easily to handle more general assumptions.

Application of the Wagner-Whitin Model

Cutfast Lawnmowers, Inc., retails Cutfast lawnmowers and is now planning its procurement/inventory for the months of May, June, and July. Currently, at the start of May, Cutfast's inventory is 0, and it forecasts demand over the next three months to be 50, 100, and 40 lawnmowers, respectively. The fixed cost to place an order for stock replenishment is $100, and the carrying cost is $10 per lawnmower carried over from one month to the next. The wholesale cost per lawnmower is $60 and is expected to increase to $75 at the start of July. How should Cutfast plan its procurement/inventory to meet demand over the next three months at minimum cost?

Solution. We will formulate a dynamic program having three stages: stage 1, May; stage 2, June; and stage 3, July. The state at each stage will be 0 if the beginning inventory is 0, and 1 otherwise. From the discussion above, orders will only be placed when $s_1 = 0$.

The objective is to minimize total costs—that is, procurement plus fixed ordering costs plus carrying costs.

To derive the recursion for this problem, let us make precise definitions of f_1 and f_1^*. We shall do so without using elaborate notation. When $s_i = 1$, we do not define a value for f_i. When $s_i = 0$, $f_i(s_i, d_i)$ equals the sum of the following four cost components, where $d_i =$ the order quantity at stage i (in units of product):

1. The fixed ordering cost of $100.
2. The purchase cost of $75d_i$ (if $i = 3$) or $60d_i$ (if $i = 1$ or 2).
3. The total carrying costs resulting from the stock replenishment of d_i units at the start of stage i.
4. The minimum cost to go to the end of July *after* the quantity d_i is depleted. This will be expressed as some term of the form $f_k^*(0)$ for $k > i$, as you will soon see.

We record this as Eq. (15–2):

$$f_i(0, d_i) = \left(\begin{array}{c} \text{Fixed} \\ \text{ordering} \\ \text{cost} \end{array}\right) + \left(\begin{array}{c} \text{Purchase} \\ \text{cost} \end{array}\right)$$

$$+ \left(\begin{array}{c} \text{Total} \\ \text{carrying} \\ \text{costs} \end{array}\right) \qquad (15\text{–}2)$$

$$+ \left(\begin{array}{c} \text{The minimum cost to go} \\ \text{to the end of July after} \\ \text{the supply, } d_i, \text{ is depleted} \end{array}\right)$$

Also, $f_i^*(0) =$ the minimum cost to go to the end of July if we start stage i with 0 inventory. We define f_4^* to be 0. The goal is to compute $f_1^*(0)$, which will then solve the problem. Of course

$$f_i^*(0) = \min_{d_i} f_i(0, d_i)$$

Let us begin with the last stage, stage 3, the start of July. If $s_i = 1$, there is no decision to make. If $s_i = 0$, we have only one choice—namely, to order the one-month July requirement of 40 lawnmowers. Equation (15–2) then becomes

$$f_3(0, 40) = \$100 + \$75(40) + 0 + f_4^*(0)$$

$$= \$100 + \$3,000 + 0 + 0$$

$$= \$3,100$$

Thus $f_3^*(0) = \$3,100$ with $d_3^* = 40$ (order 40 units). This is recorded in Table 15.9(a).

Next we move back to stage 2 (the start of June). If $s_2 = 1$, there is no decision to make. If $s_2 = 0$, d_2 may be 100 (order for June only) or d_2 may be 140 (order for June and July). If $d_2 = 100$, we have

$$f_2(0, 100) = \left(\begin{array}{c}\text{Ordering}\\\text{cost}\end{array}\right) + \left(\begin{array}{c}\text{Purchase}\\\text{cost}\end{array}\right) + \left(\begin{array}{c}\text{Carrying}\\\text{cost}\end{array}\right)$$

$$+ \left(\begin{array}{c}\text{Cost to continue at}\\\text{the end of June, } f_3^*(0)\end{array}\right)$$

$$= \$100 + \$60(100) + 0 + \$3,100$$

$$= \$9,200$$

Recall that $f_3^*(0)$ is the minimum cost to go to the end of July if we start stage 3 (July) with 0 inventory, as computed in Table 15.9(a).

If $d_2 = 140$, the ordering cost is \$100, the purchase cost is $\$60(140) = \$8,400$, the carrying cost is $40(\$10) = \$400$ (since 40 units must be carried over to July), and the cost to continue at the end of July is $f_4^*(0) = 0$ by definition. Thus

$$f_2(0, 140) = \$100 + \$60(140) + \$40(10) + 0$$

$$= \$8,900$$

and

$$f_2^*(0) = \min \begin{cases} 9,200 & d_2 = 100 \\ 8,900 & d_2 = 140 \end{cases}$$

$$= 8,900 \text{ with } d_2^* = 140$$

We see then that beginning with 0 inventory for June, the optimal decision to minimize June and July costs is to order 140 units. [See Table 15.9(b).]

TABLE 15.9(a) *Wagner-Whitin Dynamic Program: Stage 3*

s_3	$f_3(s_3, d_3)$ / d_3 / 40	d_3^*	$f_3^*(s_3)$
0	3,100	40	3,100
1	—	—	—

TABLE 15.9(b)

Stage 2

s_2	$f_2(s_2, d_2)$ d_2		d_2^*	$f_2^*(s_2)$
	100	140		
0	9,200	8,900	140	8,900
1	—	—	—	—

Also note that the above equations illustrate a type of recursion where f_2 is defined in terms of f_4 (instead of f_3).

Finally, moving back to stage 1, there is only one possible state, $s_1 = 0$, since we assume a 0 beginning inventory. The decision alternative may take one of three values:

$d_1 = \ \ 50$ Order for May only

$d_1 = 150$ Order for May and June

$d_1 = 190$ Order for May, June, and July

If $d_1 = 50$, Eq. (15–2) becomes

$f_1(0, 50) = \$100 + \$60(50) + 0 + f_2^*(0)$

$= \$100 + \$3,000 + 0 + \$8,900$

$= \$12,000$

[Note that $f_2^*(0)$ is the minimum cost to go, starting at the beginning of June (stage 2) with 0 inventory, as computed in Table 15.9(b).]

If $d_1 = 150$, we must carry 100 units over to June; also, we will then begin July (stage 3) with 0 inventory. Thus

$f_1(0, 150) = \$100 + \$60(150) + \$10(100) + f_3^*(0)$

$= \$100 + \$9,000 + \$1,000 + \$3,100$

$= \$13,200$

If $d_1 = 190$, we must carry 100 units over to June, and 40 units must be carried *two months* to the start of July. Then the cost to continue at the end of July, $f_4^*(0)$, is 0. Thus

$f_1(0, 190) = \$100 + \$60(190) + \$10(100) + \$10(40)(2) + 0$

$= \$13,300$

and

$$f_1^*(0) = \min \begin{cases} 12{,}000 & d_1 = 50 \\ 13{,}200 & d_1 = 150 \\ 13{,}300 & d_1 = 190 \end{cases}$$

$$= 12{,}000 \text{ with } d_1^* = 50 \text{ [see Table 15.9(c)]}$$

The Optimal Policy

From Table 15.9(c), starting in May (stage 1) with 0 inventory, the optimal decision is to order a one-month supply of 50 units for May. At the beginning of June (stage 2), the inventory will be 0. So $s_2 = 0$, and from Table 15.9(b), $d_2^* = 140$; that is, the optimal decision is to order a two-month supply to cover June and July. From Table 15.9(c), the minimum total cost of this optimal policy over the three-month planning horizon is given by $f_1^*(s_1^*) = f_1^*(0) = \$12{,}000$.

6. CONCLUDING REMARKS

Much of the early progress in dynamic programming is due to Richard Bellman. The interested student may wish to consult his two early books, which are still popular reading: *Dynamic Programming* (Princeton, N.J.: Princeton University Press, 1957); and, with S. Dreyfus, *Applied Dynamic Programming* (Princeton, N.J.: Princeton University Press, 1962).

This chapter presents an introduction to basic dynamic programming concepts, and illustrates how the dynamic programming method can be used to solve several practical management science problems.

A remark on notation: We have presented solutions to the shortest-path, investment, and Wagner-Whitin dynamic programming problems in terms of the general notation of Section 3. The reason for employing such notation is the ease with which the concepts of "recursion" and "the principle of optimality" can be represented. However, if you carefully study Tables 15.7(a)–(d), 15.8(a)–(c), and 15.9(a)–(c), you will discover that the dynamic program-

TABLE 15.9(c)   *Stage 1*

s_1	$f_1(0, d_1)$			d_1^*	$f_1^*(s_1)$
	d_1				
	50	150	190		
0	12,000	13,200	13,300	50	12,000

TABLE 15.10

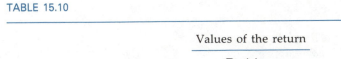

States	Values of the return — Decisions	Optimal decision	Optimal return

ming problems of this chapter can just as easily be solved without such elaborate notation. All that is required is a good understanding of how to derive the information contained in the tables. For example, the format shown in Table 15.10 can be used at each stage. To complete such a table for a given stage, the table at the previously analyzed stage must be used; thus you will actually be using the concept of "recursion" without the general notation f_i and f_i^*. In fact, this is exactly how we solved the shortest-path problem in Section 2.

TERMINOLOGY

After studying this chapter you should be familiar with the following terms:

TERM	SECTION
branches	2
decisions	2, 3
dynamic demand	5
dynamic programming	1, 3
network	2
nodes	2
optimal policy	3
path	2
principle of optimality	3
recursion	3
resource allocation problems	4
return functions	3
shortest-path	2
stages	2, 3
stage transitions	3
states	2, 3
Wagner-Whitin model	5

EXERCISES

1. *Transporting Raw Materials.* Coalamtrex, Inc., strip-mines coal at Duggin, Indiana. It transports the coal by truck to its coal-gasification plant at Eversville. Given the map in Fig. 15.5 showing alternative truck routes through intermediate cities, use dynamic programming to determine the shortest route from Duggin to Eversville.

2. *Oil Pipeline Layout.* Gushereze, Inc., has just discovered a large deposit of oil located geographically at node 1 on the map shown in Fig. 15.6. A pipeline must be constructed from node 1 to a refinery located at node 9. The branches indicate feasible routes over which the pipeline may be located; distances are shown in kilometers (km). Due to geological, political, and economic factors (such as labor availability), the average cost per km of pipeline varies along the branches as given in Table 15.11.

   Use dynamic programming to determine the minimum-cost pipeline layout.

3. *Production/Inventory Planning.* Oldebage, Inc., manufactures paper sacks for primary distribution to large food chains. Demand for the next four months is forecasted to be 20,000, 30,000, 10,000, and 40,000 for June, July, August, and September, respectively. Production costs are currently $0.04 per bag but are expected to increase to $0.05 in August.

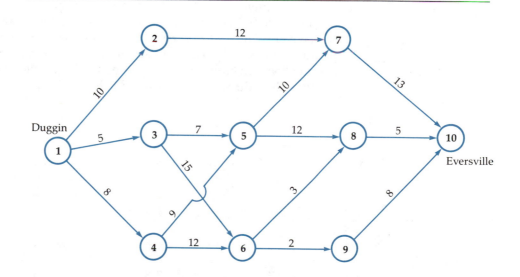

FIGURE 15.5

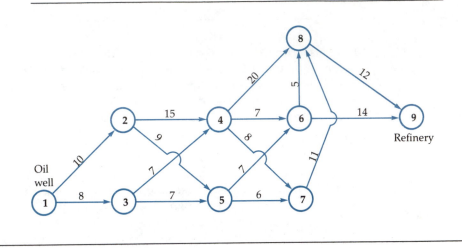

FIGURE 15.6

Carrying costs run $0.01 per bag per month, and the cost to set up for a production run is $450. Use the Wagner-Whitin dynamic program to determine the optimal production/inventory plan. Assume the starting inventory is 0.

4. *Production/Inventory Planning with Constraints.* Magnair manufactures hot-air balloons and has orders for two, four, and three balloons for the months of July, August, and September, respectively. The production cost per balloon in these months is projected to be $7,000, $7,200, $7,400, respectively. The cost to carry a balloon in inventory is 10 percent of the production cost. The storage capacity at the Magnair plant for the finished balloon inventory will accommodate three balloons. Production capacity will be three, two, and three balloons for the three months. The

TABLE 15.11

Branch	Cost/km ($000)	Branch	Cost/km ($000)
1–2	5	4–8	8
1–3	6	5–6	5
2–4	4	5–7	7
2–5	10	6–8	4
3–4	9	6–9	4
3–5	9	7–8	3
4–6	8	8–9	4
4–7	10		

August drop in capacity is caused by the fact that two key workers are scheduled for two-week vacations during August. The beginning inventory at the start of July is one balloon. Formulate a dynamic program and solve for the optimal production plan.

5. *Investment Planning.* An investor has $20,000 to invest in four projects, A, B, C, and D. The amounts that can be invested in the projects and the expected returns from the projects are given in Table 15.12. For example, the investor may place $0 in B, or the investor may place $2,500 in B and expect to regain the $2,500 plus $800, or the investor may place $7,500 in B and expect to regain $7,500 plus $2,500. The time horizon for the expected returns is assumed to be the same. Also, note that the investor may place only the amounts listed for each project. For example, the investor may put *only one* of the amounts $0, $2,500, or $7,500 in B; an investment of $5,000 in B is not allowed.

   Formulate and solve a dynamic program to determine how the $20,000 should be invested in order to maximize the return.

6. *Investment Planning.* Suppose you have $1,000 to invest in three securities. Stock A is priced at $100 and can expect to return $12 per year; stock B is priced at $200 and has an expected return $27 per year; and bond X is priced at $250 and returns $32 per year. Stock B is considered somewhat risky, and you would not purchase more than two shares. Formulate a dynamic program to determine how many issues of each security to purchase in order to maximize yearly return.

7. *Automobile Replacement.* Suppose you would like to minimize your automobile transportation costs over the next five years. Let us assume that presently you do not own a car and that over the next four years you will consider buying new cars only at the start of each year. The average price of a new car over the next four years is expected to be $5,000. You decide that you would not keep a car longer than three years. Table 15.13

TABLE 15.12

Project	Amount invested ($)	Expected return ($)
A	$ 5,000	$1,000
	10,000	3,000
B	2,500	800
	7,500	2,500
C	6,000	1,800
	8,000	2,800
D	12,000	3,750
	15,000	4,700

TABLE 15.13

Age of car	Operating costs	Trade-in value at beginning of year
Brand new	$ 600 (during year 1)	—
1 year	900 (during year 2)	$4,000 (start of year 2)
2 years	1,200 (during year 3)	3,000 (start of year 3)
3 years	—	2,200 (start of year 4)

gives operating costs and trade-in values for each type of car. There is no requirement that you dispose of your car at the end of the fifth year. Your objective is to minimize purchase plus operating costs during years 1–5. Use dynamic programming to determine an optimal policy.

Hint: Use four stages, and let the state of the system be the age of your current car. At stage 1, you have only one decision alternative—namely, to buy a new car. Use trade-in values as scrap values.

8. *Police Patrol Assignments.* The city of Runfaste has experienced a higher than average crime rate in the past few years. There are three primary crime districts in the city. The police chief must allocate five additional squad-car teams to these districts. The number of crimes that could be deterred per month by assigning additional squad cars to the districts is given in Table 15.14. It is *not* required that each district be assigned additional police support. Use dynamic programming to determine the optimal police patrol assignments.

9. *Cargo Loading.* A ship headed for Brazil, operated by Beatette, Inc., has a capacity of thirty tons. Four types of cargo may be transported by the ship. The profit and weight data for this cargo lot are given in Table 15.15. How many units of each type of cargo should the ship carry on this trip? Formulate a dynamic program to solve this problem.

TABLE 15.14   *Expected Number of Crimes Deterred per Month*

Districts	Number of additional patrol teams					
	0	1	2	3	4	5
A	0	10	12	15	22	24
B	0	15	16	19	21	23
C	0	13	13	20	21	25

TABLE 15.15

Cargo	Profit ($/unit)	Weight (tons/unit)
1	$ 60	3
2	190	9
3	270	12
4	140	6

10. *Cargo Loading: Sensitivity Analysis.* Suppose Beatette, Inc. (Exercise 9 above) learns that it has already committed six tons of its cargo capacity to another company. How does this affect the optimal cargo mix?

11. *Mining Operations.* Goldnugitt, Inc., has just purchased mining rights to mine gold in a mountainous area of a southwestern state. It has projected the expected profit per year for the next six years from the sale of the gold mined. In addition, it has estimated the profit it could obtain from the sale of the land (the mine and surrounding area) at the end of each of the six years. These data are given in Table 15.16. Formulate a dynamic program to determine when Goldnugitt should sell the land in order to maximize total profit.

   Note: If, for example, you decide to sell the mine in year 3, you will receive the profit during that year ($900,000) plus the profit from the sale ($200,000), in addition to the profits earned during years 1 and 2.

12. *Discounted Dynamic Programming.* In dynamic programming problems where the stages correspond to time periods, it is often more realistic to discount future cash flows to the present. For example, if the discount rate is 10 percent (cost of capital, interest, return on investment, etc.), a dollar received in year 3 has a *present value* of $1/(1 + 0.10)^3 = \$0.75$. Solve Exercise 11 above using *discounted profits*. Apply a discount factor

TABLE 15.16

Year	Profit during the year	Profit from sale of mine at the end of the year
1	$250,000	$100,000
2	600,000	150,000
3	900,000	200,000
4	800,000	250,000
5	600,000	350,000
6	300,000	150,000

of $1/(1 + 0.10)^i$ to year i, $i = 1, 2, \dots , 6$. For example, if you sell the mine in year 3, the \$200,000 profit received would have a present value of $\$200,000[1/(1 + 0.10)^3] = \$150,262.96$. As another example, if you operate during year 5, the \$600,000 profit received would have a present value of $\$600,000[1/(1 + 0.10)^5] = \$372,552.78$. The objective function of the problem is to maximize total *discounted* profits earned.

13. *Equipment Replacement.* A company employs a certain piece of heavy machinery in its production operations. The cost of this equipment, purchased new, is \$50,000. As the machine ages, maintenance costs increase, as shown in Table 15.17. For example, a machine that is two years old will require \$9,000 in maintenance in its third year of operation. If a new machine were purchased at the start of year 3, a purchase cost of \$50,000 would be incurred, and the maintenance cost in year 3 would be \$1,000. At the start of year 1, there is only one choice: buy a new machine and operate it during year 1 at a cost of $\$50,000 + \$1,000 = \$51,000$. We will assume that, at the *end* of year 6, the machine currently in use can be sold for \$5,000. Determine an optimal replacement policy over the six-year horizon to minimize total replacement plus maintenance costs.

   Hint: There are six stages. At stages 2–6 there are two decision alternatives: "replace" or "don't replace." Also, note that $f_7^* = -5,000$ (disposal value of the machine in use at stage 6 equals a negative cost of \$5,000).

14. *Personnel Assignments.* An independent building contractor will soon begin work on three small jobs. The contractor has ten employees to assign to the jobs, and her expected net profit from each job depends on how many people she assigns to the job. Each job must be assigned at least one employee. Table 15.18 gives the expected net profits from each job as a function of the number of employees assigned to it. Use dynamic programming to determine the optimal employee assignments.

TABLE 15.17

Age of equipment	Maintenance costs
0 (new)	\$ 1,000
1 (year old)	5,000
2	9,000
3	15,000
4	25,000
5	35,000
6	40,000

TABLE 15.18   *Profits in $000*

Job	1	2	3	4	5	6	7	8	9	10
					Number of employees assigned					
1	30	35	35	40	45	47	49	50	52	55
2	10	11	18	25	26	30	35	35	35	35
3	15	19	25	27	30	45	50	60	65	65

15. *Assigning Sales Personnel to Territories.* Revolve Cosmetics has outlined four potential sales territories. The expected net profits that can be generated from sales in each territory is a function of the number of salespeople assigned to the territory. These estimates are given in Table 15.19. It is *not* required that each territory be assigned sales personnel. If Revolve has eight salespeople to assign to the territories, use dynamic programming to determine the optimal personnel allocation.

16. *Sensitivity Analysis.* In Exercise 15 above, how would the optimal allocation change if Revolve only has five salespeople available for assignment to the territories?

   Hint: You do *not* have to re-solve the entire problem.

17. *Advertising Mix.* Revolve Cosmetics is considering how to spend its June advertising budget of $5,000 in order to maximize the number of persons exposed to its products ("person-exposures"). Three media are being considered: magazine, radio, and television. The number of potential person-exposures in these media is a function of the amount of money spent. This information is given in Table 15.20. Using dynamic programming, determine the optimal advertising budget allocation.

18. *Revolve Advertising Mix: Sensitivity Analysis.* How would Revolve's advertising mix for June change if its advertising budget were reduced to $4,000? (See Exercise 17 above.)

TABLE 15.19   *Profit in $000*

Territory	0	1	2	3	4	5	6	7	8
				Number of salespeople assigned					
1	0	5	6	9	10	15	17	19	22
2	0	6	7	9	11	14	18	20	23
3	0	3	5	5	5	15	20	25	25
4	0	4	4	8	12	13	19	20	24

TABLE 15.20   *Total Estimated June Person-Exposures in 000*

Media	$ Spent on advertising, June					
	0	1,000	2,000	3,000	4,000	5,000
Magazine	0	5	11	18	25	35
Radio	0	2	9	22	24	32
Television	0	8	10	16	27	40

TABLE 15.21

Activity	Income	Project duration
A	$7,000	3 months
B	1,500	2 months
C	5,000	4 months
D	4,000	1 month

TABLE 15.22

Job	Profit	Time required
1	$500	2 days
2	800	1 day
3	600	3 days
4	900	4 days

19. *Activity Planning.* Suzanne Rosenthal is an independent management consultant and is currently planning next year's projects. She has lined up four major opportunities: A, a state government data bank facility; B, teaching a course at a local university; C, consulting for a major steel manufacturer on a productivity analysis project; and D, acting as a consultant in a small business consulting firm. She has allocated eight months to these four projects for the coming year. The projects, the expected income from each, and the expected time requirement of each (in months) are given in Table 15.21. Use dynamic programming to determine which projects Suzanne should take on. (It is not required that she take on all four jobs.)

20. *Activity Planning—Sensitivity Analysis.* (See Exercise 19 above.) Suppose Suzanne is offered a job that would pay her $2,500 but would only leave seven months to allocate to the above four projects. Should she accept this job?

21. *Job Shop Planning.* A local job shop has five days available during the current week to process jobs. The shop has four jobs waiting to be processed. Table 15.22 lists the profit on each job and the time required for processing each job in the shop. (It is not required that all four jobs be processed during the current week.) Use dynamic programming to determine which jobs to process this week.

16 NETWORK OPTIMIZATION METHODS

CONTENTS

1. INTRODUCTION

In this chapter we present three network optimization problems. An algorithm is given to solve each type of problem. The models presented have a wide range of management applications in distribution, communication, and transportation networks, as can be seen by scanning the examples and exercises in this chapter.

A **network** is a collection of *nodes* and *branches* such as the one shown in Fig. 16.1. This network has five nodes, numbered 1, 2, 3, 4, and 5 and represented by circles. The branches are the line segments connecting the nodes. Notationally we represent the branch from node 1 to node 2 by either (1, 2) or 1–2. If a particular problem requires that we distinguish the direction of a branch, we simply reverse the "tail" and "head" nodes of the line segment. For example, if we speak of "the branch from node 2 to node 1," we would represent this branch as (2, 1) or 2–1. The tail node is 2, and the head node is 1.

Generally, in a network, we associate a quantity or activity of some kind, such as distance, time, money, or a flow (of material, liquid, traffic, electricity, and the like), with each branch.

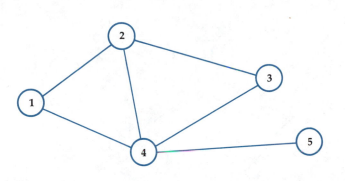

FIGURE 16.1

These network concepts are best understood by studying the specific models to be presented in the sections that follow.

2. SHORTEST-PATH ALGORITHM

The objective of a shortest-path algorithm is to identify the shortest path connecting a starting point **(initial node)** to a finishing point **(terminal node).** The path length may be measured in distance, money, or time units, as the exercises at the end of this chapter will illustrate. In this section we shall present the following shortest-route problem and its solution, using a short-est-path algorithm. You may find this approach simpler than the Dynamic Programming method in Chapter 15.

The following notation is employed:

1. Given nodes i and j, d_{ij} = the distance from node i to node j.
2. Given two numbers, a and b, min(a, b) = the minimum of a and b. For example, min(2, 7) = 2, min(4, 4) = 4, etc.

EXAMPLE 16.1. *Shortest Travel Route—A Distribution Application.* In Fig. 16.2(a), we show a map of Sunshine County's six cities. A distributor based at Hillsdale must determine the shortest route to Sullivan. Distances are shown in kilometers. The network representation of this map is given in Fig. 16.2(b). Each *node* represents a city (1, Hillsdale; 2, Caliente; 3, Jaw Bone; 4, Doston; 5, Perch; 6, Sullivan), and each *branch* represents a road. The initial node is node 1, and the terminal node is node 6. The problem is to find the shortest route from node 1 to node 6 over which the distributor can ship its product.

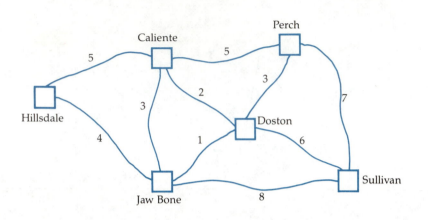

FIGURE 16.2(a)   *Sunshine County map.*

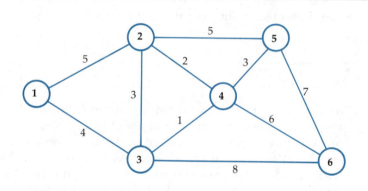

FIGURE 16.2(b)   *Network representation of Sunshine County.*

APPLICATIONS

The following applications appear in this chapter in text, examples, or problems:

Communication networks
    Road system design
    Telephone system design

Distribution networks
    Irrigation system design
    Product distribution: from manufacturer to market
    Urban planning: design of a sewer system

Solution. We shall illustrate an intuitive method of solving the shortest path problem. As the algorithm proceeds we shall speak in terms of *solved* and *unsolved* nodes. Node i is *solved* if the minimum distance from node 1 to node i has been found (that is, calculated by the algorithm); node i is *unsolved* if the minimum distance from node 1 to node i has not yet been found. Initially, all the nodes are unsolved. The algorithm terminates as soon as node 6 is solved.

We now shall illustrate the algorithm on the network of Fig. 16.2(b) above. Initially all the nodes of the network are unsolved.

As a first step it is obvious that the shortest distance from node 1 to node 1 is 0 km, so we *label* node 1 with a 0, and node 1 becomes a solved node. Nodes 2, 3, 4, 5, and 6 remain unsolved. We place a 0 above node 1. This gives us Fig. 16.3.

Next we identify the unsolved node which is closest to node 1. From Figs. 16.2(a) and 16.2(b), the candidates are clearly nodes 2 and 3, and $d_{12} = 5$ and $d_{13} = 4$. Since $\min(d_{12}, d_{13}) = d_{13} = 4$, we select node 3 to be the next solved node and place a 4 above node 3 in the diagram. (Throughout the algorithm, ties are broken arbitrarily.) We now know the following: Node 3 is a solved node; the shortest distance from node 1 to node 3 has been calculated to

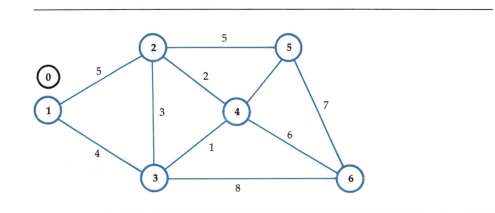

FIGURE 16.3

equal 4 km. Node 3 is *labeled* with the number 4 (see Fig. 16.3), and since node 3 was calculated *from* node 1, we place an arrow at node 3 pointing to node 1 (see Fig. 16.4). At this point, nodes 1 and 3 are solved, and nodes 2, 4, 5, and 6 are unsolved.

For the next step, we must identify the unsolved node that is closest to node 1. The candidates for this step are the unsolved nodes *that are connected directly* to a solved node. From Fig. 16.4, the candidates are clearly node 2 (connected to the solved nodes 1 and 3), node 4 (connected to the solved node 3), and node 6 (connected to the solved node 3). For each candidate node, we now compute the shortest distance from node 1 to that node.

Node 2: We must use the solved nodes to which node 2 is connected directly, nodes 1 and 3. *Using node 1,* the shortest distance from node 1 to node 2 is clearly d_{12} or 5 km. *Using node 3,* the shortest distance from node 1 to node 2 is d_{32} plus the shortest distance from node 1 to node 3, which is given by the label assigned to node 3 in Fig. 16.4. Thus, *using node 3,* the shortest distance from node 1 to node 2 equals

d_{32} + (label on node 3) = 3 + 4 = 7.

Taking the minimum of these two calculations (using node 1 and using node 3), we see that the minimum distance from node 1 to node 2 equals min(5, 7) = 5, and is calculated from node 1.

Note that it is possible to summarize these calculations more briefly as follows:

the minimum distance from node 1 to node 2

= min(d_{12}, d_{32} + label on node 3)

= min(5, 3 + 4)

= 5 km, from node 1.

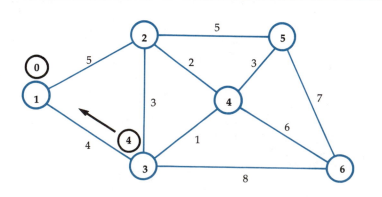

FIGURE 16.4

Node 4: Since the only solved node to which node 4 is connected is node 3, the shortest distance from node 1 to node 4 is

d_{34} + label on node 3

which equals $1 + 4 = 5$ km, from node 3.

Node 6: Since the only solved node to which node 6 is connected is node 3, the shortest distance from node 1 to node 6 is

d_{36} + label on node 3

which equals $8 + 4 = 12$ km, from node 3.

We may summarize the results of these calculations as follows:

Unsolved node i	Shortest distance from node 1 to i
2	5 km (from node 1)
4	5 km (from node 3)
6	12 km (from node 3)

We now identify the minimum distance in the second column, which is 5 km. We break the tie arbitrarily in favor of node 2. The unsolved node 2 will now become a solved node, having the label 5 (km); and since node 2 was labeled from node 1, we place an arrow at node 2 pointing to node 1. This gives us Fig. 16.5.

At this point nodes 1, 2, and 3 are solved nodes, and nodes 4, 5, and 6 are unsolved.

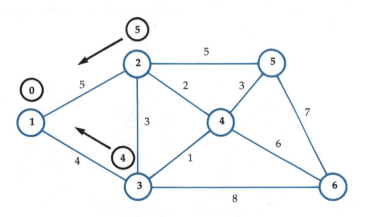

FIGURE 16.5

For the next step we must identify the unsolved node which is closest to node 1. The candidates are the unsolved nodes *which are connected directly* to a solved node. From Fig. 16.5, the candidates are clearly node 4 (connected to the solved nodes 2 and 3), node 5 (connected to the solved node 2), and node 6 (connected to the solved node 3). We now compute the shortest distance from node 1 to each candidate. These calculations are summarized in the following table, using the notation and logic employed in the previous step.

Unsolved node i	Shortest distance from node 1 to i
4	$= \min(d_{24} + $ label on node 2, $d_{34} + $ label on node 3) $= \min(2 + 5, 1 + 4)$ $= \min(7,5) = 5$, from node 3.
5	$= d_{25} + $ label on node 2. $= 5 + 5 = 10$, from node 2.
6	$= d_{36} + $ label on node 3 $= 8 + 4 = 12$, from node 3.

The unsolved node corresponding to the minimum distance in this table is node 4. The unsolved node 4 will now become a solved node, having the label 5 (km); and since node 4 was labeled from node 3, we place an arrow at node 4 pointing to node 3. This gives us Fig. 16.6.

At this point nodes 1, 2, 3, and 4 are solved nodes, and nodes 5 and 6 are unsolved.

For the next step, we must identify the unsolved node which is closest to node 1. The candidates for this step are the unsolved nodes *which are connected directly* to a solved node. From Fig. 16.6, the candidates are clearly node 5 (connected to the solved nodes 2 and 4) and node 6 (connected to the solved nodes 3 and 4). Again we summarize the required calculations in tabular form:

Unsolved node i	Shortest distance from node 1 to i
5	$= \min(d_{25} + $ label on node 2, $d_{45} + $ label on node 4) $= \min(5 + 5, 3 + 5)$ $= \min(10,8) = 8$, from node 4
6	$= \min(d_{36} + $ label on node 3, $d_{46} + $ label on node 4) $= \min(8 + 4, 6 + 5)$ $= \min(12, 11) = 11$, from node 4

The unsolved node corresponding to the minimum distance in this table is node 5. The unsolved node 5 will now become a solved node, having the

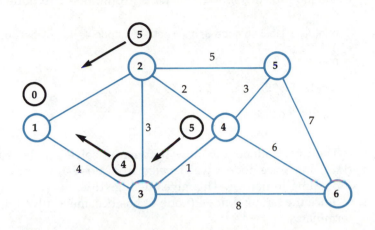

FIGURE 16.6

label 8 (km); and since node 5 was labeled from node 4, we place an arrow at node 5 pointing to node 4. This gives us Fig. 16.7.

At this point nodes 1, 2, 3, 4, and 5 are solved nodes, and node 6 is unsolved.

For the next step, we must identify the unsolved node which is closest to node 1. The candidates for this step are again the unsolved nodes which are connected directly to a solved node. From Fig. 16.7, node 6 is obviously the only candidate and is connected to solved nodes 3, 4, and 5. The required

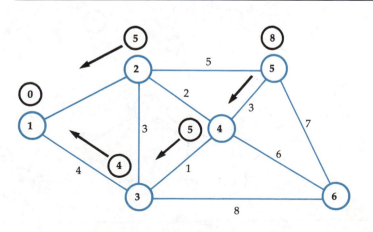

FIGURE 16.7

calculation for the shortest distance from node 1 to node 6 is the following:

$\min(d_{36} + \text{label on node 3}, d_{46} + \text{label on node 4}, d_{56} + \text{label on node 5})$

$= \min(8 + 4, 6 + 5, 7 + 8)$

$= \min(12, 11, 15)$

$= 11$, from node 4.

The unsolved node 6 now becomes a solved node, having the label 11 (km); and since node 6 was labeled from node 4, we place an arrow at node 6 pointing to node 4. This gives us Fig. 16.8.

Since the terminal node (node 6) has become a solved node, the algorithm terminates.

IDENTIFYING THE SHORTEST PATH. The length of the shortest path is given by the label on the terminal node. In our example, from Fig. 16.8, the shortest path is seen to have length 11 (km).

The nodes composing the shortest path are found by tracing the backward-pointing arrows beginning with the terminal node and finishing at the initial node. In our example, from Fig. 16.8, we have node 6 → node 4 → node 3 → node 1. Thus, the shortest path is 1 → 3 → 4 → 6, having a length of 11 km.

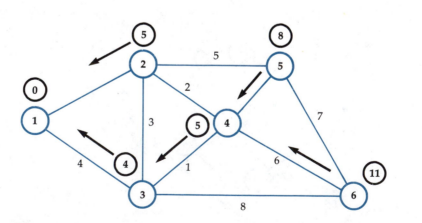

FIGURE 16.8

Notes

1. In practice, once you fully understand how the algorithm works you may work directly on Figure 16.2(b), doing all labeling on a single diagram without making explicit all of your calculations and steps. Off to the side of the diagram, you should then list the solved nodes in the order they were solved. For our example, the list would look like the following: 1, 3, 2, 4, 5, 6.
2. The interested student may wish to examine the validity of the algorithm: Why does it work? A key factor lies in understanding the definition of solved node and labeling.
3. Technically, the above algorithm is called a *dynamic program* (see Section 2 of Chapter 15). Since it moves from left to right, from the initial node to the terminal node, it is called a *forward* dynamic program. Some shortest-path algorithms are *backward* dynamic programs, moving from the terminal node backwards to the initial node.
4. We have presented an intuitive version of the algorithm. For machine computation we would need to formulate this algorithm in more formal terms.   ▲

Problems

1. In Example 16.1, using the shortest-path algorithm, find the shortest route from node 2 to node 6 in Fig. 16.2(b).
2. In the network shown in Fig. 16.9, find the shortest path(s) from the initial node 1 to the terminal node 5, using the shortest-path algorithm.

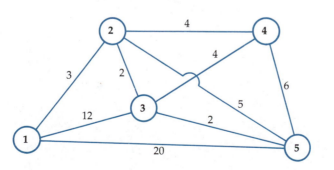

FIGURE 16.9

3. MINIMAL SPANNING TREE ALGORITHM

The objective of a minimal spanning tree algorithm is to identify the set of branches having a minimum total length that connects all nodes of the network in such a way that each node is connected to every other node by a sequence of branches. The next example will illustrate the concept of the minimal spanning tree algorithm.

EXAMPLE 16.2. *The Minimal Spanning Tree Algorithm: Facilities Design Application.* Nancy Brown, owner of a small Midwest farm, has just completed construction of the foundation, frame, and roof of a new barn for her farm. She must now plan the electrical wiring for the barn. Nancy has identified certain desirable locations for electrical outlet boxes. A schematic drawing of Nancy's layout is shown in Fig. 16.10. The main electrical service entrance is represented by node 1. Distances are shown in yards. Thus, for example, Nancy plans an electrical outlet at node 3. To get to the position in the barn represented by node 3 *directly* from node 1, the *rectilinear* path shown in Fig. 16.11 is planned. This five-yard path is shown as branch (1, 3) in the network representation, Fig. 16.10. Due to structural considerations, some nodes, such as 1 and 4, cannot be connected directly to each other.

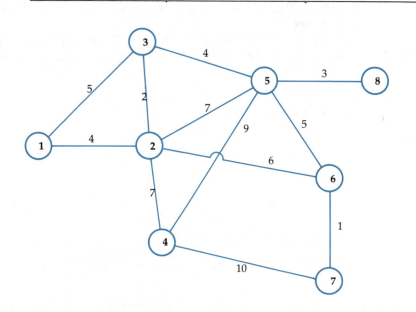

FIGURE 16.10   *A schematic of electrical layout for Nancy Brown's barn (distances shown in yards).*

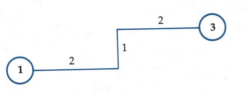

FIGURE 16.11

Nancy computes the approximate cost *per yard* of installing electrical wiring as follows:

No. 8, three-wire cable	$0.90
3/4″ metal conduit	0.80
Labor	2.50
Total	$4.20

(The cost of installing the fixtures and outlets at each of the eight locations is fixed and not affected by the connecting paths chosen, and so is ignored.) How should Nancy install the electrical wiring?

Solution. We prepare by constructing the appropriate network to use. This has been done in Fig. 16.10, but be careful to note a subtle point: Nancy's objective is to minimize *cost*, and since cost is directly proportional to distance, we can work with the distances. It would also be correct to construct a new network, converting distances to cost. Thus branch (2, 6) would have an associated cost of (6 yards) × ($4.20/yard) = $25.20. If some costs were not directly related to distance it would be *necessary* to work with a cost network. For example, branch (6, 7) might involve drilling through concrete at a cost of $9.00 per yard instead of $4.20.

We then make a list of all the network branches in *ascending order* of branch length (or cost), as shown in Table 16.1.

In case of ties, the corresponding branches can be listed in any order; for example, it would be just as correct to list (3, 5) before (1, 2).

Now we go down the list (from top to bottom) checking off each branch that, connected with the previous branches, would not cause a loop to form. (A **loop** is a closed path starting and ending at a node.) As the branches are checked off, make a tick mark on the network for that branch. If a branch would cause a loop to form, do not include it (place an X by it in the table).

The results of performing this algorithm on the network of Fig. 16.10 are shown in Table 16.2 and Fig. 16.12, where we have darkened the branches that received tick marks (that is, were included). The darkened branches

TABLE 16.1

Branch	Length
(6, 7)	1
(2, 3)	2
(5, 8)	3
(1, 2)	4
(3, 5)	4
(1, 3)	5
(5, 6)	5
(2, 6)	6
(2, 4)	7
(2, 5)	7
(4, 5)	9
(4, 7)	10

form a graph called a **tree,** which is the minimal spanning tree of the original network. The steps of the algorithm are discussed below.

In step 1 we connected branch (6, 7) to the tree. In Table 16.2, we placed a check mark ($\sqrt{}$) to indicate this action, and in Fig. 16.12, we placed a tick mark on (and later darkened) branch (6, 7). We continued this until we reached step 6. At that point, if we had included branch (1, 3), a loop would have formed with previously checked branches (1, 2) and (2, 3). Thus we excluded

TABLE 16.2   *Steps of the Minimal Spanning Tree Algorithm (Example 16.2)*

Branch	Length	Step no.		Result
(6, 7)	1	1	$\sqrt{}$	(include)
(2, 3)	2	2	$\sqrt{}$	(include)
(5, 8)	3	3	$\sqrt{}$	(include)
(1, 2)	4	4	$\sqrt{}$	(include)
(3, 5)	4	5	$\sqrt{}$	(include)
(1, 3)	5	6	X	(exclude)
(5, 6)	5	7	$\sqrt{}$	(include)
(2, 6)	6	8	X	(exclude)
(2, 4)	7	9	$\sqrt{}$	(include)
(2, 5)	7	10	X	(exclude)
(4, 5)	9	11	X	(exclude)
(4, 7)	10	12	X	(exclude)

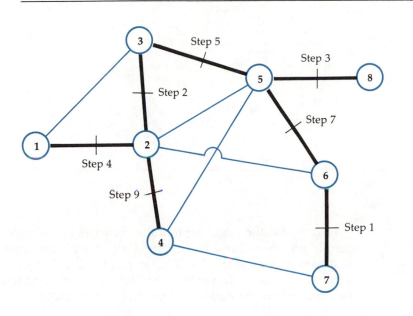

FIGURE 16.12   *The minimal spanning tree of Fig. 16.10.*

(1, 3), placing an X at step 6. Again, loops would have formed at steps 8, 10, 11, and 12, so these branches were also excluded.

Do you see the logic behind excluding loops? Look at step 6 again. If we were to include branch (1, 3), we would have the loop in the final tree, as shown in Fig. 16.13. We have connected nodes 1, 2, and 3, using eleven yards of wiring; this is not necessary because only six yards are actually required. As shown in Fig. 16.14, it is not necessary to connect nodes 1 and 3 *directly*.

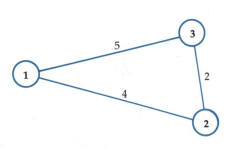

FIGURE 16.13

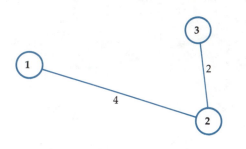

FIGURE 16.14

To compute the total length of the branches of the minimal spanning tree, simply go down Table 16.2, adding all lengths corresponding to branches that have a check mark: 1 + 2 + 3 + 4 + 4 + 5 + 7 = 26 yards, for a minimal total wiring cost of 26 yards times $4.20 per yard, or $109.20. Wiring would be installed on the darkened branches of Fig. 16.12.   ▲

Problems

1. Find the minimal spanning tree for the network shown in Fig. 16.15.

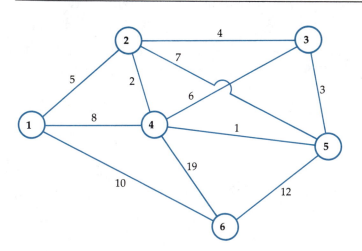

FIGURE 16.15

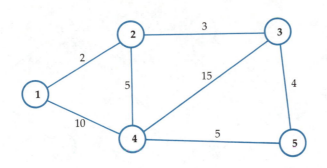

FIGURE 16.16

2. Find the minimal spanning tree for the network shown in Fig. 16.16. Is there more than one minimal spanning tree for this network?

4. MAXIMAL FLOW ALGORITHM

Suppose we have a network with a single initial node and a single terminal node (referred to as the **source** and the **sink,** respectively) in which a flow originates at the source node, travels through the branches of the network, and emerges at the sink node. The objective of a maximal flow algorithm is to determine the maximum flow the network can carry from source to sink. The **flow** might be a fluid (water or gas, for example), electricity, or traffic (vehicular, pedestrian, or air).

In the next example we shall illustrate an application of the maximal flow algorithm.

EXAMPLE 16.3. *Maximal Flow Algorithm: Product Distribution Application.* Goodroad Tire Company operates a plant at the location represented by node 1 in Fig. 16.17. The output of the plant must be shipped to one of its major retail-market centers, represented by node 6. The numbers on each branch indicate the maximum flow capacity of the branch in both directions (in 1,000 tires per month).

For example, branch (1, 2) represents an airline that supports 10 flights per month, each having a freight capacity of 300 tires. The 0 on the reverse branch (2, 1) indicates that no return flights originate at node 2 to node 1. Branch (2, 4) is a one-way railway supporting a potential freight flow of 2,000 tires per month. The return branch (4, 2) is a truck route having a monthly capacity of only 1,000 tires. From such practical considerations the rest of the branches are similarly assigned monthly flow capacities.

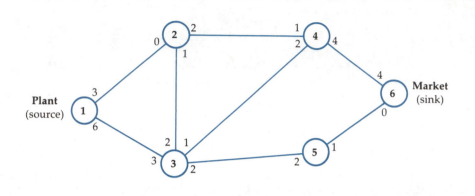

FIGURE 16.17

The Goodroad Tire Company maximal flow problem. Nodes 2, 3, 4, and 5 represent intermediate points, which may be cities, depots, or airports.

The problem is to determine how much of the current plant capacity can be shipped to the retail market and what routes should be used.

Solution. The maximal flow algorithm proceeds according to the following steps:

STEP 1. Find a path from the source node to the sink node that has a positive remaining flow capacity. If you cannot find such a path, STOP; you have reached the optimal solution (that is, the maximal flow pattern), since in performing the algorithm you have reduced all capacities to zero.

STEP 2. Select the branch on the path found in Step 1 that has the smallest positive remaining flow capacity. Call this flow *F*.

STEP 3. For each branch on this path:

a. Decrease the capacity in the direction of flow by the amount *F*.
b. Increase the reverse capacities of each branch by *F*.

The best time to read the statement of this algorithm is *after* understanding how it works. (Carefully study the discussion below.)
    To see how the algorithm works, let us solve the Goodroad Tire Company problem. (Refer to Fig. 16.17.)

ITERATION 1. Arbitrarily select a path from node 1 to node 6 that has positive flow capacity. We choose the path 1–2–3–5–6.
    The branch on this path that has the smallest remaining flow capacity is

either (2, 3) or (5, 6), each with a capacity of one.

Next, in performing the third step of the algorithm, we decrease each forward branch flow by one and increase each reverse flow by one. The results are shown in Fig. 16.18.

ITERATION 2. We (again arbitrarily) select the path 1–2–4–6, which has positive flow capacity remaining.

The branches (1, 2) and (2, 4) have the smallest flow capacity of two per month.

The new network is shown in Fig. 16.19.

ITERATION 3. The only remaining path that has positive flow capacity from source (node 1) to sink (node 6) is the path 1–3–4–6.

The branch (3, 4) has the smallest flow capacity of one per month.

Decreasing each forward flow on the path by one and increasing each reverse flow on the path by one result in the network that is shown in Fig. 16.20.

ITERATION 4. There is no path left in which a positive flow exists. To see this, try the various possibilities. For example, consider path 1–3–5–6. We can send 5 units out of node 1 to node 3, and send 1 of these on to node 5; but there it stops, because the remaining flow capacity out of node 5 is 0. Similarly, the other source-to-sink paths have 0 flow capacity. Thus the algorithm STOPS, and we have the maximal flow pattern. To determine what this flow pattern is, we can either cumulate the flow assignments made in the above steps or we can compare the final network with the original. Flow

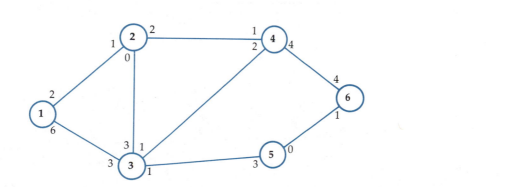

FIGURE 16.18

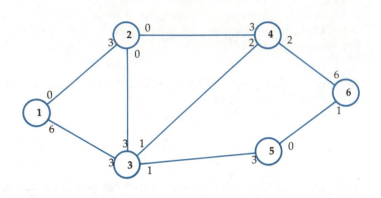

FIGURE 16.19   *Results of step 2.*

occurs in branches in which the final flows are less than the original flows. The difference is the optimal flow in the branch. Table 16.3 presents this computation, based on the final network (Fig. 16.20) and the original network (Fig. 16.17). Note that several branches, such as branch (4, 3), were excluded from consideration in the table. The reason is that the final flow (3 in this case) is not less than the initial flow, which was 2 for branch (4, 3).

The maximal flow pattern found in Table 16.3 is summarized graphically in Fig. 16.21.

Note that although the plant capacity is 9,000 tires per month, the existing

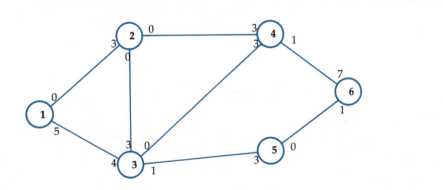

FIGURE 16.20   *Results of step 3.*

TABLE 16.3   *Finding the Optimal Flow Pattern*

Branch	Original flow	Final flow	Difference
(1, 2)	3	0	3
(1, 3)	6	5	1
(2, 3)	1	0	1
(2, 4)	2	0	2
(3, 4)	1	0	1
(3, 5)	2	1	1
(4, 6)	4	1	3
(5, 6)	1	0	1

distribution network will support only 4,000 tires per month. Assuming that the Goodroad Tire Company wishes to operate above 4,000 tires per month, the company should do one of the following three things regarding product distribution:

1. Reexamine the existing network to see if any branch capacities can be increased.
2. Study the feasibility of adding new routes between the plant and the market.
3. Examine new markets for their product (other than that represented by node 6). ▲

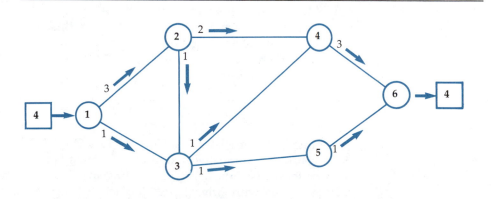

FIGURE 16.21   *Maximal flow pattern, Goodroad Tire Company. Amount shipped out of node 1 (the plant): 4,000/month. Amount received at node 6 (the market): 4,000/ month.*

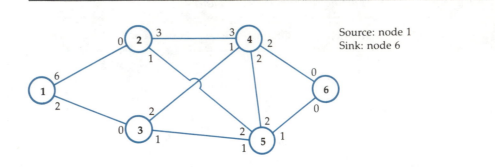

Source: node 1
Sink: node 6

FIGURE 16.22

Problems

1. Find the maximal flow pattern in the network shown in Fig. 16.22.
2. In the network of Problem 1 above, find the maximal flow pattern, assuming that node 1 is the source and node 4 is the sink.

5. COMPUTER SOLUTION OF NETWORK PROBLEMS

Another of the programs in SAS/OR is PROC NETFLOW, which implements a generalized network algorithm. PROC NETFLOW can solve problems with constrained flow (upper or lower bounds on allowable flow in each branch), and supply and demand constraints. Problem setup in PROC NETFLOW is similar to that of other SAS/OR programs (see Section 8 in Chapter 3 for an introduction to SAS/OR). In this section, the use of PROC NETFLOW for solving shortest-path, minimal spanning tree, and maximal flow problems is demonstrated.

The Shortest-Path Problem in PROC NETFLOW Format

A shortest-path problem is set up for PROC NETFLOW by listing all the node connections and the distances (or times) between them in a from-to-distance format (see the setup of the Sunshine County problem below). Nodes may be named with either letters (alphabetic) or numbers (numeric). PROC NETFLOW keywords for shortest-path problems are **ASOURCENODE** (**NSOURCENODE** if node names are numeric), which identifies the source node; **ASINKNODE** (**NSINKNODE** if node names are numeric), which identifies the sink node; **SHORTPATH,** which specifies the type of problem; **TAILNODE** which identifies the starting node of a branch; **HEADNODE,** which identifies the ending node of a branch; and **COST,** which identifies the distances. The statement **PROC PRINT** is required to print the solution.

The PROC NETFLOW Program for the Sunshine County Problem

```
 1   TITLE 'SUNSHINE COUNTY';
 2   DATA SUN;
 3       INPUT FROM$ TO$ DIST;
 4       CARDS;
 5   HILLS CALIE 5
 6   HILLS JAWBO 4
 7   CALIE PERCH 5
 8   CALIE JAWBO 3
 9   CALIE DOSTO 4
10   JAWBO DOSTO 1
11   JAWBO SULLI 8
12   DOSTO PERCH 3
13   DOSTO SULLI 6
14   PERCH SULLI 7
15   ;
16   PROC NETFLOW DATA=SUN ASOURCENODE=HILLS
17                ASINKNODE=SULLI SHORTPATH;
18       TAILNODE FROM;
19       HEADNODE TO;
20       COST DIST;
21   PROC PRINT;
```

Solution Output

The solution output from PROC NETFLOW for the Sunshine County problem is shown below. The first four columns are the input data. The column labeled **FLOW1** indicates the active nodes, that is, the branches in the shortest path. The shortest path is then: HILLS to JAWBO to DOSTO to SULLI. The column **DUAL1** lists the marginal cost of each branch. For example, including the JAWBO–SULLI branch in the path would increase the total distance by one unit. (Add up the HILLS to JAWBO to SULLI distances and see. The optimal path is eleven units long.)
NOTE: LENGTH OF SHORTEST PATH = 11
(Note: This appears on the SAS program log, not on the solution output table.)

SUNSHINE COUNTY

OBS	FROM	TO	DIST	-FLOW1-	-DUAL1-
1	HILLS	CALIE	5	0	0
2	HILLS	JAWBO	4	1	0
3	CALIE	PERCH	5	0	2
4	CALIE	JAWBO	3	0	4
5	CALIE	DOSTO	4	0	4
6	JAWBO	DOSTO	1	1	0
7	JAWBO	SULLI	8	0	1
8	DOSTO	PERCH	3	0	0
9	DOSTO	SULLI	6	1	0
10	PERCH	SULLI	7	0	4

The Minimal Spanning Tree Problem in PROC NETFLOW Format

This problem shows an interesting example of using a generalized network algorithm. A minimal spanning tree problem is a shortest-path problem. The difference between it and a minimum travel distance or time problem is that all nodes must be connected. In other words, there are multiple destinations, rather than just one. To set up a minimal spanning tree problem in PROC NETFLOW, we use its feature of being able to specify supply and demand values. The source node (node 1 in the setup of the Nancy Brown barn wiring problem below) is given a supply value equal to the number of nodes being connected (the 7 in the column for OUT in the first row of data below), and each destination node is given a demand value of one (the values in the last column—the variable IN—below). The supply and demand values should be included only once for the source node and each of the destination nodes. That is why there are so many periods in the data set below (periods are the SAS missing value symbol, here used as a "no value" symbol). So, each row in the data set below includes the names of the starting and ending nodes of a branch (here they are assigned numbers), the length of the branch, the supply at the starting node, and the demand at the ending node. The names of the variables containing these values are specified by PROC NETFLOW keywords. **TAILNODE** identifies starting points of branches, and **HEADNODE** identifies ending points. The variable containing the length values is identified with the keyword **COST**, and the supply and demand values by the keywords **SUPPLY** and **DEMAND**.

The PROC NETFLOW Program for the Nancy Brown Problem

```
1   TITLE 'NANCY BROWN BARN WIRING';
2   DATA NANCY;
```

```
 3        INPUT START END LENGTH OUT IN;
 4        CARDS;
 5    1  2  4  7  1
 6    1  3  5  .  1
 7    2  3  2  .  .
 8    2  4  7  .  1
 9    2  5  7  .  1
10    2  6  6  .  1
11    3  2  2  .  .
12    3  5  4  .  .
13    4  2  7  .  .
14    4  5  9  .  .
15    4  7  10 .  1
16    5  2  7  .  .
17    5  3  4  .  .
18    5  4  9  .  .
19    5  6  5  .  .
20    5  8  3  .  1
21    6  2  6  .  .
22    6  5  5  .  .
23    6  7  1  .  .
24    7  4  10 .  .
25    7  6  1  .  .
26    8  5  3  .  .
27   ;
28   PROC NETFLOW DATA=NANCY;
29        TAILNODE START;
30        HEADNODE END;
31        COST LENGTH;
32        SUPPLY OUT;
33        DEMAND IN;
34   PROC PRINT;
```

Solution Output

The PROC NETFLOW output is the same for all the different types of situations modeled. As shown below in the solution output for the Nancy Brown problem, the input data are included in the output, followed by the columns **FLOW1** and **DUAL1**. As before, the values in **FLOW1** indicate the flow along each branch and the values in **DUAL1** indicate the marginal cost of increasing the flow in each branch. In this context, the magnitude of flow is irrelevant; it is the presence or absence of a flow that is important.

NOTE: MINIMUM COST OF FLOW = 26

(Note: This appears on the SAS program log, not on the solution output table.)

```
                   NANCY BROWN BARN WIRING

    OBS    START    END    LENGTH    OUT    IN    -FLOW1-    -DUAL1-

     1       1       2       4        7      1       4          0
     2       1       3       5        .      1       3          0
     3       2       3       2        .      .       0          1
     4       2       4       7        .      1       1          0
     5       2       5       7        .      1       0          2
     6       2       6       6        .      1       2          0
     7       3       2       2        .      .       0          3
     8       3       5       4        .      .       2          0
     9       4       2       7        .      .       0         14
    10       4       5       9        .      .       0         11
    11       4       7      10        .      1       0         10
    12       5       2       7        .      .       0         12
    13       5       3       4        .      .       0          8
    14       5       4       9        .      .       0          7
    15       5       6       5        .      .       0          4
    16       5       8       3        .      1       1          0
    17       6       2       6        .      .       0         12
    18       6       5       5        .      .       0          6
    19       6       7       1        .      .       1          0
    20       7       4      10        .      .       0         10
    21       7       6       1        .      .       0          2
    22       8       5       3        .      .       0          6
```

Maximal Flow Problems in PROC NETFLOW Format

Maximal flow problems are set up in PROC NETFLOW in a manner similar to that of shortest-path problems. The data required are the names of starting and ending nodes, and flow capacities. The keywords for identifying the source and sink nodes, and starting and ending nodes, are the same. What differs is the use of the keywords **MAXFLOW,** which identifies the type of problem, and **CAPACITY,** which identifies the type of constraint.

The PROC NETFLOW Program for the Goodroad Tire Co. Problem

```
 1    TITLE 'GOODROAD TIRE MAXFLOW';
 2    DATA GOOD;
 3        INPUT FROM TO MAX;
 4        CARDS;
 5    1 2 3
 6    1 3 6
 7    2 3 1
 8    2 4 2
 9    3 1 3
10    3 2 2
```

```
11   3 4 1
12   3 5 2
13   4 2 1
14   4 3 2
15   4 6 4
16   5 3 2
17   5 6 1
18   6 4 4
19   ;
20   PROC NETFLOW DATA=GOOD NSOURCENODE=1
21                NSINKNODE=6 MAXFLOW;
22      TAILNODE FROM;
23      HEADNODE TO;
24      CAPACITY MAX;
25   PROC PRINT;
```

Here, the nodes are named by numbers (numeric symbols), and each data row identifies where a branch starts (FROM) and where it ends (TO), followed by the flow capacity in the branch (MAX).

Solution Output

Again, as in previous PROC NETFLOW applications, the column **FLOW1** gives the level of flow in each branch, and the column **DUAL1** indicates whether increasing the flow in that branch increases the flow through the network. Negative values in **DUAL1** mean that increasing a flow in the reverse direction in that branch would increase total flow. The solution of the Goodroad Company problem is shown below.

NOTE: MAXIMUM FLOW = 4

(Note: This appears on the SAS program log, not on the solution table.)

GOODROAD TIRE MAXFLOW

OBS	FROM	TO	MAX	-FLOW1-	-DUAL1-
1	1	2	3	2	0
2	1	3	6	2	0
3	2	3	1	0	0
4	2	4	2	2	1
5	3	1	3	0	0
6	3	2	2	0	0
7	3	4	1	1	1
8	3	5	2	1	0
9	4	2	1	0	-1
10	4	3	2	0	-1
11	4	6	4	3	0
12	5	3	2	0	0
13	5	6	1	1	1
14	6	4	4	0	0

6. CONCLUDING REMARKS

In this chapter you studied the following three network optimization algorithms:

Example 16.1, p. 587, shortest-path algorithm
Example 16.2, p. 596, minimal spanning tree algorithm
Example 16.3, p. 601, maximal flow algorithm

The shortest-path algorithm is a method for determining the shortest path (through a network) connecting an initial node to a terminal node.

The minimal spanning tree algorithm is used to connect all nodes of a network, using the minimum total branch length.

The maximal flow algorithm is a method of determining the maximum flow a network can carry from a source node to a sink node.

The exercises at the end of this chapter will illustrate the wide applicability of these methods in solving various management science problems.

TERMINOLOGY

After studying this chapter you should be familiar with the following terms:

TERM	SECTION
backward dynamic program	2
branches	1
dynamic program	2
flow	4
forward dynamic program	2
initial node	2
loop	3
maximal flow algorithm	4
minimal spanning tree algorithm	3
network	1
nodes	1
shortest-path algorithm	2
sink node	4
source node	4
terminal node	2
tree	3

EXERCISES

1. *Sales Route Planning.* John Smith, a medical-products salesman, must regularly travel from his home (labeled H in Fig. 16.23) to Jonesville (labeled J). The following network represents a map of the cities through which Smith can travel to get from H to J (distances are in miles). Use the shortest-path algorithm to determine the shortest travel route from H to J.

2. *Road System Design.* The archeology department of a local university has obtained support to begin excavations of five sites where prehistoric remains are thought to be buried. The five sites ($S1$–$S5$) are located near two cities, Bonesville and Hardin (B and H). The archeology department also plans to set up two field posts ($P1$ and $P2$) to serve as offices, labs, and storage facilities for food and medical provisions. The local geographic region is fairly rough with no established usable roads. Figure 16.24 represents a map of the area, showing the five sites, two cities, and planned locations of the two field posts. The branches shown represent *potential* routes where dirt and gravel roads can be built. Numbers shown on each branch represent the cost of constructing a road on the branch. Use the minimal spanning tree algorithm to determine the least cost plan of building roads in the region in such a way that all the nodes are connected.

3. *Irrigation System Planning.* Xavier and Cathy, who own and operate a small farm, are currently planning a new irrigation system for their fields. The network in Fig. 16.25 represents their seven fields ($F1$–$F7$), the lo-

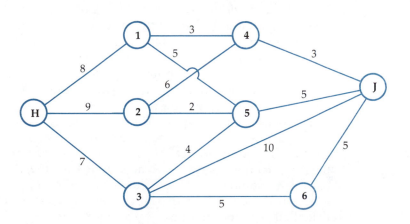

FIGURE 16.23

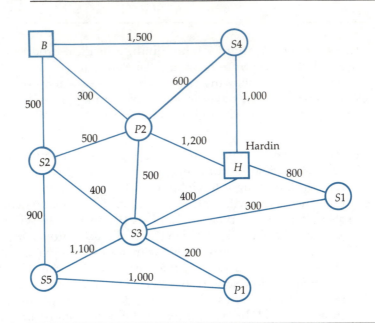

FIGURE 16.24

cation of the main pump (*P*), and the distances between feasible pipeline locations (in meters). The cost of installing the irrigation system is proportional to the length of pipe used to connect the fields to the pump. Use the minimal spanning tree algorithm to determine where the pipe should be installed in order that all fields are connected to the pump.

4. *Traffic-Flow Analysis.*   The city officials of Cranesport are making plans for the state fair to be held at the fairgrounds located in their city. Traffic must be routed from the fairground entrance (*E*) to the central fairground parking lot (*P*). The various roads winding through the fairgrounds from the entrance to the parking lot are shown in Fig. 16.26, together with the traffic flow each road can safely accommodate in either direction. For example, the road connecting the building at node 1 to that at node 2 can support 150 cars per hour; however, since that particular road is a one-way street, the reverse flow is shown as 0. The state fair officials estimate that 500 cars per hour will arrive at the fair. Use the maximal flow algorithm to determine how the Cranesport Police Department should plan to route arriving traffic from *E* to *P*. Are the existing roads located on the fairgrounds adequate to support the estimated 500 cars per hour expected to arrive?

5. *Research and Development.*   The space agency has scheduled research and development of a new lunar vehicle to take place in four phases,

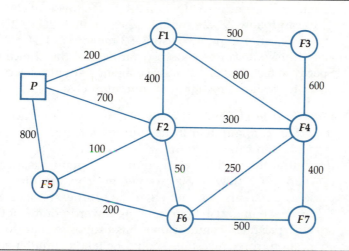

FIGURE 16.25

each phase involving various decisions regarding the vehicle's design. In phase 1, three options are available, costing $1 million, $1.5 million, and $2 million, respectively. Set up a shortest-path network, and label these options 1A, 1B, and 1C. For phase 2, four options exist: 2A, 2B, 2C, 2D, costing $4 million, $3 million, $9 million, and $7 million, respectively. However, 2A may only be followed if either 1A or 1C were chosen in phase 1; 2B can only follow 1A or 1B; 2C can only follow 1A; and 2D can be chosen regardless of the choice made in phase 1. In phase 3, three options exist: 3A, 3B, and 3C, costing $7 million, $5 million, and

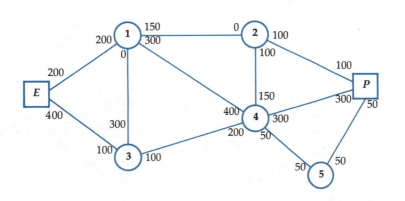

FIGURE 16.26

$3 million, respectively. Option 3A can follow any choice made in phase 2; 3B can follow 2A, 2B, or 2D; 3C can follow 2C or 2D. In phase 4, two choices exist, 4A and 4B, costing $3 million and $4 million, respectively, and either one can be chosen regardless of the choice made in phase 3. Specify which options the space agency should select at each phase in order to design the vehicle at minimum cost.

6. *Street System Design.*   The city of Townsy is reexamining the design of the street configuration in its southeast sector. The current street flow capacities (in cars per hour) are shown in Fig. 16.27. As represented in the figure, the road between point 4 and point 3 is a one-way street that can support a flow of 50 cars per hour in the direction of 4 to 3. At present, 1,000 cars per hour enter the southeast sector of the city at point 1 during evening rush hour, moving toward point 6 of the city. The city's street department commissioner has proposed that, to relieve rush-hour congestion, three measures should be taken simultaneously. First, make street 4–3 a two-way street that would support 100 cars per hour in the direction of 3 to 4 (in addition to the current flow capacity of 50 cars per hour from 4 to 3). Second, widen street 4–5 to support an additional 60 cars per hour. Third, widen street 5–6 to support an additional 60 cars per hour.
a. Evaluate the current extent of the traffic congestion at rush hour.
b. Evaluate the commissioner's recommendation.

7. *Urban Planning.*   The town of Hielo is planning to install a sewer system to meet the requirements of six new subdivisions. The subdivisions must be connected to each other and to the sewer treatment plant (STP). The network shown in Fig. 16.28 gives distances in 100-meter lengths between the subdivisions and the plant along pathways where sewer pipe can be installed. Use the minimal spanning tree algorithm to determine how the pipe should be installed so that the total length is minimized.

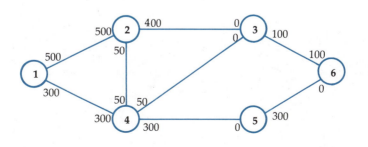

FIGURE 16.27

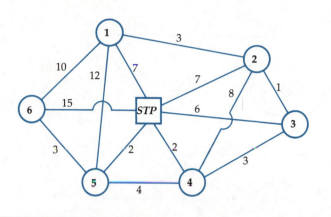

FIGURE 16.28

8. *Distribution Planning.* The Shakyleg Furniture Company must deliver a load of furniture from their location at Escondida to the town of Jaw Bone. The county map is shown in Fig. 16.29, where the nodes represent intermediate cities and the branches represent roads. Distances are in miles. Find the shortest travel route from Escondida to Jaw Bone, using the shortest-path algorithm.

9. *Design of an Irrigation System—Distribution Network.* A corporate food producer, Chemtrex, has purchased eight fields for planting vegetables. Each field must be irrigated with water from a central pump. The pump, feasible pipelines, fields, and distances (in meters) are given in Fig. 16.30.

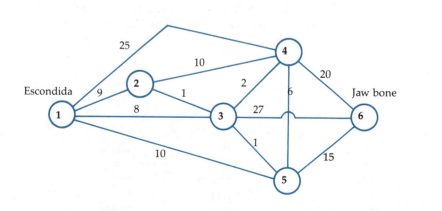

FIGURE 16.29

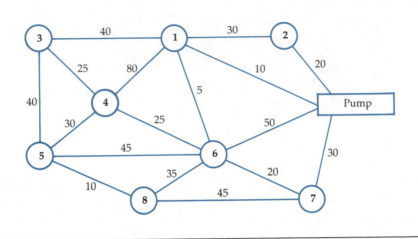

FIGURE 16.30

Use the minimal spanning tree algorithm to determine where pipe should be placed to minimize total length of pipe used.

10. *Equipment Replacement.*   Coaltrex uses a large crane in its coal mining operations. It is currently studying a purchasing plan for the next 15 years. It will consider purchasing a new crane at the beginning of years 1, 6, and 11. Projected purchase costs are: $300,000 if purchased at year 1; $450,000 if purchased at years 6 or 11. Salvage value and annual operating costs are shown in Table 16.4. (The annual operating costs rise because of increasing maintenance requirements.) In Table 16.4, if the machine is 0–4 years old, the annual operating cost is $15,000; if the machine is 5–9 years old, the annual operating cost is $20,000; and the annual operating cost in years 11–14 is $30,000. The vice-president of Coaltrex has proposed the plan shown in Table 16.5.

   Formulate this problem as a shortest-path problem and solve. Can you offer an improved plan (that is, a lower cost plan) to Coaltrex?

TABLE 16.4

Number of years used	Salvage value	Annual operating costs
5	$75,000	$15,000
10	50,000	20,000
15	20,000	30,000

TABLE 16.5

Action	Cost
Buy a new machine at the beginning of year 1	$300,000
Use it for 10 years:	175,000
Operating cost = 5(15,000) + 5(20,000)	
Sell it: Salvage value	−50,000
Buy a new machine	450,000
Use it for 5 years: 5(15,000)	75,000
Sell the second machine	−75,000
Total cost of this plan	$875,000

Note: Although this is a small problem and could be solved manually, you should appreciate the value of the shortest-path algorithm in solving the same problem if Coaltrex were allowing for possible machine replacement at the beginning of *each* of years 1 through 15.

11. *National Forest Management—A Communications Network.* The government has recently established a new wilderness area to be set aside for preservation. At present the government is planning to set up five forest ranger/tourist stations. A map of the proposed sites (1–5) and the distances between them (in kilometers) is presented in Fig. 16.31. The cost to link each given pair of stations by telephone cable depends on various factors (such as terrain) and is given in Table 16.6. Using the minimal spanning tree algorithm, determine the least cost plan for installing telephone cable so that each station is connected to all other stations.

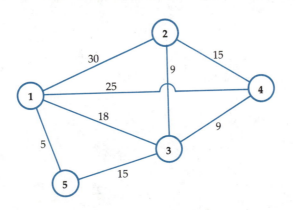

FIGURE 16.31

TABLE 16.6

From station	To station	Cost (in $/km)
1	2	$2,500
1	3	3,000
1	4	500
1	5	3,500
2	4	1,900
2	3	2,200
3	4	1,800
3	5	4,000

12. Refer to the National Forest Management problem (Exercise 11). The government must also plan a system of gravel roads to connect each station to every other station at minimum cost. The road construction costs per kilometer vary, depending on terrain, geologic factors, and other considerations. These costs are given in Table 16.7. Determine the least cost configuration of roads for this system.

13. *Oil Refining—A Distribution Network.* Skyhi Oil has operated a field of oil wells for several years and has distributed its refined product through several storage tanks to various destinations. Recently the city of Chikeger has experienced oil shortages. Prior to this time, Skyhi Oil had *not* been one of the suppliers of oil for Chikeger. However, Joanne Eastside, the mayor of Chikeger, has asked Skyhi Oil to indicate the maximum supply of oil (in gallons per hour) that could be sent from their refinery to the city. Figure 16.32 shows the refinery (R), Chikeger (C), and intermediate storage tanks (numbered 1–5). The numbers on the branches specify the maximum flow capacity along the pipelines of the branches

TABLE 16.7

From station	To station	Cost ($000/km)
1	2	$35
1	3	25
1	4	15
1	5	18
2	4	30
2	3	25
3	4	14
3	5	9

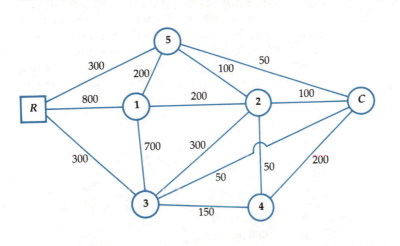

FIGURE 16.32

that can be pumped in either direction. The output of the refinery is
1,000 gallons per hour. Determine the maximum oil flow that could be
sent to Chikeger.

14. *Product Distribution.* Boxex is a small company that manufactures a
chemical food additive that improves nutritional content. Boxex's current
production rate is 150 pounds per day. Its distribution system is represented by the network shown in Fig. 16.33. The Boxex manufacturing

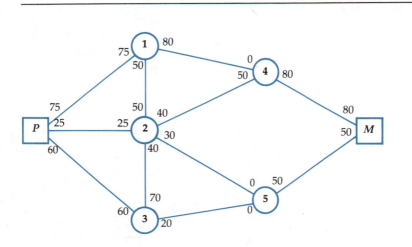

FIGURE 16.33

plant is labeled P, its major market area is labeled M, and the branches represent various alternative modes of product shipment. Each of these network elements is defined in Table 16.8 (nodes 1, 2, 3, 4, and 5 represent cities). The numbers shown on the network branches specify the maximum flow capacities. For example, the truck route from city 2 to city 3 can be relied upon to carry 40 pounds per day. The railway going

TABLE 16.8

Branch	Description
P–1, 1–P	Air lane (air-freight carrier)
P–2, 2–P	Truck route
P–3, 3–P	Railway
1–4	Air lane
4–1	Truck route
1–2, 2–1	Truck route
2–4, 4–2	Railway
2–5, 5–2	Truck route
2–3	Truck route
3–2	Railway
3–5	Truck route
4–M	Railway
5–M	Truck route

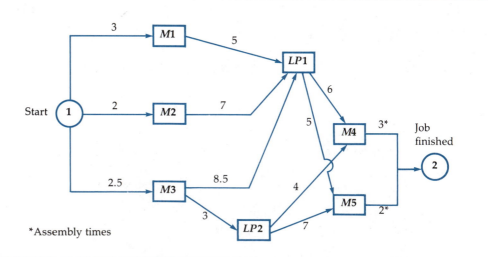

*Assembly times

FIGURE 16.34

from city 3 to city 2 can be used to transport as much as 70 pounds per day. Note that the air lane from 1 to 4 has no scheduled reverse flight (from 4 to 1). Similar interpretations can be given to the rest of the network.

Determine the maximum supply of food additive that can be shipped from Boxex's plant, P, to its market, M.

15. *Routing Jobs for Processing.*   Jobenrun, a small job shop, just received a high-priority order for a special job that requires processing on several machines as well as a few manual operations. The various routes that can be used to complete production on the order are shown in Fig. 16.34, where $M1$–$M5$ represent machine processes, $LP1$ and $LP2$ represent labor processes, and time is given in hours.

Thus, for example, one possible routing might be as follows:

Operation	Time
Machine $M1$	3
Labor process $LP1$	5
Machine $M5$	5
Assembly	2
1–$M1$–$LP1$–$M5$–2	15 hours

Use the shortest-path algorithm to determine the routing that would result in the minimum processing time to produce the product.

17 BRANCH-AND-BOUND METHODS

CONTENTS

1. INTRODUCTION

In this chapter we shall present a solution technique referred to as **branch-and-bound.** This term does not refer to a specific solution procedure but, rather, refers to a more general approach to solving various types of problems. In fact, there may be more than one branch-and-bound algorithm for solving the *same* problem. Each such algorithm would differ in the specific criteria employed in the steps of the solution procedure. However, *all* branch-and-bound algorithms do share a general "algorithmic philosophy," as we shall see.

Although branch-and-bound methods are a somewhat specialized branch of management science, we have chosen to include this brief chapter because the methods are gaining popularity and their use is spreading to more general problems. Recently, branch-and-bound methods have been applied to solve certain dynamic programs (Chapter 15). The primary value of the branch-and-bound method is in solving so-called **combinatorial problems**—problems that involve a large number of solution combinations, too many, in fact, to list easily. In addition, *most of the existing integer programming methods employ the branch-and-bound philosophy.*

To demonstrate the branch-and-bound method, we shall solve two problems: (1) an assignment problem (see Chapter 5) and (2) a pure integer program (Chapter 14).

624

2. POLITICAL CAMPAIGNING: AN ASSIGNMENT PROBLEM

Susan Doright is running for County Clerk this November. Her campaign staff consists of four key people, each of whom she must assign to work one of the four main political districts vital to carry the election. During a recent strategy meeting, each of Susan's staff members made estimates of the number of people they personally knew in each district. This information is summarized in Table 17.1. The problem facing Susan is how to assign her staff members to the four districts in order to maximize the total number of personal contacts.

This is an example of a combinatorial problem. There are 4! ("four factorial"—see Appendix C) different ways the assignments can be made: 4! = (4)(3)(2)(1) = 24. Exercise 1 at the end of this chapter asks you to enumerate each of these and to select the best one. If there were ten workers and ten districts, there would be 10! = 3,628,800 possible assignments. The branch-and-bound method *implicitly enumerates* possibilities without actually listing each and every one; thus the computational effort is greatly reduced.

Solution of the Assignment Problem

We shall now apply a branch-and-bound algorithm to solve the above assignment problem. We shall label each major phase of analysis as a step and number the procedures under each step.

STEP 1: DISTRICT A ASSIGNMENT.

1. Initialize the Problem. We start with the set of all possible assignments and represent this set (of twenty-four assignments) by a square, called a **node,** which we label as node 0. A lower bound on the final solution to the assignment problem is 0; that is, at least 0 persons will be contacted during the political campaigning. Thus we write "LB = 0" next to node 0 ("the *lower bound* to the problem equals 0"). This gives us the first node of a *tree* that

TABLE 17.1

| Staff member | Political district | | | |
	A	B	C	D
1	7	15	20	14
2	8	16	30	25
3	32	20	18	20
4	15	25	15	20

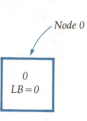

Node 0

0
LB = 0

FIGURE 17.1(a)   *Initial node.*

we shall progressively enlarge. [See Fig. 17.1(a).] We say that the current **incumbent** solution is 0.

2. Branching. We now partition the set of twenty-four possible assignments into four subsets. The first subset consists of all those assignments in which person 1 is assigned to district *A*; the second subset consists of all those assignments in which person 2 is assigned to district *A*; the third in which person 3 is assigned to district *A*; and the fourth in which person 4 is assigned to district *A*. Each of these will be represented by a node that branches off node 0 as in Fig. 17.1(b). The upper bound (UB) values will be explained below.

APPLICATIONS

The following applications appear in this chapter in text, examples, or problems:

Advertising mix

Cargo loading

Crime prevention

Job shop work assignments

Military planning

Personnel assignments

Political campaigning

Portfolio selection: An MIP

Product mix

Television programming

Traveling salesman problem

Vacation planning

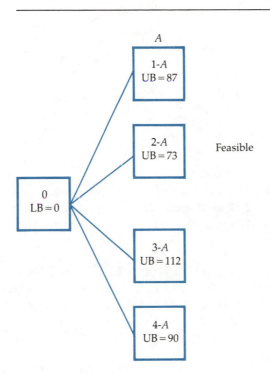

A

1-A
UB = 87

2-A
UB = 73   Feasible

0
LB = 0

3-A
UB = 112

4-A
UB = 90

FIGURE 17.1(b)   *Branching and bounding*

3. Bounding. The nodes at the tips of the branches of the tree are called **tip nodes** (surprisingly enough). Thus, currently there are four tip nodes. We must now compute an **upper bound** (UB) associated with each tip node, which will represent the most optimistic solution to the problem we can expect to obtain if we make the assignment(s) suggested by the tip node designation.

Let us start with node 1, which represents assigning person 1 to district A. This will give an immediate value of seven person-contacts (refer to Table 17.1). Now cross out row 1 and column A. This results in Table 17.2. The most optimistic value we could expect from this reduced table would be obtained by adding the largest entries in each column: 25 + 30 + 25 = 80. This is then added to the value of the assignment 1–A to give an upper bound associated with node 1: 7 + 80 = 87. Do not be concerned that the number 87 corresponds to an *infeasible* assignment—namely, 1–A, 4–B, 2–C, and 2–D, which is infeasible because person 2 has two assignments and person 3 has none. An upper bound (such as UB = 87 for node 1) is used only as an indication of the most promising value that the node *might* represent. The beauty of this approach is the *ease* with which we obtained the upper bound: almost no detailed analysis was required.

TABLE 17.2

Staff member	Political district		
	B	C	D
2	16	30	25
3	20	18	20
4	25	15	20

Examine Fig. 17.1(b) to see how we have recorded the results obtained for node 1. Nodes 2, 3, and 4 are similarly evaluated for an upper bound, and the results are shown in the figure. We summarize the calculations for these nodes below:

- *Node 2:* (2–A: 8) + 25 + 20 + 20 = 73. (Cross out row 2 and column A to obtain 25 + 20 + 20.) Also note that UB = 73 corresponds to a *feasible* assignment, namely, 2–A, 4–B, 1–C, and 3–D; thus we make a notation of this fact alongside node 2 in Fig. 17.1(b).
- *Node 3:* (3–A: 32) + 25 + 30 + 25 = 112, which corresponds to an infeasible assignment.
- *Node 4:* (4–A: 15) + 20 + 30 + 25 = 90, which corresponds to an infeasible assignment.

Before proceeding, we must emphasize the meaning of the nodes in Fig. 17.1(b). Node 0 represents the set of all possible assignments of campaign staff members to political districts. Node 1 represents the **subset** of assignments that assign person 1 to district A (there are six such assignments), and so on for nodes 2, 3, and 4. Thus we have **partitioned** the set of all possible assignments (node 0) into four subsets (represented by nodes 1, 2, 3, and 4).

4. Fathoming. Fathoming is the process of deciding which nodes no longer seem promising, which ones do, and whether a new lower bound for the problem can be determined. In solving the assignment problem, the fathoming process will consist of the following:

a. Examine the newly created tip nodes to see whether one or more of them represents a feasible solution. If there are no feasible solutions among the new tip nodes, go to part (c) below; otherwise, proceed to part (b).
b. Select the feasible solution having the largest upper bound value. If this UB value exceeds the LB value of the current incumbent solution at node 0, this new solution is then stored as the current incumbent solution. We say that this new solution has been *fathomed*, and we no longer need to consider its tip node at the branching step.

c. Fathom all other tip nodes whose UB value is less than or equal to the incumbent value.

   In our case we have found a *feasible* solution to the problem, having a value of 73 as represented by node 2. This tells us that the optimal solution to the assignment problem has a value *at least* as large as 73. Node 2 has served its purpose and can now be fathomed; that is, we no longer need to consider node 2 or any branches coming out of this node. We change the lower bound of the problem from LB = 0 to LB = 73 (at node 0). Note further that the other tip nodes, 1, 3, and 4, all have upper bounds exceeding 73, so each of these offers some promise of yielding a *feasible* solution greater than 73. Thus, we cannot yet fathom these nodes. The results of this fathoming procedure are shown in an updated tree—Fig. 17.2(a).
   Node 2, with a value of 73, is called the *incumbent solution*. It will remain the incumbent until another *feasible* solution that has a higher value is found. Also note the rationale behind labeling 73 as the lower bound: A *feasible* solution to the problem has been found which has this value; thus, the *optimal* solution to the problem will be greater than or equal to 73. The value 73

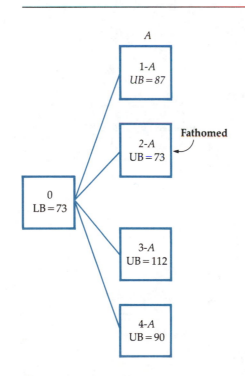

FIGURE 17.2(a)

places a lower bound on the optimal solution. (Of course, it may turn out that 73 is the optimal solution.)

STEP 2: DISTRICT B ASSIGNMENT.

1. Branching. There are three remaining subsets (nodes 1, 3, and 4) that have not yet been fathomed. We must select one of these to branch from. It seems natural to select the subset that appears to offer the highest upper bound value, which would be node 3. Thus we partition the subset represented by node 3 according to which person is assigned to district B. At node 3, person 3 is assigned to district A, so this leaves person 1, 2, or 4 to be assigned to district B.

2. Bounding. Figure 17.2(b) shows the result of branching from node 3 and then computing upper bound values for each resulting tip node. For example, in column B the node labeled "1–B" means person 1 is assigned to district B. Thus at this node, person 3 has been assigned to district A and person 1 has been assigned to district B for a value of 32 + 15 = 47; crossing out rows 3 and 1 and columns A and B of Table 17.1 gives Table 17.3.

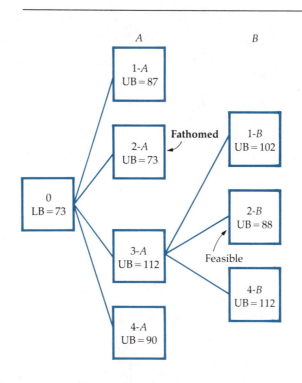

FIGURE 17.2(b)

TABLE 17.3

Staff member	Political district	
	C	D
2	30	25
4	15	20

To get an upper bound value for node 1–B we would add 47, the largest number in column C, and the largest number in column D, or UB = 47 + 30 + 25 = 102. Of course, the value 102 does *not* represent a feasible solution, since it corresponds to 3–A, 1–B, 2–C, and 2–D, which assigns person 2 to two districts and leaves person 4 with no assignment.

The upper bounds for nodes 2–B and 4–B are computed in a similar way:

- *Node 2 = B:* UB = (3–A: 32) + (2–B: 16) + 20 + 20 = 88. This represents a feasible assignment; namely, 3–A, 2–B, 1–C, and 4–D.
- *Node 4 = B:* UB = (3–A: 32) + (4–B: 25) + 30 + 25 = 112, which is an infeasible assignment.

3. Fathoming. We have found a new feasible solution, represented by node 2–B with a value 88, which exceeds the value of the incumbent (73). Thus this solution becomes the new incumbent and we have fathomed this node. Also note that the node labeled 1–A has an upper bound of 87. This means that if we assign person 1 to district A, the *best* we can hope for is a solution value of 87, and even this *may not be* feasibly attainable. In any case, our current incumbent *is feasible* and has a value of 88, which exceeds 87. Thus, we can fathom the 1–A node by eliminating it from any further consideration. Figure 17.3(a) shows the results of this fathoming.

STEP 3: DISTRICT C ASSIGNMENT.

1. Branching. There are three **unfathomed** tip nodes in the tree of Fig. 17.3(a) that have upper bound values of 90, 102, and 112. The most promising node, with a value of 112, is the node assigning person 4 to district B, and we choose to branch from this node. Two nodes result—namely, one for which person 1 is assigned to district C and one for which person 2 is assigned to district C.

2. Bounding. The upper bounds on the two newly created nodes are computed as usual, and are shown in Fig. 17.3(b). Both of these nodes are feasible and correspond to the following two assignments:

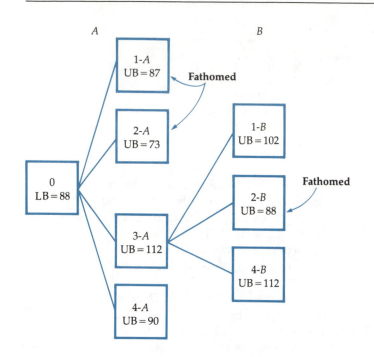

FIGURE 17.3(a)

3–A, 4–B, 1–C, 2–D = 32 + 25 + 20 + 25 = 102

3–A, 4–B, 2–C, 1–D = 32 + 25 + 30 + 14 = 101

3. Fathoming. We have found a *feasible* solution having a value of 102 and exceeding the incumbent value of 88, so we change the incumbent to 102 and fathom the node having a value of 102. We can also fathom *all* the other unfathomed tip nodes, since they each have UB values less than or equal to the incumbent (102).

4. Stop. Since there are no remaining unfathomed tip nodes, the branch-and-bound procedure terminates. The optimal assignment is the current incumbent, 3–A, 4–B, 1–C, 2–D, having a value of 102. You will note that only two *complete* assignments were fully enumerated (1–C and 2–C) out of the twenty-four possible assignments. In addition, there were some other computations, although they were rather simple in nature, involving only short additions and comparisons of nodes. In a larger problem, the computational savings over the alternative of complete enumeration is even more significant.

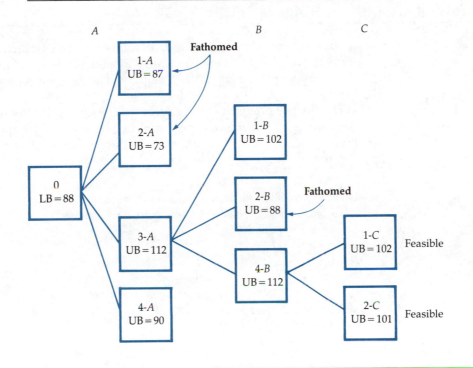

FIGURE 17.3(b)

Problems

1. List the twenty-four possible assignments in the political campaign problem of Section 2.
2. Solve the assignment problem in Table 17.4, assuming the criterion is to maximize personal contacts:

TABLE 17.4

Staff member	Political district		
	A	B	C
1	10	15	5
2	15	20	10
3	13	10	8

3. PRODUCT MIX: A PURE INTEGER PROGRAM

In this section we shall further demonstrate the branch-and-bound technique by applying it to solve a **pure integer program.** You should compare the solution procedure to that employed to solve assignment problems in Section 2.

The integer program (IP) we wish to consider is the Waveco, Inc., product mix problem, which was presented in Section 2 of Chapter 14 and solved by graphical means. You can read the description of that problem on p. 533. We restate the IP as follows:

Let x_1 = number of model A surfboards to make this week
  x_2 = number of model B surfboards to make this week
Maximize $Z = 60x_1 + 85x_2$ ($ profit this week)
Subject to:
(1) $9x_1 + 3x_2 \leq 27$ (machine-hours, machine 1)
(2) $4x_1 + 6x_2 \leq 23$ (machine-hours, machine 2)
(3) $x_1, \quad x_2 \geq 0$ (nonnegativity)
(4) x_1 and x_2 are integers

Solving the IP

We shall solve the IP for Waveco's product mix problem using a branch-and-bound algorithm.

STEP 1: PARTITION USING VALUES OF x_1.

1. Initialize the Problem. We start with the set of all solutions satisfying constraints (1), (2), and (3), but not necessarily constraint (4). This set of solutions is shown as the shaded region of Fig. 17.4. Thus we are including infeasible solutions, namely, all noninteger solutions. We denote this set of solutions by node 0. We can easily obtain a lower bound on the optimal IP solution by setting $x_1 = 0$, $x_2 = 0$, and $Z = 0$, so we set LB = 0 at node 0. [See Fig. 17.5(a).]

2. Branching. We solve the *linear program*, ignoring the integer constraint (4), to obtain the optimal LP solution $x^*_1 = 2.21$, $x^*_2 = 2.36$, $Z^* = 333.20$. If the optimal values x^*_1 and x^*_2 had turned out to be integers, we would have solved the integer program. Since they did not, we arbitrarily select the first noninteger variable, x_1, to branch on. The infeasible solution $x^*_1 = 2.21$ suggests that we should consider dividing the set of solutions into two parts, where $x_1 \leq 2$ and $x_1 \geq 3$. Remember that x_1 must be an integer in the optimal IP solution; thus this partitioning includes all possible integer x_1 values.

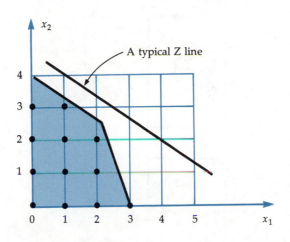

FIGURE 17.4

3. Bounding. In Fig. 17.5(b), we have displayed the tree resulting from partitioning the solution space according to whether $x_1 \leq 2$ or $x_1 \geq 3$. The upper bounds were obtained as follows: Consider node 1, $x_1 \leq 2$. If we solve the *linear program*

Maximize $Z = 60x_1 + 85x_2$
Subject to:
(1) $\quad 9x_1 + 3x_2 \leq 27$
(2) $\quad 4x_1 + 6x_2 \leq 23$
(3) $\quad x_1 \qquad \leq 2$
(4) $\quad x_1, \quad x_2 \geq 0$

we obtain $x^*_1 = 2$, $x^*_2 = 2.5$, and $Z^* = 332.50$. (You should check this by solving the LP graphically. Also, it is a good exercise for you to visual-

```
Node 0
LB = 0
x*₁ = 0
x*₂ = 0
```

FIGURE 17.5(a)

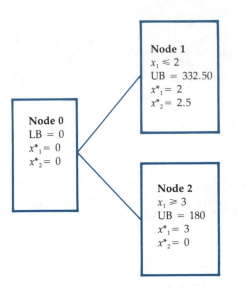

Node 1
$x_1 \leq 2$
UB = 332.50
$x^*_1 = 2$
$x^*_2 = 2.5$

Node 0
LB = 0
$x^*_1 = 0$
$x^*_2 = 0$

Node 2
$x_1 \geq 3$
UB = 180
$x^*_1 = 3$
$x^*_2 = 0$

FIGURE 17.5(b)

ize dividing the shaded region of Fig. 17.4 into the two regions $x_1 \leq 2$ and $x_1 \geq 3$.)

The meaning of these calculations for node 1 is as follows: The LP solution of the original problem with the added constraint $x_1 \leq 2$ is 332.50; so the *integer* solution to the same modified program cannot be more than 332.50. Thus 332.50 provides an *upper bound* on the set of all integer solutions to the original IP for which $x_1 \leq 2$.

Similarly, if we solve the linear program

Maximize $Z = 60x_1 + 85x_2$
Subject to:
(1) $9x_1 + 3x_2 \leq 27$
(2) $4x_1 + 6x_2 \leq 23$
(3) $x_1 \qquad \geq 3$
(4) $x_1, \quad x_2 \geq 0$

we obtain $x^*_1 = 3$, $x^*_2 = 0$, and $Z^* = 180$, which we summarize as node 2 in Fig. 17.5(b).

This bounding method uses the following fairly obvious fact: The maximum value of Z for an integer program is always less than or equal to the maximum value of Z obtained by solving the corresponding *linear* program (which ignores the integer constraints).

4. Fathoming. We have obtained a *feasible integer* solution ($x_1 = 3$, $x_2 = 0$) having a Z value (180) greater than the current incumbent solution ($x_1 = 0$, $x_2 = 0$, $Z = 0 = LB$). Thus we make this integer feasible solution the incumbent solution and fathom node 2. Since node 2 is fathomed, it need no longer be examined. The upper bound on node 1 (332.50) exceeds the best feasible solution found so far (180), so we cannot yet ignore node 1; that is, we cannot yet fathom node 1 because it still offers the promise of finding a feasible integer solution that exceeds 180.

The revised tree diagram is shown in Fig. 17.6(a). Note that 180 becomes the lower bound at node 0, meaning that the *optimal* IP solution must be *at least* as great as the incumbent feasible integer solution found so far ($x_1 = 3$, $x_2 = 0$).

Note that if the linear program of a tip node has no feasible solutions, such a node is then fathomed and therefore can be ignored in the succeeding steps.

STEP 2: PARTITION USING VALUES OF x_2.

1. Branching. There is only one unfathomed tip node to branch from, node 1, which represents all solutions for which $x_1 \leq 2$. Since $x_1 = 2$ is an integer and $x_2 = 2.5$ is noninteger, we shall branch on the x_2 variable and create two new nodes out of node 1. Node 3 will correspond to restricting $x_2 \leq 2$, and node 4 will include those solutions where $x_2 \geq 3$.

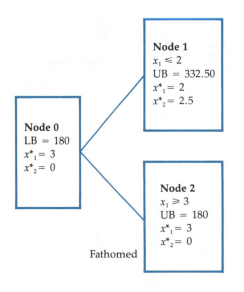

Node 1
$x_1 \leq 2$
UB = 332.50
$x^*_1 = 2$
$x^*_2 = 2.5$

Node 0
LB = 180
$x^*_1 = 3$
$x^*_2 = 0$

Node 2
$x_1 \geq 3$
UB = 180
$x^*_1 = 3$
$x^*_2 = 0$

Fathomed

FIGURE 17.6(a)

2. Bounding. Figure 17.6(b) shows the results of obtaining upper bounds for nodes 3 and 4. The linear program for node 3 is

Maximize $Z = 60x_1 + 85x_2$
Subject to:
(1) $9x_1 + 3x_2 \leq 27$
(2) $4x_1 + 6x_2 \leq 23$
(3) $x_1 \qquad \leq 2$ (from node 1)
(4) $\qquad x_2 \leq 2$
(5) $x_1, \quad x_2 \geq 0$

The solution is found to be $x^*_1 = 2$, $x^*_2 = 2$, and $Z^* = 290$. Thus 290 is an upper bound on all solutions to the IP, with $x_1 \leq 2$ and $x_2 \leq 2$.

The linear program for node 4 is the same as that for node 3, except that the constraint $x_2 \geq 3$ is used in place of the constraint $x_2 \leq 2$. The optimal LP solution is $x^*_1 = 1$, $x^*_2 = 3$, and $Z^* = 315$. Since this is the largest feasible integer solution greater than the incumbent solution, it now becomes the

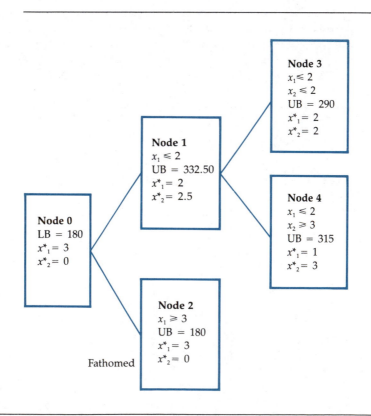

FIGURE 17.6(b)

incumbent. Furthermore, since its value of 315 exceeds the upper bound for node 3, we can fathom node 3. If we fathom nodes 4 and 3 in Fig. 17.6(b), there remain no unfathomed tip nodes, so the incumbent solution is optimal. Thus, the solution to the original Waveco IP problem is $x^*_1 = 1$, $x^*_2 = 3$, and $Z^* = 315$. This result agrees with the graphical solution obtained in Chapter 14.

Mixed Integer Programs

The above branch-and-bound algorithm easily extends to **mixed integer programs** (MIP) in which not all decision variables are restricted to be integers. For an MIP, branching would only occur on the variables that are specified to be integers in the final solution.

Minimization Problems

The branch-and-bound method for **minimization problems** is similar to that for maximization problems with the following modifications:

1. Initially, node 0 is given an upper bound of $+\infty$: UB $= +\infty$. As soon as a feasible tip node is encountered, this UB value will change as usual.
2. For each tip node, we compute a lower bound instead of an upper bound. A tip node is fathomed if its LB is greater than or equal to the UB value of node 0.

EXAMPLE 17.1. *A Minimization Assignment Problem.* Suppose we are given the following assignment problem for which the criterion is cost minimization:

TABLE 17.5

	A	B	C
1	10	8	6
2	5	4	7
3	2	6	5

The branch-and-bound solution procedure is as follows:

Step 1. Set UB $= +\infty$ for node 0.

Step 2. Branch on the assignment to A as shown in Fig. 17.7.

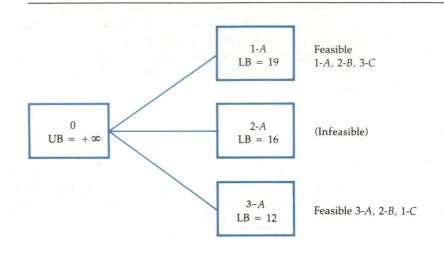

FIGURE 17.7

As an example, consider node 1–*A*. To compute the LB value, cross out row 1 and column *A*, then select the minimum column entries in columns *B* and *C*, namely, 4 and 5 (corresponding to 2–*B* and 3–*C*).

We have encountered two feasible solutions. The minimum LB value is 12, corresponding to node 3–*A*, so we can set UB = 12 at node 0 to indicate that the minimum solution to the problem cannot exceed 12.

Since 12 is less than 19, we fathom node 1–*A* (and need no longer consider it). Now node 2–*A* has an LB value of 16, which corresponds to an infeasible assignment, namely, 2–*A*, 3–*B*, and 3–*C*. In other words, 16 is the best that 2–*A* could possibly offer, and since 12 is less than 16, we need no longer consider node 2–*A*.

Thus we have found the solution to the problem as represented by node 3–*A*.   ▲

4. CONCLUDING REMARKS

Branch-and-bound refers to a general approach to solving various types of problems involving a large number of solution combinations, or so-called combinatorial problems. Essentially, a branch-and-bound method implicitly or explicitly enumerates all possible solutions in an intelligent manner. This is accomplished by dividing the set of all possible solutions into disjoint subsets ("branching"). These subsets are then evaluated to get some idea of whether or not they appear to be promising in terms of leading to an optimal solution ("bounding").

We demonstrated the branch-and-bound philosophy on two classes of problems: assignment problems and integer programs. Branch-and-bound methods have been devised to solve a wide range of problems in resource allocation, scheduling, production planning, capital budgeting, cargo-loading, and other diverse areas.

TERMINOLOGY

After studying this chapter you should be familiar with the following terms:

TERM	SECTION
assignment problems	2
bounding	2, 3
branch-and-bound	1, 4
branching	2, 3
combinational problems	1
fathoming	2, 3
incumbent solution	2
mixed integer programs (MIP)	3
node	2
pure integer program	3
tip nodes	2
upper bound (UB)	2

EXERCISES

1. *Job Shop Work Assignments.* Solve Example 5.1, p. 182, using the branch-and-bound method. Note that this is a *minimization* problem.

2. *Machine-Job Assignments.* Solve Exercise 1, p. 193, of Chapter 5, using the branch-and-bound method.

3. *Personnel Job Assignments.* Solve Exercise 3, p. 193, of Chapter 5, using the branch-and-bound method.

4. *Military Combat Effectiveness.* Solve Exercise 4, p. 194, of Chapter 5, using the branch-and-bound method.

5. *Crime Prevention.* Solve Exercise 5, p. 194, of Chapter 5, using the branch-and-bound method.

6. *Television Programming.* Solve Exercise 13, p. 198, of Chapter 5, using the branch-and-bound method.

7. *The Traveling Salesman Problem.*   The traveling salesman problem is a classic management science problem. Suppose John, a sales representative for Impact Hammer, Inc. (a manufacturer of jack hammers), must visit five clients, located in cities 1, 2, 3, 4, and 5. John's home-base location is in city 1, where he will start out. A map of the five-city region is given in Fig. 17.8 (distances are in km). John must start at city 1, *visit each city just one time,* and return to city 1. Such a travel route is called a **tour.** The objective is to select the travel route having the minimum total distance. We have recorded the distances in Table 17.6 (in km). For example, one feasible route would be 1–3–5–2–4–1 (70 km); an infeasible route would be 1–2–3–4–2–5–1, since city 2 is visited twice. Of course, city 1 will appear twice, because we start and stop there.

   Use the branch-and-bound method to determine a minimum-distance travel route.

   Hint: Use a bounding technique similar to that used in the assignment problem. This problem is also a minimization problem, so you will have to use a minimization branch-and-bound procedure. Finally, begin at node 0 with any feasible tour, such as the one given above (70 km).

8. *Bounding Methods.*   (Refer to Exercise 7 above.) Can you state two different methods for obtaining a lower bound (LB) for the tip nodes of the tree for the branch-and-bound solution to the traveling salesman problem?

9. *Vacation Planning.*   Carol is planning a vacation tour of various sites in the United States. These sites (identified by number) and the distances between them (computed from the *Travel Road Atlas* charts) are given in Table 17.7 (in miles). Carol's husband, who will be traveling with her,

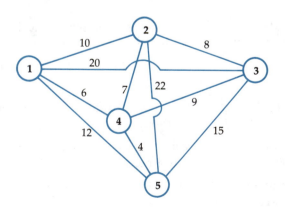

FIGURE 17.8

TABLE 17.6

			City		
City	1	2	3	4	5
1	0	10	20	6	12
2	10	0	8	7	22
3	20	8	0	9	15
4	6	7	9	0	4
5	12	22	15	4	0

sat up all night and planned the following tour—starting at site 1, their home location: 1–6–3–4–2–5–1 (5,700 miles). Their car is EPA-rated at 38 miles per gallon for highway driving, and the average price per gallon of gasoline is $1.00. Also, as a rule of thumb, for each 600 miles on the road, they will spend one evening at a motel and purchase three meals at an estimated daily cost of $60 for the two of them.

If Carol applies the branch-and-bound technique to solve this "traveling salesman" problem, how much could she and her husband save by using her solution?

10. *Product Mix.* In Exercise 1, p. 58, of Chapter 2, formulate Rustle's Bakery problem as a pure IP and solve it by using the branch-and-bound method. Check your answer by solving graphically.

11. *Portfolio Selection.* Michael has $2,000 to invest in stocks and savings. The stock he is considering is priced at $100 per share and returns 10 percent annually. Any amount of money can be put into savings to earn 6 percent annually. Michael would like to limit his investment in the stock to fifteen shares or less and his savings to $1,500 or less.

TABLE 17.7

			Site			
Site	1	2	3	4	5	6
1	0	300	500	700	400	1,000
2	300	0	1,200	1,000	500	900
3	500	1,200	0	1,500	800	1,300
4	700	1,000	1,500	0	700	800
5	400	500	800	700	0	800
6	1,000	900	1,300	800	800	0

a. Formulate a mixed integer program (MIP) to determine the optimal financial mix.

b. Solve by using the branch-and-bound method.

12. *Advertising Mix.* Formulate Exercise 8, p. 59, of Chapter 2, as a pure IP and solve by using the branch-and-bound method.

13. *Cargo Loading.* Formulate Exercise 16, p. 62, of Chapter 2, as a pure IP and solve by using the branch-and-bound method.

14. *Military Planning.* Formulate Exercise 17, p. 62, of Chapter 2, as a pure IP and solve by using the branch-and-bound method.

18 HEURISTICS IN MANAGEMENT SCIENCE

CONTENTS

1. INTRODUCTION

In this text you have encountered several algorithms and solution techniques for solving various problems in management science. These methods have been oriented toward finding an *optimal* solution to a problem, such as minimizing cost or maximizing profit (or some measure of benefit). We shall refer to such methods as **optimal methods.** Examples of optimal methods include the simplex method (Chapter 3), the stepping-stone transportation method (Chapter 4), assignment methods (Chapter 5), EOQ methods (Chapters 6, 7), dynamic programming (Chapter 15), network optimization (Chapter 16), and branch-and-bound methods (Chapter 17).

Another class of solution procedures are **heuristic programs.** A heuristic program is a method of solving a problem that is designed to reach an approximately optimal solution, not necessarily the true optimal solution. A heuristic program uses "rules of thumb" in analyzing a given problem. In fact, a **heuristic** is often defined as a rule of thumb.

You might wonder why anyone would be interested in a method that only gives approximate solutions to problems. Whenever possible, management science analysts *do* attempt to find optimal solutions to problems; however, there are two factors that enter into consideration here:

1. Although a theoretically optimal method may exist, it may not be practically feasible or desirable to use the method. For example, the optimal method might require excessive amounts of computer time in order to be

efficient for larger, real-world problems. In some instances, an optimal algorithm may be too complicated to implement relative to the needs and resources of management.

2. In many instances, management may not require an exact or perfectly optimal solution to the problem at hand. An approximate solution may suffice, especially if it is known that the approximate solution is acceptably close to the optimal solution. In addition, managers may not be concerned with optimizing a single objective but, rather, may have multiple objectives in mind, such as cost minimization, satisfying legal requirements, and employee satisfaction. In such cases, approximate solutions to various subproblems may be adequate to guide management. The benefit from exact solutions may not justify the cost of obtaining such solutions.

In this chapter we shall present a heuristic method for an inventory problem. Our objective is to give you an idea of the use of heuristics as well as the general nature of a heuristic.

Properties of a Good Heuristic Program

A good heuristic program should satisfy the following criteria:

1. It should give results that closely approximate the optimal solution.
2. It should be reasonably easy to use and to implement in terms of computing time and cost.
3. Although not a necessary requirement, it should have some intuitive appeal; that is, it should make sense.

To summarize, a good heuristic:

- *gives approximately optimal solutions*
- *is easy to use*
- *makes sense intuitively*

2. HEURISTICS FOR DYNAMIC DEMAND INVENTORY PLANNING

The basic EOQ models of Chapters 6 and 7 are based on the assumption that the demand rate is constant from period to period. In practice, demand may vary from period to period. Such variability is referred to as **dynamic demand** or **time-varying demand.** Examples of dynamic demand are:

- A contract that covers several months
- A seasonal demand
- Planned demand variation resulting from advertising and promotion
- Orders for planned maintenance of existing plant and equipment

The planning horizon may be finite (with a well-defined end) or infinite (no clearly defined end).

An (optimal) algorithm exists that will determine when to order and how much to order to minimize total costs (carrying costs plus ordering costs) over the forecasted planning horizon. This algorithm is called the **Wagner-Whitin method** and is based on the method of dynamic programming. (Interested readers may find a presentation of this algorithm in Section 4 of Chapter 15.) The Wagner-Whitin method has received relatively little acceptance in practice because of its complexity, computational requirements, and overall system implementation costs for long planning horizons.

We present two simple heuristic methods for dealing with dynamic demand, the **Fixed EOQ method** and the **Silver-Meal method.**

In each case, we assume that ordering can only take place at the beginning of each period and that the inventory is instantly replenished. After studying the methods presented, you will easily see how to incorporate a nonzero lead time.

Fixed EOQ Method

If the demand does not vary significantly, it may be reasonable to apply a fixed EOQ, using the *average* demand rate over the remainder of the planning horizon. The next example illustrates this method.

EXAMPLE 18.1. *Dynamic Demand: Use of a Fixed EOQ.* Wagonworks retails toy wagons for children. The wholesale cost of each wagon is $11, carrying costs run $0.09/$/month, and the cost to place an order is estimated to be $50. The demand forecast for each of the next five months is given below:

Month	March	April	May	June	July
Forecast	30	32	28	31	30

The current on-hand inventory is 0. How many wagons should be ordered to start this five-month planning horizon?

Solution. Let $\bar{D}$ denote the average demand over the planning horizon. Then

$$\bar{D} = \frac{30 + 32 + 28 + 31 + 30}{5} = 30.2$$

The EOQ is calculated, using the basic EOQ formula given in Eq. (6–5), and replacing D with $\bar{D}$ as shown below:

$$EOQ = \sqrt{\frac{2F\bar{D}}{Cr}} = \sqrt{\frac{2(50)(30.2)}{11(0.09)}} = 55.2$$

We assume that a whole number of months' supply must be ordered. The cumulative demand through March is 30 wagons, and cumulative demand through April is $30 + 32 = 62$. Since 55.2 is closer to 62 than to 30, the decision is made to place an order for 62 wagons, which we assume will arrive prior to or on the first of March.   ▲

The Fixed-EOQ heuristic of Example 18.1 gives acceptable results when the demand rate is approximately constant; however, when there is more demand variability, other methods should be used to obtain better results.

Silver-Meal Heuristic

Fortunately, a heuristic which is better than the Fixed EOQ and which is easy to use and has intuitive appeal, is available for the dynamic demand situation. This method is called the **Silver-Meal heuristic** (named after the developers, E. A. Silver and R. Meal) and can easily be understood by studying the next example.

EXAMPLE 18.2. *Dynamic Demand: Use of the Silver-Meal Heuristic.* Refer again to the problem facing Wagonworks (Example 18.1). Recall that $C = 11$, $r = 0.09$, and $F = 50$.

Suppose an order quantity is used that covers *only* the month of March, 30 units; then the ordering cost is $50 and carrying costs are 0 (we assume that carrying costs are paid only on inventory carried over from one month to the next). Thus

Cost to order 30 units = $50 *per month*

Next, we compute the cost per month of ordering a two-month supply. This quantity would equal 30 units for March and 32 units for April, for a total of 62 units. The ordering cost would be $50. To find the carrying cost, note that 32 units of the 62 total units must be carried through the single month of March. The associated carrying cost is (32 units)($11 cost/unit)($0.09/ $/month)(1 month), which equals $31.68. The total cost then is $50 + $31.68 = $81.68. To find the average cost per month, we must divide by 2 (the two months covered are March and April). Thus

$$\text{Cost to order 62 units} = \frac{\$81.68}{2 \text{ months}} = \$40.84 \text{ per month}$$

Next we compute the cost per month of ordering a three-month supply, or 30 + 32 + 28 = 90 units to cover March, April, and May demand. The ordering cost is $50. To find the carrying cost, note that 32 units must be carried one month (to April) and 28 units must be carried two months (to May). So carrying costs equal (32)(11)(0.09)(1) + (28)(11)(0.09)(2) = $87.12. The total cost for the three months then is $50 + $87.12 = $137.12, and to find the average monthly cost we divide by 3 as follows:

$$\text{Cost to order 90 units} = \frac{\$137.12}{3 \text{ months}} = \$45.71 \text{ per month}$$

The average monthly cost has risen from a low of $40.84 to $45.71. Since costs appear to be on the rise, we select the minimum-cost policy corresponding to $40.84—namely, to order a two-month supply of 62 units. ▲

It was merely a coincidence that the Silver-Meal method gave the same result as the Fixed EOQ method. Researchers have shown that in general the Silver-Meal method gives better results than the fixed EOQ method, especially when there is greater demand variability. In fact, the inventory costs resulting from the Silver-Meal heuristic are generally only one percent higher than the minimum costs computed when using the more complicated Wagner-Whitin algorithm.

The Fixed EOQ method and the Silver-Meal method can be compared simply by using each to plan the entire time horizon and then comparing resulting total costs. The next example illustrates this.

EXAMPLE 18.3. *Comparing Fixed EOQ and the Silver-Meal Methods.* Suppose that product cost is $5, carrying cost is $0.10/$/week, and fixed ordering cost is $20. The following table gives forecasted demand and cumulative demand for the next five weeks:

Week	1	2	3	4	5
Demand forecast	10	7	20	25	35
Cumulative demand	10	17	37	62	97

How would you plan inventory management over this five-week planning horizon, based on the above demand forecast?

Use of the Fixed EOQ Method

To plan the size of the first order (to arrive prior to week 1) we compute the average demand over the entire horizon as follows:

$$\bar{D} = \frac{10 + 7 + 20 + 25 + 35}{5} = 19.4$$

Then, using the basic EOQ formula we get

$$EOQ = \sqrt{\frac{2F\bar{D}}{Cr}} = \sqrt{\frac{2(20)(19.4)}{5(0.10)}} = 39.4$$

From the cumulative demand row of the forecast table above, we see that 39.4 is closest to a three-week supply. We would then plan to place the initial order for a three-week supply of 37 units.

To plan the size of the second order (to arrive prior to week 4) we have the following two-week planning horizon:

Week	4	5
Demand forecast	25	35
Cumulative demand	25	60

Thus

$$\bar{D} = \frac{25 + 35}{2} = 30$$

Again, using the basic EOQ formula we get

$$EOQ = \sqrt{\frac{2(20)(30)}{5(0.10)}} = 49$$

Since 49 is closer to 60 than to 25, our decision would be to place the second order for a two-month supply of 60 units.

In Table 18.1 we have computed the total ordering and carrying costs for the five-week horizon, using the Fixed EOQ rule. The carrying-cost row (e) is computed by multiplying each ending inventory carried over to the next period by the carrying cost per unit Cr = (\$5/unit)(\$0.10/\$/week) = \$0.50/unit/week. For example, the ending inventory for week 1 is given as 27 units. The cost to carry this inventory over to the next week (1 week) is (27 units)(\$0.50/unit/week)(1 week) = \$13.50. In short, to get row (e), multiply each entry of row (d) by \$0.50. In the last column we have summed row (e) to get a total carrying cost of \$41.

In row (f) we calculate total ordering cost as the number of orders placed (2) times the fixed cost per order (\$20) to get \$40. Finally, we add total carrying cost to total ordering cost to obtain the total cost of \$81.00 in row (g).

TABLE 18.1   *Total Costs, Using Fixed EOQ*

			Week				
		1	2	3	4	5	Totals
(a)	Initial inventory	0	27	20	0	35	
(b)	Amount ordered	37	0	0	60	0	97 units
(c)	Demand	10	7	20	25	35	97 units
(d)	Ending inventory	27	20	0	35	0	
(e)	Carrying costs ($)	13.50	10.00	0	17.50	0	$41.00
(f)	Ordering cost = number of orders × $20 = 2 × $20 =						40.00
(g)	Total cost =						$81.00

Note that this sort of analysis is based on our *forecast* of demand made prior to week 1. At this time we would *plan* to order at the beginning of weeks 1 and 4. In actual practice, as the weeks passed we would update our forecasts and even extend the horizon beyond week 5; as we did this, we would recalculate the order points based on a Fixed EOQ analysis, as above.

Use of the Silver-Meal Method

We shall now use the Silver-Meal method on the present example, compute its cost, and compare to the cost of the Fixed EOQ method.

To plan the size of the first order, proceed as follows:

1. To order only a one-week supply, the order cost is $20, the carrying cost is 0, the total cost is $20 + $0 = $20, and the average cost is $20/1 = $20 per week.
2. To order a two-week supply, the order cost is $20. The carrying cost is (7 units)($5/unit)($0.10/$/week)(1 week) = $3.50, which results from having to carry 7 units from week 1 to week 2. Total two-week cost then is $20 + $3.50 = $23.50, giving an average cost of $23.50/2 = $11.75 per week.
3. To order a three-week supply, the order cost is $20, the carrying cost is (7 units)($5/unit)($0.10/$/week)(1 week) + (20 units)($5/unit)($0.10/$/week)(2 weeks) = $3.50 + $20 = $23.50. The total three-week cost is $20 + $23.50 = $43.50, giving an average cost of $43.50/3 = $14.50 per week.

Since costs are rising, we stop at the low point of $11.75, which corresponds to the initial decision to order a two-week supply of 17 units.

To plan the size of the second order, we follow the same logic, this time on the planning horizon that extends from week 3 to week 5:

Week	3	4	5
Demand forecast	20	25	35
Cumulative demand	20	45	80

We shall now briefly summarize the calculations involved.

1. Cost to order a one-week supply:
   Order cost = $20
   Carrying cost = $0
   Total cost = $20
   Average weekly cost = $20/1 = $20
2. Cost to order a two-week supply:
   Order cost = $20
   Carrying cost = $12.50 (to carry 25 units from week 3 to week 4)
   Total cost = $32.50
   Average weekly cost = $32.50/2 = $16.25
3. Cost to order a three-week supply:
   Order cost = $20
   Carrying cost = $12.50 + $35.00 = $47.50 (to carry 25 units from week 3 to week 4 plus 35 units from week 3 to week 5)
   Average weekly cost = $67.50/3 = $22.50

The decision, then, is to place the second order at week 3 for a two-week supply of 45 units, to cover weeks 3 and 4.

This leaves no choice for the rest of the planning horizon, which consists of only week 5, so we shall place a third order at the beginning of week 5 for 35 units.

The cost summary of the policy specified by the Silver-Meal heuristic is given in Table 18.2.

Summary

From Tables 18.1 and 18.2, we see that use of the Silver-Meal heuristic results in a lower total five-week planned inventory cost. The percentage of savings over the Fixed EOQ method is

$$\left(\frac{81 - 76}{81}\right) \times 100\% = 6.2\%$$

In general, the greater the variability of demand, the greater will be the potential cost savings of using the Silver-Meal method over the Fixed EOQ method.

We might point out that the above solution, using the Silver-Meal heuristic, yields the same cost that would be obtained by using the (optimal) Wag-

TABLE 18.2   *Total Costs, Using the Silver-Meal Method*

			Week				
		1	2	3	4	5	Totals
(a)	Initial inventory	0	7	0	25	0	
(b)	Amount ordered	17	0	45	0	35	97
(c)	Demand	10	7	20	25	35	97
(d)	Ending inventory	7	0	25	0	0	
(e)	Carrying costs ($)	$3.50	0	12.50	0	0	$16.00
(f)	Ordering cost = number of orders × $20 = 3 × $20 =						60.00
(g)	Total cost =						$76.00

ner-Whitin method. Of course, this is simply a coincidence, but as we noted previously, the Silver-Meal method will result in total costs very close to the minimum Wagner-Whitin solution.   ▲

Cost versus Benefit

You will notice that the Fixed EOQ heuristic is simpler to use than the Silver-Meal heuristic in terms of the calculations involved and the time required. Thus, in some sense, the cost of implementing the Fixed EOQ heuristic is less than the cost of implementing the Silver-Meal heuristic. But it is also true that the latter method gives better results than the former method.

This is typical of solution methods in management science: Optimal methods (such as the Wagner-Whitin method) are more expensive and difficult to implement than heuristics. Similarly, the better the solution obtained by a heuristic, the more difficult and expensive the heuristic is to use relative to less reliable heuristics. The final decision as to which method to select rests with the management science analyst, who should take into account (1) past experience with the performance of the method in the specific application, and (2) an assessment of the cost/benefit analysis of using the various methods.

Problems

1. Suppose demand for the next three months is forecasted to be 100 units, 50 units, and 90 units respectively. Unit product cost is $25, fixed ordering

cost is $50, and the carrying cost rate is $0.20/$/month. Determine the size of the first order, using the Fixed EOQ heuristic.
2. Solve Problem 1, using the Silver-Meal method.
3. Suppose demand over the next three months is forecasted to be 50, 100, and 60 units, respectively. Product cost is $10 per unit, fixed ordering cost is $90, and the carrying cost rate is 10 percent. Determine the planned ordering policy over the three-month horizon, using the Fixed EOQ heuristic.
4. Solve Problem 3, using the Silver-Meal heuristic
5. Compare the costs of the two policies derived in Problems 3 and 4.

3. CONCLUDING REMARKS

A heuristic program is a solution procedure that yields results that are *approximately* optimal but, in general, are not *truly* optimal. Heuristics are used when (1) an exact optimal method does not exist, or (2) approximate solutions that can be easily obtained are sufficient. A good heuristic should (1) be easy to use, (2) make sense intuitively, and (3) give results that closely approximate the optimal solution.

Two heuristics were presented to solve the dynamic demand inventory problem: the Fixed EOQ method and the Silver-Meal method (see Section 2).

Other applications that have employed heuristic solution methods successfully include job-shop scheduling (scheduling jobs through a machine shop), warehouse location (locating warehouses relative to factories and markets), and facilities layout (such as determining the best layout of work centers in a manufacturing plant).

TERMINOLOGY

After studying this chapter you should be familiar with the following terms:

TERM	SECTION
dynamic demand	2
Fixed EOQ heuristic	2
heuristic	1
heuristic programs	1
optimal methods	1
Silver-Meal heuristic	2

EXERCISES

Parts of some of the following exercises require a knowledge of the material in Chapter 4 or 15. Readers not familiar with this material may simply omit the starred problems.

1. *Rare Metals Broker.* Jerry Lefkowitz is a dealer in rare metals. He forecasts customer demands for gold over the next four months to be 50, 70, 30, and 100 troy ounces in June, July, August, and September, respectively. His cost to acquire an order of gold is $100 (which includes telephone charges, use of teletype services, and personal time). The carrying cost per ounce is $30 per month, primarily due to the opportunity cost of the tied-up capital.
   a. Using the Fixed EOQ heuristic, determine the size of the first order Jerry should place.
   b. Repeat part (a) using the Silver-Meal heuristic.

2. *Inventory/Procurement Planning.* (Refer to Exercise 1 above.) Determine inventory and procurement for the entire four-month horizon, then summarize your results in the format of Tables 18.1 and 18.2, comparing the fixed EOQ and Silver-Meal heuristics.

*3. *Inventory/Procurement Planning.* Repeat Exercise 2, using the Wagner-Whitin algorithm.

4. *Planning for Price Changes.* (Refer to Exercise 1.) Suppose the current price of gold is $200 per troy ounce. Jerry anticipates this price will increase to $250 at the start of August. Carrying costs run $0.15/$/month.
   a. Using the Silver-Meal heuristic, indicate how Jerry should plan his purchasing.
   *b. Repeat part (a), using the Wagner-Whitin algorithm.

5. *Updating the Planning Function.* Suppose Johnson's Hardware forecasts demand for lawnmowers to be 20, 50, 70, and 30 units for April, May, June, and July, respectively. The purchase cost of each unit is $40. The ordering cost is $80, and the carrying-cost rate is 8 percent/month.
   a. Using the Fixed EOQ heuristic, determine the size of the first order.
   b. Now suppose the first order is placed [as computed in part (a)], and it is now the month of May. Sales for August are forecast to be 10 units. Determine the size and timing of the next order for planning purposes at the current time.

6. *Approximately Constant Demand.*
   a. Compare the Fixed EOQ and Silver-Meal heuristics on the following demand pattern: 40, 45, 45, 43; assume the product cost is $10, carrying cost is $0.10/$/month, and fixed ordering cost is $30. (Use table format of Tables 18.1 and 18.2.)
   *b. Repeat part (a), using the Wagner-Whitin algorithm.

7. *Seasonal Demand.*
   a. Repeat part (a) of Exercise 6 above, assuming the demand pattern is 40, 80, 150, 20 (such as for a seasonal product).
   *b. Use the Wagner-Whitin algorithm on this demand pattern.

8. *Restaurant Management.*   Montague's restaurant regularly serves three fine wines, each comparable in quality and price, and each substitutable for the other. The cost per bottle of these wines averages $20, carrying costs run 10 percent of inventory value per month, and the fixed cost to order is $20. The forecasted demand for the next eight weeks is as follows (in bottles): 5, 10, 10, 15, 50 (a convention is scheduled for this week), 5, 15, and 10. There are currently four bottles of wine in inventory. Indicate planned procurements over this time horizon, using:
   a. The Fixed EOQ heuristic.
   b. The Silver-Meal heuristic.

A REFERENCES AND BIBLIOGRAPHY

GENERAL REFERENCES: MANAGEMENT SCIENCE TEXTS

Anderson, D. R.; Sweeney, D. J.; and Williams, T. A. *An Introduction to Management Science.* 4th ed. St. Paul, Minn.: West Publishing, 1984.

Churchman, C. W.; Ackoff, R. L.; and Arnoff, E. L. *Introduction to Operations Research.* New York: John Wiley & Sons, 1957.

Levin, R. I., and Kirkpatrick, C. A. *Quantitative Approaches to Management.* 5th ed. New York: McGraw-Hill, 1982.

Trueman, R. E. *An Introduction to Quantitative Methods for Decision Making.* 2nd ed. New York: Holt, Rinehart and Winston, 1977.

Turban, E., and Meredith, J. R. *Fundamentals of Management Science.* Dallas, Tex.: Business Publications, 1981.

Wagner, H. M. *Principles of Management Science with Applications to Executive Decisions.* 2nd ed. Englewood Cliffs, N.J.: Prentice-Hall, 1975.

Whitehouse, G. E., and Wechsler, B. L. *Applied Operations Research: A Survey.* New York: John Wiley & Sons, 1976.

CHAPTER 1: INTRODUCTION

Caywood, T. E.; Berger, H. M.; Engel, J. H.; Magel, J. F.; Miser, H. J.; and Thrall, R. M. "Guidelines for the Practice of Operations Research." *Operations Research* 19 (1971): 1127–48.

Churchman, C. W. *The Systems Approach.* New York: Dell, 1968.

Crowther, J. G., and Whiddington, R. *Science at War.* New York: The Philosophical Library, 1948.

Hammond, J. S. "The Roles of the Manager and Management Scientist in Successful Implementation." *Sloan Management Review* (1974): 24.

Levinson, Horace C., and Brown, Arthur A. "Operations Research." *Scientific American* 184, No. 3 (March 1951): 15–17.

Little, J. D. C. "Models and Managers: The Concept of a Decision Calculus." *Management Science* 16 (1970): B–466–85.

McCloskey, J. F., and Trefethen, F. N., eds. *Operations Research for Management.* Baltimore: Johns Hopkins Press, 1954.

Morse, Philip M. "The Operations Research Society of America." *Operations Research* 1, No. 1 (Nov. 1952): 1.

Radnor, M., and Neal, R. D. "The Progress of Management Science Activities in Large U.S. Industrial Corporations." *Operations Research* 21 (1973): 427–50.

Turban, E. "A Sample Survey of Operations Research Activities at the Corporate Level." *Operations Research* 20 (No. 3): 708–721.

United States Army Air Force. *Operations Analysis in World War II.* Philadelphia: Stephenson-Brothers, 1948.

Wagner, H. M. "The ABC's of OR." *Operations Research* 19 (1971): 1259–81.

Whitmore, William F. "Edison and Operations Research." *Operations Research* 1 (1953): 82–85.

CHAPTERS 2 AND 3:
LINEAR PROGRAMMING

Charnes, A., and Cooper, W. W. *Management Models and Industrial Applications of Linear Programming.* Vols. I and II. New York: John Wiley & Sons, 1961.

Dantzig, G. B. *Linear Programming and Extensions.* Princeton, N.J.: Princeton University Press, 1963.

Gass, Saul I. *An Illustrated Guide to Linear Programming.* New York: McGraw-Hill, 1970.

———. *Linear Programming.* 4th ed. New York: McGraw-Hill, 1975.

Hadley, G. *Linear Programming.* Reading, Mass.: Addison-Wesley, 1962.

Levin, R. I., and Lamone, R. P. *Linear Programming for Management Decisions.* Homewood, Ill.: Richard D. Irwin, 1969.

Thompson, G. E. *Linear Programming.* New York: Macmillan, 1971.

CHAPTER 4:
THE TRANSPORTATION PROBLEM

See references for Chapters 2 and 3.

CHAPTER 5:
THE ASSIGNMENT PROBLEM

See references for Chapters 2 and 3.

CHAPTERS 6 AND 7:
INVENTORY MODELS

Arrow, K. J.; Karlin, S.; and Scarf, H., eds. *Studies in Applied Probability and Management Science.* Stanford, Calif.: Stanford University Press, 1962.

———. *Studies in the Mathematical Theory of Inventory and Production.* Stanford, Calif.: Stanford University Press, 1958.

Hadley, G., and Whiten, T. M. *Analysis of Inventory Systems.* Englewood Cliffs, N.J.: Prentice-Hall, 1963.

Holt, C. C.; Modigliani, F.; Muth, J. F.; and Simon, H. A. *Planning Production, Inventories, and Work Force.* Englewood Cliffs, N.J.: Prentice-Hall, 1960.

Orlicky, J. *Material Requirements Planning*. New York: McGraw-Hill, 1975.

Peterson, R., and Silver, E. A. *Decision Systems for Inventory Management and Production Planning*. New York: John Wiley & Sons, 1979.

Plossl, G. W. *Manufacturing Control: The Last Frontier for Profits*. Reston, Va.: Reston, 1973.

Starr, M. K., and Miller, D. W. *Inventory Control: Theory and Practice*. Englewood Cliffs, N.J.: Prentice-Hall, 1962.

CHAPTER 8: QUEUING MODELS

Cooper, R. B. *Introduction to Queuing Theory*. New York: Macmillan, 1972.

Gross, D., and Harris, C. M. *Fundamentals of Queuing Theory*. New York: John Wiley & Sons, 1974.

Hillier, F. S., and Lieberman, G. J. *Introduction to Operations Research*. 3rd ed. San Francisco: Holden-Day, Inc., 1980.

Jaiswal, N. K. *Priority Queues*. New York: Academic Press, 1968.

Saaty, T. L. *Elements of Queuing Theory*. New York: McGraw-Hill, 1961.

Taha, H. A. *Operations Research: An Introduction*. 3rd ed. New York: Macmillan, 1982.

CHAPTER 9: PROJECT MANAGEMENT: CPM AND PERT

Levin, R., and Kirkpatrick, C. *Planning and Control with PERT/CPM*. New York: McGraw-Hill, 1966.

Malcolm, D. G.; Roseboom, J. H.; Clark, C. E.; and Fazar, W. "Application of a Technique for Research and Development Program Evaluation." *Operations Research* 7 (1959): 646–69. (Discusses PERT application to the navy's Polaris submarine development.)

Pritsker, A. A., and Whitehouse, G. E. "GERT, Graphical Evaluation and Review Technique." *Journal of Industrial Engineering* 17, No. 6 (1966): 293–301.

Schoderbek, Peter B. "A Study of the Applications of PERT." *Academy of Management Journal* (September 1965): 199–206. (Surveys industrial applications of PERT/CPM.)

Taha, H. A. *Operations Research: An Introduction*. 3rd ed. New York: Macmillan, 1982.

Wiest, Jerome D., and Levy, F. K. *A Management Guide to PERT/CPM*. Englewood Cliffs, N.J.: Prentice-Hall, 1969.

CHAPTER 10: DECISION THEORY

Aitchison, J. *Choice Against Chance: An Introduction to Statistical Decision Theory*. Reading, Mass.: Addison-Wesley, 1970.

Bayes, T. "An Essay Towards Solving a Problem in the Doctrine of Chance," 1763. Reproduced in G. A. Barnard, "Studies in the History of Probability and Statistics: IX." *Biometrika* 45 (1958): 293–315.

DeGroot, M. H. *Optimal Statistical Decisions*. New York: McGraw-Hill, 1970.

Hadley, G. *Introduction to Probability and Statistical Decision Theory*. San Francisco: Holden-Day, 1967.

Schlaifer, R. *Analysis of Decisions Under Uncertainty*. New York: McGraw-Hill, 1969.
———. *Probability and Statistics for Business Decisions*. New York: McGraw-Hill, 1959.
Von Neumann, J., and Morgenstern, O. *Theory of Games and Economic Behavior*. 2nd ed. Princeton, N.J.: Princeton University Press, 1947.
Winkler, R. L. *An Introduction to Bayesian Inference and Decision*. New York: Rinehart and Winston, 1972.
Winkler, R. L., and Hays, W. L. *Statistics: Probability, Inference and Decisions*. 2nd ed. New York: Holt, Rinehart and Winston, 1975.

CHAPTER 11: MARKOV CHAINS

Derman, C. *Finite State Markov Decision Processes*. New York: Academic Press, 1970.
Howard, R. A. *Dynamic Probabilistic Systems: Vol. I, Markov Models; Vol. II, Semi-Markov and Decision Processes*. New York: John Wiley & Sons, 1971.
Howard, R. A. *Dynamic Programming and Markov Processes*. Cambridge, Mass.: The M.I.T. Press, 1960.
Kemeny, J. G., and Snell, J. L. *Finite Markov Chains*. Englewood Cliffs, N.J.: Prentice-Hall, 1970.
Ross, S. M. *Applied Probability Models with Optimization Applications*. San Francisco: Holden-Day, 1970.

CHAPTER 12: SIMULATION

Emshoff, J. R., and Sisson, R. L. *Design and Use of Computer Simulation Models*. New York: Macmillan, 1970.
IBM Corporation. *Bibliography on Simulation*. White Plains, N.Y.: IBM Corporation, 1966.
Naylor, T. H. *Computer Simulation Experiments with Models of Economic Systems*. New York: John Wiley & Sons, 1971.
Rand Corporation. *A Million Random Digits with 100,000 Normal Deviates*. New York: The Free Press, 1955.
Schmidt, J. W., and Taylor, R. E. *Simulation and Analysis of Industrial Systems*. Homewood, Ill.: Richard D. Irwin, 1970.

CHAPTER 13: GOAL PROGRAMMING

Ignizio, J. P. *Goal Programming and Extensions*. Lexington, Mass.: Lexington Books, 1976.
Lee, S. M. *Goal Programming for Decision Analysis*. Philadelphia: Averback, 1972.

CHAPTER 14: INTEGER PROGRAMMING

Garfinkel, R. S., and Nemhauser, G. L. *Integer Programming*. New York: John Wiley & Sons, 1972.

Geoffrion, A. M., and Morsten, R. E. "Integer Programming Algorithms: A Framework and State-of-the-Art Survey." *Management Science* 18 (1972).

Plane, D. R., and McMillan, C., Jr. *Discrete Optimization*. Englewood Cliffs, N.J.: Prentice-Hall, 1977.

CHAPTER 15: DYNAMIC PROGRAMMING

Bellman, R. *Dynamic Programming*. Princeton, N.J.: Princeton University Press, 1957.

Denardo, E. V. *Dynamic Programming: Theory and Application*. Englewood Cliffs, N.J.: Prentice-Hall, 1975.

Dreyfus, S., and Law, A. M. *The Art and Theory of Dynamic Programming*. New York: Academic Press, 1977.

Howard, R. A. *Dynamic Programming and Markov Processes*. Cambridge, Mass.: The M.I.T. Press, 1960.

Nemhauser, G. L. *Introduction to Dynamic Programming*. New York: John Wiley & Sons, 1967.

CHAPTER 16:
NETWORK OPTIMIZATION MODELS

Ford, L. R., and Fulkerson, D. R. *Flows in Networks*. Princeton, N.J.: Princeton University Press, 1962.

Plane, D. R., and McMillan, C., Jr. *Discrete Optimization: Integer Programming and Network Analysis for Management Decisions*. Englewood Cliffs, N.J.: Prentice-Hall, 1971.

CHAPTER 17:
BRANCH-AND-BOUND METHODS

(See also Chapter 14.)

Hillier, F. S., and Lieberman, G. J. *Introduction to Operations Research*. 3rd ed. San Francisco: Holden-Day, 1980.

Lawler, E. L., and Wood, D. E., "Branch-and-Bound Methods: A Survey." *Operations Research* 14 (1966): 699–719.

CHAPTER 18:
HEURISTICS IN MANAGEMENT SCIENCE

Budnick, F. S.; Mojena, R.; and Vollman, T. E. *Principles of Operations Research for Management*. Homewood, Ill.: Richard D. Irwin, 1977.

Peterson, R., and Silver, E. A. *Decision Systems for Inventory Management and Production Planning*. New York: John Wiley & Sons, 1979.

Simon, H. A., and Newell, A. "Heuristic Problem Solving: The Next Advance in Operations Research." *Operations Research* 6 (1958): 1–10.

Slagle, J. R. *Artificial Intelligence: The Heuristic Programming Approach.* New York: McGraw-Hill, 1971.

Tonge, F. M. "The Use of Heuristic Programming in Management Science." *Management Science 7* (1961): 231–37.

APPENDIX TO SECTION TWO:
TIME-SERIES FORECASTING

Box, G. E. P., and Jenkins, G. *Time Series Analysis: Forecasting and Control.* San Francisco: Holden-Day, 1970.

Brown, R. G. *Smoothing, Forecasting, and Prediction.* Englewood Cliffs, N.J.: Prentice-Hall, 1963.

Levin, R. I., and Kirkpatrick, C. A. *Quantitative Approaches to Management.* 4th ed. New York: McGraw-Hill, 1978.

Makridakis, S., and Wheelwright, S. C. *Forecasting Methods and Applications.* 2nd ed. Santa Barbara, Calif.: John Wiley & Sons, 1983.

APPENDICES E AND F:
CONCEPTS; PROBABILITY DENSITIES: APPLIED MODELS

Feller, W., *An Introduction to Probability Theory and Its Applications.* Vols. I and II. New York: John Wiley & Sons, 1966.

Freund, J. E. *Introduction to Probability.* Belmont, Calif.: Dickenson Publishing Co., 1973.

Levin, R. I. *Statistics for Management.* Englewood Cliffs, N.J.: Prentice-Hall, 1978.

Mosteller, F.; Rouke, R. E. K.; and Thomas, G. B. *Probability with Statistical Applications.* 2nd ed. Reading, Mass.: Addison-Wesley, 1970.

Parzen, E. *Modern Probability Theory and Its Applications.* New York: John Wiley & Sons, 1960.

Riggs, J. L. *Economic Decision Models for Engineers and Managers.* New York: McGraw-Hill, 1968.

Schlaifer, R. *Probability and Statistics for Business Decisions.* New York: McGraw-Hill, 1961.

B SOLUTIONS TO PRACTICE PROBLEMS

Section 2

1. Maximize $Z = 25x_1 + 40x_2$

Subject to:

(1)	$2x_1 + x_2 \leq 30$
(2)	$1.5x_1 + 1.8x_2 \leq 45$
(3)	$x_1 \geq 0$
(4)	$x_2 \geq 0$

a. Fifth constraint: (5) $x_2 \leq 21$
b. Sixth constraint: (6) $x_2 \geq 5$

2. x_1 = number of bookcases to produce per week
x_2 = number of writing desks to produce per week
Maximize $Z = 18x_1 + 30x_2$ (profit/week)

Subject to:

(1)	$x_1 + 2x_2 \leq 30$	(hours on table saw/week)
(2)	$1.25x_1 + 0.75x_2 \leq 15$	(hours on router/week)
(3)	$0.25x_1 + 0.1x_2 \leq 5$	(hours on belt sander/week)
(4)	$0.5x_1 + x_2 \leq 12$	(hours for assembly and finishing/week)
(5)	$x_1 \geq 0$	(nonnegativity)
(6)	$x_2 \geq 0$	

Section 3

1. The new objective function is: maximize $Z = 70x_1 + 80x_2$. Plotting a new initial objective function line and moving parallel to it, we find that point B (1,000, 2,000) is still optimal.

Thus

$$x_1 = 1,000$$
$$x_2 = 2,000$$

Maximize $Z = 70(1,000) + 80(2,000)$
$$Z^* = \$230,000$$

2. Maximize $Z = 25x_1 + 40x_2$

Subject to:

(1) $2x_1 + \quad x_2 \leq 30$
(2) $1.5x_1 + 1.8x_2 \leq 45$

We have graphed $Z = 400$ in Fig. B.1. Moving this Z line outward, we see that point A is optimal: $x_1 = 0$, $x_2 = 25$, $Z^* = \$1,000$.

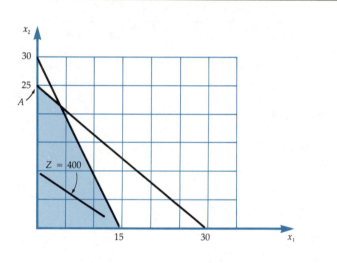

FIGURE B.1

3. Maximize $Z = 25x_1 + 40x_2$

Subject to:

(1) $2x_1 + \quad x_2 \leq 30$
(2) $1.5x_1 + 1.8x_2 \leq 45$
(3) $x_2 \leq 21$
(4) $x_2 \geq 5$

See Fig. B.2, p. 665.

Plotting an initial objective function line and moving it parallel, we find that point C is optimal.

Note: While point C *appears* to be the intersection of three constraint lines, it is actually the intersection of only two. Never rely on your graph for total accuracy.

Solving simultaneously:

(1) $2x_1 + x_2 = 30$
(3) $x_2 = 21$
$$2x_1 = 9$$
$$x_1 = 4.5$$

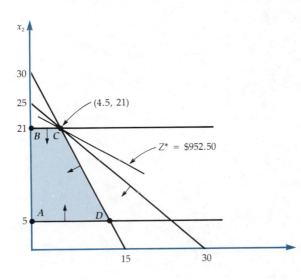

Maximize $Z = 25(4.5) + 40(21)$
$Z^* = \$952.50$

4. Maximize $Z = 18x_1 + 30x_2$
   Subject to:
   (1) $x_1 + 2x_2 \leq 30$
   (2) $1.25x_1 + 0.75x_2 \leq 15$
   (3) $0.25x_1 + 0.1x_2 \leq 5$
   (4) $0.5x_1 + x_2 \leq 12$

   See Fig. B.3. Plotting an initial objective function line of $Z = 180$ and moving it outward, we find that it will fall on point C last. We must solve for point C as the intersection of two constraint lines.

   (2) $1.25x_1 + 0.75x_2 = 15$
   (4) $-2.5(0.5x_1 + x_2 = 12)$
   $$\overline{0x_1 + 1.75x_2 = 15}$$
   $$x_2 = \underline{8.57143}$$
   $$0.5x_1 + 8.57143 = 12$$
   $$0.5x_1 = 3.42857$$
   $$x_1 = \underline{6.85714}$$

   Maximize $Z = 18(6.85714) + 30(8.57143)$
   $Z^* = \underline{\$380.57}$

5. The new objective function is: maximize $Z = 60x_1 + 100x_2$.
   Plotting a new objective function line on Fig. 2.6 and moving it outward, we find that point A (0,2666.67) is optimal.

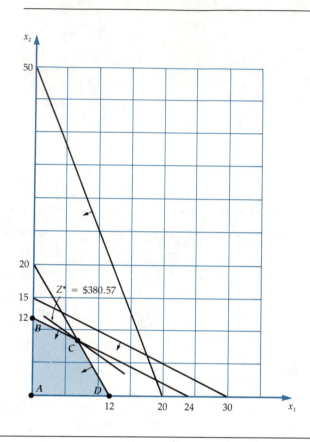

FIGURE B.3

$$\text{Maximize } Z = 60(0) + 100(2{,}666.67)$$
$$Z^* = \$266{,}667$$
$$z_1 = 0$$
$$x_2 = 2{,}666.67$$

Section 4

1. Minimize $Z = 3x + 4x_2$
Subject to:

(1)	$2x_1 + 2x_2 \geq 10$
(2)	$3x_1 + x_2 \geq 7$
(3)	$\left(\dfrac{4}{3}\right)x_1 + 2x_2 \geq 8$
(4)	$x_1 + x_2 = 8$
(5)	$x_1 \geq 2$
(6)	$x_2 \geq 3$

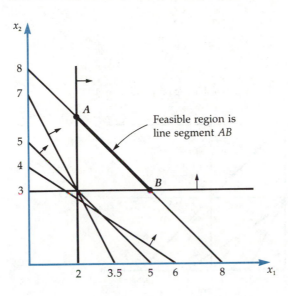

See Fig. B.4. The feasible region is simply all points falling on the line between points A and B. Plotting an initial objective function line such as $Z = 36$ and moving it *in* as far as possible yields an optimal solution at point B. Point B is the intersection of two constraints:

(4) $\qquad x_1 + x_2 = 8$

$\qquad\qquad\qquad x_2 = 3$

(4) $\qquad x_1 + 3 = 8$

$\qquad\qquad\qquad x_1 = 5$

Minimize $Z = 3(5) + 4(3)$

$\qquad Z^* = 27¢$

$\qquad F1 = 5$ ounces

$\qquad F2 = 3$ ounces

2. The two additional constraints are

(7) $\qquad x_1 \leq 5$

(8) $\qquad x_2 \leq 6$

See Fig. B.5. As demonstrated on the new graph, the two new constraints do not change the feasible solution region. Therefore, the optimal solution is the same as given in Problem 1 above.

3. See Fig. B.6. Corner points A, B, C, D, and E of the feasible solution region are found by substitution and simultaneous solving. Plotting an initial objective function line such as $Z = 100$ and moving *inward* suggests that point A is optimal. Since point E is also a strong possibility, it should be compared mathematically to point A. Do not rely on the accuracy of your graph in close cases.

Point A:

Minimize $Z = 10(8/3) + 3(22) = 92.67$

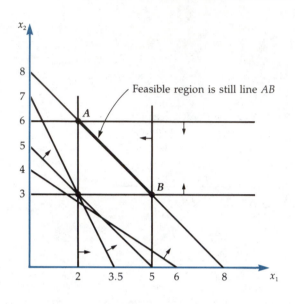

FIGURE B.5

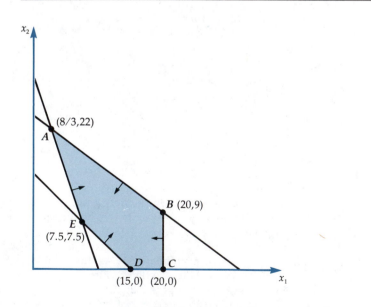

FIGURE B.6

Point E:
Minimize $Z = 10(7.5) + 3(7.5) = 97.50$
Since we are minimizing, point A is in fact our optimal solution. Thus $x_1 = 2.67$, $x_2 = 22$, and $Z^* = 92.67$.

4. Using the technique of the parallel objective function line, we find point E to be the optimal solution to this minimization problem. Thus $x_1 = 7.5$, $x_2 = 7.5$, and $Z^* = 82.50$.

5. Using the same technique, point D is now optimal. Thus $x_1 = 15$, $x_2 = 0$, and $Z^* = 150$.

Section 6

1. See Fig. B.7. This is a problem having multiple optimal solutions. The objective function line, when moved inward, falls perfectly parallel to constraint line (1).

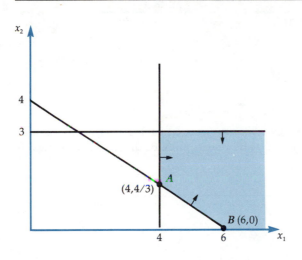

FIGURE B.7

Therefore any point on the line connecting points A and B is optimal. To prove it:

Point A:
Minimize $Z = 2(4) + 3(4/3)$
$\qquad Z^* = 12$
Point B:
Minimize $Z = 2(6) + 3(0)$
$\qquad Z^* = 12$

2. See Fig. B.8. This is a problem having an unbounded objective function. We find that x_2 cannot exceed a value of 10, but there is no limit on x_1 since we are maximizing and moving outward. This suggests an error in formulation.

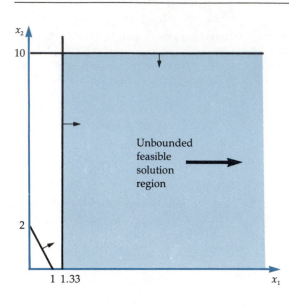

FIGURE B.8

3. See Fig. B.9. This is a problem having no feasible solutions. The feasible solution area is empty, and one or more of the constraints must be changed.

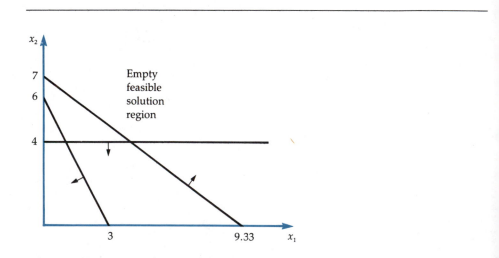

FIGURE B.9

4. See Fig. B.10. This is a problem having one optimal solution. Plotting an initial objective function line and moving it outward, we find that corner point C is the last point reached and, therefore, is optimal. To solve for point C:

$$x_1 + 2x_2 = 6$$
$$-(4.5x_1 + 2x_2 = 18)$$

$$-3.5x_1 = -12$$

$$x_1 = \underline{\underline{3.42857}}$$

$$3.42857 + 2x_2 = 6$$

$$2x_2 = 2.57143$$

$$x_2 = 1.28572$$

$$\text{Maximize } Z = 9(3.42857) + 8(1.28572)$$

$$Z^* = \underline{41.14}$$

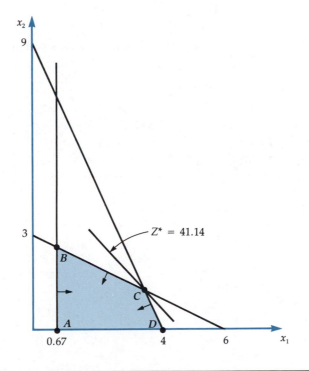

FIGURE B.10

CHAPTER 3: LINEAR PROGRAMMING: THE SIMPLEX METHOD

Section 3

1.

c_j	60	80	0	0		
Basic variable	x_1	x_2	s_1	s_2	**Right-hand side**	
s_1	1	3/2	1	0	4,000	Initial
s_2	2	1	0	1	4,000	tableau
Z					0	
z_j	0	0	0	0		
$c_j - z_j$	60	80	0	0		

c_j		60	80	0	0		
Basic variable		x_1	x_2	s_1	s_2	**Right-hand side**	
x_2		2/3	1	2/3	0	2,666.67	Second
s_2		4/3	0	−2/3	1	1,333.33	tableau
Z						213,333.33	
z_j		160/3	80	160/3	0		
$c_j - z_j$		20/3	0	−160/3	0		

c_j	60	80	0	0		
Basic variable	x_1	x_2	s_1	s_2	**Right-hand side**	
x_2	0	1	1	−1/2	2,000	Final
x_1	1	0	−1/2	3/4	1,000	tableau
Z					220,000	
z_j	60	80	50	5		
$c_j - z_j$	0	0	−50	−5		

See Fig. B.11. Step 1 involved going from point O $(0, 0)$, as represented by the initial tableau, to point A $(0, 2666.67)$, as represented by the second tableau. Step 2 involved going from point A to point B $(1000, 2000)$, as represented by the final tableau. We stop here because the values in the $c_j - z_j$ row in the final tableau are all 0 or negative. Thus our answer is: $x_1 = 1{,}000$, $x_2 = 2{,}000$, and $Z^* = 220{,}000$.

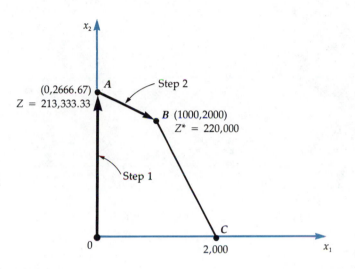

FIGURE B.11

2.

c_j	4	3	0	0	0	
Basic variable	x_1	x_2	s_1	s_2	s_3	Right-hand side
s_1	1	6/10	1	0	0	30
s_2	1	0	0	1	0	25
s_3	0	1	0	0	1	20
Z						0
z_j	0	0	0	0	0	
$c_j - z_j$	4	3	0	0	0	

Initial tableau

c_j	4	3	0	0	0	

Basic variable	x_1	x_2	s_1	s_2	s_3	Right-hand side	
s_1	0	6/10	1	−1	0	5	Second
x_1	1	0	0	1	0	25	tableau
s_3	0	1	0	0	1	20	
Z						100	
z_j	4	0	0	4	0		
$c_j - z_j$	0	3	0	−4	0		

c_j	4	3	0	0	0	

Basic variable	x_1	x_2	s_1	s_2	s_3	Right-hand side	
x_2	0	1	10/6	−10/6	0	50/6	Third
x_1	1	0	0	1	0	25	tableau
s_3	0	0	−10/6	10/6	1	70/6	
Z						125	
z_j	4	3	5	−1	0		
$c_j - z_j$	0	0	−5	1	0		

See Fig. B.12.

c_j	4	3	0	0	0	

Basic variable	x_1	x_2	s_1	s_2	s_3	Right-hand side	
x_2	0	1	0	0	1	20	Final
x_1	1	0	1	0	−6/10	18	tableau
s_2	0	0	−1	1	6/10	7	
Z						132	
z_j	4	3	4	0	6/10		
$c_j - z_j$	0	0	−4	0	−6/10		

Step 1 involved going from point O (0, 0), as represented by the initial tableau, to point D (25, 0), as represented by the second tableau. Step 2 involved going from point D to point C (25, 8.33), as represented by the third tableau. Step 3 involved going from point C to point B, as represented by the final tableau. We stop here

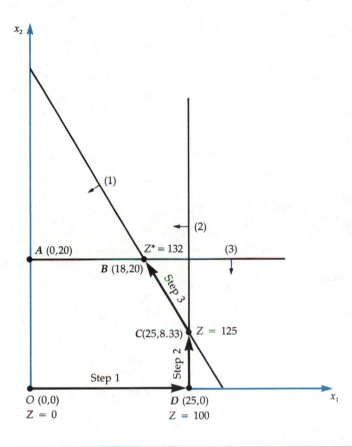

FIGURE B.12

because the values in the $c_j - z_j$ row in the final tableau are all 0 or negative. Thus our optimal solution is: $x_1 = 18$, $x_2 = 20$, and $Z^* = 132$.

3.

c_j	2	3	1	0	0	0	
Basic variable	x_1	x_2	x_3	s_1	s_2	s_3	Right-hand side
s_1	1	1	1	1	0	0	9
s_2	2	3	0	0	1	0	25
s_3	0	1	2	0	0	1	10
Z							0
z_j	0	0	0	0	0	0	
$c_j - z_j$	2	3	1	0	0	0	

Initial tableau

c_j	2	3	1	0	0	0	
Basic variable	x_1	x_2	x_3	s_1	s_2	s_3	**Right-hand side**
s_1	1/3	0	1	1	−1/3	0	2/3
x_2	2/3	1	0	0	1/3	0	25/3
s_3	−2/3	0	2	0	−1/3	1	5/3
Z							25
z_j	4/3	3	0	0	1	0	
$c_j - z_j$	2/3	0	1	0	−1	0	

Second tableau

c_j	2	3	1	0	0	0	
Basic variable	x_1	x_2	x_3	s_1	s_2	s_3	**Right-hand side**
x_3	1/3	0	1	1	−1/3	0	2/3
x_2	2/3	1	0	0	1/3	0	25/3
s_3	−4/3	0	0	−2	1/3	1	1/3
Z							25 2/3
z_j	7/3	3	1	1	2/3	0	
$c_j - z_j$	−1/3	0	0	−1	−2/3	0	

Final tableau

The optimal solution is: $x_1 = 0$, $x_2 = 25/3$, $x_3 = 2/3$, and $Z^* = 25\ 2/3$.

Section 4

1.a.

c_j	−2	−3	0	−M	0	−M	
Basic variable	x_1	x_2	s_1	a_1	s_2	a_2	**Right-hand side**
a_1	1	1	−1	1	0	0	10
s_2	0	1	0	0	1	0	20
a_2	30	8	0	0	0	1	240
Z							−250M
z_j	−31M	−9M	M	−M	0	−M	
$c_j - z_j$	31M − 2	9M − 3	−M	0	0	0	

Initial tableau

b.

c_j	-2		-3	0	$-M$	0		$-M$	
Basic variable	x_1		x_2	s_1	a_1	s_2		a_2	**Right-hand side**
a_1	0		24/30	-1	1	0		$-1/30$	2
s_2	0		1	0	0	1		0	20
x_1	1		8/30	0	0	0		1/30	8
Z									$-2M - 16$
z_j	-2		$-24/30M - 16/30$	M	M	0		$1/30M - 2/30$	
$c_j - z_j$	0		$24/30M - 74/30$	$-M$	0	0		$-31/30M + 2/30$	

Second tableau

c_j	-2	-3	0	$-M$	0		$-M$	
Basic variable	x_1	x_2	s_1	a_1	s_2		a_2	**Right-hand side**
x_2	0	1	$-10/8$	10/8	0		$-1/24$	10/4
s_2	0	0	10/8	$-10/8$	1		1/24	35/2
x_1	1	0	1/3	$-1/3$	0		4/90	22/3
Z								$-133/6$
z_j	-2	-3	37/12	$-37/12$	0		13/360	
$c_j - z_j$	0	0	$-37/12$	$-M + 37/12$	0		$-M - 13/360$	

Final tableau

Review of procedure: The objective function for this minimization problem was negated. Then the simplex algorithm for maximization was applied. The final requirement is to negate the $-Z$ found in the final tableau to give us Z^*. Thus the optimal solution is: $x_1 = 7.33$, $x_2 = 2.5$, and $Z^* = 22.167$.

c. See Fig. B.13.

2.

c_j	2	3	0	M	0	M	
Basic variable	x_1	x_2	s_1	a_1	s_2	a_2	**Right-hand side**
a_1	1	1	-1	1	0	0	10
s_2	0	1	0	0	1	0	20
a_2	30	8	0	0	0	1	240
Z							$250M$
z_j	$31M$	$9M$	$-M$	M	0	M	
$c_j - z_j$	$2 - 31M$	$3 - 9M$	M	0	0	0	

Initial tableau

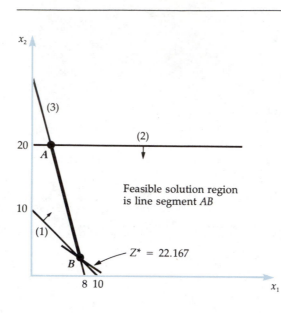

FIGURE B.13

c_j	2		3	0	M	0		M		
Basic variable	x_1		x_2	s_1	a_1	s_2		a_2	**Right-hand side**	
a_1	0		8/10	-1	1	0		$-1/30$	2	Second tableau
s_2	0		1	0	0	1		0	20	
x_1	1		4/15	0	0	0		1/30	8	
Z									$2M + 16$	
z_j	2		$8/10M + 8/15$	$-M$	M	0		$1/15 - 1/30M$		
$c_j - z_j$	0		$37/15 - 8/10M$	M	$-M$	0		$31/30M - 1/15$		

c_j	2	3	0	M	0		M		
Basic variable	x_1	x_2	s_1	a_1	s_2		a_2	**Right-hand side**	
x_2	0	1	$-10/8$	$10/8$	0		$-1/24$	10/4	Final tableau
s_2	0	0	$10/8$	$-10/8$	1		$1/24$	35/2	
x_1	1	0	$1/3$	$-1/3$	0		$4/90$	22/3	
Z								133/6	
z_j	2	3	$-37/12$	$37/12$	0		$-13/360$		
$c_j - z_j$	0	0	$37/12$	$M - 37/12$	0		$M + 13/360$		

The results using method 2 are, of course, identical to those using method 1. The only exception is that the Z given in the final tableau does not require negating.

Using method 1, we knew we had reached an optimal solution when all the values in the $c_j - z_j$ row were 0 or negative. In this problem, using method 2, we knew we were to stop when all the values in the $c_j - z_j$ row were 0 or positive. Thus the optimal solution remains: $x_1 = 7.33$, $x_2 = 2.5$, and $Z^* = 22.167$.

3.a. Maximize $Z = 5x_1 + 4x_2 + 0s_1 + Ma_1 + 0s_2 + 0s_3$.

Subject to:

(1)	$4x_1 + 5x_2 - s_1 + a_1$	$= 100$
(2)	$3x_1 + 2x_2 \qquad\qquad + s_2$	$= 60$
(3)	$\qquad x_2 \qquad\qquad\qquad + s_3 =$	15
(4)	$x_1, \quad x_2, \quad s_1, \quad a_1, \quad s_2, \quad s_3 \geq$	0

After adding the appropriate slack, surplus, and artificial variables to the original equations, we are now ready to apply the simplex method.

c_j		5	4	0	$-M$	0	0		
Basic variable		x_1	x_2	s_1	a_1	s_2	s_3	**Right-hand side**	
a_1		4	5	-1	1	0	0	100	Initial
s_2		3	2	0	0	1	0	60	tableau
s_3		0	1	0	0	0	1	15	
Z								$-100M$	
z_j		$-4M$	$-5M$	M	$-M$	0	0		
$c_j - z_j$		$5 + 4M$	$4 + 5M$	$-M$	0	0	0		

c_j	5	4	0	$-M$	0		0		
Basic variable	x_1	x_2	s_1	a_1	s_2		s_3	**Right-hand side**	
a_1	4	0	-1	1	0		-5	25	Second
s_2	3	0	0	0	1		-2	30	tableau
x_2	0	1	0	0	0		1	15	
Z								$60 - 25M$	
Z_j	$-4M$	4	M	$-M$	0		$4 + 5M$		
$c_j - z_j$	$5 + 4M$	0	$-M$	0	0		$-4 - 5M$		

c_j	5	4	0	$-M$	0	0	
Basic variable	x_1	x_2	s_1	a_1	s_2	s_3	**Right-hand side**
x_1	1	0	$-1/4$	$1/4$	0	$-5/4$	$25/4$
s_2	0	0	$3/4$	$-3/4$	1	$7/4$	$45/4$
	0	1	0	0	0	1	15
Z							91 1/4
z_j	5	4	$-5/4$	$5/4$	0	$-9/4$	
$c_j - z_j$	0	0	$5/4$	$-M - 5/4$	0	$9/4$	

Third tableau

c_j	5	4	0	$-M$	0	0	
Basic variable	x_1	x_2	s_1	a_1	s_2	s_3	**Right-hand side**
x_1	1	0	$2/7$	$-2/7$	$5/7$	0	$100/7$
s_3	0	0	$3/7$	$-3/7$	$4/7$	1	$45/7$
x_2	0	1	$-3/7$	$3/7$	$-4/7$	0	$60/7$
Z							$740/7$
z_j	5	4	$-2/7$	$2/7$	$9/7$	0	
$c_j - z_j$	0	0	$2/7$	$-M - 2/7$	$-9/7$	0	

Fourth tableau

c_j	5	4	0	$-M$	0	0	
Basic variable	x_1	x_2	s_1	a_1	s_2	s_3	**Right-hand side**
x_1	1	0	0	0	$1/3$	$-2/3$	10
s_1	0	0	1	-1	$4/3$	$7/3$	15
x_2	0	1	0	0	0	1	15
Z							110
z_j	5	4	0	0	$5/3$	$2/3$	
$c_j - z_j$	0	0	0	$-M$	$-5/3$	$-2/3$	

Final tableau

Since the $c_j - z_j$ row contains no positive values, we have reached an optimal solution: $x_1 = 10$, $x_2 = 15$, and $Z^* = 110$.

b. See Fig. B.14. Step 1 involved going from point O (0, 0) to point A (0, 15), as represented by the second tableau. The third tableau brought us to point B

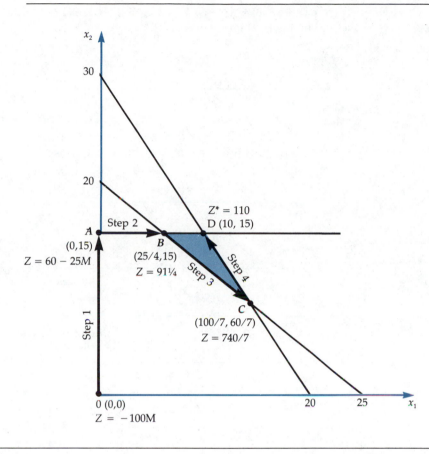

FIGURE B.14

(25/4, 15). The fourth tableau took us to point C (100/7, 60/7). The final step involved moving to point D (10, 15), as represented by the final tableau. The graphical method and the simplex method both yielded the same optimal solution.

Section 5

1. Maximize $Z = 2x_1 + 4x_2 + 0s_1 + 0s_2 + 0s_3$
Subject to:

$$
\begin{array}{llllll}
(1) & x_1 & & + s_1 & & = 8 \\
(2) & & x_2 & & + s_2 & = 3 \\
(3) & 3x_1 + 6x_2 & & & + s_3 & = 30 \\
(4) & x_1, & x_2, & s_1, & s_2, & s_3 \geq 0
\end{array}
$$

Three slack variables have been added to the original equations, and we can now set up the initial simplex tableau.

c_j	2	4	0	0	0		
Basic variable	x_1	x_2	s_1	s_2	s_3	Right-hand side	
s_1	1	0	1	0	0	8	Initial tableau
s_2	0	1	0	1	0	3	
s_3	3	6	0	0	1	30	
Z						0	
z_j	0	0	0	0	0		
$c_j - z_j$	2	4	0	0	0		

c_j	2	4	0	0	0		
Basic variable	x_1	x_2	s_1	s_2	s_3	Right-hand side	
s_1	1	0	1	0	0	8	Second tableau
x_2	0	1	0	1	0	3	
s_3	3	0	0	−6	1	12	
Z						12	
z_j	0	4	0	4	0		
$c_j - z_j$	2	0	0	−4	0		

c_j	2	4	0	0	0		
Basic variable	x_1	x_2	s_1	s_2	s_3	Right-hand side	
s_1	0	0	1	2	−1/3	4	Final tableau #1
x_2	0	1	0	1	0	3	
x_1	1	0	0	−2	1/3	4	
Z						20	
z_j	2	4	0	0	2/3		
$c_j - z_j$	0	0	0	0	−2/3		

The final tableau #1 yields an optimal solution of $x_1 = 4$, $x_2 = 3$, and $Z^* = 20$. Normally we would stop at this point, since the $c_j - z_j$ row contains no positive values. The row does contain one nonbasic variable (s_2) with 0 value, which indicates that there are multiple optimal solutions.

In the final tableau #2 below, we have introduced s_2 as a basic variable in place of s_1.

Z^* remains equal to 20, but the values for x_1 and x_2 have changed from 4 and 3 to 8 and 1, respectively.

2. Maximize $Z = 2x_1 + 5x_2 + 0s_1 + 0s_2 - Ma_1$

Subject to:

(1) $x_1 + x_2 + s_1 \qquad\qquad = 10$

(2) $2x_1 + 3x_2 \qquad - s_2 + a_1 = 48$

(3) $x_1, \quad x_2, \quad s_1, \quad s_2, \quad a_1 \geq 0$

The appropriate slack, surplus, and artificial variables have been added to the original equations of the problem. We can now proceed to the initial tableau.

c_j	2	4	0	0	0		
Basic variable	x_1	x_2	s_1	s_2	s_3	**Right-hand side**	
s_2	0	0	1/2	1	−1/6	2	Final
x_2	0	1	−1/2	0	1/6	1	tableau #2
x_1	1	0	1	0	0	8	
Z						20	
z_j	2	4	0	0	4/6		
$c_j - z_j$	0	0	0	0	−4/6		

c_j	2	5	0	0	−M		
Basic variable	x_1	x_2	s_1	s_2	a_1	**Right-hand side**	
s_1	1	1	1	0	0	10	Initial
a_1	2	3	0	−1	1	48	tableau
Z						−48M	
z_j	−2M	−3M	0	M	−M		
$c_j - z_j$	2 + 2M	5 + 3M	0	−M	0		

c_j			2	5		0	0	$-M$	
Basic variable			x_1	x_2		s_1	s_2	a_1	**Right-hand side**
x_2			1	1		1	0	0	10
a_1			-1	0		-3	-1	1	18
Z									$50 - 18M$
z_j			$5 + M$	5		$5 + 3M$	M	$-M$	
$c_j - z_j$			$-3 - M$	0		$-5 - 3M$	$-M$	0	

Final tableau

We must stop with the tableau above because all values in the $c_j - z_j$ row are 0 or negative. Note that the artificial variable remains as a basic variable in the final tableau. This indicates that the problem has no feasible solutions.

3. Maximize $Z = 3x_1 + 4x_2 + 0s_1 - Ma_1 + 0s_2$

Subject to:

(1) $9x_1 + 3x_2 - s_1 + a_1 \qquad = 54$

(2) $3x_1 \qquad\qquad\qquad + s_2 = 15$

(3) $x_1, \quad x_2, \quad s_1, \quad a_1, \quad s_2 \geq 0$

With the slack, surplus, and artificial variables added, we are ready to construct the initial tableau.

c_j		3	4	0	$-M$	0	
Basic variable		x_1	x_2	s_1	a_1	s_2	**Right-hand side**
a_1		9	3	-1	1	0	54
s_2		3	0	0	0	1	15
Z							$-54M$
z_j		$-9M$	$-3M$	M	$-M$	0	
$c_j - z_j$		$3 + 9M$	$4 + 3M$	$-M$	0	0	

Initial tableau

c_j	3	4	0	$-M$	0	
Basic variable	x_1	x_2	s_1	a_1	s_2	**Right-hand side**
a_1	0	3	-1	1	-3	9
x_1	1	0	0	0	1/3	5
Z						$15 - 9M$
z_j	3	$-3M$	M	$-M$	$3M$	
$c_j - z_j$	0	$4 + 3M$	$-M$	0	$-3M$	

Second tableau

c_j	3	4	0	$-M$	0	
Basic variable	x_1	x_2	s_1	a_1	s_2	**Right-hand side**
x_2	0	1	$-1/3$	$1/3$	-1	3	Third
x_1	1	0	0	0	$1/3$	5	tableau
Z						27	
z_j	3	4	$-4/3$	$4/3$	-3		
$c_j - z_j$	0	0	$4/3$	$-4/3 - M$	3		

c_j	3	4	0	$-M$	0	
Basic variable	x_1	x_2	s_1	a_1	s_2	**Right-hand side**
x_2	3	1	$-1/3$	$1/3$	0	18	Final
s_2	3	0	0	0	1	15	tableau
Z						72	
z_j	12	4	$-4/3$	$4/3$	0		
$c_j - z_j$	-9	0	$4/3$	$-4/3 - M$	0		

Although the $c_j - z_j$ row in the final tableau above still has a positive value within it, we are forced to stop. There are no positive entries in the column under the entering variable s_1, which indicates the LP has an unbounded solution.

Section 6

1. a. Shadow price of the machine-hours resource = $0. Shadow price of the labor-hours resource = $4.

b. *Right-hand side ranging:*

Machine-Hours Resource

RHS	÷	s_1-Column	=	a Ratio
10		1		10
16		0		$-\infty$
15		0		$-\infty$

The least positive number is $x = 10$, the least negative number is $y = -\infty$, and the current value of the machine-hours resource is $b = 10$. The range over which the shadow price of \$0 remains valid is from $b - x$ to $b - y$ or from $10 - 10$ to $10 - (-\infty)$ or from 0 to $+\infty$.

Labor-Hours Resource

RHS	$\div$	s_2-Column	$=$	a Ratio
10		-1		-10
16		$\dfrac{4}{5}$		20
15		0		$-\infty$

Here $x = 20$, $y = -10$, and $b = 16$. The range over which the shadow price of \$4 remains valid is from $16 - 20$ to $16 - (-10)$ or from -4 to 26 or from 0 to 26.

2.   *Ranging analysis on the profit coefficient of ashtrays:*

$c_j - z_j$	0	0	0	-4	-4
x_2	0	1	0	0	1
				$\uparrow$	$\uparrow$
				s_2	s_3 Nonbasic columns

$-4 \div 0 = +\infty$

$-4 \div 1 = -4$

The least positive quotient is $+\infty$, and the least negative quotient is -4. Therefore the x_2 profit coefficient can range from $5 - 4$ to $5 + \infty$ or from 1 to $+\infty$ and the current solution will remain optimal.

Section 7

1.

c_j	30	50	15	0	M	0	M		
Basic variable	y_1	y_2	y_3	s_1	a_1	s_2	a_2	Right-hand side	
a_1	5/4	5/4	0	-1	1	0	0	5	Initial
a_2	0	2	1	0	0	-1	1	12	tableau
Z								17M	
z_j	5/4M	13/4M	M	$-M$	M	$-M$	M		
$c_j - z_j$	30 − 5/4M	50 − 13/4M	15 − M	M	0	M	0		

We are minimizing, so we must choose the variable corresponding to the most negative value in the $c_j - z_j$ row as the incoming variable—that is, y_2.

c_j	30	50	15	0	M	0	M	
Basic variable	y_1	y_2	y_3	s_1	a_1	s_2	a_2	Right-hand side
y_2	1	1	0	$-4/5$	$4/5$	0	0	4
a_2	-2	0	1	$8/5$	$-8/5$	-1	1	4
Z								$200 + 4M$
z_j	$50 - 2M$	50	M	$-40 + 8/5M$	$40 - 8/5M$	$-M$	M	
$c_j - z_j$	$-20 + 2M$	0	$15 - M$	$40 - 8/5M$	$-40 + 13/5M$	M	0	

Second tableau

c_j	30	50	15	0	M	0	M	
Basic variable	y_1	y_2	y_3	s_1	a_1	s_2	a_2	Right-hand side
y_2	0	1	$1/2$	0	0	$-1/2$	$1/2$	6
s_1	$-5/4$	0	$5/8$	1	-1	$-5/8$	$5/8$	$5/2$
Z								300
z_j	0	50	25	0	0	-25	25	
$c_j - z_j$	30	0	-10	0	M	25	$-25 + M$	

Third tableau

c_j	30	50	15	0	M	0	M	
Basic variable	y_1	y_2	y_3	s_1	a_1	s_2	a_2	Right-hand side
y_2	1	1	0	$-4/5$	$4/5$	0	0	4
y_3	-2	0	1	$8/5$	$-8/5$	-1	1	4
Z								260
z_j	20	50	15	-16	16	-15	15	
$c_j - z_j$	10	0	0	16	$-16 + M$	15	$-15 + M$	

Final tableau

Interpretation: The basic variables of the dual equal the shadow prices of the primal. $y_1 = 0$, $y_2 = 4$, and $y_3 = 4$ agrees with the shadow prices found in the primal. Our shadow prices above, which are 16 and 15, agree with the basic variable values found by the primal method.

CHAPTER 4: THE TRANSPORTATION PROBLEM

Section 3

1. a.

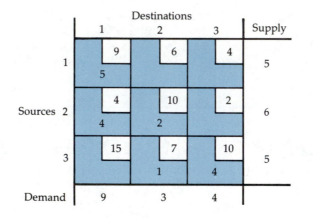

FIGURE B.15

b. Total cost of the NW-corner solution is

$$5(9) + 4(4) + 2(10) + 1(7) + 4(10) = \$128$$

c. First, we evaluate the NW-corner open squares, as follows:

Open square	Closed path	Net cost increase
1–2	+(1–2) − (2–2) + (2–1) − (1–1)	$6 - 10 + 4 - 9 = -9$
1–3	+(1–3) − (3–3) + (3–2) − (2–2) + (2–1) − (1–1)	$4 - 10 + 7 - 10 + 4 - 9 = -14$
2–3	+(2–3) − (3–3) + (3–2) − (2–2)	$2 - 10 + 7 - 10 = -11$
3–1	+(3–1) − (2–1) + (2–2) − (3–2)	$15 - 4 + 10 - 7 = 14$

The entering open square is 1–3; the exiting basic square is 2–2.

The improved solution is shown in Fig. B.16.

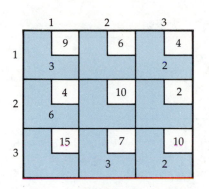

FIGURE B.16

Open square	Closed path	Net cost increase
1–2	+(1–2) − (1–3) + (3–3) − (3–2)	6 − 4 + 10 − 7 = 5
2–2	+(2–2) − (2–1) + (1–1) − (1–3) + (3–3) − (3–2)	10 − 4 + 9 − 4 + 10 − 7 = 14
2–3	+(2–3) − (2–1) + (1–1) − (1–3)	2 − 4 + 9 − 4 = 3
3–1	+(3–1) − (1–1) + (1–3) − (3–3)	15 − 9 + 4 − 10 = 0

This solution is optimal, thus the resulting minimum total cost is

$$3(9) + 2(4) + 2(10) + 3(7) + 6(4) = 100$$

2. The NW-corner initial solution is as shown in Fig. B.17.

	Destinations			
Sources	1	2	3	Supply
1	9 — 3	6	4 — 2	5
2	4 — 6	10	2	6
3	3	2 — 3	10 — 2	5
Demand	9	3	4	16

FIGURE B.17

Open square	Closed path	Net cost increase
1–2	+(1–2) − (1–3) + (3–3) − (3–2)	6 − 4 + 10 − 2 = 10
2–2	+(2–2) − (2–1) + (1–1) − (1–3) + (3–3) − (3–2)	10 − 4 + 9 − 4 + 10 − 2 = 19
2–3	+(2–3) − (2–1) + (1–1) − (1–3)	2 − 4 + 9 − 4 = 3
3–1	+(3–1) − (1–1) + (1–3) − (3–3)	3 − 9 + 4 − 10 = −12

The entering open square is 3–1; the exiting basic square is 3–3.

The improved solution can be shown as Fig. B.18. Note that the lower cost of $3 for square 3–1 has caused 3 units to shift from 1–1 to 3–1 (see Problem 1).

Sources	Destinations 1	2	3	Supply
1	9	6 1	4 4	5
2	4 6	10	2	6
3	3 3	2 2	10	5
Demand	9	3	4	16

FIGURE B.18

Open square	Closed path	Net cost increase
1–2	+(1–2) − (3–2) + (3–1) − (1–1)	6 − 2 + 3 − 9 = −2
2–2	+(2–2) − (3–2) + (3–1) − (2–1)	10 − 2 + 3 − 4 = 7
2–3	+(2–3) − (2–1) + (1–1) − (1–3)	2 − 4 + 9 − 4 = 3
3–3	+(3–3) − (3–1) + (1–1) − (1–3)	10 − 3 + 9 − 4 = 12

The entering open square is 1–2; the exiting basic square is 1–1.
The optimal solution is shown in Fig. B.19.

Sources	Destinations 1	2	3	Supply
1	3 9	10	8	9
2	2 2	4 15	10 3	20
3	2	9	6 10	10
4	8	5	4 7	7
Demand	11	15	20	46

FIGURE B.19

Open square	Closed path	Net cost increase
1–1	+(1–1) − (1–2) + (3–2) − (3–1)	$9 - 6 + 2 - 3 = 2$
2–2	+(2–2) − (3–2) + (3–1) − (2–1)	$10 - 2 + 3 - 4 = 7$
2–3	+(2–3) − (2–1) + (3–1) − (3–2) + (1–2) − (1–3)	$2 - 4 + 3 - 2 + 6 - 4 = 1$
3–3	+(3–3) − (3–2) + (1–2) − (1–3)	$10 - 2 + 6 - 4 = 10$

This optimal solution has a minimum total cost of

$$1(6) + 4(4) + 6(4) + 3(3) + 2(2) = \$59$$

3.

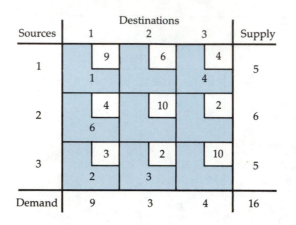

FIGURE B.20

Open square	Closed path	Net cost increase
1–2	+(1–2) − (2–2) + (2–1) − (1–1)	10 − 4 + 2 − 3 = 5
1–3	+(1–3) − (2–3) + (2–1) − (1–1)	8 − 10 + 2 − 3 = −3
3–1	+(3–1) − (2–1) + (2–3) − (3–3)	2 − 2 + 10 − 6 = 4
3–2	+(3–2) − (2–2) + (2–3) − (3–3)	9 − 4 + 10 − 6 = 9
4–1	+(4–1) − (2–1) + (2–3) − (4–3)	8 − 2 + 10 − 4 = 12
4–2	+(4–2) − (2–2) + (2–3) − (4–3)	5 − 4 + 10 − 4 = 7

The entering open square is 1–3; the exiting basic square is 2–3. The optimal solution is shown in Fig. B.21.

Destinations

Sources	1	2	3	Supply
1	3 / 6	10	8 / 3	9
2	2 / 5	4 / 15	10	20
3	2	9	6 / 10	10
4	8	5	4 / 7	7
Demand	11	15	20	46

FIGURE B.21

Open square	Closed path	Net cost increase
1–2	+(1–2) − (2–2) + (2–1) − (1–1)	10 − 4 + 2 − 3 = 5
2–3	+(2–3) − (2–1) + (1–1) − (1–3)	10 − 2 + 3 − 8 = 3
3–1	+(3–1) − (1–1) + (1–3) − (3–3)	2 − 3 + 8 − 6 = 1
3–2	+(3–2) − (2–2) + (2–1) − (1–1) + (1–3) − (3–3)	9 − 4 + 2 − 3 + 8 − 6 = 6
4–1	+(4–1) − (1–1) + (1–3) − (4–3)	8 − 3 + 8 − 4 = 9
4–2	+(4–2) − (2–2) + (2–1) − (1–1) + (1–3) − (4–3)	5 − 4 + 2 − 3 + 8 − 4 = 4

The total cost resulting from this solution is

6(3) + 3(8) + 5(2) + 15(4) + 10(6) + 7(4) = $200

4.

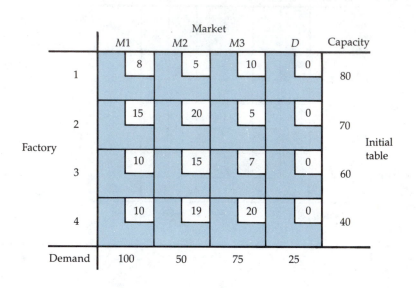

FIGURE B.22

The above figure exhibits the production capacities, market demands, and transportation costs.

Step 1: Compute the rim values:

Row 1 $5 - 0 = 5$ Column 1 $10 - 8 = 2$
Row 2 $5 - 0 = 5$ Column 2 $15 - 5 = 10$
Row 3 $7 - 0 = 7$ Column 3 $7 - 5 = 2$
Row 4 $10 - 0 = 10$ Column 4 $0 - 0 = 0$

Step 2: There is a tie for the largest rim value (10). The tie is broken by choosing row 4, since it has the lower minimum-cost entry (0). We allocate the maximum of 25 units to row 4, column 4. The following figure reflects these results. Note that the demand in column 4 and the capacity in row 4 have both been reduced by 25. Column 4 is now eliminated.

Step 1: The new rim values are included in Fig. B.23.
Step 2: The tie for largest rim value is between row 2 and column 2. The tie must be broken arbitrarily, since they both have a minimum-cost entry of 5. Row 2, column 3 has been chosen. The maximum of 70 units is assigned to that "square."

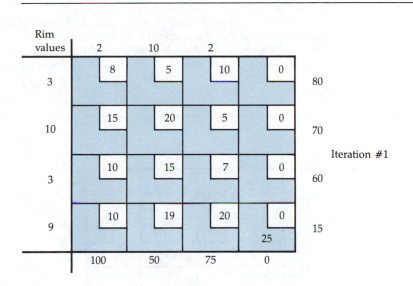

Figure B.24 reflects the results of the above computations. Demand in column 3 has been reduced by 70, and capacity in row 2 by 70 as well. Row 2 is now eliminated.

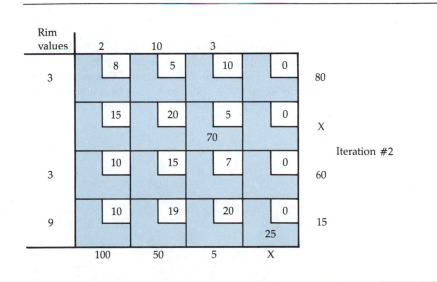

Step 1: The new rim values are included in Figure B.24.

Step 2: Column 2 has the largest rim value, and 5 is the smallest cost entry in the column. Therefore, the maximum of 50 is assigned to row 1, column 2.

Figure B.25 reflects the above computations. Demand in column 2 is reduced to 0, thus eliminating that column. Capacity in row 1 is reduced by 50 units.

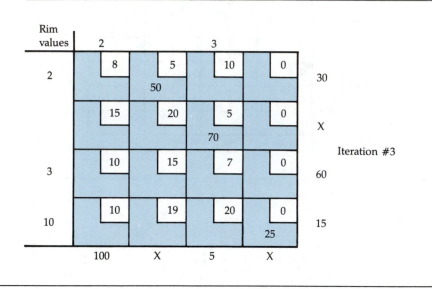

FIGURE B.25

Step 1: The new rim values are included in the above figure.

Step 2: The largest rim value is found in row 4. The minimum-cost entry is 10 in that row. Therefore the maximum of 15 units is assigned to row 4, column 1. The capacity of row 4 is reduced to 0, which eliminates the row.

The following figure reflects these computations.

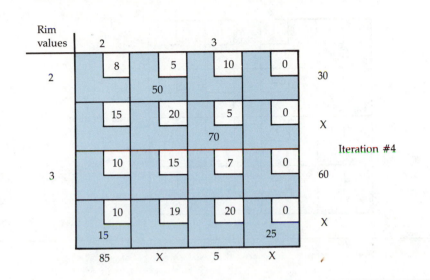

FIGURE B.26

Step 1: The new rim values are shown in Fig. B.26.

Step 2: The tie for the rim value of 3 is broken by arbitrarily choosing row 3. (Both row 3 and column 3 have the same minimum-cost entry of 7.) Therefore, the maximum of 5 units is assigned to the row 3, column 3 box.

Now we have eliminated rows 2 and 4, and columns 2, 3, and 4. It is obvious how the remaining 85 units of demand in column 1 must be distributed: 30 units will go to row 1, column 1, and 55 units will go to row 3, column 1. This reduces the four demand values to 0, and the problem is completed.

The final distribution solution is depicted in Fig. B.27. Cost of the VAM solution is

$$30(8) + 50(5) + 70(5) + 55(10) + 5(7) + 15(10) + 25(0) = \underline{\$1,575}$$

8	5	10	0	
30	50			
15	20	5	0	
		70		
10	15	7	0	
55		5		
10	19	20	0	
15			25	

Final iteration

FIGURE B.27

5.

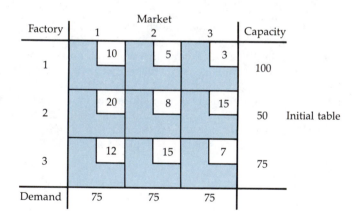

FIGURE B.28

Using the profit method, the rim values are the differences between the two *largest* values in each row and column.

Step 1:

Row 1 10 − 5 = 5   Column 1 20 − 12 = 8
Row 2 20 − 15 = 5   Column 2 15 − 8 = 7
Row 3 15 − 12 = 3   Column 3 15 − 7 = 8

We still look for the largest rim value, but ties are now broken by choosing the row or column that has the *largest* profit entry (not the smallest cost value). On this basis we choose column 1, which has the largest profit entry (20). The maximum of 50 units is assigned to the row 2, column 1 box. This eliminates row 2 and reduces the demand in column 1 from 75 to 25. These results are shown in Fig. B.29.

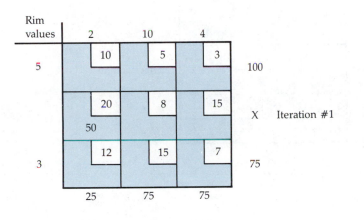

FIGURE B.29

Step 1: The new rim values are depicted above.

Step 2: Column 2 has the largest rim value. The maximum of 75 units is assigned to the row 3, column 2 box that has the largest profit entry (15). This eliminates row 3 and column 2. These changes are shown in Figure B.30.

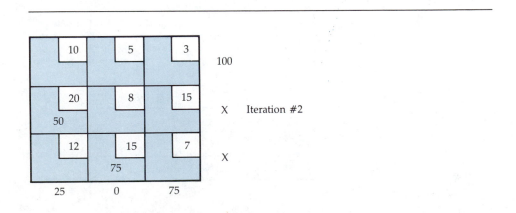

FIGURE B.30

The last iteration requires little calculation. Twenty-five units are assigned to row 1, column 1, and 75 units are given to row 1, column 3. The problem is now solved, and the final solution is given in Fig. B.31. Profit for the VAM solution is

$$25(10) + 75(3) + 50(20) + 75(15) = \underline{\$2,600}$$

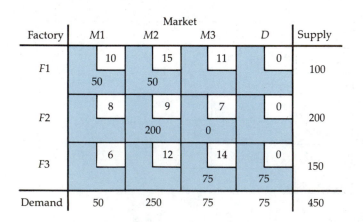

Final iteration

FIGURE B.31

Section 4

1.

Factory	M1	M2	M3	D	Supply
		Market			
F1	10 50	15 50	11	0	100
F2	8	9 200	7 0	0	200
F3	6	12	14 75	0 75	150
Demand	50	250	75	75	450

FIGURE B.32

Open square	Net cost increase
F1–M3	$11 - 7 + 9 - 15 = -2$
F1–D	$0 - 0 + 14 - 7 + 9 - 15 = 1$
F2–M1	$8 - 10 + 15 - 9 = 4$
F2–D	$0 - 0 + 14 - 7 = 7$
F3–M1	$6 - 10 + 15 - 9 + 7 - 14 = -5$
F3–M2	$12 - 9 + 7 - 14 = -4$

The entering open square is F3–M1; the exiting basic square is F1–M1.

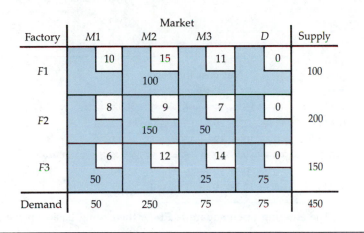

Factory	Market M1	M2	M3	D	Supply
F1	10	15 100	11	0	100
F2	8	9 150	7 50	0	200
F3	6 50	12	14 25	0 75	150
Demand	50	250	75	75	450

FIGURE B.33

Open square	Net cost increase
F1–M1	$10 - 15 + 9 - 7 + 14 - 6 = 5$
F1–M3	$11 - 7 + 9 - 15 = -2$
F1–D	$0 - 0 + 14 - 7 + 9 - 15 = 1$
F2–M1	$8 - 7 + 14 - 6 = 9$
F2–D	$0 - 0 + 14 - 7 = 7$
F3–M2	$12 - 9 + 7 - 14 = -4$

The entering open square is F3–M2; the exiting basic square is F3–M3.

	M1	M2	M3	D	Supply
F1	10	15	11	0	100
		100			
F2	8	9	7	0	200
		125	75		
F3	6	12	14	0	150
	50	25		75	
Demand	50	250	75	75	450

FIGURE B.34

Open square	Net cost increase
F1–M1	$10 - 15 + 12 - 6 = 1$
F1–M3	$11 - 7 + 9 - 15 = -2$
F1–D	$0 - 0 + 12 - 15 = -3$
F2–M1	$8 - 9 + 12 - 6 = 5$
F2–D	$0 - 0 + 12 - 9 = 3$
F3–M3	$14 - 12 + 9 - 7 = 4$

The entering open square is F1–D; the exiting basic square is F3–D.

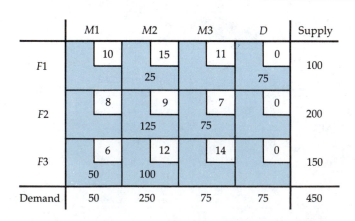

	M1	M2	M3	D	Supply
F1	10	15	11	0	100
		25		75	
F2	8	9	7	0	200
		125	75		
F3	6	12	14	0	150
	50	100			
Demand	50	250	75	75	450

FIGURE B.35

Open square	Net cost increase
F1–M1	$10 - 15 + 12 - 6 = 1$
F1–M3	$11 - 7 + 9 - 15 = -2$
F2–M1	$8 - 9 + 12 - 6 = 5$
F2–D	$0 - 9 + 15 - 0 = 6$
F3–M3	$14 - 12 + 9 - 7 = 4$
F3–D	$0 - 12 + 15 - 0 = 3$

The entering open square is F1–M3; the exiting basic square is F1–M2.

	M1	M2	M3	D	Supply
F1	10	15	11 (25)	0 (75)	100
F2	8	9 (150)	7 (50)	0	200
F3	6 (50)	12 (100)	14	0	150
Demand	50	250	75	75	450

FIGURE B.36

Open square	Net cost increase
F1–M1	$10 - 11 + 7 - 9 + 12 - 6 = 3$
F1–M2	$15 - 11 + 7 - 9 = 2$
F2–M1	$8 - 9 + 12 - 6 = 5$
F2–D	$0 - 7 + 11 - 0 = 4$
F3–M3	$14 - 12 + 9 - 7 = 4$
F3–D	$0 - 12 + 9 - 7 + 11 - 0 = 1$

Hence the solution is given by last chart. The minimum total cost is

$$25(11) + 75(0) + 150(9) + 50(7) + 50(6) + 100(12) = \$3,475$$

2. a.

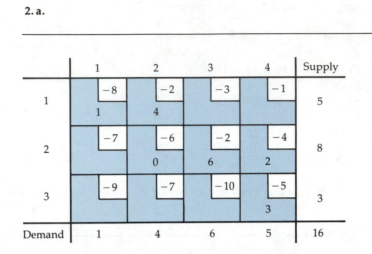

FIGURE B.37

Open square	Net cost increase	
1–3	$-3 + 2 - 6 + 2 = -5$	or $+(-3) - (-2) + (-6) - (-2)$
1–4	$-1 + 4 - 6 + 2 = -1$	
2–1	$-7 + 8 - 2 + 6 = 5$	
3–1	$-9 + 8 - 2 + 6 - 4 + 5 = 4$	
3–2	$-7 + 6 - 4 + 5 = 0$	
3–3	$-10 + 2 - 4 + 5 = -7$	

The entering open square is 3–3; the exiting basic square is 3–4.

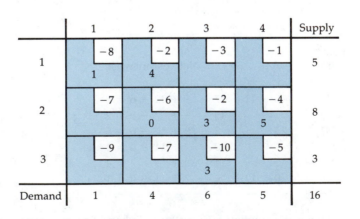

FIGURE B.38

Open square	Net cost increase
1–3	$-3 + 2 - 6 + 2 = -5$
1–4	$-1 + 4 - 6 + 2 = -1$
2–1	$-7 + 8 - 2 + 6 = 5$
3–1	$-9 + 8 - 2 + 6 - 2 + 10 = 11$
3–2	$-7 + 6 - 2 + 10 = 7$
3–4	$-5 + 10 - 2 + 4 = 7$

The entering open square is 1–3; the exiting basic square is 2–3.

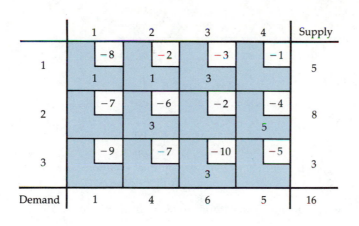

FIGURE B.39

Open square	Net cost increase
1–4	$-1 + 4 - 6 + 2 = -1$
2–1	$-7 + 8 - 2 + 6 = 5$
2–3	$-2 + 6 - 2 + 3 = 5$
3–1	$-9 + 8 - 3 + 10 = 6$
3–2	$-7 + 2 - 3 + 10 = 2$
3–4	$-5 + 10 - 3 + 2 - 6 + 4 = 2$

The entering open square is 1–4; the exiting basic square is 1–2.

706

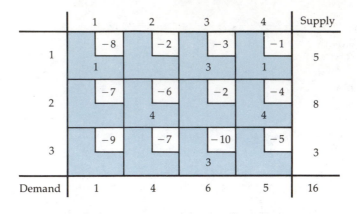

FIGURE B.40

Open square	Net cost increase
1–2	$-2 + 1 - 4 + 6 = 1$
2–1	$-7 + 8 - 1 + 4 = 4$
2–3	$-2 + 3 - 1 + 4 = 4$
3–1	$-9 + 8 - 3 + 10 = 6$
3–2	$-7 + 6 - 4 + 1 - 3 + 10 = 3$
3–4	$-5 + 10 - 3 + 1 = 3$

Hence the last chart gives the optimal solution. The minimum total cost is

$1(-8) + 3(-3) + 1(-1) + 4(-6) + 4(-4) + 3(-10) = -88$

The corresponding maximum total profit is $-(-88)$ or \$88.

2.b.

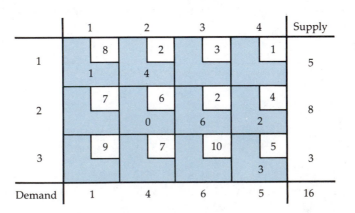

FIGURE B.41

Open square	Net profit increase
1–3	$3 - 2 + 6 - 2 = 5$
1–4	$1 - 4 + 6 - 2 = 1$
2–1	$7 - 8 + 2 - 6 = -5$
3–1	$9 - 8 + 2 - 6 + 4 - 5 = -4$
3–2	$7 - 6 + 4 - 5 = 0$
3–3	$10 - 2 + 4 - 5 = 7$

The entering open square is 3–3; the exiting basic square is 3–4.

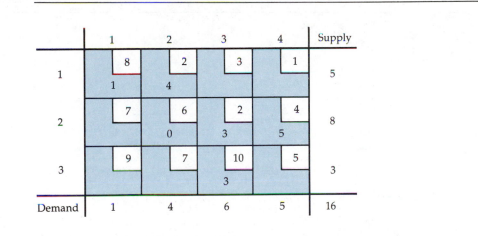

FIGURE B.42

Open square	Net profit increase
1–3	$3 - 2 + 6 - 2 = 5$
1–4	$1 - 4 + 6 - 2 = 1$
2–1	$7 - 8 + 2 - 6 = -5$
3–1	$9 - 8 + 2 - 6 + 2 - 10 = -11$
3–2	$7 - 6 + 2 - 10 = -7$
3–4	$5 - 10 + 2 - 4 = -7$

The entering open square is 1–3 (highest profit increase); the exiting basic square is 2–3.

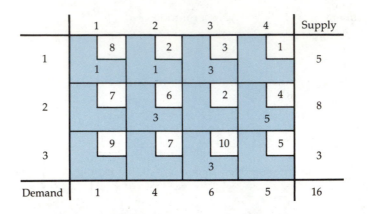

FIGURE B.43

Open square	Net profit increase
1–4	$1 - 4 + 6 - 2 = 1$
2–1	$7 - 8 + 2 - 6 = -5$
2–3	$2 - 6 + 2 - 3 = -5$
3–1	$9 - 8 + 3 - 10 = -6$
3–2	$7 - 2 + 3 - 10 = -2$
3–4	$5 - 10 + 3 - 2 + 6 - 4 = -2$

The entering open square is 1–4; the exiting basic square is 1–2.

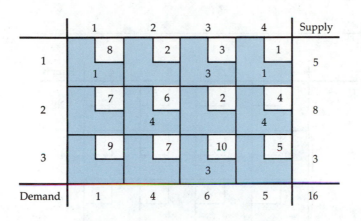

FIGURE B.44

Open square	Net profit increase
1–2	2 − 1 + 4 − 6 = −1
2–1	7 − 8 + 1 − 4 = −4
2–3	2 − 3 + 1 − 4 = −4
3–1	9 − 8 + 3 − 10 = −6
3–2	7 − 6 + 4 − 1 + 3 − 10 = −3
3–4	5 − 10 + 3 − 1 = −3

Hence the last chart gives the optimal solution. The corresponding maximum profit is

1(8) + 3(3) + 1(1) + 4(6) + 4(4) + 3(10) = $88

3.

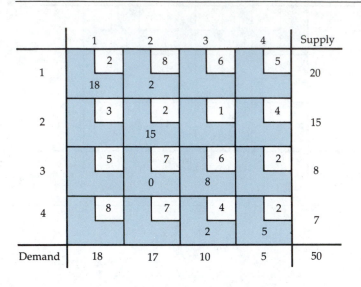

FIGURE B.45

Open square	Net cost increase
1–3	$6 - 6 + 7 - 8 = -1$
1–4	$5 - 2 + 4 - 6 + 7 - 8 = 0$
2–1	$3 - 2 + 8 - 2 = 7$
2–3	$1 - 6 + 7 - 2 = 0$
2–4	$4 - 2 + 4 - 6 + 7 - 2 = 5$
3–1	$5 - 2 + 8 - 7 = 4$
3–4	$2 - 2 + 4 - 6 = -2$
4–1	$8 - 2 + 8 - 7 + 6 - 4 = 9$
4–2	$7 - 7 + 6 - 4 = 2$

The entering open square is 3–4; the exiting basic square is 4–4.

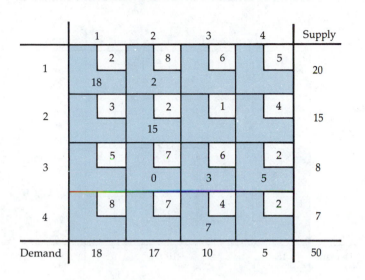

Open square	Net cost increase	
1–3	$6 - 6 + 7 - 8 =$	-1
1–4	$5 - 2 + 7 - 8 =$	2
2–1	$3 - 2 + 8 - 2 =$	7
2–3	$1 - 6 + 7 - 2 =$	0
2–4	$4 - 2 + 7 - 2 =$	7
3–1	$5 - 2 + 8 - 7 =$	4
4–1	$8 - 2 + 8 - 7 + 6 - 4 =$	9
4–2	$7 - 7 + 6 - 4 =$	2
4–4	$2 - 4 + 6 - 2 =$	2

The entering open square is 1–3; the exiting basic square is 1–2.

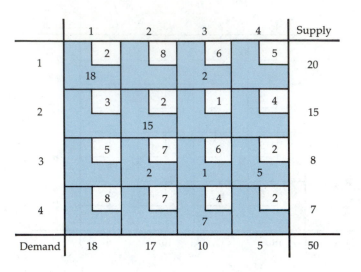

FIGURE B.47

Open square	Net cost increase
1–2	$8 - 6 + 6 - 7 = 1$
1–4	$5 - 2 + 6 - 6 = 3$
2–1	$3 - 2 + 6 - 6 + 7 - 2 = 6$
2–3	$1 - 6 + 7 - 2 = 0$
2–4	$4 - 2 + 7 - 2 = 7$
3–1	$5 - 2 + 6 - 6 = 3$
4–1	$8 - 2 + 6 - 4 = 8$
4–2	$7 - 7 + 6 - 4 = 2$
4–4	$2 - 4 + 6 - 2 = 2$

Hence the last chart gives the optimal solution. The minimum total cost is

$$18(2) + 2(6) + 15(2) + 2(7) + 1(6) + 5(2) + 7(4) = \$136$$

4.

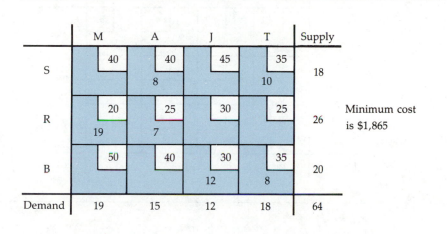

FIGURE B.48

Open square	Net cost increase
S–M	40 − 40 + 25 − 20 = 5
S–J	45 − 35 + 35 − 30 = 15
R–J	30 − 25 + 40 − 35 + 35 − 30 = 15
R–T	25 − 25 + 40 − 35 = 5
B–M	50 − 20 + 25 − 40 + 35 − 35 = 15
B–A	40 − 40 + 35 − 35 = 0

The entering open square is B–A; the exiting basic square is S–A or B–T—we will choose B–T.

	M	A	J	T	Supply
S	40	40 0	45	35 18	18
R	20 19	25 7	30	25	26
B	50	40 8	30 12	35	20
Demand	19	15	12	18	64

FIGURE B.49

Total cost in this case is

18(35) + 19(20) + 7(25) + 8(40) + 12(30) = $1,865

Hence the last chart gives an alternate optimal production/distribution plan.

5.

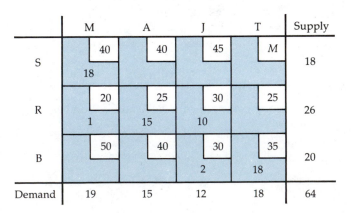

	M	A	J	T	Supply
S	40 18	40	45	M	18
R	20 1	25 15	30 10	25	26
B	50	40	30 2	35 18	20
Demand	19	15	12	18	64

FIGURE B.50

Open square	Net cost increase
S–A	$40 - 25 + 20 - 40 = -5$
S–J	$45 - 30 + 20 - 40 = -5$
S–T	$M - 35 + 30 - 30 + 20 - 40 = M - 55$
R–T	$25 - 35 + 30 - 30 = -10$
B–M	$50 - 20 + 30 - 30 = 30$
B–A	$40 - 25 + 30 - 30 = 15$

Since M is a very large penalty cost, $M > 55$ and $M - 55 > 0$. The entering open square is R–T; the exiting basic square is R–J.

	M	A	J	T	Supply
S	40 __18__	40	45	M	18
R	20 __1__	25 __15__	30	25 __10__	26
B	50	40	30 __12__	35 __8__	20
Demand	19	15	12	18	64

FIGURE B.51

Open square	Net cost increase
S–A	$40 - 25 + 20 - 40 = -5$
S–J	$45 - 30 + 35 - 25 + 20 - 40 = 5$
S–T	$M - 25 + 20 - 40 = M - 45 \ (M - 45 > 0)$
R–J	$30 - 25 + 35 - 30 = 10$
B–M	$50 - 20 + 25 - 35 = 20$
B–A	$40 - 25 + 25 - 35 = 5$

The entering open square is S–A; the exiting basic square is R–A.

	M	A	J	T	Supply
S	40 3	40 15	45	M	18
R	20 16	25	30	25 10	26
B	50	40	30 12	35 8	20
Demand	19	15	12	18	64

FIGURE B.52

Open square		Net cost increase
S–J	$45 - 30 + 35 - 25 + 20 - 40 =$	5
S–T	$M - 25 + 20 - 40 = M - 45 \ (>0)$	
R–A	$25 - 20 + 40 - 40 =$	5
R–J	$30 - 25 + 35 - 30 =$	10
B–M	$50 - 20 + 25 - 35 =$	20
B–A	$40 - 40 + 40 - 20 + 25 - 35 =$	10

Hence the optimal solution is given by the last chart. Note the effect of prohibiting an allocation to S–T. The 10 units placed in the optimal solution to the original Whiting problem have been shifted to R–T. (Compare with Fig. 4.10.) The cost of the modified solution is

$$3(40) + 15(40) + 16(20) + 10(25) + 12\,(30) + 8(35) = \$1{,}930$$

which is higher than the cost of the unrestricted problem ($1,865).

6. The transportation problem of Problem 1, Section 3, does have multiple optimal solutions because the net cost increase associated with the open square 3–1 is 0. We let 3–1 be the entering open square and 3–3 be the exiting basic square to obtain the alternate optimal solution given below:

1		4
6		
2	3	

CHAPTER 5: THE ASSIGNMENT PROBLEM

Section 3

1. The total weekly cost in the initial solutions is

1($210) + 0($150) + 1($160) + 0($200) + 1($220) + 0($200) + 1($190) = $780

The stepping-stone method requires five iterations.

Iteration	Entering square	Exiting square	Total cost
1	J3–M1	J2–M2	$690
2	J4–M3	J3–M3	$690
3	J1–M4	J1–M1	$690
4	J4–M2	J4–M4	$595
5	J3–M2	J1–M2	$595

The final table is as follows:

Job	Machine			
	M1	M2	M3	M4
J1				1
J2			1	
J3	1	0		
J4		1	0	

Section 4

1.

6	17	3	0	6	0
2	5	0	0	3	0
5	14	8	2	4	0
4	M	7	1	3	0
6	7	14	4	0	0
0	0	17	5	7	0

6	17	3	0	6	1
2	5	0	0	3	1
4	13	7	1	3	0
3	M	6	0	2	0
6	7	14	4	0	1
0	0	17	5	7	1

Step 1: Initial cost table:
Given in Table 5.7.
Step 2: Column reduction:
Given in table above.
Step 3: Row reduction:
Yielded same table as step 2 because there was a 0 in every row.
Step 4: Test for optimal solution:
Minimum number of cross-out lines (5) does not equal number of rows (6). Go to Step 5.

    Step 5: a. Minimum uncovered entry is 1.
            b. Subtract 1 from each uncovered entry.
            c. Add 1 to each entry crossed by two lines.
               All other entries remain unchanged.
            d. Go to step 4.

Step 4: Test for optimal solution:
Minimum number of cross-out lines (5) still does not equal number of rows (6). Go to step 5.
    Step 5: a. Minimum uncovered entry is 2.
            b. Subtract 2 from each uncovered entry.
            c. Add 2 to each entry crossed by two lines.
            d. Go to step 4.
Step 4: Test for optimal solution:
Minimum number of cross-out lines (5) still does not equal number of rows (6). Go to step 5.

4	15	3	0	6	1
0	3	0	0	3	1
2	11	7	1	3	0
1	M	6	0	2	0
4	5	14	4	0	1
0	0	19	7	9	3

    Step 5: a. Minimum uncovered entry is 1.
            b. Subtract 1 from each uncovered entry.
            c. Add 1 to each entry crossed by two lines.
            d. Go to step 4.
Step 4: Test for optimal solution:
Minimum number of cross-out lines (6) equals number of rows (6). Go to step 6.

3	14	2	0	6	1
0	3	0	1	4	2
1	10	6	1	3	0
0	M	5	0	2	0
3	4	13	4	0	1
0	0	19	8	10	4

			Machine			
Job	M1	M2	M3	M4	M5	M6
J1				1		
J2			1			
J3						1
J4	1					
J5					1	
J6		1				

Step 6: A 1 is placed on a 0 in such a way that only one 1 appears in each row and each column.

Optimal assignment: J1 to M4, J2 to M3, J3 to M6, J4 to M1, J5 to M5, and J6 to M2.

Minimum total cost:

$14 + $7 + $0 + $18 + $15 + $13 = $67

Note: Job 3 was assigned to a nonexistent machine and, therefore, was chosen as the job that would not be done. Also note that job 4 was not assigned to machine 2 in the optimal solution, which was a stipulation in the original problem.

2. *Step 1:* Initial cost table:
Given in problem statement.

Step 2: Column reduction:
Given in table that follows.

1	4	7
0	0	0
0	4	8

Step 3: Row reduction:
Given in table below.

Step 4: Test for optimal solution:
Minimum number of cross-out lines (2) does not equal number of rows (3). Go to step 5.

0	3	6
0	0	0
0	4	8

Step 5: a. Minimum uncovered entry is 3.
   b. Subtract 3 from each uncovered entry.
   c. Add 3 to each entry crossed by two lines.
      All other entries remain unchanged.
   d. Go to step 4.
Step 4: Test for optimal solution:
Minimum number of cross-out lines (3) equals number of rows (3). Go to step 6.

0	0	3
3	0	0
0	1	5

Step 6: A 1 is placed on a 0 in such a way that only one 1 appears in each row and each column.
   Optimal assignment: *A* to 2, *B* to 3, and *C* to 1.
   Minimum total cost: \$6 + \$1 + \$3 = \$10

	1	2	3
A		1	
B			1
C	1		

3. *Step 1:* Initial cost table:
Since we are maximizing profit, the original values in the problem are converted (negated) to negative costs. The table below gives these costs.

−4	−6	−8
−3	−2	−1
−3	−6	−9

Step 2: Column reduction:
Given in table below. Example:

Column 1
−4 − (−4) = 0
−3 − (−4) = 1
−3 − (−4) = 1

0	0	1
1	4	8
1	0	0

Step 3: Row reduction:
Given in table below. Example:

Row 2
1 − 1 = 0
4 − 1 = 3
8 − 1 = 7

0̶	0̶	1̶
0̶	3̶	7̶
1̶	0̶	0̶

Step 4: Test for optimal solution:
Minimum number of cross-out lines (3) equals number of rows (3). Go to step 6.
Step 6: A 1 is placed on a 0 in such a way that only one 1 appears in each row and each column.
Optimal assignment: A to 2, B to 1, and C to 3.
Optimal total profit: \$6 + \$3 + \$9 = \$18

	1	2	3
A		1	
B	1		
C			1

CHAPTER 6: INVENTORY MODELS: PART I

Section 4

1.a. D = 6(12 months) = 72 units per year
F = \$5
C = \$110 (always use wholesale price unless otherwise stated)
r = 0.12

b.

Q	TOC	TCC	TC	Q	TOC	TCC	TC
1	$360.00	$ 6.60	$366.60	7	51.43	46.20	97.63
2	180.00	13.20	193.20	8	45.00	52.80	97.80
3	120.00	19.80	139.80	9	40.00	59.40	99.40
4	90.00	26.40	116.40	10	36.00	66.00	102.00
5	72.00	33.00	105.00				
6	60.00	39.60	99.60				

    c. Based on the table in part b, EOQ = 7.

2. a. Number of orders per year = D/Q = 72/7 = 10.286.

    b. Average inventory level = $Q/2$ = 7/2 = 3.5.

    c. Cycle length = Q/D = 7/72 = 0.0972 years, or 29.17 days. Optimal policy: Order seven easels every 29.17 days at a total annual cost of $97.63.

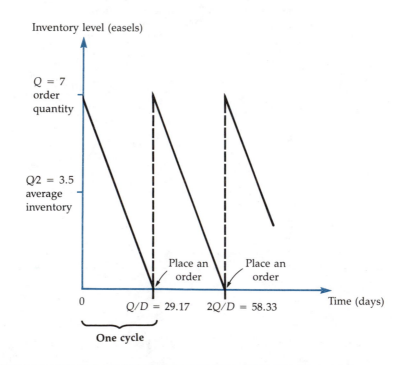

Inventory level (easels)

Q = 7 order quantity

Q2 = 3.5 average inventory

Place an order

Place an order

0

Q/D = 29.17   2Q/D = 58.33

Time (days)

One cycle

FIGURE B.53

3.

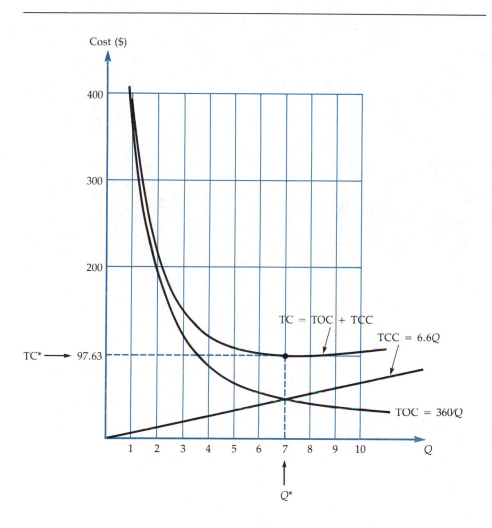

Section 5

1. $D = 72$
   $F = 5$
   $C = 110$
   $r = 0.12$

$$\text{EOQ} = \sqrt{\frac{2DF}{Cr}} = \underline{\underline{7.385}}$$

The answer does not agree precisely. The true Q^* is a noninteger, and only integers were considered earlier.

2. $TC^* = F(D/Q^*) + Cr(Q^*/2)$

$\qquad = 5(72/7.385) + 110(0.12)(7.385/2)$

$\qquad = 48.75 + 48.74 = \$97.49$

TOC and TCC differ by \$0.01 due to rounding.

3. No, she should *not* increase her EOQ by a factor of four.

$\qquad D = 288$

$\qquad F = 5$

$\qquad C = 110$

$\qquad r = 0.12$

$\qquad \text{EOQ} = \sqrt{\dfrac{2(288)(5)}{110(0.12)}} = \underline{\underline{14.771}}$

Based on a 300-day work-year:

$T^* = \text{optimal cycle length} = Q^*/D$

$\qquad = 14.771/288 = 0.051288 \text{ year}$

$0.051288 \text{ year } (300 \text{ days/year})$

$\qquad = 15.386 \text{ days}$

Optimal policy: Order 14.771 easels every 15.386 days.

4. $\quad D = 520/\text{month} \times 12 \text{ months} = 6{,}240$

$\qquad C = 1.50$

$\qquad F = 9.00$

$\qquad Cr = 0.50$

$\qquad r = 0.33$

$\qquad \text{EOQ} = \sqrt{\dfrac{2(6{,}240)(9)}{0.50}} = \underline{\underline{473.962}}$

$\qquad TC^* = F(D/Q^*) + Cr(Q^*/2)$

$\qquad\qquad = 9(6{,}240/473.962) + 0.5(473.962/2)$

$\qquad\qquad = 118.49 + 118.49$

$\qquad TC^* = \underline{\underline{\$236.98}}$

$\qquad TOC = \underline{\underline{\$118.49}}$

$\qquad TCC = \underline{\underline{\$118.49}}$

5. Optimal number of orders/year $= D/Q^* = 6{,}240/473.962 = 13.17$.

6. Optimal number of days of inventory to order $= 350/13.17 = 26.58$ days.

Section 6

1. a. $D = 2,500$

  $C = 110$

  $F = 16$

  $r = 0.20$

$$\text{EOQ} = \sqrt{\frac{2(2,500)(16)}{110(0.20)}} = \underline{\underline{60.3}}$$

b. $TC^* = F(D/Q^*) + Cr(Q^*/2)$

  $= 16(2,500/60.3) + 110(0.2)(60.3/2)$

  $= 663.45 + 663.30 = \underline{\$1,326.65}$

c. Q^* is rounded to 60.0.

  $TC° = 16(2,500/60) + 110(0.2)(60/2)$

  $= 666.67 + 660.00 = \underline{\$1,326.67}$

$$\frac{TC° - TC^*}{TC^*} \times 100\% = \frac{1,326.67 - 1,326.65}{1,326.65} \times 100\% = 0.0015\%$$

2. $Q = 60.3(1.5) = 90.45$

  $TC° = 16(2,500/90.45) + 110(0.2)(90.45/2)$

  $= 442.23 + 994.95 = \underline{\$1437.18}$

$$\frac{1,437.18 - 1,326.65}{1,326.65} \times 100\% = 8.33\%$$

Thus a 50 percent increase in the EOQ causes an 8.33 percent increase in TC.

3. a.

  $e = 0.10$

$$e_t = \left(\frac{1}{1 + 0.10} + 0.10 - 1\right) \times 50\%$$

$$= \left(\frac{1}{1.10} - 0.9\right) \times 50\% = 0.45\%$$

Thus a $+10$ percent error in Q causes a 0.45 percent increase in TC.

b.

  $e = -0.10$

$$e_t = \left(\frac{1}{1 - 0.10} - 0.10 - 1\right) \times 50\%$$

$$= \left(\frac{1}{0.90} = 1.10\right) \times 50\% = 0.55\%$$

Thus a -10 percent error in Q causes a 0.55 percent increase in TC.

Section 7

1.

$D = 50(12) = 600$

$C = 200$

$F = 11$

$r = 0.13$

L = (2 days transportation) + (1 day preparation)

       + (1 day mailing) + (3 days order filling)

    = 7 days

a. $\text{EOQ} = \sqrt{\dfrac{2(600)(11)}{200(0.13)}} = 22.53$

b. $TOC = F(D/Q^*) = 11(600/22.53)$
        $= \$292.94$

c. $TCC = CR(Q^*/2)$
        $= 200(0.13)(22.53/2)$
        $= \$292.89$

d. $TC^* = TOC + TCC$
        $= 292.94 + 292.89$
        $= \$585.53$

e. Demand/day $= 600/350 = 1.714$ units
        R = (demand/day)(lead time)
        $= 1.714(7) = 11.998 = 12$ units

Optimal policy: When the inventory level reaches 12 units, order 22.53 units.

f.

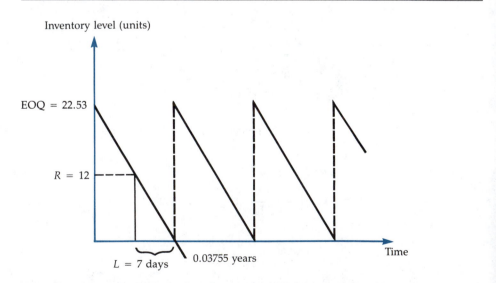

Section 8

1. $D = 150$
   $C = 375$
   $F = 10$
   $r = 0.12$

EOQ was already calculated to equal 8.16. Rounding Q up to 9 yielded a lower TC than did rounding Q down to 6.
   Next, we must determine if $Q = 9$ satisfies the $4,000 minimum order constraint:

$9(375) = \$3,375$

It does not.
   Incrementing Q by 3, we get 12 as the next feasible Q:

$12(375) = \$4,500$

The constraint is satisfied. Thus EOQ = 12 refrigerators.

$TC^* = 10(150/12) + 375(0.12)(12/2)$

$\quad = 125 + 270 = \$395.00$

Section 10

1. $D = 5,000$
   $F = 10$
   $r = 0.25$

Cost per unit	Quantity ordered
$144	$0 \leq Q < 250$
138	$250 \leq Q < 500$
130	$500 \leq Q$

a. $Q = 110$, $C = 144$:
$$TC = F(D/Q) + Cr(Q/2) + DC$$
$$= 10(5,000/110) + 144(0.25)(110/2) + 5,000(144)$$
$$= 454.55 + 1,980 + 720,000$$
$$= \$722,434.55$$
$Q = 270$, $C = 138$:
$$TC = 10(5,000/270) + 138(0.25)(270/2) + 5,000(138)$$
$$= 185.19 + 4,657.50 + 690,000$$
$$= \$694,842.69$$

$Q = 502, C = 130$:

$TC = 10(5,000/502) + 130(0.25)(502/2) + 5,000(130)$

$= 99.60 + 8,157.50 + 650,000$

$= \underline{\$658,257.10}$

b.

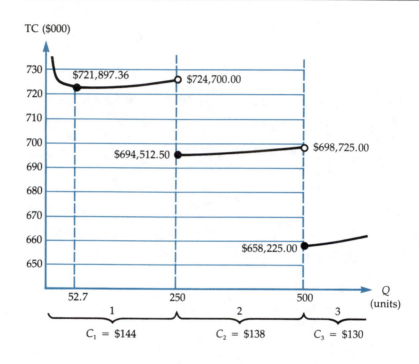

TC ($000)

730 $721,897.36   ○ $724,700.00

720

710

700   ○ $698,725.00

        $694,512.50 ●

690

680

670

660        $658,225.00 ●

650

        52.7   250   500 Q
                                              (units)

            1   2   3

        $C_1 = \$144$ $C_2 = \$138$ $C_3 = \$130$

FIGURE B.56

c. Using only Fig. B.56, the optimum order size appears to be 500 cases.

2. Working first with the rightmost region (3):

$$Q_3^* = \sqrt{\frac{2(5,000)(10)}{130(0.25)}} = 55.47$$

Since 55.47 does not belong to region 3, we need to calculate TC when $Q = 500$ and $C = 130$:

$$TC_3 = 10(5,000/500) + 130(0.25)(500/2) + 5,000(130) = \underline{\$658,225.00}$$

Now find the EOQ for region 2:

$$Q_2^* = \sqrt{\frac{2(5,000)(10)}{138(0.25)}} = 53.84$$

Since 53.84 does not belong to region 2, we need to calculate TC when $Q = 250$ and $C = 138$:

$$TC_2 = 10(5,000/250) + 138(0.25)(250/2) + 5,000(138) = \underline{\$694,512.50}$$

Now find the EOQ for region 1:

$$Q_1^* = \sqrt{\frac{2(5,000)(10)}{144(0.25)}} = 52.70$$

Thus

$$TC_1 = 10(5,000/52.70) + 144(0.25)(52.70/2) + 5,000(144) = \underline{\$721,897.36}$$

Region	Minimum cost	Order quantity
3	$658,225.00	500
2	$694,512.50	250
1	$721,897.36	52.7

Conclusion: The global minimum of the TC curve occurs at 500 units having a total annual cost of $658,225.

3. a. Cycle length $= Q^*/D = 500/5,000 = 0.10$ year $= 36$ days.
  b. Number of orders per year $= D/Q^* = 5,000/500 = 10$ orders.

4. $D = 12(300) = 3,600$
  $F = 10$
  $r = 0.12$
  $C_1 = 5.00$ each for 50 units
  $C_2 = 4.00$ each for 100 units
  $C_3 = 3.50$ each for 150 units
  $C_1 = 5.00$ and $Q = 50$:
  $TC_1 = 10(3,600/50) + 5(0.12)(50/2) + 3,600(5) = \underline{\$18,735.00}$
  $C_2 = 4.00$ and $Q = 100$:
  $TC_2 = 10(3,600/100) + 4(0.12)(100/2)$
    $+ 3,600(4) = \underline{\$14,784.00}$
  $C_3 = 3.50$ and $Q = 150$:
  $TC_3 = 10(3,600/150) + 3.5(0.12)(150/2) + 3,600(3.5) = \underline{\$12,871.50}$

Optimal inventory policy: Order 150 units at $3.50 each for a total annual cost of $12,871.50.
  Minimum total monthly cost $= \$12,871.50/12 = \$1,072.63$.
  Number of orders per month $= (D/Q^*) \div 12 = (3,600/150) \div 12 = 2$ orders.
  Time supply $=$ cycle length $= Q^*/D = 150/3,600 = 0.04167$ year $= 0.5$ month $= 15$ days.

CHAPTER 7: INVENTORY MODELS: PART II

Section 2

1. a. $Q^*_{PROD} = \sqrt{\dfrac{2(100)(10)}{25(0.10)(1 - 100/200)}} = 40$

$Q^*_{EOQ} = \sqrt{\dfrac{2(100)(10)}{25(0.10)}} = 28.28$

b. $Q^*_{PROD} = \sqrt{\dfrac{2(100)(10)}{25(0.10)(1 - 100/1,000)}}$

$= 29.81$

$Q^*_{EOQ} = 28.28$

Q^*_{EOQ} remains the same since only P is changing.

c. $Q^*_{PROD} = \sqrt{\dfrac{2(100)(10)}{25(0.10)(1 - 100/5,000)}}$

$= 28.57$

$Q^*_{EOQ} = 28.28$

d. $Q^*_{PROD} = \sqrt{\dfrac{2(100)(10)}{25(0.10)(1 - 100/10,000)}}$

$= 28.43$

$Q^*_{EOQ} = 28.28$

Comparison: This exercise demonstrates that as P approaches positive infinity, Q^*_{PROD} gets closer to equaling Q^*_{EOQ}. The larger P is in relation to D, the more appropriate it is to use the basic EOQ model to derive Q^*.

2. a. $Q^* = \sqrt{\dfrac{2(250)(50)}{25(0.25)(1 - 250/400)}} = 103.28$

$TC^* = F(D/Q) + Cr(Q/2)(1 - D/P)$

$= 50(250/103.28) + 25(0.25)(103.28/2)(1 - 250/400)$

$= 121.03 + 121.03 = \$242.06/\text{year}$

Demand/day = 250/250 = 1 unit.
R = reorder point = (lead time)(demand per day) = 4(1) = 4 units.
Optimal cycle length = Q^*/D = 103.28/250 = 0.413 year, or 103.28 days.
Optimal number of production runs per year = D/Q^* = 250/103.28 = 2.42 runs.
Length of production runs = Q^*/P = 103.28/400 = 0.2582 year, or 64.55 days.
Optimal inventory policy: When the inventory level falls to four units, place a production order for 103.28 units.

b. D is doubled to 500 units, and P is doubled to 800 units.

$$Q^* = \sqrt{\frac{2(500)(50)}{25(0.25)(1 - 500/800)}} = 146.06$$

$$TC^* = 50(500/146.06) + 25(0.25)(146.06/2)(1 - 500/800)$$

$$= 171.16 + 171.16 = \$342.32/\text{year}$$

Demand per day = 500/250 = 2 units
R = reorder point = (lead time)(demand per day) = 4(2) = 8 units.
Optimal inventory policy: When the inventory level falls to eight units, place a production order for 146.04 units. (Doubling D and P does *not* mean that Q^* is doubled.)

$$3. \; Q^*_{\text{PROD}} = \sqrt{\frac{2DF}{Cr(1 - D/P)}}$$

$$Q^*_{\text{EOQ}} = \sqrt{\frac{2DF}{Cr}}$$

Let $P \to \infty$. Then $D/P \to 0$, $(1 - D/P) \to 1$, and $Cr(1 - D/P) \to Cr(1)$. Thus $Q^*_{\text{PROD}} \to Q^*_{\text{EOQ}}$ because the denominators approach equality.

Section 4

1. $D = 2500$ $L = 5$ days
$C = 12$ $\mu = 50$ units
$r = 0.20$ $\sigma = 10$ units
$F = 25$

a.

$$Q^* = \sqrt{\frac{2(2,500)(25)}{12(0.20)}} = 228.22 \text{ units}$$

b. $s = 0.95$. From Appendix K, $k = 1.64$; therefore,

Q_s = safety stock level = $k\sigma$ = 1.64(10)

= 16.4 units

c. CrQ_s = 12(0.20)(16.4) = \$39.36 per year to carry
d. Reorder point = $\mu + k\sigma$ = 50 + 16.4 = 66.4 units

e. $TC = F(D/Q^*) + Cr(Q^*/2) + CrQ_s$

$$= 25(2,500/228.22) + 12(0.2)(228.22/2) + 39.36$$

$$= 273.86 + 273.86 + 39.36$$

$$= \$587.08 \text{ per year}$$

Optimal policy: Place an order for 228.22 units when the inventory level falls to 66.4 units. The mean demand during lead time is 50 units, and 95 percent of the time 66.4 units will be sufficient to cover lead time demand variability.

2. $D = 1{,}000$ $F = 30$
      $C = 20$ $\mu = 12$ days
      $r = 0.25$ $\sigma = 3$ days

a.

$$Q^* = \sqrt{\frac{2(1{,}000)(30)}{20(0.25)}} = 109.54 \text{ units}$$

b. $s = 0.95$. From Appendix K, $k = 1.64$; therefore,

Q_s = safety stock level = $k\sigma$(demand/day)

$= 1.64(3 \text{ days}) (4 \text{ units/day})$

$= 19.68$ units

c. $CrQ_s = 20(0.25)(19.68) = \$98.40$ per year to carry

d. Reorder point = (mean lead time)(demand/day) + (safety stock)

$= \mu(\text{demand/day}) + Q_s$

$= (12 \text{ days})(4 \text{ units/day}) + 19.8 \text{ units}$

$= 48 + 19.68 = 67.68$ units

e. $TC = F(D/Q^*) + Cr(Q^*/2) + CrQ_s$

$= 30(1{,}000/109.54) + 20(0.25)(109.54/2) + 98.40$

$= 273.87 + 273.85 + 98.40$

$= \$646.12$ per year

Optimal policy: Place an order for 109.54 units when the inventory level falls to 67.68 units. The average lead time is 12 days, during which 48 units will be used. The extra 19.68 units will be sufficient to cover lead time variability 95 percent of the time.

Section 5

1. $c = 2$, $p = 3.50$ $n = 0.25$

Number of Bushels	Probability of occurrence	Cumulative probability
10	$18/51 = 0.353$	0.353
11	$15/51 = 0.294$	0.647
12	$8/51 = 0.157$	0.804
13	$6/51 = 0.118$	0.922
14	$4/51 = 0.078$	1.000

$$\frac{p - c}{p + h} = \frac{3.50 - 2}{3.50 + 0.25} = .40$$

The first Q satisfying $P[D \leq Q^* - 1] \leq (p - c)/(p + h) \leq P[D \leq Q^*]$ is $Q = Q^* = 11$.

$$P[D \leq 11 - 1] = 0.353$$
$$P[D \leq 11] = 0.647$$

Thus, at the beginning of each week Fruitcake's Fresh Produce should stock 11 bushels of onions.

2. $c = 10¢$ $\qquad p = 25¢$ $\qquad h = 1.9¢$

$$\frac{p - c}{p + h} = \frac{25 - 10}{25 + 1.9} = 0.5576$$

The cumulative probability value of 0.5596, which corresponds to 0.15 standard deviations above the mean, is the first normal value to satisfy

$$P[D \leq Z] \geq 0.5576$$

Thus $\mu + 0.15\sigma = 50 + 0.15(16) = 52.4$ papers per day.

3. $c = 10¢$ $\qquad p = 25¢$ $\qquad h = 2¢ - 1.5¢ = 0.5¢$

$$\frac{p - c}{p + h} = \frac{25 - 10}{25 + 0.5} = 0.5882$$

The cumulative probability value of 0.5910, which corresponds to 0.23 standard deviations above the mean, is the first normal value to satisfy

$$P[D \leq Z] \geq 0.5882$$

Thus $\mu + (0.23) = 50 + 0.23(12) = 52.76$ papers per day, or approximately 53 papers per day. The order quantity is slightly higher than that of Example 7.7, because the holding cost is lower.

4. In Example 7.6, we saw that Fruitcake's should stock three bushels of onions. If the initial inventory is two bushels, this means that Fruitcake's should purchase one additional bushel at the start of the week.

CHAPTER 8: QUEUING MODELS

Section 3

1. $\lambda = 5$; mean service time $= 1/\mu = 1/7$, so $\mu = 7$. Use an $(M/M/1)$ system:
   a. $\rho = 5/7 = 0.714$, or 71.4 percent busy time
   b. $L = 5/(7 - 5) = 2.5$ trucks idle
   c. $W_q = 5 \div 7(7 - 5) = 0.357$ hour (21.4 minutes)
   d. $W = 1/(7 - 5) = 1/2$ hour (waiting plus service time)
2. $250 \times L_q$; $L_q = 5^2 \div 7(7 - 5) = 1.78$, so space needed for waiting is $(250)(1.78) = 445$ square feet.
3. b. $\rho = 5/10 = 1/2$, or busy 50 percent of the time.
   c. Use Eq. (8–1): $L = 1$, $L_q = 0.5$, $W = 0.2$ hour, $W_q = 0.1$ hour, and mean service time equals $1/\mu = 0.1$ hour (or 6 minutes).

d. If $\lambda = 9$ and $\mu = 10$, then busy time $= \rho = 0.9$ (or 90 percent of the time), $L = 9$, $L_q = 8.1$, $W = 1$ hour, $W_q = 0.9$, and mean service time $= 0.1$ hour (or 6 minutes).

Section 4

1.

λ	μ	ρ	L
1	20	0.050	0.053
5	20	0.250	0.333
10	20	0.500	1.000
15	20	0.750	3.000
16	20	0.800	4.000
17	20	0.850	5.667
19	20	0.950	19.000
19.9	20	0.995	199.000

2. See Fig. 8.5.

Section 5

1. $W = L/\lambda = 0.5/5 = 0.1$
$\quad W_q = W - 1/\mu = 0.1 - 0.067 = 0.033$
$\quad\quad L_q = L - \rho = 0.5 - 0.333 = 0.167$

2. $L = \rho/(1 - \rho)$ Solve this for ρ:

$$(1 - \rho)L = \rho$$
$$L - \rho L = \rho$$
$$L = \rho + \rho L$$
$$L = \rho(1 + L)$$
$$\rho = \frac{L}{1 + L}$$

Thus when $L = 4$, $\rho = 4/(4 + 1) = 0.80$.

Section 6

1. $\lambda = 10$, $\mu = 5$, and $s = 3$. Use an $(M/M/3)$ system:

a. $\rho = 10/15 = 0.667 = 0.67$
b. $p_0 = 0.110$ (from Appendix L)
c. $L_q = 0.889$ from Eq. (8–10c)
d. $L = 0.889 + (10/15) = 2.889$,
$W_q = 0.889/10 = 0.0889$, and
$W = 0.0889 + 1/5 = 0.2889$
e. The time that a patient must wait *before being treated* either by a doctor or by a nurse is more critical than the total time a patient must spend at the hospital.

2. $\lambda = 100$, $\mu = 40$, and $s = 4$. Use an $(M/M/4)$ system:
 a. $p_0 = 0.0737$
 b. Need to know W. First, find L_q from Eq. (8–10c): $L_q = 0.533$. Then $W_q = 0.533/100 = 0.00533$ hour, so $W = 0.00533 + 1/40 = 0.03$ hour (1.8 minutes).
 c. $L_q = 0.533$
 d. $W_q = 0.00533$ hour (about 20 seconds)
 e. The waiting area will be adequate if there are 0, 1, 2, ... , 8, or 9 students in the center. The probability of this is

$$p_0 + p_1 + p_2 + p_3 + p_4 + p_5 + p_6 + p_7 + p_8 + p_9$$

Students will be lined up outside the building if there are ten or more students inside the center, and the probability of this event occurring is 1 minus the above sum.
 Use Eq. (8–10b):

$$p_n \begin{cases} \dfrac{(100/40)^n}{n!}\,(0.0737) & \text{if } 0 \le n \le 4 \\[2ex] \dfrac{(100/4)^n}{4!\,4^{n-4}}\,(0.0737) & \text{if } n \ge 4 \end{cases}$$

Using these data, we compute the following values: $p_0 = 0.0737$, $p_1 = 0.1842$, $p_2 = 0.2303$, $p_3 = 0.1919$, $p_4 = 0.1200$, $p_5 = 0.0750$, $p_6 = 0.0468$, $p_7 = 0.0293$, $p_8 = 0.0183$, and $p_9 = 0.0114$. The sum of these terms is 0.9809, which equals the proportion of time that the waiting area will be adequate. The percentage of time the waiting area will be inadequate is $1 - 0.9809 = 0.0191$, or 1.91 percent of the time.

Section 7

1. In order for $\rho < 1$, there must be *at least* three doctor-nurse teams. Let s = number of doctor-nurse teams. They need $W_q \le 4/60 = 0.0667$ hour, $\lambda = 10$, and $\mu = 5$.

s	p_0	L_q	W_q	System
3	0.1111	0.889	0.0889	$M/M/3$
4	0.130	0.173	0.017	$M/M/4$

Thus, at least four teams are required.

2. $\lambda = 15$ and $\mu = 8n$. Use an $M/M/1$ system to find n so that $W_q \leq 4/60 = 0.0667$ hour. In order for $\rho < 1$, we need n to be at least 2.

n	μ	W_q	(Eq. 8–1f)
2	16	0.9375	
3	24	0.0694	
4	32	0.0276	

They must hire at least four workers.

Section 8

1. $\lambda = 1$ and $\mu = (0.8)(3) = 2.4$. Use an $(M/M/1)$ system:

  a. $SC = 105n = 105(3) = \$315/\text{day}$
    $WC = LC_w = (0.7143)(300) = \$214.29/\text{day}$

  b. $p_0 = 1 - \rho = 1 - 1/2.4 = 0.583$, or 58.3%

  c. $L = 0.7143$

  d. $W = L/\lambda = 0.7143/1 = 0.7143$ hour, or 42.86 minutes (key relationship)

2. $\lambda = 3$ and $\mu = 2n$. Use an $(M/M/1)$ system:

    $SC = 20n$

    $WC = L_q C_w = L_q \times 5$ [Use Eq. (8–1d) for L_q.]

    $TC = SC + WC = 20n + L_q \times 5$ (\$/day)

In order for $\rho < 1$, we need $n \geq 2$.

n	SC	μ	L_q	WC	$TC = SC + WC$
2	40	4	2.250	11.25	\$51.25
3	60	6	0.500	2.50	62.50
4	80	8	0.225	1.12	81.12

The cost is increasing. Minimum cost occurs when $n = 2$, $TC = \$51.25/\text{day}$ (hire two workers).

3.

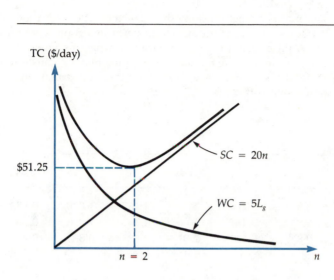

FIGURE B.57

4.

n	SC	WC	TC	
2	30	31.50	61.50	
3	45	7.00	52.00	*minimum
4	60	3.15	63.15	

Thus three workers should be hired. The graph of TC versus n is similar to Fig. 8.8.

Section 9

1. $p_0 = 1 - 1.5/2.03 = 1 - 0.739 = .261$

$$L_q = \frac{(1.5)^2(0.001) + (0.739)^2}{2(1 - 0.739)} = \frac{0.548}{0.522}$$

$= 1.050$

$W_q = 1.050/1.5 = 0.700$

$W = 0.700 + 1/2.03 = 0.700 + 0.493$

$= 1.193$

$L = 1.5(1.193) = 1.789$

2. a. Variance is 0.
   b. In Eq. (8–13b) set $\sigma^2 = 0$: $L_q = \rho^2/2(1 - \rho)$.
   c. The examples might include the following: (1) certain production processes where it takes a fixed amount of time to perform a routine operation on a part or machine; (2) public school immunization programs where the amount of time required to innoculate a student is (approximately) constant; and (3) a concession stand at a state fair that serves only fountain drinks and where each customer orders one soft drink.

3.

	ρ	p_0	L	L_q	W	W_q
A	0.833	0.167	5	4.167	1.000	0.833
B	0.833	0.167	5	4.167	1.000	0.833
C	0.833	0.167	2.92	2.083	0.584	0.417

Note that L_q for system C is half that for the other two systems. The fact that systems A and B have the same steady-state characteristics emphasizes the fact that only the mean and service time variance are important, *not* the probability density of service times.

Section 10

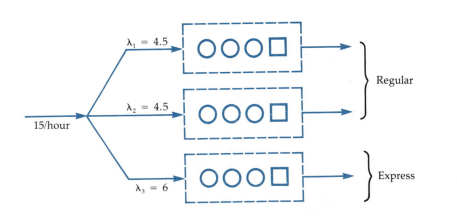

1.

	λ	μ	ρ	p_0	L	L_q	W	W_q
Regular–1	4.5	11	0.409	0.591	0.692	0.283	0.154	0.063
Regular–2	4.5	11	0.409	0.591	0.692	0.283	0.154	0.063
Express	6	15	0.400	0.600	0.667	0.267	0.111	0.044
					2.051	0.833		

$P\{$no customers in store$\} = (0.591)(0.591)(0.600)$

$= 0.210$

2. In this problem we have a system consisting of one $(M/M/2)$ model ($\lambda = 9$, $\mu = 11$) and one $(M/M/1)$ model ($\lambda = 6$, $\mu = 15$):

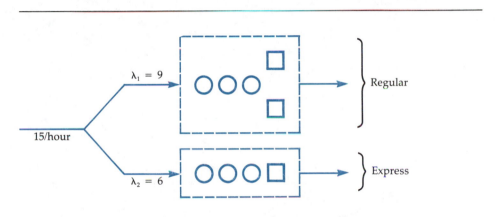

FIGURE B.59

	λ	μ	ρ	p_0	L	L_q	W	W_q
Regular	9	11	0.409	0.419	0.982	0.164	0.109	0.018
Express	6	15	0.400	0.600	0.667	0.267	0.111	0.044
					1.649	0.431		

The probability that there are no customers in the store is $(0.419)(0.600) = 0.251$.

Section 11

1. $\lambda = 100$ and $\mu = 2$ (since $1/\mu = 30/60$ hours):

    a. $L = \rho = 100/2 = 50$

b. Using Eq. (8–14b), with $n = 0$, we have

$$p_0 = \frac{e^{-p}p^0}{0!} = \frac{e^{-50}(1)}{1}$$

which is approximately 0 (1.9×10^{-22}).

CHAPTER 9: PROJECT MANAGEMENT: CPM AND PERT

Section 2

1.

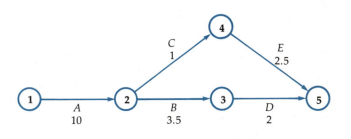

FIGURE B.60

2.

Activity	Duration	ES	EF	LS	LF	Slack	On critical path
A	10	0	10	0	10	0	*
B	3.5	10	13.5	10.0	13.5	0	*
C	1	10	11.0	12.0	13.0	2	
D	2	13.5	15.5	13.5	15.5	0	*
E	2.5	11	13.5	13.0	15.5	2	

Critical path, A–B–D; 15.2 weeks.

3.

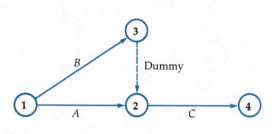

4.

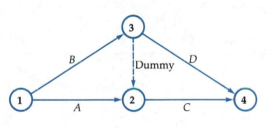

5.

Activity symbol	Time required (weeks)	Immediate predecessors
A	2	–
B	3	–
C	1	–
D	1	A
E	2	B
F	5	C
G	6	D, E, F

6.

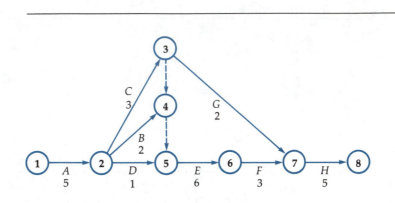

Critical path, A–C–E–F–H.

Activity	Duration	ES	EF	LS	LF	Slack	On critical path
A	5	0	5	0	5	0	*
B	2	5	7	6	8	1	
C	3	5	8	5	8	0	*
D	1	5	6	7	8	2	
E	6	8	14	8	14	0	*
F	3	14	17	14	17	0	*
G	2	8	10	15	17	7	
H	5	17	22	17	22	0	*

Section 3

1. Activity *C* would be crashed by *one* week only. At this point there are *two* critical paths: *A–C* and *B–D*. Thus, both paths would have to be crashed by the same amount *if* the crash points allowed it.
2. There are two critical paths: *A–D–G* and *B–E–G*.
   a. Since activity *G* is common to both paths and also has the lowest "cost to crash," *G* is chosen as the answer.

b. Both activities D and E would be crashed by one week, at a total cost of 100 and 250 = $350, which is less than the cost of $375 to crash G alone.

3.a.

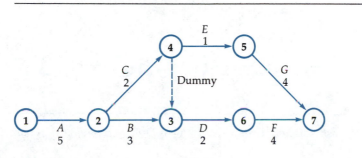

FIGURE B.64

Normal CPM schedule. Critical path, A–B–D–F; duration, 14 weeks; cost $1,900 (the sum of all normal costs).

b.

Activity	Cost to crash/week
A	100
B	50
C	125
D	50
E	∞
F	200
G	100

Example: For activity F, the cost to crash is

$$\left| \frac{\text{Crash cost} - \text{normal cost}}{\text{Crash time} - \text{normal time}} \right| = \left| \frac{900 - 500}{2 - 4} \right| = 200$$

c.

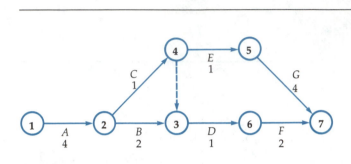

Crash schedule. Critical path, A–B–D-F; total project duration, 9 weeks; total project cost, $2,825.

d. Start with the normal schedule, part (a). First we must crash either B or D, since the two tie for the minimum crash cost ($50/week). Let us then choose B, arbitrarily.

Crash activity B by one week (at a cost of $50). The new critical paths are A–B–D–F and A–C–D–F, each with a duration of 13 weeks. Activity B is at its crash point and cannot be further crashed.

Crash activity D by one week (at a cost of $50). Now all three paths are critical: A–B–D–F, A–C–D–F, and A–C–E–G, at 12 weeks each. Activities B, D, and E cannot be further crashed. This leaves A, C, F, and G to crash, and we must shorten all three paths by one week. The least expensive possibility is to crash A by one week.

Crash activity A by one week (at a cost of $100). Now A, B, D, and E are at their crash points, and again, all three paths are critical at 11 weeks.

If we crash F, the cost would be $200 and we would shorten both A–B–D–F and A–C–D–F. Then to shorten A–C–E–G, we could crash G by one week at a cost of $100 for a total cost of $200 + $100 = $300.

Or we could crash C by one week at a cost of $125, which would shorten A–C–D–F and A–C–E–G by one week. To shorten A–B–D–F, we would then crash F by one week at a cost of $200 for a total cost of $125 + $200 = $325.

These are the only two reasonable options, so we would select the first: crash F and G each by one week at a cost of $300.

Again, all three paths are critical, each with a duration of 10 weeks. A, B, D, and E are all at their crash points. The situation is the same as it was in the previous step, so we would again crash F and G by one week each at a cost of $300.

All three paths remain critical at 9 weeks, but now A, B, D, E, F, and G are

all at their crash points. Thus, since path *A–B–D–F* cannot be further shortened, it would do no good to try to crash the other two paths.
  The minimum cost crash schedule is given in Fig. B.66.

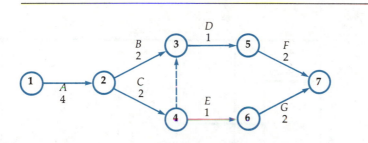

Time: 9 weeks
Total crashing cost: $50 + $50 + $100 + $300 + $300 = $800
Cost of this schedule: $1,900 + $800 = $2,700

e. Crash schedule cost: $2,825
Minimum-cost crash schedule: $2,700

Section 6

1. a. The critical path is *A–C–E*, with a length of 11 weeks.

Activity	Duration	ES	EF	LS	LF	Slack	On critical path
A	3	0	3	0	3	0	*
B	2	0	2	2	4	2	
C	4	3	7	3	7	0	*
D	3	2	5	4	7	2	
E	4	7	11	7	11	0	*
F	1	2	3	10	11	8	

b.

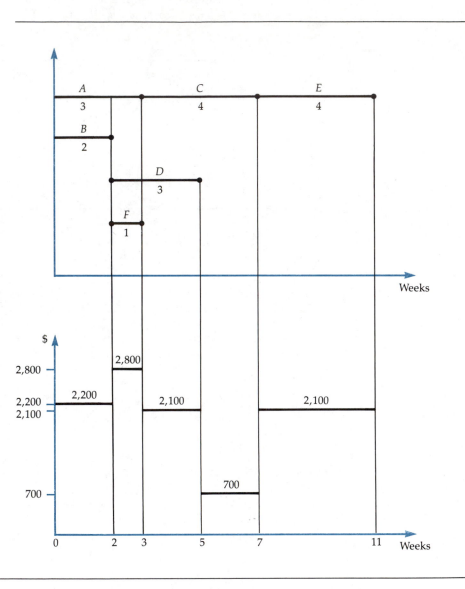

Scheduling according to ES times.

c.

Scheduling according to LS times.

d. No, activities *A* and *B* must always be conducted with some degree of overlap.

Section 7

1. G's standard deviation:

$$\frac{b - a}{6} = \frac{13 - 5}{6} = 1.33$$

Variance of project completion time:

$$(0.67)^2 + (0.83)^2 + (0.50)^2 + (1.33)^2 = 3.1567$$

Standard deviation of critical path time:

$$\sqrt{3.1567} = 1.78$$

G's mean:

$$\frac{a + b + 4m}{6} = \frac{5 + 13 + 4(7)}{6} = 7.67 \text{ weeks}$$

Mean expected project completion time:

$$3.3 + 7.5 + 7.2 + 7.7 = 25.7 \text{ weeks}$$

Number of standard deviations that 27 weeks is to the right of the 25.7-week mean:

$$\frac{27 - 25.7}{1.78} = 0.73$$

From Appendix K, the probability is seen to be 77 percent.

APPENDIX TO SECTION TWO:
TIME-SERIES FORECASTING

Section 3

1. Figure B.69.
2. The 2-period MA forecast has a lag of 1/2 period; the 5-period MA forecast has a lag of 2 periods.

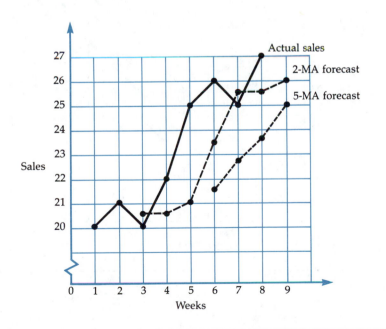

3.

Month	1	2	3	4	5	6	7	8	9	10	11	12	13
Sales	20	22	21	19	23	23	24	26	23	20	?		
Part A. 3-MA				21	20.7	21	21.7	23.3	24.3	24.3	23		
Part B. 6-MA							21.3	22	22.7	23	23.2	(lag = 2.5	
											months)		
Part C. 6-MA											23.2	23.2	23.2

4.a. Trend model.

b.

Week	1	2	3	4	5	6	7	8	9	10
Sales	3	5	7	9	11	13	15	17	19	21
3-MA				5	7	9	11	13	15	17
5-MA						7	9	11	13	15

c. Figure B.70.

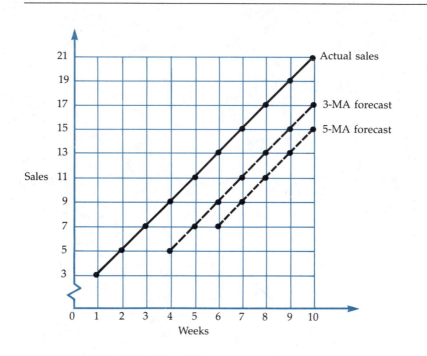

FIGURE B.70

c.

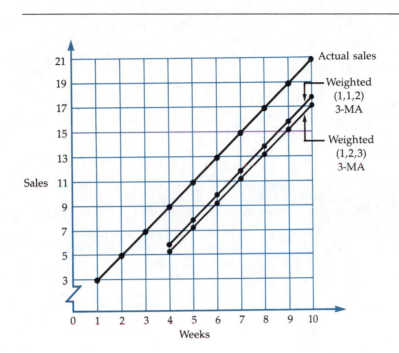

FIGURE B.71

d. Lag for the 3-MA system is one week; lag for the 5-MA system is two weeks. Select the 3-MA system, since it better responds to the trend.

5.

Week	1	2	3	4	5	6	7	8	9	10
Sales	3	5	7	9	11	13	15	17	19	21 (weights)

a. Weighted 3-MA				5.5	7.5	9.5	11.5	13.5	15.5	17.5 (1, 1, 2)
b. Weighted 3-MA				5.7	7.7	9.7	11.7	13.7	15.7	17.7 (1, 2, 3)

The weighted three-week MA system of part (b), with weights of (1, 2, 3) seems to "track" more closely.

Section 4

1.a.

Week	Actual data	3-MA	4-MA	3-MA absolute error	4-MA absolute error
1	20				
2	22				
3	18				
4	19				
5	23	19.67	19.75	3.33	3.25
6	23	20.00	20.50	3.00	2.50
7	21	21.67	20.75	0.67	0.25
8	20	22.33	21.50	2.33	1.50
9	19	21.33	21.75	2.33	2.75
10	23	20.00	20.75	3.00	2.25
11	25	20.67	20.75	4.33	4.25

$$\Sigma|e_i| = 18.99 \qquad 16.75$$
$$\text{MAD} = 2.71 \qquad 2.39$$
$$\text{3-MA} \qquad \text{4-MA}$$

---

b. The 4-MA forecast system seems to give better forecasts, since the mean absolute deviation value is smaller.

c. Using the 4-MA system, the forecast for week 12 is

$$\frac{20 + 19 + 23 + 25}{4} = 21.75$$

2. Forecast errors that are consistently positive suggest the following:

a. A rather constant trend exists, and it could be upward or downward.

b. The lag of your chosen forecast system is too great (that is, N is too large). Reduce your N, and possibly even employ some weights in your system.

Section 5

1.

Month	1	2	3	4	5	6	7	8
Actual sales	12	11	12	14	15	17	16	?
Forecast $\alpha = 0.1$	12	12	11.90	11.91	12.12	12.41	12.87	13.18
Forecast $\alpha = 0.6$	12	12	11.40	11.76	13.10	14.24	15.90	15.96

The system using $\alpha = 0.6$ responds to the apparent sales level increase more rapidly than the $\alpha = 0.4$ system does.

2.

Month	1	2	3	4	5	6	7	8
Actual sales	12	11	12	10	19	10	11	?
Forecast $\alpha = 0.1$	12	12	11.90	11.91	11.72	12.45	12.21	12.09
Forecast $\alpha = 0.6$	12	12	11.40	11.76	10.70	15.68	12.27	11.51

The system using $\alpha = 0.1$ is more stable.

3.

Month	Actual sales	$\alpha = 0.1$ forecast	$\alpha = 0.6$ forecast	$\alpha = 0.1$ absolute error	$\alpha = 0.6$ absolute error
1	12	12	12	0	0
2	11	12	12	1.00	1.00
3	12	11.90	11.40	0.10	0.60
4	14	11.91	11.76	2.09	2.24
5	15	12.12	13.10	2.88	1.90
6	17	12.41	14.24	4.59	2.76
7	16	12.87	15.90	3.13	0.10
				$\Sigma|e_i| = 13.79$	8.60
				MAD = 1.97	1.23

On the basis of the MAD values, the system using $\alpha = 0.6$ seems more appropriate.

4.

Month	Actual sales	$\alpha = 0.1$ forecast	$\alpha = 0.6$ forecast	$\alpha = 0.1$ absolute error	$\alpha = 0.6$ absolute error
1	12	12	12	0	0
2	11	12	12	1.00	1.00
3	12	11.90	11.40	0.10	0.60
4	10	11.91	11.76	1.91	1.76
5	19	11.72	10.70	7.28	8.30
6	10	12.45	15.68	2.45	5.68
7	11	12.21	12.27	1.21	1.27
				$\Sigma|e_i| = 13.95$	18.61
				MAD = 1.99	2.66

The $\alpha = 0.1$ system is more appropriate.

Section 7

1. a.

t	X_t	tX_t	t_2
1	10	10	1
2	12	24	4
3	15	45	9
4	14	56	16
5	16	80	25
$\Sigma = 67$		215	55

$$\bar{t} = \frac{n+1}{2} = 3$$

$$\bar{X} = \frac{\Sigma X_t}{n} = \frac{67}{5} = 13.4$$

$$a = \bar{X} - b\bar{t} = 13.4 - 1.4(3) = 9.2$$

$$b = \frac{\Sigma tX_t - n\bar{t}\bar{X}}{\Sigma t^2 - n(\bar{t})^2}$$

$$= \frac{215 - 5(3)(13.4)}{55 - 5(3)^2} = 1.4$$

Regression line: $F_t = 9.2 + 1.4t$

b.

t	X_t	F_t	$X_t - F_t$	$(X_t - F_t)^2$
1	10	10.60	−0.60	0.36
2	12	12.00	0.00	0.00
3	15	13.40	1.60	2.56
4	14	14.80	−0.80	0.64
5	16	16.20	−0.20	0.04
				$\Sigma = 3.60$

$$\sigma = \sqrt{\frac{\Sigma X_i - F_t)^2}{n-2}}$$

$$= \sqrt{\frac{3.60}{5-2}}$$

$$= 1.10$$

c. $F_b = 9.2 + 1.4(6) = 17.6$
d.

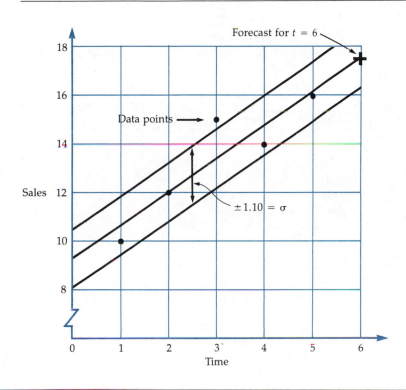

Forecast for $t = 6$

Data points →

$\pm 1.10 = \sigma$

Sales

Time

FIGURE B.72

Section 8

1.

Period t	Actual X_t	Forecast F_t	Error e_t	Error sum S	MAD	Tracking signal T
1	18	20	−2.00	−2.00	2.00	1.00
2	23	19.80	3.20	1.20	2.60	0.46
3	25	20.12	4.88	6.08	3.36	1.81
4	26	20.61	5.39	11.47	3.87	2.96
5	22	21.15	0.85	12.32	3.26	3.78
6	29	21.24	7.76	20.08	4.01	5.01
7	24	22.02	1.98	22.06	3.72	5.93

Since $k = 2$, T must satisfy:

$$T < 2(1.25)\sqrt{\frac{1}{2(0.1)}}$$

$T < 5.59$

Since $5.93 \not< 5.59$, the forecast system is subject to question and should be carefully examined. Perhaps a higher value of α should be considered.

CHAPTER 10: DECISION THEORY

Section 4

1. a. row 1 minimum = 100
row 2 minimum = 0
max(100, 0) = 100, choose action a_1
   b. row 1 minimum = −10
row 2 minimum = 0
max(−10, 0) = 0, choose action a_2
You would probably not want to abide by either of the maximin decisions.
2. a. row 1 maximum = 5,000
row 2 maximum = 4,000
max(5,000, 4,000) = 5,000, choose action a_1
   b. row 1 maximum = 5,000
row 2 maximum = 5,001
max(5,000, 5,001) = 5,001, choose action a_2
Both of these maximax decisions are probably too risky for you.
3. a. Loss table:

	s_1	s_2	s_3	s_4
a_1	4	3	2	2
a_2	10	1	0	0
a_3	0	0	9	35

   b. max(38, 40, 5) = 40, choose action 2
   c. max(46, 40, 50) = 50, choose action 3
   d. min(4, 10, 35) = 4, choose action 1
   e. A pessimistic decision maker would use the maximin rule and choose action 2. An optimistic decision maker would use the maximax rule and choose action 3. If a decision maker is risk averse, action 2 is the most appealing. A risk taker would prefer action 3.

Section 6

1.a. $ER(a_1) = 0.5(20) + 0.2(20) + 0.2(14) + 0.1(15)$
$\qquad\quad = 18.3$
$\qquad ER(a_2) = 0.5(21) + 0.2(18) + 0.2(14) + 0.1(16)$
$\qquad\qquad\quad = 18.5$
$\qquad ER(a_3) = 0.5(18) + 0.2(20) + 0.2(15) + 0.1(15)$
$\qquad\qquad\quad = 17.5$
$\qquad ER(a_4) = 0.5(19) + 0.2(16) + 0.2(17) + 0.1(20)$
$\qquad\qquad\quad = 18.1$

Hence the Bayes decision is a_2, and the expected payoff is 18.5

b. EPPI $= 0.5(21) + .02(20) + 0.2(17) + 0.1(20)$
$\qquad\qquad = 19.9$
$\qquad$ EVPI $= 19.9 - 18.5 = 1.4$

2.a.

	s_1	s_2	s_3	s_4
a_1	1	0	3	5
a_2	0	2	3	4
a_3	3	0	2	5
a_4	2	4	0	0

b. $EL(a_1) = 0.5(1) + 0.2(0) + 0.2(3) + 0.1(5) = 1.6$
$\quad EL(a_2) = 0.5(0) + 0.2(2) + 0.2(3) + 0.1(4) = 1.4$
$\quad EL(a_3) = 0.5(3) + 0.2(0) + 0.2(2) + 0.1(5) = 2.4$
$\quad EL(a_4) = 0.5(2) + 0.2(4) + 0.2(0) + 0.1(0) = 1.8$
The minimum expected loss is 1.4.

Section 8

1. See Fig. B.73. The optimal sequence of decisions involves purchasing $M1$ and then, if demand is high or moderate in year 1, capacity should be expanded.
2. The modified diagram consists of the tree of Fig. 10.7, together with a third decision branch out of node 1 (see Fig. B.74). If we fold back the node evaluated to be 64.85, we get

$$64.85 - \text{(cost of } M3) = 64.85 - 25 = 39.85$$

3. Since 39.85 is less than the 45.95 of Fig. 10.7, node 1 evaluation remains 45.95, and the optimal sequence of decisions is the same as for that figure.

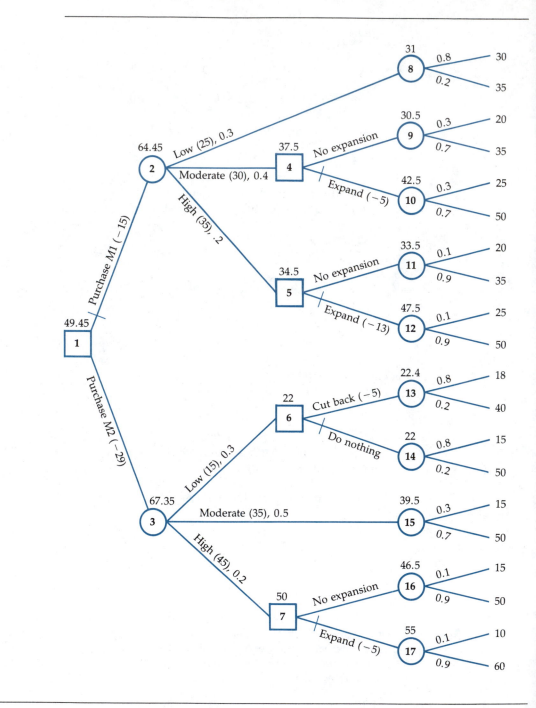

FIGURE B.73

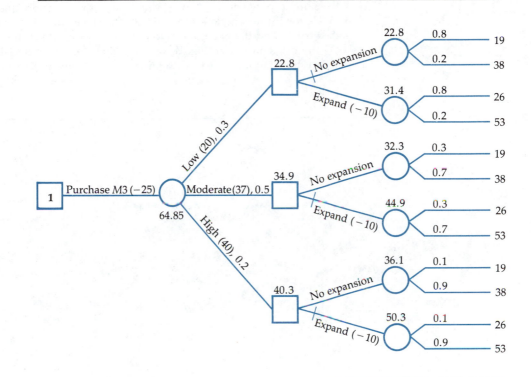

FIGURE B.74

Section 9

1.a.

$P(O_1) = 0.2(0.10) + 0.35(0.25) + 0.3(0.80) + 0.15(0.95) = 0.49$

$P(O_2) = 0.2(0.90) + 0.35(0.75) + 0.3(0.20) + 0.15(0.05) = 0.51$

$P(s_1|O_1) = 0.2(0.10)/0.49 = 0.041$

$P(s_2|O_1) = 0.35(0.25)/0.49 = 0.179$

$P(s_3|O_1) = 0.3(0.80)/0.49 = 0.490$

$P(s_4|O_1) = 0.15(0.95)/0.49 = 0.291$

$P(s_1|O_2) = 0.2(0.90)/0.51 = 0.353$

$P(s_2|O_2) = 0.35(0.75)/0.51 = 0.515$

$P(s_3|O_2) = 0.3(0.20)/0.51 = 0.118$

$P(s_4|O_2) = 0.15(0.05)/0.51 = 0.015$

b. If the sample outcome is O_1, we would have the decision tree shown in Fig. B.75. Hence if the sample outcome is O_1, the Bayes decision is to purchase the flatbed truck, and the expected payoff would be $24,625. If the sample outcome is O_2, the decision tree in Fig. B.76 shows that the Bayes decision would be to purchase the standard truck, with an expected payoff of $19,886.

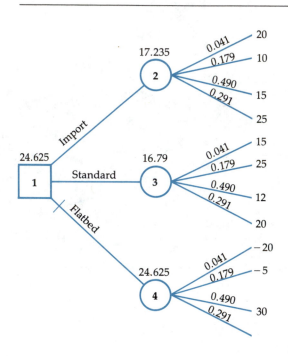

FIGURE B.75

Section 10

1. The predictive probabilities are calculated as follows:

$P(O_1) = 0.2(0.05) + 0.35(0.10) + 0.3(0.75) + 0.15(0.95) = 0.4125$

$P(O_2) = 0.2(0.95) + 0.35(0.90) + 0.3(0.25) + 0.15(0.05) = 0.5875$

The posterior probabilities are:

$P(s_1|O_1) = 0.2(0.05)/0.4125 = 0.024$

$P(s_2|O_1) = 0.35(0.10)/0.4125 = 0.085$

$P(s_3|O_1) = 0.3(0.75)/0.4125 = 0.545$

$P(s_4|O_1) = 0.15(0.95)/0.4125 = 0.345$

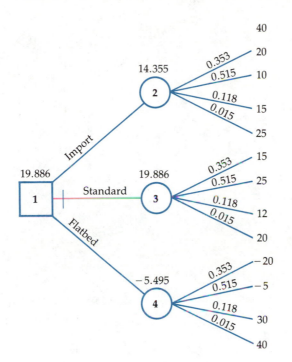

FIGURE B.76

$P(s_1|O_2) = 0.2(0.95)/0.5875 = 0.323$

$P(s_2|O_2) = 0.35(0.90)/0.5875 = 0.536$

$P(s_3|O_2) = 0.3(0.25)/0.5875 = 0.128$

$P(s_4|O_2) = 0.15(0.05)/0.5875 = 0.013$

The decision tree for the preposterior decision problem is shown in Fig. B.77. We then have

EVSI = (expected payoff with the sample information)

      − (expected payoff without sample information)

    = 23.84 − 18.35   (see Fig. 10.2)

    = 5.49, or $5,490

2. If Blockwood employs Andrite and the outcome of the sample information is O_2, the Bayes decision is to purchase the standard truck. The expected payoff is $19,194. If Andrite's fee is subtracted, the result is $18,244, which is less than the expected payoff without sample information ($18,350). If the outcome of the sample information is O_1, the Bayes decision is to purchase the flatbed truck. The expected

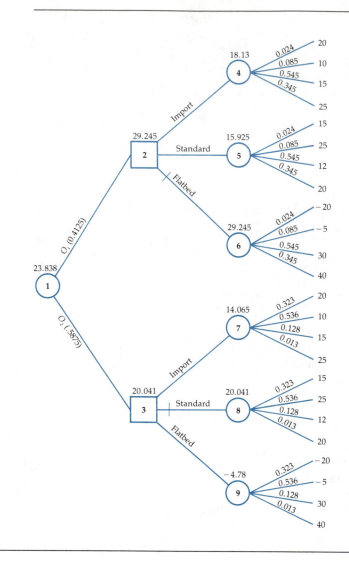

payoff is $23,850. If Andrite's fee is subtracted, the result is $22,900, which is greater than the expected payoff without sample information.

ENGS = EVSI − (cost of sampling)
= $5,490 − $900 = $4,590 > 0

Therefore, the sample information should be purchased.

CHAPTER 11: MARKOV CHAINS

Section 2

1. *Event*   *Probability*

$A \xrightarrow{2 \text{ steps}} B \xrightarrow{1 \text{ step}} B$ $(0.61)(0.3) = 0.183$

$A \xrightarrow{2 \text{ steps}} B \xrightarrow{1 \text{ step}} B$ $(0.39)(0.6) = \underline{0.234}$

$\qquad\qquad\qquad\qquad\qquad\qquad 0.417$

$B \xrightarrow{2 \text{ steps}} A \xrightarrow{1 \text{ step}} A$ $(0.52)(0.7) = 0.364$

$B \xrightarrow{2 \text{ steps}} B \xrightarrow{1 \text{ step}} A$ $(0.48)(0.4) = \underline{0.192}$

$\qquad\qquad\qquad\qquad\qquad\qquad 0.556$

$B \xrightarrow{2 \text{ steps}} A \xrightarrow{1 \text{ step}} B$ $(0.52)(0.3) = 0.156$

$B \xrightarrow{2 \text{ steps}} B \xrightarrow{1 \text{ step}} B$ $(0.48)(0.6) = \underline{0.288}$

$\qquad\qquad\qquad\qquad\qquad\qquad 0.444$

2. a. $P^4 = P \cdot P \cdot P \cdot P = P^3 \cdot P$

$$P^4 = \begin{bmatrix} 0.583 & 0.417 \\ 0.556 & 0.444 \end{bmatrix}\begin{bmatrix} 0.7 & 0.3 \\ 0.4 & 0.6 \end{bmatrix}$$

$$= \begin{bmatrix} (0.583)(0.7) + (0.417)(0.4) & (0.583)(0.3) + (0.417)(0.6) \\ (0.556)(0.7) + (0.444)(0.4) & (0.556)(0.3) + (0.444)(0.6) \end{bmatrix}$$

$$= \begin{bmatrix} 0.575 & 0.425 \\ 0.567 & 0.433 \end{bmatrix}$$

b. $[0.3 \quad 0.7]\begin{bmatrix} 0.575 & 0.425 \\ 0.567 & 0.433 \end{bmatrix}$

$= [(0.3)(0.575) + (0.7)(0.567) \quad (0.3)(0.425) + (0.7)(0.433)]$

$= [0.569 \quad 0.431]$, or 56.9% for A and 43.1% for B

3. a. $P^2 = \begin{bmatrix} 0.30 & 0.70 \\ 0.14 & 0.86 \end{bmatrix}$

$P^3 = \begin{bmatrix} 0.220 & 0.780 \\ 0.156 & 0.844 \end{bmatrix}$

$P^4 = \begin{bmatrix} 0.188 & 0.812 \\ 0.162 & 0.838 \end{bmatrix}$

Note: $P^3 = P^2 \cdot P$ and $P^4 = P^3 \cdot P$.

b. $[0.45 \quad 0.55]P^2 = [0.45 \quad 0.55]$

$\begin{bmatrix} 0.30 & 0.70 \\ 0.14 & 0.86 \end{bmatrix} = [0.212 \quad 0.788]$

$[0.45 \quad 0.55]P^3 = [0.45 \quad 0.55]$

$\begin{bmatrix} 0.220 & 0.780 \\ 0.156 & 0.844 \end{bmatrix} = [0.185 \quad 0.815]$

$[0.45 \quad 0.55]P^4 = [0.45 \quad 0.55]$

$\begin{bmatrix} 0.188 & 0.812 \\ 0.162 & 0.832 \end{bmatrix} = [0.174 \quad 0.826]$

We summarize these calculations as follows:

Brand	Initial (%)	Brand Shares, start of week (%)		
		2	3	4
C	45	21.2	18.5	17.4
D	55	78.8	81.5	82.6

c. *Sales revenue, week 3*

Brand C: (0.212)(2,000)(15) = $ 6,360
Brand D: (0.788)(2,000)(10) = $15,760

Sales revenue, week 4

Brand C: (0.185)(2,000)(15) = $ 5,550
Brand D: (0.815)(2,000)(10) = $16,300

Sales revenue, week 5

Brand C: (0.174)(2,000)(15) = $ 5,220
Brand D: (0.826)(2,000)(10) = $16,520

Total revenue

Brand C: $ 6,360 + $ 5,550 + $ 5,220 = $17,130
Brand D: $15,760 + $16,300 + $16,520 = $48,580
Total = $65,710

Note: The brand shares that govern purchasing *during* week 3 are given by $[0.45 \quad 0.55]P^2$, *not* $[0.45 \quad 0.55]P^3$, and are given similarly for weeks 4 and 5.

Section 3

1.

$$\pi_c = \pi_c(0.5) + \pi_D(0.1)$$
$$\pi_D = \pi_c(0.5)\pi_D(0.9)$$
$$\pi_c + \pi_D = 1$$
$$\pi_D = (1 - \pi_D)(0.5) + \pi_D(0.9)$$
$$= 0.5 - 0.5\pi_D + 0.9\pi_D$$
$$\pi_D = 0.5 + 0.4\pi_D$$
$$0.6\pi_D = .5$$

$$\pi_D = 5/6, \text{ so } \pi_c = 1 - \pi_D = 1/6$$

$$\pi = [1/6 \quad 5/6]$$

and the long-run brand shares are 1/6 and 5/6 regardless of the initial brand shares.

2. The transition matrix is

$$P = \begin{array}{c} \\ E \\ N \end{array} \begin{array}{cc} E & N \\ \left[\begin{array}{cc} 0.03 & 0.97 \\ 0.05 & 0.95 \end{array} \right] \end{array}$$

where the state E represents "error on current character" and N denotes "no error." The steady-state equations are

$$\pi_E = \pi_E(0.03) + \pi_N(0.05)$$

$$\pi_N = \pi_E(0.97) + \pi_N(0.95)$$

$$\pi_E + \pi_N = 1$$

Solving as usual:

$$\pi_N = (1 - \pi_N)(0.97) + \pi_N(0.95)$$

$$= 0.97 - 0.02\pi_N$$

$$1.02\pi_N = 0.97, \text{ so } \pi_N = 97/102$$

$$= 0.951$$

$$\pi_E = 1 - \pi_N = 0.049$$

Hence, on the average, 4.9 percent of the characters will be incorrectly typed.

Section 4

1. The P matrix would become

$$P = \left[\begin{array}{cc} 0.70 & 0.30 \\ 0.55 & 0.45 \end{array} \right]$$

The steady-state equations are

$$\pi_A = \pi_A(0.70) + \pi_B(0.55)$$

$$\pi_B = \pi_A(0.30) + \pi_B(0.45)$$

$$\pi_A + \pi_B = 1$$

Solving the above equations, we obtain $\pi_A = 11/17$ and $\pi_B = 6/17$. So brand A's expected weekly net profit would be

(11/17)(4,500)($0.18 per box) = $524.12

Minus cost of advertising = 125.00

Net profit = $399.12

Without the advertising, $\pi_A = 4/7$ (Example 11.4), and brand A's expected weekly profit is $462.86. Thus brand A should not implement the proposed strategy.

2.

$$P = \begin{bmatrix} 0.80 & 0.20 \\ 0.55 & 0.45 \end{bmatrix}$$

$$\pi_A = \pi_A(0.80) + \pi_B(0.55)$$

$$\pi_B = \pi_A(0.20) + \pi_B(0.45)$$

$$\pi_A + \pi_B = 1$$

Solving the above equations, we obtain $\pi_A = 11/15$ and $\pi_B = 4/15$. So brand A's expected net weekly profit would be

$(11/15)(4,500)(\$0.18 \text{ per box}) - \$110 = \$484$

Since this exceeds the current expected weekly profit of $462.86, the proposed campaign does appear profitable.

Section 5

1. $F(3, 1) + F(3, 2)$ must equal one, given the fact that if a receivable is 0–30 days old, it must eventually end up being paid or classified as a bad debt. Also, $F(4, 1) + F(4, 2) = 1$, because a receivable 31–60 days old must eventually end up being paid or classified as a bad debt.

2.

$$S = (I - Q)^{-1} = \begin{bmatrix} 0.70 & -0.10 \\ -0.30 & 0.95 \end{bmatrix}^{-1} = \begin{bmatrix} 1.4961 & 0.1575 \\ 0.4724 & 1.1024 \end{bmatrix}$$

We then have that $[7,000 \quad 5,200]SQ_1$ equals

$$[7,000 \quad 5,200] \begin{bmatrix} 1.4961 & 0.1575 \\ 0.4724 & 1.1024 \end{bmatrix} \begin{bmatrix} 0.60 & 0 \\ 0.50 & 0.15 \end{bmatrix} = [7,000 \quad 5,200] \begin{bmatrix} 0.9764 & 0.0236 \\ 0.8346 & 0.1654 \end{bmatrix}$$

$$= [11,175 \quad 1,025]$$

The bad debts ratio is

$(1.025/12,200) \times 100\% = 8.4\%$

CHAPTER 14: INTEGER PROGRAMMING

Section 2

1. Let x_1 = number of style A tables to manufacture per week
   x_2 = number of style B tables to manufacture per week
   Maximize $Z = 150x_1 + 225x_2$ ($ profit per week)

Subject to:

(1) x_1 $\leq$ 3 (sales potential limit)
(2) $x_2 \leq$ 4 (sales potential limit)
(3) $5x_1 + 6x_2 \leq$ 30 (labor-hour capacity)

See Fig. B.78. Plotting an initial objective function line and moving it outward, point A is the last point touched and, therefore, is optimal. To find the coordinates of point A, simply plug constraint (2) into constraint (3), since point A is the intersection of those two constraints.

(2) $x_2 = 4$
(3) $5x_1 + 6x_2 = 30$
          $5x_1 + 6(4) = 30$
                    $5x_1 = 6$
                      $x_1 = 1.2$

Maximize $Z = 150(1.2) + 225(4)$
          $Z^* = \$1,080$

2. Since x_2^* is already an integer, we are only concerned with rounding x_1 up to 2 or down to 1. When $x_1 = 2$, constraint (3) is violated, so $x_1 = 1$ is the only possible choice. Therefore, using the rounding technique, the optimal solution is $x_1 = 1$, $x_2 = 4$, and $Z = \$1,050$.

3. See Fig. B.79. Moving the Z line parallel to itself until it touches the leftmost integer (we are maximizing), we find the optimal feasible integer solution to be $x_1 = 1$, $x_2 = 4$, and $Z^* = \$1,050$. This, coincidentally, agrees with our solution to Problem 2 above. *Note:* The IP is the LP stated in Problem 1 above, with two additional constraints: x_1 and x_2 are integers.

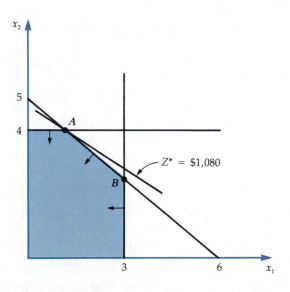

FIGURE B.78

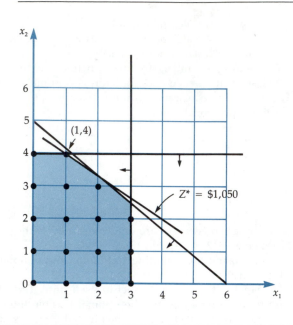

FIGURE B.79

CHAPTER 15: DYNAMIC PROGRAMMING

Section 4

1. Four-stage dynamic program:

    Stage 1—How many $100 investments to choose.
    Stage 2—How many $200 bonds to purchase.
    Stage 3—How many $250 lots of rare coins to buy.
    Stage 4—How many $320 antique purchases to make.
Goal: Compute f_1^* (1,000).

    The fourth investment alternative has been placed ahead of the existing three alternatives for a very good reason. If it had been made the stage 4 choice, it would have required recalculating *all* of the other tables. By placing it first, the tables corresponding to coins and antiques need not be recalculated. This demonstrates another advantage (or property) of dynamic programs.

    Working backwards, as the procedure specifies, we find that stage 4, formerly labeled as stage 3, is already given in Table 15.6(a). Our new stage 3, formerly labeled stage 2, is already given in Table 15.6(b). Our calculations begin by making a new stage 2 table. From this we then calculate a stage 1 table.

New Stage 2 Table

	$f_2(s_2, d_2)$							
	d_2							
s_2	0	1	2	3	4	5	d_2^*	$f_2^*(s_2)$
0	0						0	0
100	0						0	0
200	0	20					1	20
300	35	20					0	35
400	56	20	40				0	56
500	70	55	40				0	70
600	91	76	40	60			0	91
700	112	90	75	60			0	112
800	112	111	96	60	80		0	112
900	147	132	110	95	80		0	147
1,000	168	132	131	116	80	100	0	168

Derived from

$$f_2(s_2, d_2) = 20d_2 + f_3^*(s_2 - 200d_2)$$

$$f_2^*(s_2) = \max\{20d_2 + f_3^*(s_2 - 200d_2): \text{all feasible } d_2\}$$

Stage 1

	$f_1(s_1, d_1)$												
	d_1												
s_1	0	1	2	3	4	5	6	7	8	9	10	d_1^*	$f_1^*(s_1)$
1,000	168	161	140	154	147	140	140	133	132	126	140	0	168

$$f_1(s_1, d_1) = 14d_1 + f_2^*(s_1 - 100d_1)$$

$$f_1^*(1,000) = \max\{14d_1 + f_2^*(1,000 - 100d_1): \text{all feasible } d_1\}$$

Optimal policy: Read from stage 1, stage 2, stage 3, and stage 4 tables, in that order.

$$s_1 = 1,000 \qquad d_1^* = 0 \qquad f_1^*(1,000) = \$168$$
$$s_2 = 1,000 \qquad d_2^* = 0$$
$$s_3 = 1,000 \qquad d_3^* = 0$$
$$s_4 = 1,000 \qquad d_4^* = 3$$

Summary: Purchase no $100 investments; purchase no bonds; purchase no rare coins; purchase three groups of antiques; retain $40 cash. Annual return = $168.

2. Yes, the investment strategy and the annual return would change.

New Stage 1 Table

	$f_1(s_1, d_1)$						
	d_1						
s_1	0	1	2	3	4	d_1^*	$f_1^*(s_1)$
900	147	132	110	95	80	0	147

The other tables do *not* need to be changed.
Derived from

$f_1(s_1, d_1) = 20d_1 + f_2^*(s_1 - 200d_1)$

$f_1^*(900) = \max\{20d_1 + f_2^*(900 - 200d_1)$: all feasible $d_1\}$

$s_1 = 900 \qquad d_1^* = 0 \qquad f_1^*(900) = \$147$

$s_2 = 900 \qquad d_2 = 1$

$s_3 = 650 \qquad d_3 = 2$

Strategy: Purchase no bonds; purchase one lot of rare coins; purchase two groups of antiques; retain $10 cash. Annual return = $147.

3. Yes, the investment strategy would change.

New Stage 1 Table

	$f_1(s_1, d_1)$							
	d_1							
s_1	0	1	2	3	4	5	d_1^*	$f_1^*(s_1)$
1,000	168	148	163	164	144	180	5	180

Derived from

$f_1(s_1, d_1) = 36d_1 + f_2^*(s_1 - 200d_1)$

$f_1^*(1,000) = \max\{36d_1 + f_2^*(1,000 - 200d_1)$: all feasible $d_1\}$

$s_1 = 1000 \qquad d_1^* = 5 \qquad f_1^*(1000) = \$180$

$s_2 = 0 \qquad d_2^* = 0$

$s_3 = 0 \qquad d_3^* = 0$

Optimal policy: Purchase five bonds; purchase no rare coins; purchase no antiques; retain $0 cash. Annual return = $180.

CHAPTER 16: NETWORK OPTIMIZATION MODELS

Section 2

1.

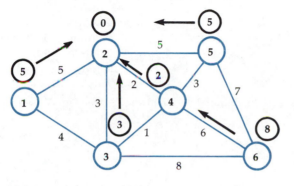

FIGURE B.80

Nodes solved in the following order: 2, 4, 3, 1, 5, 6

Step 1:

$d_{22} = 0$

Step 2:

Unsolved node i	Shortest distance from node 2 to i
1	$d_{21} = 5$
3	$d_{23} = 3$
4	$d_{24} = 2$
6	$d_{25} = 5$

Step 3:

Unsolved node i	Shortest distance from node 2 to i
1	$d_{21} = 5$
3	$\min(d_{23}, d_{43} + 2) = \min(3, 1 + 2) = \min(3,3) = 3$ (from node 2) arbitrary
5	$\min(d_{25}, d_{45} + 2) = \min(5, 3 + 2) = \min(5,5) = 5$ (from node 2) arbitrary
6	$d_{46} + 2 = 6 + 2 = 8$

Step 4:

Unsolved node i	Shortest distance from node 2 to i
1	$\min(d_{21}, d_{31} + 3) = \min(5, 4 + 3) = \min(5,7) = 5$ (from node 2)*
5	$\min(d_{25}, d_{45} + 2) = \min(5, 3 + 2) = \min(5,5) = 5$ (from node 2) arbitrary
6	$\min(d_{46} + 2, d_{36} + 3) = \min(6 + 2, 8 + 3) = \min(8,11)$ $= 8$ (from node 4)

*Node 1 is chosen arbitrarily over node 5.

Step 5:

Unsolved node i	Shortest distance from node 2 to i
5	$\min(d_{25}, d_{45} + 2) = \min(5, 3 + 2) = \min(5,5) = 5$ (from node 2) arbitrary
6	$\min(d_{36} + 3, d_{46} + 2) = \min(8 + 3, 6 + 2) = \min(8,11)$ $= 8$ (from node 4)

Step 6:

Unsolved node i	Shortest distance from node 2 to i
6	$\min(d_{36} + 3, d_{46} + 2, d_{56} + 5) = \min(8 + 3, 6 + 2, 7 + 5)$ $= \min(11,8,12)$ $= 8$ (from node 4)

2.

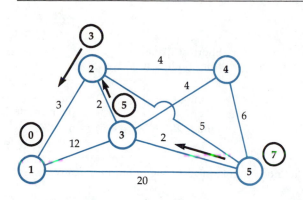

FIGURE B.81

Nodes solved in the following order: 1, 2, 3, 5

Step 1:

$d_{11} = 0$

Step 2:

Unsolved node i	Shortest distance from node 1 to i
2	$d_{12} = 3$
3	$d_{13} = 12$
5	$d_{15} = 20$

Step 3:

Unsolved node i	Shortest distance from node 1 to i
3	$\min(d_{13}, d_{23} + 3) = \min(12, 2 + 3) = \min(12,5) = 5$ (from node 2)
4	$d_{24} + 3 = 4 + 3 = 7$ (from node 2)
5	$d_{15} = 20$

Step 4:

Unsolved node i	Shortest distance from node 1 to i
4	$\min(d_{24} + 3, d_{34} + 5) = \min(4 + 3, 4 + 5) = \min(7,9) = 7$ (from node 2)
5	$\min(d_{15}, d_{25} + 3, d_{35} + 5) = \min(20, 5 + 3, 2 + 5) = \min(20,8,7)$ $= 7$ (from node 3)*

*By choosing node 5 arbitrarily, the algorithm terminates.

Section 3

1.

Branch	Length	Result
(4, 5)	1	✓
(2, 4)	2	✓
(3, 5)	3	✓
(2, 3)	4	X
(1, 2)	5	✓
(3, 4)	6	X
(2, 5)	7	X
(1, 4)	8	X
(1, 6)	10	✓
(5, 6)	12	X
(4, 6)	19	X

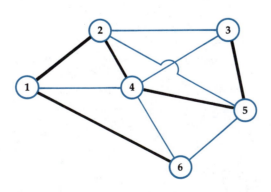

Minimum total length = 1 + 2 + 3 + 5 + 10 = 21

2.

Branch	Length	Result
(1, 2)	2	✓
(2, 3)	3	✓
(3, 5)	4	✓
(2, 4)	5	✓ or X
(4, 5)	5	X or ✓
(1, 4)	10	X
(3, 4)	15	X

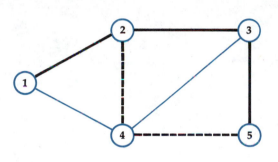

Minimum total length = 2 + 3 + 4 + 5 = 14

Section 4

1.

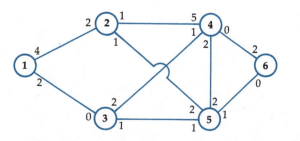

Step 1. Path, 1–2–4–6; minimum capacity, 2.

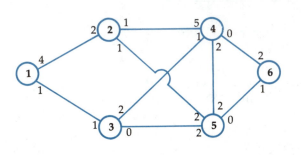

FIGURE B.85

Step 2. Path, 1–3–5–6; minimum capacity, 1.

Branch	Original flow	Final flow	Difference
(1, 2)	6	4	2
(1, 3)	2	1	1
(2, 4)	3	1	2
(2, 5)	1	1	0
(3, 4)	2	2	0
(3, 5)	1	0	1
(4, 5)	2	2	0
(4, 6)	2	0	2
(5, 6)	1	0	1

The optimal flow pattern is shown in Fig. B.86.

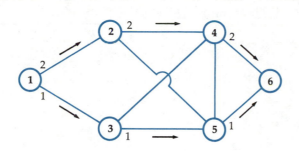

FIGURE B.86

Maximal flow pattern.

2. Solution:

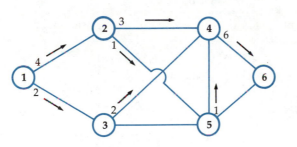

FIGURE B.87

A flow of 6 units can be sent from node 1 to node 4.

		Minimal flow on path		
Path chosen	Branch(es)	Flow	Decrease flow on:	Increase flow on:
1–2–4	(2, 4)	3	(1, 2), (2, 4)	(2, 1), (4, 2)
1–3–4	(1, 3), (3, 4)	2	(1, 3), (3, 4)	(3, 1), 4, 3)
1–2–5–4	(2, 5)	1	(1, 2), (2, 5), (5, 4)	(2, 1), (5, 2), (4, 5)

CHAPTER 17: BRANCH-AND-BOUND METHODS

Section 2

1.

Assignment	District				Assignment	District			
	A	B	C	D		A	B	C	D
1	1	2	3	4	13	3	1	2	4
2	1	2	4	3	14	3	1	4	2
3	1	3	2	4	15	3	2	1	4
4	1	3	4	2	16	3	2	4	1
5	1	4	2	3	17	3	4	1	2
6	1	4	3	2	18	3	4	2	1
7	2	1	3	4	19	4	1	2	3
8	2	1	4	3	20	4	1	3	2
9	2	3	1	4	21	4	2	1	3
10	2	3	4	1	22	4	2	3	1
11	2	4	1	3	23	4	3	1	2
12	2	4	3	1	24	4	3	2	1

2. *Step 1:* The current incumbent solution is 0, and the lower bound (LB) is 0.

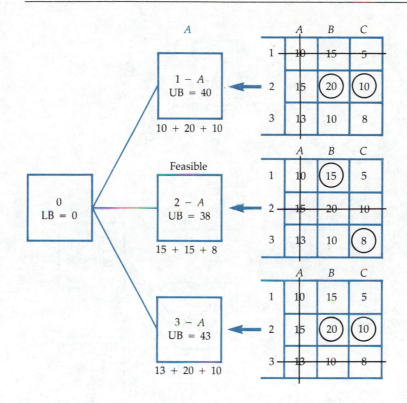

FIGURE B.88

Step 2: Node 2 has now been fathomed, so we can change the LB of node 0 from 0 to 38; that is, the optimal solution will be greater than or equal to 38. We cannot yet fathom the tip nodes 1 and 3, since they may still offer a feasible solution greater than 38.

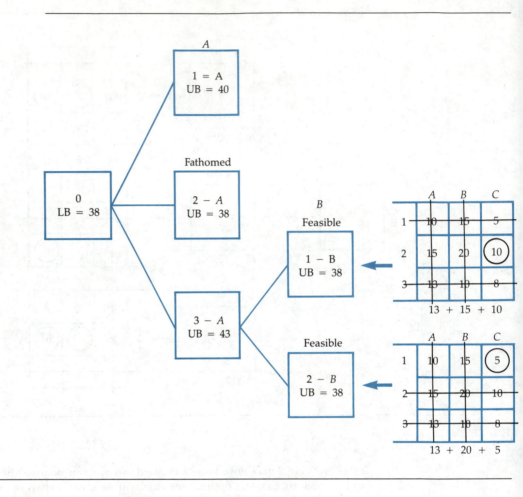

Step 3: We branch on node 3 because it offers the highest upper bound (UB) value of 43. We now have a three-way tie for the optimal solution; however, we cannot stop because there is still an unfathomed tip node with a UB value of 40, which is greater than the current incumbent value of 38. Actually, we can fathom 1–B and 2–B since their UB values do not exceed the incumbent LB value of 38.

Step 4: We branch node 1 and find a feasible solution that gives a four-way tie for the optimal solution, as shown in Fig. B.90. We fathom 2–B and 3–B, since their UB values do not exceed the node 0 LB value of 38.

The optimal solution was encountered in Step 2: 2–*A*, 1–*B*, and 3–*C*; profit = 38. (Other solutions were also found: 3–*A*, 1–*B*, 2–*C*; 3–*A*, 2–*B*, 1–*C*; and 1–*A*, 2–*B*, 3–*C*.)

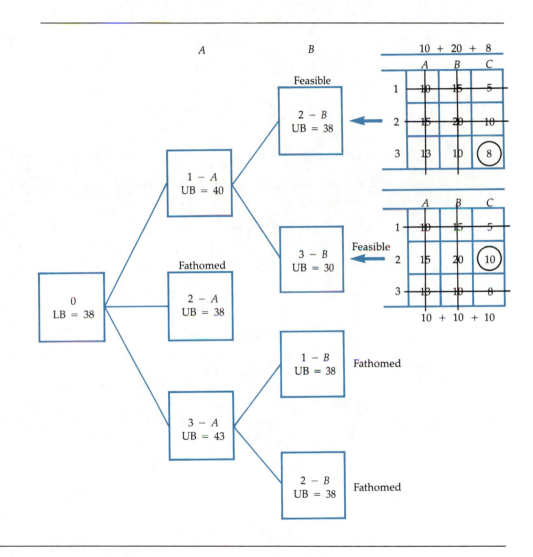

CHAPTER 18: HEURISTICS IN MANAGEMENT SCIENCE

Section 2

1. $C = \$25$
    $F = \$50$
    $r = \$0.20/\$/month$
    $\bar{D} = (100 + 50 + 90)/3 = 80$

    $$EOQ = \sqrt{\frac{2(50)(80)}{25(0.2)}}$$
    $$= \sqrt{1,600}$$
    $$= 40$$

    To meet the first month's demand, the first order will obviously have to be 100 units.

2. Ordering one month only: $50.00 average cost per month (there is no carrying cost incurred).

    Ordering for two months:

    | Ordering cost: | $= \$50$ |
    | Carrying cost: | $= 50(\$25)(\$0.20)$ |
    | | $= \$250$ |
    | Total cost: | $= \$50 + \$250 = \$300$ |
    | Per month cost: | $= \dfrac{\$300}{2} = \underline{\underline{\$150}}$ |

    Ordering for three months: Not necessary to compute, since costs are rising.
      The *first order*, using this heuristic, will also be 100 units. It is merely a coincidence that the two heuristics give the same ordering policy.

3. Fixed EOQ:

	Month 1	Month 2	Month 3	Totals
Initial inventory	0	100	0	—
Amount ordered	150	0	60	210
Demand	50	100	60	210
Ending inventory	100	0	0	—
Carrying costs ($)	100	0	0	$100

Ordering cost = 2 orders × $90 = 180

$280 = $ Total cost

$\bar{D} = 70$ units

$C = \$10$

$F = \$90$

$r = 0.10$

$$EOQ = \sqrt{\frac{2(90)(70)}{10(0.1)}} = 112.25$$

Of the three cumulative demands (50, 150, and 210), 112.25 is closest to 150. Therefore, the first order is for two months, and the second is for one month.

4. Silver-Meal:

	Month			
	1	2	3	Totals
Initial inventory	0	0	60	—
Amount ordered	50	160	0	210
Demand	50	100	60	210
Ending inventory	0	60	0	—
Carrying costs ($)	0	60	0	$60

Ordering cost = 2 orders × $90 = 180

$240 = Total cost

One-month order: $90.00 average cost

Two-month order:

Ordering cost: = $90.00

Carrying cost: = (100 units)($10)(0.10)

                  = $100.00

Total cost: = $190.00

Average cost: $= \dfrac{\$190}{2} = \$95.00$

Three-month order: Not necessary to compute, since costs are rising.

The second order is determined as follows:

One-month order: $90.00 average cost.

Two-month order:

Ordering cost: = $90.00

Carrying cost: = (60 units)($10)(0.10) = $60.00

Total cost: = $150.00

Average cost: $= \dfrac{\$150}{2} = \$75.00$ (minimum)

5. From the two preceding tables, it is evident that the Silver-Meal heuristic yielded the lower total cost with a saving of $40 ($280 − 240 = $40).

C ALGEBRAIC AND MATHEMATICAL NOTATION

The following symbols and notation are used in this text:

1. **Summation sign,** "Σ," uppercase Greek letter sigma. In the expression $\Sigma_{i=1}^{n} x_i$, "i" is called the index of summation, $i = 1$ indicates the start of the sum, and $i = n$ indicates the range of the sum. This expression is shorthand notation for the sum $x_1 + x_2 + x_3 + \cdots + x_n$. The following examples illustrate this notation:

$$\sum_{i=1}^{5} x_i = x_1 + x_2 + x_3 + x_4 + x_5$$

$$\sum_{i=0}^{3} p_i = p_0 + p_1 + p_2 + p_3$$

$$\sum_{i=1}^{4} c_i x_i = c_1 x_1 + c_2 x_2 + c_3 x_3 + c_4 x_4 \tag{C-1}$$

The index i is a "dummy variable," and the letter itself has no significance. The letters k or j, for example, could serve the same purpose. For example, $\Sigma_{i=1}^{4} c_i x_i$ means the same as $\Sigma_{j=1}^{4} c_j x_j$ or $\Sigma_{k=1}^{4} c_k x_k$. If $c_1 = 1$, $c_2 = 3$, $c_3 = 2$, $c_4 = 10$, $x_1 = 3$, $x_2 = 5$, $x_3 = 7$, and $x_4 = 10$, then Eq. (C–1) equals $(1)(3) + (3)(5) + (2)(7) + (10)(10) = 132$.

2. **Factorial,** "!". The expression $n!$ means $n(n - 1)(n - 2) \ldots (2)(1)$ 0! is defined to be 1.
Thus:

0! = 1

1! = 1

2! = (2)(1) = 2

3! = (3)(2)(1) = 6

4! = (4)(3)(2)(1) = 24

5! = (5)(4)(3)(2)(1) = 120

6! = (6)(5)(4)(3)(2)(1) = 720

7! = (7)(6)(5)(4)(3)(2)(1) = 5,040

and so on.

3. Inequalities

">" means "strictly greater than." Thus $4 > 2$.

"≥" means "greater than or equal to." Thus $4 \geq 2$, $2 \geq 2$, $10 \geq 0$, $6 \geq 4$, etc.

"<" means "strictly less than." Thus $2 < 4$, and $0 < 10$, $-2 < -1$, etc.

"≤" means "less than or equal to." Thus $2 \leq 4$, $0 \leq 10$, $2 \leq 2$, $-10 \leq 20$, etc.

4. Approximately equal, "≈." For example, $4.26 \approx 4.3$; $0.0001 \approx 0$; $1{,}001 \approx 1{,}000$; and so on.

5. Infinity, "+∞," means "plus infinity" or infinitely large in the positive direction. Thus if we want to express the fact that x is a variable which takes on larger and larger values without limit, we write $x \to +\infty$ read "x approaches plus infinity." The expression "$-\infty$" means "negative infinity" or arbitrarily negative. If we write simply "∞," we mean "$+\infty$."

6. Greek letters

α	alpha	π	pi
β	beta	ρ	rho
λ	lambda	σ	lower case sigma
μ	mu	Σ	upper case sigma (summation)

D

MATRIX ALGEBRA: A REVIEW

A **matrix** is a rectangular array of numbers. The following are examples of matrices.

$$A = \begin{bmatrix} 2 & 4 & -1 \\ 0.5 & 0 & 12.3 \end{bmatrix} \qquad B = \begin{bmatrix} 2 & 3 \\ 6 & 1 \end{bmatrix} \qquad C = [2]$$

$$D = \begin{bmatrix} 21 & 7 \\ -4 & 6 \\ 8 & -4 \end{bmatrix} \qquad E = \begin{bmatrix} 6 \\ 1 \\ -2 \end{bmatrix} \qquad F = [1 \quad 4 \quad 9]$$

We shall represent the **dimension** of a matrix in the form (m, n), where m equals the number of rows and n equals the number of columns of the matrix. For example, the dimension of A is $(2, 3)$, B is a $(2, 2)$ matrix, C is $(1, 1)$ and so on. B and C are **square** matrices since $m = n$. A **column vector** is a matrix having $n = 1$, and a **row vector** has $m = 1$. Thus E is a column vector, and F is a row vector.

ADDITION

When two matrices have the same dimension, we add (subtract) them by adding (subtracting) corresponding entries. For example, if

$$A = \begin{bmatrix} a_{11} & a_{12} \\ a_{21} & a_{22} \end{bmatrix} \quad \text{and} \quad B = \begin{bmatrix} b_{11} & b_{12} \\ b_{21} & b_{22} \end{bmatrix}$$

then

$$A + B = \begin{bmatrix} a_{11} + b_{11} & a_{12} + b_{12} \\ a_{21} + b_{21} & a_{22} + b_{22} \end{bmatrix} \quad \text{and} \quad A - B = \begin{bmatrix} a_{11} - b_{11} & a_{12} - b_{12} \\ a_{21} - b_{21} & a_{22} - b_{22} \end{bmatrix} \qquad \text{(D–1)}$$

Example D.1

If $A = \begin{bmatrix} 2 & 1 \\ -1 & 4 \end{bmatrix}$, $B = \begin{bmatrix} 10 & 1 \\ 2 & -2 \end{bmatrix}$, then $A + B = \begin{bmatrix} 12 & 2 \\ 1 & 2 \end{bmatrix}$

787

Example D.2

If $A = \begin{bmatrix} 2 & 4 & 0.5 \\ 6 & -1 & 0 \end{bmatrix}$, $B = \begin{bmatrix} -1 & 2 & 1.5 \\ 0 & 1 & 2 \end{bmatrix}$

then $A + B = \begin{bmatrix} 1 & 6 & 2 \\ 6 & 0 & 2 \end{bmatrix}$, $A - B = \begin{bmatrix} 3 & 2 & -1 \\ 6 & -2 & -2 \end{bmatrix}$

MULTIPLICATION

For a matrix A having dimension (m, n) and a matrix B with dimension (n, r), we can define the **product** $A \times B$ as a matrix having dimension (m, r). Note that the number of columns A must equal the number of rows of B. To calculate the entry in the ith row and jth column of the product matrix, multiply the elements of the ith row of A one-by-one by the elements of the jth column of B and add the results.

Example D.3

For A and B given by Eq. (D–1),

$$A \times B = \begin{bmatrix} a_{11}b_{11} + a_{12}b_{21} & a_{11}b_{12} + a_{12}b_{22} \\ a_{21}b_{11} + a_{22}b_{21} & a_{21}b_{12} + a_{22}b_{22} \end{bmatrix}$$

Example D.4

If $A = \begin{bmatrix} 2 & 4 & 3 \end{bmatrix}$ and

$$B = \begin{bmatrix} -1 & 4 \\ 2 & 0 \\ 10 & 3 \end{bmatrix}, \text{ then } A \times B = \begin{bmatrix} 2 & 4 & 3 \end{bmatrix} \begin{bmatrix} -1 & 4 \\ 2 & 0 \\ 10 & 3 \end{bmatrix}$$

$$= [(2)(-1) + (4)(2) + (3)(10) \quad (2)(4) + (4)(0) + (3)(3)] = \begin{bmatrix} 36 & 17 \end{bmatrix}$$

Example D.5

For A and B defined as in Example D.1,

$$A \times B = \begin{bmatrix} (2)(10) + (1)(2) & (2)(1) + (1)(-2) \\ (-1)(10) + (4)(2) & (-1)(1) + (4)(-2) \end{bmatrix} = \begin{bmatrix} 22 & 0 \\ -2 & -9 \end{bmatrix}$$

Example D.6. The Powers of a Matrix

If A is a square matrix, A^n ("the nth power of A") is simply A multiplied n times. For example, if A is defined as in Example D.1,

$$A^2 = A \times A = \begin{bmatrix} 2 & 1 \\ -1 & 4 \end{bmatrix} \begin{bmatrix} 2 & 1 \\ -1 & 4 \end{bmatrix} = \begin{bmatrix} 3 & 6 \\ -6 & 15 \end{bmatrix}$$

MATRIX EQUATIONS

Matrix multiplication is useful for representing systems of equations. For example, suppose we have the following system of equations:

$$\pi_1 = \pi_1 p_{11} + \pi_2 p_{21}$$

$$\pi_2 = \pi_1 p_{12} + \pi p_{22} \qquad \text{(D–2)}$$

We can express this system in an equivalent matrix equation:

$$[\pi_1 \quad \pi_2] = [\pi_1 \quad \pi_2] \begin{bmatrix} p_{11} & p_{12} \\ p_{21} & p_{22} \end{bmatrix} \qquad \text{(D–3)}$$

To see why Eq. (D–3) is equivalent to Eq. (D–2), we multiply out the right side of Eq. (D–3):

$$[\pi_1 \quad \pi_2] \begin{bmatrix} p_{11} & p_{12} \\ p_{21} & p_{22} \end{bmatrix} = [\pi_1 p_{11} + \pi_2 p_{21} \quad \pi_1 p_{12} + \pi_2 p_{22}]$$

Thus, Eq. (D–3) becomes

$$[\pi_1 \quad \pi_2] = [\pi_1 p_{11} + \pi_2 p_{21} \quad \pi_1 p_{12} + \pi_2 p_{22}]$$

Two matrices are **equal** when they have the same dimension and corresponding entries are equal. Thus the above equation, which states the equality of two (1, 2) row vectors, means that

$$\pi_1 = \pi_1 p_{11} + \pi_2 p_{21} \quad \text{and} \quad \pi_2 = \pi_1 p_{12} + \pi_2 p_{22},$$

and this is exactly (D–2).

THE DETERMINANT

If A is defined as in (D–1), the **determinant** of A, denoted $|A|$ is defined by $|A| = a_{11}a_{22} - a_{21}a_{12}$ (D–4)

Example D.7

For A and B defined in Example D.1,

$$|A| = (2)(4) - (-1)(1) = 8 - (-1) = 9$$

and $|B| = (10)(-2) - (2)(1) = -22$

MATRIX INVERSION

If a square matrix A has a nonzero determinant, then its **inverse**, denoted A^{-1} is the matrix which satisfies $A \times A^{-1} = A^{-1} \times A = I$, where I is the **identity** matrix; that is, I is the matrix having ones on the diagonal running from the upper left to the lower right and zeros elsewhere.

$$\text{If } A = \begin{bmatrix} a_{11} & a_{12} \\ a_{21} & a_{22} \end{bmatrix}, \quad \text{then} \quad A^{-1} = \begin{bmatrix} \dfrac{a_{22}}{|A|} & \dfrac{-a_{12}}{|A|} \\ \dfrac{-a_{21}}{|A|} & \dfrac{a_{11}}{|A|} \end{bmatrix} \tag{D-5}$$

Example D.8

If A is defined as in Example D.1, then $|A| = 9$ and

$$A^{-1} = \begin{bmatrix} \dfrac{4}{9} & \dfrac{-1}{9} \\ \dfrac{-(-1)}{9} & \dfrac{2}{9} \end{bmatrix} = \begin{bmatrix} \dfrac{4}{9} & \dfrac{-1}{9} \\ \dfrac{1}{9} & \dfrac{2}{9} \end{bmatrix}$$

then $A \times A^{-1} = A^{-1} \times A = I = \begin{bmatrix} 1 & 0 \\ 0 & 1 \end{bmatrix}$. Check this!

E PROBABILITY CONCEPTS

CONTENTS

1. INTRODUCTION

Probability theory is the branch of mathematics that makes precise the notion of chance. In the jargon of management, the word "chance" is more commonly thought of as uncertainty or risk. Uncertainty enters into virtually every decision-making problem confronting managers. For example, consider the broad process of new product development, which involves research and development; product prototype development; design of a production and inventory system; marketing functions, such as forecasting sales, pricing and distribution decisions; and financial functions, such as acquiring funds. Each of these aspects of product development involves uncertainties concerning costs; timing; level of activity; and, in general, degrees of success. If each of these factors were known for certain, management would have no problem. A simple arithmetic computation or the straightforward use of so-called deterministic algorithms would indicate the profitability of the project. In practice it is more common that all of these factors are uncertain and subject to chance events.

This appendix will give a brief introduction to the notions of probability theory.

2. SAMPLE SPACE AND EVENTS

In a given experiment or situation, the set of all possible outcomes that may occur is called the **sample space.** An **event** is simply a subset of the sample space. For example, consider the experiment of rolling a die. The sample space consists of all possible outcomes, or {1, 2, 3, 4, 5, 6}. We can then speak of the event "the result is 4," or the event "the result is either 2 or 4," and so on. Other examples of sample space and events are as follows:

1. Flipping a coin twice. Letting H denote heads and T tails, the sample space is {HH, HT, TH, TT}.
2. Measuring the time until a machine breaks down. If we label the current time as 0, the sample space consists of all numbers $L > 0$, where L denotes machine lifetime and could be measured in hours and fractions of hours.
3. Projecting sales demand. The sample space consists of all possible sales levels that may occur during a certain time interval.
4. Examining a component of a machine to determine whether it has failed or not. The sample space consists of the two outcomes {failed, not failed}.
5. Measuring the time to complete a project. If project completion time is measured to the nearest half week, the sample space consists of {0, 0.5, 1.0, 2.0, ...}. In practice there would be some upper limit to the project completion time.

Types of Events

Two events that cannot both occur at the same time are called **mutually exclusive.** For example, in rolling a die, the events E = {2, 4, 6} ("the result is even") and F = {1, 3, 5} ("the result is odd") are mutually exclusive. However, if we define G to be the event that the result is 3 or greater, then E and G are not mutually exclusive, since they have {4, 6} in common.

The **union** of two events is simply all outcomes that are included in *at least one* of the two events. Thus the union of E and G is written $E \cup G$ = {2, 3, 4, 5, 6}. The **intersection** of two events is the set of all outcomes that are contained in *both* the events. For example, the intersection of E and G is written $E \cap G$ = {4, 6}. When two events are mutually exclusive, their intersection is **empty,** denoted $\emptyset$. Thus $E \cap F = \emptyset$. The union symbol, $\cup$, is read "or"; the intersection symbol, $\cap$, is read "and."

A collection of events is **exhaustive** if its union contains all possible outcomes—that is, if its union equals the sample space. A collection of events which is mutually exclusive *and* exhaustive is said to form a **partition** of the sample space. For example, E and F are mutually exclusive, since $E \cap F = \varnothing$, and they are exhaustive, since $E \cup F = \{1, 2, 3, 4, 5, 6\}$. Thus E and F form a partition of the sample space. However, E, F, and G do *not* form a partition. Even though their union equals $\{1, 2, 3, 4, 5, 6\}$ (that is, they are exhaustive), they are not mutually exclusive, since E and G are not mutually exclusive. Also, note that F and G are not mutually exclusive.

3. PROBABILITIES

The **probability** of an event is the chance of it occurring. The formal picture is the following: We have a sample space S consisting of various events. To each event E we associate the probability that the event will occur, denoted $P(E)$. $P(E)$ is a number that must satisfy the following properties:

1. $P(E)$ must be between 0 and 1: $0 \le P(E) \le 1$.

APPLICATIONS

The following applications appear in this appendix in the text, examples, or problems.

Coin toss

Consumption patterns

Detecting two-headed coins

Dice games

Gambling

Guessing on exams

Job hunting

Manufacturing: estimating scrap

Medical diagnosis

Military defense

Recruiting costs

Rework in manufacturing processes

Sales analysis

Student performance

Student populations

Tax audits

Television viewer responses

2. The probability of the entire sample space is one: $P(S) = 1$. This is the mathematician's way of saying that S must include *all* possibilities, or all possible outcomes.
3. If E and F are mutually exclusive, then the probability of their union simply equals the probability of E plus the probability of F:

if $E \cap F = \varnothing$, then $P(E \cup F) = P(E) + P(F)$

Another probability rule that can be proved from the above properties gives us the following formula for calculating $P(E \cup F)$ *when E and F are not necessarily mutually exclusive:*

$$P(E \cup F) = P(E) + P(F) - P(E \cap F) \tag{E-1}$$

EXAMPLE E.1. Consider the experiment of rolling a die (see Fig. E.1). The sample space is $S = \{1, 2, 3, 4, 5, 6\}$. Define events E, F, G as above: $E = \{2, 4, 6\}$, $F = \{1, 3, 5\}$, and $G = \{3, 4, 5, 6\}$. Also, define the event $H = \{1\}$ ("the outcome is one"). Using the classical definition of probability, we define the probability of an event to be the number of outcomes favorable to that event divided by the total number of possible outcomes. Thus since there are six possible outcomes, $P(E) = 3/6$, $P(F) = 3/6$, $P(G) = 4/6$, and $P(H) = 1/6$. For example, $P(E) = 3/6$ says, "there is a 3/6 probability that the roll of the die will turn up a 2, 4, or 6." Intuitively this is a "50 percent chance." We can now check that properties 1, 2, and 3 are satisfied.

1. Property (1) is satisfied, since these probabilities are all numbers between 0 and 1.
2. Property (2) holds, since $P(S) = 6/6 = 1$.
3. To illustrate property (3), E and F are mutually exclusive, $E \cup F = S$, and so $P(E \cup F) = P(S) = 1$. Also, $P(E) + P(F) = 3/6 + 3/6 = 1$. Thus, $P(E \cup F) = P(E) + P(F)$. As another illustration of property (3), E and H are

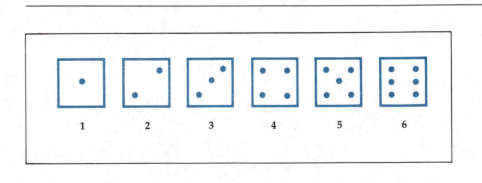

mutually exclusive and $E \cup H = \{1, 2, 4, 6\}$, so $P(E \cup H) = 4/6$. We must check that $P(E) + P(H)$ also equals $4/6$: $P(E) + P(H) = 3/6 + 1/6 = 4/6$. Thus, $P(E \cup H) = P(E) + P(H)$.

4. To illustrate Eq. (E–1), let us compute $P(E \cup G)$. Note that $E \cap G = \{4, 6\}$. So $P(E) + P(G) - P(E \cap G) = 3/6 + 4/6 - 2/6 = 5/6$, which is the right side of Eq. (E–1). To check the equation, note that $E \cup G = \{2, 3, 4, 5, 6\}$, so $P(E \cup G) = 5/6$. Thus $P(E \cup G) = P(E) + P(G) - P(E \cap G)$. ▲

Three commonly used definitions or interpretations of probability are discussed below.

1. Classical Probability

Given an event, E, containing outcomes of a sample space S, the **classical definition** of the probability of E is

$$P(E) = \frac{\text{Number of outcomes contained in } E}{\text{Total number of outcomes in } S} \qquad \text{(E–2)}$$

This is the definition we used in Example E.1. For example, when $S = \{1, 2, 3, 4, 5, 6\}$ and $E = \{2, 4, 6\}$, there are three outcomes in E and six in the total sample space S, so Eq. (E–2) becomes $P(E) = 3/6$.

2. Frequency Interpretation

The probability of an event is sometimes thought of as the **relative frequency of occurrence** of the event if the experiment or situation could be observed repeatedly over a large number of times.

For example, in rolling a die we could use Eq. (E–2) to calculate that the probability of rolling a one equals $1/6$. We can interpret this in two ways. Using the classical definition of probability, we would say that before the die is rolled there is a $1/6$ probability that the outcome will be a one. Using the frequency interpretation of probability, we would expect that if the die were to be rolled a large number of times, the number one should appear on $1/6$ of these trials. You might wish to try such an experiment. Roll a die several times (100 to 500 trials, say). At each trial, record the relative frequency of a one appearing. After 150 such trials conducted by the author, the relative frequency of a one was 23 out of 150 trials, or 0.1533. If this experiment were to be continued to 500 trials, we would expect the relative frequency to approach $1/6 = 0.1667$. In fact, there is a theorem in probability, called the Law of Large Numbers, which ensures that, as the number of rolls of the die approaches infinity, the relative frequency of a one appearing will converge to $1/6$.

A useful managerial application of the frequency interpretation is employed to compute probabilities from historical records. Suppose weekly demand for a product has been recorded over the past fifty-two weeks as follows: A weekly demand of 10 units of product occurred during seventeen of the fifty-two weeks, a demand of 11 units occurred twenty-two times, a demand of twelve occurred nine times, and a demand of thirteen occurred four times. Then for planning purposes (inventory, work force, sales, cash flow, and so on), we could compute the following demand probabilities for a typical week: P (demand $= 10$) $= 17/52 = 0.327$; P(demand $= 11$) $= 22/52 = 0.423$; P(demand $= 12$) $= 9/52 = 0.173$; and P(demand $= 13$) $= 4/52 = 0.077$. The calculations are based on the relative frequency interpretation of probability. Thus if asked what is the probability that demand next week will be 11 units, we would respond that there is a 0.423 probability, or a 42.3 percent chance.

3. Subjective Probabilities

A **subjective probability** is based on the decision maker's judgment or *degree of belief* concerning the chance that a given event will occur. In specifying a subjective probability, the decision maker may take into account classical probabilities as well as frequency probabilities. But in the final analysis, the primary determinant is the person's judgment, or degree of belief.

This method of determining probabilities is particularly applicable to situations that are either nonrepetitive or to situations that are to some extent repetitive but in which the circumstances of each repetition are nonidentical.

Examples of situations calling for a subjective probability assessment are the following:

1. You are asked, "What is the probability that you will become a middle-level manager within seven years of graduation?"
2. A manager is asked to assess the probability that her company's sales will increase by 25 percent in the upcoming quarter.
3. A government economic advisor must assess the probability that the closing annual national inflation rate will not exceed 12 percent.
4. A company must assess the probabilities of various sales levels for a new product it is planning to introduce.

4. MARGINAL, JOINT, AND CONDITIONAL PROBABILITIES

Suppose a survey is taken of television viewers following a nationally televised speech by the President on the administration's inflation policies. The responses are classified as either favorable to the President (F) or not favorable (N), and survey respondents are asked their party affiliation: Republican (R), Democratic (D), or other (X). The responses to the survey are summarized in Fig. E.2. Since there is a total of 15 responses (or 15,000) we can divide each entry by 15 to obtain frequency probabilities, as shown in Fig. E.3.

Party affiliation of respondent	D: Democrat
	R: Republican
	X: Other

| Response to President's speech | F: Favorable to the speech |
| | N: Not favorable to the speech |

		Response		
		F	N	Total
	D	2	3	5
Party	R	3	4	7
	X	2	1	3
	Total	7	8	15

(in 000s)

FIGURE E.2   *Survey results.*

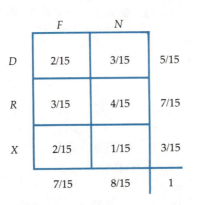

	F	N	
D	2/15	3/15	5/15
R	3/15	4/15	7/15
X	2/15	1/15	3/15
	7/15	8/15	1

FIGURE E.3   *Frequency probabilities.*

Marginal Probabilities

We can think of D, R, X, F, and N as representing outcomes or events of the experiment (the survey). We can then compute the probabilities $P(D)$, $P(R)$, $P(X)$, $P(F)$, and $P(N)$ simply by computing row and column sums in Fig. E.3. These probabilities are, in fact, shown along the *margins* of the figure. For example, the probability that a respondent selected at random from the survey is a Republican is $P(R) = 7/15$ (see the right margin of row 2). These five probabilities are called **marginal probabilities.**

Since a respondent must be a Democrat, Republican, or of some other affiliation, the events D, R, and X form a *partition* of the sample space, and therefore, $P(D) + P(R) + P(X)$ must equal one, which checks in Fig. E.3. Similarly, the events F and N form a partition, so that $P(F) + P(N) = 1$ ($= 7/15 + 8/15$).

Joint Probabilities

What is the probability that a respondent is a Democrat favorable to the President's speech? This question involves finding the probability of the joint event D and F, or $P(D \cap F)$. This probability is found in Fig. E.3, row D, column F, to be 2/15. A **joint event** is the combination of two or more events occurring at the same time or in succession. The table contains five other joint events: D and N, R and F, R and N, X and F, X and N, having respective **joint probabilities** of 3/15, 3/15, 4/15, 2/15, and 1/15.

We can use joint probabilities to compute marginal probabilities. To compute $P(D)$, note that the event "Democrat" can occur in one of two ways: the person is a Democrat and is favorable to the President, or the person is a Democrat and is not favorable to the President. The two events "favorable" (F) and "not favorable" (N) are disjoint and exhaustive; that is, they form a partition of all possible events. Thus we can use the partition $F \cup N$ to "partition" event D:

$$D = (D \cap F) \cup (D \cap N)$$

This notation says that D can occur in two ways: with F or with N.

Since $D \cap F$ and $D \cap N$ are mutually exclusive, property (3) defining probabilities (see p. 794) allows us to compute $P(D)$ as follows:

$$P(D) = P[(D \cap F) \cup (D \cap N)]$$

$$= P(D \cap F) + P(D \cap N) = \frac{2}{15} + \frac{3}{15} = \frac{5}{15} = \frac{1}{3}$$

View these calculations in terms of Fig. E.3.

The general equation follows below. Suppose the events B_1, B_2, ... , B_n form a partition of the sample space, and let A be another event. Then

$$P(A) = P(A \cap B_1) + P(A \cap B_2) + \cdots + P(A \cap B_n) \tag{E-3}$$

This equation will be used later in this appendix and in Section 9 of Chapter 10. As an exercise, use Eq. (E–3) to compute the other five marginal probabilities. For example, using the partition $\{D, R, X\}$, we obtain

$$P(N) = P(N \cap D) + P(N \cap R) + P(N \cap X)$$

$$= \frac{3}{15} + \frac{4}{15} + \frac{1}{15}$$

$$= \frac{8}{15}$$

Conditional Probabilities

What is the probability that a respondent is favorable to the President's speech *given* that the respondent is a Democrat? In other words, you are told (or "given") that a respondent is a Democrat and asked what the probability is that the person is favorable to the President's speech. Notationally we write this probability as $P(F|D)$, read "the probability of F *given* D," where the vertical bar is read "given." The formula for computing a conditional probability is

$$P(A|B) = \frac{P(A \cap B)}{P(B)} \tag{E-4}$$

The joint probability is divided by the marginal. Using Eq. (E–4) and thinking in terms of row D of Fig. E.3, we have

$$P(F|D) = \frac{P(F \cap D)}{P(D)} = \frac{\dfrac{2}{15}}{\dfrac{5}{15}} = \frac{2}{5}$$

Also,

$$P(N|D) = \frac{P(N \cap D)}{P(D)} = \frac{\dfrac{3}{15}}{\dfrac{5}{15}} = \frac{3}{5}$$

Note that $P(F|D) + P(N|D) = 2/5 + 3/5 = 1$, as it *should:* Given that the repondent is a Democrat, he or she *must* be either favorable or not favorable to the speech (according to Fig. E.3).

As an exercise, use Eq. (E–4) to check the computations of the other conditional probabilities:

$$P(F|R) = \frac{3}{7}; \quad P(N|R) = \frac{4}{7}$$

$$P(F|X) = \frac{2}{3}; \quad P(N|X) = \frac{1}{3}$$

$$P(D|F) = \frac{2}{7}; \quad P(R|F) = \frac{3}{7}; \quad P(X|F) = \frac{2}{7}$$

$$P(D|N) = \frac{3}{8}; \quad P(R|N) = \frac{4}{8}; \quad P(X|N) = \frac{1}{8}$$

5. INDEPENDENT AND DEPENDENT EVENTS

Independent Events

Two events are **independent** if the occurrence of one is not affected by the occurrence of the other. If A and B are independent, their joint probability is the product of their marginal probabilities:

$$P(A \cap B) = P(A) \times P(B) \tag{E–5}$$

Also, since knowledge of the occurrence of B does not affect the probability of A and vice versa, $P(A|B) = P(A)$ and $P(B|A) = P(B)$.

As an example, toss two coins, coin 1 and coin 2. Let $H1$ be the event that coin 1 turn up heads and $H2$ be the event that coin 2 turns up heads. Similarly, let $T1$ and $T2$ denote tails. Since the event $H1$ is clearly independent of event $H2$,

$$P(H1 \cap H2) = P(H1) \times P(H2) = \frac{1}{2}\left(\frac{1}{2}\right) = \frac{1}{4}$$

Similarly

$$P(H1 \cap T2) = \frac{1}{4}$$

$$P(T1 \cap H2) = \frac{1}{4}$$

$$P(T1 \cap T2) = \frac{1}{4}$$

If two events are not independent, they are **dependent**.

Equation (E–5) can be used to determine whether two events are independent. In the case of the survey responses to the President's speech (Section 4), is the event that a respondent is a Democrat independent of whether he or she is favorable to the President's speech? To check this, note that $P(D \cap F) = 2/15$ (see row D, column F of Fig. E.3). However, $P(D) \times P(F) = (5/15)(7/15) = 35/225$, which does not equal $2/15$. That is, Eq. (E–5) does not hold; therefore, D and F are not independent. Check to see if any other pair of events in Fig. E.3 is independent.

In general, n events $B_1, B_2, \ldots, B_n$ are independent if *every* joint probability factors into the products of the marginal probabilities.

For example, three events A, B, and C are independent if

$P(A \cap B) = P(A)P(B)$

$P(A \cap C) = P(A)P(C)$

$P(B \cap C) = P(B)P(C)$

and if

$P(A \cap B \cap C) = P(A)P(B)P(C)$

How many equations must be satisfied to determine whether four events are independent? The answer is eleven. There are six pairs, four combinations of three events, and one joint event involving all four events.

For example, if we roll a die and toss two coins, there are $(6)(2)(2) = 24$ possible outcomes in the sample space. Can you list these? Let E be the event that the value of the die is 2, let F be the event that coin number 1 is heads, and let G be the event that coin number 2 is tails. The probability of the joint event "E and F and G occurs" is

$$P(E \cap F \cap G) = P(E)P(F)P(G) = \left(\frac{1}{6}\right)\left(\frac{1}{2}\right)\left(\frac{1}{2}\right) = \left(\frac{1}{24}\right)$$

since the three events are independent.

Dependent Events

In the case of dependent events, their joint probability is computed by the formula:

$$P(A \cap B) = P(B)P(A|B) \tag{E–6}$$

This formula is obtained by multiplying both sides of Eq. (E–4) by $P(B)$. When A and B are independent, $P(A|B) = P(A)$ and Eq. (E–6) becomes Eq. (E–5). The use of this formula is illustrated in the next section. Note that since

$A \cap B = B \cap A$, using Eq. (E–6), we also have

$$P(A \cap B) = P(B \cap A) = P(A)P(B|A) \qquad \text{(E–7)}$$

6. BAYES' THEOREM

Bayes' theorem is a major tool in decision analysis (Chapter 10). It is essentially a more specialized form of Eq. (E–4).

Suppose we have an experiment whose outcomes can be partitioned by the events E_1 and E_2. We conduct the experiment, obtain the result A, and then ask the question: What is the probability that event E_1 has occurred? We can calculate this probability, using Eq. (E–4), as follows:

$$P(E_1|A) = \frac{P(E_1 \cap A)}{P(A)} \qquad \text{(E–8)}$$

Since $\{E_1, E_2\}$ is a partition, we can write out the denominator, using Eq. (E–3):

$$P(A) = P(A \cap E_1) + P(A \cap E_2)$$

Now use Eq. (E–6) to express each term on the right as follows:

$$P(A) = P(E_1)P(A|E_1) + P(E_2)P(A|E_2)$$

Similarly, we can reexpress the numerator using Eq. (E–7):

$$P(E_1 \cap A) = P(E_1)P(A|E_1)$$

Finally, Eq. (E–8) can be written as

$$P(E_1|A) = \frac{P(E_1)P(A|E_1)}{P(E_1)P(A|E_1) + P(E_2)P(A|E_2)} \qquad \text{(E–9)}$$

In the general case where $\{E_1, E_2, \ldots, E_n\}$ is a partition of the sample space, the above formula easily generalizes to

$$P(E_i|A) = \frac{P(E_i)P(A|E_i)}{\displaystyle\sum_{i=1}^{n} P(E_i)P(A|E_i)} \qquad \text{(E–10)}$$

Equation (E–10) is called Bayes' theorem. The following example illustrates the use of this formula.

EXAMPLE E.2. *Bayes' Theorem.* Suppose you have in a box a fair coin and a two-headed coin. You select one of the coins at random (without seeing which one), and it comes up heads. What is the probability that the coin is the fair coin?

Solution. Let H be the event that the coin turns up heads. Also, let $\{F, D\}$ partition the possibilities of what type of coin you flipped, where F denotes a fair coin and D denotes a double-headed coin. The answer to the problem is given by the conditional probability $P(F|H)$, which by Bayes' theorem (E–10) is

$$P(F|H) = \frac{P(F)P(H|F)}{P(F)P(H|F) + P(D)P(H|D)}$$

Now since you selected the coin at random from the box, $P(F) = 1/2$ and $P(D) = 1/2$. Also, if the coin is fair, the chance of heads appearing equals $1/2$, so $P(H|F) = 1/2$. Similarly, for a double-headed coin, $P(H|D) = 1$. Substituting these values into the above equation, we have

$$P(F|H) = \frac{\left(\frac{1}{2}\right)\left(\frac{1}{2}\right)}{\left(\frac{1}{2}\right)\left(\frac{1}{2}\right) + \left(\frac{1}{2}\right)(1)} = \frac{1}{3}$$

Using a similar formula, we could calculate $P(D|H) = 2/3$. However, it is easier to note that $P(D|H) = 1 - P(F|H) = 1 - 1/3 = 2/3$. ▲

7. CONCLUDING REMARKS

We have given a basic review of probability theory—the branch of mathematics that deals formally with the notion of chance. This notion is very important in the study of managerial decision making. In virtually every decision facing management, some or all aspects of the problem situation are subject to chance events. Management must assess not only expected outcomes (such as costs and profits) but also degrees of *risk*. Management science employs techniques of probability to express risk in precise terms.

In the next appendix, you will be introduced to some of the more widely used probability models in management science.

TERMINOLOGY

After studying this appendix you should be familiar with the following terms:

TERM	SECTION
Bayes' theorem	6
conditional probabilities	4
definitions of probability:	
frequency	3
classical	3
subjective	3
dependent events	5
empty	2
event	2
exhaustive	2
independent events	5
intersection	2
joint event	4
joint probabilities	4
marginal probabilities	4
mutually exclusive events	2
partition	2
probability	1, 3
relative frequency of occurrence	3
sample space	2
union	2

EXERCISES

1. *Rolling Two Dice.*   List the events of the sample space for the experiment of rolling a red die and a blue die together.

2. Refer to Exercise 1 above. Compute:
    a. The probability that a 3 appears on at least one die.
    b. The probability that the total value of the two dice is 7.

3. Refer to Exercise 1 above. Are the following two events independent?
    a. Exactly one 3 appears (on one of the two dice).
    b. The total value of the two dice is 7.

4. *Guessing on Exams.*   Suppose you were to take a multiple-choice exam having five questions. Each question has four multiple-choice alternatives. It happens to be a bad day for you, and you are unable to answer any of the five questions, so you decide to guess at random on each one. What is the probability that you will get a perfect paper?

5. *Gambling.* Suppose a roulette wheel has thirty-eight compartments (eighteen black numbers, eighteen red ones, and two compartments for the "house"). You use the following gambling strategy. You place a bet of $10 on red; if a red number comes up, you will quit. If a black number or "house" slot comes up, you will play again, betting $20 on red. If red shows this time, you will quit; otherwise you will bet just once more on red, this time betting $40. What is the probability that you will end up a winner?

6. *Sales Analysis.* Suppose weekly sales of a business appear to be fairly random. You examine past sales records and note that in the past twenty-five weeks, sales were 100 units in five of those weeks, 125 units during ten weeks, 150 units during seven weeks, and 175 units during three weeks. What is the probability that sales during the upcoming four weeks will exceed 125 units each week?

7. *Consumption Patterns.* A large television manufacturer conducted a survey of 1,500 households selected at random throughout the country. Each household surveyed was asked if it owned no television sets (0), one television set (1), or more than one television set (M). In addition, the survey determined whether there were children living in the household. The results of the survey are given below:

	Television sets		
	0	1	M
No children	60	400	150
With children	40	250	600

a. Compute the marginal and joint probabilities for households selected at random from this sample.
b. Given that a household has no children, what is the probability that it owns two or more television sets?
c. Given that a household has children, what is the probability that it owns two or more television sets?

8. *Rework—AAA Manufacturing.* A machine shop subcontracts certain cutting jobs to another shop. Twenty percent of the time it must send jobs back to the subcontractor for rework. If AAA sends out four jobs, what is the probability that none of the jobs will require rework?

9. *Student Performance.* A teacher knows that, on the average, 65 percent of the students in the school have part-time jobs. Students working part-time jobs tend to drop the teacher's course 30 percent of the time compared to a 20 percent drop rate for nonworking students. If a student

drops the teacher's course, what is the probability that the student has a part-time job?

10. *Recruiting Personnel.*   Bob Crabtree, the personnel manager of a medical products supply firm, must hire a person to fill a somewhat specialized position. Bob is considering advertising the position in the local newspaper. He knows from past experience that 20 percent of the time he gets three or more responses to such an ad, in which case he has a 95 percent chance of filling the position. Forty percent of the time he gets two responses, in which case he has an 80 percent chance of filling the position. Twenty-five percent of the time he gets only one response, in which case he has only a 50 percent chance of filling the position. If Bob runs the ad, what is the probability of his filling the position?

11. *Recruiting Costs.*   Refer to Exercise 10 above. The data given apply to each time an ad is placed. If each ad costs $50, what is the probability that recruiting costs could run as high as $200 in advertising expenses alone? (Assume that he will readvertise until he fills the position.)

12. *Military Defense.*   In a war-simulation study conducted by the armed forces, plans must be made to counter an offensive movement made by enemy forces. The enemy could deploy two types of missiles, $T1$ or $T2$. It is estimated that there would be a 70 percent chance that the enemy would use $T1$ in the given situation. If $T1$ is deployed, the enemy has a 75 percent chance of a successful offensive; whereas if $T2$ is used, the enemy's chance of success is 80 percent. What is the probability that the enemy will be successful?

13. *Military Strategy.*   Refer to Exercise 12 above. Suppose the armed forces do not know for certain beforehand that the enemy will deploy a missile. The enemy's tactics will depend on the actions of the armed forces. If the armed forces first launch an offensive movement against the enemy, there is an 85 percent chance that such a mission would be successful. In this case, the chance that the enemy could retaliate would be only 10 percent. If the armed force's mission is not successful, there is a 95 percent chance that the enemy would retaliate. If the armed forces conducts an offensive movement against the enemy, what is the probability that the enemy will successfully retaliate?

14. *Medical Diagnosis.*   Doctor Allen estimates that there is a 60 percent chance that her patient has disease condition A and a 40 percent chance that the patient has disease condition B. She prescribes a certain medication for the patient. Condition A is known to respond favorably to the prescribed drug 85 percent of the time; condition B responds favorably to the prescribed drug only 35 percent of the time. If the patient's condition improves favorably after taking the medication, what is the revised diagnosis of the patient's condition?

15. *Tax Audits.*   It is estimated that 20 percent of the people in a given state cheat on their income tax returns. The State Bureau of Revenue computes an indicator value for each tax return it processes. An indicator value of zero means that the tax return appears to be honest; a value of one suggests that the return should be examined more closely to detect cheating on the part of the taxpayer. It is estimated that of the people who actually cheat, 90 percent of them are assigned a one in the review process. It is also estimated that if in fact a taxpayer is not cheating, the taxpayer will be assigned a zero 75 percent of the time. If a tax examiner assigns a one to a given tax return, what is the probability that the taxpayer is cheating?

16. *Student Populations.*   The student population of Greensville High School is tabulated below by ethnic classification and class level:

Ethnic classification	Class			
	Freshman	Sophomore	Junior	Senior
Hispanic	100	95	93	90
Indian	50	50	40	60
Black	70	60	65	75
Oriental	30	25	20	20
Caucasian	300	280	250	200
Other	10	2	5	3

Each week the principal selects a student at random to interview concerning the student's satisfaction with the school's operation.
a. Compute the marginal and joint probabilities for a given selection made at random.
b. If the principal decides to restrict her selection during a given week to the freshman and senior classes, what is the probability that the student selected will be black? Hispanic?

17. *Manufacturing Processes.*   Westwind, Inc., manufactures hang gliders. It inspects each hang glider immediately upon completion of the unit. Ninety percent of the gliders pass this first inspection. Prior to packaging for shipment, each hang glider is inspected again. Of the gliders passing the first inspection, 95 percent also pass the second inspection, and the rest must go through rework. Of the gliders not passing the first inspection, 85 percent are sent to rework and 15 percent must be scrapped. Ninety-seven percent of the hang gliders that passed the first inspection but were later sent to rework can be successfully reworked; the rest must be scrapped. Eighty percent of the gliders sent to rework on the first inspection can be successfully reworked, and the remaining 20 per-

cent must be scrapped. Compute the percentage of glider units that end up as scrap.

18. *Job Hunting.*   Robert is about to enter the job market as he finishes up his senior year of college. He is planning to send out fifty copies of his résumé to various companies. For each résumé sent out he estimates that there is a 60 percent chance the company will contact him. Eighty percent of such contacts lead to a job interview. Twenty-five percent of all job interviews lead to getting a job offer, and two-thirds of all job offers are expected to be acceptable for serious consideration. Robert collected these facts from a cheerful employment counselor at the school's placement office.

a. How many acceptable job offers can Robert expect to get?

b. If Robert would like to get at least ten offers, how many résumés should he send out?

F PROBABILITY DENSITIES: APPLIED MODELS

CONTENTS

1. RANDOM VARIABLES

Let us consider again the basic framework used in the previous appendix. We have some situation or experiment that results in a set of outcomes, S, called the sample space. We now introduce the notion of a random variable. A **random variable** is a function that associates or assigns a number to each possible outcome.

For example, consider the experiment of tossing a coin twice. The sample space S equals {HH, HT, TH, TT}, which includes all possible outcomes of the two tosses. Define a random variable on S, and call it Y, which equals the number of heads which appears. Then for the outcome TT, $Y = 0$; for HT or TH, $Y = 1$; and for the outcome HH, $Y = 2$.

As another example, suppose the daily sales of a company have been observed over the past thirty days. On ten days sales were $100, on fifteen days sales were $150, and on five days sales were $200. If we believe sales to be more or less random, with these values we can define a random variable X that equals the daily sales of the company. Thus X equals $100, $150, or $200.

Discrete Random Variables

Some random variables take on only a *finite number of values*, such as the random variable Y, which equals the number of heads defined in the coin-toss experiment above, or the random variable X (daily sales) defined above. Other random variables can take on an infinite number of values, which can be listed one by one. For example, if we define a random variable Z to be the year in which a major ice age will next occur (measured relative to the current time, time zero), then Z could take on any of the values in the infinite set $\{0, 1, 2, 3, 4, \ldots\}$. Such a set is said to be **countable,** since we can list its elements.

A **discrete random variable** is a random variable that can only take on either a finite number of values or a countable number of values.

Continuous Random Variables

A **continuous random variable** is a random variable that can take on a continuum, or continuous range, of values. Examples would include the lifetime of a machine, the length of time between successive customer arrivals at a supermarket, and the length of time between successive vehicles arriving at a toll booth.

It is common practice to treat certain discrete random variables as if they were continuous. For example, if sales of a product are expected to be between 100 units and 500 units per month and if D is the sales random variable, then D should take on values in $\{100, 101, 102 \ldots, 499, 500\}$ and, therefore, is a discrete random variable. However, in many applications of this sort, management scientists often assume that D can take on *any* value in the range from 100 to 500 (including fractional values) and then treat D as a continuous random variable using some continuous probability model (see Section 3). With use of a standard continuous model, the analysis is often simplified.

2. PROBABILITY DENSITIES AND DISTRIBUTIONS

Given a random variable X, we define its **probability density** function, P_X, by

$$P_x(x) = P\{X = x\}$$

The **cumulative distribution** function F_X is defined by

$$F_x(x) = P\{X \le x\}$$

For example, in a coin toss experiment (Fig. F.1) where a coin is tossed twice, we have

(1) Outcomes	(2) Value of $Y = y$	(3) $P_Y(y)$	(4) $F_Y(y)$
TT	0	1/4	1/4
TH or HT	1	1/2	3/4
HH	2	1/4	1

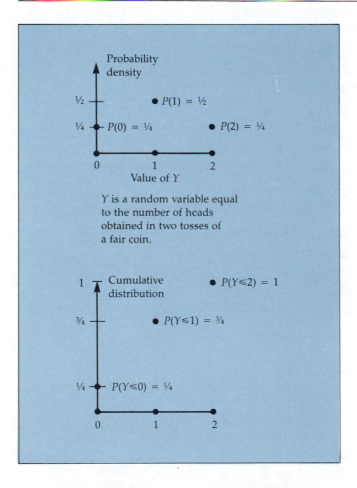

Coin toss experiment.

The outcomes are listed in column 1, the value of the random variable Y (which equals number of heads) is given in column 2, the probability density of Y is given in column 3, and the cumulative distribution of Y appears in column 4. Note that the entries in column 4 are just cumulative sums of the entries in column 3.

APPLICATIONS

The following applications appear in this appendix in the text, examples, or problems:

Bank teller service times

Breakeven analysis

Building construction

Coin toss

Computing system reliability

Customer arrivals

Drug abuse

Employment testing

Hospital E/R arrivals

Light bulb lifetimes

Machine adjustments: Bayesian analysis

Maintenance analysis:
  Maintenance of equipment for furniture manufacturing
  Police vehicle maintenance
  Public school system management

Manufacturing processes

Marketing new products

Military training

Multiple-choice exams

Predicting employee performance

Preventive maintenance

Quality control

Recreation planning

Reliability

Remedial maintenance

Replacement analysis

Sales analysis

Sports

Stock returns

Referring to the daily sales example in Section 1, we can use the historical sales data to derive a probability density for the random variable X, which equals daily sales:

(1) $X = x$ (sales)	(2) Number of days observed	(3) $P_X(x)$	(4) $F_X(x)$
$100	10	10/30 = 0.333	0.333
150	15	15/30 = 0.500	0.833
200	5	5/30 = 0.167	1.000
	30		

Column 3 is obtained by dividing each entry of column 2 by the total number of days, 30.

3. EXPECTATION

The **expectation** or **expected value** (also called the **mean**) of a random variable corresponds intuitively to the average value the random variable assumes. For a discrete random variable X, the expected value of X, denoted $E(X)$, is calculated as follows:

$$E(X) = \sum_{\text{all } x} xP(X = x) \tag{F-1}$$

That is, simply weight each value that X can assume by its probability density value and sum the results. For continuous random variables, the idea is the same except we must replace the summation sign in Eq. (F–1) by an integral sign:

$$E(X) = \int_{\text{all } x} xP_X(x)dx \tag{F-2}$$

To illustrate (F–1), we calculate the expected values of Y (in the coin toss example) and X (in the sales example) whose densities are given in Section 2 above:

(1) Value of Y(= y)	(2) P(Y = y)	(3) (1) × (2)
0	0.25	0.00
1	0.50	0.50
2	0.25	0.50
		E(X) = Σ = 1.00

So on the average we would expect to get one head on two tosses of a coin. For the sales example:

(1) Value of X(= x)	(2) P(X = x)	(3) (1) × (2)
100	0.333	33.3
150	0.500	75.0
200	0.167	33.4
		E(X) = Σ = 141.7

So, on the average we would expect sales to be 141.7 units per day.

Interpreting Expected Values

The expected value (mean) of a random variable is a measure of central tendency. A random variable will take on values on either side of its mean. Over a large number of repeated trials or experiments, the mean indicates the average value assumed by the random variable.

For example, in tossing a die, six equally likely outcomes are possible: 1, 2, 3, 4, 5, or 6. The average outcome is $(1 + 2 + 3 + 4 + 5 + 6)/6 = 3.5$. Of course, the number 3.5 can never physically appear on the toss of a die, but this number does give a measure of central tendency of the values possible, as shown in Fig. F.2.

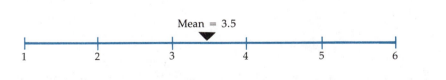

FIGURE F.2   *Values of a die.*

As another example, the mean in the sales example above was found to be 141.7; that is, average daily sales are $141.70. Thus in ten days *we would expect* total sales to be $1,417.

4. DISCRETE PROBABILITY DENSITIES

In this section we shall present some special discrete random variables and their probability densities. These densities are commonly used in management science.

The Bernoulli Random Variable

Consider an experiment that can result in only one of two possible outcomes, which we label as 0 and 1, and commonly refer to as failure (0) and success (1). Let X denote the outcome of the experiment and let p be the probability that the outcome is 1. Then the probability density function of X is given by

Value of X	$P_X(x)$
0	$1 - p$
1	p

The variable X is called a **Bernoulli random variable.**

EXAMPLE F.1: *Coin Toss.* Consider the experiment of tossing a coin once. Let the random variable X be the result of the toss. If the result is heads, we will set $X = 1$ (success); if the result is tails (failure), we will set $X = 0$. Then X is a Bernoulli random variable for which $p = 1/2$: $P(X = 1) = 1/2$. Also, $P(X = 0) = 1/2$. ▲

The Binomial Density

Another useful random variable in management science is the binomial random variable. It not only is useful in fairly general problems but also plays a major role in certain specific models such as quality control.

Consider a Bernoulli experiment that is repeated n times in such a way that, first, the n trials are independent of each other (that is, outcomes of successive trials have no effect on each other) and, second, the parameter p (which equals the probability of a success on a given trial) does not change from trial to trial. Let X equal the total number of successes which occurred in the n trials. Then X is said to be a **binomial random variable** with parameters n and p.

Let $P(r)$ denote the binomial probability of getting r successes in n trials when the probability of success on any given trial is p. It can be shown that

$$P(r) = \frac{n!}{r!\,(n-r)!}\,p^r(1-p)^{n-r} \qquad\qquad\qquad \text{(F–3)}$$

The sign "!" is read "factorial" and is explained fully in Appendix C.

The *expected value* of X is np; that is, $E(X) = np$.

EXAMPLE F.2. *Coin Toss.* A coin is tossed seven times. What is the probability that exactly two heads appear?

Solution. The Bernoulli random variable equals "success" if heads appears and "failure" if tails appears; $n = 7$, $p = 0.5$ (the probability of heads), and $r = 2$. Using Eq. (F–3), we obtain

$$P(2) = \frac{7!}{2!\,5!}\,(0.5)^2(1 - 0.5)^5$$

$$7! = (7)(6)(5)(4)(3)(2)(1) = 5040$$

$$2! = (2)(1) = 2$$

$$5! = (5)(4)(3)(2)(1) = 120$$

So the above equation becomes

$$P(2) = \frac{5040}{(2)(120)}\,(0.25)(0.03125)$$

$$= 0.1641 \qquad\qquad\qquad\qquad\qquad\qquad\qquad \blacktriangle$$

EXAMPLE F.3. *Test Results.* Weldite, Inc., is about to give welding tests to six job applicants. From historical test results the personnel office notes that the probability of a typical applicant passing the test is 0.4.

1. Compute the probabilities that exactly 0, 1, 2, 3, 4, 5, and 6 applicants will pass the test.
2. Compute the cumulative probability density function for this "experiment."
3. Graph the results of parts 1 and 2.

TABLE F.1

(1) Number passing*	(2) Probability	(3) Cumulative distribution
0	0.0467	0.0467
1	0.1866	0.2333
2	0.3110	0.5443
3	0.2765	0.8208
4	0.1382	0.9590
5	0.0369	0.9959
6	0.0041	1.0000

*The expected number passing equals $np = (6)(0.4) = 2.4$ persons.

Using $n = 6$; $r = 0, 1, 2, 3, 4, 5, 6$; and $p = 0.4$ in Eq. (F–3), we have (recall that $0! = 1$)

$$P(0) = \frac{6!}{0!6!}(0.4)^0(0.6)^6 = 0.0467$$

$$P(1) = \frac{6!}{1!5!}(0.4)^1(0.6)^5 = 0.1866$$

$$P(2) = \frac{6!}{2!4!}(0.4)^2(0.6)^4 = 0.3110$$

$$P(3) = \frac{6!}{3!3!}(0.4)^3(0.6)^3 = 0.2765$$

$$P(4) = \frac{6!}{4!2!}(0.4)^4(0.6)^2 = 0.1382$$

$$P(5) = \frac{6!}{5!1!}(0.4)^5(0.6)^1 = 0.0369$$

$$P(6) = \frac{6!}{6!0!}(0.4)^6(0.6)^0 = 0.0041$$

Table F.1 summarizes parts 1 and 2, and the graphs (part 3) are given in Figs. F.3 (a) and (b). For example, from column 3 of Table F.1 we see that the probability of no more than two people passing is 0.5443. The probability of five or more passing is

$$1 - P(4 \text{ or less passing}) = 1 - 0.9590 = 0.0410$$

Figure F.3(a) is constructed from column 2 of Table F.1, and Fig. F.3(b) is constructed from column 3 of the table. Also note that the expected number of persons passing the exam is $E(X) = np = (6)(0.4) = 2.4$. Thus, before the test is administered, it would be reasonable to expect that 2.4 persons will pass it. This should be interpreted using the frequency interpretation of probability (see Appendix E, Section 3). Thus if we repeatedly gave the test to groups of six people, in the long run we would expect that the *average* number passing would be 2.4.   ▲

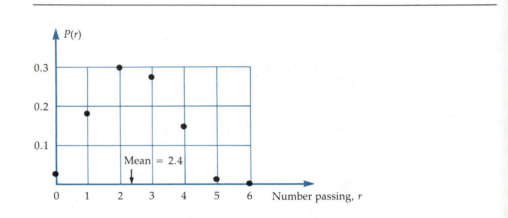

 FIGURE F.3(a)   *Probability density.*

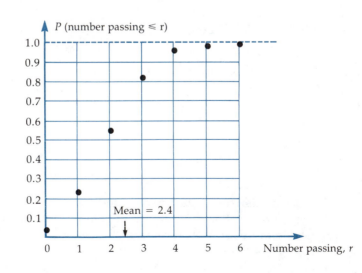

FIGURE F.3(b)   *Cumulative distribution.*

Binomial Tables, Appendix H

In Appendix H on page 849, you will find a table of binomial probabilities for $n = 1$ to $n = 10$ trials. To use the table, first locate the value of n. Then in the table for n locate the p and r values. Check your understanding of how to use the table by locating the six binomial probabilities calculated in Example F.3, Weldtite test results. Be sure to note that $r = i$ in Appendix H.

For example, to find $P(3)$ (see Example F.3), we use the following values: $n = 6$, $p = 0.4$, $i = 3$. First find the table in Appendix H headed $n = 6$. Values of p are listed across the top of the table, and values of i are listed down the left margin. Thus in the table "$n = 6$," we look in the $i = 3$ row and $p = 0.4$ column to find 0.2765, which agrees with the calculation made in Example F.3. The other probabilities for $i = 0$, 1, 2, 4, 5, and 6 can be located by reading down the $p = 0.4$ column.

The Poisson Density

The Poisson density is useful for modeling traffic flow situations (such as the number of cars arriving at a toll booth per hour), queuing or waiting line problems (such as the number of customers arriving per hour at a gas station, grocery store, or some other service center), the number of machines breaking down per day in a manufacturing plant, the number of typographical errors made per page of a printed book, communications systems (such as the number of telephone calls arriving at a police switchboard per hour), and many more similar situations.

In each of these examples there is a "counting process" involved. Certain events are assumed to occur in a *purely random manner* over time, and the decision maker is concerned with counting these events. The events may be automobile arrivals, customer arrivals, machine breakdowns, printing errors, incoming telephone calls, and so on.

To more formally define a Poisson process let us suppose we have a process that involves events occurring randomly over time at the mean rate of λ per unit time. Assume that the following conditions hold:

1. In a *very small* time interval, the probability of exactly one event occurring is very small and does not change from interval to interval.
2. In a very small time interval, the probability of two or more events occurring is approximately zero.
3. The number of events occurring in a given time interval depends only on the *length* of that time interval and not on when it occurs.
4. Successive events occur independently of each other.

Then if we let X be the random variable equal to the number of events that actually occur per unit time in a process that satisfies the above properties,

X has a **Poisson density** given by

$$P(X = i) = e^{-\lambda}\frac{\lambda^i}{i!}, \; i = 0, 1, 2, \ldots \tag{F-4}$$

where $e = 2.71828$. The expected number of events occurring in the unit time interval is λ; that is, $E(X) = \lambda$.

Poisson Probability Table, Appendix I

In computing Poisson probabilities you may use Eq. (F–4) and a pocket calculator, or you may use the tables in Appendix I. The next example will provide an opportunity to gain some practice with the Poisson density.

EXAMPLE F.4. The number of customers arriving at a supermarket checkout counter (Fig. F.4) is a random variable that has been determined to follow a Poisson density with a mean of six customers per hour.

1. Compute the probabilities that exactly 0, 1, 2, 3, 4, 5, 6, 7 customers arrive per hour.
2. Compute the cumulative probability density function for the number of customer arrivals.

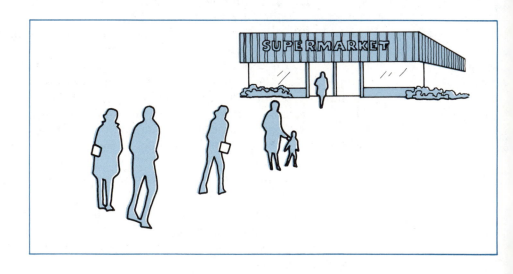

FIGURE F.4   *Customers arriving at a supermarket according to a Poisson process at an average rate of six per hour.*

3. Graph the results of parts 1 and 2.

Solution. In this application the mean λ equals 6 (customers per hour). From Appendix I, we see that

$$P(X = 0) = e^{-6} \frac{6^0}{0!} = 0.00248$$

$$P(X = 1) = e^{-6} \frac{6^1}{1!} = 0.01488$$

$$P(X = 2) = e^{-6} \frac{6^2}{2!} = 0.04464$$

Continuing in this manner, using Eq. (F–4), we obtain the results shown in Table F.2. Note that the sample space for this example is *countable* (or countably infinite): $\{0, 1, 2, 3, \ldots\}$. We have computed values only up to $X = 14$, but in theory the computation of the probabilities continues forever.

TABLE F.2

(1) Number of customers	(2) Probability	(3) Cumulative probability
0	0.00248	0.00248
1	0.01488	0.01736
2	0.04464	0.06200
3	0.08928	0.15128
4	0.13392	0.28520
5	0.16070	0.44590
6	0.16070	0.60660
7	0.13775	0.74435
8	0.10331	0.84766
9	0.06887	0.91653
10	0.04132	0.95785
11	0.02254	0.98039
12	0.01127	0.99166
13	0.00520	0.99686
14	0.00223	0.99909
.	.	.
.	.	.
.	.	.

$$\sum_{\text{all } i} = 1.00000$$

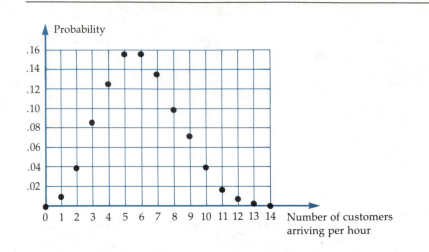

FIGURE F.5(a)   *Probability density.*

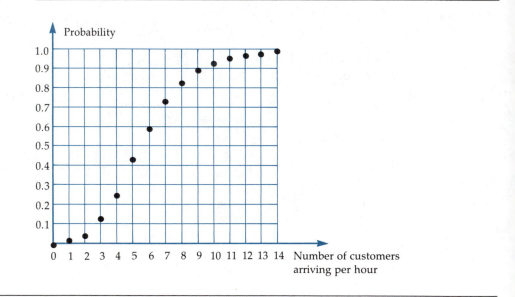

FIGURE F.5(b)   *Cumulative distribution.*

If we were to compute the sum of column 2, we would obtain the number one:

$$P(X = 0) + P(X = 1) + P(X = 2) + \cdots = 1$$

The density and cumulative distribution functions are graphed in Figs. F.5 (a) and (b). ▲

EXAMPLE F.5. In the supermarket checkout counter system, Example F.4 above, compute

1. the probability that six customers or less arrive per hour,
2. the probability that ten or more customers arrive per hour.

Solution.

1. This is given in column 3 of Table F.2:

$$P(X \le 6) = P(X = 0) + P(X = 1) + P(X = 2) + P(X = 3) + P(X = 4)$$

$$+ P(X = 5) + P(X = 6) = 0.60660.$$

2. $P(X \ge 10) = 1 - P(X \le 9) = 1 - 0.91653 = 0.08347.$ ▲

The Poisson density will play a major role in the queuing models of Chapter 8.

5. CONTINUOUS DENSITIES

We shall now discuss a few continuous densities that will appear in various chapters throughout the text. For continuous densities we do not interpret probability density values as being probabilities. However, the area under a continuous probability density curve will equal one, corresponding to the property of discrete densities where the sum of the probabilities must equal one.

Uniform Density

The **uniform density** is perhaps the simplest density to understand. Let X be a random variable that can take on values in the range from a number a to a number b: $a \le X \le b$. If each value in the range is equally likely to occur, X is said to be a uniform random variable having the probability density function p defined by

$$P(x) = \begin{cases} \dfrac{1}{b-a} & \text{if } a \le x \le b \\ 0 & \text{otherwise} \end{cases}$$

A graph of this density is given in Fig. F.6. Note that the area under the density function equals one. The expected value of X is simply the midpoint of the interval from a to b: $E(X) = (a + b)/2$, and the cumulative distribution, F_X, is given by areas under the density function:

$$F_x(x) = P(X \leq x) = \text{area under } P \text{ from } a \text{ to } x = (x - a)\,\frac{1}{b - a} \qquad \text{(F–5)}$$

EXAMPLE F.6. *The Uniform Density.* George has purchased a block of stock and estimates that each possible rate of return on the stock between 0 and 30 percent held for three months is equally likely to occur.

1. What is his expected rate of return?
2. What is the probability that the rate of return will be less than 5 percent?
3. Greater than 10 percent?

Solution. Let X = the return on the stock over three months expressed as a decimal. Then X has a uniform density on the interval from 0 to 0.30; $a = 0$; $b = 0.30$; $1/(b - a) = 10/3$. So for any value x in the interval, the probability density $p(x)$ equals $10/3$.

1. The $E(X)$ equals $(b + a)/2 = (0.30 + 0)/2 = 0.15$, or 15 percent.
2. $P(X \leq 0.05) = (0.05 - 0)(10/3) = 0.1667$.
3. $P(X \geq 0.10) = 1 - P(X \leq 0.10) = 1 - (0.10 - 0)(10/3) = 0.6667$. ▲

The uniform density on the interval from 0 to 1 (defined by $P(x) = 1$ for $0 \leq x \leq 1$) is used extensively in Chapter 12 ("Simulation").

The Exponential Density

The **exponential probability** density with parameter μ is given by

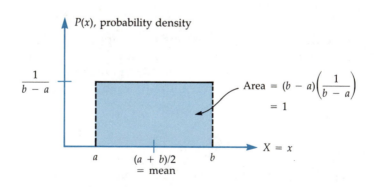

Uniform density, $P(x) = \dfrac{1}{(b - a)}$.

$$P(t) = \begin{cases} \mu e^{-\mu t} & \text{if } t \geq 0 \\ 0 & \text{if } t < 0 \end{cases}$$

($e = 2.71828$; some powers of e are given in Appendix J.) If a random variable T has an exponential probability density, its mean is $E(T) = 1/\mu$, and its cumulative distribution is given by

$$F_T(t) = P(T \leq t) = 1 - e^{-\mu t} \qquad \text{(F–6)}$$

A graph of the exponential density is given in Fig. F.7.

The exponential density is extensively used in management science in fields of reliability, quality control, life-testing, and queuing theory (see Chapter 8, where it plays a major role in the various queuing models). More specifically, the following events are often assumed to be random variables having exponential densities: the lifetime of a machine; the lifetime of electronic components; the lifetime of a light bulb; the length of a telephone conversation; the time between successive customer arrivals at a gas station, store, or other service facility; the time between job arrivals at a machine shop; the length of time it takes a person working at a checkout counter to complete service for a customer; and the length of time between successive arrivals of vehicles at a highway toll booth or at a street intersection in a city.

EXAMPLE F.7. *Lifetimes.* Suppose the lifetime of a light bulb (in hours) is found through statistical testing to be exponentially distributed with parameter 0.10.

1. What is the mean life of the light bulb?
2. What is the probability that the bulb will fail in two hours or less?
3. What is the probability that the light bulb will last ten hours or more?

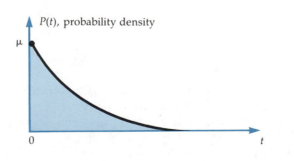

FIGURE F.7 $\qquad$ *Exponential density, $P(t) = \mu e^{-\mu t}$.*

Solution. Let T = the lifetime of the light bulb. Then $\mu = 0.10$, and

1. $E(T) = 1/\mu = 1/0.10 = 10$ hours = average lifetime of the bulb.
2. From Eq. (F–6), $P(T \leq 2) = 1 - e^{-(0.10)(2)} = 1 - 0.8187 = 0.1813$.
3. $P(T \geq 10) = 1 - P(T \leq 10) = 1 - (1 - e^{(-.10)(10)}) = e^{-1} = 0.3679$. ▲

EXAMPLE F.8. *Service Times.* Suppose the time it takes for a bank teller to serve a customer has been found to be exponentially distributed with a mean of 1.5 minutes. What is the probability that service for a customer will be completed in one minute or less?

Solution. Letting T be the service time, $E(T) = 1.5$. But we also know that $E(T) = 1/\mu$. Thus $1/\mu = 1.5$, so $\mu = 2/3$. Then we can use Eq. (F–6): $P(T \leq 1) = 1 - e^{-(2/3)(1)} = 1 - 0.5134 = 0.4866$, or a 48.66 percent chance. ▲

An important property of the exponential distribution is the following:

Suppose events occur randomly according to a Poisson density at the mean rate of λ per unit time. Then the time *between* the occurrence of successive events is an exponential random variable having a mean of $1/\lambda$ time units.

EXAMPLE F.9. *Traffic Flow.* Suppose vehicles arrive at a toll booth according to a Poisson density at the mean rate of twenty per hour.

1. What is the mean time between successive vehicle arrivals at the toll booth?
2. If a vehicle has just arrived at the toll booth, what is the probability that the next vehicle will arrive within one minute?

Solution. Let T = the time *between successive vehicle arrivals* (in hours) at the toll booth. Then from the property stated above, T is a random variable having an exponential density with a mean of $1/20$ hour. So the parameter of this exponential density is 20 (solve the equation $1/\mu = 1/20$). Then

1. $E(T) = 1/20$ hour = 3 minutes.
2. And since 1 minute = $1/60$ hour, $P(T \leq 1/60) = 1 - e^{-(20)(1/60)} = 1 - 0.7165 = 0.2835$. ▲

The Normal Density

Perhaps one of the most widely used densities in management science applications is the **normal probability density.** It is useful for describing the distribution of sales, projected profits, and project completion times. The normal density is used in Chapters 7, 8, and 9.

A normal density curve is determined by two parameters, the *mean* μ and the *standard deviation* σ. The mean, of course, gives the average value. The standard deviation measures the spread of possible values around the mean.

In Figs. F.8 (a) and (b), we show four normal density curves. The following properties of the normal density curve are illustrated.

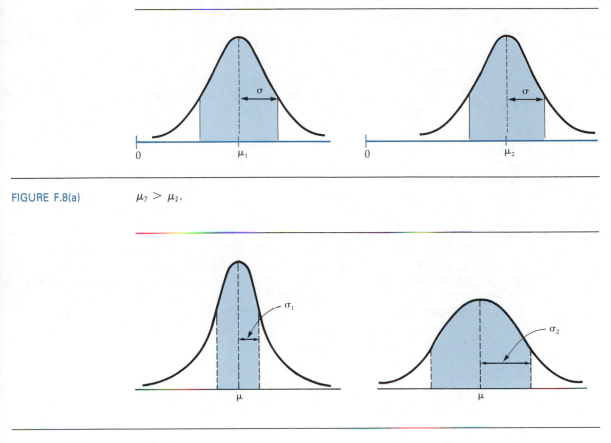

FIGURE F.8(a) $\mu_2 > \mu_1$.

FIGURE F.8(b) $\sigma_2 > \sigma_1$.

1. A normal density curve is symmetric about the mean and has a "bell shape."
2. A standard deviation's distance from the mean gives the point of inflection of the curve. That is, at a distance of σ from the mean the curve changes from being concave down to concave up.
3. The mean locates the curve on the horizontal axis. In Fig. F.8(a), μ_2 is greater than μ_1 (but the standard deviations are the same).
4. The larger the value of σ, the greater the spread of values about the mean, and the lower is the mode (or high point) of the curve. In Fig. F.8(b), the means are the same, but σ_2 is greater than σ_1.

Estimating the Mean and Standard Deviation

It is easy in practice to estimate the mean and standard deviation of a set of data points. Suppose we observe various values of demand (in units per day), and these values turn out to be $d_1, d_2, d_3, \ldots, d_n$. Assume we have computed the frequency probabilities of these demand levels to be $P(d_1)$, $P(d_2)$,

$P(d_3)$, . . . , and $P(d_n)$ (see Appendix E, Section 3). Then an estimate of the mean $\bar{D}$ is given by

$$\bar{D} = \sum_{i=1}^{n} d_i P(d_i) \qquad \text{(F–7)}$$

To estimate the standard deviation, we must first estimate the *variance* of the d_is Var(D):

$$\text{Var}(D) = \sum_{i=1}^{n} (d_i - \bar{D})^2 P(d_i) \qquad \text{(F–8)}$$

Then the standard deviation, Std Dev, is the square root of the variance:

$$\text{Std Dev}(D) = \sqrt{\text{Var}(D)} \qquad \text{(F–9)}$$

EXAMPLE F.10. *Estimating Mean and Standard Deviation.* Suppose we observe sales over a fifty-six-day period and find that sales of 20 units per day occurred five times, 25 units occurred twelve times, 30 units occurred twenty times, 35 occurred thirteen times, 40 occurred four times, and 45 occurred two times. Estimate the mean and standard deviation.

Solution. From the relative frequency interpretation of probability, we can compute probabilities by dividing each frequency by 56; $d_1 = 20$, $d_2 = 25$, $d_3 = 30$, $d_4 = 35$, $d_5 = 40$, and $d_6 = 45$. Then the probabilities $P(d_i)$ are $P(20) = 0.0893$, $P(25) = 0.2143$, $P(30) = 0.3571$, $P(35) = 0.2321$, $P(40) = 0.0714$, and $P(45) = 0.0357$. (These sum to 0.9999 instead of to one due to rounding.)

Using Eqs. (F–7), (F–8), and (F–9), we can calculate the mean and standard deviation as shown in Table F.3. ▲

TABLE F.3

(1) d_i	(2) $P(d_i)$	(3) $(1) \times (2)$	(4) $d_i - \bar{D}$	(5) $(d_i - \bar{D})^2$	(6) $(2) \times (5)$
20	.0893	1.786	−10.443	109.06	9.739
25	.2143	5.358	−5.443	29.63	6.349
30	.3571	10.713	−0.443	0.20	0.701
35	.2321	8.124	4.557	20.77	4.820
40	.0714	2.856	9.557	91.34	6.521
45	.0357	1.606	14.557	211.91	7.565

$$\bar{D} = \Sigma d_i P(d_i) = 30.443$$

$$\Sigma(d_i - \bar{D})^2 P(d_i) = 35.065$$
$$\text{Var}(D) = 35.065$$
$$\text{Std Dev}(D) = \sqrt{35.065}$$
$$= 5.921$$

Using the Normal Distribution Table

Appendix K gives a table of normal distribution values. The table gives values for a normal random variable having mean 0 and standard deviation 1. This random variable is called the **standard normal random variable.** The table gives cumulative probability values for values of the random variable ranging from 0 standard deviations to 3.69 standard deviations to the *right of the mean*. For example, if Z is normally distributed with mean 0 and standard deviation 1, the table shows that $P(Z \leq 0.2) = 0.5792$. This probability is represented by the shaded area in Fig. F.9. (Note that since the standard deviation equals one, we can interpret 0.2 to be $(0.2)(1) = 0.2$ *standard deviations.*)

The basis for the procedures listed below is the fact that if X is normally distributed with mean μ and standard deviation σ, the random variable Z defined by $(X - \mu)/\sigma$ is normally distributed with mean 0 and standard deviation 1.

Procedures for Calculating Normal Probabilities

We will now illustrate how to use the normal probability table of Appendix K. Assume that X is a random variable having a normal probability density with mean 10 and standard deviation 2. We will demonstrate four different types of calculations.

CASE 1: *Find P(X ≤ 13)* A graph of the normal density having mean 10 and standard deviation 2 is given in Fig. F.10(a). The shaded area under the curve equals the probability that X is less than or equal to 13.

To use Appendix K, we must first find how many standard deviations 13 is to the right of the mean 10:

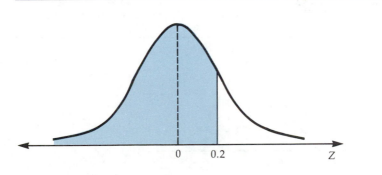

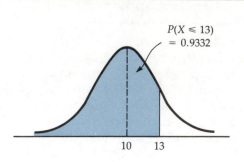

$P(X \leq 13)$
$= 0.9332$

10   13

Case 1.

$$Z = \frac{X - \mu}{\sigma} = \frac{13 - 10}{2} = 1.5$$

Thus 13 lies 1.5 standard deviations to the right of the mean. Looking up Z = 1.5 in the table, we get 0.9332; thus $P(X \leq 13) = 0.9332$.

CASE 2: *Find P(X ≥ 12)* The shaded area in Fig. F.10(b) represents $P(X \geq 12)$. The table in Appendix K only gives areas extending to the left. Thus we can find $P(X \leq 12)$ using the table and then note that

$P(X \geq 12) = 1 - P(X \leq 12)$

First find the Z value for 12:

$$Z = \frac{X - \mu}{\sigma} = \frac{12 - 10}{2} = 1$$

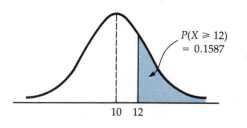

$P(X \geq 12)$
$= 0.1587$

10   12

Case 2.

That is, 12 is one standard deviation to the right of the mean. From the table, $P(X \leq 12) = P(Z \leq 1) = 0.8413$. From this we have

$$P(X \geq 12) = 1 - P(X \leq 12) = 1 - 0.8413 = 0.1587$$

CASE 3: *Find $P(X \leq 6)$* The shaded area in Fig. F.10(c) represents $P(X \leq 6)$. The table in Appendix K gives values only for $P(X \leq a)$ when a is to the right of the mean. In the present case, 6 lies to the left of the mean 10.

In order to find $P(X \leq 6)$, we use the symmetry of the normal density to see that $P(X \leq 6) = P(X \geq 14)$, as illustrated in Fig. F.10(c). From case 2, we know how to find $P(X \geq 14)$. The Z value for 14 is $(14 - 10)/2 = 2$, and looking up $Z = 2$ in the table gives us $P(X \leq 14) = P(Z \leq 2) = 0.9772$. Finally,

$$P(X \geq 14) = 1 - P(X \leq 14) = 1 - 0.9772 = 0.0228$$

from which we get the desired result:

$$P(X \leq 6) = P(X \geq 14) = 0.0228$$

CASE 4: *Find $P(X \geq 9)$* Once again, the table in Appendix K does not give us $P(X \geq 9)$ directly. However, the probability $P(X \geq 9)$ can be determined using the symmetry of the normal curve. From Fig. F.10(d), it is clear that $P(X \geq 9)$ represents the same area as $P(X \leq 11)$. (The values 9 and 11 are located symmetrically about the mean 10.) Thus $P(X \geq 9) = P(X \leq 11)$.

To find $P(X \leq 11)$, refer to case 1. The Z value corresponding to $X = 11$ is $Z = (X - \mu)/\sigma = (11 - 10)/2 = 0.50$. From the table we see that $P(X \leq 11) = P(Z \leq 0.5) = 0.6915$. Therefore

$$P(X \geq 9) = P(X \leq 11) = 0.6915$$

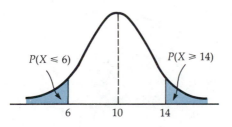

FIGURE F.10(c) *Case 3.*

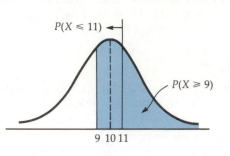

$P(X \leqslant 11)$

$P(X \geqslant 9)$

9 10 11

FIGURE F.10(d)   *Case 4.*

Some Useful Normal Probabilities

Suppose X is a random variable having normal probability density with mean
μ and standard deviation σ. To get an intuitive feeling for how σ gives a
measure of variability around the mean, it is useful to keep the following
probabilities in mind (see Fig. F.11):

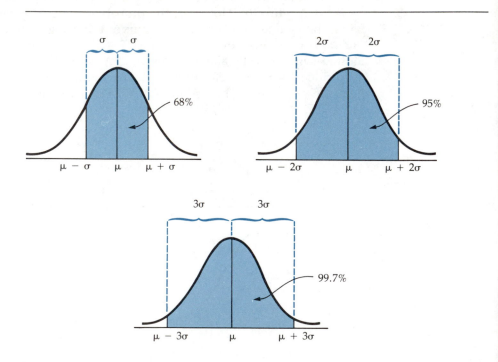

FIGURE F.11   *Some useful probabilities for the normal density.*

- Approximately 68 percent of the values of X fall within one standard deviation σ from the mean μ.
- Approximately 95 percent of the values of X fall within two standard deviations from the mean.
- Three standard deviations about the mean include approximately 99.7 percent of the values of X.

6. THE CENTRAL LIMIT THEOREM

The Central Limit Theorem is useful for calculating probabilities involving large sums of independent random variables having the same probability density.

Suppose $X_1, X_2, \ldots, X_n$ are independent random variables having the *same* probability density with mean μ and standard deviation σ. Then if n is large, the sum $Y = X_1 + X_2 + \cdots + X_n$ is approximately normal with mean $n\mu$ and standard deviation $\sigma\sqrt{n}$. Notes: (1) It does not matter what the probability density of the X_i is; (2) in practice, "large" generally means $n \geq 30$ or $n \geq 40$.

The use of this theorem is illustrated in Chapter 9, where it is a primary tool in PERT analysis.

7. APPLIED PROBABILITY MODELS

Various probability models are presented throughout this text (Chapters 7–12). In this section we briefly present four additional probabilistic models that are well known in the field of management science. We have chosen to present only the basics of each model in order to give you a general idea of the application without delving too deeply into more advanced probabilistic versions of the problem areas.

Reliability

Reliability is the field of study which is concerned with computing the probability that a given system will work. In fact, we define the **reliability** of a system to be the probability that the system is functioning.

A **series system** functions only if all of its components are functioning. A **parallel system** is a system that functions if at least one of its components is functioning.

Diagrammatically, we can review these systems as in Figs. F.12(a) and (b). *We will assume throughout this section that the components of a given system function independently of each other.*

Suppose a system consists of n independent components. Let p_i be the probability that component i is functioning. If the system is a series system, then the system will function only if all n components are functioning:

$$
\begin{aligned}
\text{The reliability of} \atop \text{a series system} =\ &\left(\text{Probability that component 1} \atop \text{functions}\right) \times \\
&\left(\text{Probability that component 2} \atop \text{functions}\right) \times \dots \times \\
&\left(\text{Probability that component } n \atop \text{functions}\right) \\
=\ & P_1 \times P_2 \times P_3 \dots \times P_n
\end{aligned}
$$

$$(\text{F--}10)$$

The fact that the components are assumed to operate independently of each other enabled us to multiply the p_is in Eq. (F–10). (See Appendix E, Section 5.)

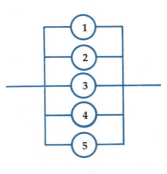

A series system of five components.

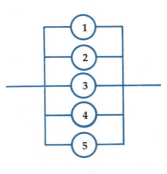

A parallel system of five components.

If the system is a parallel system, the reliability of S equals the probability that at least one of the n components is working, and this equals one minus the probability that *all* components have failed. Since the probability of failure for component i is $1 - p_i$, we have

$$\binom{\text{Reliability of the}}{\text{system}} = [1 - (1 - p_1)(1 - p_2) \dots (1 - p_n)] \tag{F-11}$$

EXAMPLE F.11. *Military Training.* A team of three pilots is required to operate a jet aircraft during Air Force training maneuvers. Team A's three pilots show up for daily training 98, 92, and 99 percent of the time (independently of each other). Compute the probability that the jet used by team A will be participating in maneuvers on any given day.

Solution. Since all three pilots are needed before the jet can be flown, the team functions as a series system: $p_1 = 0.98$, $p_2 = 0.92$, and $p_3 = 0.99$. Thus from Eq. (F-10), the reliability of the team equals $(0.98)(0.92)(0.99) = 0.89$; that is, team A will be functioning 89 percent of the time.   ▲

EXAMPLE F.12. Suppose in the above example that if at least one pilot is present, the jet can be flown. Compute the reliability of the team.

Solution. The system is now a parallel system. From Eq. (F-11), we have

(Reliability of the team) $= 1 - (1 - 0.98)(1 - 0.92)(1 - 0.99)$

$$= 1 - 0.000016$$

$$= 0.999984$$

So the team would function 99.9984 percent of the time!   ▲

EXAMPLE F.13. Refer to Example F.11. Suppose in addition to the three pilots, the team consists of one coordinator (who shows up 99 percent of the time) and two maintenance mechanics (one shows up 80 percent of the time and the other shows up 95 percent of the time). Assume that the coordinator must be present, at least one mechanic must be present, and all three pilots must be present. Determine the reliability of the team.

Solution. The system (that is, the team) consists of three subsystems in series, as shown in Fig. F.13. Since each subsystem functions independently, the reliability of the system equals the products of the reliabilities of the three subsystems.

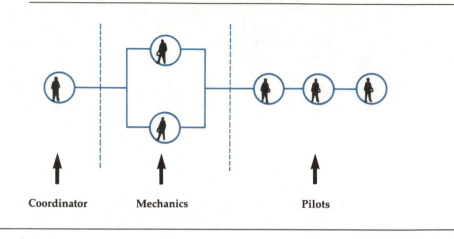

FIGURE F.13

The reliability of the mechanic subsystem is computed from Eq. (F–11):

Reliability (mechanics) = 1 − (1 − 0.80)(1 − 0.95) = 0.99

From Example F.11, the reliability of the "pilot subsystem" equals 0.89. Thus the reliability of the team equals (the reliability of the coordinator) × (the reliability of the mechanics) × (the reliability of the pilots) = (0.99)(0.99)(0.89) = 0.87. Thus the team will function 87 percent of the time.   ▲
  Other applications of these techniques are given in the chapter exercises.

Quality Control

Quality control is a field of application concerned with determining whether a given system is functioning according to acceptable standards. The next example illustrates a quality control problem concerned with machine operation in a manufacturing environment.

EXAMPLE F.14. *Manufacturing Processes: Bayesian Analysis.* A machine is used to manufacture round-head bolts in Boltcom's manufacturing plant. Ninety-five percent of the time the machine is in adjustment. When the machine is in adjustment, only 3 percent of the bolts produced are defective. When the machine is out of adjustment, 7 percent of the bolts produced are defective. A sample of ten bolts is taken and one is found to be defective. What is the probability that the machine is in adjustment?

Solution. Let E_1 be the event that the machine is in adjustment, E_2 the event that the machine is out of adjustment, and A the event that one out of ten bolts is found to be defective. The problem is to calculate the probability that the machine is in adjustment *given* that one bolt out of the sample of ten was found to be defective. In symbols this is simply the conditional probability $P(E_1|A)$. To find this value we use Bayes' theorem, Eq. (E–9) of Appendix E:

$$P(E_1|A) = \frac{P(E_1)P(A|E_1)}{P(E_1)P(A|E_1) + P(E_2)P(A|E_2)}$$

Now, from the statement of the problem, $P(E_1) = 0.95$ and $P(E_2) = 1 - P(E_1) = 1 - 0.95 = 0.05$.

Let us look at the other terms of the above expression. $P(A|E_1)$ is the probability of getting one defective in a sample of ten when the probability of getting a defective is 0.03. But this is simply the binomial probability $P(1)$ when $n = 10$ and $p = 0.03$, which from Appendix H equals 0.2281. Similarly $P(A|E_2)$ is the binomial probability $P(1)$ when $n = 10$ and $p = 0.07$, which equals 0.3643. Substituting all these values into Bayes' formula above, we have

$$P(E_1|A) = \frac{(0.95)(0.2281)}{(0.95)(0.2281) + (0.05)(0.3643)} = 0.92$$

Thus there is a 92 percent chance that the machine is in adjustment.   ▲

Breakeven Analysis

Breakeven analysis is a financial tool useful for screening proposed investments. Suppose the profitability of a proposed new product is being examined. A fixed cost of F dollars per year will be required to manufacture the product, independent of the number of units produced. This cost includes a yearly equivalent of the cost of the new production facilities required, an overhead allocation, and costs of management and clerical support. Each unit costs c dollars to make (a variable cost component) and will sell for p dollars. The breakeven volume V_{BE} (measured in units per year) is given by

$$V_{BE} = \frac{F}{p - c} \qquad\qquad\qquad \text{(F–12)}$$

If sales exceed V_{BE}, a net profit is made (above recovering the fixed-cost F); below V_{BE}, a loss is incurred; and when sales equal V_{BE}, the operation "breaks even."

For example, if the annualized fixed cost of facilities required to manufacture a product is $2 million, if the product costs $20 to manufacture and sells for $30, the breakeven volume is (see Fig. F.14)

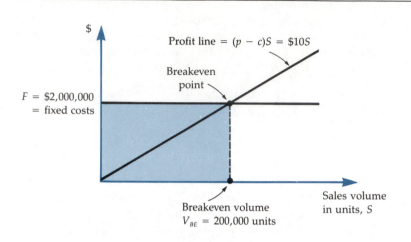

Breakeven analysis.

$$V_{BE} = \frac{2,000,000}{30 - 20} = 200,000 \text{ units per year}$$

In practice, it is not realistic to project a single level of sales for a new prod-uct. A more reasonable approach would be to estimate various probabilities of different sales volumes. The next example illustrates this approach.

EXAMPLE F.15. Gameco, Inc., is planning to market a new board game. The game will cost $3 to manufacture and will sell for $8. A new machine will be required to manufacture certain game tokens. In addition, the company must commit a yearly amount of funds to support the administrative, pro-duction, and marketing functions required to produce the game. The total of these fixed expenses is expected to be $60,000 per year irrespective of how many games are produced. The marketing manager's research suggests that sales of the new game can be expected to follow a normal probability density with a mean of 15,000 games per year. He says that the odds are four to one that sales will fall within 2,000 units of this figure. Analyze the break-even possibility of the new game.

Solution. The breakeven volume is V_{BE} = 60,000/(8 − 3) = 12,000 games per year. The normal probability density curve, according to the marketing man-ager's description, should be as shown in Fig. F.15. Thus

$$P(\text{sales} \le 17,000) = \frac{4 + 4 + 1}{1 + 4 + 4 + 1} = 0.90$$

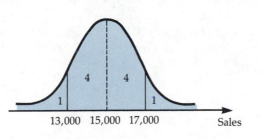

FIGURE F.15

The table in Appendix K indicates that the point having a cumulative probability of 0.90 is about 1.28 standard deviations to the right of the mean. Therefore

$1.28\sigma = (17,000 - 15,000)$,   so $\sigma = 1562.50$

or σ is approximately 1562. Since $\mu = 15,000$, we can now make probabilistic statements concerning the level of sales such as the following:

1. The probability of at least breaking even equals $P(\text{sales} \geq 12,000)$. Using case 4, Section 5, p. 831, this equals $P(\text{sales} \leq 18,000)$. $Z = (18,000 - 15,000)/1,562 = 1.92$, so $P(\text{sales} \leq 18,000) = P(Z \leq 1.92) = 0.9726$. Thus, there is a 97.26 percent chance of at least breaking even.

2. Compute the probability of exceeding the breakeven point by 30 percent. Thirty percent above breakeven equals $12,000 + .3(12,000) = 15,600$.

$P(\text{sales} \geq 15,600) = 1 - P(\text{sales} \leq 15,600)$

$$= 1 - P\left(Z \leq \frac{15,600 - 15,000}{1,562}\right)$$

$$= 1 - P(Z \leq 0.38)$$

$$= 1 - 0.6480 = 0.352$$

(or a 35.2 percent chance). Note that there is a 50 percent chance that sales will exceed the breakeven point by 25 percent: $P(\text{sales} \geq 15,000) = 0.5$, since 15,000 is the mean and the normal curve is symmetric. This would translate into (3,000 units)($5 profit/unit) or $15,000 above the breakeven, a 25 percent return on the $60,000 fixed investment.

Overall the product looks promising from a breakeven point of view. At least we could say that at this point the product would not be deleted from further consideration and certainly warrants a detailed financial analysis. ▲

It would be more reasonable, perhaps, to treat *all* the parameters (*F, p, c, and* sales) as random variables. Using the technique of simulation (Chapter 12), such an approach is possible. We could then generate (using simulation) a probability distribution of the expected profits or rates of return.

Replacement Analysis

Replacement analysis deals with determining the minimum-cost replacement policy for items in use which fail over time, such as light bulbs, mechanical parts on a fleet of city vehicles, and plumbing parts in the fixtures of a large building.

Let us suppose Lincoln Elementary School System uses 1,000 light bulbs in its buildings. Each bulb costs $0.20. There are two policies being considered for replacing bulbs:

- *Policy 1:* Replace bulbs as they burn out (this is called **remedial maintenance**).
- *Policy 2:* Replace all the bulbs at the same time in addition to replacing individual bulbs as they burn out (this is called **preventive maintenance**).

If the bulbs are replaced individually, the labor cost is $1.50 per bulb; if the entire 1,000 bulbs are replaced all at once, the labor cost per bulb is $0.35. The following data (called **life-testing data**) has been collected:

Age of bulb in use (months)	Probability of burnout
1	0.35
2	0.15
3	0.20
4	0.30

Thus a bulb which has burned for one month has a 35 percent chance of burning out at the end of that month. Note the high burn-out rate for new bulbs (0.35). If the bulbs do not fail at first, there is a low probability of failure soon after (0.15) then, as the bulbs burn they wear out and the failure rate increases (0.20 to 0.30).

We now compute the costs of the two replacement policies.

POLICY 1. From the above probability density we can compute the expected lifetime, L, of a bulb:

$$L = (1)(.35) + 2(.15) + 3(.20) + 4(.30) = 2.45 \text{ months}$$

Thus if we are using 1,000 bulbs, we will be replacing (on the average) 1,000/ 2.45 = 408.2 bulbs per month as they burn out at a cost of (408.2 bulbs/mo.) × ($1.50 + $0.20 per bulb) = $693.94 per month, which includes labor ($1.50 per bulb) plus the cost of the bulbs ($0.20 per bulb).

POLICY 2. For policy 2, we have four options: to replace all 1,000 bulbs every month, every two months, every three months, or every four months.
Let's use the following notation for this analysis. Define:

N = number of original bulbs (= 1,000)

R_1 = number replaced at the end of month 1

R_2 = number replaced at the end of month 2

R_3 = number replaced at the end of month 3

R_4 = number replaced at the end of month 4

Also denote the burn-out probabilities by p_1, p_2, p_3, and p_4. Then if we start out with all new bulbs at a given time, we can compute the values of the R_i, as in Table F.4.
The calculation of R_1 is clear. For R_2, the original bulbs are now two months old, so $N \times p_2$ of these will fail. Also the R_1 bulbs replaced at the end of month 1 are now one month old, so $R_1 \times p_1$ of these will fail in month 2. Thus $R_2 = (N \times p_2) + (R_1 \times p_1)$. You should similiarly reason through the expressions for R_3 and R_4. As an example of how to read the table, suppose at the start of month 1 all 1,000 bulbs are brand new. Then if we replace bulbs only as they fail, at the end of month 3, for example, we can expect (on the average) to replace 348 bulbs. The expected cumulative number of bulbs replaced through the end of month 3 would be 970.

TABLE F.4*

(1)				(2) R_i	(3) ΣR_i
$R_1 = N \times p_1$ $= 1{,}000 \times 0.35$				= 350	350
$R_2 = (N \times p_2)$ $= (1{,}000 \times 0.15)$	$+ (R_1 \times p_1)$ $+ (350 \times 0.35)$			= 272	622
$R_3 = (N \times p_3)$ $= (1{,}000 \times 0.20)$	$+ (R_2 \times p_1)$ $+ (272 \times 0.35)$	$+ (R_1 \times p_2)$ $+ (350 \times 0.15)$		= 348	970
$R_4 = (N \times p_4)$ $= (1{,}000 \times 0.30)$	$+ (R_3 \times p_1)$ $+ (348 \times 0.35)$	$+ (R_2 \times p_2)$ $+ (272 \times 0.15)$	$+ (R_1 \times p_3)$ $+ (350 \times 0.20)$	= 533	1,503

*All calculations rounded to nearest whole number.

The four options for policy 2 are listed in Table F.5, together with their expected cost per month. For policy 2, the third plan has the minimum expected monthly cost ($733).

SELECTING A REPLACEMENT POLICY. The expected monthly cost using policy 1 would be about $694; if all 1,000 bulbs are replaced every three months, the expected monthly cost would be $733. Thus using policy 1 would save $39 per month in replacement costs; that is, the remedial policy, *in this case*, is better than the preventive maintenance policy.

TABLE F.5

(1) Option: Replace all 1,000 bulbs	(2) Cost of replacing 1,000 bulbs at once ($0.35 + $0.20) × 1,000	(3) Cost of replacing the bulbs that fail since last replacement ($1.50 + $0.20 = $1.70 each)	(4) Total cost (2) + (3)	(5) Average cost per month
Every month	$550	$ 595 (350 × $1.70)	$1,145	$1,145
Every 2 months	550	1,057 (622 × $1.70)	1,607	804
Every 3 months	550	1,649 (970 × $1.70)	2,199	733
Every 4 months	550	2,555 (1,503 × $1.70)	3,105	776

8. CONCLUDING REMARKS

In this appendix, we have continued our discussion of probability begun in Appendix E. The notion of random variables and their densities was introduced. The expected value of a random variable makes precise the notion of "average value."

The two types of probability densities are discrete and continuous, for example:

Discrete densities	Continuous densities
Bernoulli	Uniform
Binomial	Exponential
Poisson	Normal

Finally, we discussed four well-known probability models of management science: (1) reliability, (2) quality control, (3) breakeven analysis, and (4) replacement analysis.

TERMINOLOGY

After studying this appendix, you should be familiar with the following terms:

TERM	SECTION
Bernoulli random variable	4
binomial density	4
breakeven analysis	7
Central Limit Theorem	5
continuous densities	6
continuous random variable	1
cumulative distribution	2
discrete random variable	1
expected value	3
exponential density	5
geometric random variable	8
life-testing data	7
mean	3,5
normal density	5
parallel system	7
Poisson density	4
preventive maintenance	7
probability density	2
quality control	7
random variable	1
reliability	7
remedial maintenance	7
replacement analysis	7
standard normal random variable	5
series system	7
standard deviation	5
uniform density	5

EXERCISES

1. *Geometric Random Variable.* Suppose an experiment can result in "success" or "failure." Let p be the probability of a success occurring on any given trial. Define a random variable X whose value equals the number

of times the experiment is conducted before the *first* success occurs. Write an algebraic expression for the probability density of X. Such a random variable is called a **geometric random variable** (or is said to have a **geometric density**). The expected value of X, $E(X)$, equals $1/p$.

2. *Sports—Baseball.*   A baseball player has a 0.1 probability of hitting a home run on any given time up to bat. What is the probability that the player hits his/her first home run in the first five times at bat of the season? What is the expected number of times at bat for this player before he/she will hit a home run? (Refer to Exercise 1.)

3. *Employee Performance.*   The Navy has observed that 85 percent of the personnel who pass screening tests for submarine duty later perform satisfactorily. If five enlistees have just passed these tests, what is the probability that
   a. all of them will perform satisfactorily?
   b. none of them will perform satisfactorily?
   c. three or more will perform satisfactorily?

4. *Manufacturing Processes.*   A manufacturing process produces 5 percent defective items. What is the probability that a random sample of four items contains two or more defectives?

5. *Hospital Emergency Room Arrivals.*   Statistical analysis has shown that patient arrivals at the St. Mary's Hospital emergency room occur at an average rate of five per hour and follow a Poisson distribution.
   a. What is the probability that five or more patients will arrive in any given hour?
   b. What is the probability that no patients arrive in a two-hour interval?
   c. What is the expected time between successive patient arrivals?
   d. If a patient has just arrived, what is the probability that the next patient will arrive within ten minutes?

6. *Recreation Planning.*   The weather bureau indicates that the probability of rain on each of the next five days will be 30 percent. You are planning a five-day camp out and other outdoor activities that will require at least three days of clear weather to be fully enjoyed. What is the probability that your five-day outing will be completely successful?

7. *Building Construction.*   The number of days having weather conditions suitable for building construction in the Ranchero area approximately follows a normal distribution with a mean of 170 days per year and a standard deviation of 20 days. What is the probability that at least 200 days of the year will favor the building construction industry?

8. *Stock Returns.*   The annual dividend return on Ramjam common stock tends to be normally distributed, with a mean of 10 percent and standard deviation of 1-1/2 percent. What is the probability that a given year's return falls below 7 percent? Exceeds 11 percent?

9. *Sales Analysis.*   Sales records for Caltron Calculators are given below for last year's sales:

Sales (units)	Number of weeks	Sales (units)	Number of weeks
35	1	40	10
36	3	41	7
37	6	42	5
38	8	43	2
39	9	44	1

a. Compute the probability density of these data, and plot this density on a graph.
b. Compute the mean and variance of the density.
c. Fit a normal curve to the data [using the results of part (b)]. Using the normal probability density, compute the probabilities shown in the table below. Compare these to the probabilities you would obtain using the original discrete density of part (a):

Event	Normal probability	Discrete probability
Sales $\geq$ 42		
Sales $\leq$ 38		
Sales $\leq$ 40		

10. *Reliability of a Computing System.*   To run a batch computer program at the university, a student must punch the program card deck on a key-punch machine and submit the deck to one of two card-readers. The program is then processed by the computer on one of three peripheral processors, and the results are sent to a printer terminal to be printed out. The keypunch machine functions properly 98 percent of the time. The down time on each of the card-readers is 10 percent. Each of the three processors is functioning 99 percent of the time, and the printer works 90 percent of the time. On a typical day, if a student prepares a correctly written program, what is the probability that he or she can suc-cessfully run the program on the system?

11. *Reliability of Nonidentical Parallel Components.*   Suppose a parallel sys-tem consists of three components, the first of which functions 98 percent of the time, the second functions 95 percent of the time, and the third functions 96 percent of the time. An arriving job must be processed by any one of the three components. However, there is a device that assigns

the arriving jobs to one of the three components. The probabilities that a job will be assigned to each of the above three components are 0.3, 0.5, and 0.2, respectively. What is the probability that an arriving job will be successfully processed by this parallel system? Do you see an application of such a system in Exercise 10 above?

12. *Who Made the Pizza?*   Jane and Bob regularly order a pizza from Chen's Potluck Pizza Mill. They have two good friends who work at Chen's, Raphael and Cindy, who work at different times. Cindy works four days a week, and Raphael works three days a week, although the particular days each works change constantly. Raphael tends to make excellent pizzas 80 percent of the time, and Cindy's pizzas turn out excellent only 60 percent of the time. If Jane and Bob order a pizza and it turns out to be good, what is the probability that Cindy is working that day?

13. *Police Vehicle Maintenance.*   Claysville operates twenty police cars. Tires for these vehicles cost the city $45. If a tire blows out and requires changing, it is estimated that the cost incurred is $10. However, all eighty tires on the fleet could be replaced at a single vehicle maintenance check for an average cost of $1 per tire. Experience with the tires indicates the following lifetime probabilities for a tire: $P(\text{failure in one month}) = 0.10$, $P(\text{failure in two months}) = 0.60$, $P(\text{failure in three months}) = 0.30$. Determine whether the city should use a remedial or a preventive maintenance plan for changing the tires.

14. *Equipment Maintenance for Furniture Manufacturer.*   A furniture manufacturer uses seven large shapers in its manufacturing operations. If one of these breaks down, an average repair cost of $350 is incurred. The cost of performing preventive maintenance if done on all seven machines at the same time would be $40 per machine and would include cleaning, oiling, and adjustments. The lifetime data on the machines indicate the following breakdown probabilities:

Number of months since maintenance:	1	2	3	4
Probability of breakdown:	0.20	0.15	0.30	0.35

What type of maintenance policy would you recommend for this manufacturer?

15. *Typographical Errors.*   A typist averages one error every ten words. The occurrence of such errors can reasonably be assumed to satisfy the conditions for a Poisson process. What is the probability that the typist will make two or more errors in a twenty-word paragraph? What is the probability that he makes one or more errors in a ten-word sentence?

16. *Concession-Booth Management.* Sally Jones is looking into the profitability of setting up a concession stand at a one-day arts and crafts fair coming up soon. The costs to construct the booth out of plywood, rent a soda fountain to dispense soft drinks, obtain a permit, and pay a fee for the electrical hook-up would total $250. She would sell only soft drinks at the stand. Each drink would be priced at $0.50 and would cost her $0.20 to prepare (which includes the soft drink mix and the paper cups). Sally estimates that sales of soft drinks will be normally distributed with a mean of 1,000 and standard deviation of 150. Sally does not feel it would be worth the effort to set up the stand unless she has at least a 70 percent chance of clearing $400 above all expenses.
    a. Should she plan to go ahead or not (a "go, no go" decision)?
    b. What is the probability that she would break even?

17. *Machine Adjustment.* An automatic machine for stamping steel forms is self-adjusting to a great extent. Based on the machine manufacturer's data and past experience with the machine, the machine is in adjustment 95 percent of the time. When in proper adjustment, the machine produces 7 percent defectives; when the machine is out of adjustment, the defective rate jumps to 15 percent. If a sample of ten items is found to contain one defective item, what is the probability that the machine is out of adjustment?

18. *Multiple-Choice Exams.* An exam contains ten questions, each of which has four multiple-choice alternatives. A student must get nine or ten questions correct to get an A and seven or eight correct for a B. If the student guesses randomly at each question, what is the probability of getting an A? Of getting a B?

19. *Drug Abuse.* It is estimated that 30 percent of the students at Highcrest High School are drug abusers. In a class of ten students, what is the probability that three or more students use drugs? What assumptions did you make in calculating this probability?

G TABLE OF RANDOM NUMBERS

Line	Column									
	1	2	3	4	5	6	7	8	9	10
1	00980	50494	72116	66409	63874	70064	70037	05153	22611	42042
2	62556	56710	27465	55032	14126	96688	33701	60938	13879	87320
3	91837	25339	63295	88259	22805	49676	59454	75413	37960	67037
4	02160	26968	61043	54410	23380	52730	66680	47191	83005	07791
5	37556	50165	82205	84342	25140	99615	98311	46063	08024	48901
6	24798	21048	81299	81642	08063	40310	08710	39049	68201	98931
7	37150	28140	78234	03327	89902	71238	57780	88034	49059	22770
8	00065	33137	75573	89710	85463	25949	51544	79685	85817	89330
9	86056	19101	78094	27251	35512	44406	82702	70601	83913	75122
10	42806	36314	34904	95311	04283	96773	45387	50287	61963	37537
11	28746	48446	26403	24016	87286	29091	37469	82796	45383	12393
12	35645	00384	10885	43012	03656	77445	44052	82057	13627	11656
13	50890	30261	11369	06368	69123	25090	07348	75673	50692	54198
14	45924	37110	28711	99782	67057	67100	10129	48435	72478	23803
15	05263	29156	93619	31576	24353	94987	71911	41888	61011	32081
16	21676	72897	57032	88151	78404	48090	53658	92842	70549	68890
17	65986	90339	22178	34250	67343	93356	09798	02560	35637	18839
18	87587	21234	74719	79145	55180	92173	37559	24224	07355	22283
19	84182	88178	90799	83549	52260	61271	52229	28020	26774	85733
20	63834	52603	04699	57149	16655	29227	95948	80262	96576	71564
21	99795	04828	85059	20508	83237	64268	01549	03836	62832	10282
22	23280	63083	30733	62998	69072	73664	02524	41291	72008	18988
23	74066	77435	21072	86251	06238	49211	95503	91374	60701	60884
24	10724	49489	99327	43863	79151	49413	20295	01816	42311	18136

H BINOMIAL PROBABILITIES, $P(i) = \binom{n}{i}p^i(1 - p)^{n-i}$

N = 1 to 10
P = 0.01 to 0.5

N = 1
Values of P

i	.01	.02	.03	.04	.05	.06	.07	.08	.09	.10
0	.9900	.9800	.9700	.9600	.9500	.9400	.9300	.9200	.9100	.9000
1	.0100	.0200	.0300	.0400	.0500	.0600	.0700	.0800	.0900	.1000
	.11	.12	.13	.14	.15	.16	.17	.18	.19	.20
0	.8900	.8800	.8700	.8600	.8500	.8400	.8300	.8200	.8100	.8000
1	.1100	.1200	.1300	.1400	.1500	.1600	.1700	.1800	.1900	.2000
	.21	.22	.23	.24	.25	.26	.27	.28	.29	.30
0	.7900	.7800	.7700	.7600	.7500	.7400	.7300	.7200	.7100	.7000
1	.2100	.2200	.2300	.2400	.2500	.2600	.2700	.2800	.2900	.3000
	.31	.32	.33	.34	.35	.36	.37	.38	.39	.40
0	.6900	.6800	.6700	.6600	.6500	.6400	.6300	.6200	.6100	.6000
1	.3100	.3200	.3300	.3400	.3500	.3600	.3700	.3800	.3900	.4000
	.41	.42	.43	.44	.45	.46	.47	.48	.49	.50
0	.5900	.5800	.5700	.5600	.5500	.5400	.5300	.5200	.5100	.5000
1	.4100	.4200	.4300	.4400	.4500	.4600	.4700	.4800	.4900	.5000

H. BINOMIAL PROBABILITIES, $P(i) = \binom{n}{i} p^i (1-p)^{n-i}$

$N = 2$
Values of P

i	.01	.02	.03	.04	.05	.06	.07	.08	.09	.10
0	.9801	.9604	.9409	.9216	.9025	.8836	.8649	.8464	.8281	.8100
1	.0198	.0392	.0582	.0768	.0950	.1128	.1302	.1472	.1638	.1800
2	.0001	.0004	.0009	.0016	.0025	.0036	.0049	.0064	.0081	.0100

	.11	.12	.13	.14	.15	.16	.17	.18	.19	.20
0	.7921	.7744	.7569	.7396	.7225	.7056	.6889	.6724	.6561	.6400
1	.1958	.2112	.2262	.2408	.2550	.2688	.2822	.2952	.3078	.3200
2	.0121	.0144	.0169	.0196	.0225	.0256	.0289	.0324	.0361	.0400

	.21	.22	.23	.24	.25	.26	.27	.28	.29	.30
0	.6241	.6084	.5929	.5776	.5625	.5476	.5329	.5184	.5041	.4900
1	.3318	.3432	.3542	.3648	.3750	.3848	.3942	.4032	.4118	.4200
2	.0441	.0484	.0529	.0576	.0625	.0676	.0729	.0784	.0841	.0900

	.31	.32	.33	.34	.35	.36	.37	.38	.39	.40
0	.4761	.4624	.4489	.4356	.4225	.4096	.3969	.3844	.3721	.3600
1	.4278	.4352	.4422	.4488	.4550	.4608	.4662	.4712	.4758	.4800
2	.0961	.1024	.1089	.1156	.1225	.1296	.1369	.1444	.1521	.1600

	.41	.42	.43	.44	.45	.46	.47	.48	.49	.50
0	.3481	.3364	.3249	.3136	.3025	.2916	.2809	.2704	.2601	.2500
1	.4838	.4872	.4902	.4928	.4950	.4968	.4982	.4992	.4998	.5000
2	.1681	.1764	.1849	.1936	.2025	.2116	.2209	.2304	.2401	.2500

$N = 3$
Values of P

i	.01	.02	.03	.04	.05	.06	.07	.08	.09	.10
0	.9703	.9412	.9127	.8847	.8574	.8306	.8044	.7787	.7536	.7290
1	.0294	.0576	.0847	.1106	.1354	.1590	.1816	.2031	.2236	.2430
2	.0003	.0012	.0026	.0046	.0071	.0102	.0137	.0177	.0221	.0270
3	.0000	.0000	.0000	.0001	.0001	.0002	.0003	.0005	.0007	.0010

	.11	.12	.13	.14	.15	.16	.17	.18	.19	.20
0	.7050	.6815	.6585	.6361	.6141	.5927	.5718	.5514	.5314	.5120
1	.2614	.2788	.2952	.3106	.3251	.3387	.3513	.3631	.3740	.3840
2	.0323	.0380	.0441	.0506	.0574	.0645	.0720	.0797	.0877	.0960
3	.0013	.0017	.0022	.0027	.0034	.0041	.0049	.0058	.0069	.0080

N = 3 (continued)

i	.21	.22	.23	.24	.25	.26	.27	.28	.29	.30
0	.4930	.4746	.4565	.4390	.4219	.4052	.3890	.3732	.3579	.3430
1	.3932	.4015	.4091	.4159	.4219	.4271	.4316	.4355	.4386	.4410
2	.1045	.1133	.1222	.1313	.1406	.1501	.1597	.1693	.1791	.1890
3	.0093	.0106	.0122	.0138	.0156	.0176	.0197	.0220	.0244	.0270

i	.31	.32	.33	.34	.35	.36	.37	.38	.39	.40
0	.3285	.3144	.3008	.2875	.2746	.2621	.2500	.2383	.2270	.2160
1	.4428	.4439	.4444	.4443	.4436	.4424	.4406	.4382	.4354	.4320
2	.1989	.2089	.2189	.2289	.2389	.2488	.2587	.2686	.2783	.2880
3	.0298	.0328	.0359	.0393	.0429	.0467	.0507	.0549	.0593	.0640

i	.41	.42	.43	.44	.45	.46	.47	.48	.49	.50
0	.2054	.1951	.1852	.1756	.1664	.1575	.1489	.1406	.1327	.1250
1	.4282	.4239	.4191	.4140	.4084	.4024	.3961	.3894	.3823	.3750
2	.2975	.3069	.3162	.3252	.3341	.3428	.3512	.3594	.3674	.3750
3	.0689	.0741	.0795	.0852	.0911	.0973	.1038	.1106	.1176	.1250

N = 4
Values of P

i	.01	.02	.03	.04	.05	.06	.07	.08	.09	.10
0	.9606	.9224	.8853	.8493	.8145	.7807	.7481	.7164	.6857	.6561
1	.0388	.0753	.1095	.1416	.1715	.1993	.2252	.2492	.2713	.2916
2	.0006	.0023	.0051	.0088	.0135	.0191	.0254	.0325	.0402	.0486
3	.0000	.0000	.0001	.0002	.0005	.0008	.0013	.0019	.0027	.0036
4	.0000	.0000	.0000	.0000	.0000	.0000	.0000	.0000	.0001	.0001

i	.11	.12	.13	.14	.15	.16	.17	.18	.19	.20
0	.6274	.5997	.5729	.5470	.5220	.4979	.4746	.4521	.4305	.4096
1	.3102	.3271	.3424	.3562	.3685	.3793	.3888	.3970	.4039	.4096
2	.0575	.0669	.0767	.0870	.0975	.1084	.1195	.1307	.1421	.1536
3	.0047	.0061	.0076	.0094	.0115	.0138	.0163	.0191	.0222	.0256
4	.0001	.0002	.0003	.0004	.0005	.0007	.0008	.0010	.0013	.0016

i	.21	.22	.23	.24	.25	.26	.27	.28	.29	.30
0	.3895	.3702	.3515	.3336	.3164	.2999	.2840	.2687	.2541	.2401
1	.4142	.4176	.4200	.4214	.4219	.4214	.4201	.4180	.4152	.4116
2	.1651	.1767	.1882	.1996	.2109	.2221	.2331	.2439	.2544	.2646
3	.0293	.0332	.0375	.0420	.0469	.0520	.0575	.0632	.0693	.0756
4	.0019	.0023	.0028	.0033	.0039	.0046	.0053	.0061	.0071	.0081

i	.31	.32	.33	.34	.35	.36	.37	.38	.39	.40
0	.2267	.2138	.2015	.1897	.1785	.1678	.1575	.1478	.1385	.1296
1	.4074	.4025	.3970	.3910	.3845	.3775	.3701	.3623	.3541	.3456
2	.2745	.2841	.2933	.3021	.3105	.3185	.3260	.3330	.3396	.3456
3	.0822	.0891	.0963	.1038	.1115	.1194	.1276	.1361	.1447	.1536
4	.0092	.0105	.0119	.0134	.0150	.0168	.0187	.0209	.0231	.0256

N = 4 (continued)

i	.41	.42	.43	.44	.45	.46	.47	.48	.49	.50
0	.1212	.1132	.1056	.0983	.0915	.0850	.0789	.0731	.0677	.0625
1	.3368	.3278	.3185	.3091	.2995	.2897	.2799	.2700	.2600	.2500
2	.3511	.3560	.3604	.3643	.3675	.3702	.3723	.3738	.3747	.3750
3	.1627	.1719	.1813	.1908	.2005	.2102	.2201	.2300	.2400	.2500
4	.0283	.0311	.0342	.0375	.0410	.0448	.0488	.0531	.0576	.0625

N = 5
Values of P

i	.01	.02	.03	.04	.05	.06	.07	.08	.09	.10
0	.9510	.9039	.8587	.8154	.7738	.7339	.6957	.6591	.6240	.5905
1	.0480	.0922	.1328	.1699	.2036	.2342	.2618	.2866	.3086	.3280
2	.0010	.0038	.0082	.0142	.0214	.0299	.0394	.0498	.0610	.0729
3	.0000	.0001	.0003	.0006	.0011	.0019	.0030	.0043	.0060	.0081
4	.0000	.0000	.0000	.0000	.0000	.0001	.0001	.0002	.0003	.0004
5	.0000	.0000	.0000	.0000	.0000	.0000	.0000	.0000	.0000	.0000

i	.11	.12	.13	.14	.15	.16	.17	.18	.19	.20
0	.5584	.5277	.4984	.4704	.4437	.4182	.3939	.3707	.3487	.3277
1	.3451	.3598	.3724	.3829	.3915	.3983	.4034	.4069	.4089	.4096
2	.0853	.0981	.1113	.1247	.1382	.1517	.1652	.1786	.1919	.2048
3	.0105	.0134	.0166	.0203	.0244	.0289	.0338	.0392	.0450	.0512
4	.0007	.0009	.0012	.0017	.0022	.0028	.0035	.0043	.0053	.0064
5	.0000	.0000	.0000	.0001	.0001	.0001	.0001	.0002	.0002	.0003

i	.21	.22	.23	.24	.25	.26	.27	.28	.29	.30
0	.3077	.2887	.2707	.2536	.2373	.2219	.2073	.1935	.1804	.1681
1	.4090	.4072	.4043	.4003	.3955	.3898	.3834	.3762	.3685	.3601
2	.2174	.2297	.2415	.2529	.2637	.2739	.2836	.2926	.3010	.3087
3	.0578	.0648	.0721	.0798	.0879	.0962	.1049	.1138	.1229	.1323
4	.0077	.0091	.0108	.0126	.0146	.0169	.0194	.0221	.0251	.0283
5	.0004	.0005	.0006	.0008	.0010	.0012	.0014	.0017	.0021	.0024

i	.31	.32	.33	.34	.35	.36	.37	.38	.39	.40
0	.1564	.1454	.1350	.1252	.1160	.1074	.0992	.0916	.0845	.0778
1	.3513	.3421	.3325	.3226	.3124	.3020	.2914	.2808	.2700	.2592
2	.3157	.3220	.3275	.3323	.3364	.3397	.3423	.3441	.3452	.3456
3	.1418	.1515	.1613	.1712	.1811	.1911	.2010	.2109	.2207	.2304
4	.0319	.0357	.0397	.0441	.0488	.0537	.0590	.0646	.0706	.0768
5	.0029	.0034	.0039	.0045	.0053	.0060	.0069	.0079	.0090	.0102

i	.41	.42	.43	.44	.45	.46	.47	.48	.49	.50
0	.0715	.0656	.0602	.0551	.0503	.0459	.0418	.0380	.0345	.0313
1	.2484	.2376	.2270	.2164	.2059	.1956	.1854	.1755	.1657	.1563
2	.3452	.3442	.3424	.3400	.3369	.3332	.3289	.3240	.3185	.3125
3	.2399	.2492	.2583	.2671	.2757	.2838	.2916	.2990	.3060	.3125
4	.0834	.0902	.0974	.1049	.1128	.1209	.1293	.1380	.1470	.1562
5	.0116	.0131	.0147	.0165	.0185	.0206	.0229	.0255	.0282	.0312

N = 6
Values of P

i	.01	.02	.03	.04	.05	.06	.07	.08	.09	.10
0	.9415	.8858	.8330	.7828	.7351	.6899	.6470	.6064	.5679	.5314
1	.0571	.1085	.1546	.1957	.2321	.2642	.2922	.3164	.3370	.3543
2	.0014	.0055	.0120	.0204	.0305	.0422	.0550	.0688	.0833	.0984
3	.0000	.0002	.0005	.0011	.0021	.0036	.0055	.0080	.0110	.0146
4	.0000	.0000	.0000	.0000	.0001	.0002	.0003	.0005	.0008	.0012
5	.0000	.0000	.0000	.0000	.0000	.0000	.0000	.0000	.0000	.0001
6	.0000	.0000	.0000	.0000	.0000	.0000	.0000	.0000	.0000	.0000

i	.11	.12	.13	.14	.15	.16	.17	.18	.19	.20
0	.4970	.4644	.4336	.4046	.3771	.3513	.3269	.3040	.2824	.2621
1	.3685	.3800	.3888	.3952	.3993	.4015	.4018	.4004	.3975	.3932
2	.1139	.1295	.1452	.1608	.1762	.1912	.2057	.2197	.2331	.2458
3	.0188	.0236	.0289	.0349	.0415	.0486	.0562	.0643	.0729	.0819
4	.0017	.0024	.0032	.0043	.0055	.0069	.0086	.0106	.0128	.0154
5	.0001	.0001	.0002	.0003	.0004	.0005	.0007	.0009	.0012	.0015
6	.0000	.0000	.0000	.0000	.0000	.0000	.0000	.0000	.0000	.0001

i	.21	.22	.23	.24	.25	.26	.27	.28	.29	.30
0	.2431	.2252	.2084	.1927	.1780	.1642	.1513	.1393	.1281	.1176
1	.3877	.3811	.3735	.3651	.3560	.3462	.3358	.3251	.3139	.3025
2	.2577	.2687	.2789	.2882	.2966	.3041	.3105	.3160	.3206	.3241
3	.0913	.1011	.1111	.1214	.1318	.1424	.1531	.1639	.1746	.1852
4	.0182	.0214	.0249	.0287	.0330	.0375	.0425	.0478	.0535	.0595
5	.0019	.0024	.0030	.0036	.0044	.0053	.0063	.0074	.0087	.0102
6	.0001	.0001	.0001	.0002	.0002	.0003	.0004	.0005	.0006	.0007

i	.31	.32	.33	.34	.35	.36	.37	.38	.39	.40
0	.1079	.0989	.0905	.0827	.0754	.0687	.0625	.0568	.0515	.0467
1	.2909	.2792	.2673	.2555	.2437	.2319	.2203	.2089	.1976	.1866
2	.3267	.3284	.3292	.3290	.3280	.3261	.3235	.3201	.3159	.3110
3	.1957	.2061	.2162	.2260	.2355	.2446	.2533	.2616	.2693	.2765
4	.0660	.0727	.0799	.0873	.0951	.1032	.1116	.1202	.1291	.1382
5	.0119	.0137	.0157	.0180	.0205	.0232	.0262	.0295	.0330	.0369
6	.0009	.0011	.0013	.0015	.0018	.0022	.0026	.0030	.0035	.0041

i	.41	.42	.43	.44	.45	.46	.47	.48	.49	.50
0	.0422	.0381	.0343	.0308	.0277	.0248	.0222	.0198	.0176	.0156
1	.1759	.1654	.1552	.1454	.1359	.1267	.1179	.1095	.1014	.0938
2	.3055	.2994	.2928	.2856	.2780	.2699	.2615	.2527	.2436	.2344
3	.2831	.2891	.2945	.2992	.3032	.3065	.3091	.3110	.3121	.3125
4	.1475	.1570	.1666	.1763	.1861	.1958	.2056	.2153	.2249	.2344
5	.0410	.0455	.0503	.0554	.0609	.0667	.0729	.0795	.0864	.0937
6	.0048	.0055	.0063	.0073	.0083	.0095	.0108	.0122	.0138	.0156

H. BINOMIAL PROBABILITIES, $P(i) = \binom{n}{i}p^{i}(1 - p)^{n-i}$

N = 7
Values of P

i	.01	.02	.03	.04	.05	.06	.07	.08	.09	.10
0	.9321	.8681	.8080	.7514	.6983	.6485	.6017	.5578	.5168	.4783
1	.0659	.1240	.1749	.2192	.2573	.2897	.3170	.3396	.3578	.3720
2	.0020	.0076	.0162	.0274	.0406	.0555	.0716	.0886	.1061	.1240
3	.0000	.0003	.0008	.0019	.0036	.0059	.0090	.0128	.0175	.0230
4	.0000	.0000	.0000	.0001	.0002	.0004	.0007	.0011	.0017	.0026
5	.0000	.0000	.0000	.0000	.0000	.0000	.0000	.0001	.0001	.0002
6	.0000	.0000	.0000	.0000	.0000	.0000	.0000	.0000	.0000	.0000
7	.0000	.0000	.0000	.0000	.0000	.0000	.0000	.0000	.0000	.0000

	.11	.12	.13	.14	.15	.16	.17	.18	.19	.20
0	.4423	.4087	.3773	.3479	.3206	.2951	.2714	.2493	.2288	.2097
1	.3827	.3901	.3946	.3965	.3960	.3935	.3891	.3830	.3756	.3670
2	.1419	.1596	.1769	.1936	.2097	.2248	.2391	.2523	.2643	.2753
3	.0292	.0363	.0441	.0525	.0617	.0714	.0816	.0923	.1033	.1147
4	.0036	.0049	.0066	.0086	.0109	.0136	.0167	.0203	.0242	.0287
5	.0003	.0004	.0006	.0008	.0012	.0016	.0021	.0027	.0034	.0043
6	.0000	.0000	.0000	.0000	.0001	.0001	.0001	.0002	.0003	.0004
7	.0000	.0000	.0000	.0000	.0000	.0000	.0000	.0000	.0000	.0000

	.21	.22	.23	.24	.25	.26	.27	.28	.29	.30
0	.1920	.1757	.1605	.1465	.1335	.1215	.1105	.1003	.0910	.0824
1	.3573	.3468	.3356	.3237	.3115	.2989	.2860	.2731	.2600	.2471
2	.2850	.2935	.3007	.3067	.3115	.3150	.3174	.3186	.3186	.3177
3	.1263	.1379	.1497	.1614	.1730	.1845	.1956	.2065	.2169	.2269
4	.0336	.0389	.0447	.0510	.0577	.0648	.0724	.0803	.0886	.0972
5	.0054	.0066	.0080	.0097	.0115	.0137	.0161	.0187	.0217	.0250
6	.0005	.0006	.0008	.0010	.0013	.0016	.0020	.0024	.0030	.0036
7	.0000	.0000	.0000	.0000	.0001	.0001	.0001	.0001	.0002	.0002

	.31	.32	.33	.34	.35	.36	.37	.38	.39	.40
0	.0745	.0672	.0606	.0546	.0490	.0440	.0394	.0352	.0314	.0280
1	.2342	.2215	.2090	.1967	.1848	.1732	.1619	.1511	.1407	.1306
2	.3156	.3127	.3088	.3040	.2985	.2922	.2853	.2778	.2698	.2613
3	.2363	.2452	.2535	.2610	.2679	.2740	.2793	.2838	.2875	.2903
4	.1062	.1154	.1248	.1345	.1442	.1541	.1640	.1739	.1838	.1935
5	.0286	.0326	.0369	.0416	.0466	.0520	.0578	.0640	.0705	.0774
6	.0043	.0051	.0061	.0071	.0084	.0098	.0113	.0131	.0150	.0172
7	.0003	.0003	.0004	.0005	.0006	.0008	.0009	.0011	.0014	.0016

	.41	.42	.43	.44	.45	.46	.47	.48	49	.50
0	.0249	.0221	.0195	.0173	.0152	.0134	.0117	.0103	.0090	.0078
1	.1211	.1119	.1032	.0950	.0872	.0798	.0729	.0664	.0604	.0547
2	.2524	.2431	.2336	.2239	.2140	.2040	.1940	.1840	.1740	.1641
3	.2923	.2934	.2937	.2932	.2918	.2897	.2867	.2830	.2786	.2734
4	.2031	.2125	.2216	.2304	.2388	.2468	.2543	.2612	.2676	.2734
5	.0847	.0923	.1003	.1086	.1172	.1261	.1353	.1447	.1543	.1641
6	.0196	.0223	.0252	.0284	.0320	.0358	.0400	.0445	.0494	.0547
7	.0019	.0023	.0027	.0032	.0037	.0044	.0051	.0059	.0068	.0078

i	.01	02	.03	.04	.05	.06	.07	.08	.09	.10
0	.9227	.8508	.7837	.7214	.6634	.6096	.5596	.5132	.4703	.4305
1	.0746	.1389	.1939	.2405	.2793	.3113	.3370	.3570	.3721	.3826
2	.0026	.0099	.0210	.0351	.0515	.0695	.0888	.1087	.1288	.1488
3	.0001	.0004	.0013	.0029	.0054	.0089	.0134	.0189	.0255	.0331
4	.0000	.0000	.0001	.0002	.0004	.0007	.0013	.0021	.0031	.0046
5	.0000	.0000	.0000	.0000	.0000	.0000	.0001	.0001	.0002	.0004
6	.0000	.0000	.0000	.0000	.0000	.0000	.0000	.0000	.0000	.0000
7	.0000	.0000	.0000	.0000	.0000	.0000	.0000	.0000	.0000	.0000
8	.0000	.0000	.0000	.0000	.0000	.0000	.0000	.0000	.0000	.0000

i	.11	.12	.13	.14	.15	.16	.17	.18	.19	.20
0	.3937	.3596	.3282	.2992	.2725	.2479	.2252	.2044	.1853	.1678
1	.3892	.3923	.3923	.3897	.3847	.3777	.3691	.3590	.3477	.3355
2	.1684	.1872	.2052	.2220	.2376	.2518	.2646	.2758	.2855	.2936
3	.0416	.0511	.0613	.0723	.0839	.0959	.1084	.1211	.1339	.1468
4	.0064	.0087	.0115	.0147	.0185	.0228	.0277	.0332	.0393	.0459
5	.0006	.0009	.0014	.0019	.0026	.0035	.0045	.0058	.0074	.0092
6	.0000	.0001	.0001	.0002	.0002	.0003	.0005	.0006	.0009	.0011
7	.0000	.0000	.0000	.0000	.0000	.0000	.0000	.0000	.0001	.0001
8	.0000	.0000	.0000	.0000	.0000	.0000	.0000	.0000	.0000	.0000

i	.21	.22	.23	.24	.25	.26	.27	.28	.29	.30
0	.1517	.1370	.1236	.1113	.1001	.0899	.0806	.0722	.0646	.0576
1	.3226	.3092	.2953	.2812	.2670	.2527	.2386	.2247	.2110	.1977
2	.3002	.3052	.3087	.3108	.3115	.3108	.3089	.3058	.3017	.2965
3	.1596	.1722	.1844	.1963	.2076	.2184	.2285	.2379	.2464	.2541
4	.0530	.0607	.0689	.0775	.0865	.0959	.1056	.1156	.1258	.1361
5	.0113	.0137	.0165	.0196	.0231	.0270	.0313	.0360	.0411	.0467
6	.0015	.0019	.0025	.0031	.0038	.0047	.0058	.0070	.0084	.0100
7	.0001	.0002	.0002	.0003	.0004	.0005	.0006	.0008	.0010	.0012
8	.0000	.0000	.0000	.0000	.0000	.0000	.0000	.0000	.0001	.0001

i	.31	.32	.33	.34	.35	.36	.37	.38	.39	.40
0	.0514	.0457	.0406	.0360	.0319	.0281	.0248	.0218	.0192	.0168
1	.1847	.1721	.1600	.1484	.1373	.1267	.1166	.1071	.0981	.0896
2	.2904	.2835	.2758	.2675	.2587	.2494	.2397	.2297	.2194	.2090
3	.2609	.2668	.2717	.2756	.2786	.2805	.2815	.2815	.2806	.2787
4	.1465	.1569	.1673	.1775	.1875	.1973	.2067	.2157	.2242	.2322
5	.0527	.0591	.0659	.0732	.0808	.0888	.0971	.1058	.1147	.1239
6	.0118	.0139	.0162	.0188	.0217	.0250	.0285	.0324	.0367	.0413
7	.0015	.0019	.0023	.0028	.0033	.0040	.0048	.0057	.0067	.0079
8	.0001	.0001	.0001	.0002	.0002	.0003	.0004	.0004	.0005	.0007

i	.41	.42	.43	.44	.45	.46	.47	.48	.49	.50
0	.0147	.0128	.0111	.0097	.0084	.0072	.0062	.0053	.0046	.0039
1	.0816	.0742	.0672	.0608	.0548	.0493	.0442	.0395	.0352	.0313
2	.1985	.1880	.1776	.1672	.1569	.1469	.1371	.1275	.1183	.1094
3	.2759	.2723	.2679	.2627	.2568	.2503	.2431	.2355	.2273	.2188
4	.2397	.2465	.2526	.2580	.2627	.2665	.2695	.2717	.2730	.2734
5	.1332	.1428	.1525	.1622	.1719	.1816	.1912	.2006	.2098	.2187
6	.0463	.0517	.0575	.0637	.0703	.0774	.0848	.0926	.1008	.1094
7	.0092	.0107	.0124	.0143	.0164	.0188	.0215	.0244	.0277	.0312
8	.0008	.0010	.0012	.0014	.0017	.0020	.0024	.0028	.0033	.0039

H. BINOMIAL PROBABILITIES, $P(i) = \binom{n}{i}p^i(1 - p)^{n-i}$

$N = 9$
Values of P

i	.01	.02	.03	.04	.05	.06	.07	.08	.09	.10
0	.9135	.8337	.7602	.6925	6302	.5730	.5204	.4722	.4279	.3874
1	.0830	.1531	.2116	.2597	.2985	.3292	.3525	.3695	.3809	.3874
2	.0034	.0125	.0262	.0433	.0629	.0840	.1061	.1285	.1507	.1722
3	.0001	.0006	.0019	.0042	.0077	.0125	.0186	.0261	.0348	.0446
4	.0000	.0000	.0001	.0003	.0006	.0012	.0021	.0034	.0052	.0074
5	.0000	.0000	.0000	.0000	.0000	.0001	.0002	.0003	.0005	.0008
6	.0000	.0000	.0000	.0000	.0000	.0000	.0000	.0000	.0000	.0001
7	.0000	.0000	.0000	.0000	.0000	.0000	.0000	.0000	.0000	.0000
8	.0000	.0000	.0000	.0000	.0000	.0000	.0000	.0000	.0000	.0000
9	.0000	.0000	.0000	.0000	.0000	.0000	.0000	.0000	.0000	.0000

	.11	.12	.13	.14	.15	16	.17	.18	.19	.20
0	.3504	.3165	.2855	.2573	.2316	.2082	.1869	.1676	.1501	.1342
1	.3897	.3884	.3840	.3770	.3679	.3569	.3446	.3312	.3169	.3020
2	.1927	.2119	.2295	.2455	.2597	.2720	.2823	.2908	.2973	.3020
3	.0556	.0674	.0800	.0933	.1069	.1209	.1349	.1489	.1627	.1762
4	.0103	.0138	.0179	.0228	.0283	.0345	.0415	.0490	.0573	.0661
5	.0013	.0019	.0027	.0037	.0050	.0066	.0085	.0108	.0134	.0165
6	.0001	.0002	.0003	.0004	.0006	.0008	.0012	.0016	.0021	.0028
7	.0000	.0000	.0000	.0000	.0000	.0001	.0001	.0001	.0002	.0003
8	.0000	.0000	.0000	.0000	.0000	.0000	.0000	.0000	.0000	.0000
9	.0000	.0000	.0000	.0000	.0000	.0000	.0000	.0000	.0000	.0000

	.21	.22	.23	.24	.25	.26	.27	.28	.29	.30
0	.1199	.1069	.0952	.0846	.0751	.0665	.0589	.0520	.0458	.0404
1	.2867	.2713	.2558	.2404	.2253	.2104	.1960	.1820	.1685	.1556
2	.3049	.3061	.3056	.3037	.3003	.2957	.2899	.2831	.2754	.2668
3	.1891	.2014	.2130	.2238	.2336	.2424	.2502	.2569	.2624	.2668
4	.0754	.0852	.0954	.1060	.1168	.1278	.1388	.1499	.1608	.1715
5	.0200	.0240	.0285	.0335	.0389	.0449	.0513	.0583	.0657	.0735
6	.0036	.0045	.0057	.0070	.0087	.0105	.0127	.0151	.0179	.0210
7	.0004	.0005	.0007	.0010	.0012	.0016	.0020	.0025	.0031	.0039
8	.0000	.0000	.0001	.0001	.0001	.0001	.0002	.0002	.0003	.0004
9	.0000	.0000	.0000	.0000	.0000	.0000	.0000	.0000	.0000	.0000

	.31	.32	.33	.34	.35	.36	.37	.38	.39	.40
0	.0355	.0311	.0272	.0238	.0207	.0180	.0156	.0135	.0117	.0101
1	.1433	.1317	.1206	.1102	.1004	.0912	.0826	.0747	.0673	.0605
2	.2576	.2478	.2376	.2270	.2162	.2052	.1941	.1831	.1721	.1612
3	.2701	.2721	.2731	.2729	.2716	.2693	.2660	.2618	.2567	.2508
4	.1820	.1921	.2017	.2109	.2194	.2272	.2344	.2407	.2462	.2508
5	.0818	.0904	.0994	.1086	.1181	.1278	.1376	.1475	.1574	.1672
6	.0245	.0284	.0326	.0373	.0424	.0479	.0539	.0603	.0671	.0743
7	.0047	.0057	.0069	.0082	.0098	.0116	.0136	.0158	.0184	.0212
8	.0005	.0007	.0008	.0011	.0013	.0016	.0020	.0024	.0029	.0035
9	.0000	.0000	.0000	.0001	.0001	.0001	.0001	.0002	.0002	.0003

i	.41	.42	.43	.44	.45	.46	.47	.48	.49	.50
0	.0087	.0074	.0064	.0054	.0046	.0039	.0033	.0028	.0023	.0020
1	.0542	.0484	.0431	.0383	.0339	.0299	.0263	.0231	.0202	.0176
2	.1506	.1402	.1301	.1204	.1110	.1020	.0934	.0853	.0776	.0703
3	.2442	.2369	.2291	.2207	.2119	.2027	.1933	.1837	.1739	.1641
4	.2545	.2573	.2592	.2601	.2600	.2590	.2571	.2543	.2506	.2461
5	.1769	.1863	.1955	.2044	.2128	.2207	.2280	.2347	.2408	.2461
6	.0819	.0900	.0983	.1070	.1160	.1253	.1348	.1445	.1542	.1641
7	.0244	.0279	.0318	.0360	.0407	.0458	.0512	.0571	.0635	.0703
8	.0042	.0051	.0060	.0071	.0083	.0097	.0114	.0132	.0153	.0176
9	.0003	.0004	.0005	.0006	.0008	.0009	.0011	.0014	.0016	.0020

i	.01	.02	.03	.04	.05	.06	.07	.08	.09	.10
0	.9044	.8171	.7374	.6648	.5987	.5386	.4840	.4344	.3894	.3487
1	.0914	.1667	.2281	.2770	.3151	.3438	.3643	.3777	.3851	.3874
2	.0042	.0153	.0317	.0519	.0746	.0988	.1234	.1478	.1714	.1937
3	.0001	.0008	.0026	.0058	.0105	.0168	.0248	.0343	.0452	.0574
4	.0000	.0000	.0001	.0004	.0010	.0019	.0033	.0052	.0078	.0112
5	.0000	.0000	.0000	.0000	.0001	.0001	.0003	.0005	.0009	.0015
6	.0000	.0000	.0000	.0000	.0000	.0000	.0000	.0000	.0001	.0001
7	.0000	.0000	.0000	.0000	.0000	.0000	.0000	.0000	.0000	.0000
8	.0000	.0000	.0000	.0000	.0000	.0000	.0000	.0000	.0000	.0000
9	.0000	.0000	.0000	.0000	.0000	.0000	.0000	.0000	.0000	.0000
10	.0000	.0000	.0000	.0000	.0000	.0000	.0000	.0000	.0000	.0000

i	.11	.12	13	.14	.15	.16	.17	.18	.19	.20
0	.3118	.2785	.2484	.2213	.1969	.1749	.1552	.1374	.1216	.1074
1	.3854	.3798	.3712	.3603	.3474	.3331	.3178	.3017	.2852	.2684
2	.2143	.2330	.2496	.2639	.2759	.2856	.2929	.2980	.3010	.3020
3	.0706	.0847	.0995	.1146	.1298	.1450	.1600	.1745	.1883	.2013
4	.0153	.0202	.0260	.0326	.0401	.0483	.0573	.0670	.0773	.0881
5	.0023	.0033	.0047	.0064	.0085	.0111	.0141	.0177	.0218	.0264
6	.0002	.0004	.0006	.0009	.0012	.0018	.0024	.0032	.0043	.0055
7	.0000	.0000	.0000	.0001	.0001	.0002	.0003	.0004	.0006	.0008
8	.0000	.0000	.0000	.0000	.0000	.0000	.0000	.0000	.0001	.0001
9	.0000	.0000	.0000	.0000	.0000	.0000	.0000	.0000	.0000	.0000
10	.0000	.0000	.0000	.0000	.0000	.0000	.0000	.0000	.0000	.0000

i	.21	.22	.23	.24	.25	.26	.27	.28	.29	.30
0	.0947	.0834	.0733	.0643	.0563	.0492	.0430	.0374	.0326	.0282
1	.2517	.2351	.2188	.2030	.1877	.1730	.1590	.1456	.1330	.1211
2	.3011	.2984	.2942	.2885	.2816	.2735	.2646	.2548	.2444	.2335
3	.2134	.2244	.2343	.2429	.2503	.2563	.2609	.2642	.2662	.2668
4	.0993	.1108	.1225	.1343	.1460	.1576	.1689	.1798	.1903	.2001
5	.0317	.0375	.0439	.0509	.0584	.0664	.0750	.0839	.0933	.1029
6	.0070	.0088	.0109	.0134	.0162	.0195	.0231	.0272	.0317	.0368
7	.0011	.0014	.0019	.0024	.0031	.0039	.0049	.0060	.0074	.0090
8	.0001	.0002	.0002	.0003	.0004	.0005	.0007	.0009	.0011	.0014
9	.0000	.0000	.0000	.0000	.0000	.0000	.0001	.0001	.0001	.0001
10	.0000	.0000	.0000	.0000	.0000	.0000	.0000	.0000	.0000	.0000

$$N = 10$$
Values of P (continued)

i	.31	.32	.33	.34	.35	.36	.37	.38	.39	.40
0	.0245	.0211	.0182	.0157	.0135	.0115	.0098	.0084	.0071	.0060
1	.1099	.0995	.0898	.0808	.0725	.0649	.0578	.0514	.0456	.0403
2	.2222	.2107	.1990	.1873	.1757	.1642	.1529	.1419	.1312	.1209
3	.2662	.2644	.2614	.2573	.2522	.2462	.2394	.2319	.2237	.2150
4	.2093	.2177	.2253	.2320	.2377	.2424	.2461	.2487	.2503	.2508
5	.1128	.1229	.1332	.1434	.1536	.1636	.1734	.1829	.1920	.2007
6	.0422	.0482	.0547	.0616	.0689	.0767	.0849	.0934	.1023	.1115
7	.0108	.0130	.0154	.0181	.0212	.0247	.0285	.0327	.0374	.0425
8	.0018	.0023	.0028	.0035	.0043	.0052	.0063	.0075	.0090	.0106
9	.0002	.0002	.0003	.0004	.0005	.0006	.0008	.0010	.0013	.0016
10	.0000	.0000	.0000	.0000	.0000	.0000	.0000	.0001	.0001	.0001

i	.41	.42	.43	.44	.45	.46	.47	.48	.49	.50
0	.0051	.0043	.0036	.0030	.0025	.0021	.0017	.0014	.0012	.0010
1	.0355	.0312	.0273	.0238	.0207	.0180	.0155	.0133	.0114	.0098
2	.1111	.1017	.0927	.0843	.0763	.0688	.0619	.0554	.0494	.0439
3	.2058	.1963	.1865	.1765	.1665	.1564	.1464	.1364	.1267	.1172
4	.2503	.2488	.2462	.2427	.2384	.2331	.2271	.2204	.2130	.2051
5	.2087	.2162	.2229	.2289	.2340	.2383	.2417	.2441	.2456	.2461
6	.1209	.1304	.1401	.1499	.1596	.1692	.1786	.1878	.1966	.2051
7	.0480	.0540	.0604	.0673	.0746	.0824	.0905	.0991	.1080	.1172
8	.0125	.0147	.0171	.0198	.0229	.0263	.0301	.0343	.0389	.0439
9	.0019	.0024	.0029	.0035	.0042	.0050	.0059	.0070	.0083	.0098
10	.0001	.0002	.0002	.0003	.0003	.0004	.0005	.0006	.0008	.0010

POISSON PROBABILITIES,

$$P(i) = \frac{e^{-\lambda}\lambda^i}{i!}$$

					Value of λ					
i	1	2	3	4	5	6	7	8	9	10
0	.3679	.1353	.0498	.0183	.0067	.0025	.0009	.0003	.0001	.0000
1	.3679	.2707	.1494	.0733	.0337	.0149	.0064	.0027	.0011	.0005
2	.1839	.2707	.2240	.1465	.0842	.0446	.0223	.0107	.0050	.0023
3	.0613	.1804	.2240	.1954	.1404	.0892	.0521	.0286	.0150	.0076
4	.0153	.0902	.1680	.1954	.1755	.1339	.0912	.0573	.0337	.0189
5	.0031	.0361	.1008	.1563	.1755	.1606	.1277	.0916	.0607	.0378
6	.0005	.0120	.0504	.1042	.1462	.1606	.1490	.1221	.0911	.0631
7	.0001	.0034	.0216	.0595	.1044	.1377	.1490	.1396	.1171	.0901
8		.0009	.0081	.0298	.0653	.1033	.1304	.1396	.1318	.1126
9		.0002	.0027	.0132	.0363	.0688	.1014	.1241	.1318	.1251
10			.0008	.0053	.0181	.0413	.0710	.0993	.1186	.1251
11			.0002	.0019	.0082	.0225	.0452	.0722	.0970	.1137
12			.0001	.0006	.0034	.0113	.0263	.0481	.0728	.0948
13				.0002	.0013	.0052	.0142	.0296	.0504	.0729
14				.0001	.0005	.0022	.0071	.0169	.0324	.0521
15					.0002	.0009	.0033	.0090	.0194	.0347
16						.0003	.0014	.0045	.0109	.0217
17						.0001	.0006	.0021	.0058	.0128
18							.0002	.0009	.0029	.0071
19							.0001	.0004	.0014	.0037
20								.0002	.0006	.0019
21								.0001	.0003	.0009
22									.0001	.0004
23										.0002
24										.0001
25										.0000

I. POISSON PROBABILITIES, $P(i) = \dfrac{e^{-\lambda}\lambda^i}{i!}$

	Value of λ									
i	11	12	13	14	15	16	17	18	19	20
0	.0000	.0000	.0000	.0000	.0000	.0000	.0000	.0000	.0000	.0000
1	.0002	.0001	.0000	.0000	.0000	.0000	.0000	.0000	.0000	.0000
2	.0010	.0004	.0002	.0001	.0000	.0000	.0000	.0000	.0000	.0000
3	.0037	.0018	.0008	.0004	.0002	.0001	.0000	.0000	.0000	.0000
4	.0102	.0053	.0027	.0013	.0006	.0003	.0001	.0001	.0000	.0000
5	.0224	.0127	.0070	.0037	.0019	.0010	.0005	.0002	.0001	.0001
6	.0411	.0255	.0152	.0087	.0048	.0026	.0014	.0007	.0004	.0002
7	.0646	.0437	.0281	.0174	.0104	.0060	.0034	.0019	.0010	.0005
8	.0888	.0655	.0457	.0304	.0194	.0120	.0072	.0042	.0024	.0013
9	.1085	.0874	.0661	.0473	.0324	.0213	.0135	.0083	.0050	.0029
10	.1194	.1048	.0859	.0663	.0486	.0341	.0230	.0150	.0095	.0058
11	.1194	.1144	.1015	.0844	.0663	.0496	.0355	.0245	.0164	.0106
12	.1094	.1144	.1099	.0984	.0829	.0661	.0504	.0368	.0259	.0176
13	.0926	.1056	.1099	.1060	.0956	.0814	.0658	.0509	.0378	.0271
14	.0728	.0905	.1021	.1060	.1024	.0930	.0800	.0655	.0514	.0387
15	.0534	.0724	.0885	.0989	.1024	.0992	.0906	.0786	.0650	.0516
16	.0367	.0543	.0719	.0866	.0960	.0992	.0963	.0884	.0772	.0646
17	.0237	.0383	.0550	.0713	.0847	.0934	.0963	.0936	.0863	.0760
18	.0145	.0255	.0397	.0554	.0706	.0830	.0909	.0936	.0911	.0844
19	.0084	.0161	.0272	.0409	.0557	.0699	.0814	.0887	.0911	.0888
20	.0046	.0097	.0177	.0286	.0418	.0559	.0692	.0798	.0866	.0888
21	.0024	.0055	.0109	.0191	.0299	.0426	.0560	.0684	.0783	.0846
22	.0012	.0030	.0065	.0121	.0204	.0310	.0433	.0560	.0676	.0769
23	.0006	.0016	.0037	.0074	.0133	.0216	.0320	.0438	.0559	.0669
24	.0003	.0008	.0020	.0043	.0083	.0144	.0226	.0328	.0442	.0557
25	.0001	.0004	.0010	.0024	.0050	.0092	.0154	.0237	.0336	.0446
26		.0002	.0005	.0013	.0029	.0057	.0101	.0164	.0246	.0343
27		.0001	.0002	.0007	.0016	.0034	.0063	.0109	.0173	.0254
28			.0001	.0003	.0009	.0019	.0038	.0070	.0117	.0181
29			.0001	.0002	.0004	.0011	.0023	.0044	.0077	.0125
30				.0001	.0002	.0006	.0013	.0026	.0049	.0083
31					.0001	.0003	.0007	.0015	.0030	.0054
32					.0001	.0001	.0004	.0009	.0018	.0034
33						.0001	.0002	.0005	.0010	.0020
34							.0001	.0002	.0006	.0012
35								.0001	.0003	.0007
36								.0001	.0002	.0004
37									.0001	.0002
38									.0000	.0001

VALUES OF e^{-x}

The table below gives values of e^{-x}. The number e is the base of the natural logarithm and equals 2.718281828. . . . Values in the table are rounded to five places. For example, to find e^{-6}, $x = 6$, so the value is $e^{-6} = 0.00248$. Some values not given in the table are easily calculated from the values given. For example,

$$e^{-6.2} = e^{-(6+0.2)} = e^{-6-0.2} = e^{-6}e^{-0.2}$$

$$= (0.00248)(0.81873) = 0.00203$$

$$e^{-6.12} = e^{-(6+0.1+0.02)} = e^{-6}e^{-0.1}e^{-0.02}$$

$$= (0.00248)(0.90484)(0.98020) = 0.00220$$

x	e^{-x}
0.01	0.99005
0.02	0.98020
0.03	0.97044
0.04	0.96079
0.05	0.95123
0.06	0.94176
0.07	0.93239
0.08	0.92312
0.09	0.91393
0.10	0.90484
0.20	0.81873
0.30	0.74082
0.40	0.67032
0.50	0.60653
0.60	0.54881
0.70	0.49658
0.80	0.44933
0.90	0.40657

x	e^{-x}
1.0	0.36790
1.1	0.33287
1.2	0.30119
1.3	0.27253
1.4	0.24660
1.5	0.22313
1.6	0.20190
1.7	0.18268
1.8	0.16530
1.9	0.14957
2.0	0.13534
2.1	0.12246
2.2	0.11080
2.3	0.10026
2.4	0.09072
2.5	0.08208
2.6	0.07427
2.7	0.06720
2.8	0.06081
2.9	0.05502
3.0	0.04979
3.1	0.04505
3.2	0.04076
3.3	0.03688
3.4	0.03337
3.5	0.03020
3.6	0.02732
3.7	0.02472
3.8	0.02237
3.9	0.02024
4.0	0.01832
4.1	0.01657
4.2	0.01450
4.3	0.01357
4.4	0.01228
4.5	0.01111
4.6	0.01005
4.7	0.00910
4.8	0.00823
4.9	0.00745
5.0	0.00674
5.1	0.00610
5.2	0.00552
5.3	0.00499
5.4	0.00452
5.5	0.00409
5.6	0.00370
5.7	0.00334
5.8	0.00303
5.9	0.00274
6.0	0.00248
7.0	0.00091
8.0	0.00034
9.0	0.00012
10.0	0.00004

K CUMULATIVE NORMAL DISTRIBUTION VALUES

Table of Normal Probabilities

Z	.00	.01	.02	.03	.04	.05	.06	.07	.08	.09
.00	.5000	.5040	.5080	.5120	.5160	.5199	.5239	.5279	.5319	.5358
.10	.5398	.5438	.5478	.5517	.5557	.5596	.5636	.5675	.5714	.5753
.20	.5792	.5832	.5871	.5910	.5948	.5987	.6026	.6064	.6103	.6141
.30	.6179	.6217	.6255	.6293	.6331	.6368	.6406	.6443	.6480	.6517
.40	.6554	.6591	.6628	.6664	.6700	.6736	.6772	.6808	.6844	.6879
.50	.6915	.6950	.6985	.7019	.7054	.7088	.7123	.7157	.7190	.7224
.60	.7257	.7291	.7324	.7356	.7389	.7422	.7454	.7486	.7517	.7549
.70	.7580	.7611	.7642	.7673	.7704	.7734	.7764	.7794	.7823	.7852
.80	.7881	.7910	.7939	.7967	.7995	.8023	.8051	.8078	.8106	.8133
.90	.8159	.8186	.8212	.8238	.8264	.8289	.8315	.8340	.8364	.8389
1.00	.8413	.8438	.8461	.8485	.8508	.8531	.8554	.8577	.8599	.8621
1.10	.8643	.8665	.8686	.8708	.8728	.8749	.8770	.8790	.8810	.8830
1.20	.8849	.8869	.8888	.8906	.8925	.8944	.8962	.8980	.8997	.9015
1.30	.9032	.9049	.9066	.9082	.9099	.9115	.9131	.9146	.9162	.9177
1.40	.9192	.9207	.9222	.9236	.9251	.9265	.9278	.9292	.9306	.9319
1.50	.9332	.9345	.9357	.9370	.9382	.9394	.9406	.9418	.9429	.9441
1.60	.9452	.9463	.9474	.9484	.9495	.9505	.9515	.9525	.9535	.9545
1.70	.9554	.9564	.9573	.9582	.9591	.9599	.9608	.9616	.9625	.9633
1.80	.9641	.9648	9656	.9664	.9671	.9678	.9686	.9692	.9699	.9706
1.90	.9713	.9719	.9726	.9732	.9738	.9744	.9750	.9756	.9761	.9767
2.00	.9772	.9778	.9783	.9788	.9793	.9798	.9803	.9808	.9812	.9817
2.10	.9821	.9826	.9830	.9834	.9838	.9842	.9846	.9850	.9854	.9857
2.20	.9861	.9864	.9868	.9871	.9874	.9878	.9881	.9884	.9887	.9890
2.30	.9893	.9896	.9898	.9901	.9904	.9906	.9909	.9911	.9913	.9916
2.40	.9918	.9920	.9922	.9924	.9926	.9928	.9930	.9932	.9934	.9936
2.50	.9938	.9940	.9941	.9943	.9944	.9946	.9948	.9949	.9951	.9952
2.60	.9953	.9955	.9956	.9957	.9958	.9960	.9961	.9962	.9963	.9964
2.70	.9965	.9966	.9967	.9968	.9969	.9970	.9971	.9972	.9973	.9974
2.80	.9974	.9975	.9976	.9977	.9977	.9978	.9979	.9979	.9980	.9981
2.90	.9981	.9982	.9982	.9983	.9984	.9984	.9985	.9985	.9986	.9986
3.00	.9986	.9987	.9987	.9988	.9988	.9988	.9989	.9989	.9990	.9990
3.10	.9990	.9991	.9991	.9991	.9992	.9992	.9992	.9992	.9993	.9993
3.20	.9993	.9993	.9994	.9994	.9994	.9994	.9994	.9995	.9995	.9995
3.30	.9995	.9995	.9996	.9996	.9996	.9996	.9996	.9996	.9996	.9996
3.40	.9997	.9997	.9997	.9997	.9997	.9997	.9997	.9997	.9997	.9998
3.50	.9998	.9998	.9998	.9998	.9998	.9998	.9998	.9998	.9998	.9998
3.60	.9998	.9998	.9998	.9998	.9999	.9999	.9999	.9999	.9999	.9999

L P_0 FOR MULTIPLE–CHANNEL QUEUES

Number of Channels, S

$\dfrac{\lambda}{S\mu}$	1	2	3	4	5	6	7
.01	0.9900	0.9802	0.9704	0.9608	0.9512	0.9418	0.9324
.02	0.9800	0.9608	0.9418	0.9231	0.9048	0.8869	0.8694
.03	0.9700	0.9417	0.9139	0.8869	0.8607	0.8353	0.8106
.04	0.9600	0.9231	0.8869	0.8521	0.8187	0.7866	0.7558
.05	0.9500	0.9048	0.8607	0.8187	0.7788	0.7408	0.7047
.06	0.9400	0.8868	0.8353	0.7866	0.7408	0.6977	0.6570
.07	0.9300	0.8692	0.8106	0.7558	0.7047	0.6570	0.6126
.08	0.9200	0.8519	0.7866	0.7261	0.6703	0.6188	0.5712
.09	0.9100	0.8349	0.7633	0.6977	0.6376	0.5827	0.5326
.10	0.9000	0.8182	0.7407	0.6703	0.6065	0.5488	0.4966
.11	0.8900	0.8018	0.7188	0.6440	0.5769	0.5169	0.4630
.12	0.8800	0.7857	0.6975	0.6188	0.5488	0.4868	0.4317
.13	0.8700	0.7699	0.6769	0.5945	0.5220	0.4584	0.4025
.14	0.8600	0.7544	0.6568	0.5712	0.4966	0.4317	0.3753
.15	0.8500	0.7391	0.6373	0.5487	0.4724	0.4066	0.3499
.16	0.8400	0.7241	0.6184	0.5272	0.4493	0.3829	0.3263
.17	0.8300	0.7094	0.6000	0.5065	0.4274	0.3606	0.3042
.18	0.8200	0.6949	0.5821	0.4866	0.4065	0.3396	0.2837
.19	0.8100	0.6807	0.5648	0.4675	0.3867	0.3198	0.2645
.20	0.8000	0.6667	0.5479	0.4491	0.3678	0.3012	0.2466
.21	0.7900	0.6529	0.5316	0.4314	0.3499	0.2836	0.2299
.22	0.7800	0.6393	0.5157	0.4145	0.3328	0.2671	0.2144
.23	0.7700	0.6260	0.5002	0.3981	0.3165	0.2515	0.1999
.24	0.7600	0.6129	0.4852	0.3824	0.3011	0.2369	0.1864
.25	0.7500	0.6000	0.4706	0.3673	0.2863	0.2231	0.1738
.26	0.7400	0.5873	0.4564	0.3528	0.2723	0.2101	0.1620
.27	0.7300	0.5748	0.4426	0.3389	0.2590	0.1978	0.1510
.28	0.7200	0.5625	0.4292	0.3255	0.2463	0.1863	0.1408
.29	0.7100	0.5504	0.4161	0.3126	0.2343	0.1754	0.1313
.30	0.7000	0.5385	0.4035	0.3002	0.2228	0.1652	0.1224
.31	0.6900	0.5267	0.3911	0.2882	0.2118	0.1555	0.1141
.32	0.6800	0.5152	0.3791	0.2768	0.2014	0.1464	0.1064
.33	0.6700	0.5038	0.3675	0.2657	0.1915	0.137	0.0992

Number of Channels, S *(continued)*

$\dfrac{\lambda}{S\mu}$	1	2	3	4	5	6	7
.34	0.6600	0.4925	0.3561	0.2551	0.1821	0.1298	0.0925
.35	0.6500	0.4815	0.3451	0.2449	0.1731	0.1222	0.0862
.36	0.6400	0.4706	0.3343	0.2351	0.1646	0.1151	0.0804
.37	0.6300	0.4599	0.3238	0.2256	0.1565	0.1083	0.0749
.38	0.6200	0.4493	0.3137	0.2165	0.1487	0.1020	0.0698
.39	0.6100	0.4388	0.3038	0.2077	0.1413	0.0960	0.0651
.40	0.6000	0.4286	0.2941	0.1993	0.1343	0.0903	0.0606

Number of Channels, S

$\dfrac{\lambda}{S\mu}$	8	9	10	11	12	13	14	15
.01	0.9231	0.9139	0.9048	0.8958	0.8869	0.8781	0.8694	0.8607
.02	0.8521	0.8353	0.8187	0.8025	0.7866	0.7711	0.7558	0.7408
.03	0.7866	0.7634	0.7408	0.7189	0.6977	0.6771	0.6570	0.6376
.04	0.7262	0.6977	0.6703	0.6440	0.6188	0.5945	0.5712	0.5488
.05	0.6703	0.6376	0.6065	0.5770	0.5488	0.5220	0.4966	0.4724
.06	0.6188	0.5827	0.5488	0.5169	0.4868	0.4584	0.4317	0.4066
.07	0.5712	0.5326	0.4966	0.4630	0.4317	0.4025	0.3753	0.3499
.08	0.5273	0.4868	0.4493	0.4148	0.3829	0.3535	0.3263	0.3012
.09	0.4868	0.4449	0.4066	0.3716	0.3396	0.3104	0.2837	0.2592
.10	0.4493	0.4066	0.3679	0.3329	0.3012	0.2725	0.2466	0.2231
.11	0.4148	0.3716	0.3329	0.2982	0.2671	0.2393	0.2144	0.1921
.12	0.3829	0.3396	0.3012	0.2671	0.2369	0.2101	0.1864	0.1653
.13	0.3535	0.3104	0.2725	0.2393	0.2101	0.1845	0.1620	0.1423
.14	0.3263	0.2837	0.2466	0.2144	0.1864	0.1620	0.1409	0.1225
.15	0.3012	0.2592	0.2231	0.1921	0.1653	0.1423	0.1225	0.1054
.16	0.2780	0.2369	0.2019	0.1720	0.1466	0.1249	0.1065	0.0907
.17	0.2567	0.2165	0.1827	0.1541	0.1300	0.1097	0.0926	0.0781
.18	0.2369	0.1979	0.1653	0.1381	0.1153	0.0963	0.0805	0.0672
.19	0.2187	0.1809	0.1496	0.1237	0.1023	0.0846	0.0699	0.0578
.20	0.2019	0.1653	0.1353	0.1108	0.0907	0.0743	0.0608	0.0498
.21	0.1864	0.1511	0.1225	0.0993	0.0805	0.0652	0.0529	0.0429
.22	0.1720	0.1381	0.1108	0.0889	0.0714	0.0573	0.0460	0.0369
.23	0.1588	0.1262	0.1003	0.0797	0.0633	0.0503	0.0400	0.0317
.24	0.1466	0.1153	0.0907	0.0714	0.0561	0.0442	0.0347	0.0273
.25	0.1353	0.1054	0.0821	0.0639	0.0498	0.0388	0.0302	0.0235
.26	0.1249	0.0963	0.0743	0.0573	0.0442	0.0340	0.0263	0.0202
.27	0.1153	0.0880	0.0672	0.0513	0.0392	0.0299	0.0228	0.0174
.28	0.1064	0.0805	0.0608	0.0460	0.0347	0.0263	0.0198	0.0150
.29	0.0983	0.0735	0.0550	0.0412	0.0308	0.0231	0.0172	0.0129
.30	0.0907	0.0672	0.0498	0.0369	0.0273	0.0202	0.0150	0.0111
.31	0.0837	0.0614	0.0450	0.0330	0.0242	0.0178	0.0130	0.0096
.32	0.0773	0.0561	0.0408	0.0296	0.0215	0.0156	0.0113	0.0082
.33	0.0713	0.0513	0.0369	0.0265	0.0191	0.0137	0.0099	0.0071
.34	0.0658	0.0469	0.0334	0.0238	0.0169	0.0120	0.0086	0.0061
.35	0.0608	0.0428	0.0302	0.0213	0.0150	0.0106	0.0074	0.0052
.36	0.0561	0.0391	0.0273	0.0191	0.0133	0.0093	0.0065	0.0045
.37	0.0518	0.0358	0.0247	0.0171	0.0118	0.0081	0.0056	0.0039
.38	0.0478	0.0327	0.0224	0.0153	0.0105	0.0072	0.0049	0.0033
.39	0.0441	0.0299	0.0202	0.0137	0.0093	0.0063	0.0043	0.0029
.40	0.0407	0.0273	0.0183	0.0123	0.0082	0.0055	0.0037	0.0025

Number of Channels, s

$\dfrac{\lambda}{S\mu}$	1	2	3	4	5	6	7
.41	0.5900	0.4184	0.2847	0.1912	0.1276	0.0850	0.0565
.42	0.5800	0.4085	0.2756	0.1834	0.1213	0.0800	0.0527
.43	0.5700	0.3986	0.2667	0.1758	0.1152	0.0753	0.0491
.44	0.5600	0.3889	0.2580	0.1686	0.1094	0.0708	0.0457
.45	0.5500	0.3793	0.2496	0.1616	0.1039	0.0666	0.0426
.46	0.5400	0.3699	0.2414	0.1549	0.0987	0.0626	0.0397
.47	0.5300	0.3605	0.2333	0.1484	0.0937	0.0589	0.0370
.48	0.5200	0.3514	0.2255	0.1422	0.0889	0.0554	0.0344
.49	0.5100	0.3423	0.2179	0.1362	0.0844	0.0521	0.0321
.50	0.5000	0.3333	0.2105	0.1304	0.0801	0.0490	0.0298
.51	0.4900	0.3245	0.2033	0.1249	0.0760	0.0460	0.0278
.52	0.4800	0.3158	0.1963	0.1195	0.0721	0.0432	0.0259
.53	0.4700	0.3072	0.1894	0.1143	0.0683	0.0406	0.0241
.54	0.4600	0.2987	0.1827	0.1094	0.0648	0.0381	0.0224
.55	0.4500	0.2903	0.1762	0.1046	0.0614	0.0358	0.0208
.56	0.4400	0.2821	0.1699	0.0999	0.0581	0.0336	.00194
.57	0.4300	0.2739	0.1637	0.0955	0.0551	0.0315	0.0180
.58	0.4200	0.2658	0.1576	0.0912	0.0521	0.0296	0.0167
.59	0.4100	0.2579	0.1517	0.0870	0.0493	0.0277	0.0155
.60	0.4000	0.2500	0.1460	0.0831	0.0466	0.0260	0.0144
.61	0.3900	0.2422	0.1404	0.0792	0.0441	0.0244	0.0134
.62	0.3800	0.2346	0.1349	0.0755	0.0417	0.0228	0.0124
.63	0.3700	0.2270	0.1296	0.0719	0.0394	0.0214	0.0115
.64	0.3600	0.2195	0.1244	0.0685	0.0372	0.0200	0.0107
.65	0.3500	0.2121	0.1193	0.0651	0.0350	0.0187	0.0099
.66	0.3400	0.2048	0.1143	0.0619	0.0330	0.0175	0.0092
.67	0.3300	0.1976	0.1095	0.0588	0.0311	0.0163	0.0085
.68	0.3200	0.1905	0.1048	0.0559	0.0293	0.0152	0.0079
.69	0.3100	0.1834	0.1002	0.0530	0.0276	0.0142	0.0073
.70	0.3000	0.1765	0.0957	0.0502	0.0259	0.0132	0.0067
.71	0.2900	0.1696	0.0913	0.0475	0.0243	0.0123	0.0062
.72	0.2800	0.1628	0.0870	0.0450	0.0228	0.0114	0.0057
.73	0.2700	0.1561	0.0828	0.0425	0.0214	0.0106	0.0053
.74	0.2600	0.1494	0.0788	0.0401	0.0200	0.0099	0.0048
.75	0.2500	0.1429	0.0748	0.0377	0.0187	0.0091	0.0044
.76	0.2400	0.1364	0.0709	0.0355	0.0174	0.0085	0.0041
.77	0.2300	0.1299	0.0671	0.0333	0.0162	0.0078	0.0037
.78	0.2200	0.1236	0.0634	0.0313	0.0151	0.0072	0.0034
.79	0.2100	0.1173	0.0597	0.0292	0.0140	0.0066	0.0031

Number of Channels, s

$\dfrac{\lambda}{S\mu}$	8	9	10	11	12	13	14	15
.41	0.0376	0.0249	0.0166	0.0110	0.0073	0.0048	0.0032	0.0021
.42	0.0347	0.0228	0.0150	0.0098	0.0065	0.0043	0.0028	0.0018
.43	0.0320	0.0208	0.0136	0.0088	0.0057	0.0037	0.0024	0.0016
.44	0.0295	0.0190	0.0123	0.0079	0.0051	0.0033	0.0021	0.0014
.45	0.0272	0.0174	0.0111	0.0071	0.0045	0.0029	0.0018	0.0012
.46	0.0251	0.0159	0.0100	0.0063	0.0040	0.0025	0.0016	0.0010
.47	0.0232	0.0145	0.0091	0.0057	0.0035	0.0022	0.0014	0.0009
.48	0.0214	0.0132	0.0082	0.0051	0.0031	0.0019	0.0012	0.0007
.49	0.0197	0.0121	0.0074	0.0045	0.0028	0.0017	0.0010	0.0006
.50	0.0182	0.0110	0.0067	0.0041	0.0025	0.0015	0.0009	0.0006
.51	0.0167	0.0101	0.0061	0.0036	0.0022	0.0013	0.0008	0.0005
.52	0.0154	0.0092	0.0055	0.0033	0.0019	0.0012	0.0007	0.0004
.53	0.0142	0.0084	0.0050	0.0029	0.0017	0.0010	0.0006	0.0004
.54	0.0131	0.0077	0.0045	0.0026	0.0015	0.0009	0.0005	0.0003
.55	0.0121	0.0070	0.0040	0.0023	0.0014	0.0008	0.0005	0.0003
.56	0.0111	0.0064	0.0037	0.0021	0.0012	0.0007	0.0004	0.0002
.57	0.0102	0.0058	0.0033	0.0019	0.0011	0.0006	0.0003	0.0002
.58	0.0094	0.0053	0.0030	0.0017	0.0009	0.0005	0.0003	0.0002
.59	0.0087	0.0048	0.0027	0.0015	0.0008	0.0005	0.0003	0.0001
.60	0.0080	0.0044	0.0024	0.0013	0.0007	0.0004	0.0002	0.0001
.61	0.0073	0.0040	0.0022	0.0012	0.0007	0.0004	0.0002	0.0001
.62	0.0068	0.0037	0.0020	0.0011	0.0006	0.0003	0.0002	0.0001
.63	0.0062	0.0033	0.0018	0.0010	0.0005	0.0003	0.0001	0.0001
.64	0.0057	0.0030	0.0016	0.0009	0.0005	0.0002	0.0001	0.0001
.65	0.0052	0.0028	0.0015	0.0008	0.0004	0.0002	0.0001	0.0001
.66	0.0048	0.0025	0.0013	0.0007	0.0004	0.0002	0.0001	0.0000
.67	0.0044	0.0023	0.0012	0.0006	0.0003	0.0002	0.0001	0.0000
.68	0.0040	0.0021	0.0011	0.0005	0.0003	0.0001	0.0001	0.0000
.69	0.0037	0.0019	0.0010	0.0005	0.0002	0.0001	0.0001	0.0000
.70	0.0034	0.0017	0.0009	0.0004	0.0002	0.0001	0.0001	0.0000
.71	0.0031	0.0015	0.0008	0.0004	0.0002	0.0001	0.0000	0.0000
.72	0.0028	0.0014	0.0007	0.0003	0.0002	0.0001	0.0000	0.0000
.73	0.0026	0.0013	0.0006	0.0003	0.0001	0.0001	0.0000	0.0000
.74	0.0024	0.0011	0.0006	0.0003	0.0001	0.0001	0.0000	0.0000
.75	0.0021	0.0010	0.0005	0.0002	0.0001	0.0001	0.0000	0.0000
.76	0.0019	0.0009	0.0004	0.0002	0.0001	0.0000	0.0000	0.0000
.77	0.0018	0.0008	0.0004	0.0002	0.0001	0.0000	0.0000	0.0000
.78	0.0016	0.0008	0.0004	0.0002	0.0001	0.0000	0.0000	0.0000
.79	0.0015	0.0007	0.0003	0.0001	0.0001	0.0000	0.0000	0.0000

L. P_0 FOR MULTIPLE-CHANNEL QUEUES

Number of Channels, s

$\dfrac{\lambda}{S\mu}$	1	2	3	4	5	6	7
.80	0.2000	0.1111	0.0562	0.0273	0.0130	0.0061	0.0028
.81	0.1900	0.1050	0.0527	0.0254	0.0120	0.0056	0.0026
.82	0.1800	0.0989	0.0493	0.0236	0.0111	0.0051	0.0023
.83	0.1700	0.0929	0.0460	0.0219	0.0102	0.0047	0.0021
.84	0.1600	0.0870	0.0428	0.0202	0.0093	0.0042	0.0019
.85	0.1500	0.0811	0.0396	0.0186	0.0085	0.0038	0.0017
.86	0.1400	0.0753	0.0366	0.0170	0.0077	0.0035	0.0015
.87	0.1300	0.0695	0.0335	0.0155	0.0070	0.0031	0.0014
.88	0.1200	0.0638	0.0306	0.0140	0.0063	0.0028	0.0012
.89	0.1100	0.0582	0.0277	0.0126	0.0056	0.0024	0.0011
.90	0.1000	0.0526	0.0249	0.0113	0.0050	0.0021	0.0009
.91	0.0900	0.0471	0.0222	0.0099	0.0043	0.0019	0.0008
.92	0.0800	0.0417	0.0195	0.0087	0.0038	0.0016	0.0007
.93	0.0700	0.0363	0.0168	0.0075	0.0032	0.0014	0.0006
.94	0.0600	0.0309	0.0143	0.0063	0.0027	0.0011	0.0005
.95	0.0500	0.0256	0.0118	0.0051	0.0022	0.0009	0.0004
.96	0.0400	0.0204	0.0093	0.0040	0.0017	0.0007	0.0003
.97	0.0300	0.0152	0.0069	0.0030	0.0012	0.0005	0.0002
.98	0.0200	0.0101	0.0045	0.0019	0.0008	0.0003	0.0001
.99	0.0100	0.0050	0.0022	0.0010	0.0004	0.0002	0.0001

$\dfrac{\lambda}{S\mu}$	8	9	10	11	12	13	14	15
.80	0.0013	0.0006	0.0003	0.0001	0.0001	0.0000	0.0000	0.0000
.81	0.0012	0.0005	0.0002	0.0001	0.0001	0.0000	0.0000	0.0000
.82	0.0011	0.0005	0.0002	0.0001	0.0000	0.0000	0.0000	0.0000
.83	0.0010	0.0004	0.0002	0.0001	0.0000	0.0000	0.0000	0.0000
.84	0.0009	0.0004	0.0002	0.0001	0.0000	0.0000	0.0000	0.0000
.85	0.0008	0.0003	0.0001	0.0001	0.0000	0.0000	0.0000	0.0000
.86	0.0007	0.0003	0.0001	0.0001	0.0000	0.0000	0.0000	0.0000
.87	0.0006	0.0003	0.0001	0.0000	0.0000	0.0000	0.0000	0.0000
.88	0.0005	0.0002	0.0001	0.0000	0.0000	0.0000	0.0000	0.0000
.89	0.0005	0.0002	0.0001	0.0000	0.0000	0.0000	0.0000	0.0000
.90	0.0004	0.0002	0.0001	0.0000	0.0000	0.0000	0.0000	0.0000
.91	0.0003	0.0001	0.0001	0.0000	0.0000	0.0000	0.0000	0.0000
.92	0.0003	0.0001	0.0000	0.0000	0.0000	0.0000	0.0000	0.0000
.93	0.0002	0.0001	0.0000	0.0000	0.0000	0.0000	0.0000	0.0000
.94	0.0002	0.0001	0.0000	0.0000	0.0000	0.0000	0.0000	0.0000
.95	0.0002	0.0001	0.0000	0.0000	0.0000	0.0000	0.0000	0.0000
.96	0.0001	0.0000	0.0000	0.0000	0.0000	0.0000	0.0000	0.0000
.97	0.0001	0.0000	0.0000	0.0000	0.0000	0.0000	0.0000	0.0000
.98	0.0001	0.0000	0.0000	0.0000	0.0000	0.0000	0.0000	0.0000
.99	0.0000	0.0000	0.0000	0.0000	0.0000	0.0000	0.0000	0.0000

INDEX